Visit classzone
and get connected

Online resources for students and parents

ClassZone resources provide instruction, practice, and learning support.

Online Workbook

Interactive, leveled practice supports skill development.

WebQuests

Guided Web activities introduce students to real-world French.

Flashcards

Interactive review of vocabulary and pronunciation includes audio prompts.

Online Self-Check

Self-scoring quizzes help students assess their comprehension.

Writing Center

Unit-level writing workshops invite students to share their compositions online.

Now it all clicks!™

CLASSZONE.COM

McDougal Littell

FLORIDA
EDITION

3
Rouge

Discovering
FRENCH
Nouveau!

Jean-Paul Valette
Rebecca M. Valette

McDougal Littell
A DIVISION OF HOUGHTON MIFFLIN COMPANY
Evanston, Illinois • Boston • Dallas

Cover Photography

Cover design by Studio Montage **Front cover** Port Al-Kantaoui, Sousse, Tunisia;
Back cover Level 1a: Palace of Versailles, Versailles, France; Level 1b: Martinique;
Level 1: Eiffel Tower illuminated at night, Paris, France; Level 2: Chateau Frontenac,
Quebec Old Town, Quebec, Canada; Level 3: Port Al-Kantaoui, Sousse, Tunisia

Photography credits appear on page R75.

Illustrations

Francis Back, Pierre Ballouhey, Gilles-Marie Bauer, Jean-Louis Besson, Dave Clegg,
Véronique Deiss, Chris Demarest, Patrick Deubelbeiss, Philippe Dumas, Jacques Ferrandez,
Caroline Finadri, Michel Garneau, Paul Giambarba, Carol Inouye, Louise-Andrée Laliberte,
Winslow Pinney Pels, Mike Reagan, John Rumery, Dave Shepherd, Lorraine Silvestri,
Anna Vojtech, Laura Wallace, Fabrice Weiss, YAYO

Copyright © 2007 McDougal Littell, a division of Houghton Mifflin Company. All rights reserved.

Warning: No part of this work may be reproduced or transmitted in any form or by any means, electronic or
mechanical, including photocopying and recording, or by any information storage or retrieval system without the
prior written permission of McDougal Littell unless such copying is expressly permitted by federal copyright law.
With the exception of not-for-profit transcription in Braille, McDougal Littell is not authorized to grant permission for
further uses of copyrighted selections reprinted in this text without the permission of their owners. Permission must
be obtained from the individual copyright owners as identified herein. Address inquiries to Supervisor, Rights and
Permissions, McDougal Littell, P.O. Box 1667, Evanston, IL 60204.

Printed in the United States of America

ISBN-13: 978-0-618-73544-0
ISBN-10: 0-618-73544-5   X 2 3 4 5 6 7 8 9 10 - VJM - 12 11 10 09 08 07 06

Internet: www.mcdougallittell.com

MERCI!

We would like to thank the many teachers across the country who have responded to surveys and sent suggestions for this new program. In particular, we would like to thank the following people who participated in the development process and provided guidance and encouragement:

Susan Arandjelovic
Dobson High School
Mesa, AZ

Joseph Giorgio Arias
James "Niki" Rowe High School
McAllen, TX

Pat Barr-Harrison
Prince George's County Public Schools
Landover, MD

Beth Bossong
Vestal High School
Vestal, NY

Celeste Carr
Howard County Public Schools
Ellicott City, MD

Betty C. Clough
McCallum High School
Austin, TX

Linda Crecca
Hampton Bays Junior/Senior High School
Hampton Bays, NY

Kay Dagg
Washburn Rural High School
Topeka, KS

Dorothy Davis
Royal High School
Simi Valley, CA

Deborah DeMelfi
Central Columbia High School
Bloomsburg, PA

Janice Dowd
Teaneck High School
Teaneck, NJ

Christiane Fabricant
The Winsor School
Boston, MA

Susan Fritz
Reading Memorial High School
Reading, MA

Susan Hennessey
Reading Memorial High School
Reading, MA

Mary Sue Hoffman
Upper Moreland High School
Willow Grove, PA

Barbara Holohan
Princeton High School
Princeton, NJ

Sheila (Ray) Hutchinson
Kimball High School
Dallas, TX

Belinda Kuck
Clearfield High School
Clearfield, UT

Myrella LeBlanc
Sam Rayburn High School
Pasadena, TX

Lula Lewis
Hyde Park Academy
Chicago, IL

Virginia Mayer
Padua Academy
Wilmington, DE

Patricia McCann
Lincoln-Sudbury High School
Sudbury, MA

William Price
Day Junior High School
Newton, MA

Susan Redd
Mt. Vernon High School
Mt. Vernon, WA

Barbara Reeback
Albuquerque Academy
Albuquerque, NM

T. Jeffrey Richards
Roosevelt High School
Sioux Falls, SD

Virginia Rossy
Simi Valley High School
Simi Valley, CA

Dr. Judith Smith
Baltimore, MD

Kathy Withington
McCluer Senior High School
Florissant, MO

We would also like to thank the following persons for helping us acquire a better insight into their areas of the French-speaking world:

Thierry Gustave *(Martinique)*   **Kouadio Konan** *(Ivory Coast)*

Yasmina Hacien-Bey *(Algeria)*   **Ourida Mostefai** *(Algeria)*

CONTENTS

Reprise

UNITÉ 2

Soyons utiles!

UNITÉ 3

Vive la nature!

Aspects de la vie quotidienne

UNITÉ 5

Bon voyage!

UNITÉ 6 · Séjour en France

UNITÉ 9 Les relations personnelles

Vous êtes fantastiques!

You are terrific! We would like to welcome you back to DISCOVERING FRENCH, but first and foremost we congratulate you on your decision to continue your study of French. As you have discovered, French is a language that broadens your horizons and opens doors to a world of new experiences and opportunities. French offers you the chance to communicate with new people and learn about their culture, the opportunity to explore the wonderful variety of the French-speaking world, and maybe one day the possibility to travel, study or even work in a country where French is spoken... knowing French gives you that extra little "plus" that makes life richer and more enjoyable!

With DISCOVERING FRENCH–ROUGE you will learn to communicate on a variety of topics useful when you travel abroad: making a train reservation, staying in a youth hostel, shopping for things you need, asking for services, etc. But you will learn much more than that. First, you will expand your communication and reading skills. You will also learn to express your thoughts more naturally and more effectively. You will increase your awareness of the francophone world and become more familiar with the many contributions that French-speaking people have made in the world of arts, sciences and great ideas.

As you progress in your study of French, we hope that you will be able to put your knowledge into practice. Perhaps you will have the opportunity to visit Quebec on a school trip. Maybe in the summer you will be able to go bicycling in Belgium or study in France or participate in a home stay program in the Ivory Coast. Even if travel is not in your immediate future, you may have the chance to meet French speakers in the region where you live: new American citizens from Haiti, tourists from Quebec or France, foreign students who have studied French. Remember that in the world there are millions of young people who, like you, are learning French! Don't be shy! Use your French! It's a great language!

Jean-Paul Valette   Rebecca M. Valette

Sunshine State Standards

Florida Course Requirements for French III

This chart provides an overview of where the *Course Requirements for French III* are addressed in **Discovering French, Nouveau! Rouge.** The page references refer to the Pupil Edition or Teacher's Edition. Teacher's Edition pages are denoted with "TE."

SUNSHINE STATE STANDARDS		COMMUNICATION
STANDARD 1	The student engages in conversation, expresses feelings and emotions, and exchanges opinions.	
Benchmark FL.A.1.4.1	The student interacts in the target language in a number of true-life situations chosen from a variety of contexts (e.g., asking for information).	
Course Requirement FL.A.1.2.3	Recognize and appropriately use oral syntax (grouping of words into sentences and phrases) and inflection in spoken target language.	p. 5, Act. 4; p. 23, Act. 1; **p. 25, Act. 1**; p. 39, Act. 2; p. 45, Act. 6; p. 77, Act. 4; **p. 79, Act. 3**; p. 86, Act. 1; p. 88, Act. 6; p. 89, Act. 8; p. 117, Act. 7; p. 118, Act. 11; p. 131, Act. 7; **p. 165, Acts. 5–6, 8**; p. 193, Act. 3; p. 202, Act. 3; p. 206, Act. 9; p. 237, Act. 6; p. 243, Act. 3; p. 245, Act. 5; p. 273, Act. 3; p. 280, Act. 1; p. 309, Act. 1; p. 316, Act. 6; p. 323, Acts. 2–3; p. 324, Act. 5; **p. 355, Act. 7**; p. 357, Acts. 11–12; **p. 362, Act. 1**; p. 365, Act. 5; p. 388, Act. 2; p. 391, Act. 7; p. 399, Act. 3; p. 400, Acts. 4, 6; p. PA3, *Unité* 2 Pair Act.
Course Requirement FL.A.1.3.1	Exchange information with peers and familiar adults orally and in writing about topics of common interest and about the target culture (e.g., personal relationships, events in the past, or academic and cultural interests).	p. 3, *À votre avis*; p. 4, Act. 2; p. 10, Acts. 1, 2, 4–7; p. 15, Act. 2; p. 16, Act. 2; p. 19, Acts. 1–8; p. 23, Act. 2; p. 25, Act. 2; p. 26, Acts. 2–4; 6, 7; **p. 37, Conversations libres**; p. 43, Act. 3; p. 50, Act. 1; p. 52 TE, Teaching strategy: Dialog development; p. 77, Act. 5; p. 85, Act. 1; **p. 87, Acts. 4–5**; p. 114, Act. 1; p. 115, Act. 2; p. 125, Act. 2; p. 129, Act. 3; p. 157, Act. 2; p. 167, Act. 1; **p. 202, Act. 1**; p. 203, Act. 4; p. 235, Act. 3; p. 237, Act. 7; p. 243, Act. 1; p. 267, Act. 2; **p. 278, Act. 1**; p. 306, Act. 1; p. 312, Act. 1; p. 313, Act. 2; **p. 315, Act. 2**; p. 351, Act. 5; p. 389, Act. 5; **p. 395, Act. 2**; p. 400, Act. 5; p. PA11, *Unité* 10 Pair Act.
Course Requirement FL.A.1.3.2	Interact with fluent native or neo-native users of the target language, with sufficient skill to gather information necessary for a simple project.	p. 304 TE, Teaching strategy; p. 351 TE, Teaching suggestion; p. 386 TE, Teaching suggestion; p. 392 TE, Teaching strategy; p. 395, Act. 1

SUNSHINE STATE STANDARDS — COMMUNICATION

Course Requirement FL.A.1.4.1	**Interact in the target language in a number of true-life situations chosen from a variety of contexts (e.g., asking for information).**	p. 4, Act. 1; p. 8 TE, Teaching strategy: Groups; p. 10, Act. 3; p. 10 TE, Inclusion; **p. 26, Acts. 1, 5**; p. 81, Act. 7; p. 83 TE, Teaching strategy: Expansion; **p. 155, Acts. 4–5**; p. 160 TE, Teaching strategy: Expansion; p. 161, Act. 1; **p. 191, Act. 2**; p. 199, Act. 3; p. 200, *Conversations libres*; **p. 232, Act. 2**; p. 239, *Expression orale*; p. 241, Act. 1; p. 268, Acts. 3–4; **p. 279, Act. 2**, *Conversations libres*; p. 395 TE, Teaching strategy; p. PA5, *Unité* 4 Pair Act.; p. PA6, *Unité* 5 Pair Act.; p. PA7, *Unité* 6 Pair Act.; p. PA9, *Unité* 8 Pair Act.
Benchmark FL.A.1.4.2	The student rephrases and uses indirect expressions to communicate a message in the target language.	
Course Requirement FL.A.1.4.2	**Rephrase and use indirect expressions to communicate a message in the target language.**	p. 53, Act. 3; p. 158, Act. 4; p. 159, Act. 5; p. 163, Acts. 2–3; p. 244, Act. 4; p. 245, Acts. 6–7; p. 281, Act. 2
STANDARD 2	The student understands and interprets written and spoken language on a variety of topics.	
Benchmark FL.A.2.4.1	The student obtains and processes information in spoken or written form on topics of academic, cultural, and historical interest, near the level of an educated native speaker of the language.	
Course Requirement FL.A.2.2.7	**Recognize the multiple ways in which an idea may be expressed in the target language and use them appropriately.**	p. 24 TE, Teaching strategy: Direct object pronouns; p. 55, Act. 1; p. 85 TE, Teaching strategy: Vocabulary practice; p. 200, Act. 4; p. 267, Act. 1; p. 277, *Et vous?: Définitions*; p. 351, Act. 3; p. 356, Act. 8; p. 361, Act. 3
Benchmark FL.A.2.4.2	The student understands the main ideas and significant details of extended discussions, presentations, and feature programs on radio and television, in movies, and in other forms of media designed for use by native speakers.	
Course Requirement FL.A.2.2.4	**Listen and read in the target language for leisure and personal enrichment (e.g., listen to, read, or view age-appropriate stories, plays, poems, films, or visual works of art).**	pp. 27–31, *Lecture: Les trois bagues*; pp. 46–47, *Info magazine: À la residence Bon Repos*; pp. 56–59, *Lecture: Conte pour enfants de moins de trois ans*; pp. 92–97, *Lecture: La Couverture*; pp. 134–139, *Lecture: King*; pp. 170–175, *Lecture: Une histoire de cheveux*; pp. 208–215, *Lecture: Le mystérieux homme en bleu*; pp. 246–251, *Lecture: Une étrange aventure*; pp. 282–291, *Lecture: En voyage*; pp. 326–333, *Lecture: Les pêches*; pp. 366–371, *Lecture: Le bracelet*; p. 378 TE, Teaching strategy; pp. 402–409, *Lecture: Le portrait*
Course Requirement FL.A.2.3.2	**Comprehend and interpret the main ideas and details from television, movies, videos, radio, or live presentations produced in the target language.**	p. 145 TE, Teaching strategy: Challenge; p. 167 TE, Teaching suggestion; p. 240 TE, Teaching suggestion: Video/DVD Program; p. 249 TE, Teaching suggestions; p. 343 TE, Teaching suggestions

Course Requirement FL.A.2.3.4	Recognize the relationship between verbal and nonverbal signals in communication, while listening to a live speaker of the target language or while viewing and listening to a mass-media product (i.e., film, video, or concert).	p. 24 TE, Teaching strategy; p. 74 TE, Teaching suggestion; p. 144 TE, Teaching strategy: Expansion; p. 241 TE, Teaching suggestion; p. 264 TE, Teaching suggestion

Benchmark FL.A.2.4.3	The student reads authentic written materials and analyzes them orally or in writing (e.g., describes characters, plot, personal reactions, and feelings).	
Course Requirement FL.A.2.3.1	Comprehend and interpret the content of authentic, written materials selected according to the familiarity of the topic and the scope of vocabulary and structure (e.g., personal letters and notes, pamphlets, newspapers and magazine articles, and advertisements).	pp. 2–3, *Vive les vacances!*; p. 6 TE, Teaching strategy: Challenge; **p. 8, Act. 1**; p. 12, Act. 1; **p. 14, Act. 1**; **pp. 33–35, *Info magazine: L'importance du "look"***; **p. 41, *Et vous?***; pp. 71–72, *Info magazine: Les passe-temps actifs*; pp. 82–83, *Info magazine: Le travail, ça paie!*; pp. 109–111, ***Info magazine: Oui à la nature!***; p. 142 TE, Teaching strategy: Expansion; pp. 187–188, *Info magazine: La Passion des voyages*; p. 199 TE, Teaching strategy: Groups; p. 321 TE, Inclusion; p. 383 TE, Teaching strategy; p. PA10, *Unité* 9 Pair Act.
Course Requirement FL.A.2.3.3	Formulate and answer questions about the literary elements (e.g., plot, characters, main ideas, and supporting details) of authentic target-language literary selections.	pp. 28–30, *Avez-vous compris?*; p. 31, *Expression orale: Discussion*; **p. 31, *Expression écrite: Les trois neveux, Jules Larivière***; pp. 57–59, *Avez-vous compris?*; p. 94, *Avez-vous compris?*; p. 96, *Avez-vous compris?*; **p. 97, *Expression orale: Discussion***; pp. 136–138, *Avez-vous compris?*; **p. 139, *Expression écrite: Le sens de l'humour***; pp. 171–174, *Avez-vous compris?*; pp. 211–214, *Avez-vous compris?*; p. 215, *Expression écrite: Le rapport de l'inspecteur de police*; pp. 247–250, *Avez-vous compris?*; p. 257 TE, Teaching strategies; pp. 283–290, *Avez-vous compris?*; pp. 328–332, *Avez-vous compris?*; p. 332, *Expression orale: La morale de l'histoire*; **pp. 367–370, *Avez-vous compris?***; pp. 405–408, *Avez-vous compris?*

STANDARD 3	The student presents information, concepts, and ideas to an audience of listeners or readers on a variety of topics.	
Benchmark FL.A.3.4.1	The student effectively communicates orally in the target language regarding a past, present, or future event.	
Course Requirement FL.A.3.4.1	Effectively communicate orally in the target language regarding a past, present, or future event.	p. 13, Acts. 2–3; p. 14 TE, Teaching strategy: Oral/Aural Practice; p. 15, Act. 3; **p. 16, Act. 1**; p. 18, Act. 4; p. 43, Act. 2; p. 45, Act. 4; p. 51, Act. 2; p. 76, Act. 3; p. 116, Acts. 5–6; p. 117, Acts. 8–9; p. 118, Act. 10; p. 119, Act. 14; p. 125, Act. 1; p. 128, Act. 1; p. 129, Act. 2; **p. 130, Acts. 5–6**; p. 132, Acts. 8–10; p. 154, Acts. 2–3; p. 199, Acts. 1–2; p. 202, Act. 2; **p. 205, Acts. 7–8**; p. 207, Act. 12; p. 234, Act. 1; **p. 309, Acts. 2–4**; p. 361, Act. 2; **p. 391, Acts. 8–9**; p. PA4, *Unité* 3 Pair Act.

SUNSHINE STATE STANDARDS		COMMUNICATION
Benchmark FL.A.3.4.2	The student communicates in writing using a variety of vocabulary for past, present, and future events and feelings about those events (e.g., by writing a letter to a native speaker of the target language.)	
Course Requirement FL.A.3.3.1	**Write various types of texts (e.g., simple letters and essays) for a defined audience (e.g., teacher, peers, or pen pal) about topics of personal interest or experience (in terms of, e.g., ideas, opinions, attitudes, and feelings).**	p. 31, *Expression écrite: L'héritage*; **p. 41, *Expression écrite***; p. 45, Act. 5; p. 47, *Expression écrite*; p. 59, *Expression écrite: Un peu d'humour*; p. 73, *Et vous?: Expression écrite*; p. 80, Act. 4; p. 97, *Expression écrite: En famille*; **p. 110, *Et vous?: Expression écrite***; p. 123, *Et vous?: Expression écrite*; p. 154, Act. 1; p. 175, *Expression écrite: Imaginons un peu*; p. 188, *Et vous?: Composition*; p. 189, *Et vous?: Composition*; p. 203, Act. 5; p. 206, Act. 11; **p. 215, *Expression écrite: Article de journal***; p. 233, Act. 3; p. 237, Act. 9; p. 251, *Expression écrite: Une étrange aventure*; **p. 277, *Et vous? Expression écrite***; p. 284 TE, Teaching strategy: Expansion; p. 291, *Expression écrite: Notice nécrologique*; p. 315, Act. 4; p. 317, Act. 8; **p. 333, *Expression écrite: Sujets de composition***; p. 339 TE, Student portfolios; p. 359, *Et vous?: Expression écrite*; p. 361, Act. 4; p. 371, *Expression écrite: Une autre conclusion*
Course Requirement FL.A.3.3.2	**Provide information in spoken and written form on a variety of topics of personal, academic, and cultural interest (e.g., descriptions of popular or historical characters, expressions of opinion, personal conclusions about general-interest topics, and comparisons and contrasts between the target culture and his or her own culture).**	p. 3, *À votre tour*; **p. 5, Act. 3**; p. 7, Act. 1; p. 9, Acts. 2–3; p. 18, Act. 3; p. 35, *Et vous?*; p. 37, Acts. 1–2; p. 38, Act. 1; p. 41, *Expression orale*; p. 43, Act. 1; p. 47, *À votre tour*; p. 49, Act. 1; **p. 53, Acts. 1–2**; p. 55, Act. 3; p. 72, *Et vous?*; p. 73, *Et vous?: Expression orale*; p. 75, Act. 1; p. 76, Act. 2; p. 80, Act. 5; p. 81, Act. 6; **p. 83, *Et vous?: Expression orale***; p. 86, Acts. 2–3; p. 89, Acts. 7, 9–11; p. 91, Act. 2; p. 110, *Et vous?: Expression orale*; p. 111, *Et vous?*; p. 113, Act. 1; p. 121, *Et vous?*; p. 123, *Et vous?: Débat*; p. 127, Act. 3; p. 139, *Expression orale: Expérience personelle*; p. 150, *Situations*; p. 190, Act. 1; p. 200, Act. 5; p. 214, *Et vous?*; p. 232, Act. 1; p. 235, Act. 2; p. 237, Act. 8; p. 251, *Expression orale: Débat*; **p. 261, *Et vous?***; p. 275, Act. 7; p. 281, Act. 4; p. 301 TE, Teaching strategy; p. 305 TE, Teaching strategy; p. 311, *Et vous?*; p. 315, Act. 3; p. 317, Acts. 7, 9; p. 325, Act. 6; p. 346 TE, Teaching strategy; p. 347, *Et vous?*; **p. 348, Act. 1**; p. 349, Act. 2; p. 351, Act. 4; p. 354, Act. 5; p. 356, Act. 9; p. 359, *Et vous?: Expression orale*; p. 361, Act. 1; p. 363, Act. 4; p. 371, *Expression écrite: Frédéric Cottet*; **p. 384, *Et vous?***; p. 385, *Et vous?*; p. 387, Acts. 1–2; p. 388, Act. 3; p. 391, Act. 10; p. 395, Act. 3; p. PA2, *Unité* 1 Pair Act.

| Course Requirement FL.A.3.4.2 | Communicate in writing using a variety of vocabulary for past, present, and future events and feelings about those events (e.g., by writing a letter to a native speaker of the target language). | p. 7, Act. 2; p. 12 TE, Teaching strategy: Warm-up; p. 31, *Expression écrite: Le testament*; p. 51, Acts. 3–4; **p. 59, *Expression écrite: Une lettre***; p. 83, *Et vous?: Expression écrite*; p. 97, *Expression écrite: D'un autre point de vue*; p. 115, Acts. 3–4; p. 130, Act. 4; p. 139, *Expression écrite: Une lettre, Le rapport du gardien*; **p. 175, *Expression écrite: Page de journal***; p. 194, *Et vous?: Composition*; p. 215, *Expression écrite: Journal d'un prisonnier*; p. 239, *Expression écrite*; p. 273, Acts. 4–5; p. 291, *Expression écrite: Journal intime, Lettre d'adieu*; p. 321, *Et vous?: Expression écrite*; **p. 333, *Expression écrite: Lettre à une ami(e)***; **p. 353, Act. 4**; p. 371, *Expression écrite: Une lettre*; **p. 384, *Expression écrite***; p. 393, *Expression écrite*; p. 409, *Expression écrite* |

STANDARD 1	The student demonstrates an understanding of the relationship between the perspectives and products of culture studied and uses this knowledge to recognize cultural practices.

Benchmark FL.B.1.4.1	The student interacts in a variety of situations that reflect the activities of teenagers in the target culture, using appropriate verbal and nonverbal communication.

| Course Requirement FL.B.1.3.2 | Participate in age-appropriate cultural activities (e.g., sports-related activities, music, television, and games). | p. 31, *Expression orale: Dramatisation, Situations*; p. 59, *Expression orale*; p. 97, *Expression orale: Dramatisation, Situations*; **p. 175, *Expression orale: Dramatisation***; **p. 183 TE, Teaching strategy: Expansion**; p. 215, *Expression orale: Dramatisation, Situations*; **p. 227, *Et vous?***; p. 251, *Expression orale: Situations*; p. 291, *Expression orale: Dramatisation, Situations*; p. 333, *Expression orale: Situations*; **p. 371, *Expression orale: Situations***; p. 409, *Expression orale: Situations* |
| Course Requirement FL.B.1.4.1 | Interact in a variety of situations that reflect the activities of teenagers in the target culture, using appropriate verbal and nonverbal communication. | p. 49, *Conversations libres*; p. 83, *Et vous?: Expression orale*; **p. 85, *Conversations libres***; p. 113, *Conversations libres*; p. 127, *Conversations libres*; p. 151 TE, Teaching strategy: Dialog development; **p. 155, *Conversations libres***; p. 167, Act. 2; **p. 175, *Expression orale: Situations***; p. 227, *Et vous?*; p. 233, *Conversations libres*; p. 269, *Conversations libres*; **p. 307, *Conversations libres***; **p. 319, Acts. 10–11**; p. 385, *Expression orale*; p. 397, *Conversations libres*; p. PA8, *Unité* 7 Pair Act. |

SUNSHINE STATE STANDARDS — CULTURE

Benchmark FL.B.1.4.2	The student identifies and discusses various patterns of behavior or interaction and the values and mindsets typical of youth in the target culture.	
Course Requirement FL.B.1.3.3	**Recognize simple themes, ideas, or viewpoints on social behavior or social interaction in various settings (e.g., school, family, and immediate community).**	p. 262 TE, Teaching strategy: Warm-up; p. 276 TE, Teaching strategy; p. 300 TE, Teaching strategy; p. 345 TE, Teaching strategy; p. 347, *Et vous?*
Course Requirement FL.B.1.4.2	**Identify and discuss various patterns of behavior or interaction and the values and mindsets typical of youth in the target culture.**	p. 34 TE, Teaching strategy: Warm-up; p. 41, *Et vous?*; p. 73, *Et vous?: Expression écrite*; p. 298, *Djamila ou le dilemme de l'intégration*; p. 348 TE, Teaching suggestion: Video/DVD Program; p. 349 TE, Teaching strategy: Warm-up; p. 385, *Et vous?*
Benchmark FL.B.1.4.3	The student identifies and discusses various aspects of the target culture (e.g., social and political institutions and laws).	
Course Requirement FL.B.1.3.4	**Identify and discuss various aspects of the target culture (e.g., educational systems or institutions, means of transportation, and various rules).**	p. 20, *Faits culturels*; p. 194, *Et vous?: Discussion*; p. 195, *Questions*; p. 261 TE, *Débats*; p. 384, *Expression orale*
Benchmark FL.B.1.4.4	The student identifies and discusses artistic expressions and forms of the target culture (e.g., books, periodicals, videos, commercials, music, dance, design, and art).	
Course Requirement FL.B.1.3.5	**Know various expressive forms of the target culture such as popular music, dance, children's magazines, comic books, children's literature, and common or everyday artwork (e.g., designs typical of the culture and used in clothing, pottery, ceramics, paintings, and architectural structures) and the influence of these forms on the larger community.**	**p. 62 TE, Teaching strategy: Groups**; p. 68 TE, Teaching strategy: Games; **p. 100 TE, Teaching suggestion: Video/DVD program**; p. 139, *Expression écrite: Le sens de l'humour*; **p. 176 TE, Teaching strategy: Cultural connection**; p. 222 TE, Teaching strategy: Expansion; p. 256 TE, Teaching strategy; p. 340 TE, Teaching note, Teaching strategy; p. 381 TE, Teaching strategy; **p. 419 TE, Teaching strategy**

STANDARD 1	The student reinforces and furthers knowledge of other disciplines through foreign language.	
Benchmark FL.C.1.4.1	The student conducts research on a topic of interest from an academic discipline (e.g., an event, a historical figure, or a scientific concept) using a variety of target-language sources (e.g., print, audio, and CD-ROM).	
Course Requirement FL.C.1.3.1	Use new information from a target language class (e.g., knowledge gained through a film or discussion in language class) to enhance study of a topic in another class.	p. 11 TE, Teaching strategy: Expansion; p. 20, *Faits culturels*; p. 21, *Situations culturelles*; **p. 62 TE, Teaching strategy: Groups**; p. 105 TE, Teaching strategy: Expansion; p. 107 TE, Teaching strategy: Game; **p. 110, *Et vous?: Expression orale***; p. 120, Teaching strategy; p. 194 TE, Interdisciplinary connection: Mathematics; **p. 216 TE, Interdisciplinary/Community Connections**; p. 263, *Le savez-vous?*; p. 303, *Et vous?*; p. 310 TE, Interdisciplinary/ Community Connections; p. 393, *Et vous?: Curriculum vitae*; p. 416 TE, Teaching strategy; **p. 417 TE, Teaching strategy: Interdisciplinary/Community Connections**
Course Requirement FL.C.1.3.2	Use sources in the target language to assemble specific information about topics of personal interest in connection with ideas being studied in another class.	p. 115 TE, Student portfolios; p. 140 TE, Interdisciplinary/ Community Connections; p. 263, *Le Savez-vous?*; p. 296 TE, Teaching strategy: Projects; p. 401 TE, Interdisciplinary/ Community Connections: Art/Music
STANDARD 2	The student acquires information and perspectives that are available only through the foreign language and within the target culture.	
Benchmark FL.C.2.4.1	The student uses research information as a basis for expressing opinions that reflect knowledge of the target culture.	
Course Requirement FL.C.2.2.1	Use information from a story being studied in the target language and connect elements from the story (e.g., color symbolism, geographic setting, and genre characteristics) to similar life situations.	p. 56, *Avant de lire*; **p. 92, Teaching strategy**; p. 120, Teaching strategy; p. 146 TE, Teaching strategy: Expansion; p. 170, *Avant de lire*; **p. 246, *Avant de lire***; p. 250 TE, Teaching strategies; p. 254 TE, Teaching strategy; **p. 282, *Anticipons un peu!***; p. 331, *Et vous?*; p. 371, *Expression orale: Débat: L'amour éternel*; p. 381 TE, Teaching strategy; p. 402, *Avant de lire*
Benchmark FL.C.2.4.3	The student uses target-language skills to obtain information and perspectives from speakers of the target language.	
Course Requirement FL.C.2.4.3	Use target-language skills to obtain information and perspectives from speakers of the target language.	p. 155 TE, Teaching suggestion; p. 203 TE, Expansion: Activity 4; p. 207 TE, Interdisciplinary/Community Connections: Technology; p. 229, *Comment lire le Guide Michelin*; p. 365 TE, Interdisciplinary/Community Connections: Technology

SUNSHINE STATE STANDARDS		CONNECTIONS
Benchmark FL.C.2.4.4	The student uses target-language sources (e.g., members of the target culture) to obtain information (in person or via the Internet) about a hobby, sport, or topic of personal, community, or world interest.	
Course Requirement FL.C.2.3.1	**Use the target language to establish contact with members of the target culture (e.g., to obtain information about a hobby, sport, or topic of general interest).**	p. 115 TE, Expansion: Activity 4; p. 203 TE, Expansion: Activity 4; p. 365 TE, Interdisciplinary/Community Connections: Technology & Community; p. 401 TE, Interdisciplinary/Community Connections: Community
Course Requirement FL.C.2.4.4	**Use target-language sources (e.g., members of the target culture) to obtain information (in person or via the Internet) about a hobby, sport, or topic of personal, community, or world interest.**	p. 6 TE, Expansion; p. 49 TE, Teaching suggestion; p. 110 TE, Expansion: *Expression écrite*; p. 300 TE, Additional information; p. 365 TE, Interdisciplinary/Community Connections: Community
Benchmark FL.C.2.4.5	The student uses the target language to access, process, and discuss information that is only available through the target language or within the target culture (e.g., by using technology such as databases and CD-ROMs produced in the target language or consulting target-language sources to gain information on a topic of personal, community, or global concern).	
Course Requirement FL.C.2.2.4	**Restate and share information acquired from written texts in the context of a group discussion.**	**p. 31, *Expression orale: Discussion***; p. 72 TE, General teaching strategy: *Info magazines*; p. 97, *Expression orale: Discussion*; **p. 188, *Et vous?: Discussion***; p. 189, *Et vous?: Sujet de discussion*; **p. 251, *Expression orale: Discussion***; p. 286 TE, Teaching strategy; p. 291, *Expression orale: Sujets de discussion*; **p. 333, *Expression orale: Débat***; p. 368 TE, Teaching strategy; p. 393, *Et vous?*; p. 402 TE, Teaching strategy
Course Requirement FL.C.2.3.2	**Use the target language to gain access to information and perspectives that are only available through the target language or within the target culture (e.g., target-language tourism publications or target-language sources about the target-language community).**	p. 4, Act. 2; p. 14, Act. 1; p. 189, *Et vous?: Sujet de discussion*; p. 229, *Et vous?*; p. 300 TE: Teaching strategy; p. 359, *Comment se sont-ils rencontrés?*
Course Requirement FL.C.2.3.3	**Use films or texts produced in the target language to gain knowledge and understanding of various aspects of the arts, music, literature, history, or economics of the target culture.**	p. 142 TE, Teaching note; p. 251, *Expression écrite: Un peu d'histoire*; p. 259 TE, Teaching strategy; p. 333, *Expression écrite: La Belle époque*; p. 343 TE, Teaching note; p. 378 TE, Teaching strategy; p. 416 TE, Teaching strategy; p. 417 TE, Teaching strategy

STANDARD 1	The student recognizes that languages have different patterns of communication and applies this knowledge to his or her own culture.	
Benchmark FL.D.1.4.1	The student knows elements of the target language that signify time, and the similarities and differences between comparable linguistic markers in the target language and in his or her own language.	
Course Requirement FL.D.1.4.1	**Know elements of the target language that signify time, and the similarities and differences between comparable linguistic markers in the target language and in his or her own language.**	p. 19 TE, Inclusion; p. 96 TE, Teaching strategy; p. 119, Acts. 12–13; p. 128 TE, Teaching strategy: Warm-up; p. 133, Act. 11; p. 206, Act. 10
Benchmark FL.D.1.4.2	The student understands and applies the target-language pronunciation, intonation, stress patterns, and writing conventions in a variety of contexts.	
Course Requirement FL.D.1.3.2	**Identify and use typical patterns of communication in the target language (e.g., cognates and syntax variations) both orally and in written form.**	p. 23 TE, Inclusion; p. 73 TE, Teaching strategy: Challenge; p. 79, Acts. 1–2; p. 80 TE, Inclusion; p. 86 TE, Teaching strategy: Warm-up; **p. 88 TE, Teaching strategy: Warm-up**; p. 139, *Expression orale: Situations*; **p. 157, Acts. 1, 3**; p. 163, Acts. 1, 4; p. 165, Act. 7; p. 165, Act. 7; **p. 172 TE, Teaching strategy: Expansion**; p. 182 TE, Teaching strategy: Challenge; p. 193, Acts. 1–2; p. 205, Act. 6; p. 235, Act. 4; p. 236, Act. 5; p. 243, Act. 2; p. 271, Acts. 1–2; **p. 275, Act. 6**; p. 281, Act. 3; p. 314, Act. 1; p. 316, Act. 5; p. 323, Act. 1; p. 324, Act. 4; p. 325, Acts. 7–8; p. 352, Act. 1; p. 353, Acts. 2–3; p. 355, Act. 6; p. 356, Act. 10; p. 362, Act. 2; p. 363, Act. 3; p. 365, Act. 6; p. 367 TE, Inclusion; **p. 388, Act. 1**; p. 389, Act. 4; p. 390, Act. 6; p. 399, Acts. 1–2; p. 401, Acts. 7–8
Benchmark FL.D.1.4.3	The student recognizes how languages differ in the way they can be used to communicate similar ideas (e.g., through oral, written, or artistic expression).	
Course Requirement FL.D.1.3.1	**Understand how idiomatic expressions have an impact on communication and reflect culture, by using them correctly in both oral and written form.**	p. 39, Act. 3; p. 55, Acts. 2, 4; p. 169, Acts. 1–2

SUNSHINE STATE STANDARDS		COMPARISONS
STANDARD 2	**The student recognizes that cultures have different patterns of interaction and applies this knowledge to his or her own culture.**	
Benchmark FL.D.2.4.1	The student uses the target language to discuss how aspects of the target culture are reflected in his or her own culture.	
Course Requirement FL.D.2.3.1	**Understand cultural traditions and celebrations that exist in the target culture and in the native culture (e.g., holidays, birthdays, "coming of age" celebrations, and recreational gatherings).**	p. 96 TE, *Note culturelle*; p. 150, *Situations*; p. 151 TE, Teaching strategy: Dialog development; pp. 358–359, *Le mariage en France*; p. 359, *Et vous?: Discussion*
Benchmark FL.D.2.4.3	The student demonstrates knowledge and understanding of the similarities and differences between his or her own culture and the target culture as represented in the media and/or literature.	
Course Requirement FL.D.2.3.2	**Recognize the similarities and differences between music and songs from the target culture and those in the native culture.**	p. 176 TE, Teaching strategy: Cultural connection; p. 181 TE, Teaching suggestion & Teaching strategy: Community connections; p. 223 TE, Teaching strategy; p. 418 TE, Teaching suggestion
Course Requirement FL.D.2.3.3	**Recognize the similarities and differences between attitudes about various topics found among teenagers in American culture and attitudes among teenagers in the target culture (e.g., surveys conducted through face-to-face contact or written exchanges).**	p. 34 TE, Teaching strategy: Warm-up; p. 41, *Et vous?*; p. 121 TE, Teaching strategy: Expansion; p. 188 TE, Teaching strategy: Cultural comparisons; p. 345 TE, Teaching strategy
Benchmark FL.D.2.4.4	The student recognizes the contributions of other parallel cultures (e.g., Native American, African, and European) to the target culture.	
Course Requirement FL.D.2.3.4	**Understand selected economic, political, and social events that have shaped the target culture and its relationship with the United States across time.**	pp. 410–416, *L'histoire franco-américaine en dix questions*; p. 414 TE, *Notes historiques*; p. 417, *Villes américaines–noms français*; p. 417 TE, Teaching strategy: Interdisciplinary/ Community Connections; p. 418, *Les héritiers de la Louisiane française*
Course Requirement FL.D.2.4.4	**Recognize the contributions of other parallel cultures (e.g., Native American, African, and European) to the target culture.**	p. 298, *L'influence maghrébine en France*; p. 300 TE, Teaching strategy; p. 336, *Deux Martiniquais célèbres & Qu'est-ce que la négritude?*; p. 379, *L'art africain*; p. 419 TE, *Notes culturelles*

STANDARD 1	The student uses the language within and beyond the school setting.
Benchmark FL.E.1.4.1	The student understands that knowing more than one language allows people to function effectively in multilingual communities.

Course Requirement FL.E.1.4.1	**Understand that knowing more than one language allows people to function effectively in multilingual communities.**	p. 281 TE, Interdisciplinary/Community Connections: Social Studies & Community; p. 401 TE, Interdisciplinary/Community Connections: Science & Technology; p. 418 TE, Teaching suggestion: Video/DVD Program

Benchmark FL.E.1.4.2	The student knows the benefits that being able to communicate in more than one language can have on one's career.

Course Requirement FL.E.1.3.2	**Know professional organizations or individuals who use the target language (e.g., foreign consulates, corporations, and educational institutions) that he or she could contact to request information about possible employment opportunities.**	p. 293 TE, Teaching suggestion; p. 392 TE, Teaching suggestion; p. 401 TE, Interdisciplinary/Community Connections: Language Arts, Math, Social Studies, & Community
Course Requirement FL.E.1.4.2	**Know the benefits that being able to communicate in more than one language can have on one's career.**	p. 45, Act. 5; p. 91 TE, Interdisciplinary/Community Connections; p. 125 TE, Teaching suggestions: Warm-up; pp. 392–393, *Comment se présenter à une entrevue*; p. 397, *Conversations libres*

Discovering FRENCH Nouveau!

Florida Comprehensive Assessment Test

FCAT Support by Unit

The strategies and activities listed in the chart below will support success on the Florida Comprehensive Assessment Test. All units support the development of reading, writing, and grammar skills.

	Reading	Writing
Reprise		
	Vive les vacances!, pp. 2–3 *Lettre de Valérie*, p. 6 **Lecture** *Les trois bagues*, pp. 27–30	*À votre avis*, p. 3 *Activité 2, Une lettre à Valérie*, p. 7 **Lecture** *Expression écrite*, p. 31
Unité 1		
	L'importance du «Look», pp. 33–34 *Les visages de la beauté*, p. 35 *Entre nous*, pp. 40–41 *À la Résidence Bon Repos*, pp. 46–47 **Lecture** *Conte pour enfants de moins de trois ans* pp. 56–59 **Interlude culturel: Le monde des arts** *La Révolution impressionniste*, pp. 60–61 *Claude Monet: le peintre de la lumière*, pp. 62–63 *Après l'Impressionnisme*, pp. 64–65 *Le surréalisme*, pp. 66–67 *La fourmi*, p. 67 *Pour faire le portrait d'un oiseau*, p. 68 *L'art dans la rue*, p. 69	*Et vous?*, p. 35 *Activité 2*, p. 37 *Expression écrite*, p. 41 *À votre tour*, p. 47 *Expression écrite*, p. 47 *Activité 4, Ma routine personnelle*, p. 51 **Lecture** *Expression écrite*, p. 59

	Reading	Writing
Unité 4		
	En France, faites comme les Français!, pp. 150–151 *Scènes de la vie courante*, p. 151 **Lecture** *Une histoire de cheveux*, pp. 170–175 **Interlude culturel: Vive la musique!** *L'histoire de la chanson française*, pp. 176–177 *Les vedettes d'hier*, pp. 177–178 *Les vedettes d'aujourd'hui*, p. 179 *La musique des jeunes*, pp. 180–181 *La musique francophone en Amérique*, p. 183 *Une chanson: Mon pays*, p. 183 *Et la musique classique?*, pp. 184–185	*Situations*, p. 150 **Lecture** *Expression écrite*, p. 175
Unité 5		
	La Passion des voyages, pp. 187–188 *Impressions d'Amérique*, p. 189 *La France en train*, p. 194 *L'Eurotunnel*, p. 195 **Lecture** *Le mystérieux homme en bleu*, pp. 208–215 **Interlude culturel: Les grands moments de l'histoire de France (1715–1870)** *Les dates*, p. 216 *Les événements*, p. 216 *Les personnes*, p. 217 *L'héritage de la Révolution*, pp. 218–221 *L'histoire de la «Marseillaise»*, pp. 222–223 *Documents: «Les Misérables»*, pp. 224–225	*Composition*, p. 188 *Composition: Une lettre*, p. 189 *Composition: Une lettre*, p. 194 *Activité 11, Bienvenue chez nous!*, p. 206 **Lecture** *Et vous?*, p. 214 *Expression écrite*, p. 215
Unité 6		
	Les jeunes touristes en France, p. 227 *Le Guide Michelin*, pp. 228–229 *À l'Hôtel de la Plage*, pp. 238–239 **Lecture** *Une étrange aventure*, pp. 246–251	*Et vous?*, p. 229 *Activité 3, Une lettre de réservation*, p. 233 *Activité 9, Au Syndicat d'Initiative*, p. 237 *Expression écrite*, p. 239 **Lecture** *Expression écrite*, p. 251

Reprise

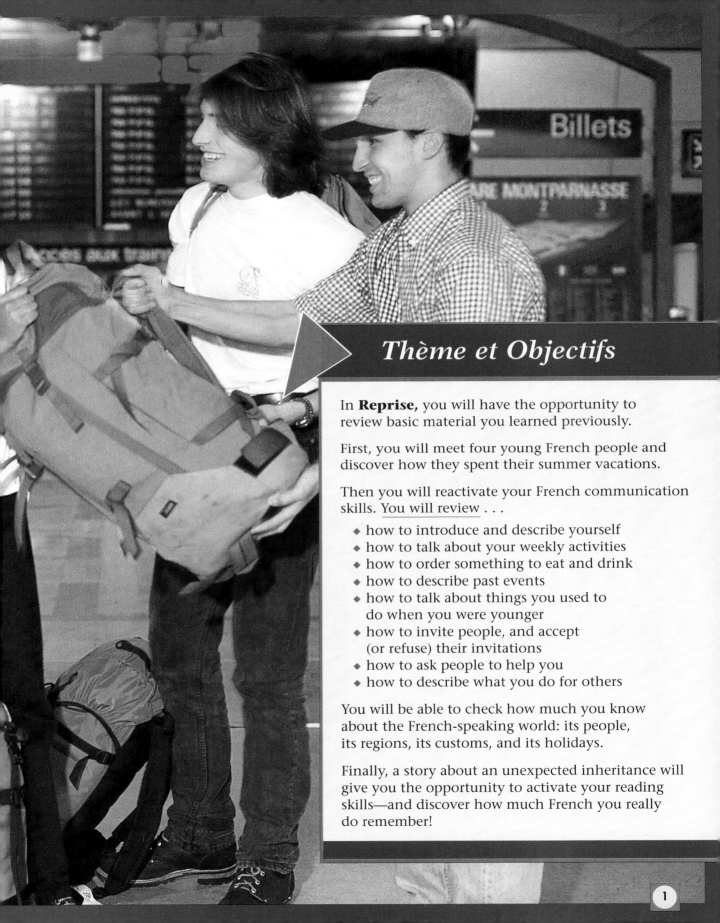

Thème et Objectifs

In **Reprise,** you will have the opportunity to review basic material you learned previously.

First, you will meet four young French people and discover how they spent their summer vacations.

Then you will reactivate your French communication skills. You will review . . .

◆ how to introduce and describe yourself
◆ how to talk about your weekly activities
◆ how to order something to eat and drink
◆ how to describe past events
◆ how to talk about things you used to do when you were younger
◆ how to invite people, and accept (or refuse) their invitations
◆ how to ask people to help you
◆ how to describe what you do for others

You will be able to check how much you know about the French-speaking world: its people, its regions, its customs, and its holidays.

Finally, a story about an unexpected inheritance will give you the opportunity to activate your reading skills—and discover how much French you really do remember!

Vive les vacances!...

C'est la rentrée. Quatre jeunes Français (deux garçons et deux filles) parlent de ce qu'ils ont fait pendant les vacances.

Jean-Michel Renaudin (15 ans et demi)

Comme d'habitude,° j'ai passé les vacances avec ma famille. Chaque année, nous allons dans un endroit différent. Cette année, nous sommes allés à Sanary-sur-Mer où nous avons fait du camping. J'ai fait un stage° dans un club de planche à voile. À la fin° du stage, j'ai participé à un championnat et je suis arrivé troisième. Pas mal pour un débutant!°

comme d'habitude *as usual* **faire un stage** = *suivre des leçons*
la fin *end* **un débutant** *beginner*

Ali Belkacem (18 ans)

Je suis allé au Québec avec un programme d'échange. Nous étions quatre Français dans notre groupe. Nous avons passé les deux premières semaines à la ferme Pouliot sur l'Île d'Orléans. Là, on a cueilli° les framboises et on a fait la récolte° du maïs.° (On dit «blé° d'Inde» en québécois.)

Après notre séjour° sur l'Île d'Orléans, nous avons visité la ville de Québec où nous avons loué° un camping-car. Puis, nous avons fait le tour de la Gaspésie. Partout nous avons été accueillis° dans les familles québécoises. Les Québécois sont vraiment des gens formidables!° J'espère bien retourner un jour dans la «Belle Province»!

cueillir *to pick* **faire la récolte** *to harvest* **le maïs** *corn* **blé** *wheat*
un séjour *stay* **louer** *to rent* **être accueilli** = *être invité* **formidable** *great, terrific*

FLASH d'information

Sanary-sur-Mer
C'est une petite ville de la Côte d'Azur° située près de Toulon.

Le Jura
Le Jura est une région montagneuse située à l'est de la France.

La Gaspésie
C'est une région située à l'est de la province de Québec. Cette région est connue° pour ses petits villages de pêcheurs° et son parc naturel.

L'Auvergne
C'est une région du centre de la France, célèbre pour ses volcans, ses stations thermales,° ses eaux minérales, ses chapelles romanes et ses vieux châteaux.

la Côte d'Azur *French Riviera [blue coast]*
connu(e) *known* **un pêcheur** *fisherman*
une station thermale *hot springs resort*

Laurence Legarec (16 ans et demi)

J'ai passé l'été en Auvergne avec les «Chantiers° Histoire et Architecture Médiévales». C'est une organisation qui recrute des volontaires pour restaurer les monuments anciens. Le projet de notre groupe était de restaurer une chapelle romane du XIIe siècle.°

D'abord, on a reconstruit° un mur° qui tombait en ruines. Puis, on a refait le toit°. Le travail était dur, c'est vrai, mais il y avait beaucoup d'avantages. Pour moi, l'avantage principal de cette expérience a été de faire la connaissance° de jeunes d'autres pays européens. Notre groupe était, en effet, très international. Il y avait des Allemands, des Belges, des Hollandais, des Anglais . . . et un jeune Italien très sympathique avec qui je continue à correspondre!

un chantier *worksite*   **un siècle** = 100 ans
reconstruire *to rebuild*   **un mur** *wall*   **le toit** *roof*
faire la connaissance = rencontrer

Valérie Laroze (17 ans)

En juillet je suis restée chez moi. En août, je suis allée dans le Jura où j'ai travaillé comme animatrice° dans une colonie de vacances pour jeunes handicapés mentaux. Nous étions trois animatrices pour accompagner un groupe de vingt jeunes.

Chaque jour, on faisait une randonnée° de 10 à 15 kilomètres dans la montagne. Pendant les haltes, on étudiait la faune° locale. (Je devais° être bien préparée, parce que les jeunes voulaient tout connaître sur les animaux et les oiseaux de la région.) Le soir, j'organisais des activités et des jeux pour le groupe.

Pour moi qui habite dans une grande ville, j'ai bien profité de ces vacances en plein air.° Mais surtout, en aidant ces jeunes handicapés à avoir une vie° normale, j'ai fait un travail utile et intéressant. Et en plus,° j'ai gagné un peu d'argent!

une animatrice *counselor*   **une randonnée** *long hike*   **la faune** = les animaux
je devais *I had to*   **en plein air** = dans la nature   **une vie** *life*   **en plus** *in addition*

À votre avis *(In your opinion)*

Avec un(e) ou plusieurs partenaires, discutez des questions suivantes.

◆ Qui a fait le voyage le plus long?
◆ Qui a passé les vacances les plus intéressantes? Pourquoi?
◆ Qui a fait la chose la plus utile? Pourquoi?
◆ Vous avez la possibilité de passer les vacances comme ces quatre jeunes Français. Qu'est-ce que vous choisissez de faire? Pourquoi?

À votre tour!

Maintenant parlez de vos vacances.
1. Êtes-vous resté(e) chez vous ou avez-vous fait un voyage? Si vous avez fait un voyage, où êtes-vous allé(e)? Avec qui? Combien de temps êtes-vous resté(e) là-bas? Qu'est-ce que vous avez vu?
2. Est-ce que vous vous êtes reposé(e) ou est-ce que vous avez travaillé? Si vous avez travaillé, quel travail avez-vous fait? Où? Est-ce que vous avez gagné de l'argent?
3. Qu'est-ce que vous avez fait d'intéressant?
4. Qu'est-ce que vous avez fait d'utile?

Rappel ① Bonjour!

1 À l'Institut de Touraine

L'Institut de Touraine est une école où beaucoup d'étudiants viennent apprendre le français en été. Vous allez passer un mois à l'Institut de Touraine.

Donnez oralement les renseignements demandés.

INSTITUT D'ÉTUDES FRANÇAISES
DE TOURAINE
1, Rue de la Grandière, 37000 TOURS

BULLETIN D'INSCRIPTION

Prénoms et Nom..

Né(e) le ....

à...

Nationalité:...

Profession:..

Adresse (dans le pays d'origine):................................

École ou collège d'origine:..

Nombre d'années d'étude du français:.........................

---

2 Les parents idéaux

Quelles sont les qualités les plus importantes pour la mère idéale ou le père idéal? Un magazine québécois, le *Bulletin Pacijou*, a posé cette question à des jeunes de 13 à 18 ans. Voici les résultats de cette enquête.

LA MÈRE IDÉALE: QUALITÉS ESSENTIELLES

selon les filles		selon les garçons	
compréhensive	29%	gentille	39%
gentille	29%	compréhensive	17%
attentive	15%	joyeuse	17%
confiante°	11%	généreuse	11%
tolérante	9%	patiente	8%
patiente	7%	confiante	8%

LE PÈRE IDÉAL: QUALITÉS ESSENTIELLES

selon les filles		selon les garçons	
gentil	31%	gentil	31%
compréhensif	30%	compréhensif	31%
tolérant	23%	riche et généreux	21%
affectueux	16%	drôle	17%

confiant(e) *trusting*

Maintenant faites une enquête dans votre classe:
- Quelles sont les qualités essentielles pour être la mère idéale?
- Quelles sont les qualités essentielles pour être le père idéal?

Les adjectifs réguliers et irréguliers

Révision ▶ p. R7

Pratique ▶  p. 3

3 Notre personnalité

Nous avons tous des qualités, mais nous avons aussi des petits défauts. Choisissez une des personnes suivantes (ou une autre personne de votre choix). Décrivez deux qualités—au moins—et un petit défaut de cette personne.

- moi
- mon copain
- ma copine
- mon cousin
- ma cousine
- mes profs
- mes parents
- mes voisins
- les élèves de cette classe
- ??

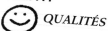

En général . . .

☺ **QUALITÉS**

actif
aimable
amusant
attentif
brillant
compréhensif
consciencieux
courageux
discret
drôle
dynamique
énergique
gentil
généreux
honnête

imaginatif
intéressant
joyeux
optimiste
organisé
patient
poli
ouvert
sensible *(sensitive)*
sérieux
spirituel *(witty)*
spontané
sympathique
tolérant
??

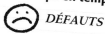

mais de temps en temps . . .

☹ **DÉFAUTS**

bête
distant
égoïste
ennuyeux
impoli
inactif
incompréhensif
indifférent
indiscret
indiscipliné
méchant

paresseux
pénible
pessimiste
prétentieux
renfermé
(uncommunicative)
sévère
stupide
timide
triste
vaniteux *(vain)*
??

Avoir et les expressions avec avoir

Révision ▶ 📖 p. R3

Pratique ▶ 📝 p. 4

▶ En général, ma cousine Élisabeth est très gentille. Elle est aussi drôle et optimiste. De temps en temps elle est un peu prétentieuse.

4 Que faire?

Choisissez une expression de la colonne A et décrivez votre situation à votre partenaire.
Votre partenaire va vous dire ce qu'il faut faire, en utilisant les suggestions de la colonne B.

J'ai chaud!

Eh bien, tu peux ouvrir la fenêtre!

A. Votre situation
- faim
- soif
- chaud
- froid
- sommeil
- besoin d'un livre
- envie de voir un film
- besoin de ??
- envie de ??

B. Conseils
- mettre un pull
- ouvrir la fenêtre
- aller au ciné
- passer à la bibliothèque
- manger un sandwich
- boire un soda
- dormir
- prendre un café
- ??

RAPPEL!

TO DESCRIBE . . .
- what you ARE GOING TO DO
- what you ARE DOING RIGHT NOW
- what you HAVE JUST DONE

USE . . .
aller + infinitive
être en train de + infinitive
venir de + infinitive

Je vais sortir.
Je suis en train de téléphoner.
Je viens de dîner.

Aller, être, venir

Révision ▶ 📖 p. R3

Pratique ▶ 📝 p. 4

Il va dîner.   Il est en train de dîner.   Il vient de dîner.

Bonjour,

Je m'appelle Valérie Dussart. J'ai 17 ans et j'habite à Lyon. Je suis élève de première au Lycée Saint-Exupéry où je prépare le bac.

J'ai beaucoup de travail, mais je ne travaille pas tout le temps. Le samedi, par exemple, est un jour que je me réserve entièrement. L'après-midi je vais en ville et je fais du shopping. Quand il y a une bonne exposition, je vais au musée. Le soir, je sors en bande° (J'ai beaucoup de copains et de copines, mais je n'ai pas de «copain» en particulier.) En général, on va voir un film. De temps en temps, on va danser dans une «boîte°».

J'ai d'autres loisirs. Je fais du théâtre depuis un an à la Maison des Jeunes. En juin, nous allons présenter «La leçon» une pièce de l'écrivain° Ionesco dans laquelle° je joue le rôle de l'Élève... Je suis° aussi des cours de danse africaine. C'est excellent pour la forme!

Pendant l'année, je n'ai pas l'occasion de faire beaucoup de sport, mais en été je me rattrape°. Ma passion, c'est la planche à voile. Il y a d'autres sports que j'aimerais faire, comme le parapente. Malheureusement, mes parents ne sont pas d'accord!

Et vous, quels sont vos loisirs préférés?

Valérie

Moi, avec mes amies.

en bande = en groupe   **une boîte** club, nightspot   **un écrivain** = une personne qui écrit
laquelle which   **suivre** to take [a class]   **se rattraper** to catch up with

J'ATTENDS MON COPAIN DEPUIS TROIS HEURES!

RAPPEL!

To describe what you <u>have</u> <u>been</u> <u>doing for</u> or <u>since</u> some time, you use:

present + **depuis** + time

Depuis

Pratique ▶  p. 5

RAPPEL!

- In French, there are three groups of regular verbs: **-er, -ir, -re**.
- **Vouloir, pouvoir, devoir** and verbs like **sortir** are irregular.
- **Faire**, an irregular verb, is used in many expressions.

Verbes réguliers

Révision ▶ p. R2

Pratique ▶ p. 6

Quelques verbes irréguliers

Révision ▶ p. R2

Pratique ▶ p. 6

Faire et expressions avec faire

Révision ▶ p. R3

Pratique ▶ p. 7

1 Et vous?

Répondez au questionnaire suivant. Si vous voulez, comparez vos réponses avec les réponses de votre partenaire ou de votre groupe.

1. À la maison, quand j'ai du temps libre *(free time)*, je préfère . . .
   - regarder la télé
   - écouter de la musique
   - lire un bon livre
   - ??

2. Quand je suis en ville, je préfère . . .
   - faire du shopping
   - faire du lèche-vitrine *(window-shopping)*
   - voir une exposition
   - ??

3. Avec mon argent, je préfère . . .
   - aller au cinéma
   - acheter des vêtements
   - acheter des CD
   - ??

4. Le samedi soir, je préfère . . .
   - sortir seul(e) *(by myself)*
   - sortir avec mes copains
   - regarder une cassette vidéo à la maison
   - ??

5. Quand je sors avec mes copains, je préfère . . .
   - assister à un concert
   - voir un film
   - aller au restaurant
   - ??

6. Pour rester en forme, je préfère . . .
   - courir
   - faire du vélo
   - faire des exercices de gymnastique
   - ??

7. L'après-midi, quand il fait beau, je préfère . . .
   - faire du jogging
   - faire du roller *(roller blades)*
   - jouer au basket
   - ??

8. Quand je suis à la plage, je préfère . . .
   - nager
   - jouer au volley
   - prendre des bains de soleil
   - ??

9. Pendant les vacances, je préfère . . .
   - faire un voyage
   - rendre visite à des amis ou à des parents
   - travailler et gagner de l'argent
   - ??

10. Je voudrais apprendre à . . .
    - jouer de la clarinette
    - faire du parapente
    - piloter un avion
    - ??

2 Une lettre à Valérie

Écrivez une lettre à Valérie où vous expliquez . . .
- qui vous êtes
- à quelle école vous allez
- ce que vous faites le samedi
- quels sont vos loisirs
- quels sports vous pratiquez
- ce que vous faites en été

Puis comparez votre lettre avec celle de votre partenaire.

1 Le bon choix

Regardez les illustrations pour compléter les phrases avec l'option qui convient. Soyez logique.

Nourriture et boissons

Révision ▶ p. R11

Pratique ▶ p. 8

Le Grenier de Notre Dame

RESTAURANT VÉGÉTARIEN

18, rue de la Bûcherie
75005 PARIS ☎ 01 43 29 98 29 +
Métro St. Michel   NATURESTO

On va dans ce restaurant si on aime . . .
- les légumes
- la viande de porc
- la cuisine chinoise

La Langouste

*Poissons - Fruits de mer -
Langouste - Homard - Bouillabaisse*

FORMULE HOMARD 30 euros s.c. + CARTE (ouvert dimanche)
Place des Ternes (1, av. des Ternes) - Tél. 01 43 80 15 83

Dans ce restaurant, on peut commander . . .
- du saumon grillé
- du poulet rôti
- une omelette aux champignons

IZRAEL

L'ÉPICERIE DU MONDE

PRODUITS DES AMÉRIQUES
DES INDES ET DE LA MEDITERRANÉE

Fermé en Août
30, rue François Miron - Paris 4ᵉ

01 42 72 66 23

On va dans ce magasin si on veut acheter . . .
- des côtelettes de veau
- du poivre
- des croissants

Au Prince Gourmand

pâtisserie - traiteur - réception

magasins:

122, rue Saint-Dominique 75007 PARIS - 01 45 51 68 64
2, impasse des Noisetiers-Chamblean 28500 Garnay - 02 37 42 14 93

On va dans ce magasin si on veut acheter . . .
- une tarte aux fraises
- des pommes de terre
- une douzaine d'oeufs

RAPPEL!

- To refer to things you like in general, use: **le (l'), la (l'), les.**
  J'aime le poulet, la salade, les frites.

- To refer to a CERTAIN, UNDEFINED QUANTITY or AMOUNT of something, use: **du (de l'), de la (de l'), des.**
  Je voudrais du poulet, de la salade, des frites.

Note: In negative sentences: **du, de la, des → de**
  Je ne vais pas prendre de fromage.

Les articles définis et partitifs

Révision ▶ p. R6

Pratique ▶ p. 9

② Et vous?

Répondez au questionnaire suivant. Si vous voulez, comparez vos réponses avec celles de votre partenaire ou de votre groupe.

> **Prendre** (to take, to have), **boire** (to drink)
> ___
> **Révision** ▶ p. R2; pp. R24–R29
> **Pratique** ▶ p. 10

1. Mon repas préféré est . . .
   - le petit déjeuner
   - le déjeuner
   - le dîner

2. Au petit déjeuner, je prends généralement . . .
   - des céréales
   - des oeufs
   - du pain avec du beurre et de la confiture
   - ??

3. Avec ça, je bois . . .
   - du lait
   - du chocolat chaud
   - du jus d'orange
   - ??

4. Je préfère les sandwichs avec . . .
   - du jambon
   - du fromage
   - du beurre de cacahuète *(peanut)*
   - ??

5. Quand je dîne au restaurant, je commande généralement . . .
   - de la viande
   - du poisson
   - des spaghetti
   - ??

6. En général, sur mes hamburgers, je mets . . .
   - du ketchup
   - de la moutarde
   - de la mayonnaise
   - ??

7. Mon plat favori est . . .
   - le steak-frites
   - le poulet rôti
   - le filet de sole
   - ??

8. Il y a certaines choses que je n'aime pas, par exemple, . . .
   - les brocolis
   - les carottes
   - les épinards *(spinach)*
   - ??

9. Comme dessert, je préfère manger . . .
   - de la glace
   - du gâteau au chocolat
   - de la tarte aux pommes
   - ??

10. Ma cuisine favorite est . . .
    - la cuisine italienne
    - la cuisine chinoise
    - la cuisine mexicaine
    - ??

③ À Monoprix

Votre partenaire et vous, vous faites les courses à Monoprix, un supermarché français.

Vous passez par les rayons suivants. Chacun va faire une liste des articles qu'il/elle va acheter.

Achetez deux (2) articles par rayon. Puis comparez vos listes:
- Quels produits identiques avez-vous achetés?
- Quels produits différents avez-vous choisis?

MONOPRIX

← BOISSONS	PRODUITS LAITIERS →
BOUCHERIE CHARCUTERIE FRUITS	↓	BOULANGERIE PÂTISSERIE LÉGUMES

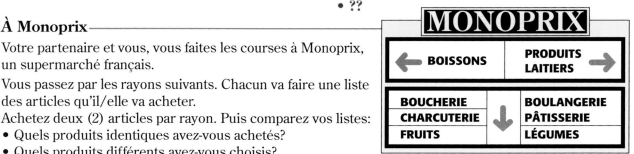

RAPPEL!

- **Y** replaces a NAME OF A PLACE introduced by **à, dans, chez . . .**

  Je vais <u>au restaurant</u>. → J'<u>y</u> vais.
  Je ne vais pas <u>chez Paul</u>. → Je n'<u>y</u> vais pas.

- **En** replaces **de, du, de la, des** + NOUN.
  Je mange <u>du pain</u>. → J'<u>en</u> mange.
  Je ne bois pas <u>de limonade</u> → Je n'<u>en</u> bois pas.

TU VEUX DU LAIT?

OUI, J'EN VEUX!

.....À votre tour! ....

Imagine you are in the following situations.
Your partner will take the role of the other person
in the dialogue and answer your questions.

4 You are visiting Quebec City with your friend. It is about one o'clock.

Ask your friend . . .
- if he/she is hungry
- if he/she feels like going to a French restaurant
- what he/she feels like eating.

1 While on an errand, you see a friend waiting at the bus stop.

Ask your friend . . .
- where he/she is going
- what he/she is going to do there
- how long he/she has been waiting for the bus.

5 You are making weekend plans with your friend.

Ask your friend . . .
- if he/she is going to go out
- what he/she is going to do
- if he/she feels like going to the movies on Sunday.

2 At a party last weekend, your friend met a French-speaking girl named Juliette. You want to know more about Juliette.

Ask your friend . . .
- how old Juliette is
- if she is French or Canadian
- what she is doing in the United States.

6 You have invited your friend for dinner next Saturday and want to find out if your friend has any special food preferences.

Ask your friend . . .
- if he/she eats meat
- what desserts he/she likes
- what he/she does not eat.

3 You are new in town and you would like some information.

Ask your friend . . .
- to which supermarket he/she goes shopping
- where he/she buys her clothes
- what sports one can do in the summer.

7 You have been invited to spend a week at the home of your French friend. You are asking about meals.

Ask your friend . . .
- at what time they have breakfast
- what they eat
- what they drink.

Rappel Culturel

**Utilisez vos connaissances du monde francophone
pour compléter les portraits suivants.**

1 Virginie habite à la Martinique. En classe elle parle français, mais avec ses copains elle parle souvent . . .

   a. créole
   b. italien
   c. espagnol
   d. alsacien

2 Nathalie est née à Bruxelles. Elle parle français, mais elle n'est pas française. Elle est de nationalité . . .

   a. belge
   b. suisse
   c. allemande
   d. luxembourgeoise

3 Aya parle français. Elle est d'Abidjan, une grande ville de 2,5 millions d'habitants. Son pays est . . .

   a. l'Algérie
   b. le Nigéria
   c. le Sénégal
   d. la Côte d'Ivoire

4 Albert Bilodeau est un homme de 60 ans. Il habite dans la paroisse d'Iberville où ses ancêtres sont venus il y a plus de deux cents ans. Albert Bilodeau comprend le français et il le parle un peu. Il adore aller aux festivals de musique «cajun» de la région. Albert Bilodeau habite . . .

   a. en Floride
   b. en Louisiane
   c. en Nouvelle-
      Angleterre
   d. dans la province
      de Québec

5 Yasmina habite en France avec sa famille. Ses parents qui sont immigrés sont d'origine algérienne. Ils pratiquent la religion de leur pays qui est la religion . . .

   a. catholique
   b. protestante
   c. bouddhiste
   d. musulmane

6 Jean-Philippe habite à Boston, mais il n'est pas américain. Il comprend le français mais il n'est pas français. Il vient d'un pays qui est une ancienne colonie française et qui est devenu indépendant en 1804. Jean-Philippe est . . .

   a. haïtien
   b. martiniquais
   c. portoricain
   d. cubain

7 Gilles habite à Montana dans une région très montagneuse. En hiver, il est moniteur de ski. Là où il habite, on parle français. À l'est, on parle un dialecte allemand. Plus à l'est, on parle italien. Gilles est . . .

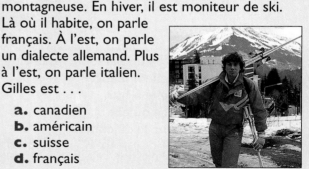

   a. canadien
   b. américain
   c. suisse
   d. français

8 Mai Van Lee vient d'un pays d'Asie où beaucoup de gens parlaient *(used to speak)* français. Il est . . .

   a. coréen
   b. vietnamien
   c. thaïlandais
   d. japonais

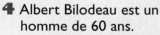

Answers: 1-a; 2-a; 3-d; 4-b; 5-d; 6-a; 7-c; 8-b

Hier et avant

Rappel Le week-end

1 Êtes-vous bon(ne) détective?

Le week-end dernier, vous avez trouvé
un portefeuille dans la rue.
Dans ce portefeuille
il n'y a pas d'argent,
mais il y a les choses
suivantes. Regardez
bien ces choses.
Pouvez-vous décrire
ce qu'a fait la personne
qui a perdu
le portefeuille?

```
** NOUVELLES GALERIES **

  COMPACT       18€
  LIVRE          9€
  TOTAL         27€

  CB 5201001190741190
  000000002809717 VIV
      ************
         MERCI
```

- Où est-ce que cette personne est allée?
- Qu'est-ce qu'elle a acheté?
- Combien a-t-elle payé chaque objet?

Chez Jacqueline

CAFÉ – RESTAURANT
21, RUE BERTHELOT
01-47-05-69-34

Table n° 4	
1 steak-frites	6€
1 salade mixte	3€
1 eau minérale	2€
Total	11€

- Où est-ce que cette personne a déjeuné?
- Qu'est-ce qu'elle a mangé?
- Qu'est-ce qu'elle a bu?
- Combien est-ce qu'elle a dépensé pour le déjeuner?

CINÉ-VOX

Festival Belmondo
Les films de la semaine

lundi-vendredi
CARTOUCHE

samedi-dimanche
L'HOMME DE RIO

Séances à 14h30 et 17h

CINÉ-VOX
ENTRÉE
7€
350717

- Où est-elle allée après le déjeuner?
- Qu'est-ce qu'elle a vu?
- À quelle heure est-ce que le film a commencé?

JE N'AI PAS ÉTUDIÉ PENDANT LES VACANCES.

RAPPEL!

To describe what people DID in the past, use the PASSÉ COMPOSÉ.

- For most verbs,
   passé composé = **avoir** + PAST PARTICIPLE
   Tu as étudié hier. Je n'ai pas étudié.

- For a few verbs like **aller**,
   passé composé = **être** + PAST PARTICIPLE
   Je suis allé(e) au cinéma.

Le passé composé des verbes réguliers avec avoir

Révision ▶ p. R4

Pratique ▶ p. 11

2 Oui ou non?

Décrivez deux choses que vous avez faites et une chose que
vous n'avez pas faite le week-end dernier. Utilisez les activités
suggérées ou d'autres activités de votre choix.

Les participes passés irréguliers

Révision ▶ p. R4

Pratique ▶ p. 12

- ■ dormir
- ■ ranger ma chambre
- ■ travailler dans le jardin
- ■ acheter des vêtements
- ■ déjeuner dans un restaurant
- ■ visiter un musée
- ■ assister à un concert
- ■ rendre visite à des copains

- ■ lire un livre
- ■ voir un film
- ■ faire des achats
- ■ avoir un rendez-vous
- ■ faire une promenade à la campagne
- ■ faire du camping
- ■ prendre des photos
- ■ ??

3 Un week-end à la campagne

Ces personnes ont passé le week-end à la campagne. Dites ce qu'elles ont fait.

RAPPEL!

To express HOW LONG AGO
you did something, use:
il y a + time

J'AI ACHETÉ MA VOITURE IL Y A 70 ANS!

Il y a

Pratique ▶ p. 12

1 Un voyage au Maroc

L'été dernier, Gabrielle a fait un voyage au Maroc avec un voyage organisé. Voici le programme de ce voyage. Regardez bien ce programme et répondez aux questions.

- Comment est-elle allée au Maroc?
- Quel jour est-elle partie?
- À quelle heure est-elle arrivée à Rabat?
- Qu'est-ce qu'elle a visité dans cette ville?
- Dans quelle ville est-elle allée ensuite?

- Qu'est-ce qu'elle a fait dans cette ville?
- Quelle est la dernière ville qu'elle a visitée?
- Qu'est-ce qu'elle a vu dans cette ville?
- Quel jour est-elle rentrée en France?
- À quelle heure a-t-elle pris son avion?
- À quelle heure est-elle arrivée à Paris?

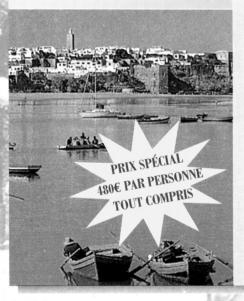

Agence Maroc-Tours

PRIX SPÉCIAL
480€ PAR PERSONNE
TOUT COMPRIS

5 jours au Maroc
✦ PROGRAMME DU VOYAGE ✦

✦ VENDREDI, 10 JUIN

matin	Départ de Paris, vol Air Maroc 104, 8h35 Arrivée à Rabat, 11h18
après-midi	Tour de Rabat en autocar

✦ SAMEDI, 11 JUIN

matin	Visite de la Kasbah Musée des Arts marocains
après-midi	Libre

✦ DIMANCHE, 12 JUIN

matin	Départ pour Fès en autobus, 8h00
après-midi	Libre

✦ LUNDI, 13 JUIN

matin	Visite guidée de Fès-el-Boli (vieille ville)
après-midi	Départ pour Marrakech en avion, 18h35

✦ MARDI, 14 JUIN

matin	Marrakech, Visite de la Médina Mosquée de la Koutoubia
après-midi	Visite des souks: shopping

✦ MERCREDI, 15 JUIN

matin	Libre
après-midi	Départ pour Paris, vol Air Maroc 121, 12h35 Arrivée à Paris, 15h21

FLASH d'information

Le Maroc est un pays de 30 millions d'habitants situé au nord-ouest de l'Afrique. La majorité des Marocains sont arabes et pratiquent la religion musulmane.

La capitale du Maroc est Rabat, mais la plus grande ville est Casablanca. Marrakech et Fès sont des villes traditionnelles avec des monuments anciens.

Ancien protectorat français, le Maroc est devenu indépendant en 1956. C'est une monarchie constitutionnelle avec un roi, le Roi Mohammed VI.

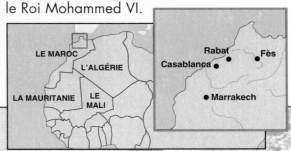

RAPPEL!

When the passé composé of a verb is formed with **être**, the past participle AGREES WITH THE SUBJECT.

> Julien **est arrivé** ce matin.
> Pauline et Claire <u>sont arrivées</u> hier soir.

Le passé composé

Révision ▶ p. R4

Pratique ▶ p. 13

---

2 Dialogues

Avec votre partenaire, composez et jouez l'un des dialogues suivants.

> Tu **as étudié** hier soir?
>
> Non, je **suis allée** au ciné.
>
> Qu'est-ce que tu **as vu**?
>
> Un film policier.

1. • rester chez toi ce week-end
   • aller à la campagne
   • faire
   • une promenade à vélo

2. • sortir avec ton copain samedi
   • faire des achats
   • acheter
   • un blouson

3. • rentrer chez toi à midi
   • déjeuner au restaurant
   • manger
   • ??

4. • venir à la boum dimanche
   • aller au théâtre
   • voir
   • ??

---

3 Pendant les vacances

Pendant les vacances, ces personnes ont fait des choses différentes. Avec un(e) partenaire, choisissez une des illustrations et décrivez-la ensemble. Faites trois ou quatre phrases et utilisez votre imagination.

Où sont allées les personnes? Qu'est-ce qu'elles ont fait?

Paul et Robert

Juliette

Monsieur Ramirez

Alice et Julien

Caroline

Cécile et Sophie

Thomas

Olivier

Rappel ⬥6⬥ Qu'est-ce qui se passe?

1 Plus de peur que de mal

En général, Monsieur Léveillé dort très bien, mais la nuit dernière, il n'a pas bien dormi.
Expliquez pourquoi. Avec votre partenaire, décrivez l'histoire en répondant aux questions
correspondant à chaque illustration.

Scène A ⟶

1. **Quelle heure était-il?**
   - Il était onze heures.
   - Il était minuit.
   - Il était une heure du matin.

2. **Où était Monsieur Léveillé?**
   - Il était au salon.
   - Il était dans la salle à manger.
   - Il était dans sa chambre.

3. **Qu'est-ce qu'il faisait?**
   - Il dormait.
   - Il lisait le journal.
   - Il écoutait son baladeur.

Scène B

4. **Pourquoi est-ce que Monsieur Léveillé s'est réveillé?**
   - Il avait chaud.
   - Il avait mal à la tête.
   - Il a entendu un bruit.

Scène C

5. **Qu'est-ce qu'il a fait?**
   - Il est resté au lit.
   - Il est descendu.
   - Il a téléphoné à la police.

6. **Qu'est-ce qu'il avait à la main?**
   - Il avait un revolver.
   - Il avait une batte de baseball.
   - Il avait une raquette de tennis.

Scène D

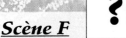

7. Qu'est-ce qu'il a vu?
   - Il a vu un homme armé.
   - Il a vu une ombre *(shadow)* dans le jardin.
   - Il a vu des traces sur le sol.

Scène F

Maintenant racontez la fin de l'histoire.
   - Qu'a fait Monsieur Léveillé?
   - Et les ratons laveurs?
   - Et le chat?

Scène E

8. Qu'est-ce qu'il y avait dans la cuisine?
   - Il y avait un fantôme.
   - Il y avait un cambrioleur *(burglar)*.
   - Il y avait des ratons laveurs *(raccoons)*.

9. Qu'est-ce qu'ils faisaient là?
   - Ils dormaient.
   - Ils jouaient avec le chat.
   - Ils mangeaient la nourriture du chat.

10. Où était le chat?
    - Il était sur la table.
    - Il était sous la table.
    - Il mangeait avec les ratons laveurs.

RAPPEL!

To describe what you USED TO DO, what you WERE DOING, or to describe the CIRCUMSTANCES of an event, use the **imperfect** tense.

J'allais au ciné.	I *used to go* to the movies.
	I *was going* to the movies.
Il était six heures.	It *was* 6 o'clock.

→ You will learn more about the use of the imperfect in Unit 3.

L'imparfait

Révision ▶ p. R5

Pratique ▶ p. 13

---

2 **Dialogue**

Avec votre partenaire, composez et jouez l'un des dialogues suivants.

▶ — Où étais-tu hier soir?
  — J'étais dans ma chambre.
  — Qu'est-ce que tu faisais?
  — Je lisais un livre.
  — Et qu'est-ce que tu as fait après?
  — J'ai fini mes devoirs.

1. • cet après-midi
   • au café
   • attendre un copain
   • aller au ciné

2. • à deux heures
   • à la bibliothèque
   • étudier
   • rentrer chez moi

3. • samedi matin
   • au centre commercial
   • faire du shopping
   • ??

4. • samedi après-midi
   • dans le jardin
   • aider mon père
   • ??

3 Au café

Vous avez passé l'après-midi à la terrasse d'un café. Vous avez vu les personnes suivantes passer dans la rue. Décrivez chacune de ces personnes.

- Il était (quelle heure?)
- J'ai vu (un homme? une dame? . . . ?)
- Il/elle était (jeune? grand(e)? . . . ?)

- Il/elle portait (quels vêtements?)
- Il/elle avait aussi (quoi?)
- Il/elle allait (où?)
- Il/elle allait faire (quoi?)

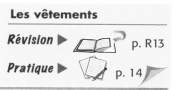

Les vêtements

Révision ▶ p. R13

Pratique ▶ p. 14

4 Photos de vacances

Vous avez passé les vacances en France avec votre partenaire. Pendant votre voyage, vous avez pris les photos suivantes. Choisissez deux photos et décrivez ce qui se passait *(what was going on)* quand vous avez pris ces photos. Utilisez l'imparfait.

.....À votre tour!...

SITUATIONS

Imagine you are in the following situations.
Your partner will take the role of the other person
in the dialogue and answer your questions.

1 Your friend just told you that he/she saw a great movie last Saturday.

Ask your friend . . .
• with whom he/she went to the movies
• what movie they saw
• what they did afterwards.

2 For his/her birthday, your friend was invited to a French restaurant.

Ask your friend . . .
• if he/she went to this restaurant for lunch or dinner
• what he/she ate
• what he/she drank.

3 You are phoning your French friend Valérie. Her brother/sister answers the phone and says that Valérie is not at home.

Ask Valérie's brother/sister . . .
• what time Valérie left
• where she went
• when she is coming back home.

4 Your friend came back from spring vacation with a tan and looks great.

Ask your friend . . .
• where he/she went
• what he/she did there
• when he/she came back.

5 Last summer your friend traveled through France with his/her family. You want to know more about their trip.

Ask your friend . . .
• how long they stayed in France
• if they traveled by *(en)* car or by train
• what cities they visited.

6 Last night your friend went to a concert by a French rock group.

Ask your friend . . .
• if the group *(le groupe)* sang in French or in English
• what clothes they were wearing
• how many people there were at the concert.

7 After supper last night you called your friend but nobody answered the phone.

Ask your friend . . .
• where he/she was
• what he/she was doing
• what his/her family was doing.

8 You and your friend are talking about your childhood — when you were eight years old.

Ask your friend . . .
• where he/she used to live
• to which school he/she used to go
• what programs *(quelles émissions)* he/she used to watch on TV.

Rappel Culturel

A. FAITS CULTURELS

1. La devise *(motto)* de la France est . . .
   a. Paix et Prospérité
   b. Liberté, Égalité, Fraternité
   c. Je me souviens

2. La France métropolitaine est divisée administrativement en 96 . . .
   a. cantons
   b. départements
   c. provinces

3. Le TGV est . . .
   a. un avion supersonique
   b. une voiture électrique
   c. un train très rapide

4. Si on veut faire du ski en hiver, on peut aller . . .
   a. à Monaco
   b. en Normandie
   c. en Savoie

5. La «Belle Province» est le nom que l'on donne à . . .
   a. la Touraine
   b. la Louisiane
   c. la province de Québec

6. La Polynésie française est un groupe d'îles qui font partie de la France d'outre-mer. La plus grande de ces îles est . . .
   a. Tahiti
   b. la Martinique
   c. Madagascar

7. En 1803, la France a vendu aux États-Unis un vaste territoire pour la somme de 15 millions de dollars. Ce territoire était . . .
   a. la Louisiane
   b. la Caroline du Sud
   c. l'Alaska

8. Ce Français est un héros de la Révolution américaine. Il s'appelle . . .
   a. Cavelier de la Salle
   b. Champlain
   c. La Fayette

9. Le continent où il y a le plus grand nombre de pays qui utilisent le français comme langue officielle est . . .
   a. l'Europe
   b. l'Afrique
   c. l'Amérique du Sud

10. L'Algérie est une ancienne colonie française. Ce pays est situé . . .
   a. en Asie
   b. en Afrique noire
   c. en Afrique du Nord

11. En Afrique, les masques sont considérés comme des objets . . .
   a. religieux
   b. de collection
   c. de la vie courante

12. Au Sénégal, la religion principale est . . .
   a. la religion musulmane
   b. la religion catholique
   c. la religion protestante

13. La population de la France est de . . .
   a. 40 millions d'habitants
   b. 60 millions d'habitants
   c. 100 millions d'habitants

14. La «Nouvelle France» est le nom . . .
   a. d'un grand magasin à Paris
   b. d'un satellite français
   c. de l'ancien empire français en Amérique du Nord

Answers: 1-b; 2-b; 3-c; 4-c; 5-c; 6-a; 7-a; 8-c; 9-b; 10-c; 11-a; 12-a; 13-b; 14-c

1. Les Smith, des touristes anglais, ont visité la France en voiture. À Paris ils ont vu Notre-Dame. En Normandie, ils ont vu le Mont-Saint-Michel. En Provence, ils ont vu le Pont du Gard. *Qu'est-ce qu'ils ont vu en Alsace?*
   a. *Le Futuroscope.*
   b. *Le château de Chambord.*
   c. *La cathédrale de Strasbourg.*

2. Patrick et Jérôme ont passé leurs vacances dans les Alpes. Un jour, ils ont assisté à un grand événement sportif. Pour voir cet événement, ils sont allés sur une route de montagne et là ils ont attendu patiemment avec des milliers d'autres personnes. Enfin, ils ont vu des voitures, des motos, et finalement les coureurs parmi lesquels ils ont reconnu le «maillot jaune».
   À quel événement sportif ont-ils assisté?
   a. *Le Grand Prix de Monaco.*
   b. *Les 24 Heures du Mans.*
   c. *Le Tour de France.*

3. Catherine est une étudiante française. À Noël, elle va généralement faire du ski, mais cette année elle n'a pas fait de ski. Elle a fait un grand voyage, mais elle n'est pas allée à l'étranger. Là où elle est allée, elle a fait de la planche à voile et du ski nautique. Elle est rentrée chez elle très bronzée.
   Où est-elle allée?
   a. *En Savoie.*
   b. *En Normandie.*
   c. *À la Guadeloupe.*

4. Chaque année Claire attend patiemment la période de Carnaval. Finalement le Carnaval est arrivé. Le premier jour, Claire a assisté au couronnement de la reine par «Bonhomme». Les jours suivants, Claire a assisté à la course des canoës sur le Saint-Laurent et elle a admiré les sculptures de glace et de neige.
   Où habite Claire?
   a. *À Québec.*
   b. *À Nice.*
   c. *En Guyane française.*

5. Hier c'était un jour férié *(holiday)*. Le matin, Julien est allé sur les Champs-Élysées où il a assisté au défilé militaire. L'après-midi, il est sorti avec sa copine Véronique. Le soir, les deux amis ont vu les feux d'artifice *(fireworks)*. Ensuite, ils ont dansé dans les rues comme des millions de Français.
   Quelle fête est-ce qu'on célébrait hier?
   a. *La fête du Travail.*
   b. *La fête nationale.*
   c. *La fête de Mardi Gras.*

6. Philippe montre les photos qu'il a prises pendant les vacances. Il explique: «Cet arbre géant est un baobab . . . Le vêtement que porte cette jeune fille s'appelle un boubou . . . Cet homme qui raconte une histoire est un griot.» *Où Philippe est-il allé pendant les vacances?*
   a. *Au Sénégal.*
   b. *En Algérie.*
   c. *À Tahiti.*

7. Il y a environ deux cents ans, Jean-Baptiste Point du Sable, un Français d'ascendance africaine, arrivait dans la région des Grands Lacs. Il a construit la première maison d'un petit village qui allait devenir l'une des plus grandes villes du continent américain.
   Quelle est cette ville?
   a. *Détroit.*
   b. *Chicago.*
   c. *Montréal.*

8. Monsieur Dutour est ingénieur pour une compagnie de prospection pétrolière. Dans sa profession, il voyage beaucoup. La semaine dernière, il est allé dans un pays d'Afrique du Nord qui produit beaucoup de pétrole et de gaz naturel.
   Où est allé Monsieur Dutour?
   a. *Au Congo.*
   b. *En Algérie.*
   c. *En République Centrafricaine.*

Answers: 1-c; 2-c; 3-c; 4-a; 5-b; 6-a; 7-b; 8-b

Rappel **Vive l'amitié!**

Dans la vie, l'amitié est peut-être la chose la plus importante. Mais attention, il y a toutes sortes d'amis! Par exemple . . .

RAPPEL!

When we ask someone to do something for us, we often use OBJECT PRONOUNS:

Téléphone-**moi** ce soir. Prête-**moi** dix dollars.

Note also the constructions:

Tu **me** donnes ton numéro de téléphone?	Tu **nous** invites?
Je **te** donne aussi mon adresse.	Je **vous** invite à ma boum.

- **me, te → m', t'** before a vowel sound.

 Tu **m'**invites? Oui, je **t'**invite.

Les pronoms compléments

Révision ▶ p. R8-R9

Pratique ▶ p. 15

1 S'il te plaît

Vous venez d'arriver en France. Demandez à votre copain français (copine française) trois services et expliquez-lui pourquoi.

S'il te plaît, présente-moi à tes copains.

Pourquoi?

Je voudrais rencontrer des jeunes Français.

QUELS SERVICES?

- amener dans une boutique de vêtements
- amener à la banque
- présenter à tes copains
- prêter ton plan *(map)* de la ville
- prêter ton appareil-photo
- donner l'adresse d'un bon restaurant
- montrer où est la poste
- ??

POURQUOI?

- envoyer une lettre
- changer de l'argent
- dîner en ville
- faire une promenade
- prendre des photos
- rencontrer des jeunes Français
- acheter un blouson
- ??

2 Échanges

Demandez certains services à votre partenaire. Il/elle va proposer un échange. Acceptez ou refusez.

Dis, Éric, prête-moi ton VTT.

D'accord! Je te prête mon VTT si tu me prêtes tes rollers.

D'accord!

(Non, merci!)

prêter . . .	tes notes
	tes CD
	ton VTT *(mountain bike)*
inviter . . .	chez toi
	à ta fête d'anniversaire
aider . . .	avec le devoir de français
	avec le devoir de maths
présenter . . .	à ton copain
	à ta copine
montrer . . .	tes photos
	tes magazines

TU CONNAIS QUELQU'UN ICI?

NON, JE NE CONNAIS PERSONNE. JE NE SAIS PAS OÙ NOUS SOMMES.

RAPPEL!

Although **connaître** and **savoir** both mean *to know*, they are used differently:

Nous **connaissons** Yasmina.
Nous **savons** où elle habite.

Connaître et savoir

Révision ▶ p. R8-R9

Pratique ▶ p. 16

RAPPEL!

| **quelqu'un** *(someone)* | Je vois **quelqu'un**. | **ne . . . personne** *(no one)* Je **ne** vois **personne**. |
| **quelque chose** *(something)* | Je vois **quelque chose**. | **ne . . . rien** *(nothing)* Je **ne** vois **rien**. |

Dans la classe, il y a une nouvelle élève. Elle s'appelle Catherine. Pierre la trouve sympathique, mais il est trop timide pour lui parler.

Je la trouve vraiment très sympa . . .

Qui est ce garçon? Pourquoi est-ce qu'il me regarde tout le temps?

Après la classe, Pierre et Catherine attendent le bus . . .

Je voudrais bien lui parler . . . Oui, mais qu'est-ce que je vais lui dire?

Pourquoi est-ce qu'il ne me parle pas?

Chez lui, Pierre pense toujours à Catherine. Il prend le guide et regarde le programme des films de la semaine.

Il y a un bon film ce soir. Je pense que Catherine aime le cinéma. Est-ce que je l'invite? Courage, je vais lui téléphoner!

Mais Pierre ne téléphone pas à Catherine.

Et si elle me dit qu'elle n'est pas libre . . . Bon . . . Je vais lui téléphoner samedi prochain. C'est promis!

Pierre met sa veste et il va seul au cinéma.

Pendant ce temps, Catherine regarde aussi le journal.

Tiens, il y a un bon film ce soir en ville . . . Je voudrais bien le voir, mais je n'ai pas envie d'aller seule au cinéma . . . Si je téléphonais à ce garçon qui me regarde tout le temps en classe. Après tout, je le trouve bien sympathique.

Catherine cherche le numéro de Pierre sur l'Internet. Puis elle lui téléphone . . .

. . . mais chez Pierre, personne ne répond au téléphone.

DRIN . . .
DRIN . . .

Le lendemain après la classe.

Pierre, il y a un bon film au Rex. Est-ce que tu l'as vu?

Euh oui . . . je l'ai vu. C'est un film vraiment super!

Est-ce que tu veux le revoir avec moi ce soir?

Mais oui, avec plaisir.

Et maintenant, avec votre partenaire, imaginez la suite de l'histoire. Par exemple . . .

• Quand est-ce que Pierre et Catherine sont allés au cinéma?
• Qu'est-ce qu'il lui a dit?
• Qu'est-ce qu'elle lui a dit?
• Est-ce qu'ils ont eu d'autres rendez-vous?

RAPPEL!

To refer to people previously mentioned, use:

le / la / les	
Je regarde **Marc**.	Je **le** regarde.
Tu connais **Claire**.	Tu **la** connais.
J'invite **mes** amis.	Je **les** invite.

lui / leur	
Je téléphone **à Marc**.	Je **lui** téléphone.
Tu parles **à Claire**.	Tu **lui** parles.
J'écris **à mes amis**.	Je **leur** écris.

• **le/la/les** may also refer to things.
 Je regarde **la photo**. Je **la** regarde.
• **le/la** → **l'** before a vowel sound
 Nous écoutons **le CD**. Nous **l'**écoutons.

Les compléments d'objet direct et indirect

Révision ▶ p. R8-R9

Pratique ▶ p. 17

Voir *(to see)*, **écrire** *(to write)*

Révision ▶ pp. R26,–R30

Pratique ▶ p. 18

1 Relations personnelles

Demandez à votre partenaire de décrire ses relations avec l'une des personnes indiquées.

▶ — **Tu as une cousine?**
— **Oui, bien sûr.**
— **Tu la vois souvent?**
— **Oui, je la vois de temps en temps.**
— **Tu lui écris?**
— **Non, je ne lui écris jamais.**

QUI?
un copain
des copines
une tante
des cousins
une cousine
des voisins

QUOI?
voir
inviter
téléphoner (à)
écrire (à)
aider
rendre visite (à)
donner des cadeaux (à)
donner des conseils *(advice)* (à)
demander des conseils (à)

QUAND?
souvent
de temps en temps
rarement
jamais
toujours

2 La boum

Vous préparez une boum. Demandez à votre partenaire s'il (si elle) peut vous aider avec les choses suivantes. Votre partenaire va accepter ou refuser.

▶ — **Tu peux préparer les sandwichs?**
— **Oui, d'accord, je vais les préparer.**
  (Je suis désolé(e) mais je ne peux pas les préparer.)

• faire les courses
• acheter les boissons
• laver les verres
• ranger la cuisine
• mettre la table
• préparer les sandwichs
• décorer le salon
• apporter ta mini-chaîne
• choisir la musique
• inviter nos amis
• téléphoner aux voisins

·····À votre tour! ···

SITUATIONS

Imagine you are in the following situations.
Your partner will take the role of the other person
in the dialogue and answer your questions.

1 You are an exchange student in a French lycée. It is your first day at school and you need help.

Ask another student (who, of course, is willing to help you) . . .
- to loan you a notebook
- to give you a pencil
- to show you where the cafeteria is
- to take you *(amener)* to the library.

2 You are spending two weeks at the home of your French cousin who lives in Paris.

Ask your cousin (who will accept or refuse) . . .
- to introduce you to his/her friends
- to loan you something you need
- to show you a place in Paris you would like to visit
- to take you to a show or an event that you are interested in.

3 Your friend has a Belgian neighbor named Béatrice. You would like to know more about their relationship.

Ask your friend . . .
- how long he/she has known Béatrice
- if he/she knows her parents
- if he/she invites her often
- what he/she is going to give Béatrice for her birthday.

4 Your friend has a Canadian penpal, Jean, who is coming to visit next weekend. You want to know what your friend has planned for Jean's visit.

Ask your friend . . .
- to what restaurant he/she is going to invite Jean
- what places *(quels endroits)* he/she is going to show him
- what gift *(un cadeau)* he/she is going to give him.

5 You are the manager of a tourist shop in Montreal. You are hiring students for the summer and are interviewing one of the candidates.

Ask the candidate . . .
- if he/she knows how to speak French well
- What other languages he/she knows how to speak
- if he/she knows how to answer the phone in French
- what other things he/she knows how to do.

6 You and your friend are planning a party for next Friday night. You are checking if your friend has done his/her share of the work.

Ask your friend . . .
- if he/she sent the invitations
- if he/she called the neighbors
- if he/she chose the music
- if he/she bought the beverages *(les boissons)*.

7 You are visiting Paris with your friend. It is your first trip but your friend has visited Paris before.

Ask your friend . . .
- what monuments he/she knows
- if he/she knows how to get to the Eiffel Tower
- if he/she knows if the Louvre is open *(ouvert)* this afternoon
- if he/she knows a good restaurant.

LECTURE

Les trois bagues

AVANT DE LIRE

Quand on lit une histoire, il est utile d'anticiper ce qui va se passer d'après les éléments que l'on connaît déjà. Lisez d'abord la **Note culturelle** et **Une annonce**. D'après vous, pourquoi est-ce que les neveux vont aller chez le notaire?

- pour assister à un mariage
- pour vendre la maison familiale
- pour recevoir une somme d'argent
- pour régler *(to settle)* une dispute

Maintenant, continuez votre lecture pour vérifier votre réponse.

NOTE CULTURELLE

Le notaire

Le notaire joue un rôle important dans la vie des familles françaises. Son rôle est d'officialiser un grand nombre d'actes et de contrats de la vie civile (contrat de mariage, testaments,° ventes° de biens immobiliers,° etc.). Un notaire a le titre de **Maître,** Maître Durand, par exemple. Son bureau° s'appelle **une étude.**

testament *will*   **vente** *sale*
biens immobiliers *real estate*
bureau *office*

LES TROIS BAGUES

Une annonce

Un jour l'annonce suivante a paru dans *La Nouvelle République* de Tours.

Héritage

Les neveux de Jules Larivière, né le 18 octobre 1930 à Amboise, sont invités à se présenter le 21 janvier à l'étude de Maître Durand, notaire à Tours.

Mots utiles

un neveu	*nephew*
un propriétaire	*owner*
un ouvrier	*worker*
gagner sa vie	*to earn one's living*

Les trois neveux

Le 21 janvier, trois hommes se sont présentés° à l'étude de Maître Durand. Neveux de Jules Larivière, ils étaient cousins, mais de condition sociale très différente.

Le premier neveu, Roland Larivière, avait 45 ans et était célibataire.° Propriétaire d'un grand hôtel dans le centre de Tours, il était président de la Chambre de Commerce de la ville. C'était un homme riche et influent.

Le second neveu, Henri Larivière, 38 ans, exerçait la profession de pharmacien et gagnait bien sa vie. Marié, mais sans enfants, il habitait avec sa femme dans une jolie maison située en banlieue.°

Le troisième neveu, Jean-Marc Larivière, 28 ans, était un simple ouvrier agricole. Il habitait dans une petite ferme à la campagne° avec sa femme et ses trois enfants.

La secrétaire de Maître Durand a pris le nom, la profession et l'adresse des trois neveux, puis elle les a introduits° dans le bureau du notaire.

se sont présentés = sont venus   **célibataire** = non-marié   **banlieue** *suburbs*
campagne *country*   **les a introduits** *led, introduced them*

Avez-vous compris?

1. Quand et pourquoi les trois neveux vont-ils chez le notaire?
2. Qui est le plus riche des trois neveux? le moins riche?
3. À votre avis, lequel des trois neveux exerce la profession la plus intéressante? Pourquoi?
4. À vos yeux, lequel est le plus sympathique? Pourquoi?

Anticipons un peu!

D'après vous, qu'est-ce qui va se passer à la fin de l'histoire?
- Les trois neveux vont recevoir la même somme d'argent.
- Le neveu le plus riche va donner sa part *(share)* à ses cousins.
- Le neveu le moins riche va recevoir plus d'argent que ses cousins.
- Autre possibilité? Expliquez votre opinion.

Maintenant, finissez l'histoire et vérifiez si vous aviez raison.

Le Testament

Maître Durand a serré la main° des trois neveux et puis il a commencé à parler.

Me Durand
J'ai le regret de vous annoncer le décès° de votre oncle Jules Larivière. Il est mort le 12 décembre dernier au Mexique dans la ville de Cuernavaca où il habitait depuis son départ de France, il y a quinze ans. Il n'avait pas d'enfants. Vous êtes, par conséquent, ses héritiers.

20

Roland L.
Qu'est-ce qu'il nous a laissé?

Me Durand
Il vous a laissé trois bagues.

Roland L.
Trois bagues? C'est tout?!

25 Me Durand
Non, il vous a laissé aussi une très belle photo de lui.

Roland L.
Est-ce qu'on peut voir les bagues?

Me Durand
Oui, bien sûr.

Maître Durand a pris une grande enveloppe dans laquelle il y avait les trois bagues. Il les a mises sur une table et il a continué . . .

30

Me Durand
Voilà les trois bagues. Comme vous pouvez voir, ces bagues sont très différentes. Il y a une bague de diamant, une bague en or et une bague en argent . . .

Roland L.
Mais ces bagues n'ont pas la même valeur.° Le partage° est impossible.

35

Me Durand
Au contraire! Le testament de votre oncle est très explicite. Il stipule que c'est à l'aîné de ses neveux de choisir d'abord.

Roland L.
Alors là, mon oncle a eu une bonne idée!

Me Durand
Monsieur Roland Larivière, vous êtes l'aîné! Quelle bague voulez-vous?

40

Roland L.
Eh bien, c'est facile! Je prends la bague de diamant! Quel merveilleux souvenir de mon oncle!

Me Durand
Voulez-vous aussi la photo de votre oncle?

Roland L.
Euh, non. Je crois que je me souviendrai° mieux de mon oncle avec la bague. Et puis, j'ai assez de vieilles choses chez moi.

45

Maître Durand s'est tourné° ensuite vers Henri Larivière.

Me Durand
Monsieur Henri Larivière, vous êtes le second neveu. C'est votre tour maintenant.

50 Henri L.
Eh bien, moi, je proteste! Je ne suis peut-être pas l'aîné, mais c'était moi le neveu préféré de mon oncle. Pourquoi est-ce qu'il ne m'a pas donné la bague de diamant? Oui, je proteste!

Me Durand
Choisissez, s'il vous plaît! La bague en or ou la bague en argent?

55

Henri L.
Bon, je prends la bague en or, mais . . .

Me Durand
Voulez-vous la photo de votre oncle?

Henri L.
Ah ça, certainement pas! Mon oncle a été trop injuste avec moi!

Mots utiles	
un testament	*will*
un héritier	*heir*
laisser	*to leave*
une bague	*ring*
l'or	*gold*
l'argent	*silver*
l'aîné	*= le plus âgé*
une clé	*key*
un coffre	*safe*
juste ≠ injuste	*fair ≠ unfair*

a serré la main de *shook hands with* **décès** *death* **valeur** *value* **le partage** = la division
je me souviendrai *I will remember* **s'est tourné** *turned*

Finalement Maître Durand s'est tourné vers le troisième neveu.

Me Durand	Alors, Monsieur Jean-Marc Larivière, il vous reste° la bague en argent . . . Je suppose que vous non plus, vous ne désirez pas la photo de votre oncle.
Jean-Marc L.	Au contraire. Je me souviens bien de lui. C'était un homme très bon et très juste. Je l'aimais beaucoup!
Me Durand	Eh bien, voilà votre bague, et voici la photo de votre oncle.

60

Anticipons un peu!

D'après vous, qu'est-ce qui va se passer à la fin?

Maître Durand s'est levé,° puis il a serré très fort° la main de Jean-Marc Larivière.

65

Me Durand	Félicitations, vous êtes maintenant un homme très riche!
Jean-Marc L.	Mais non, je suis seulement un pauvre ouvrier agricole . . .
Me Durand	Oui, mais vous avez la photo.
Jean-Marc L.	La photo?
Me Durand	Retournez-la . . . Il y a la clé du coffre de votre oncle. Quand il était au Mexique, votre oncle a fait des investissements très profitables. Il est mort multi-millionnaire et c'est vous qui héritez de sa fortune!

70

75

il vous reste = vous avez   **s'est levé** got up   **très fort** = avec beaucoup de force

Avez-vous compris?

1. Pourquoi les neveux de Jules Larivière étaient-ils ses héritiers?
2. Quels objets est-ce que Jules Larivière a laissés à ses neveux?
3. En quoi ces bagues étaient-elles différentes?
4. Pourquoi est-ce que les deux premiers neveux n'ont pas pris la photo de leur oncle?
5. Pourquoi est-ce que le troisième neveu a pris la photo?
6. Comment est-ce qu'il a été récompensé (rewarded)?

EXPRESSION ORALE

■ Discussion

Voici plusieurs morales possibles pour l'histoire que vous avez lue. Avec votre partenaire, déterminez quelle est la meilleure morale et expliquez pourquoi. (Si vous préférez, vous pouvez suggérer une autre morale.)

- Il y a toujours une justice.
- L'avarice (*greed*) ne paie pas.
- Les riches ont souvent tort.
- L'argent ne fait pas le bonheur.

■ Dramatisation

Avec vos camarades de classe, jouez la scène du **Testament**. Chaque personne va adopter la personnalité correspondant à son rôle et jouer ce rôle avec beaucoup d'expression.

■ Situations

Avec votre partenaire, choisissez l'une des situations suivantes. Composez le dialogue correspondant et jouez-le en classe.

1 La bonne nouvelle

Jean-Marc Larivière rentre chez lui et annonce la bonne nouvelle à sa femme qui veut des détails.

Rôles: Jean-Marc Larivière, sa femme

2 Au café

Roland Larivière va au café où il rencontre un(e) ami(e). Il lui raconte l'histoire du testament.

Rôles: Roland Larivière, un(e) ami(e)

3 Un procès

Henri Larivière, très mécontent de ce qui s'est passé, va voir un(e) avocat(e) (*lawyer*), dans l'intention de faire un procès (*suit*) à son cousin Jean-Marc. Il explique l'injustice de la situation à l'avocat(e) qui veut des détails.

Rôles: Henri Larivière, l'avocat(e)

EXPRESSION ÉCRITE

■ L'héritage

Dans un petit paragraphe, décrivez ce que Jean-Marc Larivière va faire avec l'argent de l'héritage.

■ Les trois neveux

Sur la base de l'histoire que vous avez lue, faites le portrait des trois neveux (leurs qualités, leurs défauts, ce qu'ils aiment, ce qu'ils n'aiment pas, etc.).

■ Jules Larivière

Écrivez une courte biographie de Jules Larivière. Utilisez votre imagination. Vous pouvez considérer les questions suivantes:

- Que faisait Jules Larivière avant d'aller au Mexique?
- Pourquoi a-t-il quitté la France?
- Qu'est-ce qu'il a fait à Cuernavaca?

■ Le testament

Choisissez l'un des personnages suivants:

Maître Durand, Roland Larivière, Henri Larivière, Jean-Marc Larivière

Écrivez une lettre dans laquelle vous décrivez l'histoire du point de vue de la personne que vous avez choisie. Comparez votre lettre avec celles que vos camarades ont écrites.

Thème et Objectifs

Culture

In this unit, you will discover . . .

- what French people call "le look" and why it is important to them
- how French teenagers care for their personal appearance
- how different artists have expressed the concept of beauty
- what constitutes the daily routine for different French people

Communication

You will learn how . . .

- to describe what a person looks like
- to explain what you do to make yourself look good
- to talk about your daily activities
- to describe how you feel in different circumstances

Langue

You will learn how . . .

- to describe what people do for themselves
- to describe certain aspects of your daily routine
- to express feelings and changes of mood

L'importance du

« LOOK »

Il y a deux semaines, Cédric, **16 ans,** avait les cheveux longs. Maintenant, il les a courts.° Cédric change de coiffure° tous les° trois mois. Véronique, **17 ans,** dépense son argent en «fringues»° qu'elle achète au moment des soldes.° Pour se composer un «look», Sandrine préfère utiliser sa vaste collection d'accessoires.

Pour les jeunes Français, le «look» est extrêmement important. En fait, l'importance du look marque le passage de l'enfance° à l'adolescence. Avant l'âge de 12 ou 13 ans, ils ne s'intéressent° pas beaucoup à leur apparence. Après, ils y font très attention.

Le look, c'est une façon de personnaliser son apparence physique, de se créer un style. S'il est difficile de modifier son corps,° on peut facilement changer son look. Il suffit° de choisir les vêtements, les accessoires, la coupe° de cheveux correspondant à l'impression qu'on veut donner. Voici, par ordre d'importance, les éléments du look pour les «ados» (les adolescents) français.

■ Les vêtements

Avec le choix de ses vêtements, on détermine son style général: sport, classique, romantique, etc. . . Pour les ados, les vêtements les plus importants sont d'abord le jean, uniforme de la jeunesse internationale, et ensuite le blouson, le sweat et le tee-shirt. La marque des vêtements est capitale. On n'achète pas un blouson, mais un Naf Naf ou un Chevignon. On ne porte pas un sweat, mais Go Sport ou un Kookaï. Parce que la marque coûte cher, les ados mélangent° les vêtements de marque avec des vêtements moins chers qu'ils achètent dans les grandes surfaces.°

■ Les chaussures

Les Français sont les plus grands acheteurs de chaussures d'Europe: ils en achètent en moyenne cinq paires par an. Là aussi, la forme, le style et surtout la marque sont très importants.

"C'est la première impression qui compte"

---

courts *short* **coiffure** *hairstyle* **tous les** *every* **fringues** *= vêtements (slang)* **soldes** *sales* **l'enfance** *childhood* **ne s'intéressent** *= ne sont pas intéressés*
corps *body* **suffit** *= il est suffisant* **coupe** *cut* **marques** *designer (boutique) brand names* **mélangent** *mix* **grandes surfaces** *shopping centers*

■ Les accessoires

Colliers, bracelets, boucles d'oreille, bijoux, chapeaux permettent aux filles de se créer un look ou d'en changer rapidement. Pour leur look, les garçons utilisent casquettes,° ceintures, bretelles,° et parfois des boucles d'oreilles. Le sac à dos° est un élément du look plus important pour les filles que pour les garçons. Et n'oublions pas les lunettes. Suivant leur forme et leur couleur, on peut avoir un look sérieux, intelligent, drôle, rétro . . .

■ Le maquillage et les produits de beauté

Aujourd'hui, les jeunes Françaises préfèrent un style naturel. Leur maquillage° et aussi leur parfum restent généralement discrets. Quant° aux jeunes Français, ils utilisent de plus en plus° de produits de beauté: eaux de toilette, crèmes et lotions pour les mains, gels pour les cheveux.

■ La coiffure

La coiffure fait partie° intégrale du look. C'est aussi une façon° de manifester ses opinions. Les cheveux longs des années 1970 ou le style «punk» des années 1980 marquaient le refus de s'intégrer à la société des adultes.

Les ados aujourd'hui sont retournés à un style assez classique de coiffure avec des cheveux ni° trop longs, ni trop courts. Courts ou longs, frisés, bouclés° ou souples, l'important c'est que les cheveux soient propres et faciles à entretenir.°

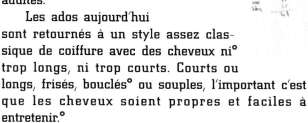

et vous?

LE LOOK ET VOUS

D'après vous, quelles sont les trois choses les plus importantes pour le look d'un garçon et le look d'une fille?

	POUR UN GARÇON	POUR UNE FILLE
• avoir beaucoup de vêtements différents	☐	☐
• avoir des vêtements qui vous vont bien	☐	☐
• avoir une coiffure originale	☐	☐
• porter des accessoires exotiques	☐	☐
• porter des couleurs vives°	☐	☐
• être naturel(le)	☐	☐
• avoir l'air décontracté°	☐	☐
• se sentir° bien physiquement	☐	☐

---

casquettes caps **bretelles** suspenders **sac à dos** backpack **fait partie** is a component **façon** = une manière **ni** neither **bouclés** wavy **entretenir** to take care of **maquillage** makeup **Quant à** as for **plus en plus** more and more **vives** bright **l'air décontracté** to look relaxed **se sentir** to feel

Les artistes ont toujours voulu représenter leur idée de la beauté. La beauté a des visages différents à travers les âges et les cultures.

Les visages de la beauté

La beauté, c'est . . .

Pour Léonard de Vinci (1452-1519)

. . . un visage tranquille
. . . des traits° réguliers
. . . un sourire° énigmatique
. . . la discrétion et le mystère

Pour ce sculpteur du Moyen Âge

. . . un visage ovale
. . . des cheveux bouclés
. . . un sourire d'ange
. . . la douceur° et la discrétion

Pour Pierre Auguste Renoir (1841-1919)

. . . un visage rond
. . . des joues° pleines°
. . . un teint° frais
. . . la joie de vivre

Pour Amedeo Modigliani (1884-1920)

. . . un visage ovale
. . . un nez long et fin
. . . des traits symétriques
. . . la délicatesse

Pour Paul Gauguin (1848-1903)

. . . un visage rond
. . . des cheveux abondants
. . . une bouche pleine
. . . la bonté° et la générosité

Pour Pablo Picasso (1881-1973)

. . . un regard profond
. . . des traits marqués
. . . une attitude fière
. . . la personnalité

Pour ce sculpteur anonyme du Bénin

. . . une coiffure° élaborée
. . . un visage altier°
. . . des traits fermes
. . . la noblesse° de caractère

**Et ça!
C'est le contraire de la beauté!**

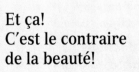

- Parmi les huit visages représentés, lesquels correspondent le mieux à votre idéal de la beauté? Expliquez pourquoi.
- Apportez en classe des photos ou des portraits de personnes que vous considérez être belles. Décrivez ces portraits.

---

traits *features*   **sourire** *smile*   **douceur** *kindness*   **joues** *cheeks*   **pleines** *full*   **teint** *complexion*
bonté *goodness*   **coiffure** *hairdo*   **altier** *proud*   **noblesse** *nobility*

LE FRANÇAIS PRATIQUE

La description physique

La figure, le visage

- les cheveux
- le front
- un oeil (les yeux)
- la joue
- le cou
- le nez
- une oreille
- la bouche
- le menton

	Un garçon / une fille . . .		
LES CHEVEUX	est **brun(e)**	ou	**blond(e)** **roux (rousse)** *(redhead)*
	a les cheveux bruns	ou	**blonds** **châtain** *(chestnut)* **noirs** **châtain clair** *(gold)* **roux** **châtain foncé** *(brown)*
	a les cheveux longs **lisses** *(straight)*	ou ou	**courts** *(short)* **frisés** *(curly, frizzy)* **bouclés** *(curly, wavy)*
LES YEUX	**a les yeux noirs**	ou	**bleus** **verts** **gris** **marron** *(brown)*
LE VISAGE (LA FIGURE)	**a le visage ovale**	ou	**rond** **rectangulaire** **carré** *(square)*
LA TAILLE	**est grand(e)**	ou	**petit(e)** **de taille moyenne** *(average)*
L'APPARENCE GÉNÉRALE	est **mince** *(thin)* **maigre** *(skinny)*	ou	**gros(se)** *(heavyset, fat)*
	est **athlétique** **fort(e)** *(strong)* **costaud(e)** *(solid, well-built)*	ou	**faible** *(weak)*
LES SIGNES PARTICULIERS	**porte des lunettes**	ou	**des verres de contact** **des lentilles** *(lenses)* **de contact**

▶ **À noter**   **la taille** *(height)*   **Je mesure** 1 mètre 75.   *I am 5 feet 10 inches tall.*
           le poids *(weight)*   **Je pèse** 65 kilos.   *I weigh 143 pounds (65 kilos).*

Ce monsieur. . .

 **est chauve**

 **est barbu; a une barbe**

 **a une moustache**

 **a une cicatrice** *(scar)*

Ce garçon . . .
Cette fille . . .

 a les cheveux en brosse *(crew-cut)*

 a une queue de cheval *(ponytail)*

 **a des taches de rousseur** *(freckles)*

 **a un grain de beauté** *(beauty mark)* sur le menton

1 Dix ans après

Dix ans séparent ces deux photos.
Entre temps, les élèves du lycée
Descartes ont beaucoup changé.
Choisissez un(e) élève sur la photo
de l'école et décrivez-le(la).
Votre partenaire va décrire cette
personne maintenant.

Au lycée Descartes, il y a 10 ans

Alice   Marc   Sophie   Isabelle   Julien   Jérôme

Maintenant

Alice   Marc   Sophie   Isabelle   Julien   Jérôme

2 Autoportrait

Faites votre autoportrait en donnant le maximum de détails sur votre aspect physique.

Conversations libres

Avec votre partenaire, choisissez l'une des situations suivantes.
Composez le dialogue correspondant et jouez-le en classe.

1 Rendez-vous

Votre partenaire vous propose
d'aller au cinéma avec un(e)
jeune Français(e) qu'il/elle
a rencontré(e) récemment.
Vous voulez avoir des détails
sur cette personne.

2 Un(e) enfant perdu(e)

Vous faites du shopping aux Galeries Lafayette
avec votre petit(e) cousin(e). Pendant que
vous êtes au rayon des jouets *(toys)*, votre
cousin(e) disparaît *(disappears)*. Faites une
description de votre cousin(e) au détective
du magasin (votre partenaire). Il va vous
demander des détails.

A. L'usage de l'article avec les parties du corps

Catherine a **les yeux** bleus.   *Catherine has blue eyes. (= **Her eyes** are blue.)*
Qu'est-ce que tu as dans **la main**?   *What do you have in **your hand**?*
J'ai une cicatrice sur **le menton**.   *I have a scar on **my chin**.*

In French the DEFINITE ARTICLE **(le, la, l', les)** is generally used with parts of the body.
(In English, we use possessive adjectives.)

1 Monsieur et Madame Dupont

Monsieur et Madame Dupont sont des touristes français. Complétez la description
de Monsieur Dupont et ensuite faites la description de Madame Dupont.

Monsieur Dupont a . . . frisés.

Il porte un chapeau sur . . .
Il a une pipe dans . . .
Il a un foulard autour (de) . . .
Il porte son appareil-photo sur . . .
Il a un magazine (à) . . .
Il porte des sandales (à) . . .

Madame Dupont a . . .

la bouche
les cheveux
le cou
l'épaule
la main
les pieds
la tête

RAPPEL!

à + le → au   de + le → du
à + les → aux   de + les → des

Avoir mal à + les parties du corps

Révision ▶  p. R3;
p. R12

❷ Dommage!

Aujourd'hui ça ne va pas! Choisissez une chose que vous ne pouvez pas faire et expliquez pourquoi.

Je ne peux pas <u>travailler dans le jardin</u>.

Mon/ma pauvre! Qu'est-ce que tu as?

J'ai mal <u>au dos</u>.
<u>(aux pieds)</u>.

Dommage!

QUELLE ACTIVITÉ?	POURQUOI?
parler	le genou
sortir avec toi	les pieds
dîner avec toi	la main
faire du jogging	le dos
jouer au foot	la gorge *(throat)*
jouer au ping-pong	les jambes
manger des bonbons	le ventre
transporter cette table	les dents
écouter ce CD de rap	la tête
travailler dans le jardin	les oreilles
??	??

❸ Enrichissez votre vocabulaire!

Voici certaines expressions que vous pouvez utiliser avec vos amis. Faites correspondre ces expressions avec leurs équivalents anglais.

1. Ne fais pas la tête!
2. Ne mets pas les pieds dans le plat!
3. Tu as un poil *(hair)* dans la main!
4. Tu as les yeux plus gros que le ventre!
5. Tu as le coeur sur la main!
6. Tu coupes les cheveux en quatre.
7. J'ai l'estomac dans les talons *(heels)*.

a. I am very hungry.
b. You are too greedy. (Your eyes are bigger than your stomach.)
c. You are really lazy.
d. Don't look so upset.
e. Don't put your foot in your mouth.
f. You are very finicky. (You are splitting hairs.)
g. You are a very generous person. (You wear your heart on your sleeve.)

Usages de l'article défini

Pratique ▶  p. 19

ALLONS PLUS LOIN: Autres usages de l'article défini

The definite article is used . . .

- with dates
  le 18 juin   **le samedi 3 avril**

- with days of the week (or parts of the day) to refer to a repeated or habitual action
  Compare:
  Que fais-tu **le samedi**?   *What do you do **on Saturdays?***
  Que fais-tu **samedi**?   *What are you doing **on (this) Saturday?***

- with geographical names (countries, states, rivers, mountains, etc.), except cities
  le Canada   les États-Unis   but   **Israël, Cuba, Tahiti, Haïti**
  la Virginie   le Mississippi   les Alpes

- with names of languages, colors, and school subjects
  J'étudie **le français** et **les maths**.
  Mes couleurs préférées sont **le bleu** et **le rouge**.

- with certain titles
  le docteur Mercat   **la princesse** Diane   **la reine** Élizabeth

- with nouns indicating a weight, measure, or quantity
  L'essence coûte un euro **le litre**.   *Gas costs one euro **a liter**.*

Juliette a l'impression de ne pas être belle.
Elle parle de son problème dans *Le Journal
des Copains*. Lisez ce que les lecteurs de
ce journal lui ont répondu.

Chers copains,

Quand je me regarde dans la glace,
je ne suis pas satisfaite de moi. J'ai le nez
trop long, les oreilles trop grandes, le front
trop large, les cheveux trop raides.° En un mot,
je ne suis pas très belle. J'ai 15 ans, et pour moi,
c'est un grave problème.

Juliette

Valérie (Grenoble),
17 ans

Ne t'inquiète pas!° à 15 ans, toutes les filles
pensent qu'elles ne sont pas assez belles.
C'était mon cas quand j'avais ton âge.
Je me suis trouvée° beaucoup plus belle
le jour où un garçon m'a invitée. Patiente
un peu! Un jour, ça va être ton tour.

Valérie

---

raides *straight* **ne t'inquiète pas** *don't worry* **Je me suis trouvée** *I found myself*

Cécile *(Pau),*
16 ans

La beauté, c'est une chose, mais il y a aussi le look. Ça aussi, c'est important. Tu peux changer de coiffure, te maquiller° un peu, porter des accessoires marrants,° choisir des vêtements qui correspondent à ta personnalité... L'essentiel, c'est de se créer un style. Essaie!° Ce n'est pas si difficile!

Cécile

Guillaume *(Bruxelles),*
18 ans

Tu sais, je ne suis pas très beau non plus, mais ce n'est pas si grave que tu penses. En fait, j'ai des tas° de copains et de copines. La clé° du succès, c'est de se sentir° bien dans sa peau°. La vraie beauté n'est pas physique. Elle dépend des qualités que tu as. Mets les tiennes° en valeur. Et n'oublie pas que la beauté ne fait pas nécessairement le bonheur.° Regarde donc Marilyn Monroe!

Guillaume

Philippe *(Nice),*
17 ans

La beauté est importante, mais ce n'est pas tout. Ce qui compte aussi, c'est le charme et la personnalité. Quand j'invite une fille, ce n'est pas parce qu'elle est super-jolie, mais parce qu'elle est sympa, drôle, et qu'elle aime rire!° Cultive ton sens de l'humour et tu auras toujours des amis!

Philippe

Et vous?

Expression orale

D'après vous, quelle lettre offre les meilleurs conseils à Juliette? Expliquez pourquoi.

Expression écrite

Écrivez votre propre *(own)* réponse à la lettre de Juliette.

---

te maquiller *put on makeup* **marrants** = drôles *(slang)* **essaie** *try* **des tas** = quantités
la clé *key* **se sentir** *to feel* **dans sa peau** *inside (in one's skin)* **les tiennes** = tes qualités
le bonheur *happiness* **rire*** *to laugh*

La toilette et les soins personnels

Les parties du corps

Révision ▶ p. R12

Olivier utilise . . .   pour . . .

le rasoir	**se raser**	**se raser** *to shave*
le savon	**se laver la figure**	
la brosse à dents	**se brosser les dents**	**se brosser** *to brush*
la serviette	**s'essuyer les mains**	**s'essuyer** *to (wipe) dry*
les ciseaux	**se couper les ongles** (nails)	**se couper** *to cut*

Charlotte utilise . . .   pour . . .

le shampooing	**se laver les cheveux**	
le séchoir	**se sécher les cheveux**	**se sécher** *to dry*
le peigne	**se peigner**	**se peigner** *to comb one's hair*
le rouge à lèvres	**se maquiller**	**se maquiller** *to apply makeup*
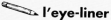 **l'eye-liner**	**se maquiller les yeux**	

Quelques autres articles de toilette et produits de beauté

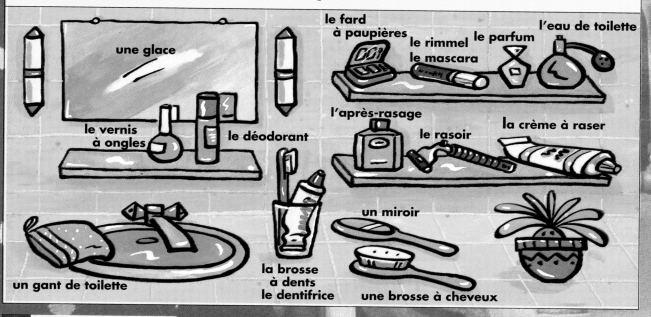

une glace

le fard à paupières

le rimmel
le mascara

le parfum

l'eau de toilette

le vernis à ongles

le déodorant

l'après-rasage

le rasoir

la crème à raser

un gant de toilette

la brosse à dents
le dentifrice

un miroir

une brosse à cheveux

1 La trousse de toilette *(toiletry kit)*

Ce week-end vous n'allez pas rester chez vous.
Mentionnez cinq articles—ou plus—que
vous allez mettre dans votre trousse de toilette . . .

- si vous allez faire du camping
- si vous allez passer le week-end chez vos cousins.

Maintenant imaginez que vous allez en France cet été.
Faites une liste de dix articles ou produits
que vous allez emporter *(take along)* avec vous.

Comparez vos listes avec celles de votre partenaire.
Combien de choses identiques avez-vous prises?
Combien de choses différentes?

2 Qu'est-ce qu'ils vont faire?

Lisez les descriptions suivantes. Puis mentionnez deux ou trois choses que
chaque personne va faire.

▶ **Philippe vient de jouer au foot. Il va dans la douche du stade.**
Il va prendre une douche.
Il va se laver les cheveux.
Ensuite, il va se sécher et se mettre du déodorant.

1. Il est sept heures du matin. Monsieur Lebot, président
de la Banque Industrielle, se lève et va dans la salle de bains.

2. Il est onze heures du soir. Jérôme va se coucher. D'abord il va dans la salle de bains.

3. Ce soir, la fameuse chanteuse d'opéra va jouer le rôle de Carmen. Elle est dans sa
loge *(dressing room)* où elle se prépare pour la représentation *(performance)*.

4. Caroline va dîner avec Vincent, son nouveau copain, dans un restaurant très élégant.
Elle se prépare pour l'occasion.

3 En voyage ▶

Vous êtes en voyage avec un groupe.
Demandez à votre partenaire l'un des objets
suivants et expliquez pourquoi vous
en avez besoin.

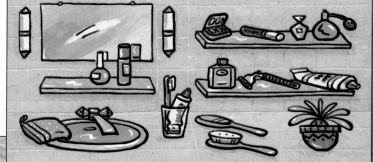

A. Les verbes réfléchis

REFLEXIVE VERBS are formed with a REFLEXIVE PRONOUN that represents the same person as the subject.

Je **me** lave.   Monsieur Martin **se** rase.

FORMS

Review the forms of **se laver** in the present and the imperative.

	PRESENT
AFFIRMATIVE	je **me** lave tu **te** laves il/elle/on **se** lave nous **nous** lavons vous **vous** lavez ils/elles **se** lavent
NEGATIVE	**je ne me lave pas**
INTERROGATIVE	**est-ce que tu te laves?** **te laves-tu?**

IMPERATIVE	
AFFIRMATIVE	**NEGATIVE**
lave-toi!	**ne te lave pas!**
lavons-nous!	**ne nous lavons pas!**
lavez-vous!	**ne vous lavez pas!**

INFINITIVE CONSTRUCTIONS

Je vais **me** laver. Nous allons **nous** brosser les dents.	Je **ne** vais **pas me** laver les cheveux. Vous **n'**allez **pas vous** raser.

➡ In an infinitive construction, the reflexive pronoun comes immediately before the verb and represents the same person as the subject.

USES

Reflexive verbs are very common in French. They are used:

- to describe actions that the subject is performing on or for himself/herself.

  Catherine **se regarde** dans la glace.   *Catherine **is looking at herself** in the mirror.*
  Je **me fais** un sandwich.   *I **am fixing myself** a sandwich.*

- to describe many aspects of one's DAILY ROUTINE.

  Je **me lève** à sept heures.   *I get up at seven.*

➡ Note the use of the DEFINITE ARTICLE after reflexive verbs.

  Tu te brosses **les** dents.   *You are brushing **your** teeth.*
  Alice se coupe **les** ongles.   *Alice is cutting **her** nails.*

Le présent des verbes

Révision p. R2

comme préférer: se sécher
pp. R20-21

comme payer: s'essuyer
pp. R20-21

Pratique  p. 21

4 Le matin

Choisissez une personne et dites ce qu'elle fait et
ce qu'elle va faire après. Soyez logique!

QUI?	
moi	Jean-Philippe
toi	Madame Lescure
nous	Monsieur Dupont
vous	Éric et Thomas
Alice	Sylvie et Catherine

QUOI?	
• se laver	• se brosser les dents
• se raser	• se laver la figure
• se maquiller	• se laver les mains
• se peigner	• se laver les cheveux
• s'essuyer	• se couper les ongles
• se regarder dans la glace	• se brosser les cheveux
	• se sécher les cheveux

▶ **Tu te sèches les cheveux. Après, tu vas te peigner.**

5 Publicité

Composez des slogans publicitaires pour
les produits suivants.

Radio-Symphonie	se raser
le savon SAMBON	se laver
le dentifrice SOURIRE	se laver les cheveux
l'eau de toilette VÉSUVE	se maquiller
le shampooing CAPILLO	se couper les ongles
le séchoir SAHARA	se couper les cheveux
le rasoir BLIP	se brosser les dents
les ciseaux CLIP	se parfumer
la brosse à dents BRIL	se sécher les cheveux
le fard CLÉOPÂTRE	se réveiller en musique

▶ **Mesdemoiselles, maquillez-vous avec
le fard Cléopâtre!**

6 Baby-sitting

Vous faites du baby-sitting pour l'enfant de vos
voisins français. Dites-lui de faire les choses
suivantes. L'enfant (votre partenaire) va vous
répondre qu'il/elle ne peut pas. Puis, il/elle
va vous donner une excuse.

ACTIONS
• se peigner
• se laver les mains
• se laver les cheveux
• s'essuyer les mains
• se brosser les dents
• se sécher les cheveux

EXCUSES POSSIBLES
Je ne trouve pas . . .
Je ne sais pas où est . . .
Je ne peux pas trouver . . .
J'ai perdu . . .

▶ — **Brosse-toi les dents!**
— **Je ne peux pas me brosser les dents!**
— **Et pourquoi donc?**
— **J'ai perdu ma brosse à dents.**
  (Je ne trouve pas le dentifrice.)

ALLONS PLUS LOIN

To express what you or other people can do by themselves,
use the construction:

STRESS PRONOUN + **même(s)**

J'ai réparé mon vélo **moi-même.** *I fixed my bike by myself.*

→ **Même** is also used to reinforce a stress pronoun referring to the subject.
Jérôme parle toujours **de lui-même**. *Jérôme always talks about himself.*

**Moi-même,
toi-même, etc.**

Pratique ▶ p. 22

À LA RÉSIDENCE
BON REPOS

Aujourd'hui, les gens des villes habitent généralement dans des immeubles.° Ces immeubles ont beaucoup d'avantages . . . et quelques petits inconvénients.

Un jour comme un autre à la résidence° «Bon Repos» dans la banlieue° parisienne. Il est six heures du matin. Tout est calme. . . Tout d'un coup°. . .

SIXIÈME ÉTAGE

Drin. . . Drin . . . Un réveil° sonne° chez Monsieur Léveillé. Drin. . .Drin. . . Monsieur Léveillé se réveille en sursaut°. . . Puis il se lève, met sa robe de chambre° et va dans la salle de bains. Il se regarde dans la glace, se brosse les dents. Ensuite, il branche° son rasoir électrique et commence à se raser. Zzz. . . Zzz. . .

CINQUIÈME ÉTAGE

Le bruit° du rasoir électrique de Monsieur Léveillé réveille Madame Dumoulin. Elle ouvre un oeil, puis l'autre, et attend deux ou trois minutes. Finalement, elle se lève et va dans la cuisine pour se préparer une tasse de café. Elle branche son nouveau moulin° électrique. Grr. . . Grr. . .

QUATRIÈME ÉTAGE

Le moulin à café de Madame Dumoulin réveille Mademoiselle Lasouplesse. Elle se lève, enfile° un short et un tee-shirt, met une cassette vidéo de gymnastique et commence ses exercices. Une, deux. . . une, deux. . . une, deux . . .

TROISIÈME ÉTAGE

Quand il entend Mademoiselle Lasouplesse faire sa gymnastique, Monsieur Trémolo se réveille. Il va dans la salle de bains et prend une douche. Quand il se lave, Monsieur Trémolo adore chanter ses airs d'opéra favoris: «Toréador, toréador. . .»*

* «Toréador» is a well-known aria from Bizet's **Carmen**.

DEUXIÈME ÉTAGE

La belle voix de Monsieur Trémolo réveille Madame Bellamy. Elle se lève, prend un bain, et se lave les cheveux. Puis, elle s'habille, se peigne et se maquille. . .

À huit heures et demie, tous les locataires° de la résidence «Bon Repos» sont partis pour leurs occupations de la journée. . . Tous sauf° un. C'est Monsieur Morphée, le locataire du premier étage. Il travaille comme portier° de nuit dans un grand hôtel. À l'heure où les autres locataires se rendent° à leur travail, lui, il rentre chez lui. Là, il se déshabille et prend un bon bain. «Quelle chance d'habiter dans une résidence si calme» pense-t-il. Puis, il va dans sa chambre, met son pyjama, se couche et s'endort° d'un profond sommeil.

Une journée comme les autres vient de commencer.

---

immeubles *apartment buildings* **résidence** = l'immeuble **banlieue** *suburbs* **Tout d'un coup** *all of a sudden*
réveil *alarm clock* **sonne** *rings* **en sursaut** *with a start* **robe de chambre** *bathrobe* **branche** *plugs in*
bruit *noise* **moulin** *coffee grinder* **enfile** = met **locataires** *tenants* **sauf** = excepté **portier** *doorman*
se rendent = vont **s'endort** *falls asleep*

et vous?

À VOTRE TOUR

- Dites à quelle heure vous vous levez d'habitude et ce que vous faites après.
- Dites comment vous trouvez l'histoire que vous avez lue: réaliste? amusante? triste? exagérée? Expliquez pourquoi.

EXPRESSION ÉCRITE

Décrivez les habitudes des personnes de votre famille. Dites à quelle heure chaque personne se lève et ce qu'elle fait ensuite. (Votre description peut être réaliste ou imaginaire.)

LE FRANÇAIS PRATIQUE

La routine quotidienne

> Je me réveille à 7 heures et quart. Je me lève, et puis je me lave.

Il y a beaucoup de choses qu'on fait tous les jours. Ces choses font partie de la routine quotidienne *(daily).* Ici Stéphanie explique sa routine quotidienne:

Le matin . . .
> **Je me réveille** à 7 heures et quart.
> **Je me lève.**
> **Je me lave.**
> Je prends **un bain** *(bath)* ou **une douche** *(shower).*
> **Je m'habille.**

se réveiller	*to wake up*
se lever	*to get up*
se laver	*to wash*
s'habiller	*to get dressed*

Après le petit déjeuner . . .
> **Je me prépare.**
> Puis, **je me rends** à l'école.
> **Je me dépêche** pour être à l'heure.
> (Si je suis en retard, **je m'excuse.**)

se préparer	*to get ready*
se rendre à	*to go to*
se dépêcher	*to hurry*
s'excuser	*to apologize*

En classe . . .
> J'étudie.
> À midi, **je m'amuse** avec mes copains.

s'amuser	*to have fun*

L'après-midi, après les cours . . .
> **Je me promène** en ville.
> **Je m'arrête** parfois chez le marchand de glaces, et **je m'achète** une glace.
> Je rentre et **je me repose** un peu.

se promener	*to take a walk*
s'arrêter	*to stop*
s'acheter	*to buy (oneself)*
se reposer	*to rest*

À sept heures et demie . . .
> **Je me mets à table**
> et je dîne avec ma famille.
> Puis je fais mes devoirs.

se mettre à table	*to sit down to eat*

Le soir, **vers** *(at about)* onze heures . . .
> **Je me déshabille.**
> **Je me couche.**
> Et finalement **je m'endors.**

se déshabiller	*to get undressed*
se coucher	*to go to bed*
s'endormir	*to go to sleep*

Verbes comme acheter
se lever, se promener

Révision ▶ 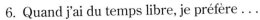 pp. R20-21

Pratique ▶ p. 23

① Et vous? ....

Décrivez certains aspects de votre vie. Comparez
vos réponses avec celles de votre partenaire.

1. En semaine, je me réveille . . .
   - avant sept heures
   - à sept heures
   - ??

2. Je me rends à l'école . . .
   - à pied
   - en bus
   - à vélo
   - ??

3. Le soir, je me couche . . .
   - avant dix heures
   - après onze heures
   - ??

4. Généralement, je m'endors . . .
   - vite *(fast)*
   - assez vite
   - difficilement
   - ??

5. Le dimanche, je ne me lève
   jamais . . .
   - avant huit heures
   - avant neuf heures
   - ??

6. Quand j'ai du temps libre, je préfère . . .
   - me reposer
   - me promener en ville
   - me rendre chez mes amis
   - ??

7. Quand je me promène en ville,
   j'aime mieux m'arrêter . . .
   - dans les magasins
   - dans un fast-food
   - ??

8. Avec mon argent, je préfère m'acheter . . .
   - des cassettes
   - des vêtements
   - des magazines
   - ??

9. Je me dépêche le plus pour aller . . .
   - à l'école
   - à un rendez-vous
   - à un concert
   - ??

10. En général, je m'excuse quand . . .
    - j'ai tort
    - je suis en retard
    - ??

Conversations libres

Avec votre partenaire, choisissez l'une des situations suivantes.
Composez le dialogue correspondant et jouez-le en classe.

1 — **Camarade de chambre**

Vous êtes étudiant(e) à l'université de
Montréal. Vous cherchez un(e) camarade
de chambre pour le trimestre prochain.
Expliquez votre routine quotidienne à un(e)
autre étudiant(e) (votre partenaire). Ensuite,
posez-lui des questions sur sa routine.

2 — **Activités du dimanche**

Vous avez invité un(e) camarade français(e)
(votre partenaire) à passer le week-end chez
vous. Expliquez-lui ce que vous faites le
dimanche. Demandez-lui s'il/si elle fait les
mêmes choses.

A. Le passé composé des verbes réfléchis

The PASSÉ COMPOSÉ of reflexive verbs is formed with **être.**

AFFIRMATIVE	je **me suis lavé** tu **t'es lavé** il/on **s'est lavé** nous **nous sommes lavés** vous **vous êtes lavé(s)** ils **se sont lavés**	je **me suis lavée** tu **t'es lavée** elle **s'est lavée** nous **nous sommes lavées** vous **vous êtes lavée(s)** elles **se sont lavées**
NEGATIVE	je **ne me suis pas lavé**	je **ne me suis pas lavée**
INTERROGATIVE	**est-ce que tu t'es lavé?** **t'es-tu lavé?**	**est-ce que tu t'es lavée?** **t'es-tu lavée?**

Usually, <u>but not always</u>, the past participle agrees with the subject.

> **Éric s'est promen**é. **Anne et Claire se sont promen**ées avec lui.

➡ There is <u>no agreement</u> when the reflexive verb is directly followed by a NOUN. Compare:

> Stéphanie **s'est lav**ée. Elle **s'est lav**é <u>les mains.</u>

Note also:

> Catherine et Sophie **se sont achet**é <u>des vêtements.</u>

1 Samedi dernier

Demandez à votre partenaire s'il/si elle a fait les choses suivantes samedi dernier. Votre partenaire peut donner des précisions correspondant aux questions.

> ▶ se lever tard (à quelle heure?)

> 1. se promener (où?)
> 2. s'acheter des vêtements (quels vêtements?)
> 3. s'acheter autre chose (quoi?)
> 4. s'amuser (comment?)
> 5. se reposer (quand?)
> 6. se coucher tard (à quelle heure?)

Est-ce que tu t'es levée tard samedi dernier?

Non, je ne me suis pas levée tard. Je me suis levée à 8 heures.

2 Qu'est-ce qu'ils ont fait?

Informez-vous sur les personnes suivantes et dites
ce qu'elles ont fait. Pour cela, utilisez les verbes suggérés.

▶ Monsieur Marty a pris son rasoir.   **Il s'est rasé.**

1. Caroline a pris le dentifrice.
2. Tu as pris tes vêtements.
3. Nous avons entendu le réveil *(alarm clock)*.
4. À minuit, tu es allé dans ta chambre.
5. Vous avez pris une semaine de vacances.
6. Nous sommes allées à la campagne.
7. Marc et Philippe ont vu un film très drôle.
8. Dans le bus, j'ai marché *(stepped)* sur les pieds
   de quelqu'un.
9. Le chauffeur de bus a vu le feu-rouge *(red light)*.
10. Tu as pris les ciseaux.
11. Vous avez voulu être à l'heure au rendez-vous.

s'amuser
s'arrêter
se brosser les dents
se coucher
se couper les ongles
se dépêcher
s'excuser
s'habiller
se promener
se raser
se reposer
se réveiller

3 La journée d'un mannequin

Christine est mannequin *(model)* pour un magazine de mode. Lisez comment elle
décrit sa journée:

Je me réveille à huit heures. Je ne me lève pas immédiatement.
J'attends dix minutes. Ensuite je me lève et je vais dans la salle de bains.
Là, je prends une douche et je me lave les cheveux. Ensuite je me maquille
et je m'habille. Vers neuf heures, je descends dans la cuisine et
je me prépare un petit déjeuner très léger *(light)*. Après, je regarde
le journal. Je téléphone à mon magazine pour faire mes rendez-vous.
Je réponds à mon courrier *(mail)*.

Vers dix heures et demie, je sors et je fais les courses. Je rentre
chez moi, mais je ne déjeune pas. À une heure, je prends un taxi. Je vais
directement au magazine pour les séances *(sessions)* de photo.
Je travaille tout l'après-midi.

À sept heures, je rentre chez moi et je dîne. Ensuite je regarde un film
à la télé. À onze heures je me couche et je m'endors.

Chaque jour, Christine suit la même routine. Décrivez ce qu'elle a fait hier.
▶ **Hier, Christine s'est réveillée à huit heures . . .**

4 Ma routine personnelle

Décrivez votre routine personnelle. Pour cela, composez un petit paragraphe où vous
racontez ce que vous avez fait hier. (Si nécessaire, utilisez votre imagination!) Ensuite,
comparez votre journée avec celle de votre partenaire.

▶ **Hier, c'était samedi [dimanche]. Je me suis réveillé(e) à . . .**

La condition physique et les sentiments

Comment te sens-tu?

Je me sens bien.

Qu'est-ce qu'il y a?

Je me sens fatigué.

COMMENT DEMANDER DES NOUVELLES À UN(E) AMI(E)

Ça va?
Comment te sens-tu? *How do you feel?*
Qu'est-ce que tu as? | *What's the matter?*
Qu'est-ce qu'il y a? | *What's wrong?*

se sentir *to feel*

COMMENT RÉPONDRE

Ça va. ☺

Je me sens | **bien.**
| **en forme** *(in shape)*
|
| **décontracté(e)** *(relaxed)*

Je suis | **heureux (heureuse).**
| **content(e)**
| **de bonne humeur**
| *(in a good mood)*

Ça ne va pas. ☹

Je me sens | **mal.**
| **malade**
| **fatigué(e)** *(tired)*
| **tendu(e)** *(tense, uptight)*

Je suis | **malheureux (malheureuse).**
| **triste** *(sad)*
| **de mauvaise humeur** *(in a bad mood)*
| **énervé(e)** *(upset)*
| **furieux (furieuse)**
| **en colère** *(angry)*

COMMENT DÉCRIRE QUELQU'UN

Ton ami(e) | **semble** | **calme.**
| **a l'air** |

Il/Elle | **semble** | **perplexe.**
| **a l'air** | **préoccupé(e)** *(worried)*
| | **inquiet (inquiète)** *(worried)*
| | **déçu(e)** *(disappointed)*

sembler *to seem*
avoir l'air *to look, appear*

▶ À noter

Sentir is conjugated like **dormir**.

sentir	*to smell*	Est-ce que **tu sens** cette bonne odeur?
se sentir (+ adjective or expression)	*to feel*	Est-ce que **tu te sens** fatigué? **Je me sens** en forme.
ressentir (+ noun)	*to feel (a pain or an emotion)*	**Je ressens** beaucoup d'admiration pour cette personne.

1 Ça va?

Choisissez trois des situations suivantes. Décrivez votre condition ou vos sentiments dans chacun des cas.

- Vous êtes en vacances.
- Vous avez un examen.
- Vous avez un rendez-vous.
- Vous faites du sport.
- Vous mangez trop.
- Vous étudiez trop.
- Vous avez une bonne note à un examen.
- Vous étudiez beaucoup mais vous avez une mauvaise note.

- Vous vous disputez avec votre copain (copine).
- Votre copain (copine) n'est pas à l'heure à un rendez-vous.
- Votre frère (soeur) oublie votre anniversaire.
- Le professeur est malade.
- Votre cousin(e) vous téléphone à une heure du matin.
- Vos professeurs sont contents de vous.
- Vos amis vous critiquent.

▶ **Quand j'ai un examen, je me sens malade (je me sens tendu(e), décontracté(e) . . .)**

2 Qu'est-ce qu'ils ont?

Décrivez les personnes suivantes. Avec votre partenaire, trouvez deux raisons pour cette situation.

▶ **— Monsieur Moreau a l'air en colère.**
— C'est parce qu'il a eu un accident de voiture.
— Non, je ne suis pas d'accord. C'est parce que son fils est rentré à deux heures du matin.

| M. Moreau | Thomas | Pauline | Juliette |
| Jean-Philippe | Mme Tessier | Charlotte | Christophe |

3 Créa-dialogue

C'est lundi matin. D'habitude votre partenaire est toujours de bonne humeur. Mais aujourd'hui il/elle est de mauvaise humeur. Vous voulez savoir pourquoi.

— Ça va?
— Non, ça ne va pas.
— Qu'est-ce que tu as?
— Je suis triste.
— Et pourquoi donc?
— Mon copain a oublié la date de mon anniversaire.

- *Use another expression.*
- *Express another feeling: anger, disappointment, worry . . .*
- *Give an original and appropriate reason.*

A. L'usage idiomatique des verbes réfléchis

Reflexive verbs are used:

- to describe certain MOVEMENTS

  se rendre à   *to go to*   Mme Meunier **se rend à** son bureau.

- to describe FEELINGS or changes in feelings

  s'impatienter   *to get impatient*   Pourquoi est-ce que tu **t'impatientes?**

- to describe certain other actions and situations

  s'excuser   *to apologize*   Tu as tort! **Excuse-toi!**

  se trouver   *to be (located)*   Où **se trouve** la pharmacie?

NE T'INQUIÈTE PAS!

Vocabulaire: Quelques verbes réfléchis

MOVEMENT

s'asseoir	*to sit down*		**s'approcher (de)**	*to come closer*
se lever	*to stand up*		**s'arrêter**	*to stop*
			s'en aller	*to go away*

FEELINGS

s'amuser	*to have fun*		**s'inquiéter**	*to worry*
s'embêter	*to get bored*		**se mettre en colère**	*to get angry*
s'impatienter	*to get impatient*		**se sentir (triste . . .)**	*to feel (sad)*
s'énerver	*to get upset*			

OTHER MEANINGS

s'appeler	*to be called, named*		**se rappeler**	*to remember; to recall*
se trouver	*to be (located)*		**se souvenir (de)**	*to remember*
s'intéresser à	*to be interested in*		**se tromper**	*to make a mistake*
s'occuper de	*to be busy with;*		**se taire**	*to be quiet; to shut up*
	to take care of			

➡ The verb **se souvenir** is conjugated like **venir.**

      PRESENT: **je me souviens**   **nous nous souvenons**   **elles se souviennent**

PASSÉ COMPOSÉ: **je me suis souvenu(e)**

➡ The following irregular verbs are commonly used in the imperative:

s'en aller	se taire	s'asseoir
Va-t'en!	Tais-toi!	Assieds-toi!
Allez-vous-en!	Taisez-vous!	Asseyez-vous!

➕ Transports Québec

AU QUÉBEC, LA PRUDENCE FAIT TOUTE LA DIFFÉRENCE!

⚜ Je me souviens

Le présent des verbes **s'appeler, se rappeler (comme appeler)**

Révision ▶ pp. R20-21

Pratique ▶ p. 25

ALLONS PLUS LOIN

Reflexive verbs are also used to express a reciprocal action, that is, an action in which two or more people interact with one another.

Philippe et Claire **se téléphonent.**	*Philippe and Claire **phone each other.***
Marc et moi, **nous nous voyons** souvent.	*Marc and I often **see each other.***
Où est-ce que vous allez **vous retrouver?**	*Where are you going **to meet (each other)?***

1 Une question de personnalité

Analysez la personnalité des personnes suivantes et dites si oui ou non elles font les choses entre parenthèses.

▶ Tu es toujours calme. (s'inquiéter?)
Tu ne t'inquiètes pas.

1. Tu as une excellente mémoire. (se souvenir de tout?)
2. Vous n'aimez pas attendre. (s'impatienter?)
3. Alice est optimiste. (se sentir triste?)
4. Philippe est très irritable. (se mettre souvent en colère?)
5. Nous sommes curieux. (s'intéresser à tout?)
6. J'aime étudier. (s'embêter en classe?)
7. Tu es très patient. (s'énerver?)
8. Nous avons toujours raison. (se tromper?)

2 Que dire?

Qu'est-ce que vous allez dire à votre ami français dans les circonstances suivantes?
Utilisez l'impératif affirmatif ou négatif des verbes de la liste. Soyez logique dans votre choix!

▶ Votre ami est furieux. **Ne te mets pas en colère!**
▶ Il a tort. **Excuse-toi!**

- Il parle trop.
- Il attend sa copine depuis une heure.
- Il est insupportable *(unbearable)* avec vous.
- Il a un problème avec ses parents.
- Il va à une boum.
- Il a un examen de maths.
- Il est fatigué.
- Il a une entrevue professionnelle dans une semaine.

s'amuser
s'asseoir sur cette chaise
s'en aller
s'excuser
s'impatienter
s'inquiéter
se mettre en colère
se souvenir de la date
se taire
se tromper dans les calculs

3 Et vous?

Complétez les phrases suivantes avec une expression personnelle.
Ensuite, comparez vos réponses avec celles de votre partenaire.

1. Je m'intéresse à . . .
2. Je me souviens toujours de . . .
3. Je m'amuse quand . . .
4. Je m'embête quand . . .
5. Je m'inquiète quand . . .
6. Je me sens triste quand . . .
7. Je me sens heureux (heureuse) quand . . .
8. Je me mets en colère quand . . .
9. Je me sens fatigué(e) quand . . .
10. Je ne me tais pas quand . . .

4 Zut alors!

Aujourd'hui les personnes suivantes ont eu des problèmes. Expliquez leurs problèmes.
Attention: les phrases peuvent être affirmatives ou négatives!

▶ Philippe / s'amuser à la boum
Philippe ne s'est pas amusé à la boum.

1. vous / s'énerver pendant l'examen
2. moi / se souvenir de mon rendez-vous
3. les élèves / se tromper dans l'exercice
4. Alice / se mettre en colère
5. nous / s'impatienter
6. toi / s'embêter pendant la classe
7. Pierre et Robert / se sentir malades au restaurant
8. Isabelle / se sentir en forme

Conte pour enfants
de moins de trois ans

Eugène Ionesco

Eugène Ionesco (1912-1994) est né en Roumanie. Il fait des études de français à l'université de Bucarest, et devient lui-même professeur de français. En 1938, il quitte son pays menacé par le nazisme et vient s'installer en France. Il commence alors une brillante carrière littéraire qui lui vaudra d'être nommé à l'Académie française.

Ionesco est l'auteur de 33 pièces de théâtre. Dans ses pièces, il dénonce la banalité ou l'angoisse de l'existence avec une arme très puissante: l'humour. Combattant l'absurde par l'absurde, Ionesco a créé un théâtre entièrement nouveau que ses critiques ont justement appelé «Le Théâtre de l'Absurde».

AVANT DE LIRE

Dans ce conte, Ionesco met en scène un père et sa petite fille, âgée de deux ans et demi, dans une situation ordinaire de l'existence. Un matin, papa et sa fille se trouvent seuls à la maison. Pour une raison inexpliquée, la maman est partie chez sa mère. (Il y a peut-être eu une dispute dans le couple.) La petite fille, inquiète° de l'absence de sa mère, veut rester tout près de son père, mais celui-ci, qui veut se laver, n'a pas besoin d'elle. Pour être seul, il joue sur la psychologie des enfants: ce qui est absurde ou illogique pour un adulte peut sembler tout à fait° naturel et logique pour un enfant.

Pour mieux comprendre une histoire, il est utile de savoir quel genre° d'histoire c'est. À votre avis, d'après le titre, les illustrations et la note biographique sur Ionesco, quel genre d'histoire allez-vous lire?

- une histoire réaliste?
- une histoire humoristique?
- un drame psychologique?
- un conte fantastique?
- un récit d'aventures?

inquiète *worried*   **tout à fait** = complètement   **genre** = sorte

NOTE CULTURELLE

L'Académie française

Créée en 1635, l'Académie française a pour but° de préserver la langue française. Cette prestigieuse institution a 40 membres, appelés les «Immortels». Ce sont généralement des écrivains français très connus. Eugène Ionesco est l'un des rares Académiciens d'origine étrangère.

but = objectif

Mots utiles

avoir mal à l'estomac	*to have an upset stomach*
avoir mal à la tête	*to have a headache*
empêcher de	*to stop, keep from (doing)*
frapper	*to knock*
pleurer	*to cry*
profiter de	*to take advantage of*

Conte pour enfants de moins de trois ans

Ce matin, comme d'habitude,° Josette frappe à la porte de la chambre à
coucher de ses parents. Papa n'a pas très bien dormi. Maman est partie à
la campagne* pour quelques jours. Alors papa a profité de cette absence pour
manger beaucoup de saucisson, pour boire de la bière, pour manger du pâté
5   de cochon,** et beaucoup d'autres choses que maman l'empêche de manger
parce que c'est pas bon pour la santé.° Alors, voilà, papa a mal au foie,** il a mal
à l'estomac, il a mal à la tête, et ne voudrait pas se réveiller. Mais Josette frappe
toujours° à la porte. Alors papa lui dit d'entrer. Elle entre, elle va chez son papa.
Il n'y a pas maman. Josette demande:
10   — Où elle est maman?
     Papa répond: «Ta maman est allée se reposer à
                 la campagne chez sa maman à elle.»
     Josette répond: «Chez Mémée?»°
     Papa répond: «Oui, chez Mémée.»
15   — Écris à maman, dit Josette. Téléphone à maman, dit Josette.
     Papa dit: «Faut pas téléphoner.»
     Josette dit: «Raconte une histoire avec maman et toi, et moi.»
       — Non, dit papa, je vais aller au travail. Je me lève, je vais m'habiller.
Et papa se lève. Il met sa robe de chambre° rouge, par-dessus° son pyjama, il
20   met dans les pieds ses *poutouffles*.° Il va dans la salle de bains. Il ferme la porte
de la salle de bains. Josette est à la porte de la salle de bains. Elle frappe avec ses
petits poings,° elle pleure.
     Josette dit: «Ouvre-moi la porte.»
     Papa répond: «Je ne peux pas. Je suis tout nu,° je me lave, après je me rase.»
25   Josette dit: «Tu laves ta figure, tu laves tes épaules,° tu laves tes bras, tu laves
               ton dos, tu laves ton *dérère*,° tu laves tes pieds.
       — Je rase ma barbe, dit papa.
       — Tu rases ta barbe avec du savon, dit Josette. Je veux entrer. Je veux voir.

   * **La campagne.** In French, the term **la campagne** (the country) is used to refer to any area outside **la ville** (the city).
 ** **Mal au foie.** The French believe that eating too many fatty foods, such as **saucisson** (sausage) and **pâté de
    cochon** (a type of meatloaf made of ground pork and served cold), and drinking too much wine or beer leads to **mal
    au foie** (abdominal pain indicating liver trouble).

comme d'habitude *as usual* **santé** *health* **toujours** = sans arrêter **Mémée** = grand-mère **robe de chambre**
bathrobe **par-dessus** = sur **poutouffles** = pantoufles *slippers* **poings** *fists* **nu** *naked, nude* **épaules** *shoulders*
dérère = derrière *behind, rear end*

Avez-vous compris?

1. Comment le Papa de
Josette se sent-il ce
matin-là? Pourquoi?
2. Qu'est-ce que Josette
demande d'abord à
son père?
3. Selon vous, pourquoi
est-ce que Josette
veut rester près de
son père?

Anticipons un peu!

Imaginez que vous êtes dans une situation semblable à celle du Papa. Vous
êtes dans la salle de bains où vous vous habillez pour aller à un rendez-
vous. Vous vous dépêchez parce que vous avez peur d'être en retard . . .
Votre petit(e) frère (soeur) veut entrer dans la salle de bains. Il/elle pleure,
mais vous savez que ce n'est pas trop grave. Qu'est-ce que vous allez faire?

- fermer la porte à clé?
- dire à votre petit(e) frère (soeur) de se taire?
- ouvrir la porte et lui donner une sucette *(lollypop)*?
- sortir de la salle de bains pour lui raconter une histoire?
- trouver une autre solution plus originale? laquelle?

Maintenant, lisez la deuxième partie pour voir ce que le papa de Josette a fait.

II

un canapé

un buffet

les casseroles

le four

Papa dit: «Tu ne peux pas me voir, parce que je ne suis plus dans
   la salle de bains.»
Josette dit (derrière la porte): «Alors, où tu es?»
Papa répond: «Je ne sais pas, va voir. Je suis peut-être dans la salle
   à manger, va me chercher.»
Josette court dans la salle à manger, et papa commence sa toilette. Josette
court avec ses petites jambes, elle va dans la salle à manger.
Papa est tranquille, mais pas longtemps. Josette arrive de nouveau devant
la porte de la salle de bains, elle crie à travers la porte:
Josette: «Je t'ai cherché. Tu n'es pas dans la salle à manger.»
Papa dit: «Tu n'as pas bien cherché. Regarde sous la table.»
Josette retourne dans la salle à manger. Elle revient.
   Elle dit: «Tu n'es pas sous la table.»
Papa dit: «Alors va voir dans le salon. Regarde bien si je suis sur le
   fauteuil, sur le canapé, derrière les livres, à la fenêtre.»
Josette s'en va. Papa est tranquille, mais pas pour longtemps.
Josette revient.
   Elle dit: «Non, tu n'es pas dans le fauteuil, tu n'es pas à la fenêtre,
      tu n'es pas sur le canapé, tu n'es pas derrière les livres, tu n'es
      pas dans la télévision, tu n'es pas dans le salon.»
Papa dit: «Alors, va voir si je suis dans la cuisine.»
Josette dit: «Je vais te chercher dans la cuisine.»
Josette court à la cuisine. Papa est tranquille, mais pas pour longtemps.
Josette revient.
   Elle dit: «Tu n'es pas dans la cuisine.»
Papa dit: «Regarde bien, sous la table de la cuisine, regarde bien si je
   suis dans le buffet, regarde bien si je suis dans les casseroles,
   regarde bien si je suis dans le four avec le poulet.»
Josette va et vient. Papa n'est pas dans le four, papa n'est pas dans les
casseroles, papa n'est pas dans le buffet, papa n'est pas sous le paillasson,
papa n'est pas dans la poche de son pantalon. Dans la poche du pantalon,
il y a seulement le mouchoir.
Josette revient devant la porte de la salle de bains.
   Josette dit: «J'ai cherché partout. Je ne t'ai pas trouvé. Où tu es?»

le paillasson

Mots utiles

aller voir	*to go look*
courir*	*to run*
crier	*to yell, shout*
embrasser	*to kiss*
être tranquille	*to be alone, undisturbed*
revenir*	*to come back*
sauter	*to jump*
à travers	*across, through*
de nouveau	*again*
ne . . . plus	*no longer, not anymore*

la poche, le mouchoir

une armoire

un tapis

une poubelle

Papa dit: «Je suis là.» Et papa, qui a eu le temps de faire sa toilette, qui s'est rasé, qui s'est habillé, ouvre la porte.

65 Il dit: «Je suis là.» Il prend Josette dans ses bras, et voilà aussi la porte de la maison qui s'ouvre, au fond du couloir,° et c'est maman qui arrive. Josette saute° des bras de son papa, elle se jette° dans les bras de sa maman, elle l'embrasse, elle dit:

— Maman, j'ai cherché papa sous la table, dans l'armoire, sous
70 le tapis, derrière la glace, dans la cuisine, dans la poubelle, il n'était pas là.

Papa dit à maman: «Je suis content que tu sois revenue. Il faisait beau à la campagne? Comment va ta mère?»

Josette dit: «Et Mémée, elle va bien? On va chez elle?»

au fond du couloir *at the end of the hall*   **saute** *jump*   **se jette** *throws herself*

Avez-vous compris?

1. Quel stratagème est-ce que le père utilise pour être tranquille?
2. Est-ce que ce stratagème réussit? Pourquoi, selon vous?
3. Comment se termine l'histoire?

APRÈS LA LECTURE

EXPRESSION ORALE

■ Situation
Avec votre partenaire, composez un dialogue correspondant à la situation suivante. Utilisez votre imagination.

Au bureau
Le papa de Josette parle de son week-end avec un(e) collègue de bureau qui veut des détails. Il décrit . . .
• pourquoi sa femme n'était pas là (il ne dit pas la vérité), et où elle était
• ce qu'il a bu et mangé
• ce qu'il a fait avec sa petite fille
• ce qu'il a fait d'autre

Rôles: le papa, le/la collègue

■ Théâtre
Avec votre partenaire, composez une scène semblable au conte que vous avez lu sur le thème suivant: Stéphanie (18 ans) fait du baby-sitting pour Dominique (3 ans). Elle veut téléphoner à son copain, mais Dominique ne la laisse pas tranquille. Pour se libérer, Stéphanie utilise un stratagème semblable à celui de l'histoire. (Variation: c'est Stéphane qui fait du baby-sitting, et il veut téléphoner à sa copine.)

EXPRESSION ÉCRITE

■ Un peu d'humour
Décrivez brièvement les éléments de l'histoire que vous avez trouvés drôles.

■ Une lettre
Imaginez que vous êtes la mère de Josette. Vous écrivez à votre cousine pour lui expliquer les événements du week-end. Vous pouvez mentionner. . .
• la raison de votre dispute avec votre mari (Inventez!)
• où vous êtes allée et ce que vous avez fait (Inventez!)
• quand vous êtes rentrée chez vous et pourquoi vous étiez heureuse de rentrer

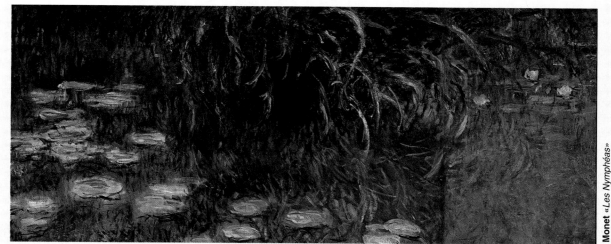

Monet *«Les Nymphéas»*

■ *La Révolution impressionniste* ■

L'art moderne est né en France dans les années 1870. C'est à cette époque, en effet, qu'un groupe d'artistes, nommés «les **Impressionnistes**», a présenté au monde une nouvelle façon° de concevoir la peinture. Avant eux, la peinture° était très traditionnelle. Les artistes essayaient d'imiter la réalité en reproduisant de façon très exacte et avec beaucoup de détails les sujets qu'ils peignaient. Ils apprenaient leur métier° dans des «académies», c'est-à-dire dans des écoles où ils copiaient minutieusement des modèles sous la direction de maîtres sans grande imagination. Pour ces artistes, l'essentiel dans la peinture était la forme.

Au lieu de° s'intéresser à la forme, les Impressionnistes se sont intéressés à la couleur, et surtout aux effets de la lumière° sur les objets qu'ils représentaient. Au lieu de peindre des scènes de bataille ou des héros de l'Antiquité, ils ont peint des scènes de la vie courante,° des portraits d'amis, et surtout la nature. Au lieu de travailler dans des ateliers,° ils ont travaillé en plein air.° Cette façon simple et naturelle de peindre a révolutionné le monde des arts.

À l'origine, cependant, les Impressionnistes n'ont eu aucun° succès. C'est par dérision° qu'un journaliste leur a donné le nom d'«impressionnistes». Ces peintres ne pouvaient même pas exposer leurs toiles° dans les salons officiels patronnés par le gouvernement. Ils ont donc organisé leurs propres° expositions chez des amis. Il y a eu huit expositions impressionnistes entre 1874 et 1886, mais ces expositions ont été des échecs.°

La peinture impressionniste choquait trop le sens esthétique de l'époque!

Peu à peu, les critiques d'art ont finalement compris l'importance de la «révolution» impressionniste. Les collectionneurs ont commencé à acheter les tableaux° de ces peintres. Aujourd'hui, ces tableaux valent° des fortunes. On peut les admirer dans les plus grands musées du monde: à Paris, à New York, à Londres, à Chicago, à Boston, à Saint Pétersbourg.

Les peintres impressionnistes sont considérés parmi° les plus grands artistes de tous les temps: **Monet**, **Manet**, **Cézanne**, **Renoir**, **Degas** . . . Parmi ces artistes, il y avait des femmes: **Berthe Morisot** et une Américaine, **Mary Cassatt**. Mary Cassatt, fille d'un riche banquier de Philadelphie, était venue étudier l'art à Paris. En faisant connaître° l'impressionnisme aux États-Unis, elle en a assuré le triomphe dans le monde.

---

façon *manner* **peinture** *painting* **métier** *trade* **au lieu de** *instead of* **lumière** *light* **vie courante** *daily life* **ateliers** *studios* **en plein air** *outdoors* **aucun** *no* **dérision** *mockery* **toiles** *paintings (canvases)* **propres** *own* **échecs** *failures* **tableaux** *paintings* **valent** *are worth* **parmi** *among* **en faisant connaître** *by making known*

■ *Quelques peintres impressionnistes*

Degas *«Répétition d'un ballet»*

■ Edgar Degas (1834-1917)

Degas était le fils d'un banquier. Sa mère était issue d'une riche famille de La Nouvelle-Orléans. Degas a étudié le droit°, mais il a abandonné ses études pour se consacrer à la peinture. C'était aussi un sculpteur. Ses sujets préférés étaient les danseuses de l'Opéra, les scènes de café et les chevaux.

Manet *«Le fifre»*

■ Édouard Manet (1832-1883)

Manet voulait être officier de marine, mais après un voyage au Brésil, il a décidé de se consacrer à la peinture. Ses premiers tableaux, de couleurs violentes, ont provoqué l'hostilité du public et des critiques, mais l'admiration de jeunes peintres alors inconnus: Monet, Renoir, Cézanne. C'est ainsi qu'il est devenu le chef d'un nouveau mouvement qui allait être l'impressionnisme. Manet a peint toutes sortes de sujets: portraits de ses amis, scènes de la vie courante et familière, paysages° divers.

■ Pierre-Auguste Renoir (1841-1919)

Renoir a commencé par peindre des devantures° de café, puis il est allé à l'École des Beaux-Arts. Ce peintre aimait les couleurs chaudes. Ses sujets principaux sont les enfants, les jeunes filles, les femmes, les fleurs, les scènes de café et les bals populaires.

Renoir *«La Danse à Bougival»*

■ Berthe Morisot (1841-1895)

Berthe Morisot était la belle-sœur d'Édouard Manet. Elle s'est intéressée très jeune à la peinture. Comme beaucoup d'artistes de l'époque, elle a commencé à copier les tableaux du musée du Louvre. C'est là qu'elle a fait la connaissance de Manet. Elle a alors rejoint le groupe des peintres impressionnistes. Elle a peint avec eux et elle a participé à leurs expositions. Berthe Morisot aimait utiliser les couleurs claires.° Ses sujets principaux sont les fleurs, les paysages, les scènes de la vie champêtre° et les portraits de jeunes filles.

Morisot *«Fillette lisant / La lecture»*

---

droit *law* **devantures** *store fronts* **paysages** *landscapes* **claires** *light* **champêtre** = *rurale*

■ *Claude Monet: le peintre de la lumière*

C'est un tableau de **Monet** intitulé **«Impression, soleil levant»°** qui a donné son nom à l'impressionnisme. Monet (1840-1926) était fasciné par les effets de la lumière. Il pensait qu'on pouvait reconstituer les reflets de la lumière sur les objets en décomposant celle-ci° en ses couleurs fondamentales. Il a donc inventé une technique qui consistait à peindre par petites taches° de couleur: du jaune, du rouge, du bleu, du vert, de l'orange et aussi du blanc et du noir.

Monet *«Impression, soleil levant»*

Monet, *«Gare Saint Lazare»*

Claude Monet *(1840-1926)*

Monet aimait peindre et repeindre les mêmes scènes sous des lumières différentes: à midi, très tôt le matin, le soir, au printemps, en plein été, sous la neige. Il a ainsi exécuté des séries entières d'un seul° sujet peint à différents moments de la journée ou de l'année. Monet a peint surtout des paysages, mais il a peint aussi des scènes urbaines très célèbres: **la cathédrale de Rouen, la Gare Saint Lazare** à Paris, **la Tamise°** à Londres.

Pendant de longues années, Monet est resté très pauvre, mais avec le succès de l'impressionnisme, il a finalement connu la célébrité, la gloire et la fortune. Après des années de misère, il est devenu un véritable héros national.

Monet, *«La cathédrale de Rouen»*

---

soleil levant *rising sun*   **celle-ci** = la lumière   **taches** *spots*   **un seul** *only one*   **la Tamise** *Thames (River)*

Monet a vécu° longtemps dans une maison de campagne située à **Giverny**, à 60 kilomètres de Paris. Devant cette maison, il avait créé un superbe jardin avec une très grande variété de fleurs qui changeait de couleur avec les saisons. C'est ce jardin aux couleurs chaudes et variées que Monet a peint dans de nombreux tableaux. À Giverny, Monet aimait recevoir ses amis et aussi beaucoup de jeunes peintres qui venaient écouter ses conseils.° Parmi ces peintres, il y avait une colonie d'artistes américains qui s'étaient installés dans un hôtel près de la maison de l'artiste. Vers° la fin° de sa vie, malheureusement, ce grand artiste de la lumière était devenu aveugle,° et ne pouvait plus peindre.

    Après la mort de Monet, la maison de Giverny et son jardin ont été abandonnés. Heureusement, grâce à° la générosité d'une riche Américaine, cette maison a été récemment restaurée et le jardin recréé dans sa splendeur originale. Aujourd'hui des centaines de milliers de visiteurs venus du monde entier viennent chaque année à Giverny saluer la mémoire du grand artiste français et admirer son merveilleux jardin.

Maison de Monet à Giverny

Renoir, *«Monet peignant dans son jardin»*

Monet, *«Le pont japonais»*

Détail, «Le pont japonais»

Le jardin de Monet à Giverny

vécu *lived* **conseils** *advice* **vers** *towards* **fin** *end* **aveugle** *blind* **grâce à** *thanks to*

■ *Après l'Impressionnisme* ■

Une conséquence importante de l'impressionnisme a été de libérer l'art des normes esthétiques traditionnelles. Ce mouvement a donc ouvert° des voies° nouvelles à d'autres artistes qui ont pu exercer librement° leur imagination et leur créativité. Après l'impressionnisme, d'autres mouvements artistiques sont nés en France. Vers 1900, Paris était devenu la capitale universelle des arts, attirant° des artistes de tous les pays du monde.

Van Gogh «*La nuit étoilée*»

■ Vincent Van Gogh (1853-1890): Le génie de la folie

Van Gogh était hollandais, mais c'est en France qu'il a peint ses tableaux les plus célèbres. Comme les Impressionnistes, il avait un sens profond de la lumière et des couleurs brillantes, mais il est allé plus loin qu'eux. Van Gogh voulait non seulement peindre ce qu'il voyait, mais cherchait aussi à exprimer les sensations° étranges qu'il éprouvait.° Pour cela, il exagérait l'intensité des couleurs et il donnait un mouvement aux choses inanimées. Ses représentations de la lune° et des étoiles° tournant dans le ciel° sont particulièrement hallucinantes.

■ Paul Gauguin (1848-1903): Le peintre de l'exotisme

Gauguin travaillait dans une banque où il gagnait bien sa vie. Un jour, à l'âge de 35 ans, il a décidé de tout abandonner, travail, famille, enfants, vie confortable, pour se consacrer totalement à la peinture. Il a rejoint les peintres impressionnistes, mais c'est dans l'exotisme qu'il a cherché son inspiration. Il est allé à Panama, à la Martinique, à Tahiti et, finalement, dans une petite île des Marquises.* Là, loin de la civilisation et en compagnie de gens simples, mais nobles et généreux, il a peint ses plus belles toiles.

* Les Marquises: a group of islands in the South Pacific

Gauguin «*Femmes de Tahiti*»

Rousseau «*La bohémienne endormie*»

■ Henri Rousseau (1844-1910): Le douanier inspiré

Pendant la semaine, **Henri Rousseau** était un bureaucrate dont° le travail consistait à contrôler le trafic des marchandises à l'entrée de Paris (d'où son surnom de «douanier»).° Le dimanche, cet employé modèle quittait la ville avec sa boîte de peintures pour aller peindre en plein air. Comme il n'avait jamais étudié dans une école d'art, Rousseau utilisait une technique très rudimentaire où la perspective n'existait pas. Si son style était simple, «naïf», son imagination était débordante.° Ses tableaux les plus célèbres représentent des paysages irréels peuplés° d'animaux exotiques.

ouvert *opened* **voies** *ways* **librement** *freely* **attirant** *attracting* **sensations** *feelings* **éprouvait** *experienced, felt*
lune *moon* **étoiles** *stars* **ciel** *sky* **dont** *whose* **douanier** *customs officer* **débordante** *overflowing* **peuplés** *populated*

Toulouse-Lautrec «Jane Avril au Jardin de Paris»

■ Toulouse-Lautrec (1864-1901): **Le peintre de la vie parisienne**

Henri de Toulouse-Lautrec est né dans une famille aristocratique très illustre et très ancienne. À l'âge de 14 ans, il a eu un accident de cheval qui l'a rendu infirme° pour le reste de sa vie. Encouragé par sa mère, il a décidé de devenir artiste et il est allé étudier à l'École des Beaux Arts à Paris. Toulouse-Lautrec aimait fréquenter° les cafés, les cabarets et les music-halls, comme le Moulin Rouge pour lequel° il a dessiné des affiches célèbres.

Dans ses tableaux, il a surtout représenté les scènes de spectacle auxquels il assistait: théâtre, music-hall, cirque, vélodrome°. . . Il a immortalisé les artistes de ces spectacles, comme Jane Avril, dans de nombreux portraits.

■ Henri Matisse (1869-1954): **Le grand Fauve**

C'est au lit que **Matisse** a découvert la peinture. Jeune homme, il étudiait le droit pour être avocat. Les complications d'une appendicite l'ont obligé à rester dans sa chambre pendant plusieurs mois. Un jour, pour le distraire°, sa mère lui a offert des pinceaux° et une boîte de couleurs.° Tout d'un coup, Matisse a eu la révélation de sa véritable° vocation. Après sa maladie, il a abandonné ses études de droit pour se consacrer uniquement et entièrement à la peinture.

Matisse est l'un des plus grands artistes du vingtième siècle. Durant sa vie, Matisse a peint dans des styles très différents. Vers 1900, il a fondé avec quelques amis un nouveau mouvement artistique, le «Fauvisme». (On appelle ces artistes les «Fauves»° non seulement parce qu'ils utilisaient des couleurs violentes — rouge, brun, orange — mais aussi parce que leurs ateliers ressemblaient à des tanières° de bêtes sauvages!)

Plus tard, Matisse a utilisé des couleurs plus claires et plus délicates pour peindre des fruits, des fleurs, des jeunes femmes d'une façon très décorative. Il s'est exprimé dans des médias divers: il a dessiné, sculpté, illustré des livres, fait des collages avec du papier découpé.° Vers la fin de sa vie, Matisse était malade et paralysé, mais il a continué à peindre en attachant des pinceaux à ses avant-bras.°

Matisse «La desserte rouge»

Matisse «Icarus, Jazz»

■ Camille Claudel (1864-1943): **L'élève, égale au maître**

Claudel «Autoportrait»

Comme beaucoup de jeunes filles de son époque, **Camille Claudel** voulait être artiste. Comme elle s'intéressait à la sculpture, elle a décidé d'aller à Paris pour étudier sous la direction d'Auguste Rodin, le plus grand sculpteur d'alors. D'élève, Camille Claudel est devenue l'assistante et l'inspiratrice du maître. Son influence est présente dans un grand nombre de sculptures de Rodin.

Camille Claudel était elle-même un grand sculpteur, mais ses oeuvres,° produites dans l'ombre° d'un homme que l'on considérait comme l'un des grands génies de son temps, sont longtemps restées ignorées. Un film sur sa vie tragique a fait redécouvrir le talent de cette artiste méconnue.°

infirme crippled **fréquenter** = visiter **lequel** which **vélodrome** bicycle racetrack **distraire** to amuse **pinceaux** brushes **boîte de couleurs** paintbox
véritable true **Fauves** wild beasts **tanières** lairs **découpé** cut out **avant-bras** forearms **oeuvres** works **ombre** shadow **méconnue** unrecognized

Le surréalisme

■ *Peinture . . .*

Regardez bien ce tableau. Il représente un homme avec un chapeau sur la tête et une pomme verte. La juxtaposition de cette personne réelle avec un objet réel constitue une situation qui n'est pas réelle. C'est une situation surréelle ou «**surréaliste**».

L'artiste qui a peint ce tableau est l'un des plus grands peintres surréalistes. Il était belge et s'appelait **René Magritte**. Magritte ressemblait beaucoup à l'homme du tableau. Il portait souvent une cravate, un manteau et un chapeau, même° quand il peignait. Il n'avait pas de studio. Il peignait ses tableaux dans sa cuisine ou dans son salon. Quand il ne travaillait pas, il aimait faire les courses ou promener son chien Loulou, comme les gens du quartier où il habitait. Cet homme à l'apparence très ordinaire faisait des tableaux absolument extraordinaires.

Les peintres surréalistes comme Magritte voulaient choquer le public en créant° des scènes bizarres à partir° d'éléments étrangement réels. Quand on regarde un tableau surréaliste, on reste perplexe et on veut savoir ce que veut représenter l'artiste. Quelle est la signification° des scènes qui apparemment n'ont pas de sens? La réponse est donnée par Magritte lui-même. Quand les gens lui demandaient d'expliquer ses tableaux, il répondait: «C'est simple! L'explication, c'est qu'il n'y a pas d'explication!»

Magritte, «La Grande Guerre»

René Magritte (1898–1967)

Magritte, «Carte Blanche»

même *even* **en créant** *by creating* **à partir de** *from* **signification** *meaning*

■ . . . *et littérature*

Le surréalisme est un mouvement à la fois° artistique et littéraire. Ce mouvement est né en Belgique et en France vers 1920, quelques années après la première guerre mondiale.* Les artistes et les écrivains surréalistes se sont révoltés contre tous les aspects de la société d'alors, responsable, selon eux, de cette terrible guerre.

Pour les surréalistes, le monde tel qu'on le connaît° est une création artificielle. La véritable réalité vient du subconscient qu'on peut atteindre° par le rêve.° Le surréalisme rejette la raison et la logique. La seule° source d'inspiration est l'imagination, mais celle-ci° doit être libre de tout contrôle et de toute convention. Comme les enfants, et comme dans les rêves, les surréalistes ont construit un monde imaginaire où tout est possible.

* La première guerre mondiale (*World War I*): 1914-1918.

à la fois *at the same time*   **tel qu'on le connaît** *as we know it*   **atteindre** *to reach*   **rêve** *dream*   **seule** *only*   **celle-ci** = l'imagination

Documents: La fourmi

LA FOURMI

Une fourmi de dix-huit mètres
Avec un chapeau sur la tête,
Ça n'existe pas, ça n'existe pas.

Une fourmi traînant un char
Plein de pingouins et de canards,
Ça n'existe pas, ça n'existe pas.

Une fourmi parlant français,
Parlant latin et javanais,
Ça n'existe pas, ça n'existe pas.

    Eh! Pourquoi pas?

Robert Desnos (1900-1945)

Robert Desnos est l'un des fondateurs du surréalisme. Pendant la deuxième guerre mondiale, il a participé à la Résistance contre les Allemands. Fait prisonnier, il est mort dans un camp en Tchécoslovaquie.

Dans ce petit poème très simple, Desnos pose la question fondamentale du surréalisme: **Où est la réalité? Dans ce que nous voyons ou dans ce que nous imaginons?**

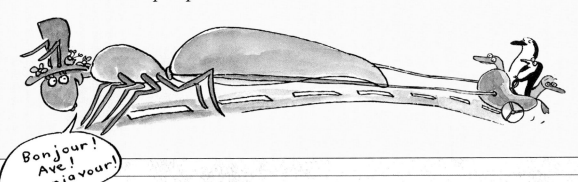

Pour faire le portrait d'un oiseau

Peindre d'abord une cage
avec une porte ouverte
peindre ensuite
quelque chose de joli
quelque chose de simple
quelque chose de beau
quelque chose d'utile
pour l'oiseau

Jacques Prévert (1900-1977)

Jacques Prévert (1900-1977) est un autre poète surréaliste. Il a aussi écrit des chansons et des scénarios° de films. Dans ce poème, il explique de façon humoristique comment peindre° un oiseau.

placer ensuite la toile° contre un arbre
dans un jardin
dans un bois°
ou dans une forêt
se cacher° derrière l'arbre
sans rien dire
sans bouger°. . .

Parfois l'oiseau arrive vite
mais il peut aussi bien mettre de
longues années
avant de se décider

Ne pas se décourager
attendre
attendre s'il le faut pendant des
années
la vitesse° ou la lenteur° de l'arrivée
de l'oiseau n'ayant aucun rapport°
avec la réussite du tableau

Quand l'oiseau arrive
s'il arrive
observer le plus profond silence
attendre que l'oiseau entre dans
la cage et quand il est entré
fermer doucement° la porte avec
le pinceau°
puis
effacer° un à un tous les barreaux
en ayant soin de ne toucher aucune
des plumes de l'oiseau

Faire ensuite le portrait de l'arbre
en choisissant la plus belle de ses branches
pour l'oiseau
peindre aussi le vert feuillage° et la fraîcheur° du vent
la poussière° du soleil
et le bruit des bêtes de l'herbe dans la chaleur° de l'été
et puis attendre que l'oiseau se décide de chanter
Si l'oiseau ne chante pas
c'est mauvais signe
signe que le tableau est mauvais
mais s'il chante c'est bon signe
signe que vous pouvez signer
alors vous arrachez° tout doucement
une des plumes de l'oiseau
et vous écrivez votre nom dans un coin° du tableau

---

scénarios *scripts*   **peindre** *to paint*   **toile** *canvas*   **bois** *woods*   **se cacher** *hide*   **sans bouger** *without moving*   **vitesse** *speed*
lenteur *slowness*   **aucun rapport** *no relationship*   **doucement** *gently*   **pinceau** *brush*   **effacer** *erase*   **feuillage** *leaves*
fraîcheur *coolness*   **poussière** *dust (visible in the rays of sunlight)*   **chaleur** *warmth*   **arracher** *pull out*   **coin** *corner*

■ *L'art dans la rue*

Quand on veut voir les oeuvres° des grands artistes, on va dans les musées. À Paris, on va au Louvre pour admirer les chefs-d'oeuvres° classiques, au Musée d'Orsay pour regarder les peintures des Impressionnistes et des grands artistes du 19e siècle, et au Centre Pompidou si on veut voir des tableaux modernes. Si on s'intéresse à l'art moderne, on peut aussi se promener dans la rue.

Cette sculpture mobile flottante se trouve° près du **Centre Pompidou**. C'est la création de **Niki de Saint-Phalle**, une artiste qui a aussi créé des bijoux très originaux.

Cette sculpture, intitulée «Hommage à Picasso», représente un centaure, créature imaginaire, mi-homme,° mi-cheval. C'est l'oeuvre du sculpteur **César Baldaccini**. Dans ses sculptures, César utilise toutes sortes de matériaux. Il est connu en particulier pour ses sculptures faites avec des voitures compressées.

Cette sculpture est l'oeuvre du peintre et sculpteur **Jean Dubuffet**. Elle est typique de son style, caractérisé par l'utilisation de lignes parallèles ou concentriques bleues et rouges sur un fond° blanc.

Cette sculpture, oeuvre du sculpteur **Arman,** se trouve près de la **Gare Saint Lazare**. Intitulée «Heure de tous», elle rappelle° peut-être aux voyageurs l'importance d'arriver à l'heure.

---

oeuvres *works*   **chefs-d'oeuvres** *masterpieces*   **se trouve** *is located*   **mi-homme** *half man*   **fond** *background*   **rappelle** *reminds*

Soyons utiles!

Thème et Objectifs

Culture

In this unit, you will discover . . .

- what the French call "bricolage"
- what types of creative activities they engage in at home
- how French young people earn spending money by performing services for their neighbors

Communication

You will learn how . . .

- to talk about various chores and activities around the home
- to ask others to help you, and to give excuses if you cannot be of service to them
- to describe objects: their shape, dimensions, weight, and construction

Langue

You will learn how . . .

- to describe what you have to do
- to ask others to do certain things for you
- to express opinions about situations and events

LES PASSE-TEMPS ACTIFS

Le samedi, Catherine, 15 ans, sort rarement avec ses copains. Avec sa soeur Mélanie, 16 ans, elle préfère passer son temps à perfectionner Gustave, un robot de leur invention qui peut se déplacer° sur simple commande vocale. Et quand il y a quelque chose à réparer à la maison, un meuble, un appareil électrique ou même° la voiture de Papa, c'est Catherine ou Mélanie qui s'en charge.° «Nous nous amusons et nous apprenons en même temps» déclare Catherine pour expliquer son goût° pour les travaux manuels.

Le cas de Catherine et de Mélanie n'est pas unique. En France il y a des milliers de jeunes qui préfèrent les passe-temps actifs aux passe-temps passifs comme la télévision et la lecture. Voici deux passe-temps qui sont à la fois créatifs et récréatifs:° le bricolage° et le jardinage.°

■ Le bricolage est une des occupations favorites des Français de tout âge.

Le bricolage

Bricoler, c'est faire toutes sortes de petits travaux manuels. Quand on est un peu créatif et pas trop maladroit,° il y a beaucoup de choses qu'on peut faire chez soi.° On peut peindre° sa chambre, construire des étagères,° installer un système hi-fi ou un système d'alarme, réparer la télé ou la machine à laver, … Mais attention, quand on démonte° quelque chose, il faut aussi savoir le remonter.° Et surtout, il ne faut pas le casser!°

Le bricolage est une des occupations favorites des Français de tout âge. Et cette occupation n'est pas l'exclusivité des hommes. Aujourd'hui, 75% des Françaises bricolent (et 85% des Français). Pour subvenir° aux besoins des bricoleurs, tous les grands magasins et beaucoup de supermarchés ont un rayon «bricolage» où on trouve l'équipement et les outils° nécessaires. Pour les spécialistes, il y a aussi des magazines comme *Bricolage-Service*. Et pour les passionnés,° il y a à Paris chaque année un Salon° du Bricolage qui attire° des milliers de visiteurs.

---

se déplacer *move around*   **même** *even*   **s'en charge** = s'en occupe   **goût** *taste*   **récréatifs** *recreational*   **le bricolage** *fixing and building things*
le jardinage *gardening*   **maladroit** *clumsy*   **chez soi** = à la maison   **peindre** ✳ *to paint*   **construire** ✳ *to build*   **étagères** *shelves*
démonte *takes apart*   **remonter** *to put back together*   **casser** *break*   **subvenir** ✳ *to meet*   **les outils** *tools*   **les passionnés** *real devotees*
un Salon *show*   **attire** *attracts*

Le jardinage

Quand on voyage en France au printemps ou en été, on peut admirer les fleurs de toutes les couleurs qui ornent° les parcs publics, les jardins privés et les balcons des maisons. Les Français adorent les fleurs et 60% d'entre° eux pratiquent le jardinage.

Ce n'est pas surprenant° dans un pays où la majorité des gens habitent une maison individuelle et disposent° d'un jardin où ils peuvent planter des fleurs et faire pousser° des légumes. Le jardinage n'est pas seulement une activité manuelle. C'est un loisir écologique qui nous rapproche de la nature et qui est aussi esthétique … et nutritif. Quoi de plus beau qu'un bouquet de fleurs et quoi de meilleur qu'un plat de tomates qui viennent de son jardin!

et vous?

DÉFINITIONS

Définissez les mots et les expressions suivants. Quand c'est possible, illustrez avec un exemple.

- un robot
- les travaux manuels
- un passe-temps
- le bricolage
- le jardinage
- un loisir écologique

EXPRESSION PERSONNELLE

- Faites-vous des petits travaux manuels chez vous? Qu'est-ce que vous aimez faire et qu'est-ce que vous n'aimez pas faire?
- À votre avis, quel est le passe-temps le plus intéressant: le jardinage ou le bricolage? Expliquez pourquoi.
- Connaissez-vous une personne qui aime bricoler comme Catherine et Mélanie? Décrivez ce que cette personne a fait.

Soyez bon pour les plantes

Les Français aiment beaucoup les plantes. Dans chaque maison française, il y a, en moyenne,° sept plantes.

Les plantes ont beaucoup d'avantages:

— Elles décorent votre chambre.
— Elles purifient l'air que vous respirez.°
— Elles demandent° une attention minime.
— Elles sont propres.°

Les plantes sont des êtres° vivants.° Comme nous, elles ont besoin qu'on s'occupe un peu d'elles. Alors, si vous avez une plante, soyez bon pour elle.

Voici quelques conseils élémentaires:

✿ Arrosez°-la régulièrement. Mais attention: certaines plantes ont très soif. D'autres ont besoin seulement d'un petit peu d'eau.
✿ Si elle aime le soleil,° mettez-la près de la fenêtre. Si elle préfère l'obscurité, ne l'exposez pas à la lumière.°
✿ De temps en temps, mettez-lui de la musique. Les plantes adorent la musique douce.° Elles aiment la musique classique, mais elles détestent le rock et le rap.
✿ Parlez-lui souvent. Chaque jour, dites-lui bonjour et bonsoir.
✿ Ne la maltraitez pas.
✿ Ne l'insultez pas.
✿ Soyez toujours poli et attentif avec elle.
✿ Dites-lui souvent «Je t'aime.»

et vous?

- Est-ce qu'il y a des plantes chez vous? Quelles plantes? Dans quelles pièces sont-elles?
- Avez-vous des plantes ou des fleurs dans votre chambre? Qu'est-ce que vous faites pour elles?
- Pensez-vous que les plantes sont des êtres sensibles *(that have feelings)*? Expliquez votre position.

---

ornent = embellissent   **d'entre** *among*   **surprenant** *surprising*   **disposent** = ont   **pousser** *to grow*   **en moyenne** *on the average*   **respirez** *breathe*
demandent = nécessitent   **propres** *clean*   **êtres** *beings*   **vivants** *living*   **arrosez** *water*   **le soleil** *sun*   **la lumière** *light*   **douce** *soft*

Ça, c'est la JUSTICE!

Aujourd'hui, Madame Chauvat a beaucoup de travail. Elle demande à ses enfants Victor et Stéphanie de l'aider, mais ce n'est pas facile de les convaincre.° Elle s'adresse° d'abord à Victor qui regarde la télé au salon.

— Dis, Victor, qu'est-ce que tu fais?
— Tu vois, je regarde la télé.
— C'est bien, mais moi, j'ai besoin de toi.
— Pourquoi donc?
— Pour passer l'aspirateur.°
— Alors ça, c'est pas juste!°
— Comment ça?
— C'est pas juste parce que c'est moi qui ai passé l'aspirateur samedi dernier. Alors, cette fois-ci, c'est pas mon tour.° C'est le tour de Stéphanie. Elle ne fait jamais rien!
— Ah oui, c'est vrai, j'ai oublié! Je vais demander à ta soeur.

Victor pousse un soupir de soulagement° pendant que sa mère monte chercher Stéphanie. Celle-ci° est dans sa chambre en train de jouer à un jeu électronique.

— Dis donc, Stéphanie. Je voudrais que tu passes l'aspirateur au salon…
— Ah non, maman. Ça, c'est pas juste… C'est moi qui fais tout dans cette maison!
— Qu'est-ce que tu as fait récemment?
— Eh bien, par exemple, j'ai fait la vaisselle hier.
— Ah oui, c'est vrai… Bon, je te laisse° le choix: la vaisselle ou l'aspirateur.

Stéphanie réfléchit° un instant.

— Mais dis, il y a beaucoup de casseroles° à laver?
— Oui, y en a plein l'évier.°
— Alors, dans ce cas, je suis d'accord pour passer l'aspirateur.

Madame Chauvat redescend au salon.

— Dis, Victor, est-ce que tu peux éteindre° la télé et faire la vaisselle?
— La vaisselle? Mais pourquoi, maman?
— Parce que c'est ton tour.
Et ça, c'est la justice!

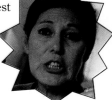

et vous?

EXPRESSION ORALE

Comment sont distribuées les tâches domestiques *(chores)* chez vous? (Décrivez les tâches de chaque personne.) À votre avis, est-ce que cette distribution est juste ou non? Expliquez.

EXPRESSION ÉCRITE

Imaginez que vous êtes Victor ou Stéphanie. Dans une lettre à un copain (une copine) vous décrivez ce qui est arrivé aujourd'hui.

---

convaincre ✴ *to convince*   **s'adresse** = *parle*   **l'aspirateur** *vacuum cleaner*   **juste** *fair*   **tour** *turn*   **un soupir de soulagement** *breathes a sigh of relief*   **celle-ci** = *Stéphanie*
laisse *leave*   **réfléchit** = *pense*   **casseroles** *pots*   **y en a plein l'évier** *the sink is full (of pots)*   **éteindre** ✴ *to turn off*

Les travaux domestiques

Oh là là,
j'ai beaucoup de travail
aujourd'hui.

Est-ce que . . .
la chambre est **propre** *(clean)* ou **sale** *(dirty)*?
le salon est **rangé** *(picked up)* ou **en désordre**?
Oh là là, j'ai beaucoup de **travail** aujourd'hui.

le travail work	
les travaux domestiques	
household chores	

Dans la chambre et la salle de bains, je dois . . .

faire le ménage *(to clean up)*	**ranger les vêtements**	**ranger** *to put away*
faire le lit	**nettoyer le lavabo** *(sink)*	**nettoyer** *to clean*

Dans le salon, je dois . . .

ranger les magazines	**nettoyer les vitres** *(windows)*	**vider** *to empty*
passer l'aspirateur *(to vacuum)*	**vider la corbeille** *(wastepaper basket)*	

Dans la salle à manger, je dois . . .

mettre la table	**débarrasser la table**	**débarrasser** *to clear*
mettre le couvert *(silverware)*		

Dans la cuisine, je dois . . .

couper le pain	**essuyer la table**	**couper** *to cut*
laver les légumes	**balayer le sol** *(floor)*	**laver** *to wash*
éplucher les carottes	**vider les ordures** *(garbage)*	**éplucher** *to peel*
faire la vaisselle	**sortir la poubelle** *(trash can)*	**essuyer** *to wipe, dry*
ranger la vaisselle		**balayer** *to sweep*
essuyer les verres		**sortir** *to take out*

Dans **la lingerie** *(laundry room)*, je dois . . .

laver le linge *(laundry)*	**repasser les chemises**	**repasser** *to iron*

Je dois aussi m'occuper des animaux.

Dehors (*outside*), dans le jardin, je dois . . .

laver la voiture

arroser | **les plantes**
| **les fleurs** (*flowers*)

couper l'herbe (*grass*)
tondre la pelouse (*lawn*)
tailler les arbustes (*shrubs*)

| **arroser** *to water* | **tondre** *to mow, to cut very short* |
| **tailler** *to prune* | |

Je dois aussi **m'occuper des animaux**. Je dois . . .

promener le chien

donner à manger | **au chat**
| **au lapin**

vider | **l'aquarium**
remplir |

nettoyer la cage | **de l'oiseau**
| **de la perruche** (*parakeet*)

| **s'occuper de** *to take care of* |

| **donner à manger à** *to feed* |

| **remplir** *to fill* |

Verbes en –ger (ranger)

Révision ▶

p.R21

1 Et vous?

Indiquez comment vous participez aux travaux domestiques.
Comparez vos réponses avec celles de votre partenaire.

1. En général, ma chambre est . . .
   - propre
   - rangée
   - en désordre
   - ??

2. Je fais mon lit . . .
   - le matin
   - le soir
   - jamais
   - ??

3. Je range ma chambre . . .
   - tous les jours
   - toutes les semaines
   - une fois par mois
   - ??

4. Quand j'aide à faire le ménage, je préfère . . .
   - passer l'aspirateur
   - vider les corbeilles
   - nettoyer les vitres
   - ??

5. Quand j'aide mon père (ma mère) dans la cuisine, je préfère . . .
   - éplucher les légumes
   - essuyer les assiettes
   - nettoyer l'évier (*kitchen sink*)
   - ??

6. Quand j'aide avec les repas, je préfère . . .
   - mettre le couvert
   - débarrasser la table
   - faire la vaisselle
   - ??

7. Quand je travaille dans le jardin, je préfère . . .
   - tondre la pelouse
   - arroser les plantes
   - tailler les arbustes
   - ??

8. Le travail que je déteste le plus est de . . .
   - balayer le garage
   - sortir les poubelles
   - vider les ordures
   - ??

2 La famille Duboulot

Aujourd'hui, tout le monde est très occupé chez les Duboulot. Choisissez deux personnes et dites où sont ces personnes et ce qu'elles font.

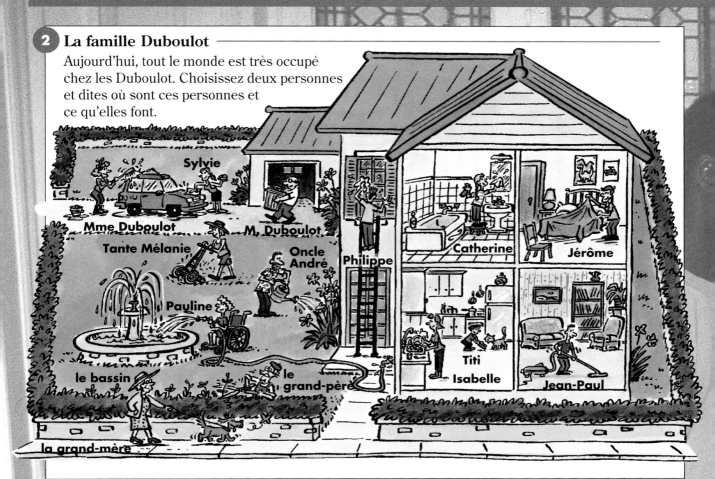

Sylvie

Mme Duboulot

Tante Mélanie

Pauline

le bassin

la grand-mère

M. Duboulot

Oncle André

Philippe

le grand-père

Catherine

Jérôme

Titi

Isabelle

Jean-Paul

3 Jobs d'été

Votre partenaire et vous, vous allez travailler cet été. Choisissez un job de la colonne A. Votre partenaire va choisir un job de la colonne B. Expliquez ce que vous allez faire. Donnez deux ou trois exemples.

▶ — **Moi, je vais travailler dans la cuisine d'un restaurant. Je vais éplucher les légumes et faire la vaisselle. Je vais aussi . . .**
— **Et moi, je vais travailler dans un zoo. Je vais . . .**

A. Vous

• travailler dans la cuisine d'un restaurant
• travailler pour les jardins publics de la ville
• travailler pour une entreprise de nettoyage (cleaning) de bureaux
• travailler chez un marchand d'animaux domestiques (pets)
• être garçon d'étage (femme de chambre) dans un hôtel

B. Votre partenaire

• travailler dans la salle (dining room) d'un restaurant
• travailler dans un zoo
• travailler comme jardinier (gardener) dans un hôtel
• être concierge dans un immeuble (building superintendent)
• travailler dans une blanchisserie (laundry)
• travailler pour les voisins

Quelques objets utiles

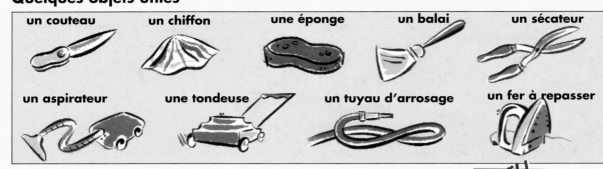

un couteau   un chiffon   une éponge   un balai   un sécateur

un aspirateur   une tondeuse   un tuyau d'arrosage   un fer à repasser

---

4 **Le bon objet**

RAPPEL!

de + le → du

J'ai besoin du couteau.

Choisissez un objet de la liste et dites pourquoi vous avez besoin de cet objet.

J'ai besoin de . . .

- l'aspirateur
- le balai
- le fer
- la tondeuse
- le sécateur
- le tuyau d'arrosage
- un chiffon
- un couteau
- une éponge

pour . . .

- essuyer la table
- nettoyer la chambre
- laver la voiture
- éplucher les carottes
- repasser cette chemise
- tondre la pelouse
- nettoyer le lavabo
- tailler le rosier *(rose bush)*
- balayer le garage

---

5 **Le chalet des Laurentides**

Vous passez l'été dans la région des Laurentides. Il y a beaucoup de travail dans le chalet que vous avez loué avec vos cousins. Malheureusement, vos cousins ne sont pas très coopératifs. Quand vous leur demandez de faire quelque chose, ils trouvent une excuse. Jouez les dialogues avec votre partenaire.

Dis, Annie, est-ce que tu peux essuyer la table?

Je voudrais bien, mais j'ai un problème.

Quoi?

Je ne trouve pas l'éponge.

TRAVAUX

- tondre la pelouse
- arroser les fleurs
- tailler les arbustes
- essuyer la table
- essuyer les assiettes
- éplucher les pommes de terre
- balayer la terrasse
- repasser les serviettes *(napkins)*
- nettoyer le salon
- ??

EXCUSES

- Le chiffon est sale.
- L'aspirateur est cassé *(broken)*.
- Le fer ne fonctionne pas.
- La tondeuse ne marche pas.
- Je ne trouve pas l'éponge.
- J'ai perdu le sécateur.
- Je n'ai pas de couteau.
- Je ne sais pas où est le balai.
- Il y a un trou *(hole)* dans le tuyau.
- ??

NOTE CULTURELLE

Située dans la province de Québec, la région des **Laurentides** est populaire à la fois pour ses stations de ski en hiver et pour ses stations d'été.

A. La formation du subjonctif (1)

The sentences below express a NECESSITY or OBLIGATION. In sentences of this type, the French use a verb form called the SUBJUNCTIVE.

Il faut que **je finisse** mon travail.	*It is necessary that **I finish** my work.* *(I have to finish my work.)*
Il faut que **vous aidiez** vos parents.	*It is necessary that **you help** your parents.* *(You have to help your parents.)*

The SUBJUNCTIVE is a verb form that occurs frequently in French. It is used after certain verbs and expressions in the construction:

VERB OR EXPRESSION	+	**que**	+	SUBJECT	+	SUBJUNCTIVE VERB . . .
Il faut		**que**		Marc		**tonde** la pelouse

➡ The subjunctive is almost always introduced by **que**.

FORMS

For all regular verbs and many irregular verbs, the subjunctive is formed as follows:

SUBJUNCTIVE STEM	+	SUBJUNCTIVE ENDINGS
ils-form of present minus **-ent**		**-e, -es, -e, -ions, -iez, -ent**

Note the subjunctive forms of the regular verbs **parler**, **finir**, **vendre**, and the irregular verb **dire**.

INFINITIVE		parler	finir	vendre	dire	SUBJUNCTIVE ENDINGS
PRESENT STEM	ils	**parlent** parl-	**finissent** finiss-	**vendent** vend-	**disent** dis-	
SUBJUNCTIVE	que je que tu qu'il/elle/on	**parle** **parles** **parle**	**finisse** **finisses** **finisse**	**vende** **vendes** **vende**	**dise** **dises** **dise**	-e -es -e
	que nous que vous qu'ils/elles	**parlions** **parliez** **parlent**	**finissions** **finissiez** **finissent**	**vendions** **vendiez** **vendent**	**disions** **disiez** **disent**	-ions -iez -ent

Dire, lire, écrire

Révision ▶ pp. R26-27

Pratique ▶ p. 28

1 Le subjonctif, s'il vous plaît!

Pour chaque verbe du tableau, donner la forme **ils** du présent. Ensuite, complétez les phrases avec le subjonctif de ces verbes.

INFINITIF	PRÉSENT	SUBJONCTIF
▶ laver	ils lavent	Il faut que (nous) lavions la voiture.
1. aider	ils . . .	Il faut que (tu, nous, vous) . . . les voisins.
2. réussir	ils . . .	Il faut que (je, vous, les élèves) . . . à l'examen.
3. répondre	ils . . .	Il faut que (je, Pauline, nous) . . . à cette lettre.
4. attendre	ils . . .	Il faut que (nous, tu, les voyageurs) . . . le train.
5. lire	ils . . .	Il faut que (je, Charlotte, vous) . . . cet article.
6. écrire	ils . . .	Il faut que (tu, nous, mes copains) . . . à Philippe.
7. partir	ils . . .	Il faut que (je, Olivier, nous) . . . à six heures.
8. mettre	ils . . .	Il faut que (je, tu, vous) . . . la table.
9. se laver	ils . . .	Il faut que (tu, vous, ce garçon) . . . les cheveux.
10. se dépêcher	ils . . .	Il faut que (Pierre, nous, vos amis) . . .

2 Avant de partir ce week-end

Expliquez ce que chacun doit faire avant de partir ce week-end.

▶ Claire   **Il faut que Claire range sa chambre. Et puis, il faut qu'elle . . .**

Claire
- ranger sa chambre
- laver son linge
- passer l'aspirateur

moi
- finir mes devoirs
- écrire une lettre
- téléphoner à mon copain

toi
- laver la cage du lapin
- remplir l'aquarium
- donner à manger au chat

Éric et Vincent
- tailler les arbustes
- tondre la pelouse
- arroser les fleurs

vous
- finir la vaisselle
- vider les ordures
- sortir la poubelle

nous
- regarder la carte *(map)*
- choisir notre itinéraire
- préparer la voiture

3 Après la fête

Votre partenaire et vous, vous avez organisé une fête chez vous. Maintenant vous devez ranger. Vous vous distribuez les tâches. Choisissez une tâche de la colonne A pour votre partenaire. Il/elle va choisir une tâche de la colonne B pour vous.

▶

Dis, Bernard, il faut que tu laves les verres.

Bon, je vais laver les verres, mais toi, il faut que tu ranges la cuisine.

D'accord!

A
• ranger le salon
• laver les assiettes
• laver les verres
• débarrasser la table
• vider les ordures
• ??

B
• ranger la cuisine
• passer l'aspirateur
• laver les casseroles *(pots)*
• mettre les chaises à leur place
• sortir la poubelle
• ??

B. Comment exprimer une obligation personnelle: l'usage du subjonctif après **il faut que**

Note the use of the subjunctive in the following sentences:

Il faut que je **parte**.   *I have to (I must)* **leave**.
Il faut que vous **travailliez**.   *You have to (you must)* **work**.

To express what people HAVE TO or MUST DO, use the construction:

> **il faut que** + SUBJUNCTIVE

➡️ Personal obligations can also be expressed with **devoir** + INFINITIVE.

Je dois **partir**.   *I have to* **leave**.

➡️ Note that **il faut** + INFINITIVE is used to express a GENERAL obligation.

Il faut **étudier**.   *One has to (one should)* **study**. *You [people in general] have to* **study**.

➡️ The negative **il ne faut pas que** + SUBJUNCTIVE expresses a PROHIBITION or INTERDICTION.

Il ne faut pas que tu **dormes** en classe.   *You should not* **sleep** *in class.*

ALLONS PLUS LOIN

The following expressions are used to express the LACK OF OBLIGATION:

Il n'est pas nécessaire que tu partes. ⎫
Tu n'es pas obligé(e) de partir.   ⎬   *You don't have to leave.*
Tu n'as pas besoin de partir.   ⎪
Tu n'as pas à partir. ⎭

---

4 Obligations?

Voici certains travaux domestiques. Faites une liste des cinq principaux travaux que vous devez faire. Classez-les par ordre d'importance. Puis comparez votre liste avec celle de votre partenaire.

- ranger le salon
- laver la vaisselle
- débarrasser la table
- laver le linge
- sortir la poubelle
- arroser les plantes
- tondre la pelouse

- passer l'aspirateur
- mettre le couvert
- ranger ma chambre
- vider les ordures
- donner à manger au chien/chat
- ??

5 C'est interdit

Vous êtes en France avec des copains. Vous voyez les panneaux *(signs)* suivants. Expliquez ce que vous ne devez pas faire.

INTERDICTION DE . . .

| fumer | marcher sur la pelouse | entrer ici | tourner à gauche | déposer des ordures | écrire sur les murs |

▶ — Il ne faut pas que nous . . .

C. La formation du subjonctif (2)

Some verbs like **venir** have different stems in the **ils**- and **nous**-forms of the present. Verbs of this type have TWO STEMS in the subjunctive. (Note that the following verbs all have regular subjunctive endings.)

INFINITIVE	venir	
PRESENT	ils	**viennent**
	nous	**venons**
SUBJUNCTIVE	que je	**vienne**
	que tu	**viennes**
	qu'il/elle/on	**vienne**
	qu'ils/elles	**viennent**
	que nous	**venions**
	que vous	**veniez**

Il faut que . . .

acheter	j'**achète**	nous **achetions**
espérer	j'**espère**	nous **espérions**
appeler	j'**appelle**	nous **appelions**
payer	je **paie**	nous **payions**
boire	je **boive**	nous **buvions**
voir	je **voie**	nous **voyions**
prendre	je **prenne**	nous **prenions**

6 Chez le médecin

Vous êtes médecin. Donnez des conseils à un patient, Monsieur Grosjean, qui n'est pas en forme. Commencez vos phrases par **il faut que vous . . .**
                ou
     il ne faut pas que vous . . .

▶ boire trop de café
   Il ne faut pas que vous buviez trop de café.

- boire beaucoup d'eau minérale?
- se lever tôt?
- se lever tard?
- dormir bien?
- acheter un vélo?
- apprendre à nager?
- prendre des vitamines?
- s'inquiéter trop?
- payer ma note *(bill)*?
- revenir dans un mois?

7 La meilleure solution

Avec votre partenaire, choisissez une des situations et décidez ensemble des choses que les personnes doivent faire **(il faut que . . .)** ou ne pas faire **(il ne faut pas que . . .)**.

1. Philippe veut rentrer chez lui, mais il n'a pas la clé.
   - attendre sa mère?
   - casser *(break)* une fenêtre?
   - retourner à l'école?
   - ??

2. Valérie a dîné au restaurant. Elle a oublié son portefeuille.
   - partir sans payer?
   - téléphoner à son copain?
   - travailler dans la cuisine?
   - ??

3. Les touristes sont à l'hôtel. Ils voient de la fumée *(smoke)*.
   - sortir par la porte?
   - sauter *(jump)* par la fenêtre?
   - attendre l'arrivée des pompiers?
   - ??

4. Marc est secrètement amoureux de Stéphanie mais il est très timide.
   - lui écrire un poème?
   - lui envoyer une lettre d'amour anonyme?
   - prendre des leçons de danse et inviter Stéphanie dans une discothèque?
   - ??

5. Hélène et Catherine ont eu un accident avec la voiture de leur mère.
   - dire la vérité à leur mère?
   - voir un garagiste?
   - payer la réparation?
   - ??

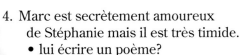

6. Thomas et Julien ont trouvé un portefeuille dans la rue.
   - apporter le portefeuille à la police?
   - mettre une annonce dans un journal?
   - garder *(keep)* le portefeuille?
   - ??

Le travail, ça paie!

Aux États-Unis, beaucoup de jeunes travaillent régulièrement dans les supermarchés, les restaurants ou les stations-service. En France, les jeunes n'ont pas de travail régulier pendant l'année scolaire. (Ils ont trop de devoirs à faire à la maison!) Mais certains ont des jobs qui leur permettent de gagner un peu d'argent. Voici le cas de cinq jeunes Français qui ont découvert° que le travail, ça paie!

Camille, 15 ans, adore les animaux. Un jour, elle espère être vétérinaire. En attendant,° elle a transformé son amour° des animaux en job.

« *Dans mon quartier, il y a beaucoup d'animaux, mais leurs propriétaires° n'ont pas toujours le temps de s'occuper d'eux. Alors, c'est moi qui le fais. Quand les gens partent le week-end, par exemple, je vais chez eux pour donner à manger à leurs chats et je promène leurs chiens. Je préfère les gros° chiens, comme les dobermans et les bergers allemands.° D'abord, ça a plus d'allure° et puis les pourboires° sont meilleurs.*

Je pourrais° gagner plus d'argent si je pouvais garder° les animaux chez moi. Malheureusement, mon père n'est pas d'accord. Il veut bien° que je gagne de l'argent, mais il refuse absolument que je transforme la maison en chenil.° Dommage! **»**

Pour Jean-François, 15 ans, la cuisine n'a pas de secret, mais c'est dans la pâtisserie qu'il excelle.

« *J'ai toujours aimé faire des gâteaux. Quand j'étais petit, je passais mon temps dans la cuisine à regarder ma mère. C'est elle qui m'a appris à faire les mousses, les brioches,* les tartes aux fruits, les gâteaux à la crème ou au chocolat, et surtout les crêpes créoles,** une spécialité de la Martinique. Je cuisine° pour m'amuser, mais aussi pour gagner un peu d'argent. Quand les gens du quartier préparent une fête, c'est souvent à moi qu'ils font appel° pour les pâtisseries. (Ils savent que mes gâteaux sont meilleurs et moins chers que ceux du boulanger du coin!°) La semaine prochaine, par exemple, je dois faire les pâtisseries pour une réception de 50 personnes. J'espère que ma mère va me donner un coup de main!°* **»**

Pendant l'année scolaire, Aïcha, 16 ans, n'a pas de job, mais en juillet et août, elle est très occupée. Aïcha explique:

« *Quand les gens sont en vacances, moi je travaille. Chaque été, je m'occupe, en effet, d'une vingtaine de jardins. Je tonds les pelouses, je taille les arbustes, j'arrose les plantes et les fleurs. Vingt jardins, ça représente beaucoup de travail. Quand j'ai trop à faire, je recrute des assistants. En général, ce sont mes copains de lycée. Ils m'appellent "Aïcha l'arrosoir,°" mais quand ils ont besoin de gagner un peu d'argent, ils sont bien contents de me trouver!* **»**

---

*Une brioche is a light, sweet pastry prepared as a bun or a round bread. **Une crêpe créole is made with coconut milk and is flavored with cinnamon and nutmeg.

découvrir ❖ *to discover* **En attendant** *In the meantime* **amour** *love* **propriétaires** *owners* **gros** *= grands* **les bergers allemands** *shepherd dogs*
plus d'allure *look more impressive* **les pourboires** *tips* **pourrais** *could* **garder** *keep* **Il veut bien** *= il est d'accord pour* **chenil** *kennel*
cuisine *= fais la cuisine* **font appel** *= appellent* **du coin** *= quartier* **un coup de main** *= m'aider* **l'arrosoir** *watering can*

Avec le premier argent qu'il a gagné, Fabien, 16 ans, a acheté l'équipement dont il a besoin pour son job: une échelle° en aluminium avec laquelle il lave les vitres. Il explique comment il a commencé:

« *Un jour de printemps, il y a deux ans, ma mère m'a demandé de laver les vitres de l'extérieur. C'était un samedi. Il faisait très beau, et j'avais l'intention de faire un tour à vélo avec mes copains. Évidemment, j'étais furieux, mais je n'avais pas le choix. Je suis allé dans le garage. J'ai pris l'échelle, une vieille échelle en bois° très lourde,° et j'ai commencé mon travail. Une voisine m'a vu et m'a demandé: "Dis, Fabien, est-ce que tu veux laver mes vitres aussi? Pour ta peine,° je te donnerai 20 euros." Quand j'ai fini chez moi, je me suis précipité° chez la voisine. Pendant que je lavais ses vitres, j'ai reçu° trois offres d'autres voisins. Depuis ce jour, je suis occupé presque tous les samedis et je vais bientôt avoir assez d'argent pour m'acheter une moto.* **»**

Danièle, 17 ans, et son frère Vincent, 16 ans, ont leur carte professionnelle, leur uniforme et leur compagnie: Ado-Services.*
Danièle explique:

« *Aujourd'hui, les adultes travaillent énormément. Quand ils rentrent chez eux le soir, ils sont trop fatigués pour passer l'aspirateur et faire le ménage. Et le week-end, ils ont des choses plus intéressantes à faire. Mais nous, les ados, nous avons du temps libre et nous avons aussi besoin d'argent. Pourquoi ne pas aider les adultes dans leurs tâches domestiques?*

Un jour, j'ai mis une annonce° dans un supermarché pour offrir mes services. J'ai attendu trois semaines avant de recevoir mon premier coup de téléphone.° Ma première cliente m'a recommandée à une amie qui m'a recommandée à une voisine… Bref,° je me suis vite constitué une petite clientèle.

Bientôt, j'ai eu trop de travail pour moi seule. Alors, j'ai demandé à mon frère Vincent s'il voulait m'aider. D'abord, il a hésité. "Je ne suis pas une femme de chambre"° m'a-t-il dit. Mais, comme il avait besoin d'argent, il a fini par accepter. Maintenant nous travaillons en équipe. Je range le salon, je passe l'aspirateur dans les chambres. Vincent, lui, s'occupe de la cuisine. Il fait la vaisselle, range les assiettes, lave le sol° et sort les poubelles.

Aujourd'hui, notre compagnie Ado-Services marche très bien. Nous refusons même des clients. À un moment, je pensais engager des employés, mais il fallait° assurer leur formation,° prendre des assurances,° acheter du matériel,° etc… J'ai renoncé° à ce projet pour le moment. Mais, si je rate° mon bac l'année prochaine, je sais que je vais faire! **»**

---

et vous?

DÉFINITIONS

Définissez, en français, les mots ou expressions suivants.

- un(e) vétérinaire
- un pourboire
- un chenil
- un buffet
- un hors-d'œuvre
- une réception
- une échelle
- une femme de chambre
- une équipe
- une pâtisserie
- un boulanger

EXPRESSION ORALE

1. Des jeunes Français décrits dans le texte, qui, selon vous, a le job le plus intéressant? Expliquez pourquoi.

2. Votre partenaire et vous, vous allez choisir d'être l'un des adolescents décrits dans le texte. Chacun va décrire le job qu'il/elle a et expliquer les avantages et les inconvénients de ce job.

3. Préférez-vous avoir un job où vous travaillez à votre compte (comme les adolescents décrits dans le texte) ou un job où vous travaillez pour quelqu'un d'autre (par exemple, pour un fast-food, une boutique, une station-service, etc.)? Expliquez votre choix. Considérez les éléments suivants:
   - l'intérêt du travail
   - le salaire
   - la flexibilité des heures de travail
   - l'indépendance

EXPRESSION ÉCRITE

Vous avez un job (réel ou imaginaire). Écrivez une lettre à votre ami(e) français(e) où vous décrivez:
- comment vous avez trouvé ce job
- ce que vous faites
- les avantages et les inconvénients de ce job

---

*Ado-Services: le terme **ado** est souvent utilisé pour désigner **un adolescent** (comparez **teen** qui désigne un **teenager**).
une échelle *ladder* **en bois** *wood* **lourde** *heavy* **peine** = *travail* **précipité** = *dépêché d'aller* **recevoir** ❋ *to get, receive* **une annonce** *notice, ad*
coup de téléphone *phone call* **Bref** *In brief* **une femme de chambre** = *chamber maid* **le sol** *floor* **il fallait** = *il était nécessaire* **formation** *training* **assurances**
insurance **du matériel** *equipment* **renoncé** *gave up* **rate** *flunk*

LE FRANÇAIS PRATIQUE

Pour rendre service

Est-ce que tu peux m'aider?

Oui, bien sûr.

COMMENT DEMANDER DE L'AIDE

Est-ce que tu peux | **m'aider?**
| **m'aider à** nettoyer le salon?
| **me donner un coup de main**
   (give me a hand)?
| **me rendre service**
   (do me a favor)?

COMMENT ACCEPTER

Oui, | **bien sûr.**
| **d'accord.**
| **je veux bien.** *(I'd love to)*
Volontiers! *(With pleasure)*
Avec plaisir!

COMMENT REFUSER . . . ET DONNER UNE EXCUSE

Non, vraiment je ne peux pas.
Écoute, | j'aimerais bien, mais . . . | je suis **occupé(e)** *(busy).*
| je voudrais bien, mais . . . | je ne suis pas **libre** *(free).*
| je suis **désolé(e)**, mais . . . | je n'ai pas **le temps** *(time).*
| **je m'excuse**, mais . . . | j'ai **d'autres choses à faire.**
| **je regrette**, mais. . . | je dois sortir/étudier.

COMMENT REMERCIER . . . ET RÉPONDRE À QUELQU'UN QUI VOUS REMERCIE

C'est | **gentil!**
| **sympa!**
Merci | **beaucoup.** | **De rien.** *(You're welcome)*
| **mille fois.** | **Il n'y a pas de quoi.**
Je te remercie. | **Je t'en prie.**

1 Créa-dialogue

C'est samedi aujourd'hui et vous passez l'après-midi chez votre cousin(e) français(e). Il/elle vous demande de l'aider. Avec votre partenaire, composez un dialogue et jouez-le en classe. Votre partenaire va jouer le rôle de votre cousin(e).

— Dis, est-ce que tu peux m'aider?
— Oui, bien sûr. Où es-tu?
— Je suis au salon.
— Qu'est-ce que je peux faire pour toi?
— Est-ce que tu peux nettoyer les vitres?
— Je voudrais bien, mais je n'ai pas de chiffon.

- *Use another expression.*
- *Use another expression.*
- *Name another part of the house or yard.*

- *Mention a chore that needs to be done there.*
- *Accept or refuse. If you refuse, give an explanation. If you accept, your partner will thank you.*

Conversations libres

Avec votre partenaire, choisissez l'une des situations suivantes. Composez ensemble un dialogue correspondant à cette situation et jouez ce dialogue en classe.

1 À l'université

Jean-Jacques et Christophe sont camarades de chambre à l'université. Jean-Jacques aime l'ordre. Christophe, au contraire, est un garçon très désordonné. Chacun critique les habitudes de l'autre.

Rôles: Jean-Jacques, Christophe

2 Après la soirée

Thomas et Isabelle ont organisé une soirée chez eux. La soirée est finie et Thomas et Isabelle doivent ranger l'appartement qui est vraiment en désordre. Ils discutent de la répartition *(distribution)* des tâches, mais ils ne sont pas d'accord!

Rôles: Thomas, Isabelle

3 Argent de poche

Jean-Philippe veut gagner de l'argent de poche cet été. Il va voir ses voisins pour leur offrir ses services. Madame Brunet répond et veut savoir ce que Jean-Philippe sait faire.

Rôles: Mme Brunet, Jean-Philippe

4 Le robot

À l'exposition de l'Électro-ménager *(household appliances)*, un vendeur présente la nouvelle invention de sa compagnie: un robot qui fait toutes sortes de travaux domestiques. Il démontre le robot à une cliente qui n'est pas convaincue *(convinced)*.

Rôles: Le vendeur, la cliente

5 La visite des grands-parents

Les grands-parents de Catherine et de Jean-François vont venir passer le week-end à la maison. Madame Thibault demande à ses enfants de l'aider pour préparer la maison et le jardin. Catherine a d'autres projets et Jean-François est un garçon paresseux.

Rôles: Mme Thibault, Catherine, Jean-François

6 «Le bistrot»

Monsieur Labouffe est propriétaire du restaurant «Le bistrot». Chaque été, il recrute des étudiants pour travailler dans la cuisine et la salle du restaurant. Il explique le travail à deux jeunes employés, Mélanie et Philippe. Ceux-ci demandent des précisions.

Rôles: M. Labouffe, Mélanie, Philippe

7 Drôles de vacances

Robert passe ses vacances chez sa tante Amélie qui a une ferme à la campagne. En réalité, ce ne sont pas de véritables vacances parce que Tante Amélie a toujours des projets pour Robert. Aujourd'hui, Tante Amélie a préparé une longue liste de choses à faire. Robert a décidé de refuser de travailler. Pour chaque chose, il a une excuse.

Rôles: Tante Amélie, Robert

A. Le subjonctif: formation irrégulière

The subjunctive forms of **être**, **avoir**, **aller**, and **faire** are irregular.

	être	**avoir**	**aller**	**faire**
que je (j')	**sois**	**aie**	**aille**	**fasse**
que tu	**sois**	**aies**	**ailles**	**fasses**
qu'il/elle/on	**soit**	**ait**	**aille**	**fasse**
que nous	**soyons**	**ayons**	**allions**	**fassions**
que vous	**soyez**	**ayez**	**alliez**	**fassiez**
qu'ils/elles	**soient**	**aient**	**aillent**	**fassent**

1 Tant pis! *(Too bad!)*

Invitez votre partenaire à faire certaines choses avec vous.
Il/elle va refuser en donnant une excuse.

Tu veux déjeuner avec moi?

Je m'excuse, mais il faut que je sois chez moi à midi.

Tant pis!

INVITATIONS
- sortir
- jouer au volley
- déjeuner
- aller au ciné
- venir chez moi
- faire une promenade
- ??

EXCUSES
- faire mes devoirs
- faire des achats
- aller au supermarché
- aller chez un copain
- être chez moi à midi
- être à un rendez-vous
- ??

2 Que faire?

Lisez ce que les personnes suivantes vont faire et dites ce qu'elles doivent faire.

▶ Tu vas ranger la cuisine. (faire la vaisselle)
Il faut que tu fasses la vaisselle.

1. Je vais voir un film. (aller au ciné / être à l'heure)
2. Tu vas organiser un pique-nique. (aller au supermarché / faire les courses)
3. Nous sommes invités à dîner. (avoir un cadeau / être polis)
4. Vous allez prendre l'avion. (faire vos valises / aller à l'aéroport)
5. Mélanie va faire du parapente. (faire attention / avoir du courage)
6. Anne et Thomas vont participer à un marathon. (être en bonne forme/ faire du jogging régulièrement)

3 Choses à faire

Choisissez une période de temps et nommez deux ou trois choses que vous devez faire en utilisant

il faut que je . . .

- ce soir
- avant le week-end
- ce week-end
- la semaine prochaine
- avant les vacances
- cet été

B. L'usage du subjonctif après certaines expressions impersonnelles

Note the use of the subjunctive in the following sentences.

Il est important **que nous soyons** à l'heure.   *It is important **that we be** on time.*
Il est bon **que vous fassiez** du sport.   *It is good **that you do** sports.*
Il est dommage **que tu partes**.   *It is too bad **that you are leaving.***

In French, the subjunctive is used after certain impersonal expressions of OPINION when they are <u>referring to specific people.</u>

➡ When the expression of opinion is used in a GENERAL sense, it is followed by **de** + INFINITIVE.
Compare:

Il est utile **de parler** français.   *It is useful (in general) **to speak** French.*
Il est utile **que Marc parle** français.   *It is useful **that Marc speaks** French.*

Vocabulaire: Quelques expressions d'opinion

il est bon que	**il est utile que**	**il est dommage que**
il est important que	**il est naturel que**	**il vaut mieux** *(it is better)* **que**
il est essentiel que	**il est normal que**	
il est indispensable que	**il est juste** *(fair)* **que**	

---

4 D'accord ou non?

Exprimez votre opinion sur l'un des sujets suivants.
Votre partenaire va être d'accord ou pas d'accord avec vous. (Ajoutez d'autres sujets à la liste si vous voulez.)

▶ — **Il est important (utile, indispensable) que j'aille à l'université.**
— **Je suis d'accord avec toi. Il est important que nous allions à l'université.**
      (Je ne suis pas d'accord avec toi.
        Il n'est pas important que
          nous allions à l'université.)

- aller à l'université
- être en bonne santé *(health)*
- aider mes parents
- être ponctuel en classe
- avoir beaucoup d'amis
- être riche
- réussir aux examens
- faire des progrès en français
- aller en France
- trouver un job cet été
- avoir mon diplôme
- ??

---

5 Pour rester en forme

Votre partenaire veut commencer un programme pour rester en forme. Il/elle hésite entre plusieurs options. Donnez-lui votre opinion en commençant votre suggestion par **il vaut mieux que . . .**

▶ jouer au volley ou au basket?

Je voudrais rester en forme. Je ne sais pas si je dois jouer au volley ou au basket.

Il vaut mieux que tu joues au volley.

1. manger des fruits ou de la viande?
2. boire du thé ou de l'eau minérale?
3. faire du jogging ou de la musculation?
4. aller à la piscine ou au club de sport?
5. acheter un vélo ou des haltères *(weights)*?
6. faire du golf ou du tennis?

C. L'usage du subjonctif après **vouloir que**

Note the use of the subjunctive in the sentences below.

Je **voudrais que tu viennes** chez moi.
Éric **veut que je sorte** avec lui.
Mon frère **ne veut pas que je prenne** sa voiture.

I would like you to come to my house.
Éric wants me to go out with him.
My brother does not want me to take his car.

▎ In French, the SUBJUNCTIVE is used after **vouloir que** to express a WISH.

➡ Note that the wish must concern someone or something OTHER THAN THE SUBJECT.
When the wish concerns the SUBJECT, the INFINITIVE is used.
Contrast:

The wish concerns the subject: INFINITIVE	The wish concerns someone else: SUBJUNCTIVE
Je veux **sortir**. **Mon père** veut **prendre** sa voiture.	**Je** veux que **tu sortes** avec moi. **Mon père** ne veut pas que **je prenne** sa voiture.

➡ The subjunctive is also used after **je veux bien (que)**.

— Est-ce que je peux sortir?
— Oui, **je veux bien que
tu sortes**.

Can I go out?
*Sure, it's OK with me
if you go out.*

> QUELQUES EXPRESSIONS DE
> DÉSIR ET DE VOLONTÉ
> *(par ordre d'intensité)*
>
> **je préfère que** . . .
> **je souhaite que** . . . *(I wish)*
> **je désire que** . . . *(I wish)*
> **je voudrais que** . . .
> **j'aimerais que** . . .
> **je veux que** . . .
> **j'insiste pour que** . . .
> **j'exige que** . . . *(I demand)*

6 Chez vous

Votre camarade français(e) (votre partenaire) est chez vous.
Il/elle vous demande la permission de faire certaines choses.
Acceptez ou refusez.

▶ regarder tes photos

> Est-ce que je peux
> regarder tes photos?

1. mettre un CD?
2. faire un sandwich?
3. lire ton journal *(diary)*?
4. téléphoner à un copain en France?
5. emprunter ton vélo?
6. aller dans la chambre de tes parents?
7. aider avec la vaisselle?
8. promener ton chien?
9. donner à manger à ton chat?

> Oui, je veux bien que
> tu regardes mes photos.

(Pas question! Je ne veux pas que
tu regardes mes photos!)

7 Oui ou non?

Décrivez les souhaits *(wishes)* des personnes suivantes. Utilisez **vouloir que**
affirmativement ou négativement. Et soyez logique!

▶ le professeur / les élèves (étudier? dormir en classe?)

Le professeur veut que les élèves étudient.
Il ne veut pas qu'ils dorment en classe.

1. nous / le professeur (être très strict? donner de bonnes notes?)
2. le médecin / ses patients (faire du sport? fumer?)
3. Caroline / son copain (être loyal? sortir avec une autre fille?)
4. tu / ton frère (lire ton journal *[diary]*? casser *[to break]* ta chaîne hi-fi?)
5. je / mes amis (dire des mensonges *[lies]*? être patients avec moi?)
6. mes parents / je (avoir de bonnes notes? être impoli?)

8 D'accord, mais . . .

Nathalie demande à son père de faire
certaines choses. Il accepte, mais avec
certaines conditions. Jouez les deux
rôles avec votre partenaire.

1. prendre la voiture
   mettre ta ceinture
   (seatbelt)

2. aller au ciné
   finir tes devoirs

3. inviter des copains
   ranger le salon

4. organiser une boum
   faire la vaisselle

5. faire du parapente
   être très prudente

6. acheter une moto
   porter un casque
   (helmet)

> Dis, Papa, je voudrais <u>sortir</u>.
> Écoute, je veux bien que tu sortes, mais à une condition!
> Quelle condition?
> D'accord, Papa.
> Il faut que <u>tu rentres</u> avant onze heures.

9 C'est vous le patron (la patronne)! *(You're the boss!)*

Choisissez l'une des situations suivantes. Donnez à un(e) jeune employé(e) deux ou trois
tâches à faire. Vous pouvez utiliser les expressions du *Français pratique* à la page 74/75.

Vous êtes . . .
- le chef d'un restaurant
- le directeur (la directrice) d'un zoo
- le chef jardinier du parc municipal
- le directeur (la directrice) d'une campagne de nettoyage *(clean-up campaign)*
- le patron (la patronne) d'une teinturerie *(dry-cleaner's)*

▶ **Je voudrais que tu . . .**   **J'aimerais aussi que tu . . .**

10 Expression personnelle

Choisissez une personne et exprimez certains
souhaits pour cette personne.

je { souhaite / désire / voudrais } que
- mes parents . . .
- le professeur. . .
- mon copain . . .
- ma cousine . . .
- les voisins . . .

11 Exigences

Expliquez les exigences *(demands)* d'une
des personnes suivantes à votre égard.

mon père
ma mère
mes profs
mon meilleur ami
ma meilleure amie

exiger
insister pour
ne pas vouloir
} que je . . .

Comment décrire un objet

Un objet peut être . . .

La forme (shape) :

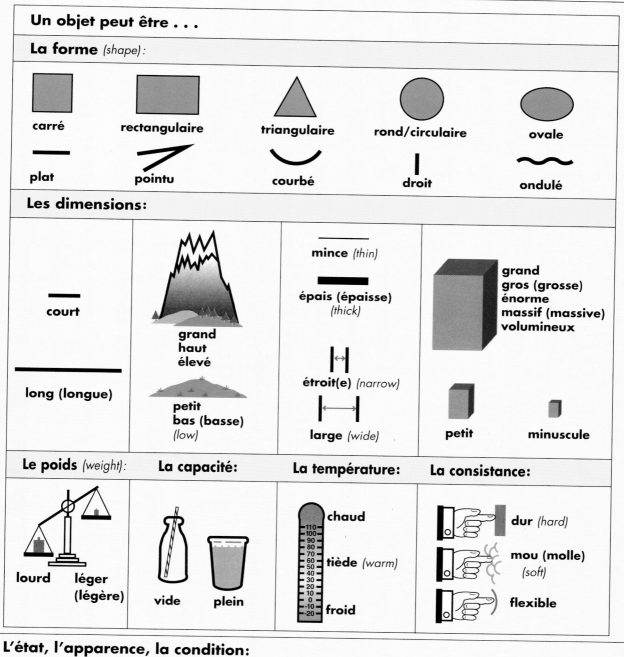

carré   rectangulaire   triangulaire   rond/circulaire   ovale

plat   pointu   courbé   droit   ondulé

Les dimensions:

court

long (longue)

grand
haut
élevé

petit
bas (basse)
(low)

mince (thin)

épais (épaisse)
(thick)

étroit(e) (narrow)

large (wide)

grand
gros (grosse)
énorme
massif (massive)
volumineux

petit   minuscule

Le poids (weight):

lourd   léger
(légère)

La capacité:

vide   plein

La température:

chaud

tiède (warm)

froid

La consistance:

dur (hard)

mou (molle)
(soft)

flexible

L'état, l'apparence, la condition:

solide	≠	fragile
sec (sèche) (dry)	≠	mouillé (wet), humide
lisse (smooth), poli (polished)	≠	rugueux (rugueuse) (rough, uneven)
brillant (shiny)	≠	terne (dull)
neuf (neuve) (new)	≠	vieux (vieille), ancien (ancienne)
		d'occasion (secondhand, used)
		usagé (worn)

Comment décrire
un objet

Pratique ▶

p. 33

La matière:

> En quoi est cet objet?

—En quoi est cet objet?
  Il est **en plastique**.

> Il est en plastique.

le papier	**le bois** *(wood)*	**le métal (les métaux)**
le carton *(cardboard)*	**la pierre** *(stone)*	**l'acier** *(steel)*
l'étoffe *(fabric)*	**la brique** *(brick)*	**le fer** *(iron)*
le caoutchouc *(rubber)*	**le verre** *(glass)*	**le cuivre** *(copper)*
le plastique		**le plomb** *(lead)*
la matière synthétique		**l'aluminium**

---

1 Qui suis-je?

Faites correspondre chaque monument avec sa description.

1. la Tour Eiffel

2. La Statue de la Liberté

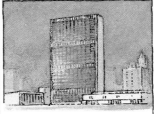

3. le bâtiment des Nations Unies

4. L'Arche de Saint Louis

(a) Je suis en métal. Je suis mince, plate et assez étroite. À l'intérieur, je suis vide. Je ne suis ni pointue, ni droite, ni ondulée. Ma caractéristique principale est que je suis courbe.

(b) Je suis élevé et droit. Je suis rectangulaire et plat. Le matin et l'après-midi, je suis plein, mais la nuit, je suis généralement vide. Je ne suis pas entièrement en métal. Je ne suis pas en pierre non plus.

(c) Mon socle *(pedestal)* est en pierre, mais je suis en métal. Je suis verte parce que je suis en cuivre. Je suis grande, mais je ne suis pas très épaisse. Ma figure n'est pas carrée. Ma couronne *(crown)* est circulaire.

(d) Je suis très haute—j'ai 300 mètres de hauteur—mais je ne suis pas grosse. Je suis plutôt mince. Je suis lourde parce que je pèse 7300 tonnes, mais je suis relativement légère. Je ne suis pas en verre. Je suis en fer.

2 Qu'est-ce que c'est?

Choisissez un de ces objets. Puis décrivez cet objet sans mentionner son nom.
Votre partenaire va deviner ce que c'est.

un clou

un fer à repasser

une bouteille

une scie

un ballon

un parachute

un réfrigérateur

LECTURE

La Couverture

fable du Moyen Âge

Le texte que vous allez lire est basé sur une fable très ancienne, puisqu'elle a été écrite au 13ᵉ siècle par un certain Bernier. Au Moyen Âge°, les fables ou **fabliaux** étaient très populaires en France, surtout dans la région du Nord. La fable est une histoire, généralement assez courte, qui a pour objet d'illustrer une vérité morale importante pour les gens de l'époque. Les personnages de fables peuvent être réels ou imaginaires. Dans *La Couverture*, les personnages sont intéressants parce qu'ils sont réels et qu'ils représentent assez bien la vie et la société au Moyen Âge.

le Moyen Âge *Middle Ages*

Anticipons un peu!

Dans la première partie de la fable, un père, qui est commerçant, apprend que son fils veut se marier avec une fille d'une classe sociale plus élevée. Malheureusement, ce fils, qui vient de terminer ses études, n'a ni argent ni maison. Que doit faire le père?

- Conseiller à son fils de trouver une femme qui soit de la même classe sociale que lui.
- Donner sa maison au jeune couple et acheter pour lui une maison plus petite, tout en continuant son commerce.
- Vendre son commerce et en donner les profits ainsi que sa maison au jeune couple.

Maintenant, lisez la première partie de la fable pour voir quelle décision le père a prise.

NOTE CULTURELLE

La noblesse

Avant la Révolution de 1789, la société française était divisée en trois groupes qui n'avaient pas les mêmes droits: **la noblesse** (militaire), **le clergé** (religieux) et **le peuple**. En général, les gens nobles ne se mariaient pas avec les gens du peuple.

Dans ce texte, la différence de classe sociale entre le marchand et le noble est reflétée dans le langage que chacun utilise pour parler à l'autre:

- **Brave homme** *(my good man)* est une expression condescendante.
- **Messire** (dérivé de **monsire** et **monseigneur**) était le terme utilisé au Moyen Âge pour parler à une personne noble. (C'est la forme ancienne de **monsieur**, qui aujourd'hui n'exprime pas la supériorité sociale.)

ABBEVILLE
PICARDIE
PARIS
LA FRANCE

LA COUVERTURE

I

À Abbeville* vivait autrefois° un homme
heureux. C'était un marchand qui avait un
commerce de tissus.° Il avait peu de biens, mais,
grâce à son travail, il gagnait honnêtement sa vie. Cet
5   homme était marié à une femme qu'il adorait. Ils avaient
un fils unique. Ce garçon était beau, fort, intelligent et
respectueux de ses parents. Chaque jour, le marchand et
sa femme rendaient grâce à Dieu° de leur bonheur. Ce
bonheur, malheureusement, n'a pas duré éternellement.
10 Un jour, la femme du marchand est tombée malade d'une
fièvre subite°. Une semaine plus tard, elle était morte . . .
Inconsolable, notre marchand continua° à travailler dur et
à s'occuper de l'éducation de son fils. Quand celui-ci eut°
dix-huit ans, il l'envoya° à Paris faire des études de droit.

15   Après deux ans d'études, le jeune homme revient à Abbeville
pour travailler comme clerc de notaire. Un dimanche, pendant la messe,°
il remarque une très belle jeune fille qui est assise au premier rang° de
l'église. Il s'enquiert° de l'identité de celle-ci. On lui dit qu'elle est orpheline
et qu'elle vient d'une famille très noble mais sans fortune.
20   Les dimanches suivants, le jeune homme revoit la jeune fille qui lui
sourit°. Il tombe éperdument amoureux° d'elle. Finalement il se décide à lui
parler et il se rend compte que la jeune fille l'aime aussi. Alors, un jour il lui
demande: «Voulez-vous m'épouser?» La jeune fille lui répond: «Je voudrais
bien vous épouser, mais vous n'êtes pas noble. Il faut donc que votre père
25 aille voir mon frère aîné et obtienne le consentement de celui-ci.»
      Le jeune homme va trouver son père pour lui expliquer la situation.
Le marchand, qui veut faire le bonheur de son fils, va chez le frère de
la jeune fille. Celui-ci écoute sa requête, hésite et finalement dit:
      — Brave homme, je veux bien que ma soeur épouse votre fils, mais
30 à deux conditions.
      — Quelles sont ces conditions, messire?
      — D'abord, je veux que vous donniez votre maison à votre fils pour que
ma soeur soit chez elle et non chez vous.

Mots utiles	
les biens	wealth
le bonheur	happiness
une couverture	blanket
un marchand	merchant
appartenir à	to belong to
avoir lieu	to take place
durer	to last
épouser	to marry
remarquer	to notice
se rendre compte	to realize
celui-ci, celle-ci	the latter
grâce à	thanks to

*__Abbeville__. Abbeville est une petite ville de Picardie, une province située dans le Nord de la France. Au Moyen Âge, cette ville avait une industrie textile très importante.

autrefois = dans le passé **tissus** _fabrics_
rendaient grâce à Dieu _gave thanks to God_ **subite** _sudden_
continua = a continué **eut** = a eu **envoya** = a envoyé
la messe _(Catholic) Mass_ **rang** _row_
s'enquiert de = pose des questions concernant
sourit _smiles_ **éperdument amoureux** _hopelessly in love_

— C'est facile! Tout ce qui m'appartient appartiendra à mon fils. Je lui
35 donnerai ma maison la veille° même de son mariage. Et la seconde condition,
messire?

— Je veux que vous me donniez 10.000 écus d'or.**

— Mais, c'est impossible, messire. Je n'ai pas cette somme sous la main.°

— Que faites-vous dans la vie, brave homme?

40 — Je suis marchand de tissu.

— Eh bien, il faut que vous vendiez votre commerce et que vous
m'apportiez le produit de cette vente°.

— Je ferai tout ce que vous voulez pour assurer le bonheur de mon fils.

Comme convenu°, le marchand vend son commerce et donne sa maison
45 à son fils. Le mariage a lieu. Les jeunes époux viennent habiter chez l'ancien
marchand qui leur laisse sa chambre, la plus belle pièce de la maison.

Au début, tout se passe bien. Le jeune couple est heureux. L'ancien
marchand, qui n'exerce plus sa profession, aide son fils et sa belle-fille dans
tous les petits travaux de la vie domestique. Il bricole, répare les ustensiles de
50 cuisine, coupe du bois pour le chauffage° de la maison, nourrit° les animaux,
s'occupe du jardin. Quand le premier enfant du couple naît, il cède° sa
chambre au bébé et va habiter dans une chambre plus petite. C'est lui qui
s'occupe de son petit-fils. Il joue avec l'enfant, il le promène, il lui apprend à
marcher et à parler.

10 000 écus d'or. L'écu était une pièce de monnaie utilisée en France jusqu'à la Révolution en 1789.
Dix mille écus d'or représentaient une somme considérable.

la veille = le jour avant   **sous la main** at hand, available   **vente** sale   **comme convenu** as agreed   **vente** sale
chauffage heating   **nourrit** = donne à manger à   **cède** = donne

Avez-vous compris?

1. Pourquoi est-ce que le marchand était un homme heureux?
2. Quels sont les sentiments du jeune homme et de la jeune fille? Quel est l'obstacle à leur mariage?
3. Pour le marchand, laquelle des deux conditions émises (expressed) par le noble est la plus difficile à réaliser? Pourquoi?
4. Que fait le marchand après le mariage de son fils? Décrivez sa vie.

Anticipons un peu!

Dans la deuxième partie de la fable, le grand-père, qui est maintenant âgé et très infirme, habite encore chez son fils. Malheureusement, la femme trouve de plus en plus difficile de s'occuper du grand-père malade. Que doit faire le fils?

- Engager une infirmière pour s'occuper du vieillard.
- Garder (keep) le grand-père à la maison et demander à toute la famille de faire le sacrifice nécessaire pour s'en occuper.
- Envoyer le grand-père dans un hospice pour gens âgés.
- Autre solution?

II

55 **L**es années ont passé et la situation a bien changé à la maison. Il y a maintenant cinq enfants. Le grand-père habite une chambre minuscule au grenier.° Il est vieux et infirme° et il ne peut plus travailler comme avant. Son fils n'a pas réussi dans ses affaires et l'argent

60 manque° à la maison. La femme de celui-ci a perdu sa beauté. Elle est devenue dure et méchante, et elle ne peut plus supporter la présence de son beau-père à la maison. Un jour, elle parle à son mari:

— Votre* père est devenu une charge inutile. Il faut qu'il quitte la maison.

65 — Mais, mon amie . . .

—Oubliez-vous qui vous avez épousé? Il faut que vous choisissiez: votre père ou moi!

Le fils est morfondu.° Il va trouver son père et essaie de trouver une excuse.

70 — Père, il faut que vous* quittiez votre chambre.

— Mais, mon fils, pourquoi veux-tu que je la quitte?

— Père, nous avons besoin d'argent. Il faut que nous louions cette chambre.

75 — Écoute, mon fils, je veux bien aller loger dans l'étable avec les chevaux…

— Père, c'est impossible!

— Et pourquoi donc me chasses-tu?

Embarrassé, le fils doit avouer la vérité: «Père, ma femme exige que

80 vous partiez.»

Le vieillard, consterné, regarde son fils. «Et où veux-tu que je loge?»

—Vous irez à l'hospice des vieillards.° Ils vous recevront.°

— Mais, il fait froid là-bas.

85 Le fils appelle son fils aîné, un garçon de quatorze ans, celui-là même que son grand-père avait élevé quand il était petit.

— Fils, va dans ma chambre. Dans l'armoire, tu trouveras une grande couverture de laine.° Prends-la et donne-la à ton grand-père.

Mots utiles	
les affaires	*business*
une charge	*burden*
un couteau	*knife*
la moitié	*half*
dur	*hard-hearted*
méchant	*mean, nasty*
allumer un feu	*to light a fire*
avouer	*to admit, avow*
élever	*to raise (children)*
exiger	*to insist*
expliquer	*to explain*
garder	*to keep*
loger	*to live, lodge*
supporter	*to bear, stand*

---

*L'usage de *vous.* Autrefois, l'usage de **vous** (au lieu de **tu**) était beaucoup plus courant que maintenant. C'était une marque de respect utilisée par les enfants pour parler à leurs parents, et par les époux quand ils se parlaient entre eux.

grenier *attic* **infirme** = invalide **l'argent manque** = il n'y a pas d'argent **morfondu** *upset*
vieillards = personnes âgées **vous recevront** = vont vous prendre **laine** wool

90 Le garçon monte dans la chambre de ses parents, ouvre l'armoire et prend la couverture. Puis, il prend son couteau et coupe la couverture en deux. Il descend dans la cour° et donne la moitié de la couverture à son grand-père.

Son père, surpris, lui demande:

— Fils, pourquoi as-tu coupé la couverture en deux? Et pourquoi
95 n'en donnes-tu que la moitié à ton grand-père?

— Parce qu'un jour, vous aurez besoin de l'autre moitié.

L'homme regarde son fils sans comprendre.

—Il faut que tu t'expliques! Quand donc aurai-je besoin de cette couverture?

100 —Quand vous serez devenu vieux et quand, à mon tour, je vous enverrai à l'hospice des vieillards.

L'homme finalement comprend son ingratitude. Il s'excuse et va embrasser son père qui fond en larmes.° Puis, il va trouver sa femme pour lui dire qu'il a décidé de garder son père à la maison. Celle-ci, qui a vu toute
105 la scène de sa fenêtre, a aussi compris. Elle monte dans la chambre de son beau-père pour allumer un bon feu de cheminée,° puis elle va préparer un grand repas. Une nouvelle vie familiale commence . . .

cour *courtyard*   **fond en larmes** *breaks into tears*   **cheminée** *fireplace*

Avez-vous compris?

1. Qu'est-ce qui a changé à la maison du marchand? Décrivez un ou deux de ces changements.

2. Quelle excuse est-ce que le fils donne à son père quand il lui demande de quitter sa chambre?

3. Qu'est-ce que le petit-fils doit faire dans la chambre de son père?
   Qu'est-ce qu'il fait en plus?

4. Qu'est-ce que le garçon explique à son père?

5. Comment finit l'histoire?

EXPRESSION ORALE

■ Dramatisation

Avec votre partenaire, choisissez une scène de la fable que vous avez trouvée intéressante et jouez-la en classe.

■ Situations

Avec votre partenaire, choisissez l'une des situations suivantes. Composez le dialogue correspondant et jouez-le en classe.

1 Rencontre

Après sa visite au noble, le marchand rencontre un(e) ami(e) qui est marchand(e) aussi. Il explique sa décision de vendre son commerce. L'autre marchand(e) essaie de le dissuader.

Rôles: le marchand de tissus, un ami(e)

2 Explication

Après la scène de la couverture, le petit-fils explique à un(e) jeune frère (soeur) ce qui s'est passé. Celui-ci (celle-ci) veut des détails.

Rôles: le petit-fils, un frère (une soeur)

■ Discussion: La morale de l'histoire

Comme nous l'avons vu, l'objet d'une fable est généralement d'illustrer un certain principe moral.

A. Voici plusieurs morales possibles pour la fable que vous avez lue.
   • Les gens riches ne sont jamais heureux.
   • Il ne faut pas se marier avec une personne d'une autre classe sociale.
   • Les jeunes sont charitables; les adultes sont égoïstes.
   • Tout est bien qui finit bien.
   • On ne peut pas compter sur ses enfants. Pour cela, toute personne raisonnable doit garder ses biens jusqu'à sa mort.
   • Il ne faut pas faire aux autres personnes ce qu'on ne voudrait pas qu'elles nous fassent à nous.

Choisissez la morale qui, selon vous, correspond le mieux au récit de *La Couverture*. (Ou, si vous voulez, trouvez une autre morale.) Expliquez votre choix à votre partenaire.

B. D'après vous, quelle était la morale de cette histoire au Moyen Âge? (Pour connaître cette réponse, allez au bas de la page.)

EXPRESSION ÉCRITE

■ D'un autre point de vue

Imaginez que vous êtes le petit-fils ou la petite-fille du marchand de tissu. Dans une lettre à un(e) ami(e), vous racontez de votre point de vue la scène de la couverture.

■ En famille

Décrivez la vie de la famille <u>après</u> l'incident. Pour cela, composez un texte où vous décrivez ce que chacun fait à la maison pour aider les autres.

■ Fable moderne

Transformez *La Couverture* en fable moderne. Pour cela, composez une nouvelle fable que vous situerez à l'époque actuelle en gardant la morale générale de l'histoire.

■ D'un oeil critique

Expliquez pourquoi *La Couverture* est une fable très ancienne. Pour cela, faites une liste de tous les détails qui indiquent que l'action de cette fable se passe autrefois plutôt que maintenant.

LA MORALE DE L'HISTOIRE
L'auteur du Moyen Âge qui a écrit cette fable voulait conseiller aux parents de garder leurs biens et leurs ressources pour leurs vieux jours.

INTERLUDE CULTUREL

■ *Les dates*

Période gallo-romaine

- **200** av. J.-C.
- **151** *Provincia Romana*
- **52** *Vercingétorix à Gergovie*
- **0**

- **450** apr. J.-C.

- **508** *Clovis, roi des Francs*

Empire de Charlemagne

- **778** *Roland à Roncevaux*
- **800** *Sacre de Charlemagne*

- **1066** *Guillaume le Conquérant: Bataille de Hastings*

- **1152** *Aliénor d'Aquitaine épouse Henri Plantagenêt*

Guerre de Cent Ans

- **1337**

- **1429** *Jeanne d'Arc délivre la ville d'Orléans*
- **1453**

■ *Les événements*

La période romaine (200 av. J.-C. - 450 apr. J.-C.)

Les premières légions romaines arrivent dans le sud de **la Gaule** (l'ancien nom de la France) au deuxième siècle avant Jésus-Christ. En 151 av. J.-C., Rome annexe cette région qui devient «Provincia Romana» ou Provence. En 58 av. J.-C., **Jules César** arrive en Gaule pour conquérir le reste du pays. Ses troupes sont victorieuses, malgré la résistance héroïque du chef gaulois, **Vercingétorix**.

Les Romains construisent de nombreux monuments, visibles encore aujourd'hui: arènes, amphithéâtres, arcs de triomphe, temples . . . Ils apportent aussi leur langue, le latin, qui est la base du français moderne.

À partir de 400, une série d'invasions met fin à la civilisation gallo-romaine. Les Francs, tribu d'origine germanique, conquièrent la Gaule. En 508, **Clovis**, leur roi, choisit Paris comme capitale. La Gaule va devenir la France.

GALLIA PROVINCIA

L'Empire de Charlemagne (800-814)

En 800, **Charlemagne**, ou Charles le Grand, roi des Francs, est sacré empereur de l'Occident. Son empire est immense: il comprend la France, l'Allemagne, la Belgique, la Hollande, l'Italie du Nord et le nord de l'Espagne. Avec Charlemagne, l'unification de l'Europe est pour la première fois réalisée.

Aix-la-Chapelle

L'empire de Charlemagne

La Guerre de Cent Ans (1337-1453)

Cette guerre représente plus de 100 ans de conflits franco-anglais. Elle commence en 1337 quand **Édouard III**, roi d'Angleterre, veut devenir roi de France. Les armées anglaises débarquent en France et remportent de brillantes victoires à **Crécy** (1346), à **Poitiers** (1356) et à **Azincourt** (1415). Les Anglais occupent une grande partie du territoire français et dévastent le pays.

Finalement la chance tourne. En 1429, **Jeanne d'Arc**, une jeune fille de 19 ans, rallie l'armée française, qui va peu à peu libérer la France.

■ *Les personnes*

Vercingétorix: un général de 20 ans

Vercingétorix (72- 46 av. J.-C.) est le premier héros national français. En gaulois, son nom signifie «chef suprême des combattants». En 52 av. J.-C., il a vingt ans. Jeune et courageux, il décide de se révolter contre l'occupant romain. Il rallie les tribus gauloises, devient leur chef et attaque les légions romaines. **César** contre-attaque. Malgré la supériorité des Romains, Vercingétorix est victorieux à **Gergovie**. Mais le combat est inégal et finalement, quelques mois plus tard, Vercingétorix est capturé. Enchaîné, il est emmené à Rome où il figure au triomphe de César, puis il est exécuté.

Pour les Français, Vercingétorix symbolise le courage, le patriotisme, l'esprit d'indépendance et la résistance contre l'ennemi.

Vercingétorix (72 - 46 av. J-C) le premier héros national français

Charlemagne: Empereur de l'Occident

Charlemagne (747-814) est un grand conquérant et un grand administrateur. Pour gouverner son très vaste empire, il établit sa capitale à **Aix-la-Chapelle** au centre de cet empire et crée une administration centralisée.

Charlemagne (742 - 814), Empereur de l'Occident

Charlemagne fonde aussi un grand nombre d'écoles, les «écoles du palais». C'est un homme cultivé qui parle latin et grec et s'intéresse aux sciences. Il encourage la littérature, la philosophie, les sciences, la médecine, les arts, l'architecture. Dans sa capitale, il fonde une Académie où viennent les plus grands savants° du monde.

Jeanne d'Arc (1412 -1431), grande héroïne française

Jeanne d'Arc: héroïne et martyre

On trouve la statue de **Jeanne d'Arc** (1412-1431) dans toutes les églises de France. C'est non seulement une sainte de l'église catholique, mais aussi la grande héroïne française. Jeanne a seulement 17 ans quand le roi de France lui donne le commandement de son armée. Elle rallie les troupes démoralisées par de nombreuses défaites. Puis, elle délivre **Orléans**, assiégée par les Anglais, et va de victoire en victoire. Elle est finalement capturée par des soldats bourguignons° qui la vendent à leurs alliés anglais. Elle est jugée, accusée de sorcellerie° et condamnée à être brûlée.° La mort héroïque de Jeanne d'Arc, à l'âge de 19 ans, ne profite pas aux Anglais qui sont définitivement chassés de France quelques années plus tard.

---

savants *scientists* **bourguignons** = de Bourgogne *(Burgundy)* **sorcellerie** *witchcraft* **brûlée** *burned at the stake*

▪ *Astérix et sa bande* ▪

Tous les Français connaissent **Astérix le Gaulois**. C'est un petit homme blond avec de grandes moustaches. Il est très petit, mais il est très musclé, très intelligent et très courageux. Il a un copain, **Obélix**, qui est très loyal, très fort, mais pas très intelligent.

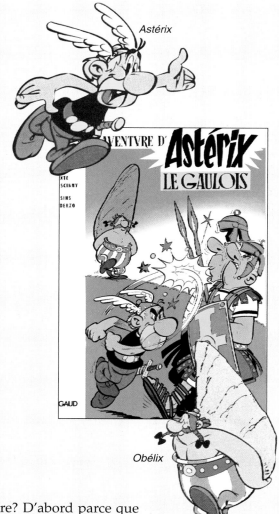

Astérix

Obélix

Astérix est d'une force° exceptionnelle. Son secret est une potion magique préparée par le druide **Panoramix**. Quand Astérix boit un peu de cette potion, ses forces sont multipliées par cent.

Bien sûr, Astérix n'est pas une personne réelle. C'est le héros d'une bande dessinée très populaire en France.

Les aventures d'Astérix ont lieu vers 50 avant Jésus-Christ. À cette époque, la Gaule entière est occupée par les Romains. Il y a un seul° village qui résiste, le village où habitent Astérix et ses copains. Astérix étant° Gaulois, les Romains sont évidemment ses ennemis mortels . . .

Une légion romaine est signalée près de son village. Notre héros prend un peu de potion magique et avec Obélix il va à l'attaque de l'ennemi. Crac! Boum! Zap! En une minute la légion romaine est décimée. Tous les Romains sont prisonniers.

Astérix connaît d'autres aventures. Toujours avec Obélix, il va à Rome où il rencontre **Jules César**. Il va en Égypte où il rencontre **Cléopâtre**. Il va en Belgique, en Angleterre, en Allemagne, en Suisse . . . Chaque aventure est le sujet d'un nouvel album et chaque album a un succès phénoménal.

Pourquoi Astérix est-il si populaire? D'abord parce que ce petit homme moustachu symbolise l'esprit de la France en lutte° contre ses ennemis. Et aussi parce qu'il représente assez bien le caractère national français. Il est aventureux, brave, astucieux.° Il est aussi irritable, impatient, agressif et vaniteux.° Avant tout, il est indépendant. Astérix correspond à l'image que les Français ont d'eux-mêmes. Il a leurs qualités . . . et leurs défauts!°

---

force *strength* **un seul** *only one* **étant** *being* **en lutte** *struggling* **astucieux** *smart* **vaniteux** *boastful* **défauts** *faults, failings*

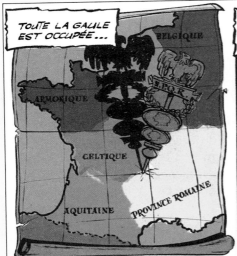

Une Aventure d'Astérix le Gaulois, Goscinny / Uderzo, Dargaud, S.A., p.5

▪ *Roland, l'homme et la légende* ▪

Roland sonne
son oliphant

Roland est à la fois un personnage historique et le héros d'une des plus grandes légendes françaises.

■ L'histoire

Nous sommes en l'an 778. **Charlemagne** est en Espagne où il fait la guerre° à des princes arabes. Une insurrection éclate° dans son royaume.° Charlemagne retourne précipitamment en France avec ses meilleures troupes, mais il ne peut pas emmener ses bagages, qui sont trop lourds.° Il confie° leur transport à **Roland**, l'un de ses officiers.

Dans les Pyrénées, le convoi de bagages est attaqué par une bande de pillards° qui capturent le butin° et tuent° Roland.

Les Francs
et les Sarrasins
en combat.

■ La légende

La légende embellit les faits historiques et le rôle de Roland. Dans la légende, Roland est le neveu préféré de Charlemagne. C'est aussi le plus noble et le plus brave de ses chevaliers.° Il accompagne l'empereur dans toutes ses expéditions militaires. Il est avec lui en Espagne où les Francs combattent les Sarrasins,* ennemis de la chrétienté.°

Comme dans l'histoire, Charlemagne doit rentrer à la hâte en France. C'est à Roland qu'il confie son arrière-garde.° Roland est trahi° par l'infâme **Ganelon**, son beau-père. À **Roncevaux**, son armée de 20 000 hommes tombe dans une embuscade° tendue par 400 000 Sarrasins. Quand **Olivier**, le loyal compagnon de Roland, voit l'arrivée des ennemis, il demande à Roland de sonner° son oliphant (un cor° en ivoire d'éléphant) pour appeler Charlemagne. Homme d'honneur, Roland refuse: il préfère se battre.°

L'infâme
Ganelon

Charlemagne et son neveu préféré, Roland

* **Sarrasins**: nom donné aux conquérants arabes venus en Europe au 8e siècle.

---

guerre *war*   **éclate** *breaks out*   **royaume** *kingdom*   **lourds** *heavy*   **confie** *entrusts*   **pillards** *looters*   **butin** *booty*   **tuent** *kill*
chevaliers *knights*   **chrétienté** *Christendom*   **arrière-garde** *rear guard*   **trahi** *betrayed*   **embuscade** *ambush*   **sonner** *to blow*
cor *horn*   **se battre** *to fight*

Roland avec son épée Durendal

Charlemagne revint avec ses troupes . . . .

La belle Aude

Toute la journée, les Francs, avec Roland et Olivier à leur tête, repoussent les ennemis. Ils multiplient les actes de courage, mais à un contre vingt le combat est inégal. Peu à peu, tous les compagnons de Roland sont massacrés. Roland voit que la bataille est perdue. Avant de mourir, il sonne son «oliphant» pour que Charlemagne vienne venger° ses compagnons. Roland essaie de briser° son épée° **Durendal** contre un rocher. Il frappe° dix fois, mais l'épée ne se brise pas.

Charlemagne revient sur ses pas.° Il détruit l'armée sarrasine, enterre° ses morts et, rempli° de tristesse, rentre dans sa capitale. Là, il donne l'épée de Roland à la fiancée de celui-ci, la belle **Aude**. La jeune fille meurt en apprenant la disparition de son bien-aimé.°

La Chanson de Roland

Au 12e siècle, c'est-à-dire plus de 300 ans après les faits historiques, un moine° anonyme écrit *La Chanson de Roland*. C'est un long poème épique de 4 000 vers qui relate en détail la légende. *La Chanson de Roland* est la première grande oeuvre littéraire écrite en langue française. Elle a un succès immédiat dans tout le monde occidental.° Pour certains historiens, les raisons de ce succès sont politiques. Au 12e siècle, en effet, les chevaliers chrétiens partent en croisade pour délivrer Jérusalem prise par les Turcs. Ils sont inspirés par *La Chanson de Roland* qui représente un épisode de la guerre sainte des Chrétiens contre les Musulmans.

Un troubadour médiéval

venger *to avenge* **briser** *to break* **épée** *sword* **frappe** *strikes* **pas** *steps* **enterre** *buries* **rempli** *filled* **bien-aimé** *beloved* **moine** *monk* **occidental** *western*

■ *Quand les rois d'Angleterre étaient français*

■ Guillaume le Conquérant et la conquête de l'Angleterre (1066)

Les ancêtres de **Guillaume le Conquérant** (1028-1087) sont scandinaves. Ce sont ces terribles **«Normands»** (homme du Nord) qui, venus de Norvège° et du Danemark sur leurs **drakkars**, ont attaqué et dévasté l'ouest de la France au 9e siècle. Ils ont pris et brûlé° Orléans, Tours et Paris. Pour avoir la paix,° le roi de France a donné à leur chef le duché de Normandie . . . et la main de sa fille. Les Normands sont devenus de bons et loyaux vassaux° du roi de France.

«Drakkar» scandinave

Guillaume est le fils de Robert Ier, duc de Normandie. Il a seulement huit ans quand son père meurt. Il devient alors lui-même duc de Normandie. Jeune homme, il fait un voyage en Angleterre pour rendre visite à son cousin, le roi **Édouard**. Celui-ci lui promet la couronne d'Angleterre à sa mort. Mais il y a un autre prétendant: **Harold le Saxon**. Un jour, Harold vient en Normandie où il est immédiatement fait prisonnier. Guillaume lui propose un échange: la liberté contre la promesse de renoncer à la couronne° d'Angleterre. Harold accepte l'échange, retourne en Angleterre, et là il oublie sa promesse.

Quand Édouard meurt en 1066, Harold se fait nommer° roi. Guillaume apprend cette trahison.° Furieux, il décide de punir Harold et de conquérir l'Angleterre par la force. Pour cela, il organise une formidable expédition. Le 23 septembre, ses bateaux chargés° de soldats arrivent en Angleterre. Le 14 octobre, il défait l'armée d'Harold à **la bataille de Hastings**. Le jour de Noël, il est couronné à Londres roi d'Angleterre sous le nom de **Guillaume Ier**.

Une conséquence de la conquête est que le français va devenir pendant plusieurs siècles la langue de la cour d'Angleterre.

L'histoire de la conquête de l'Angleterre par Guillaume est représentée graphiquement dans une très belle tapisserie° de 70 mètres de long, la tapisserie de Bayeux. C'est, en quelque sorte, la première «bande dessinée» de l'histoire.

Scène de la tapisserie de Bayeux, la première «bande dessinée»

Norvège *Norway* **brûlé** *burned* **paix** *peace* **vassaux** = sujets **couronne** *crown* **se fait nommer** *has himself named*
trahison *betrayal* **chargés** *loaded* **tapisserie** tapestry

■ Aliénor d'Aquitaine: Reine de France et Reine d'Angleterre

Elle a été reine° de France, puis reine d'Angleterre. C'est aussi la mère de deux rois d'Angleterre.

Fille et héritière° du duc d'Aquitaine, **Aliénor** (1122-1204) est une princesse d'une grande beauté. À l'âge de quinze ans, elle épouse° le roi de France, **Louis VII**, avec qui elle part en croisade contre les Turcs. Après leur retour de Terre Sainte,° Aliénor et Louis ont deux filles, mais le roi, qui veut des fils, fait annuler le mariage.

Quelques semaines plus tard, Aliénor se remarie avec **Henri Plantagenêt**, duc de Normandie, qui devient roi d'Angleterre en 1153. À leur tour, leurs fils, **Richard Coeur de Lion** et **Jean sans Terre** vont aussi être rois d'Angleterre. À cette époque, les rois d'Angleterre possèdent de vastes territoires en France: la Normandie, l'Anjou, l'Aquitaine. Cette situation est une des causes principales de la **Guerre de Cent Ans**.

Aliénor d'Aquitaine est très belle, très intelligente et très cultivée. En France et en Angleterre, elle crée une cour brillante où elle protège les poètes et les artistes. Princesse libérale, elle donne beaucoup de libertés aux habitants des villes qu'elle possède. À la fin° de sa vie, elle se retire en France, dans son abbaye de Fontevrault, où sont enterrés° deux rois d'Angleterre, son mari et son fils, Richard.

À la cour d'Aliénor d'Aquitaine

---

reine *queen*   **héritière** *heiress*   **épouse** *marries*   **Terre Sainte** *Holy Land*   **à la fin** *towards the end*   **enterrés** *buried*

Jeanne d'Arc à Chinon

Le château de Chinon

Un jour, Jeanne a entendu des voix.

Jeanne d'Arc est née en 1412 à Domrémy, un petit village de Lorraine. À cette époque, la France était occupée par les Anglais. Un jour, Jeanne a entendu des voix. Elle a reconnu Sainte Catherine, Sainte Marguerite et Saint Michel. Ces voix lui ont dit: «Jeanne, c'est toi qui vas délivrer le pays!»

«Moi? Mais je suis une paysanne° qui sait à peine° lire et écrire,» a répondu Jeanne.

Mais les voix ont insisté: «Jeanne, va chez le roi et dis-lui que c'est Dieu° qui t'envoie.»

Jeanne et le sire de Baudricourt.

Jeanne a accepté la mission, mais maintenant elle est inquiète°. «Aller chez le roi? Oui, mais comment? Le roi habite si loin et les routes sont pleines° de brigands.»°

Jeanne va trouver un seigneur° local, le sire de Baudricourt.

— Messire, donnez-moi une escorte. Je veux aller chez le roi de France.

— Et qui t'envoie?

— Le Roi du Ciel.°

Baudricourt se moque de° Jeanne et la renvoie chez elle. Jeanne revient. Elle insiste et finalement elle obtient une escorte. C'est avec cette escorte de six hommes qu'elle arrive devant le château de Chinon où réside Charles, roi de France, avec sa cour. Immédiatement elle demande d'être présentée au roi.

Jeanne et son escorte arrivent au château de Chinon.

---

paysanne *peasant girl* **à peine** *hardly* **Dieu** *God* **inquiète** *worried* **pleines** *full* **brigands** = *bandits* **seigneur** *lord*
Messire = Monsieur **Roi du Ciel** *King of Heaven* **se moque de** *makes fun of*

Jeanne a reconnu le vrai roi malgré ses humbles apparences.

Le roi Charles est un roi sans royaume.° Il a perdu sa capitale. Paris est occupé par les Anglais, qui ont choisi un autre roi de France, un roi anglais, bien sûr. Charles est un jeune homme timide et sans énergie. Il ne croit plus en la victoire et certainement pas aux miracles. «Qui est cette Jeanne et qu'est-ce qu'elle veut de moi?»

Un courtisan, Bernard de Chissay, suggère au roi de jouer un bon tour° à Jeanne. «Déguisons-nous! Je vais mettre vos vêtements et vous, vous allez vous déguiser en simple courtisan. Nous allons voir si cette petite paysanne va reconnaître le vrai roi.» Bernard de Chissay met les vêtements du roi alors que° Charles met un simple vêtement noir. Jeanne entre dans la grande salle°

du château. Il y a plusieurs centaines de dames et de chevaliers. Bernard de Chissay, magnifiquement habillé, reçoit les hommages des courtisans. Charles, le vrai roi, est au fond° de la salle, mais c'est vers lui que Jeanne s'avance.

— Gentil roi de France, le Roi du Ciel m'envoie vers vous.

— Mais ce n'est pas moi, le roi. Le roi est là-bas.

— C'est vous le roi, et pas un autre . . .

Oui, Jeanne a reconnu le vrai roi malgré° ses humbles apparences. Charles est très impressionné. Il décide d'écouter Jeanne. Jeanne et Charles ont une longue conversation secrète. Charles est maintenant convaincu.° Jeanne est l'envoyée° de Dieu.

Jeanne devant la ville d'Orléans.

Le roi lui donne une armée. Jeanne d'Arc, qui a seulement 17 ans, prend le commandement des troupes royales. Elle part délivrer Orléans, assiégée par les Anglais. Arrivée devant la ville, elle exhorte ses compagnons d'armes: «Entrez hardiment° parmi° les Anglais!» Surpris par le courage de cette jeune fille, les soldats attaquent. Le lendemain, Orléans est délivrée!

Charles est couronné roi de France.

La libération de la France vient de commencer. Jeanne d'Arc gagne d'autres batailles. Son grand triomphe a lieu quelques mois après l'entrevue de Chinon quand Charles est solennellement couronné roi de France dans la cathédrale de Reims.

---

sans royaume *without a kingdom* **tour** *trick* **alors que** *whereas* **salle** *hall* **au fond** *in the back* **malgré** *in spite of* **convaincu** *convinced* **l'envoyée** = *la messagère* **hardiment** *boldly* **parmi** *among*

Vive la nature!

Thème et Objectifs

Culture

In this unit, you will discover . . .

- why the French people feel close to their roots
- how the French incorporate «tourisme écologique» into their vacation plans
- how the French people feel about their environment
- why Jacques Cousteau is so well known and what important work he did
- what the «culte du soleil» represents for French people

Communication

You will learn how . . .

- to talk about vacation activities
- to tell people who are on vacation that they should take certain precautions and avoid dangers
- to describe weather conditions and natural phenomenon

Langue

You will learn how . . .

- to narrate a sequence of past events
- to describe the setting of these past events
- to read literary accounts of past events

OUI à la nature!

Les racines°

Cécile Pécoul, 25 ans, est infirmière. Elle habite et travaille à Paris, mais c'est à la campagne qu'elle se sent vraiment bien. Elle explique: «J'ai besoin d'air pur.° Alors, le week-end, je pars souvent en Normandie* avec mes copains. Parfois je vais faire de l'escalade° dans la forêt de Fontainebleau.** Et en été, je passe les vacances dans la ferme de mes grands-parents en Auvergne.*** C'est là d'où vient ma famille. C'est donc là où je suis vraiment chez moi, parce que c'est là où sont mes racines.»

Aujourd'hui, la majorité des Français habitent dans des grandes villes mais, comme Cécile, ils restent très attachés à leur province d'origine. Ils y retournent à l'occasion des vacances, pour retrouver leurs racines, mais surtout pour établir un contact avec la nature. Cet amour de la terre° et de la nature explique le succès du tourisme «vert» ou du tourisme «écologique».

Notre planète, ça nous concerne

■ Deux adeptes de la randonnée pédestre

Le tourisme vert

■ L'escalade en montagne

Il y a différentes façons de pratiquer le tourisme écologique. La forme la plus simple est évidemment la marche à pied.° Si on aime celle-ci,° on peut faire de la «randonnée pédestre°» le long° des milliers de kilomètres de sentiers° ruraux. On part le matin, sac au dos.° On marche pendant 35 à 40 kilomètres. On s'arrête le soir dans un gîte° rural où on passe la nuit. En dix jours, on peut ainsi visiter toute une région «de l'intérieur», sans rencontrer beaucoup de gens. Un avantage de la randonnée pédestre est qu'on peut la pratiquer à tout âge. C'est une activité très populaire en France. La Fédération Française de Randonnée Pédestre compte plus de 300.000 membres.

Quand on passe les vacances à la montagne, celle-ci offre une grande variété d'activités qui nous mettent en contact direct avec notre milieu naturel. En plus° de la randonnée pédestre, on peut faire du VTT, du ski sur l'herbe,° de l'escalade, de l'alpinisme° et, si on aime les sensations fortes, du delta-plane et du parapente.°

MINISTERE DE L'ENVIRONNEMENT

***Normandie** une région à l'ouest de Paris ****Fontainebleau** une forêt au sud de Paris où il y a des rochers *****Auvergne** une province au centre de la France
racines roots **pur** fresh **l'escalade** rock climbing **la terre** land **la marche à pied** walking **celle-ci** the latter **la randonnée pédestre** hiking **le long** along **sentiers** trails **sac au dos** with a back pack **un gîte** simple lodging **En plus** In addition **l'herbe** grass **l'alpinisme** mountain climbing **parapente** parasailing

La protection de la nature

Journées de l'environnement

Quand on aime la nature, il faut la protéger. À cet effet, le gouvernement français a créé des réserves naturelles et de grands parcs nationaux. Ces parcs sont situés principalement dans les zones de montagne (Alpes, Pyrénées, Massif Central). Là, tout est fait pour préserver la faune° et la flore° typiques de la région, et en particulier les espèces en danger. Il est interdit de camper, de faire du feu,° de toucher à la végétation et de déranger° les animaux.

Évidemment, la protection de la nature n'est pas seulement l'affaire° du gouvernement. C'est l'affaire de tout le monde. Pour 80% des Français, l'environnement est «un problème immédiat et urgent.» Cette préoccupation explique sans doute le succès des partis° écologiques. Aux élections, les «écolos» ou les «verts» obtiennent généralement 10% ou 12% des voix. Ce n'est pas beaucoup, mais c'est assez pour avoir une action politique efficace. Cette action se porte° sur beaucoup de domaines: protection de l'environnement, lutte° contre la pollution, limitation et contrôle de l'énergie nucléaire, aide et subventions° pour le développement de l'énergie solaire. Si on veut préserver la qualité de la vie de demain, c'est aujourd'hui qu'il faut agir!°

Les éco-musées

Une autre forme de tourisme écologique consiste à visiter les «éco-musées». Le but de ces musées est de préserver la vie rurale d'autrefois quand la majorité des Français habitaient à la campagne. Ces musées sont souvent des reconstructions de fermes et de villages anciens où l'on peut voir les outils,° les instruments, les ustensiles qu'on utilisait à l'époque.

et vous?

DÉFINITIONS

Définissez en français les mots et expressions suivantes:
- les racines
- le tourisme écologique
- la randonnée pédestre
- un sentier rural
- un gîte rural
- un parc national
- la faune
- un éco-musée

EXPRESSION ORALE

- À votre avis, est-ce que les Américains ont «l'amour de la terre»? Expliquez.
- Avez-vous jamais fait du camping ou de la randonnée pédestre? Décrivez cette expérience.
- Avec votre partenaire, discutez des différentes façons de protéger l'environnement. Préparez un rapport.

EXPRESSION ÉCRITE

Dans une lettre à un(e) ami(e) français(e), vous expliquez comment on peut faire du «tourisme écologique» dans la région ou l'état où vous habitez.

---

la faune *wildlife*   **la flore** *plant life*   **feu** *fire*   **déranger** *bother*   **l'affaire** *business*   **des partis** = partis politiques   **se porte** = concerne
lutte *fight*   **subventions** *subsidies*   **agir** *to act*   **outils** *tools*

Les sept commandements
du campeur

Chaque année, des millions de Français font du camping. Si vous venez un jour en France, vous aurez peut-être l'occasion d'en faire aussi. Voici quelques consignes° à observer.

*P*our protéger la terre et l'eau, restons simples...

*D*es idées pour mieux respirer

1. Respectez les règlements.°

En France le camping est en principe libre° sur le territoire public . . . sauf° là où il est interdit. Le camping est interdit sur les plages de mer, dans les réserves naturelles, près des points d'eau utilisés pour la consommation, près des monuments historiques. Et si vous campez sur un terrain privé, n'oubliez pas de demander l'autorisation au propriétaire.°

2. Faites attention au feu.

L'incendie est la plus grande menace qui existe pour la forêt. Chaque année, des milliers d'hectares de forêts sont détruits° par des incendies° causés par des campeurs imprudents.°

PARC NATUREL REGIONAL DE CAMARGUE
CIRCUITS DE DECOUVERTE

3. Préservez l'environnement.

La nature est fragile et a besoin de notre protection. Alors, préservez la végétation au lieu de° la détruire. Ne cassez° pas les branches des arbres. N'arrachez° pas les plantes. Ne cueillez° pas les fleurs, qui ne sont pas pour vous seulement, mais pour tout le monde.

4. Ne dérangez pas les animaux.

Les animaux sont chez eux et vous, vous êtes sur leur territoire. Ce sont vos hôtes. Agissez° avec eux en invité° respectueux, et non pas en barbare.

5. Ne contaminez pas l'eau.

L'eau est une ressource précieuse non seulement pour les humains, mais aussi pour tous les habitants de la nature. Pensez aux animaux qui viennent boire tous les jours dans les rivières et les lacs.

6. Ne laissez pas de déchets.°

Emportez° vos déchets avec vous. Déposez-les dans les réceptacles spéciaux que vous trouverez sur les routes. Surtout, ne laissez pas d'objets en plastique. Le plastique n'est pas biodégradable et il peut provoquer la mort° des animaux qui le mangent.

7. Ne faites pas de bruit.

Si vous avez décidé de faire du camping, c'est pour profiter du calme de la nature et non pas pour écouter de la musique. Alors, laissez votre radio chez vous et n'oubliez pas que le bruit est une forme de pollution.

et vous?

D'après vous, quels sont les trois commandements les plus importants? Expliquez pourquoi.

---

consignes *rules* **règlements** *rules* **libre** = autorisé **sauf** = excepté **propriétaire** *owner* **détruire** ✳ *to destroy* **incendies** *fires* **imprudents** = qui ne font pas attention **au lieu de** *instead of* **casser** *to break* **arracher** *pull up* **cueillir** *to pick* **agir** *to act* **invité** *guest* **déchets** *trash* **emporter** *to take along* **la mort** *death*

LE FRANÇAIS PRATIQUE

Les vacances: Plaisirs et problèmes

Quand on est en vacances, on peut faire beaucoup de choses.
Mais il faut aussi **éviter** certains dangers et faire attention!

éviter	*to avoid*

Au bord de la mer, on peut . . .

nager
se baigner

bronzer
prendre un bain de soleil
   (sunbath)

faire une promenade en bateau *(boat)*

faire de la planche à voile
faire de la plongée sous-marine *(scuba diving)*

Mais attention! Il ne faut pas . . .

se noyer

attraper un coup de soleil *(sunburn)*

avoir le mal de mer
tomber dans l'eau
perdre l'équilibre

se baigner	*to go swimming*
se noyer	*to drown*
bronzer	*to get tan*
attraper	*to catch, get*
avoir le mal de mer	*to be seasick*
perdre l'équilibre	*to lose one's balance*

À la campagne, on peut . . .

se promener
faire un tour *(walk)*
   | **dans les champs** *(fields)*
   | **dans la forêt**
   | **dans les bois** *(woods)*

faire un pique-nique sur l'herbe

faire du camping

observer les animaux

Mais attention! Il ne faut pas . . .

se perdre

être piqué par des moustiques *(mosquitos)*

mettre le feu
marcher sur un serpent

se perdre	*to get lost*
piquer	*to sting*
mettre le feu	*to set a fire*
marcher sur	*to step on*

À la montagne, on peut . . .

faire de l'escalade
   (rock climbing)

faire de l'alpinisme
   (mountain climbing)

aller à la pêche *(fishing)*

Mais attention! Il ne faut pas . . .

glisser
tomber
se blesser
se casser la jambe

glisser	*to slip*
se faire mal	*to get hurt*
se blesser	*to injure oneself*
se casser	*to break (a leg)*

Et dans tous les cas, il faut . . .

respecter | **la nature**
protéger | **l'environnement**

Il ne faut pas . . .

polluer
laisser | **des déchets** *(refuse)*
jeter | **des vieux papiers**
détruire la végétation
casser les branches des arbres
faire peur aux animaux

polluer	*to pollute*
protéger	*to protect*
laisser	*to leave*
jeter	*to throw*
détruire*	*to destroy*
casser	*to break*
faire peur à	*to scare*

Les formes des verbes:
jeter, détruire

Révision et Expansion ▶ pp. R20-23

1 Et vous?

Complétez les phrases en exprimant votre opinion personnelle.
Comparez vos réponses avec celles de votre partenaire.

1. Je préfère passer les vacances . . .
   - à la mer
   - à la montagne
   - à la campagne
   - ??

2. Quand je suis à la plage,
   je préfère . . .
   - me baigner
   - prendre des bains de soleil
   - faire de la planche à voile
   - ??

3. Pour me protéger contre les coups de soleil . . .
   - je porte un chapeau
   - je garde *(keep on)* mon tee-shirt
   - je mets de la crème solaire
   - ??

4. Quand je vais à la campagne, je préfère . . .
   - me promener dans les champs
   - faire un tour dans les bois
   - faire de l'escalade
   - ??

5. Quand on se perd à la campagne,
   l'objet le plus utile est . . .
   - une boussole *(compass)*
   - une carte de la région
   - une lampe de poche
   - ??

6. Ce que je déteste le plus est de (d') . . .
   - attraper un coup de soleil
   - être piqué(e) par les moustiques
   - me baigner dans l'eau froide
   - ??

7. Quand on fait un tour dans une forêt, la chose
   la plus stupide est de . . .
   - laisser des vieux papiers
   - casser les branches des arbres
   - faire peur aux animaux
   - ??

8. Quand on fait du camping, la chose la plus
   stupide est de . . .
   - détruire la végétation
   - jeter des déchets
   - mettre le feu à la forêt
   - ??

Conversations libres

Avec votre partenaire, choisissez l'une des situations suivantes.
Composez le dialogue correspondant et jouez-le en classe.

1 Deux week-ends différents

Samedi dernier Catherine est allée à la campagne où elle a passé
une journée très agréable. Son cousin Guillaume est allé à la plage
où il a passé une très mauvaise journée. Catherine et Guillaume
se téléphonent pour décrire leur week-end respectif.

Rôles: Catherine, Guillaume

2 Escalade

Carole, une jeune fille très sportive, adore faire
de l'escalade. Elle veut enseigner *(to teach)* ce
sport à son copain Bertrand. Bertrand, qui
n'est pas très courageux, refuse absolument,
expliquant les dangers de ce sport.

Rôles: Carole, Bertrand

3 Camping dans la forêt

Florence est monitrice dans une colonie de vacances. Elle organise
un week-end de camping dans la forêt. Maintenant elle explique
aux jeunes ce qu'ils doivent faire et ce qu'ils ne doivent pas faire.
Ils veulent savoir pourquoi. Florence répond.

Rôles: Florence, une campeuse

Les participes passés irréguliers
verbes conjugués avec être

Révision ▶ 📖 pp. R4-
(participes passés) p. R4
pp. R22-31
(verbes / être) p. R4

A. Révision: Le passé composé

The PASSÉ COMPOSÉ is used to describe what people DID, what HAPPENED.

Je **suis allé** au cinéma. **J'ai vu** une comédie. Après, je **me suis promené.**

Review the forms of the passé composé:

voyager	aller	s'amuser
j'**ai voyagé**	je **suis allé(e)**	je me **suis amusé(e)**
tu **as voyagé**	tu **es allé(e)**	tu t'**es amusé(e)**
il/elle/on **a voyagé**	il/elle/on **est allé(e)**	il/elle/on s'**est amusé(e)**
nous **avons voyagé**	nous **sommes allé(e)s**	nous nous **sommes amusé(e)s**
vous **avez voyagé**	vous **êtes allé(e)(s)**	vous vous **êtes amusé(e)(s)**
ils/elles **ont voyagé**	ils/elles **sont allé(e)s**	ils/elles se **sont amusé(e)s**
je n'**ai** pas **voyagé**	je ne **suis** pas **allé(e)**	je ne me **suis** pas **amusé(e)**
est-ce que tu **as voyagé?** **as**-tu voyagé?	est-ce que tu **es allé(e)?** **es**-tu allé(e)?	est-ce que tu t'**es amusé(e)?** t'**es**-tu **amusé(e)?**

➡ Review the following expressions:

déjà	*ever*	Est-ce que tu as **déjà** visité Paris?
ne . . . jamais	*never*	Non, je **n'ai jamais** visité Paris.
déjà	*yet, already*	Est-ce que vous avez **déjà** vu ce film?
ne . . . pas encore	*not yet*	Non, je **n'ai pas encore** vu ce film.

➡ Note the position of the following ADVERBS in the passé composé.

AFTER the past participle: Je me suis levé **tôt.**	**tôt** *(early),* **tard** *(late)* Éric s'est couché **tard.**
BEFORE the past participle: Sophie a **beaucoup** aimé ce film.	**bien, mal, souvent, beaucoup, trop, assez** Nous nous sommes **bien** amusés.

ALLONS PLUS LOIN

Depending on their meaning, the following verbs may be conjugated with **être** or **avoir**:

	(avoir)		(être)
monter	*to take or carry something up*	*or*	*to go up*
descendre	*to take or carry something down*	*or*	*to go down*
sortir	*to take something out*	*or*	*to go out*
passer	*to spend [time]*	*or*	*to pass by*

Pauline **a sorti** la poubelle. *Pauline **took** the trashcan **out**.*
Après, elle **est sortie**. *After that she **went out**.*

▶ **Est-ce que tu as déjà fait du ski nautique?**

Oui, j'ai déjà fait du ski nautique.

(Non, je n'ai jamais fa[it] de ski nautique[.]

Ah bon? Où ça?

Dans le Michigan.

1 Oui ou non?

Il y a beaucoup de choses qu'on peut faire en vacances. Demandez à votre partenaire s'il (si elle) a fait une des choses suivantes. En cas de réponse affirmative, demandez des précisions: où? quand? à quelle occasion? avec qui?

▶ faire du ski nautique?

- visiter la Floride?
- aller en Suisse?
- faire de l'alpinisme?
- voir un ours *(bear)*?
- monter dans un hélicoptère?

- descendre dans un sous-marin *(submarine)*?
- faire une promenade à cheval?
- se promener à dos de chameau *(camel)*?
- faire de la plongée sous-marine?
- avoir le mal de mer?

- attraper un coup de soleil?
- se perdre dans une forêt?
- se casser la jambe?

2 Créa-dialogue: Pas de chance!

Avec votre partenaire, composez un dialogue où vous décrivez un problème.

— Où es-tu allé(e) ce week-end?
— Je suis allé(e) à la montagne avec ma cousine.
— Ah bon? Qu'est-ce que vous avez fait?
— Nous avons fait de l'alpinisme.
— Vous vous êtes amusé(e)s?
— Oui, mais il y a eu un problème.
— Ah bon? Quoi?
— Ma cousine a glissé et elle s'est cassé le bras.
— C'est vraiment pas de chance!

Choose another time.
Choose another place: beach, city . . . *Choose another person.*
Choose an appropriate activity.
Describe another problem corresponding to the situation.

3 Une lettre de Paris

Amélie, une jeune Canadienne, vient d'arriver à Paris avec son frère Pascal. Elle écrit une lettre à son amie Gabrielle. Complétez la lettre d'Amélie avec le passé composé des verbes entre parenthèses.

Ma chère Gabrielle,

Eh bien, voilà! Je suis à Paris depuis deux jours avec mon frère Pascal. Nous _____ (arriver) avant-hier mais nous _____ (déjà faire) beaucoup de choses.

Hier matin, nous _____ (se lever tôt) et nous _____ (se promener) dans le quartier Latin. Nous _____ (prendre) le petit déjeuner dans un café où nous _____ (rencontrer) un groupe de jeunes Français. Pascal, qui ne perd pas de temps, _____ (donner) rendez-vous à une jeune fille très sympathique.

Après, nous _____ (s'arrêter) dans une boutique où j' _____ (acheter) des cartes postales. À midi, nous _____ (déjeuner) dans un restaurant algérien. J'_____ (manger) un couscous et j' _____ (boire) du thé à la menthe. C'était délicieux!

L'après-midi, nous_____ (faire) une promenade en bateau sur la Seine et ensuite nous _____(monter) à la Tour Eiffel. Du sommet on a une vue splendide sur Paris. Évidemment, j'_____ (prendre) beaucoup de photos. Quand nous _____ (descendre), Pascal _____ (vouloir) téléphoner à sa nouvelle amie. Il _____ (chercher) son portefeuille, mais il _____ (ne pas le trouver). Alors, il _____ (remonter) au sommet et heureusement il _____ (trouver) son portefeuille!

Le soir, Pascal _____ (sortir) avec la jeune fille. Moi, je_____ (ne pas sortir) avec eux. Je _____ (rester) à l'hôtel et j'_____ (écrire) des lettres. À onze heures, je _____ (se coucher) et j'_____(dormir). Ce matin, je _____ (se réveiller) à huit heures. Pascal, qui _____(rentrer) très tard hier soir, dort encore!

Je t'embrasse,   **Amélie**

4 Et vous?

Écrivez une lettre où vous décrivez une journée que vous avez passée dans une grande ville au cours *(during)* d'un voyage (réel ou imaginaire).

B. Révision: L'imparfait

The IMPERFECT is used to describe:

- what people USED TO DO, what USED TO BE
  Quand j'**étais** petit,   *When I **was** little,*
     je **jouais** au Monopoly.   *I **used to play** Monopoly.*

- what people WERE DOING, what WAS GOING ON, what WAS HAPPENING
  Hier soir, je **n'étais pas** chez moi. *Last night I **was not** home.*
  Je **dînais** avec un copain. *I **was having** dinner with a friend.*

Review the formation of the imperfect.

	dîner	faire	se promener	ENDINGS
	nous **dînons**	nous **faisons**	nous **nous promenons**	
je	**dînais**	**faisais**	me **promenais**	-ais
tu	**dînais**	**faisais**	te **promenais**	-ais
il/elle/on	**dînait**	**faisait**	se **promenait**	-ait
nous	**dînions**	**faisions**	nous **promenions**	-ions
vous	**dîniez**	**faisiez**	vous **promeniez**	-iez
ils/elles	**dînaient**	**faisaient**	se **promenaient**	-aient

➡ The imperfect stem is formed as follows:

> **nous**-form of the present minus **-ons**

➡ **Être** is the only verb with an irregular imperfect stem: ét- ➞ **j'étais**   **nous étions**

IMPERFECT STEMS	
visiter	je **visitais**
finir	je **finissais**
vendre	je **vendais**
avoir	j'**avais**
faire	je **faisais**
aller	j'**allais**
être	j'**étais**
venir	je **venais**
sortir	je **sortais**
mettre	je **mettais**
vivre	je **vivais**
savoir	je **savais**
recevoir	je **recevais**
prendre	je **prenais**
boire	je **buvais**
lire	je **lisais**
dire	je **disais**
écrire	j'**écrivais**
voir	je **voyais**
connaître	je **connaissais**

5 En 1900

Imaginez la vie en 1900. Dites ce qu'on faisait et ce qu'on ne faisait pas.

▶ on / utiliser des ordinateurs? **On n'utilisait pas d'ordinateurs.**

1. tout le monde / avoir des voitures?
2. les gens / voyager en train?
3. on / travailler beaucoup?
4. les gens / respecter l'environnement?
5. on / consommer beaucoup d'essence (*gas*)?
6. beaucoup de gens / habiter à la campagne?
7. les jeunes/ faire de la planche à voile?
8. on / être plus heureux qu'aujourd'hui?

6 En colonie de vacances

Marc est allé en colonie de vacances cet été. Il décrit ce qu'il faisait.

▶ En général, nous (se lever à 6 heures et demie) **En général, nous nous levions à 6 heures et demie.**

1. Après, je (me laver et prendre mon petit déjeuner)
2. Le matin, on (aller à la plage et se baigner)
3. De temps en temps, mes copains (faire une promenade en bateau)
4. D'habitude, on (déjeuner à midi et après faire la sieste)
5. Après la sieste, nous (nous promener dans les bois et observer les animaux)
6. Parfois, on (faire une promenade dans la montagne et faire de l'escalade)
7. Le week-end, nous (prendre nos tentes et faire du camping)
8. D'habitude, tout le monde (se coucher à 10 heures et dormir très bien)

Si vous avez été en colonie de vacances, racontez votre propre expérience en décrivant votre routine quotidienne.

7 Souvenirs d'enfance ────────────

Posez des questions à votre partenaire sur son enfance.
Il/elle va vous poser les mêmes questions.

Où est-ce que tu habitais?

J'habitais à Charleston. Et toi?

Moi, j'habitais à Savannah.

▶ où / habiter?

1. à quelle école / aller?
2. comment / aller à l'école?
3. à quelle heure / se lever?
4. à quelle heure / se coucher?
5. à quels jeux *(games)* / jouer?
6. quels sports / faire?

7. quelles émissions / regarder?
8. qui / être ton acteur favori?
9. qui / être ta chanteuse favorite?
10. quels objets / collectionner?
11. où / passer les vacances?
12. quel animal domestique / avoir?

 Si vous voulez, écrivez un petit paragraphe où vous décrivez les similarités et les différences entre votre enfance et celle de votre partenaire.

8 Pourquoi personne n'a répondu . . . ? ────────────

Hier après-midi vers deux heures, Pierre a voulu téléphoner à ses copains. Personne n'a répondu. Expliquez pourquoi en disant où chacun était et ce qu'il faisait. Soyez logique!

Qui?	Où?	Quoi?
moi	à la plage	déjeuner
toi	à la piscine	lire un livre
nous	à la campagne	jouer au basket
vous	au restaurant	tondre la pelouse
Béatrice	dans le jardin	faire des achats
Jean-Paul	en ville	faire un pique-nique
Philippe et Claire	au Club de Sport	faire de la plongée sous-marine
Marc et Alice	à la bibliothèque	prendre un bain de soleil
Jérôme et Stéphanie	dans les bois	se baigner
		se promener

▶ **Moi, j'étais à la plage. Je me baignais.**

9 Tout change! ────────────

Tout change avec le temps. Avec votre partenaire comparez les photos et décrivez les différences entre aujourd'hui et autrefois.

Maintenant. . .

Maintenant, Monsieur Lescroc est riche. Il est assez gros et . . .

Maintenant, Valérie . . .

Maintenant Madame Leblanc . . .

Autrefois. . .

Autrefois, il était jeune. Il était grand et mince . . .

Autrefois, elle . . .

Autrefois, . . .

C. L'usage du passé composé et de l'imparfait

In talking about the past, the French use the IMPERFECT and the PASSÉ COMPOSÉ.
The choice of tenses reflects the type of action or events that are being described.

IMPERFECT	PASSÉ COMPOSÉ

• HABITUAL OR REPEATED ACTIONS
*(what people **used to do**)*
Le samedi soir nous **allions** au ciné.
D'habitude on **faisait** de la planche
  à voile.
• PROGRESSIVE ACTIONS
*(what **was going on**)*
Je **me promenais** sur la plage.
Nous **faisions** du camping.
	• SPECIFIC ACTIONS
	*(what people **did**)*
	Samedi dernier, je **suis allé** à un concert.
	Un jour, on **a fait** de la plongée
	  sous-marine.
	
	J'**ai rencontré** un copain.
	Nous **avons vu** un ours *(bear)*.

➡ Depending on how the speaker interprets the action, the passé composé or the imperfect
   may be used.

Hier à 9 heures, nous **dînions**.	*Yesterday at nine we **were eating dinner**.*
Hier nous **avons dîné** à 9 heures.	*Yesterday we **ate dinner** at nine.*
Tous les jours j'**allais** à la plage.	*Every day I **used to go** to the beach.*
Tous les jours je **suis allée** à la plage.	*Every day I **went** to the beach.*

10 Une explosion

Tout le monde parle de l'explosion qui a eu lieu hier soir dans le quartier Saint Victor. Dites ce que
chaque personne faisait au moment de l'explosion et ce qu'elle a fait immédiatement après.

▶ Monsieur Duval (travailler dans le jardin / rentrer chez lui)
   Monsieur Duval travaillait dans le jardin. Il est rentré chez lui.

1. nous (dîner / regarder par la fenêtre)
2. vous (faire la vaisselle / téléphoner à la police)
3. moi (me promener / aller sur la scène de l'incident)
4. toi (rentrer chez toi / prendre des photos)
5. mes parents (regarder la télé / sortir sur le balcon)
6. mon grand-père (dormir / se réveiller)

11 Allô!

Téléphonez à votre partenaire pour lui demander ce qu'il/elle faisait à certains moments.
Il/elle va répondre avec les réponses suggérées ou des réponses de son choix.

▶ — **Où étais-tu <u>hier soir</u>?**
   — **J'étais <u>chez moi</u>.**
   — **Qu'est-ce que tu faisais?**
   — **J'<u>étudiais</u>.**
   — **Et après, qu'est-ce que tu as fait?**
   — **J'ai <u>regardé un film à la télé</u>.**

1. • ce matin
   • dans le jardin
   • tondre la pelouse
   • se promener

2. • cet après-midi
   • à la plage
   • bronzer
   • se baigner

3. • après le pique-nique
   • dans la forêt
   • observer les animaux
   • prendre des photos

4. • avant le dîner
   • chez un copain
   • regarder ses photos
   • rentrer chez moi

12 L'été dernier

Décrivez ce que les personnes ont fait ou faisaient l'été dernier. Utilisez le passé composé ou l'imparfait.

1. tous les jours / nous / aller à la plage
2. un jour où il faisait très chaud / Julien / attraper un coup de soleil
3. le samedi / mes copains / faire une promenade en bateau
4. pendant la promenade / Pierre / tomber dans l'eau
5. le 14 juillet / Catherine et Pauline / assister aux feux d'artifice (fireworks)
6. le week-end / vous / faire du camping
7. pendant la nuit / toi / être piqué par un moustique
8. nous / rentrer chez nous / à la fin de juillet

13 Souvenir de vacances

Monsieur Mercier raconte un souvenir de vacances. Complétez son histoire en mettant les verbes au passé. Utilisez l'imparfait ou le passé composé.

Quand j'_____ (être) étudiant, je _____ (passer) mes vacances à Annecy. En général, je _____ (ne pas me lever) avant dix heures du matin.

L'après-midi, je/j' _____ (aller) à la piscine où je _____ (prendre) des bains de soleil. Parfois, je/j' _____ (faire) de la planche à voile sur le lac. Le soir, je _____ (sortir) avec mes copains et je _____ (rentrer) tard chez moi.

Un jour, un copain m' _____ (inviter) à faire de l'escalade avec lui. Le lendemain, je _____ (me lever) tôt et je _____ (partir) avec mon copain. Malheureusement, pendant l'escalade, je/j' _____ (glisser) et je _____ (me casser) la jambe. À l'hôpital où je/j' _____ (aller), je/j' _____ (rencontrer) une jeune infirmière très sympathique. Un jour, je lui _____ (demander) si elle voulait se marier avec moi. Elle _____ (accepter) et aujourd'hui, c'est ma femme!

14 Photos de vacances

Pendant vos vacances en France, vous avez pris des photos de vos amis français.
Pour chaque photo, dites:
- où vous étiez
- ce que chaque personne faisait au moment de l'incident
- ce que ces personnes ont fait après

Utilisez votre imagination.

Pierre et Caroline

Juliette et Jérôme

Christine et Jean-Pierre

JACQUES-YVES COUSTEAU
champion de l'écologie marine

Jacques-Yves Cousteau
(1910-1997) était un homme
universel. À la fois° scientifique,
explorateur, inventeur, écrivain,
cinéaste, il a mis ses
innombrables talents au service
d'une seule° cause: la protection
des océans. Aujourd'hui, son
nom reste associé à la
protection de l'écologie marine.

■ Jacques-Yves Cousteau

Cousteau a d'abord été officier dans la Marine française. C'est à cette époque qu'il a inventé le scaphandre autonome (ou SCUBA* en anglais), permettant l'exploration des espaces sous-marins. Au cours de° ses expéditions sur ses fameux bateaux, la Calypso, l'Alcyone, la Calypso II, Cousteau a exploré les fonds° marins un peu partout dans le monde, en France, en Grèce, en Égypte, au Brésil, à Madagascar, dans l'Atlantique, le Pacifique et l'Océan Indien. De ces expéditions, il a rapporté° de nombreux films documentaires. Ces films, comme *Le monde du silence* et *Le monde sans soleil,* et plus tard ses séries télévisées *Découvertes du monde,* ont fait connaître° au grand public l'univers merveilleux de la mer.

> «Il faut sauver les océans!
> Il faut sauver notre
> planète, la Terre!»

Mais Cousteau ne s'est pas contenté° d'être l'un des grands explorateurs de ce siècle. Il a aussi entrepris° une croisade mondiale pour la protection de l'environnement. Son message est simple: À long terme,° l'avenir° de l'humanité dépend de la préservation de notre environnement naturel et, en particulier, du monde marin. Aujourd'hui, celui-ci° est menacé non seulement par la pollution, mais aussi par une exploitation économique incontrôlée. Il faut donc le protéger. Il faut sauver les océans! Il faut sauver notre planète, la Terre! Cousteau s'est engagé° totalement dans cette croisade. Pour cela, il a créé une fondation internationale, la Fondation Cousteau, et aussi la «Cousteau Society» qui a 200.000 membres aux États-Unis. Dans son travail, il était secondé par son fils, Jean-Michel Cousteau, qui habite en Californie.

■ Le commandant Cousteau à bord de la Calypso.

■ Jacques-Yves Cousteau et son fils, Jean-Michel

Jacques-Yves Cousteau faisait aussi partie° de l'élite littéraire. Pour son oeuvre°, il a été élu° membre de l'Académie française, le plus prestigieux groupe d'écrivains français.

à la fois *at the same time* **d'une seule** *only one* **au cours de** = *durant* **les fonds** *depths* **rapporté** *brought back* **faire connaître** *made known*
contenté = *limité* **entreprendre** ✷ *to undertake* **À long terme** *In the long run* **l'avenir** *future* **celui-ci** = *le monde marin*
engagé *committed himself* **faisait partie** = *était membre* **oeuvre** *work* **élire** ✷ *to elect*
*Un acronyme pour Self-Contained Underwater Breathing Apparatus.

L'Écologie à la maison

Préserver l'environnement, ce n'est pas difficile. Il suffit d'y penser.° L'écologie commence à la maison. Des jeunes Français expliquent comment ils pratiquent l'écologie chez eux.

Stéphanie:

❮❮Je recycle le verre. Ce n'est pas compliqué Il suffit de séparer les bouteilles et de les déposer dans les réceptacles spéciaux qu'on trouve partout dans les villes, et même à la campagne.❯❯

Danièle:

❮❮J'ai demandé à ma mère de n'acheter que° des produits favorables à l'environnement. J'ai un argument convaincant:° Je refuse de faire la vaisselle ou de laver le linge° avec des produits qui contiennent des phosphates, nocifs,° à l'environnement.❯❯

Xavier:

❮❮J'essaie de conserver l'eau au maximum. Par exemple, au lieu de° prendre des bains, je prends des douches qui utilisent moins d'eau. Quand je me lave les mains, je ferme l'évier.° Quand je me brosse les dents, je ferme le robinet.° J'économise un peu d'eau chaque fois et, à la longue,° ça compte!❯❯

Vincent:

❮❮Quand j'achète quelque chose, je fais attention aux produits qu'il contient.° En général, je donne la préférence aux produits recyclables ou recyclés. Et j'utilise toujours des emballages° en papier, jamais en plastique.❯❯

Zoé:

❮❮Je n'utilise plus d'aérosols, parce que les CFC (chlorofluorocarbures) qu'ils contiennent détruisent l'ozone de l'atmosphère. Et les savons, les shampooings, les dentifrices et les produits de beauté que j'utilise sont toujours à base de produits naturels.❯❯

et vous?

Faites une liste des choses que vous faites pour pratiquer l'écologie chez vous.

Il suffit d'y penser. *You just have to think about it.* **contenir** ❊ *to contain* **emballages** *packaging* **au lieu de** *instead of* **l'évier** *sink* **robinet** *faucet* **à la longue** *in the long run* **que** *only* **convaincant** *convincing* **linge** *laundry* **nocifs** *harmful*

Le soleil, notre bonne étoile

Chaque jour, le soleil nous donne sa lumière,° sa chaleur° et son énergie. Il est source de toute vie.° Sans lui, il n'y aurait pas° de plantes, pas de fleurs, pas d'arbres, pas d'animaux et, évidemment, pas de vie humaine. C'est lui qui cause la pluie, le vent, les différences de climat et les changements de saison. Grâce à° lui, les rivières coulent° et les plantes poussent.° Le soleil est vraiment notre bonne étoile!°

À cause de ses innombrables bienfaits,° les civilisations anciennes ont créé un culte du soleil. Pour les Égyptiens, Amon-Râ, le soleil, était le dieu° suprême. En Amérique, les Incas et les Aztèques adoraient aussi le soleil.

Aujourd'hui, le culte du soleil existe toujours, mais il a pris une forme nouvelle. Chaque année, par exemple, des millions de Français vont sur les plages de l'Atlantique et de la Méditerranée pour se baigner, mais surtout et avant tout pour bronzer au soleil. On peut aussi bronzer à la piscine, à la montagne, dans son jardin, ou même sur son balcon. En moyenne, les Français bronzent 2 heures 15 minutes par jour pendant les vacances.

Il y a différentes raisons pour lesquelles° les Français s'exposent au soleil. Selon une enquête,° 50% des personnes interrogées° trouvent que c'est agréable, 22% pensent que c'est bon pour la santé,° 18% déclarent qu'être bronzé, c'est à la mode. Le bronzage fait en effet partie du «look». Aujourd'hui la majorité des femmes déclarent préférer les hommes bronzés et, alternativement, la majorité des hommes préfèrent les femmes qui ont un joli bronzage.

Si le soleil est indispensable au succès des vacances, il peut aussi créer des problèmes pour les personnes imprudentes.° La lumière solaire contient, en effet, des rayons ultra-violets (UV). Quand ces rayons sont trop intenses, ils sont dangereux pour la peau° et pour les yeux. Si on ne fait pas attention, on peut attraper un coup de soleil ou, chose plus grave, être victime d'une insolation.° À long terme, le soleil contribue au vieillissement° de la peau. Pour les personnes qui ont une peau délicate, le soleil est aussi un facteur de risque important du cancer cutané.°

---

lumière *light* **chaleur** *heat* **vie** *life* **il n'y aurait pas** *there wouldn't be* **Grâce à** *Thanks to* **coulent** *flow* **poussent** *grow* **étoile** *star* **bienfaits** *benefits, blessings* **le dieu** *god, deity* **lesquelles** *which* **enquête** *survey* **interrogées** *asked* **santé** *health* **imprudentes** *who are not careful* **peau** *skin* **insolation** *sunstroke* **vieillissement** *aging* **cutané** *of the skin*

Avant de s'exposer au soleil, il est donc important de prendre quelques précautions élémentaires. Voici certains conseils:

* Bronzez progressivement et modérément. Le premier jour, restez seulement cinq minutes au soleil, puis augmentez° de quelques minutes par jour la durée° de vos bains de soleil. Un bronzage progressif vous donnera une photo-protection naturelle contre les rayons du soleil.

* Évitez° de vous mettre au soleil entre 11 heures du matin et 2 heures de l'après-midi. C'est à ce moment que les rayons ultra-violets sont les plus intenses.

* Protégez-vous la tête avec un chapeau à large bord° et les yeux avec de bonnes lunettes de soleil qui les recouvrent entièrement.

* Utilisez une bonne crème solaire. Les crèmes solaires filtrent les rayons ultra-violets. Choisissez une crème solaire adaptée à votre peau.

* N'utilisez pas de produits qui contiennent des substances photo-sensibilisantes, comme l'eau de cologne ou certains parfums. Ces substances sont à l'origine de réactions cutanées anormales.

* Soyez vigilants en hiver aussi bien qu'en été. La neige reflète les rayons ultra-violets plus que le sable.° Si la lumière est intense, portez des lunettes de soleil.

et vous?

DÉBAT: LE SOLEIL: AMI OU ENNEMI?

Prenez une position sur ce sujet et débattez-le avec votre partenaire (qui prendra la position contraire). Présentez vos arguments par ordre d'importance.

EXPRESSION ÉCRITE

Êtes-vous un(e) «adorateur(trice) du soleil»? Composez un paragraphe où vous allez expliquer ...

• pourquoi vous aimez le soleil
• où et quand vous bronzez
• quelles précautions vous prenez

Jacques **Prévert** (1900-1977) est un écrivain et aussi l'auteur de chansons populaires et de plusieurs scénarios de films. Dans ses poèmes, il décrit avec humour et fantaisie les thèmes simples de l'existence: la nature, l'amour, l'amitié, l'enfance, la réalité de tous les jours.

Dans cet extrait, Prévert explique:
■ pourquoi il faut être poli avec la terre et le soleil
■ les relations personnelles qui existent entre la terre, le soleil et la lune

SOYEZ POLIS

Le soleil est amoureux de la terre
La terre est amoureuse du soleil
Ça les regarde
C'est leur affaire
Et quand il y a des éclipses
Il n'est pas prudent ni discret de les regarder
Au travers de sales petits morceaux de verre fumé
Ils se disputent
C'est des histoires personnelles
Mieux vaut ne pas s'en mêler
Parce que
Si on s'en mêle on risque d'être changé
En pomme de terre gelée
Ou en fer à friser

Le soleil aime la terre
La terre aime le soleil
C'est comme ça
Le reste ne nous regarde pas
La terre aime le soleil
Et elle tourne
Pour se faire admirer
Et le soleil la trouve belle
Et il brille sur elle
Et quand il est fatigué
Il va se coucher

Et la lune se lève
La lune c'est l'ancienne amoureuse du soleil
Mais elle a été jalouse
Et elle a été punie
Elle est devenue toute froide
Et elle sort seulement la nuit
Il faut aussi être très poli avec la lune
Ou sans ça elle peut vous rendre un peu fou
Et elle peut aussi
Si elle veut
Vous changer en bonhomme de neige
En réverbère
Ou en bougie

Prévert, Histoires (Paris: Gallimard, 1963, pp. 66-69)

---

augmentez *increase*   **durée** = le temps   **Évitez** *Avoid*   **bord** *brim*   **sable** *sand*

LE FRANÇAIS PRATIQUE

Quoi de neuf?

Devine!

Quoi de neuf?

COMMENT DÉCRIRE UN ÉVÉNEMENT, COMMENT RACONTER UNE HISTOIRE

— **Quoi de neuf?** *(What's new?)*
Devine!

deviner *to guess*

— Je ne sais pas!
Qu'est-ce qui est arrivé? **Qu'est-ce qui a eu lieu?**
Qu'est-ce qui s'est passé? **Qu'est-ce qu'il y a eu?**

arriver *to happen*
se passer *to happen*
avoir lieu *to take place*
qu'est-ce qu'il y a *what's happening*
assister à *to be present at, to see*
être témoin de *to witness*

J'ai **assisté à**
J'ai **été témoin de** } quelque chose de bizarre.
J'ai **vu**

— Ah bon? Quand?
C'est arrivé } **hier**   **lundi dernier**   **il y a** deux heures
Ça s'est passé } **hier soir**   **la semaine dernière**   **il y a** dix jours
Ça a eu lieu } **avant-hier**   **le mois dernier**

— Où étais-tu?
J'étais } **dehors** *(outside)*   dans un magasin
Je me trouvais } en ville   chez un copain

se trouver *to be*

— Alors, raconte! Qu'est-ce que tu as fait?

raconter *to tell (what happened)*

Eh bien, **d'abord** *(first)*, j'ai téléphoné à . . .
puis *(then)* . . .   **enfin** *(at last)* . . .
ensuite *(next)* . . .   **finalement** *(finally)* . . .
après *(after, afterwards)* . . .

Quelques événements

un accident	**un événement** *(event)*
un incendie *(fire)*	**un fait** *(fact)*
un cambriolage *(burglary)*	**un fait divers** *(minor news item)*

Comment exprimer la surprise

Vraiment?	*Really?*	**C'est incroyable!**	*That's unbelievable!*
Pas possible!	*That's not possible!*	**Ce n'est pas croyable!**	*That's not for real!*
Mon Dieu!	*My goodness!*	**Tu plaisantes!**	*You're kidding!*

1 Journalisme

Vous êtes journaliste pour le magazine RADAR. Dites quand et où les événements
de la colonne A ont eu lieu en choisissant un élément des colonnes B et C. Soyez logique.

A: QUOI?	B: QUAND?	C: OÙ?
un cambriolage	ce matin	à l'église St. Charles
un accident	à deux heures cet après-midi	sur l'autoroute A4
un incendie	hier soir	dans une galerie d'art
un violent orage *(storm)*	vendredi dernier	dans la région de Toulouse
une avalanche	le week-end dernier	dans la forêt d'Amboise
un ouragan *(hurricane)*	la semaine dernière	dans les Alpes
le mariage de l'acteur	l'hiver dernier	à la Martinique
Georges Belhomme	en avril dernier	au zoo de Vincennes

▶ **Un accident a eu lieu ce matin (à deux heures cet après-midi)
sur l'autoroute A4 (dans la forêt d'Amboise).**

2 Créa-dialogue

Avec votre partenaire, choisissez un événement au bas de la page (ou imaginez
un événement original). Composez le dialogue où vous racontez cet événement.

— Quoi de neuf?	
— Devine!	
— Je ne sais pas! Qu'est-ce qui est arrivé?	• *Use another expression.*
— J'ai rencontré le président!	• *Imagine a different event.*
— Tu plaisantes! Quand?	• *Use another expression of surprise.*
— Ce matin.	• *Mention another time.*
— Où étais-tu?	
— Je me trouvais à l'aéroport.	• *Mention another place.*
— Qu'est-ce que tu as fait alors?	
— J'ai pris une photo et j'ai demandé un autographe.	• *Mention two things you did.*
— C'est incroyable!	• *Use another expression of surprise.*

Événements

- J'ai rencontré Oprah Winfrey.
- J'ai vu un OVNI *(UFO)*.
- J'ai été témoin d'un cambriolage.
- J'ai assisté à un accident spectaculaire.
- J'ai assisté au mariage de . . .(?)
- J'ai découvert un trésor.

Comment parler de la pluie et du beau temps

Pour le week-end, **la météo** (weather forecast) **a prédit:**

du beau temps	**du mauvais temps**	
du soleil (sun)	**de la pluie** (rain)	**de la neige** (snow)
un ciel (sky) **bleu**	**du vent** (wind)	**une tempête de neige**
des nuages (clouds)	**un orage** (thunderstorm)	**du verglas** (sheet ice)
de la brume (mist)	**une tempête** (storm)	
du brouillard (fog)	**un ouragan** (hurricane)	

> **prédire** to predict

Quand il fait beau . . .

Le soleil **brille.**
Le ciel est bleu.

Quand il fait mauvais . . .

Le ciel est **couvert** (overcast).
La pluie tombe.

Quand il y a un orage . . .

Le vent **souffle.**
On voit **des éclairs** (lightning).
On entend **le tonnerre** (thunder).

Quand il fait nuit ...

Il fait noir.
On voit **la lune** (moon).
et **les étoiles** (stars).

Quand il fait froid . . .

La neige **tombe.**
Il y a **de la glace** (ice).
Le lac est **gelé** (frozen).

> **briller** to shine
> **souffler** to blow
> **il fait noir** it is dark

AUJOURD'HUI	HIER		DEMAIN
il pleut	il pleuvait	**il a plu** le matin	il va pleuvoir
il neige	il neigeait	**il a neigé** à midi	il va neiger
il y a un orage	il y avait un orage	**il y a eu un orage** dans la nuit	il va y avoir un orage

3 Une question de temps

Complétez les phrases en décrivant
le temps (ou le moment de la journée).

1. Je mets mes lunettes de soleil quand . . .
2. Je mets mon imperméable quand . . .
3. On peut faire du ski quand . . .
4. On peut voir des éclairs quand . . .
5. On ne voit pas le soleil quand . . .
6. On voit des étoiles quand . . .
7. La visibilité sur la route est mauvaise
   quand . . .
8. On peut faire du patinage *(go skating)*
   sur un lac quand . . .

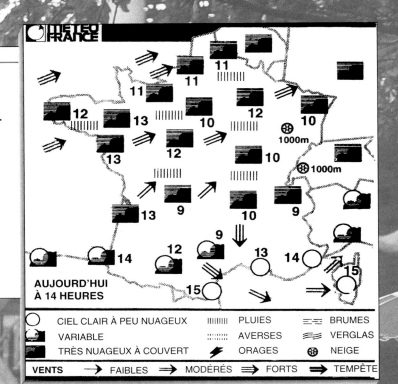

MÉTÉO FRANCE

AUJOURD'HUI
À 14 HEURES

○	CIEL CLAIR À PEU NUAGEUX	⦀	PLUIES	≡	BRUMES
	VARIABLE	⦂⦂	AVERSES	≋	VERGLAS
▨	TRÈS NUAGEUX À COUVERT	⚡	ORAGES	✹	NEIGE

VENTS → FAIBLES ⇒ MODÉRÉS ⇒ FORTS ⇒ TEMPÊTE

Conversations libres

Avec votre partenaire, choisissez l'un des sujets suivants. Composez
le dialogue correspondant à la situation et jouez-le en classe.

1 Les vacances de printemps

Béatrice passe les vacances de printemps
à la Martinique où il fait très, très beau.
Xavier les passe au Québec où il fait très,
très froid. Les deux cousins se téléphonent
et parlent du temps.

Rôles: Béatrice, Xavier

2 Un ouragan

Nous sommes en septembre. Carole,
une étudiante française, visite la
Floride. Aujourd'hui, il y a un terrible
ouragan. Elle téléphone à son père
qui veut avoir des détails.

Rôles: Carole, son père

3 Week-end

Votre partenaire et vous, vous avez
décidé de passer la journée de samedi
ensemble. La météo a prédit un temps
incertain. Discutez de ce que vous allez
faire suivant le temps.

Rôles: vous, votre partenaire

A. La description d'un événement: le passé composé et l'imparfait

The following sentences tell about an accident.

The sentences on the left give the main facts.

The sentences on the right describe the scene and the background.

MAIN EVENTS	BACKGROUND AND DESCRIPTION
J'**ai vu** un accident.	C'**était** samedi soir. Il **était** 8 heures. Il **pleuvait**. La visibilité **était** mauvaise. J'**allais** à un rendez-vous. Je **voulais** être à l'heure.
Une voiture **est rentrée** dans un arbre.	C'**était** une voiture de sport. Le conducteur **était** un jeune homme blond.
J'**ai téléphoné** à la police qui **est arrivée** immédiatement.	Le jeune homme ne **portait** pas de ceinture de sécurité. Il **était** légèrement blessé.

The PASSÉ COMPOSÉ tells
   WHAT HAPPENED and narrates
   the ACTION
	The IMPERFECT sets the SCENE and gives the BACKGROUND

It is used to describe:
• SPECIFIC EVENTS
• the ACTIONS which constitute
  the STORY LINE
	It is used to describe:
	• EXTERNAL CONDITIONS
	  date weather time scenery
	• DESCRIPTIONS OF THE CHARACTERS
	  age physical traits health attitudes
	  appearance clothing feelings intentions
	• BACKGROUND ACTIVITIES
	  what people were doing
	  what was going on

1 Une question de temps

Expliquez logiquement les actions suivantes en décrivant le temps qu'il faisait.

CE QUI EST ARRIVÉ	QUEL TEMPS?
• J'ai glissé.	Il pleut.
• Stéphanie a bien bronzé.	Il fait noir.
• Nous avons fait du ski.	Il est gelé.
• Vous avez pris vos imperméables.	Il y a du verglas.
• Patrick a pris sa lampe de poche *(flashlight)*.	Il y a de la neige.
• On n'a pas vu le sommet de la montagne.	Il y a des nuages.
• Nous avons fait du patin à glace sur le lac.	Il y a de la brume.
• J'ai entendu l'avion mais je ne l'ai pas vu.	Il y a beaucoup de soleil.

▶ **J'ai glissé parce qu'il y avait du verglas.**

2 Un mauvais témoin

Monsieur Loiseau a été témoin d'un cambriolage samedi dernier. Malheureusement il n'a pas bonne mémoire. Lisez son témoignage *(account)* et rectifiez-le.

Monsieur Loiseau:

«Il était une heure et demie de l'après-midi. Il faisait beau. Il n'y avait pas de voitures dans la rue. Le bandit est sorti par la porte. C'était un homme petit et assez gros. Il avait une barbe noire. Il portait un masque de ski. Il portait un pull. Sa complice l'attendait derrière la banque. C'était une jeune fille brune. Elle avait les cheveux courts et frisés. Elle portait un collier autour du cou. Elle n'avait pas de lunettes. Le bandit et sa complice sont partis en voiture.»

▶ **Mais non! C'est faux! Il n'était pas une heure et demie. Il était trois heures! . . .**

3 Pourquoi?

Demandez à votre partenaire pourquoi il/elle a fait les choses suivantes. Il/elle va répondre avec l'explication suggérée (ou une autre explication de son choix).

▶ aller au café   — **Pourquoi est-ce que tu es allé(e) au café?**
    (j'ai soif)   — **Parce que j'avais soif.**
                      (Parce que je voulais rencontrer mes copains, . . .)

1. aller au restaurant
  (j'ai faim)
2. aller à la plage
  (il fait beau)
3. mettre de la crème solaire
  (il y a du soleil)

4. aller à la disco
  (j'ai envie de danser)
5. rentrer chez toi
  (il est minuit)
6. se dépêcher
  (je veux être à l'heure)

7. téléphoner à ta cousine
  (c'est son anniversaire)
8. prendre de la dramamine
  (j'ai le mal de mer)

4 Une promenade romantique? ———————————————

Pierre habite à Annecy. L'été dernier, il s'est acheté un bateau. Voilà ce qui lui est arrivé un jour.

C'est samedi. Il est sept heures du soir. Il fait beau. Pierre est chez lui. Il a envie de sortir. Il téléphone à Armelle, sa nouvelle copine. Il lui propose de faire une promenade en bateau sur le lac d'Annecy. Armelle accepte. Pierre prend sa moto et il va chercher Armelle. Il arrive chez elle. Armelle l'attend. Elle porte une belle robe rouge à fleurs et ses nouvelles chaussures.

Pierre et Armelle arrivent au lac. Ils montent dans le bateau de Pierre. Pierre prend sa guitare. Il chante des chansons romantiques. Le ciel est clair. La lune et les étoiles brillent dans le ciel. Armelle écoute Pierre. Elle est très contente.

Tout d'un coup° Pierre fait un mouvement brusque. Il tombe dans l'eau. Armelle perd l'équilibre et tombe dans l'eau aussi. L'eau est très, très froide. Pierre et Armelle nagent jusqu'à la plage. Armelle est trempée° . . . et furieuse. Sa robe et ses nouvelles chaussures sont fichues°. Elle demande à Pierre de la raccompagner chez elle. Pauvre Pierre, il n'a pas de chance!

tout d'un coup (all of a sudden) **trempée** (soaked) **fichues** (ruined)

▶ Maintenant, mettez l'histoire au passé.

C'était un samedi pendant les vacances. . . .

5 Faits divers ——————————————————————

Vous avez été témoin des faits divers suivants. Votre partenaire va choisir un de ces faits et vous poser des questions comme:

- C'était quand?
- Où étais-tu?
- Qu'est-ce que tu faisais?
- Qu'est-ce qui s'est passé?
- Qu'est-ce que tu as vu?
- Qu'est-ce que tu as fait?

Répondez à ses questions en utilisant votre imagination.

INCENDIE

Un incendie a eu lieu dans la nuit du 5 février aux établissements Dumoulin. Cet incendie, provoqué,° semble-t-il, par un court-circuit, a détruit l'atelier° de constructions mécaniques et a fait un million d'euros de dégâts.°

provoqué caused
atelier workshop
dégâts damages

ACCIDENT

Un accident de la circulation a eu lieu hier après-midi vers trois heures à l'intersection de la rue Victor Hugo et l'avenue de la République. Une voiture de tourisme, conduite par Monsieur Picard, professeur au lycée Descartes, est entrée en collision avec un camion de l'armée. L'accident, provoqué par la neige, n'a pas fait de victime.

CAMBRIOLAGE

Un cambriolage a eu lieu le week-end dernier dans un magasin d'antiquités de la rue de la Paix. D'après les déclarations de Madame Durand, la propriétaire, les cambrioleurs ont emporté° quelques statues sans valeur mais ont laissé une collection de monnaies° anciennes estimée à deux cent mille euros.

emporter to carry off, steal
monnaies coins

MARIAGE PRINCIER

Le mariage de la princesse Sophie a été célébré le 15 juin dans la chapelle du château de Rambucourt. La princesse, vêtue de satin blanc, a été accompagnée à l'autel° par son père, l'archiduc Ferdinand.

autel altar

6 À votre tour ——————————————————————

Racontez un événement de votre vie. Décrivez la scène et les événements principaux. Vous pouvez décrire, par exemple . . .

- un accident
- un anniversaire
- un mariage
- une fête familiale
- un événement sportif auquel vous avez participé
- un concert ou un spectacle

B. L'imparfait et le passé composé dans la même phrase

In describing a past event, we may use both the PASSÉ COMPOSÉ and the IMPERFECT in the same sentence.

SPECIFIC ACTION *(what people did)*	ON-GOING OR PROGRESSIVE ACTION *(what was happening)*
J'**ai vu** un accident . . .	pendant que j'**attendais** le bus.
Le cambrioleur **est entré** . . .	pendant que les voisins **dormaient**.
Quand tu **as téléphoné**, . . .	je **regardais** la télé.
Quand l'orage **a commencé**, . . .	nous **nous promenions**.
J'**ai observé** un oiseau . . .	qui **chantait** dans un arbre.
Tu **as pris** une photo de ton cousin . . .	qui **faisait** de la planche à voile.

The relationship between events and the corresponding choice of the passé composé or the imperfect can be illustrated as follows:

SPECIFIC ACTION	J'**ai vu** un accident	Quand tu **as téléphoné**	J'**ai observé** un oiseau
PROGRESSIVE ACTION	pendant que j'**attendais** le bus.	je **regardais** la télé.	qui **chantait** dans un arbre.

➡ Depending on what action is being described, either the PASSÉ COMPOSÉ or the IMPERFECT may be used after **quand.**

J'ai téléphoné **quand tu regardais** la télé.	*I called **when you were watching** television.*
Je téléphonais **quand tu es parti.**	*I was talking on the phone **when you left.***

Les expressions de temps

PREPOSITION (+ noun)		
pendant	*during*	Qu'est-ce que tu as fait **pendant** les vacances?
CONJUNCTION		
pendant que	*while*	Qu'est-ce que tu as fait **pendant que** je jouais au golf?
lorsque	*when*	J'ai rencontré Paul **lorsqu'**il travaillait à Paris.
au moment où	*just as*	Je suis arrivé à la gare **au moment où** le train partait.

---

7 **Où étais-tu?**

Demandez à votre partenaire où il/elle était quand certaines choses sont arrivées. Il/elle va répondre en utilisant l'expression suggérée ou une expression de son choix.

Où étais-tu quand j'ai téléphoné?

Qu'est-ce que tu faisais?

J'étais dans ma chambre.

Je dormais.

1. • je suis passé(e)
   • au jardin
   • tondre la pelouse

2. • tu as vu l'incendie
   • dans la rue
   • me promener

3. • tu t'es cassé la jambe
   • à la montagne
   • faire de l'alpinisme

4. • tu as vu l'ours *(bear)*
   • à la campagne
   • faire du camping

5. • le cambrioleur est entré
   • dans la salle de bains
   • se laver les cheveux

6. • l'homme s'est noyé
   • à la plage
   • prendre un bain de soleil

8 **Rencontres de vacances** ─────────────────────────

Décrivez les rencontres suivantes.

▶ à la plage / Thomas / parler à une fille / prendre un bain de soleil
   À la plage, Thomas a parlé à une fille qui prenait un bain de soleil.

1. à la montagne / nous / voir des gens / faire de l'escalade
2. pendant l'excursion / Philippe / rencontrer un camarade / se promener dans les bois
3. à la mer / tu / prendre des photos d'un ami / faire de la planche à voile
4. au café / nous / écouter un étudiant / jouer de la guitare
5. au musée / vous / parler à des touristes / visiter la ville
6. dans la rue / Sophie / rencontrer des copains / aller au cinéma

9 **Zut alors!** ─────────────────────────

Certaines choses arrivent toujours au mauvais moment. Décrivez ce que les personnes faisaient quand certaines choses sont arrivées.

▶ Je visite la Guadeloupe / quand / il y a un ouragan
   Je visitais la Guadeloupe quand il y a eu un ouragan.

1. Philippe regarde les filles / quand / il tombe dans l'eau
2. Mon cousin va à 120 à l'heure / lorsque / la police l'arrête
3. Nous faisons une promenade à pied / quand / l'orage commence
4. Thomas écrit à sa copine / au moment où / le professeur lui pose une question
5. Marc gagne le match de tennis / lorsque / il glisse et se casse le bras
6. Jérôme embrasse *(kisses)* Alice / au moment où / le père d'Alice entre

10 **D'autres mésaventures** ─────────────────────────

Décrivez les mésaventures *(mishaps)* suivantes au passé.

1. Nous montons à la Tour Eiffel. Pendant que nous sommes dans l'ascenseur, il y a une panne d'électricité.
2. Caroline et Sandrine font du camping. Pendant qu'elles dorment, un raton laveur *(raccoon)* mange leurs provisions.
3. Monsieur Malchance monte sur le toit pour réparer l'antenne de télévision. Pendant qu'il la répare, un vent fort souffle et l'échelle *(ladder)* tombe. Monsieur Malchance reste toute la nuit sur le toit.
4. Roméo va sous le balcon de Juliette et lui chante une chanson d'amour. Pendant qu'il chante, le père de Juliette lui jette un seau *(bucket)* d'eau sur la tête.

C. Le passé simple

Like the PASSÉ COMPOSÉ, the PASSÉ SIMPLE is used to describe what people DID, what HAPPENED.

Although you do not need to learn how to write the passé simple, you should be able to recognize its forms since the tense is often used in written narration and literary texts.

> **Passé simple**
>
> *Expansion* ▶
>
> pp. R32-33

Note the passé simple of regular verbs:

INFINITIVE		parler	finir	répondre
PASSÉ SIMPLE	je	parl**ai**	fin**is**	répond**is**
	tu	parl**as**	fin**is**	répond**is**
	il/elle/on	parl**a**	fin**it**	répond**it**
	nous	parl**âmes**	fin**îmes**	répond**îmes**
	vous	parl**âtes**	fin**îtes**	répond**îtes**
	ils/elles	parl**èrent**	fin**irent**	répond**irent**

➡ For most irregular verbs, the stem of the passé simple is similar to the past participle:

aller (**allé**) →	il **alla**	ils **allèrent**	prendre (**pris**) →	il **prit**	ils **prirent**
avoir (**eu**) →	il **eut**	ils **eurent**	recevoir (**reçu**) →	il **reçut**	ils **reçurent**

Note the following common irregular forms:

être → il **fut** ils **furent**   venir → il **vint** ils **vinrent**
faire → il **fit** ils **firent**   voir → il **vit** ils **virent**

11 **Un peu d'histoire**

Lisez l'histoire d'une exploration importante. Puis, racontez cette histoire à votre partenaire en remplaçant le passé simple par le passé composé.

Jacques Cartier (1491–1557) est l'un des grands explorateurs français. Il naquit à Saint-Malo en 1491. Dans sa jeunesse, il alla au Portugal, au Brésil et probablement dans la région de Terre-Neuve.° En 1534, le roi de France lui donna la mission d'explorer les côtes° de l'Amérique du Nord. Cartier et ses hommes partirent de Saint-Malo le 20 avril et arrivèrent dans la région de Gaspé au Canada le 25 juillet. Cartier descendit à terre, planta une croix dans le sol et prit possession de la région au nom du roi de France. L'expédition revint en France où elle fut reçue en triomphe. Jacques Cartier fit un second voyage en 1535 avec la mission cette fois de chercher de l'or et des pierres précieuses. Il ne trouva pas d'or mais il découvrit un immense fleuve qu'il nomma Saint-Laurent. Cartier remonta le fleuve jusqu'au site d'un village indien, Hochelaga, aujourd'hui Montréal. Les premiers colons français s'installèrent au Canada 70 ans plus tard. C'est ainsi que le Canada devint un territoire français.

Terre-Neuve *(Newfoundland)*   **les côtes** *(coast)*

LECTURE

King

Sempé et Goscinny

L'histoire suivante est extraite d'un album humoristique intitulé **Les Récrés du petit Nicolas**. Le petit Nicolas est un peu l'équivalent français de «Denis la Menace». C'est un garçon de 6 ou 7 ans. Il est généreux, affectueux, vif d'esprit,° parfois turbulent, mais sans méchanceté.° Il adore ses parents, aime les animaux, et il a toute une bande de copains. Comme à tous les enfants de son âge, il lui arrive parfois de° «faire des bêtises»,° ou bien, très innocemment, de créer des situations plus ou moins embarrassantes pour ses parents, ses voisins ou ses professeurs.

Notez que dans ce récit, c'est le Petit Nicolas qui parle. Les impressions présentées et le style utilisé sont, par conséquent, ceux d'un jeune enfant français.

Les divers albums relatant les aventures du *Petit Nicolas* sont le produit de la collaboration d'un illustrateur et d'un écrivain. **Jean-Jacques Sempé** (né en 1932), l'illustrateur, a collaboré à de nombreux magazines. Il est aussi le père d'un fils qui s'appelle … Nicolas. **René Goscinny** (1926-1977), l'écrivain, a créé d'autres personnages très célèbres en France comme *Astérix* et le cow-boy *Lucky Luke*.

NOTE CULTURELLE

Le jardin public

Les villes françaises ont généralement un **jardin** ou **parc public** où les petits enfants viennent jouer, les personnes âgées se reposer, et les gens de tout âge se promener. Ces jardins publics sont généralement très bien entretenus° et très bien équipés. On y trouve généralement des massifs de fleurs,° des pelouses de gazon,° une pièce d'eau° avec une fontaine, des jeux pour les petits enfants, et des bancs.° Pour maintenir le bon usage de ces jardins, un grand nombre d'activités sont interdites.° Il est interdit, par exemple, de faire de la bicyclette dans les allées, de marcher sur les pelouses, de jouer au frisbee ou au volley, de faire des pique-niques et d'aller à la pêche dans les pièces d'eau.

Les jardins publics sont généralement placés sous la surveillance d'un gardien. Le gardien est souvent un homme âgé (un ancien militaire, par exemple). Il porte un uniforme et une casquette, del et, pour maintenir l'ordre, il utilise un sifflet.

Anticipons un peu

Pour mieux comprendre une histoire, il est parfois utile de participer indirectement à cette histoire en prenant la place d'un observateur et en essayant d'anticiper ce qui va arriver. Imaginez, par exemple, que vous êtes le frère aîné ou la soeur aînée du petit Nicolas. Vous avez appris que celui-ci est parti faire une promenade avec ses copains dans un endroit où il y a un étang.° Connaissant bien votre petit frère, vous vous doutez bien° qu'il va rapporter quelque créature vivante de cette promenade. Avant de lire l'histoire, essayez de deviner°…

- quel animal le petit Nicolas va rapporter de l'étang
- qu'est-ce qu'il a l'intention de faire avec cet animal
- comment vos parents vont réagir°

vif d'esprit *alert*   **méchanceté** = *malice*   **il lui arrive parfois de** *it sometimes happens that he*
bêtises = choses pas très intelligentes   **entretenus** *maintained*   **massifs de fleurs** *flower beds*
gazon *grass*   **pièce d'eau** *pool*   **banc** *bench*   **interdites** *forbidden*   **étang** *pond*
vous vous doutez bien = vous êtes assez sûr   **deviner** *guess*   **réagir** *to react*

King

1.

Mes copains et moi, nous avons décidé d'aller à la pêche!

Il y a un square° où nous allons jouer souvent, et dans le square il y a un chouette étang. Et dans l'étang il y a des têtards, et c'est ça que nous avons décidé de pêcher. Les têtards, ce sont de petites bêtes qui grandissent
5   et qui deviennent des grenouilles.

À la maison, j'ai pris un bocal à confitures° vide et je suis allé dans le square, en faisant bien attention que le gardien ne me voie pas. Le gardien du square a une grosse moustache, une canne, et un sifflet à roulette comme celui du papa de Raoul, qui est agent de police.° Le gardien nous
10 gronde° souvent, parce qu'il y a des tas de choses qui sont défendues dans le square: il ne faut pas marcher sur l'herbe, monter aux arbres, arracher les fleurs, faire du vélo, jouer au football, jeter des papiers par terre, et se battre.° Mais on s'amuse bien quand même!

Édouard, Raoul, et Clotaire étaient déjà au bord de l'étang avec leur
15 bocaux. Alceste est arrivé le dernier—il nous a expliqué qu'il n'avait pas trouvé de bocal vide et qu'il avait dû en vider un. Il avait encore plein de° confiture sur la figure, Alceste.

Comme le gardien n'était pas là, on s'est tout de suite mis à pêcher.

C'est très difficile de pêcher des têtards! Il faut se mettre à plat ventre°
20 sur le bord° de l'étang, plonger le bocal dans l'eau, et essayer d'attraper les têtards qui bougent et qui n'ont pas du tout envie d'entrer dans les bocaux. Le premier qui a eu un têtard, c'était Clotaire, et il était tout fier, parce qu'il n'est pas habitué° à être le premier en quoi que ce soit.°

Et puis, à la fin, nous avons tous eu notre têtard. C'est-à-dire
25 qu'Alceste n'a pas réussi à en pêcher un, mais Raoul, qui est un pêcheur formidable, en avait deux dans son bocal, et il a donné le plus petit à Alceste.

— Et qu'est-ce qu'on va faire avec nos têtards? a demandé Clotaire.

Mots utiles

un têtard

une grenouille

un étang

un bocal

un sifflet
à roulette

aller à la pêche   to go fishing
emmener   to bring
grandir   to grow (in
                 size)

se mettre à *   = commencer
                 à

pêcher   to fish
plonger   to plunge
vider   to empty

défendu   forbidden
fier (fière)   proud
vide   empty

quand même   anyhow

Langage familier

une bête = un animal
chouette = super
rigolo = amusant
des tas de = beaucoup de

square = jardin public **confitures** jam **un agent de police** policeman **gronde** scolds **se battre** to fight **plein de** = beaucoup de
se mettre à plat ventre lie down on your stomach **bord** edge **habitué à** accustomed, used to **quoi que ce soit** whatever it is

30 — Ben, a répondu Raoul, on va les emmener chez nous, on va attendre qu'ils grandissent et qu'ils deviennent des grenouilles, et on va faire des courses. Ce sera rigolo.

— Et puis, a dit Édouard, les grenouilles, c'est pratique, ça monte sur une petite échelle et ça vous dit le temps qu'il fera!

35 — Et puis, a dit Alceste, les cuisses de grenouilles, avec de l'ail, c'est très, très bon!

Et Alceste a regardé son têtard, en se passant la langue° sur les lèvres.

langue *tongue*

NOTE CULTURELLE

Les grenouilles sont des animaux très communs en France. On les trouve un peu partout: dans les étangs, dans les lacs, dans les rivières. Les grenouilles font partie du folklore français.

- ### Les grenouilles et la météo.
  D'après le folklore, on peut prédire le temps en observant les grenouilles. Si les grenouilles restent dans l'eau, il va faire beau. Si les grenouilles sortent de leur étang pour chercher un terrain sec,° il va pleuvoir. Autrefois, on mettait une grenouille dans un grand bocal avec de l'eau et une petite échelle. Si la grenouille montait à l'échelle, c'était un signe d'orage.

- ### La course de grenouilles.
  Traditionnellement, à la campagne, les enfants attrapaient des grenouilles et organisaient des courses pour voir laquelle irait le plus vite.

- ### Les cuisses de grenouilles.
  Contrairement à ce que pensent beaucoup d'Américains, les cuisses de grenouilles ne sont pas un plat typiquement français. En fait, pratiquement aucun° restaurant français ne sert ce plat.

sec *dry* **aucun** *no*

Avez-vous compris?

1. Qu'est-ce que c'est qu'un têtard?
2. En quoi consiste le travail du gardien du square?
3. Comment Nicolas et ses copains ont-ils attrapé les têtards?
4. Qu'est-ce qu'Alceste a fait pour obtenir un bocal vide?
5. Comment Alceste a-t-il eu un têtard?
6. Qu'est-ce que les enfants veulent faire avec leurs têtards?

Anticipons un peu

Quelle va être la réaction de la mère du petit Nicolas quand elle va voir le têtard?

- Elle va être heureuse que son fils s'intéresse à la nature.
- Elle va acheter un aquarium pour le têtard.
- Elle va demander à son fils de se débarrasser de *(to get rid of)* cet animal immédiatement.
- Elle va se débarrasser elle-même de l'animal.
- Autre possibilité?

2.

Et puis nous sommes partis en courant parce que nous avons vu
le gardien du square qui arrivait. Dans la rue, en marchant, je voyais mon
têtard dans le bocal, et il était très chouette. Il bougeait° beaucoup, et j'étais
40 sûr qu'il deviendrait une grenouille formidable, qui allait gagner toutes les
courses. J'ai décidé de l'appeler King; c'est le nom d'un cheval blanc que j'ai
vu jeudi dernier dans un film de cow-boys. C'était un cheval qui courait très
vite et qui venait quand son cow-boy le sifflait. Moi, je lui apprendrai à faire
des tours, à mon têtard, et quand il sera grenouille, il viendra quand je
45 le sifflerai.

Quand je suis entré dans la maison. Maman m'a regardé et elle s'est
mise à pousser des cris: «Mais regarde-moi dans quel état tu t'es mis!
Tu as de la boue° partout, tu es trempé comme une soupe! Qu'est-ce
que tu as encore fabriqué?»

50 C'est vrai que je n'étais pas très propre, surtout que j'avais oublié
de rouler° les manches° de ma chemise quand j'avais mis mes bras dans
l'étang.

— Et ce bocal? a demandé Maman, qu'est-ce qu'il y a dans ce bocal?
— C'est King, j'ai dit à Maman en lui montrant mon têtard. Il va
55 devenir grenouille, il viendra quand je le sifflerai, il nous dira le temps
qu'il fait, et il va gagner des courses!

Maman a fait une tête avec le nez tout chiffonné.°

— Quelle horreur! a crié Maman. Combien de fois faut-il que je te
dise de ne pas apporter des saletés° dans la maison?

60 — Ce n'est pas des saletés, j'ai dit, c'est propre comme tout, c'est tout
le temps° dans l'eau, et je vais lui apprendre à faire des tours!

— Eh bien, voilà ton père, a dit Maman; nous allons voir ce qu'il en
dit!

Et quand Papa a vu le bocal, il a dit: «Tiens! C'est un têtard.» Et il est
65 allé s'asseoir dans le fauteuil pour lire son journal. Maman était toute
fâchée.

— C'est tout ce que tu trouves à dire? elle a demandé à Papa. Je ne
veux pas que cet enfant ramène toutes sortes de sales bêtes à la maison!

— Bah! a dit Papa, un têtard, ce n'est pas bien gênant…

Mots utiles

faire des tours	to do tricks
pousser des cris	to scream
prévenir *	to warn
ramener	to bring back
siffler	to whistle
fâché	upset
gênant	bothersome
parfait	perfect
propre ≠ sale	clean ≠ dirty, nasty
trempé	soaking wet
partout	everywhere
puisque	since

bougeait *was moving around* **boue** *mud* **rouler** *to roll up* **manches** *sleeves* **chiffonné**
wrinkled **une saleté** *something gross, dirty* **tout le temps** = toujours

Langage familier

fabriquer = faire

Avez-vous compris?

1. Pourquoi les enfants ont-ils quitté l'étang en courant?
2. Quel nom le petit Nicolas a-t-il donné à son têtard et pourquoi?
3. Dans quel état le petit Nicolas est-il rentré chez lui?
4. Quelle a été la réaction de sa mère quand elle a vu le bocal?
5. Quelle a été la réaction de son père?

Anticipons un peu

D'après vous, que va faire le père du petit Nicolas pour résoudre le conflit?

3.

70   Eh bien, parfait, a dit Maman, parfait! Puisque je ne compte pas, je ne dis plus rien. Mais je vous préviens, c'est le têtard ou moi!

Et Maman est partie dans la cuisine.

Papa a poussé un gros soupir° et il a plié son journal.

— Je crois que nous n'avons pas le choix, Nicolas, il m'a dit. Il va falloir se débarrasser de cette bestiole.°

Moi, je me suis mis à pleurer. J'ai dit que je ne voulais pas qu'on fasse du mal à King, et que nous étions déjà copains tous les deux. Papa m'a pris dans ses bras.

— Ecoute, mon petit bonhomme,° il m'a dit. Tu sais que ce petit
75   têtard a une maman grenouille. Et la maman grenouille doit avoir beaucoup de peine d'avoir perdu son enfant. Maman ne serait pas contente si on t'emmenait dans un bocal. Pour les grenouilles, c'est la même chose. Alors, tu sais ce qu'on va faire? Nous allons partir tous les deux et nous allons remettre le têtard où tu l'as pris, et puis tous les dimanches tu
80   pourras aller le voir. Et en revenant à la maison, je t'achèterai une tablette° de chocolat.

Moi, j'ai réfléchi un moment, et j'ai dit: «Bon, d'accord.»

Alors, Papa est allé dans la cuisine et il a dit à Maman, en riant, que nous avions décidé de la garder, et de nous débarrasser du têtard.

85   Maman a ri aussi. Elle m'a embrassé et elle a dit que pour ce soir elle ferait un gâteau. J'étais très consolé.

Quand nous sommes arrivés dans le jardin, j'ai conduit Papa, qui tenait le bocal, vers le bord de l'étang. J'ai dit: «C'est là.» Alors, j'ai dit au revoir à King, et Papa a versé dans l'étang tout ce qu'il y avait dans le bocal.

90   Et puis nous nous sommes retournés pour partir et nous avons vu le gardien du square qui sortait de derrière un arbre avec des yeux ronds.

— Je ne sais pas si vous êtes tous fous, ou si c'est moi qui le deviens, a dit le gardien, mais vous êtes le septième bonhomme, y compris° un agent de police, qui vient aujourd'hui jeter le contenu d'un bocal d'eau à cet
95   endroit précis° de l'étang.

a poussé un gros soupir *let out a large sigh*   **une bestiole** = une petite bête
bonhomme = homme   **tablette** *bar*   **y compris** *including*   **cet endroit précis** *this very spot*

Mots utiles

avoir de la peine	= être triste
conduire *	to lead
se débarrasser	to get rid of
faire du mal à	to hurt
plier	to fold (up)
réfléchir	to think things over
rire *	to laugh
tenir *	to hold
verser	to pour
fou (folle)	crazy
vers	toward

Avez-vous compris?

1. Qu'est-ce que le père du petit Nicolas explique à son fils?
2. Quelle est la première réaction du petit Nicolas?
3. Quels arguments le père utilise-t-il pour convaincre son fils de remettre le têtard dans l'étang?
4. Que fait la mère lorsqu'elle apprend la bonne nouvelle?
5. Qu'est-ce que le gardien du square a vu? Pourquoi pense-t-il que ces gens sont fous?

EXPRESSION ORALE

■ Expérience personnelle

Quand vous étiez petit(e), avez-vous trouvé un jour un animal que vous avez voulu apporter à la maison? Décrivez ce qui est arrivé. Par exemple . . .

- Quel animal était-ce?
- Où l'avez-vous trouvé?
- Quelle a été la réaction de votre père/mère?
- Qu'est-ce que vous avez fait de l'animal? Est-ce que vous l'avez gardé? Sinon, qu'est-ce que vous avez fait de lui?

■ Situations

Avec votre partenaire, choisissez l'une des situations suivantes. Composez le dialogue correspondant et jouez-le en classe.

---

1 Au marché

Au marché, la mère du petit Nicolas rencontre la mère d'Alceste. Elles parlent de ce que leurs enfants ont fait hier et quelles ont été leurs réactions.

Rôles: la mère de Nicolas, la mère d'Alceste

---

2 Au café

Le père du petit Nicolas et le père de Raoul se rencontrent au café et parlent de ce qui s'est passé. Ils décrivent…

- ce que leurs enfants ont fait
- comment leurs épouses ont réagi *(reacted)*
- comment le problème a été résolu *(solved)*

Rôles: le père de Nicolas, le père de Raoul

EXPRESSION ÉCRITE

■ Le sens de l'humour

Les Récrés du petit Nicolas sont un livre humoristique. Décrivez deux ou trois scènes ou situations qui vous paraissent humoristiques dans le récit que vous avez lu et expliquez pourquoi vous les trouvez drôles.

■ Une lettre

La mère du petit Nicolas écrit une lettre à sa soeur. Elle lui explique ce qui s'est passé hier.

■ Le rapport du gardien

Le gardien écrit un rapport sur ce qu'il a vu hier dans le square. Il décrit . . .

- où il était
- ce qu'il faisait
- ce qu'il a vu
- pourquoi c'était bizarre

—> Hier, j'ai été témoin de quelque chose de bizarre. . . .

■ Les dates ■ Les événements

La Renaissance (1500-1570)

- **1453** Fin de la Guerre de Cent Ans

- **1515**

Règne de François Ier

La Renaissance

- **1547**

La cour de François Ier

Après la Guerre de Cent Ans et la reconquête de son territoire, la France est finalement en paix. La période qui commence s'appelle la «**Renaissance**», c'est-à-dire le renouvellement. C'est une période de grande activité artistique et culturelle. C'est à cette époque que les rois de France ont habité en Touraine où ils ont construit de magnifiques châteaux: **Chenonceaux, Amboise, Chambord.**

Le château de Chambord est immense, avec plus de 400 pièces et 365 cheminées.

- **1589**

Règne d'Henri IV

Le Grand Siècle (1643-1715)

- **1610**

Règne de Louis XIII

Le Grand Siècle, c'est le siècle de **Louis XIV**, ou «**Roi-Soleil**». C'est aussi la période la plus brillante de l'histoire de France. Louis XIV est devenu roi à l'âge de cinq ans et il a régné sur la France pendant 72 ans. Pendant son règne, il a encouragé les arts et les sciences. Il a créé des académies de peinture, de sculpture, de sciences, d'architecture. Avec Louis XIV, le prestige de la culture française s'est répandu° dans toute l'Europe. Mais Louis XIV était aussi un roi autoritaire et ambitieux. De son château de **Versailles** il exerçait un pouvoir absolu sur le reste du pays. C'est lui qui a dit: «L'État, c'est moi!» Louis XIV a engagé la France dans de nombreuses guerres qui ont fini par ruiner le pays.

- **1643**

Le Grand Siècle

Règne de Louis XIV

- **1715** Mort de Louis XIV

Louis XIV à la guerre

s'est répandu *spread*

■ *Les personnes*

François Ier et Mona Lisa

Jean Clouet «*François Ier*»

Léonard de Vinci *la «Joconde»*

Le roi **François Ier** (1494-1547) était très grand, très beau et très athlétique. Il aimait tous les sports de son époque, et en particulier le jeu de paume, l'ancêtre du tennis actuel. Sa grande passion était la chasse° qu'il pratiquait dans les forêts de ses châteaux de **Chambord** et d'**Amboise**.

C'était aussi un esprit fin° et cultivé qui aimait la musique, les arts et les lettres. Il a fait venir° dans son château d'Amboise le grand artiste italien **Léonard de Vinci** à qui il a acheté la «**Joconde**» ou «**Mona Lisa**», aujourd'hui le portrait le plus célèbre du monde.

La vie de cour sous François Ier

Louis XIV et sa cour

La cour de Louis XIV à Versailles

Louis XIV

Louis XIV (1638-1715) a longtemps vécu au château de **Versailles**. Il a construit ce château non seulement pour son plaisir, mais pour attirer les nobles du pays. C'était une façon de les contrôler et de les empêcher° de se révolter contre lui. Trois mille personnes vivaient au château de Versailles.

À la cour de Louis XIV, tout était organisé autour de la personne du roi. Les événements de sa vie quotidienne° étaient des cérémonies officielles, réglées par° une étiquette très stricte. C'était un privilège d'assister au lever, au dîner, au souper, au coucher du roi. Seuls les grands seigneurs° étaient invités.

Patron des arts et des lettres, Louis XIV s'intéressait personnellement à la musique, au théâtre et surtout au ballet. Parfois, il participait lui-même aux représentations. Un jour, il a paru sur scène déguisé en soleil, d'où son nom de «**Roi-Soleil**». Ce nom est avant tout° symbolique. Louis XIV brillait sur sa cour, sur la France et sur le monde. Il se considérait vraiment comme le centre de l'univers.

---

la chasse *hunting* **fin** *refined* **fait venir** *brought* **empêcher** *to prevent* **quotidienne** *daily* **réglées par** *structured according to* **seigneurs** = nobles **avant tout** *above all*

■ *Cyrano de Bergerac* ■

Cyrano de Bergerac a vraiment existé. Il a vécu à l'époque de **Louis XIV**. C'était un soldat et un écrivain qui a laissé° un curieux roman de science-fiction où il décrit un voyage dans la lune. Ce personnage historique serait cependant resté dans une tranquille obscurité s'il n'avait pas été transformé en héros de légende et immortalisé dans une comédie célèbre du 19ᵉ siècle.

Cette comédie, intitulée *Cyrano de Bergerac*, écrite il y a cent ans par Edmond Rostand, a connu un très grand succès à son époque. Depuis, elle a été mise en musique, adaptée à l'écran,° et maintes° fois transformée et parodiée.* Le dernier film en date, dans lequel l'acteur Gérard Depardieu joue le rôle principal, est une reproduction assez fidèle° de la pièce originale.

Cyrano de Bergerac est essentiellement une histoire d'amour, basée sur un gigantesque quiproquo° tragico-comique. **Cyrano** aime **Roxane** qui aime un autre homme, **Christian**. Mais si Roxane a d'abord été attirée° par la beauté physique de Christian, c'est pour la beauté de sa poésie qu'elle l'aime vraiment. Or, cette poésie n'est pas celle de Christian, mais celle de l'infortuné Cyrano.

Cyrano, le héros de l'histoire, est un vaillant soldat du régiment des Cadets de Gascogne. Il est brave, courageux, téméraire° à l'extrême. C'est aussi un poète à l'âme tendre.° Il est bon, loyal, généreux, intelligent, spirituel,° sensible et il écrit de magnifiques vers. Il a toutes les qualités possibles sauf une: il n'est pas beau.

Cyrano est en effet affligé d'une infirmité incurable: Il a un nez monstrueusement long. Cette infirmité le rend très susceptible° auprès° des hommes, et très timide auprès des femmes. Personne en sa présence ne peut mentionner le mot «nez». Cyrano est secrètement amoureux de sa cousine Roxane, mais il sait qu'il n'a aucune chance, précisément à cause de cet immense nez qui le défigure. . .

* Une parodie classique est le film américain *Roxanne* où Steve Martin joue le rôle d'un pompier (*fireman*) amoureux.

Documents: «Cyrano de Bergerac»

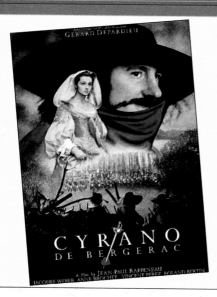

Le film Cyrano de Bergerac (1990) reproduit fidèlement la pièce de théâtre.

L'action de la pièce se passe dans la France du 17ᵉ siècle. Dans la première scène, une foule° se presse° pour assister à un spectacle de **Montfleury**, comédien en vogue, mais ennemi de Cyrano. Dans cette foule, on reconnaît tous les personnages principaux de l'histoire, et d'abord **Roxane**. Elle est belle, coquette, romanesque et éprise° de poésie. Tous les hommes sont amoureux d'elle. Ce jour-là, elle est accompagnée de **de Guiche**, un seigneur noble et puissant° qui lui fait la cour.°

---

laissé *left* **écran** *screen* **maintes** = plusieurs **fidèle** *faithful* **quiproquo** *misunderstanding* **attirée** *attracted* **téméraire** *bold*
à l'âme tendre *with a soft heart* **spirituel** *witty* **susceptible** *touchy* **auprès de** = avec **foule** *crowd* **se presse** *hurries* **éprise** *enamoured*
puissant *powerful* **lui fait la cour** *is courting her*

Mais Roxane pense secrètement à un jeune homme qu'elle a aperçu un jour et dont elle est tombée secrètement amoureuse. C'est le beau **Christian**, qui, lui aussi, est dans la foule à la recherche de Roxane. Le public s'impatiente.

Roxane 1

2 Christian

On attend Montfleury, mais on attend aussi **Cyrano** qui a promis de lancer un défi° à Montfleury. Montfleury entre en scène. Est-ce que Cyrano viendra? Oui, il arrive! D'une voix éclatante,° il ridiculise Montfleury et le chasse de scène.

Tous les spectateurs ne sont pas contents de l'interruption du spectacle, en particulier de Guiche et son neveu Valvert. Celui-ci va défier Cyrano en lui disant «Monsieur, vous avez un grand nez». Stimulé par cette insulte suprême, Cyrano se lance alors dans la fameuse tirade où il fait l'éloge de son appendice nasal. Puis, il traite Valvert de sot° et engage celui-ci dans un duel, tout en composant des vers. Tout cela se passe sous les yeux de la belle Roxane, très fière de la bravoure et de l'intelligence de son cousin.

3 Le spectacle a commencé et Cyrano vient d'arriver. En présence de sa cousine Roxane, Cyrano s'adresse à son ennemi, le comédien Montfleury, et le ridiculise.

Après le duel, Cyrano va accompagner un ami chez lui. Il tombe dans une embuscade° d'où il sort victorieux à un contre cent. L'histoire de cet exploit fait le tour° de la ville et Cyrano devient le héros du jour. Entre-temps°, Roxane lui a envoyé sa dame de compagnie° pour lui demander un rendez-vous.

Intimidé, mais reprenant espoir,° Cyrano va au rendez-vous. Après un long préambule où elle évoque leur enfance passée ensemble et leur longue amitié, Roxane déclare son amour pour . . . Le visage de Cyrano s'illumine.° Pour lui? Hélas, non! Ce n'est pas lui que Roxane aime, mais le beau Christian. Oui, c'est lui qu'elle aime et si elle est venue voir Cyrano, c'est pour lui demander de prendre Christian sous sa protection. Celui-ci va, en effet, entrer au régiment des Cadets de Gascogne, le régiment de Cyrano.

4 La querelle oratoire entre Valvert et Cyrano s'est transformée en duel. Pendant le duel, Cyrano se moque de son adversaire, tout en composant des vers.

lancer un défi *to challenge* éclatante *very loud* sot = stupide embuscade *ambush* fait le tour *goes around* entre-temps = pendant ce temps
dame de compagnie *lady-in-waiting* espoir *hope* s'illumine *brightens*

Cyrano promet de protéger Christian, mais c'est déçu° et triste qu'il va rejoindre ses compagnons d'armes. Tout le monde le salue en héros. Cyrano, trop peiné,° ne fait pas attention. Soudain, Christian, la nouvelle recrue du régiment, entre dans la salle d'armes.° Ne connaissant pas Cyrano, il se moque de lui, répétant sans cesse le mot «nez». L'assistance° est pétrifiée! Que va-t-il se passer? Est-ce que Cyrano va tuer° Christian? Non! Fidèle° à la promesse faite à Roxane, Cyrano traite son rival en ami et en frère.

Dès lors,° Cyrano va assister Christian dans toutes ses démarches amoureuses° auprès de Roxane. Christian avoue° qu'il est sot, qu'il n'a pas d'éloquence, qu'il ne sait pas parler aux femmes. Que cela ne tienne!° C'est Cyrano qui sera sa voix, son porte-parole.° C'est lui qui écrira à Roxane les lettres d'amour que Christian ne sait pas écrire. L'inspiration lui est facile puisque,° lui aussi, il aime éperdument° Roxane.

Les lettres de Cyrano, signées Christian, enflamment de plus en plus le coeur de Roxane qui consent à accorder° un rendez-vous au beau Christian. Celui-ci va seul au rendez-vous, mais sans l'éloquence de Cyrano, il ne dit que des banalités. Roxane, qui s'attendait° à des torrents de déclamations lyriques, est déçue et renvoie° le jeune homme.

Christian obtient un nouveau rendez-vous, mais cette fois, avec l'assistance de Cyrano, qui lui souffle° chaque mot de sa déclaration d'amour, il réussit à conquérir Roxane dans la célèbre scène du balcon. Au cours de° cette scène, Christian monte au balcon de Roxane, entre chez elle où les deux amants sont mariés par un prêtre envoyé par de Guiche, toujours° amoureux de Roxane.

De Guiche arrive lui-même chez Roxane où il apprend le mariage. Furieux et jaloux, il annonce qu'il vient d'être nommé commandant de l'armée française chargée de déloger les Espagnols de la ville d'Arras. Il décide d'y envoyer sur le champ° le régiment des Cadets de Gascogne, séparant ainsi Christian de sa nouvelle femme.

L'action change de lieu.° Nous sommes maintenant à Arras où le régiment de Christian et de Cyrano est cantonné.° La guerre a mal tourné pour les Français. Assiégés par les Espagnols, les fougueux° soldats de Gascogne meurent de faim.° Cyrano veut tenir la promesse qu'il a faite à Roxane. Chaque jour, elle reçoit une lettre de Christian. En réalité, c'est toujours Cyrano qui lui écrit, évidemment à l'insu de° son ami, des billets° d'un lyrisme magnifique.

Dans le camp français, la situation est maintenant désespérée. Sur les ordres de de Guiche, le régiment de Gascogne doit être sacrifié. Cyrano écrit à Roxane une dernière lettre d'adieu, toujours signée du nom de Christian. Entre-temps, émue° par l'intensité des lettres poétiques de son mari, Roxane décide de tout risquer pour le rejoindre à Arras. Elle traverse° les lignes espagnoles et arrive dans le camp quelques heures avant la bataille finale. En présence de Cyrano, elle avoue à Christian que ce n'est plus pour sa beauté qu'elle l'aime, mais pour sa poésie, et qu'elle l'aimerait même s'il était laid.° Déconcerté par cet aveu,° Christian part à l'assaut. Au cours de l'engagement,° il est blessé.° Il meurt, réconforté par l'amour de Roxane et l'amitié de Cyrano. La bataille finale a lieu. Pendant cette bataille, Cyrano et de Guiche combattent héroïquement. Christian est mort, mais sa femme et ses amis sont sauvés.

Quinze ans ont passé. Roxane a pris le deuil de° Christian et s'est retirée dans un couvent. Là, elle reçoit régulièrement la visite de ses deux amis, de Guiche, devenu duc et maréchal de France, et Cyrano, pauvre, mais toujours aussi fier.° Un jour, celui-ci arrive en retard au rendez-vous. Il a été blessé dans une embuscade tendue par ses ennemis et il va mourir.

Ce jour-là, Roxane comprend enfin que c'est bien lui l'auteur des merveilleuses lettres d'amour qu'elle recevait de Christian. Cyrano meurt dans ses bras, finalement aimé par celle qu'il avait aimée toute sa vie.

---

déçu *disappointed* **peiné** *in pain* **salle d'armes** *fencing hall* **l'assistance** = les personnes dans la salle **tuer** *to kill* **fidèle** *faithful* **dès lors** *from then on* **démarches amoureuses** *steps in his courtship* **avoue** = admet **que cela ne tienne** *that won't matter* **porte-parole** *spokesperson* **puisque** *since* **éperdument** *madly* **accorder** *to grant* **s'attendait** *was expecting* **renvoie** *sends away* **souffle** *prompts* **au cours de** = pendant **toujours** *still* **sur le champ** = immédiatement **lieu** *location* **cantonné** *quartered* **fougueux** = braves **meurent de faim** *dying of starvation* **à l'insu de** *without the knowledge of* **billets** = lettres **émue** *moved* **traverse** *crosses* **laid** *ugly* **aveu** *admission* **au cours de l'engagement** = pendant la bataille **blessé** *wounded* **a pris le deuil de** *is in mourning for* **fier** *proud*

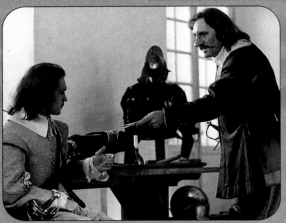

5 Dans la salle d'armes du régiment, Cyrano fait connaissance de son rival Christian qu'il a promis de protéger.

6 Cyrano et Christian deviennent amis. Malgré lui, Cyrano va aider Christian à gagner le coeur de Roxane.

7 Émue par la poésie des lettres signées Christian, mais écrites en réalité par Cyrano, Roxane a donné rendez-vous à Christian sous son balcon. C'est Christian qui parle, mais c'est Cyrano qui exprime son amour pour elle.

8 Roxane arrive devant Arras avec un chariot de vivres (food) pour les Français assiégés. Elle traverse les lignes espagnoles avec Christian et Cyrano.

9 Christian est mort héroïquement. Ses amis Cyrano et Ragueneau emmènent sa femme loin du champ de bataille.

10 Bien des années ont passé. Un jour, Cyrano arrive en retard à son rendez-vous habituel avec Roxane. Blessé, il va mourir, mais avant, Roxane apprendra enfin son secret.

Le corbeau et le renard

À l'école, tous les jeunes Français apprennent par coeur les fables de La Fontaine. Leur auteur est l'un des écrivains les plus célèbres du siècle de Louis XIV. À travers° ses portraits d'animaux, **Jean de La Fontaine** (1621-1695) voulait critiquer les défauts de ses contemporains. La morale de ses fables est en réalité éternelle.

La fameuse fable *Le corbeau et le renard*° s'adresse aux gens qui ont besoin d'être admirés.

Le corbeau et le renard

Maître Corbeau, sur un arbre perché,
　　Tenait° en son bec un fromage.
Maître Renard, par l'odeur alléché,°
　　Lui tint à peu près ce langage:°
　　　　«Hé! bonjour, Monsieur du Corbeau,
Que vous êtes joli! que vous me semblez beau!
　　　　Sans mentir,° si votre ramage°
　　　　Se rapporte° à votre plumage
Vous êtes le phénix° des hôtes de ces bois.
À ces mots, le Corbeau ne se sent pas de joie;°
　　　　Et pour montrer sa belle voix,
Il ouvre un large bec, laisse tomber° sa proie.°
Le Renard s'en saisit,° et dit: «Mon bon Monsieur,
　　　　Apprenez que tout flatteur
　　　　Vit° aux dépens° de celui qui l'écoute:
Cette leçon vaut° bien un fromage, sans doute.»
　　　　Le Corbeau, honteux° et confus,°
Jura,° mais un peu tard, qu'on ne l'y prendrait plus.°

(*Fables choisies*, Livre I, 1688)

à travers = avec　**le corbeau et le renard** *the crow and the fox*　**tenait** = avait　**alléché** = attiré　**lui tint à peu près ce langage** = lui parla ainsi
sans mentir = en vérité　**ramage** = chant　**se rapporte** = est égal　**le phénix** = l'oiseau le plus fabuleux　**ne se sent pas de joie** = est transporté de joie
laisse tomber *drops*　**proie** = le fromage qu'il a trouvé　**s'en saisit** = la prend　**vit** *lives*　**aux dépens** *at the expense*　**vaut** *is worth*
honteux *ashamed*　**confus** *upset*　**jura** *swore*　**on ne l'y prendrait plus** *he wouldn't be taken in again*

■ L'histoire de France à travers ses châteaux

Carcassonne

Comme beaucoup de villes médiévales, Carcassonne était entourée de hauts ramparts qui la protégeaient contre d'éventuels envahisseurs.° Elle résista aux Anglais pendant la Guerre de Cent Ans.

Chenonceaux

Le château de Chenonceaux est de pur style Renaissance. Sur ses murs on peut y lire encore des graffiti (en anglais) laissés par les gardes écossais° du roi Henri II.

Angers

Angers était la capitale des Plantagenêts, ducs d'Anjou et futurs rois d'Angleterre. Avec ses grosses tours rondes, le château est un bel exemple d'architecture féodale.

Fontainebleau

Maintes fois transformé, Fontainebleau a servi de résidence à plus de 20 rois de France, parmi lesquels François Ier et Louis XIII, père de Louis XIV. C'est ici que Napoléon a fait ses adieux avant de partir en exil.

Château-Gaillard

Construit en 1196 par Richard Coeur de Lion, Château-Gaillard dominait la Seine et barrait la route entre Paris et Rouen. Dix ans plus tard, le château tomba dans les mains des Français et il n'en reste aujourd'hui que d'imposantes ruines.

Vaux-le-Vicomte

Le château de Vaux-le-Vicomte a été construit par Nicolas Fouquet, surintendant des finances du royaume de France. Un jour, Fouquet eut la mauvaise idée d'y inviter le jeune roi Louis XIV. Celui-ci, jaloux de la richesse de son ministre, le fit emprisonner.

Amboise

Le château d'Amboise est situé sur un rocher qui domine la Loire. Sa grosse tour ronde permettait aux cavaliers° et aux carrosses° d'accéder directement au château. C'est au château d'Amboise que le roi François Ier recevait Léonard de Vinci.

Versailles

Toute la majesté de Louis XIV et la puissance de la France sont exprimées dans la splendeur du château de Versailles et de ses magnifiques jardins. C'est ici que vivait le roi, entouré de milliers de courtisans.

---

envahisseurs *invaders* **cavaliers** *horsemen* **carrosses** *horse-drawn carriages* **écossais** *Scottish*

Aspects de la vie quotidienne

Thème et Objectifs

Culture

In this unit, you will discover . . .
- where to buy various items and obtain various services
- how shopping habits differ in France and the United States

Communication

You will learn how . . .
- to buy stamps and mail letters
- to purchase small items you might need
- to have items fixed or cleaned
- to get a haircut
- to ask for various services

Langue

You will learn how . . .
- to answer questions using one or more pronouns
- to talk about numbers of people and things without specifying exact quantities
- to describe actions that people have others do for them

EN FRANCE, FAITES COMME
les Français!

Il y a beaucoup d'endroits où nous devons aller régulièrement pour répondre aux besoins de la vie quotidienne.° Nous allons au centre commercial pour faire nos achats, au supermarché pour faire les courses, à la poste pour acheter des timbres,° à la banque pour déposer ou retirer° de l'argent. Et de temps en temps, nous allons chez le coiffeur pour nous faire couper les cheveux.° Si les Français font les mêmes choses que les Américains, ils les font parfois un peu différemment.

Un jour vous irez peut-être en France. Voilà quelques conseils pour vivre° «à la française».°

■ Avant de faire votre shopping, surfez sur l'Internet. Avec l'Internet, vous trouverez les magasins qui vendent ce que vous cherchez. Vous pourrez étudier les catalogues, comparer les prix, et vous découvrirez peut-être des soldes° extraordinaires. Si vous ne voulez pas vous déplacer,° vous pourrez passer° votre commande° directement sur l'Internet.

■ Si vous allez au supermarché, n'oubliez pas de prendre de la monnaie.° Pour obtenir° un chariot,° vous devrez, en effet, déposer une pièce d'un euro. Quand vous passerez à la caisse,° n'attendez pas° à ce que la caissière empaquette° vos achats. Vous devrez faire cela vous même. Et si vous voulez récupérer l'euro que vous avez déposé pour votre chariot, n'oubliez pas de rapporter votre chariot à l'endroit où vous l'avez pris.

■ Si vous préférez un service plus personnalisé, allez chez les petits commerçants du quartier où vous habitez. Là, les prix sont plus élevés,° mais la qualité est souvent meilleure. Et vous pouvez faire la connaissance des gens de votre quartier. Évidemment n'oubliez pas de dire bonjour et au revoir à la marchande et aux clients qui se trouvent dans la boutique. Sinon, vous serez considéré comme une personne mal élevée.°

---

quotidienne *daily* **timbres** *stamps* **retirer** *to withdraw* **faire couper les cheveux** *to get a haircut* **vivre** *to live* **«à la française»** = comme les Français
soldes *sales* **ne voulez pas vous déplacer** = quitter votre maison **passer** = donner **commande** *order* **monnaie** *change* **obtenir** *to get*
chariot *cart* **caisse** *check-out* **n'attendez pas** *don't expect* **empaquette** *bag* **élevés** *high* **mal élevée** = impolie

■ Si vous allez chez le coiffeur, n'oubliez pas de donner un pourboire° à la personne qui vous a coupé les cheveux, même si vous n'êtes pas très satisfait du résultat. Mais au café et au restaurant, vous n'êtes pas obligé de laisser de pourboire. Il est compris° dans l'addition.

■ Si vous avez besoin d'une photo d'identité, ne perdez pas votre temps à chercher un photographe. Allez dans un grand magasin. Là vous trouverez un «Photomaton» où vous aurez votre photo en cinq minutes. Dans ce même magasin, vous trouverez aussi d'autres services très pratiques: une photocopieuse, un service de réparation de chaussures, un service de reproduction de clés.°

■ Si vous avez besoin de timbres un jour où la poste est fermée, allez alors dans un bureau de tabac.° Là, vous pourrez acheter des timbres ordinaires, et aussi des télécartes, indispensables si vous voulez téléphoner d'une cabine° publique.

Maintenant vous savez comment vivre en France. C'est simple. Faites comme les Français!

et vous?

DÉFINITIONS

Donnez une définition des mots et expressions suivantes.

- un centre commercial
- un supermarché
- un coiffeur
- une poste
- un chariot
- un pourboire
- une banque
- la caisse
- l'addition
- des soldes
- une télécarte

SITUATIONS

1. Vous habitez en France. Vous faites les courses avec un(e) ami(e) américain(e) qui vous rend visite. Expliquez à votre ami(e) — votre partenaire — les différences entre un supermarché en France et aux États-Unis.

2. Un(e) ami(e) français(e) vous rend visite. Expliquez à votre ami(e) — votre partenaire — dans quelles circonstances on donne un pourboire aux États-Unis.

3. Imaginez que vous allez passer deux ou trois mois en France. Est-ce que vous pourrez vous adapter facilement à la vie quotidienne décrite dans le texte?
   - Quels aspects vous semblent pratiques et intéressants?
   - Avec quels aspects auriez-vous des difficultés?

pourboire *tip* **compris** = inclus **clés** *keys*
bureau de tabac *tobacco shop* **cabine** *booth*

Scènes de la vie courante

Au supermarché

une touche

Si on veut utiliser un chariot, il faut payer une caution.° Pour cela, on introduit une pièce dans un petit réceptacle qui se trouve sur le chariot. Celui-ci se débloque° automatiquement. Quand on a fini ses courses, on rapporte le chariot à l'endroit où on l'a trouvé et on récupère son argent.

Au rayon des fruits et légumes, tout est «self-service». Le client doit peser° les différentes choses qu'il achète. Pour cela, on met chaque produit sur une balance° automatique et on appuie° sur une touche correspondant à ce produit. La balance imprime° un ticket qu'on colle° sur le produit.

la balance

le ticket

Chez les petits commerçants

Chez les petits commerçants, le service est plus personnel. En parlant avec les gens, on y apprend les nouvelles du quartier où on habite.

Au café

Partout° en France, il y a des cafés. On va au café non seulement pour prendre une boisson ou un sandwich, mais aussi pour bavarder.°

Pour téléphoner

Signal d'Appel

France Telecom

TELECARTE 50 UNITES

France Telecom

puce

TELECARTE 50

télécarte, (carte à puce)

Si on veut téléphoner d'une cabine téléphonique, on doit avoir une télécarte. Les télécartes sont des «cartes à puce»° qui permettent de téléphoner pendant un certain nombre de minutes. Créées il y a vingt ans seulement, les télécartes sont devenues des objets de collection, comme les timbres.

L'usage des télécartes est très simple! On décroche° le récepteur,° on introduit la télécarte dans l'appareil, et on compose° le numéro. Quand on a terminé son appel, on reprend la carte. Les télécartes s'achètent dans les postes ou dans les bureaux de tabac.

---

caution *deposit* **se débloque** *unlocks* **peser** *to weigh* **balance** *scale* **appuie** *pushes* **imprime** *prints* **colle** *sticks* **partout** *everywhere*
bavarder *to chat* **puce** *microchip* **décroche** *picks up* **récepteur** *receiver* **compose** *dials*

LE FRANÇAIS PRATIQUE

Comment faire des achats

PAPETERIE

À la papeterie

— Vous désirez?

Je voudrais	
Pouvez-vous me donner	**du papier à lettres.**
S'il vous plaît, donnez-moi	

— Vous désirez | **quelque chose d'autre** *(something else)*?
autre chose?

Oui, | **donnez-moi aussi** | **un stylo à bille.**
j'ai besoin d'
il me faut *(I need)*

— **Et avec ça?**
    C'est tout, merci!
    Ça fait combien?
    Combien est-ce que je vous dois?
— **Ça fait 6 euros cinquante.**
    Voici 10 euros.
— Et voici **votre monnaie** *(change).*
    Merci.

> **Vous désirez?**

> **Pouvez-vous me donner du papier à lettres?**

> **C'est tout?**

> **Oui, c'est tout, merci!**

devoir	*to owe*

LA POSTE
Guichet automatique

À la poste

— **C'est votre tour** *(it's your turn)*, **Mademoiselle.**
    Je voudrais **des timbres** *(stamps)* à 67 centimes.
— **Combien en voulez-vous?**
    Donnez-m'en dix, s'il vous plaît.
— **Voilà. C'est tout?**
    Non, je voudrais aussi . . .

        envoyer | **cette lettre.**
                cette carte postale.
                ce colis *(package).*
                ce paquet *(package).*
        faire **des photocopies.**
        prendre **mon courrier** *(mail)* **à la poste restante** *(general delivery).*

> **C'est votre tour, Mademoiselle.**

> **Je voudrais des timbres à 67 centimes.**

> **Combien en voulez-vous?**

> **Donnez-m'en dix, s'il vous plaît.**

Quelle boutique? Quel rayon (department)?	Quels articles (items)?	Quelles quantités?
À la papeterie Au rayon «Papeterie»	**un carnet** (notebook) **un crayon** **un stylo à bille** (ballpoint pen) **du papier, du papier à lettres** **des enveloppes** **de la colle** (glue) **du scotch** (scotch tape) **un trombone** (paper clip) **un élastique** (rubber band)	**un bloc** de papier **un paquet** d'enveloppes **un tube** de colle **un rouleau** de scotch **une boîte** de trombones d'élastiques
Chez le photographe Au rayon «Photo»	**une pellicule** (film) en noir et blanc **une pellicule-couleurs** **des diapos** (slides) **une pile** (battery)	**un rouleau** de diapos
À la pharmacie Chez le pharmacien Chez la pharmacienne Au rayon «Produits d'Hygiène»	**du dentifrice** **de l'aspirine, des vitamines** **du shampooing** **de l'eau de toilette** **un coton-tige** (cotton swab) **un mouchoir en papier** (tissue) **de l'ouate** (cotton) **un pansement adhésif** (Band-aid)	**un tube** de dentifrice d'aspirine **une bouteille** de shampooing d'eau de toilette de parfum **une boîte** de coton-tiges de mouchoirs **un paquet** d'ouate de pansements
À la supérette Au rayon «Produits d'entretien» «Produits de maison»	**du savon** **de la lessive** (detergent) **du papier hygiénique** (toilet paper) **du Sopalin** (paper towels) **de la ficelle** (string) **une allumette** (match) **une épingle** (pin) **une épingle de sûreté** (safety pin)	**un paquet** de lessive **un rouleau** de papier hygiénique de Sopalin **une pelote** (ball) de ficelle **une boîte** d'allumettes d'épingles

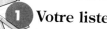

1 Votre liste

Vous allez passer les vacances de printemps à la Martinique avec votre partenaire. Chacun va faire une liste de dix articles qu'il va emporter *(take along)* avec lui. Utilisez le tableau qui figure à la page 153.

Puis comparez vos listes:

- Qu'est-ce que vous avez pris de semblable *(similar)*?
- Qu'est-ce que vous avez pris de différent?

2 À la Samaritaine

Vous êtes allé(e) à la Samaritaine, un grand magasin à Paris. Là, vous avez acheté l'un des articles suivants. Dites . . .

- à quel rayon vous êtes passé(e)
- ce que vous avez acheté (nommez l'article)
- deux autres choses que vous avez achetées à ce rayon.

▶ **Je suis passé(e) au rayon «Papeterie». J'ai acheté une boîte de trombones. J'ai aussi acheté . . .**

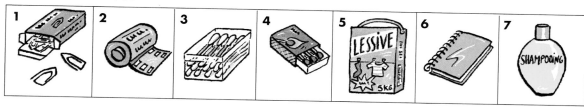

3 Achats

Un groupe d'étudiants américains visite la France. Ces étudiants passent dans un grand magasin. Déterminez les besoins de chacun. Dites à quel rayon il passe et ce qu'il achète.

▶ Betty veut prendre des photos du groupe.
Elle passe au rayon «Photo» où elle achète une pellicule-couleurs (un rouleau de diapos).

1. John veut écrire à ses parents.
2. Jim veut laver ses chemises.
3. Elizabeth a perdu sa trousse de toilette *(toiletry kit)*.
4. Anne a mal à la tête.
5. Jacqueline a des ampoules *(blisters)* aux pieds.
6. Cindy éternue *(sneezes)* constamment.
7. Alice veut se laver les cheveux.
8. Robert veut faire un paquet qu'il va envoyer à ses parents.

4 À la poste

C'est votre première semaine à Paris. Vous allez à la poste pour certaines choses. Composez le dialogue suivant avec votre partenaire qui va jouer le rôle de l'employé(e) de poste.

Employé(e):	*Say hello.*
Client(e):	Say hello and ask for stamps at 50 centimes.
Employé(e):	*Ask how many stamps the client wants.*
Client(e):	Mention a number.
Employé(e):	*Ask if that is all.*
Client(e):	Say that you have something to mail (mention the item: a letter? a postcard? a package?).
Employé(e):	*Determine the price of the items requested and ask the client for the money.*
Client(e):	Pay the postal clerk the sum requested.

5 Créa-dialogue

C'est samedi aujourd'hui et vous avez beaucoup d'achats à faire. Choisissez une boutique où vous allez faire quelques achats. Avec votre partenaire, composez un dialogue pour cette boutique et jouez-le en classe. Votre partenaire va jouer le rôle du vendeur (de la vendeuse).

▶ — Vous désirez, <u>mademoiselle</u>?
— Je voudrais <u>un tube de dentifrice</u>.
— Et avec ça?
— <u>J'ai besoin</u> aussi <u>d'une bouteille de shampooing</u>.
— Voici <u>le dentifrice et le shampooing</u>.
— Merci. <u>C'est combien</u>, s'il vous plaît?
— <u>11 euros cinquante centimes</u>.
— Voici <u>vingt euros</u>.
— Et voici votre monnaie: <u>8 euros et cinquante centimes</u>.

- *Use appropriate greeting.*
- *Mention another product.*
- *Use another expression.*
- *Use another expression and name another product.*
- *Give client the items requested.*
- *Use another expression.*
- *Give a price under 100 euros.*
- *Give a bill to cover the amount.*
- *Return the correct change.*

Conversations libres

Avec votre partenaire, choisissez l'une des situations suivantes. Composez le dialogue correspondant et jouez-le en classe.

1   Shopping

Vous êtes un(e) étudiant(e) français(e). Vous venez d'arriver à cette école avec un programme d'échange. Faites une liste de trois ou quatre choses dont vous avez besoin et demandez à votre partenaire où vous pouvez les acheter.

2   Une erreur

Vous êtes allé(e) dans un grand magasin où vous avez acheté plusieurs articles. Quand vous rentrez chez vous, vous vous rendez compte *(realize)* que vous avez pris le sac d'une autre personne. Téléphonez au magasin pour expliquer la situation. L'employé(e) va vous demander ce que vous avez acheté et ce qu'il y a dans le sac que vous avez ramené chez vous.

3   Camping

Ce week-end vous allez faire du camping avec votre partenaire. Pour la préparation de cette expédition, votre partenaire veut acheter toutes sortes d'articles. Vous dites que ce n'est pas nécessaire et vous donnez des raisons *(reasons)*.

A. Révision: Le pronom y

The object pronoun **y** replaces a noun or noun phrases introduced by a preposition of place (**à, en, dans, chez, sur, sous,** etc.). It is the equivalent of *there*.

Tu vas **au supermarché**?	Oui, j'**y** vais.
Tu es passé **chez le pharmacien**?	Non, je n'**y** suis pas passé.

➡ **Y** is also used to replace **à** + NOUN referring to a THING.

Tu vas participer **au championnat**?   Oui, je vais **y** participer.

> **Verbs used with à**
>
> **jouer à**
> **participer à**
> **croire à**
> **penser à**
> **assister à**
> **faire attention à**

B. Révision: Le pronom en

The object pronoun **en** replaces **du, de la, de l', des, de** + NOUN. It is the equivalent of *some, any*.

Tu prends **des vitamines**?	Non, je n'**en** prends pas.
Tu as acheté **du dentifrice**?	Oui, j'**en** ai acheté.

➡ **En** is also used to replace:

- the preposition **de** + NOUN

Tu viens **de la pharmacie**?	Oui, j'**en** viens.
Tu as besoin **de ton stylo à bille**?	Non, je n'**en** ai pas besoin.

- a noun introduced by **un** or **une**

Tu as **une guitare**?   Oui, j'**en** ai **une**.

- a noun introduced by a NUMBER

Marc a acheté **deux cartes postales**.   Moi, j'**en** ai acheté **trois**.

> **Verbs used with de**
>
> **venir de**
> **parler de**
> **avoir besoin de**
> **avoir envie de**
> **avoir peur de**

- **de** + NOUN after an expression of quantity

Tu as **beaucoup d'argent**?	Non, je n'**en** ai pas **beaucoup**.
Vous voulez **deux kilos d'oranges**?	Oui, j'**en** veux **deux kilos**.
Combien de rouleaux de diapos as-tu pris?	J'**en** ai pris **un rouleau**.

➡ Note the use of **en** with **il y a** and **donnez-moi**.

Il y a une papeterie dans mon quartier.	Il y **en** a une.
Donnez-moi deux blocs de papier.	Donnez-m'**en** deux.

RAPPEL!

The pronouns **y** and **en** come BEFORE the verb, <u>except</u> in affirmative commands. Compare:

Tu vas à la papeterie?	Tu **y** vas?	Vas-**y**.
Tu achètes des enveloppes?	Tu **en** achètes?	Achètes-**en**.

1 La vie de star

Vous interviewez un(e) star de cinéma français(e) sur sa vie. Votre partenaire va vous répondre affirmativement en donnant des précisions et en utilisant **y** ou **en**.

> **Vous allez souvent au concert?**
>
> **Oui, j'y vais souvent avec mes amis.**

▶ aller souvent au concert? (avec mes amis)

1. aller au cinéma? (de temps en temps)
2. jouer au tennis? (pendant les vacances)
3. faire du jogging? (tous les matins)
4. faire attention à votre santé? (tout le temps)
5. boire de l'eau minérale? (à tous les repas)
6. manger des fruits? (beaucoup)
7. donner des interviews? (de temps en temps)
8. participer au festival de Cannes? (tous les ans)
9. avoir une voiture de sport? (une)
10. avoir des admirateurs? (beaucoup)
11. avoir besoin d'encouragement? (souvent)

2 Les courses

Vous passez les vacances dans un petit village de Normandie. Votre partenaire a fait les courses ce matin. Demandez-lui ce qu'il/elle a acheté.

▶ — **Tu es allé(e) à la papeterie?**
— **Oui, j'y suis allé(e).**
— **Tu as acheté des enveloppes?**
— **Oui, j'en ai acheté un paquet.**

1. • à la poste
   • des timbres
   • vingt

2. • chez le photographe
   • des diapos
   • deux rouleaux

3. • à la pharmacie
   • du shampooing
   • une bouteille

4. • au marché
   • des tomates
   • deux kilos

5. • chez le crémier
   • des oeufs
   • une douzaine

6. • à la boulangerie
   • des croissants
   • six

3 Camping

Maintenant vous allez faire du camping. Votre partenaire vous demande ce qu'il/elle doit prendre. Répondez-lui en lui donnant des quantités. Soyez logique!

> ▶ **Je prends des allumettes?**
>
> **Oui, prends-en une boîte.**

(deux boîtes)

QUOI?	QUELLE QUANTITÉ?
du dentifrice	un paquet
de la lessive	un tube
du shampooing	une boîte
des coton-tiges	une bouteille
de la ficelle	une pelote
de l'ouate	un rouleau
des pansements	
du Sopalin	
des allumettes	
du papier hygiénique	

C. Expressions indéfinies de quantité

Indefinite expressions of quantity refer to an undetermined number of people or things.

ADJECTIVE (+ NOUN)		PRONOUN	
quelques . . .	some, a few	**quelques-uns** **quelques-unes** }	some, a few
un(e) autre . . . **d'autres . . .**	another other, some other	**un(e) autre** **d'autres**	another one others, some others, other ones
plusieurs . . .	several	**plusieurs**	several
certain(e)s . . .	some, several	**certain(e)s**	some, certain ones
la plupart de . . .	most of	**la plupart**	most (of them)

The above expressions of quantity can be used either as subjects or as objects.

ADJECTIVE	PRONOUN
SUBJECT	
Quelques amies sont venues. **Plusieurs** lettres sont arrivées ce matin.	**Quelques-unes** sont venues. **Plusieurs** sont arrivées ce matin.
OBJECT	
J'ai invité **quelques** amis. Nous avons visité **plusieurs** monuments.	J'en ai invité **quelques-uns**. Nous en avons visité **plusieurs**.

➡ Note that **en** is used with the indefinite <u>pronouns</u> of quantity when these expressions are the direct object of the verb.

4 S'il te plaît!

Vous êtes chez votre partenaire. Il/elle vous offre à nouveau certaines choses.
Acceptez-les (ou refusez, en expliquant pourquoi).

▶ une limonade
 — **Tu veux une limonade?**
 — **Oui, donne-m'en une autre,**
  s'il te plaît.
  (Non, merci, je n'ai pas soif.)

1. un hamburger
2. un jus d'orange
3. une part de pizza
4. un sandwich
5. une tasse de café
6. un thé glacé

5 **Un après-midi à Montréal**

Vous êtes à Montréal avec votre partenaire. Cet après-midi, vous êtes resté(e) à votre hôtel, mais votre partenaire est sorti(e). Demandez-lui ce qu'il/elle a fait.

▶ acheter des souvenirs (quelques-uns)
1. prendre des photos (quelques-unes)
2. écrire des lettres (quelques-unes)
3. envoyer des cartes postales (plusieurs)
4. acheter un guide de la ville (un autre)
5. acheter des CD (plusieurs)
6. rencontrer des jeunes Canadiens (quelques-uns)

▶ **Tu as acheté des souvenirs?**

Oui, j'en ai acheté quelques-uns.

À chacun son

style

D ans notre apparence personnelle, nous sommes tous un peu différents. Chacun peut choisir son style de vêtements, son style de chaussures et son style de coiffure.

Quel style de coiffure demanderiez-vous à votre coiffeur si vous étiez en France? Aimeriez-vous avoir . . .

les cheveux en brosse

les cheveux au carré

une raie sur le côté

un style punk

une frange sur le devant

des tresses très serrées

des mèches

une permanente

LE FRANÇAIS PRATIQUE

Au salon de coiffure

> Pouvez-vous me couper les cheveux?

> Oui, bien sûr.

JORDI COIFFURE

JORDI COIFFURE

Coiffure Hommes et Dames
Spécialiste des Enfants
Garçons et Filles

20 av de Breteuil
75007 Paris _ _ _ _ _ _ 01 45 51 47 05

ZINZIUS ALAIN

ALAIN ZINZIUS

Haute Coiffure Création
Visagiste Ouvrier de France 1982

108 av Gambetta
75020 Paris_ _ _ _ _ _ _ _ _ 01 40 30 55 57
1 r Paris (face au RER)
94340 Joinville le Pont_ _ _ _ _ 01 42 83 86 15

— **C'est votre tour**, monsieur (mademoiselle).

Pouvez-vous **me couper les cheveux**?

Est-ce que vous pouvez me faire

une coupe de cheveux *(haircut)*?
une coupe-brushing *(haircut and blow-dry)*?
un shampooing?
une permanente?
une mise en pli *(set)*?

— Comment est-ce que je vous coupe les cheveux?

Dégagez-les	**sur les côtés** *(on the sides).*
Coupez-les-moi courts	**sur le devant** *(in front).*
Laissez-les-moi longs	**sur le dessus** *(on top).*
Ne me les coupez pas trop courts	**derrière** *(in back).*

dégager to cut back, shorten (hair)

laisser to leave

---

1 **Chez le coiffeur** *(At the hairdresser)* —————

Vous êtes dans un salon de coiffure. Votre partenaire va jouer le rôle
du coiffeur (de la coiffeuse). Inventez votre dialogue.

Coiffeur(se): *Tell the client that it is his/her turn.*
   Client(e): Ask for a haircut.
Coiffeur(se): *Ask if the client wants something else (for example, a shampoo).*
   Client(e): Accept or refuse politely.
Coiffeur(se): *Ask how the client wants his/her hair cut.*
   Client(e): Tell the hairdresser how to cut your hair.

A. Révision: les pronoms **le**, **la**, **les** et **lui**, **leur**

LE, LA, LES

Le, la, les are direct-object pronouns.
They replace PEOPLE or THINGS.

Tu vois **cette fille** là-bas?	Oui, je **la** vois.
Tu vois **ces maisons**?	Oui, je **les** vois.

➡ Compare the use of **en** and **le, la, les**.

Tu achètes **le journal**?	Oui, je **l'**achète.
Tu achètes **du pain**?	Oui, j'**en** achète.

➡ In the passé composé, the past participle agrees with **le, la, les**, but not with **en**.

Tu as pris **la carte postale**?	Oui, je **l'**ai pris<u>e</u>.
Tu as pris **mes photos**?	Oui, je **les** ai pris<u>es</u>.
BUT: Tu as pris **des photos**?	Non, je n'**en** ai pas **pris**.

L'accord du participe passé

Pratique ▶ p.49

LUI, LEUR

Lui and **leur** are indirect-object pronouns.
They replace **à** + NOUN designating PEOPLE.

Tu as écrit **à tes cousins**?	Non, je ne **leur** ai pas écrit.

➡ Compare the use of **y** and **lui, leur**.

Tu as répondu **à Pauline**?	Oui, je **lui** ai répondu.
Tu as répondu **à cette lettre**?	Oui, j'**y** ai répondu.

➡ Note that **lui, leur** are not used with **penser**.

Tu penses **à tes amis**?	Oui, je pense **à eux**.

RAPPEL!

Object pronouns always come BEFORE the verb, <u>except</u> in affirmative commands.
Compare:

Je prends ces magazines?	Ne **les** prends pas.	Oui, prends-**les**.
Je téléphone à Christine?	Ne **lui** téléphone pas.	Oui, téléphone-**lui**.

C'EST TOI QUI L'AS INVITÉ?

OUI, MAIS JE LUI AVAIS DIT QUE CE N'ÉTAIT PAS UN BAL COSTUMÉ!

1 Au revoir!

Vous avez visité Genève avec vos amis. C'est bientôt *(soon)* le départ. Dites que vos amis ont fait les choses suivantes en répondant affirmativement aux questions. Utilisez le pronom qui convient (**l', les, lui, leur, en, y**).

▶ Catherine a acheté du parfum?　**Oui, elle en a acheté.**

1. Julien a fait ses valises?
2. Pauline a téléphoné à sa mère?
3. Pierre est allé à l'agence de voyages?
4. Marc et Éric ont acheté leurs billets?
5. Claire a trouvé son passeport?
6. Thomas a pris des photos?
7. Isabelle a acheté des souvenirs?
8. Antoine a dit au revoir à ses amis?
9. Alice a acheté un foulard?
10. Véronique a écrit plusieurs cartes postales?

2 Le week-end dernier

Demandez à votre partenaire s'il/si elle a fait l'une des choses suivantes le week-end dernier. Il/elle va répondre affirmativement ou négativement en utilisant le pronom qui convient (**l', les, lui, leur, en**).

▶ — **Est-ce que tu as écouté de la musique classique le week-end dernier?**
　— **Oui, j'en ai écouté. (Non, je n'en ai pas écouté.)**

- lire le journal du dimanche?
- regarder les bandes dessinées?
- acheter des vêtements?
- voir un film?
- voir tes voisins?
- téléphoner à ton copain/ta copine?
- ranger ta chambre?
- écouter de la musique classique?
- écouter du rap?
- faire du jogging?
- écrire à ta cousine?
- rendre visite à tes grands-parents?
- aider tes parents?
- ??

3 Pourquoi pas?

Demandez à votre partenaire s'il/si elle a fait les choses suivantes, et ensuite pourquoi pas. Il/elle va vous répondre avec l'excuse suggérée ou une autre excuse.

▶ inviter Pauline
　(elle est trop snob)

— **Tu as invité Pauline?**
— **Non, je ne l'ai pas invitée.**
— **Mais pourquoi est-ce que tu ne l'as pas invitée?**
— **Elle est trop snob.**

1. téléphoner à tes copains
   (ils ne sont pas chez eux)
2. laver ta voiture
   (elle n'était pas sale)
3. acheter de la limonade
   (je n'avais pas soif)
4. faire les courses
   (j'ai dîné au restaurant)
5. aller chez le coiffeur
   (je n'ai pas les cheveux longs)
6. écrire à Catherine
   (j'ai perdu son adresse)
7. prendre des photos
   (je n'avais pas mon appareil)
8. finir tes devoirs
   (j'avais mal à la tête)
9. tondre la pelouse
   (la tondeuse est cassée)
10. aller à la pharmacie
    (elle est fermée aujourd'hui)

4 L'assistant(e)

Vous êtes l'assistant(e) du président (de la présidente) d'une compagnie française. Demandez-lui si vous devez faire les choses suivantes. Votre partenaire va répondre affirmativement ou négativement.

▶ téléphoner à Madame Simon (oui)

1. téléphoner à Monsieur Lamy (non)
2. répondre à ces clients (oui)
3. copier ces documents (oui)
4. répondre à cette lettre (non)
5. écrire à Madame Susuki (oui)
6. inviter Monsieur Schmidt (non)
7. passer à la poste (oui)
8. acheter des timbres (oui)
9. envoyer ce chèque (non)
10. aller à la papeterie (oui)
11. commander du papier à lettres (oui)
12. acheter des enveloppes (non)
13. acheter votre billet d'avion (oui)
14. réserver une chambre d'hôtel (oui)
15. confirmer la réservation (non)

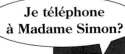

Je téléphone à Madame Simon?

Oui, téléphonez-lui!

B. L'ordre des pronoms

Sometimes a sentence may contain <u>two</u> object pronouns. Note the sequence of these pronouns in the following sentences:

DIRECT- AND INDIRECT-OBJECT PRONOUNS

le la les	before	lui leur	Je prête **mon vélo à Alice.**	Je **le lui** prête.
			Tu envoies **cette carte à tes cousins.**	Tu **la leur** envoies.
			Nous montrons **nos diapos à Éric.**	Nous **les lui** montrons.

➡ This order is also used in affirmative commands.

Montre **la photo à Catherine.**   Montre-**la-lui.**

me te nous vous	before	le la les	Vous **me** donnez **le journal.**	Vous **me le** donnez.
			Le coiffeur **te** coupe **les cheveux.**	Il **te les** coupe.
			Paul **nous** vend **sa chaîne-stéréo.**	Paul **nous la** vend.
			Sylvie **vous** prête **ses CD.**	Elle **vous les** prête.

➡ Note the order in affirmative commands:

le la les	before	moi nous	Donne-**moi ton adresse.**	Donne-**la-moi.**
			Montre-**nous ces photos.**	Montre-**les-nous.**

OBJECT PRONOUNS AND **Y, EN**

le/la/les lui/leur me/te/nous/vous	before	y en	J'amène **mes amis au concert.**	Je **les y** amène.
			Je donne **des conseils à Marc.**	Je **lui en** donne.
			Alice **me** prête **de l'argent.**	Elle **m'en** prête.
			L'employé **nous** vend **des timbres.**	Il **nous en** vend.

➡ This order is also used in affirmative commands.

Donne **des timbres à Catherine.**   Donne-**lui-en.**
Donne-**moi du papier à lettres.**   Donne-**m'en.**

ALLONS PLUS LOIN

When two pronouns are used with a reflexive verb, the reflexive pronoun always comes first.

Je m'achète des vêtements.   Je **m'en** achète.
Alice s'est coupé les cheveux.   Elle **se les** est coupés.

Comment est ce que je vous les coupe?

5 Conversation

Demandez à votre partenaire s'il/si elle fait les choses suivantes. Il/elle va répondre affirmativement ou négativement.

▶ prêter ton portable à ton copain?
  — **Est-ce que tu prêtes ton portable à ton copain?**
  — **Oui, je le lui prête. (Non, je ne le lui prête pas.)**

1. prêter de l'argent à tes copains?
2. montrer ton journal *(diary)* à ta copine?
3. montrer tes notes *(grades)* à tes parents?
4. emprunter la tondeuse à tes voisins?
5. demander des conseils à ton prof?
6. donner de l'argent aux pauvres?
7. dire la vérité à tes amis?
8. couper les cheveux à ton petit frère?

6 Échanges

Votre partenaire va vous demander de lui prêter une des choses suivantes. Négociez un échange avec lui/elle. Votre partenaire va accepter ou refuser.

▶ — **Dis, prête-moi <u>ton baladeur</u>.**
  — **D'accord, je vais te le prêter si tu me prêtes ta bicyclette.**
  — **Bon, je vais te la prêter.**
      (Non, je ne veux pas te la prêter.)

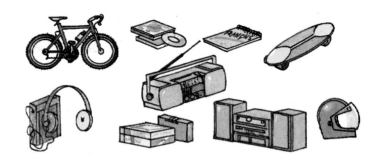

7 Oui ou non?

Répondez aux questions suivantes, affirmativement ou négativement. Utilisez les pronoms **lui/leur** et **en**. Soyez logique!

▶ Est-ce qu'on donne de l'aspirine à un malade?
    Oui, on lui en donne.

1. Est-ce qu'on donne des allumettes aux enfants?
2. Est-ce qu'on parle de ses problèmes à ses amis?
3. Est-ce qu'on offre du chocolat à une personne qui est au régime *(on a diet)*?
4. Est-ce qu'on demande des conseils à ses parents?
5. Est-ce qu'on raconte des histoires de fantômes à une personne impressionnable?
6. Est-ce qu'on envoie des cartes de voeux *(season's greetings)* à ses amis?
7. Est-ce qu'on donne un bon pourboire à un serveur désagréable?
8. Est-ce qu'on sert de la viande à un végétarien?
9. Est-ce qu'on écrit des poèmes à une personne qu'on aime?

8 À Paris

Vous travaillez à Paris dans l'un des endroits suivants. Offrez certains services à votre partenaire, qui va accepter. (S'il/si elle refuse, votre partenaire va vous donner une explication.)

▶ — **Je vous apporte le menu?**
  — **Oui, apportez-le-moi, s'il vous plaît.**
      (Non, pas maintenant! Je vais attendre un peu.)

AU RESTAURANT
• apporter le menu
• décrire le plat du jour
• donner du pain
• servir du café

CHEZ LE COIFFEUR
• faire un shampooing
• couper les cheveux très courts
• mettre du gel

DANS UN MAGASIN DE DISQUES
• montrer nos nouveaux CD
• faire un paquet
• donner un sac en plastique

À L'HÔTEL
• montrer votre chambre
• monter vos bagages
• préparer votre note *(bill)*
• commander un taxi

Services

> Est-ce que vous pouve
> réparer ces chaussure

> Oui, bien sûr.

> Quand est-ce que
> ce sera prêt?

> D'ici
> une semaine.

Chez le cordonnier
(At the shoe repair shop)

— Est-ce que vous pouvez | **réparer** ces chaussures?
                     | **changer les talons** *(heels)*?

réparer *to fix*

— Quand est-ce que **ce sera prêt** *(when will it be ready)*?
    Tout à l'heure! *(In a little while!)*
    Dans deux jours.
    D'ici une semaine. *(A week from now.)*

> Est-ce que vous pouvez
> enlever cette tache?

Chez le teinturier *(At the cleaners)*

— Est-ce que vous pouvez | **nettoyer** cette veste?
                          | **laver** ces chemises?
                          | **repasser** ce pantalon?
                          | **enlever** cette tache
                          | *(spot, stain)*?

repasser *to iron*
enlever *to remove*

> Oui,
> mademoiselle.

Chez le photographe

> Est-ce que vous pouvez
> développer ces photos?

— Est-ce que vous pouvez **développer ces photos**?
Est-ce que vous pouvez aussi **réparer mon appareil-photo**?

    Oui, quel est le problème?
    Qu'est-ce qu'il y a?
    Qu'est-ce qui ne marche pas?

> Oui, monsieur

Le flash | **est cassé.**
         | **ne fonctionne pas.**
         | **ne marche pas.**

marcher *to work,*
to function

La pile est **usée** *(worn out)*.

le flash
le téléobjectif
le bouton
la lentille
l'objectif
le filtre

1 Réparations

Vous avez un objet à réparer et vous allez chez un spécialiste. Avec votre partenaire, choisissez un des objets suivants et composez le dialogue correspondant.

▶ — S'il vous plaît, est-ce que vous pouvez réparer __ma montre__?
   — Oui, bien sûr. Quel est le problème?
   — __Le ressort__ *(spring)* est cassé.
   — Bon, je vais voir ça.

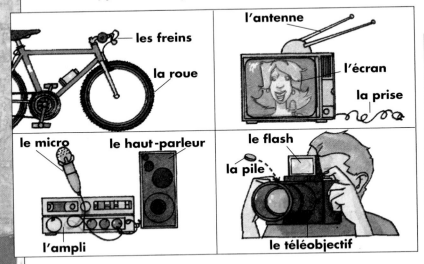

- __mon appareil-photo__
  le flash? la pile? le téléobjectif?
- __ma chaîne stéréo__
  le micro? l'ampli?
  le haut-parleur?
- __ma télé__
  l'antenne? l'écran?
  la prise?
- __mon vélo__
  les freins? la roue?

2 Créa-dialogue

Lisez le dialogue «Chez l'électricien». Puis, avec votre partenaire, choisissez une autre boutique et préparez un nouveau dialogue. Par exemple, vous allez chez le teinturier, chez le photographe, ou chez le cordonnier.

«CHEZ L'ÉLECTRICIEN»

— Bonjour, madame. Est-ce que vous pouvez changer cette prise *(plug)*?	• *Use the appropriate form of address.* • *Ask for a service available at the shop.*
— Bien sûr, monsieur. Ce sera tout?	• *Use the appropriate form of address.*
— Non, est-ce que vous pouvez aussi réparer cette lampe?	• *Ask for another service.*
— D'accord, je vais faire ça.	
— Quand est-ce que ce sera prêt?	
— D'ici dix jours.	• *Give the number of days from now.*
— Ce n'est pas possible avant?	
— Si, peut-être. Revenez lundi prochain.	• *Give another day closer in time.*

A. La construction **faire** + infinitif

Note the use of the construction **faire** + INFINITIVE.

Je **fais développer** les photos.	*I **am having** the pictures **developed**.*
Tu **as fait réparer** ton vélo.	*You **had** your bicycle **fixed**.*
Nous allons **faire laver** notre voiture.	*We are going **to have** our car **washed**.*

> The construction **faire** + INFINITIVE is used to describe actions that people have <u>done by someone else.</u>

➡ In this construction, it is the verb **faire** that is used:
- in the negative

  Je fais réparer ma télé.   Je **ne fais pas** réparer mon portable.
- with pronouns

  Ma montre était cassée.   Je **l'**ai fait réparer.
  Ta voiture est sale.   Fais-**la** laver.

> The construction **faire** + INFINITIVE is also used to describe actions that we make or have other people do.

  Le professeur **fait étudier** les élèves.   *The teacher **makes** the students **study**.*

Faire + infinitif

Pratique ▶ 🗒️ p.51

ALLONS PLUS LOIN
- The construction **faire** + INFINITIVE is used in certain expressions:

  faire cuire *to cook*   **faire frire** *to fry*   **faire bouillir** *to boil*

  Also: **faire marcher** *to operate (equipment)*   **faire voir** *to show*
- Note the use of **se faire** + INFINITIVE to describe actions that people are having done for themselves.

  Je vais **me faire couper les cheveux**.   *I am going **to have my hair cut**.*

1 Services

Demandez à votre partenaire pourquoi il va à certains endroits. Il/elle va répondre logiquement.

▶ — **Tu vas à la teinturerie?**
— **Oui, je vais faire nettoyer mon blazer.**

OÙ?
• à la station-service
• chez le mécanicien
• à la teinturerie
• chez le photographe
• à la laverie *(laundry)*
• à la boutique d'appareils électriques
• chez le serrurier *(locksmith)*
• chez le vétérinaire

POURQUOI?
• réparer mon vélo ✓
• réparer mon séchoir
• changer cette serrure *(lock)* ✓
• nettoyer mon blazer ✓
• laver mon linge
• laver ma voiture ✓
• vacciner mon chien ✓
• développer mes diapos ✓

2 Que faire?

Votre partenaire vous explique certains problèmes. Dites-lui ce qu'il/elle doit faire.

▶ — **Ma montre est cassée.**
— **Fais-la réparer.**

PROBLÈMES
• Ma montre est cassée.
• Ma veste a une tache *(spot)*.
• Mes cheveux sont trop longs.
• Mon baladeur ne marche pas.
• Les piles de ma radio cassette sont usées *(worn out)*.
• Mon chien n'a pas eu ses piqûres *(shots)*.

QUE FAIRE?
changer . . .
couper . . .
nettoyer . . .
réparer . . .
vacciner . . .

«Ma montre est cassée.»

«Mes cheveux sont trop longs.»

«Mon baladeur ne marche pas.»

«Les piles de ma radio cassette sont usées.»

«Ma veste a une tache.»

«Mon chien n'a pas eu ses piqûres.»

Langue et communication 169

LECTURE

Une histoire de cheveux

Comédie en 4 scènes

AVANT DE LIRE

Le titre et le sous-titre de ce texte indiquent qu'il s'agit° d'une histoire plutôt humoristique avec pour sujet un événement assez ordinaire de la vie quotidienne: une coupe de cheveux.

Pour vous mettre dans l'esprit de cette histoire, répondez aux questions suivantes.

- Est-ce que vous attachez beaucoup d'importance à votre coiffure? Pourquoi ou pourquoi pas?
- Quel style de coiffure préférez-vous?
- Est-ce que vos parents sont toujours d'accord avec ce style? (Si non, pourquoi pas?)
- Quel coiffeur vous coupe les cheveux habituellement? Combien de fois par an (ou par mois) y allez-vous?
- Si votre coiffeur était indisponible° un jour, est-ce que vous permettriez à quelqu'un d'autre (un copain ou une copine, votre soeur ou votre frère, votre mère ou votre père…) de vous couper les cheveux? Pourquoi ou pourquoi pas?

il s'agit de *it is about* **indisponible** *unavailable*

Alain
MAITRE BARBIER COIFFEUR
"SALON MUSEE"
DU MARDI AU SAMEDI DE 9H15 A 19H
8 rue St Saint-Claude 01 42 77 55 80
75003 Paris

MARC DELACRE
Coiffure et Soins Esthétiques
Pour Hommes
Soins Cheveux Corps Visage
Manucure Pédicure Médicale
UV, Sauna, Hammam
Restaurant, Cireur, Voiturier
17 av George V
75008 Paris.......................01 40 99 77 70

Une histoire de cheveux

Comédie en 4 scènes

Scène 1

Patrick, 15 ans, a un problème commun à tous les jeunes de son âge.
Il n'a jamais assez d'argent. Alors, de temps en temps, il en demande à son père.
Malheureusement, aujourd'hui, celui-ci n'est pas d'humeur généreuse.

—Dis, Papa, tu peux me donner un peu d'argent?

5 —Mais, je t'ai donné vingt euros la semaine dernière.

—S'il te plaît, papa, c'est la dernière fois que je t'en demande.

—N'insiste pas, Patrick, la dernière fois, c'était la dernière
fois…

Le père de Patrick examine son fils de plus près.

10 —Dis donc, Patrick, tourne-toi un peu.

Patrick se retourne.

— Tu as les cheveux drôlement longs.

— Mais Papa, c'est la mode.

— Eh bien, moi, je n'aime pas tellement la mode des cheveux longs…

15 Il faut absolument que tu ailles chez le coiffeur.

— Tu oublies que je n'ai pas d'argent.

— Ah oui, c'est vrai. Combien est-ce que ça coûte, une coupe de cheveux?

— Dans les° quinze euros.

— Bon. Eh bien, voilà. Je te donne vingt euros, mais je ne veux plus voir

20 cette horrible tignasse!

— Merci, papa, à ce soir!

dans les = approximativement

une tignasse

Mots utiles	
l'humeur	*mood*
se tourner	*to turn around*
de près	*closely, from close up*
de temps en temps	*from time to time*

Langage familier
drôlement = vraiment
tellement = beaucoup

Avez-vous compris?

1. Qu'est-ce que Patrick demande à son père?
2. Pourquoi est-ce que le père refuse?
3. Qu'est-ce qu'il remarque quand il examine Patrick de près?
4. Qu'est-ce qu'il demande à son fils de faire?
5. Combien d'argent lui donne-t-il?

Anticipons un peu!

Selon vous, est-ce que Patrick va aller chez le coiffeur ou non? Expliquez pourquoi.

Scène 2

25   Patrick prend le billet de vingt euros que son
père a sorti de son portefeuille, puis il met son
blouson et quitte la maison. En route, il
rencontre Béatrice, une nouvelle élève du lycée
où il va. C'est une grande fille brune avec de
30   merveilleux yeux bleus. Patrick la trouve très
sympa et très mignonne, mais jusqu'ici, il n'a pas
eu vraiment l'occasion de lui parler.

— Salut, Béatrice! Ça va?

— Oui, ça va.

35   — Dis donc, où est-ce que tu vas comme ça?

— Je vais au ciné.

— Qu'est-ce que tu vas voir?

— Le dernier film de Depardieu. Il paraît° que c'est génial... Si tu
veux, on peut y aller ensemble.

40   Patrick voudrait bien accepter la proposition de Béatrice.
Malheureusement, il y a cette maudite° coupe de cheveux.

— Euh, c'est que je dois aller chez le coiffeur.

— Mais, pourquoi? Je t'aime bien comme ça avec tes cheveux longs...

Patrick rougit.

45   — Malheureusement, j'ai un père qui préférerait me voir avec les
cheveux courts.

— Ah bon, je comprends... Écoute, j'ai une idée!

— Quoi donc?

— On peut aller au ciné, et puis après, on peut aller chez moi. Mon
50   père est coiffeur. Il va te faire une coupe super... Et, en plus, tu
économiseras ton argent.

— Ben, oui, c'est une idée! Tu es bien sûre que ton père sera chez
toi tout à l'heure?

— Absolument! C'est son jour de congé aujourd'hui.

55   — Alors, dans ce cas, j'accepte!

il paraît que = on dit que   **maudite** *darned*

Mots utiles

un jour de congé	*day off*
rougir	*to blush*
jusqu'ici	*until now*
tout à l'heure	*in a while*

Avez-vous compris?

1. Qui est Béatrice et qu'est-ce que Patrick pense d'elle?
2. Pourquoi Patrick n'accepte-t-il pas immédiatement la proposition de Béatrice?
3. Selon vous, pourquoi Patrick rougit-il?
4. Quelle solution Béatrice propose-t-elle à Patrick?

Anticipons un peu!

Selon vous, qu'est-ce qui va se passer après le film?

Scène 3

60   Patrick et Béatrice sont allés au cinéma. Après le film, Patrick a invité Béatrice dans un petit restaurant italien où ils ont mangé une pizza. Ensuite, ils sont allés chez Béatrice. Là, ils ont une mauvaise surprise: il n'y a personne à la maison. Patrick s'inquiète.

65   — Où est ton père?

       — Je ne sais pas! Il a dû faire un tour en ville avec ma mère. Ne t'inquiète pas. Je suis sûre qu'ils rentreront bientôt.

    Une heure passe, et toujours personne. Finalement, le téléphone sonne. C'est la mère de Béatrice qui lui dit de ne pas l'attendre. Elle
70 et son mari sont invités à dîner chez des amis. Ils ne vont pas rentrer avant onze heures. Béatrice se rend compte du problème.

       — Dis, Patrick, mes parents ne vont pas rentrer ce soir.

       — Et ma coupe de cheveux?

       — T'en fais pas! C'est moi qui vais te les couper.

75   — Comment? Tu sais couper les cheveux, toi?

       — Ben oui, tu sais, j'ai souvent regardé mon père.

    Patrick n'est pas très rassuré, mais il n'a pas le choix. Il est bien obligé d'accepter l'offre de Béatrice.

    Béatrice va chercher les ciseaux de son père. Elle demande à Patrick
80 de s'asseoir sur un tabouret. Puis, elle commence à lui couper les cheveux. Clic, une mèche par ci! Clac, une mèche par là. Clic! Clac! Clic! Clic! Il est bien évident que Béatrice n'a jamais coupé de cheveux de sa vie et le résultat est un véritable désastre. Elle a beau° passer° de l'eau et du gel fixatif sur les cheveux de Patrick, elle n'arrive pas à masquer
85 les échelles qu'elle a faites de tous les côtés.

    Patrick se regarde dans la glace. Il comprend alors l'ampleur° de la catastrophe.

       — Mon Dieu, qu'est-ce que je vais faire?

    Béatrice essaie de le rassurer.

90   — Écoute, c'est pas si mal que ça! Mets-toi un peu dans l'obscurité°... Non, ce n'est pas trop mal. Un conseil: quand tu seras chez toi, ne te mets pas trop près de la lumière, et personne ne verra rien.

    Mais Patrick n'écoute pas. Il prend son blouson et sort de chez
95 Béatrice, très inquiet...

Mots utiles	
un côté	side
un désastre	= une catastrophe
la lumière	light
arriver à	to manage to
sonner	to ring

Langage familier
t'en fais pas = ne t'inquiète pas

un tabouret

une mèche

des échelles

elle a beau = c'est en vain qu'elle essaie de
passer = mettre
ampleur *extent*
l'obscurité = un endroit où il fait noir

Avez-vous compris?

1. Pourquoi est-ce que Patrick s'inquiète?
2. Qu'est-ce que la mère de Béatrice annonce à sa fille quand elle lui téléphone?
3. Qu'est-ce que Béatrice fait pour résoudre le problème de Patrick?
4. Comment réussit-elle dans ce projet? Expliquez.
5. Qu'est-ce qu'elle conseille à Patrick de faire pour ne pas être trop visible?

Anticipons un peu!

Selon vous, quelle va être la réaction du père de Patrick quand il va voir son fils? Est-ce qu'il va être heureux? furieux? perplexe? Expliquez pourquoi.

Scène 4

Vingt minutes après, Patrick arrive chez lui. 100
Il a l'air vraiment pitoyable. Sa mère ne peut
pas s'empêcher de rire.

— Mon pauvre Patrick! Tu as l'air d'un
chat qui est tombé dans l'eau...
Qui est-ce qui t'a coupé les cheveux? 105
Allez, dis-moi la vérité.

Patrick hésite un peu. Puis, il raconte à sa
mère ce qui s'est passé.
Celle-ci essaie de le consoler.

—Tu as de la chance! Ton père n'est pas encore rentré! En 110
attendant qu'il rentre, je vais essayer d'arranger cela!

Elle va dans la salle de bains chercher la tondeuse qu'elle utilisait
quand Patrick était petit. Puis elle commence l'opération... En cinq
minutes, elle a complètement tondu le crâne de Patrick.

— C'est un peu court, mais au moins ça peut passer... 115

la tondeuse

Puis elle va ranger la tondeuse pendant que Patrick va se regarder
dans la glace.

— J'ai la boule à zéro! Qu'est-ce que mes copains vont penser
de moi?

— Ils vont trouver ça très bien. Je suis sûre que tu vas lancer 120
une nouvelle mode... Tiens, voilà ton père.

le crâne

Le père de Patrick vient en effet de rentrer. Il regarde Patrick avec
surprise.

— Bravo, mon garçon! Tu as beaucoup de courage... Je te
félicite! Tiens, pour te récompenser, je vais t'emmener au 125
cinéma ce soir. Est-ce que tu veux aller voir le dernier film de
Depardieu? Il paraît que c'est très bon!

— Merci, Papa, ...mais j'ai des devoirs à faire!

— Comme tu veux! Et excuse-moi d'avoir été un peu brusque
avec toi cet après-midi. 130

avoir la boule à
zéro

Mots utiles

arranger	to fix
s'empêcher de	to stop, prevent oneself from
lancer	to launch
récompenser	to reward
rire *	to laugh
tondre	to clip very short
pitoyable	pitiful

Avez-vous compris?

1. Quelle est la réaction de la mère de Patrick quand elle voit son fils?
2. Qu'est-ce qu'elle fait pour aider Patrick?
3. Quel est le résultat de cette action?
4. Quelle est la réaction du père de Patrick?
5. Qu'est-ce qu'il propose à son fils?
6. Qu'est-ce que Patrick répond à l'invitation de son père? Quelle est la véritable raison de son refus?

EXPRESSION ORALE

■ Dramatisation

En petits groupes, préparez une lecture dramatique de cette histoire. Chaque groupe présentera une scène.

- D'abord, choisissez un narrateur et distribuez les autres rôles.
- Pendant les parties «narratives», les acteurs feront les gestes et montreront les émotions indiquées.
- Pendant les dialogues, chaque acteur lira son texte avec beaucoup d'expression.

■ Situations

Avec votre partenaire, choisissez l'une des situations suivantes. Composez le dialogue correspondant et jouez-le en classe.

1. Au téléphone

Le soir, après le dîner, Béatrice téléphone à Patrick pour lui demander ce qui est arrivé quand il est rentré chez lui. Patrick le lui explique.

Les rôles: Béatrice, Patrick

2. En classe

Le lendemain, un(e) camarade de classe de Patrick est très étonné(e) de voir son ami avec «la boule à zéro». Il/Elle lui demande ce qui s'est passé. Patrick lui répond. (Patrick peut lui dire la vérité ou bien il peut inventer une histoire complètement différente.)

Les rôles: le/la camarade de classe, Patrick

3. La nouvelle mode

Maintenant, Patrick est très fier de sa nouvelle coiffure. Il explique à un autre copain les avantages d'avoir «la boule à zéro» et il essaie de le convaincre de faire la même chose. Le copain n'est pas tellement convaincu.

Les rôles: Patrick, le copain

EXPRESSION ÉCRITE

■ Imaginons un peu

Quelle va être la réaction des copains de Patrick quand celui-ci ira au lycée demain matin? Qu'est-ce que Patrick va leur dire? À vous d'écrire la Scène 5.

■ Page de journal

Imaginez que vous êtes Patrick ou Béatrice. Écrivez une page ou deux dans votre journal intime (diary) où vous ferez un résumé des événements de la journée.

INTERLUDE CULTUREL

• *Histoire de la chanson française* •

Un proverbe français dit que «tout finit par des chansons». On pourrait° dire aussi que tout a commencé par une chanson. L'histoire de la chanson française est en effet un peu l'histoire de France. La première grande oeuvre° littéraire française date du douzième siècle.° C'était une chanson: *La Chanson de Roland*.

Troubadour du Moyen Âge

Au Moyen Âge,° les **«troubadours»** allaient de cour° en cour en chantant des poèmes qu'ils composaient. Sous **Louis XIV**, les soldats allaient à la guerre en chantant des chansons comme «Malbrough s'en va-t-en guerre»° ou «Auprès° de ma blonde». En 1789, les Français ont fait la Révolution en chantant «Ça ira!»° Pendant la guerre de 1940, le «Chant des partisans» était le cri de ralliement° de la Résistance contre les troupes allemandes.

Mais la chanson n'est pas seulement un phénomène historique. C'est aussi un art populaire et un spectacle. Les premiers chanteurs populaires chantaient dans la rue. Ils recevaient un peu d'argent si leurs chansons étaient bonnes . . . et parfois un seau° d'eau sur la tête si leurs chansons étaient mauvaises.

Plus tard, la chanson a fait son entrée dans les **«cabarets»**. Le cabaret le plus célèbre était un cabaret de Montmartre qui s'appelait le «Chat noir». C'était un cabaret artistique où se réunissaient° les peintres, les musiciens, les poètes, les étudiants pour écouter les «chansonniers» de l'époque. Ces chansonniers chantaient surtout des chansons politiques, des chansons satiriques et parfois des chansons comiques.

Picasso *«Femme à la Mandoline»*

Le «Chat Noir», cabaret artistique à Montmartre.

pourrait *could* **oeuvre** *work* **siècle** *century* **au Moyen Âge** *in the Middle Ages* **cour** *court* **s'en va-t-en guerre** *goes off to war* **auprès de** *next to* **ça ira** *things will go well* **cri de ralliement** *rallying cry* **seau** *bucket* **se réunissaient** *used to get together*

Leurs grands succès
Édith Piaf:
La vie en rose
Mon légionnaire, Milord
Non, je ne regrette rien
Yves Montand:
Les feuilles mortes
Les grands boulevards
À Paris
Mon manège à moi
Georges Brassens:
Chanson pour l'Auvergnat
Une jolie fleur
Auprès de mon arbre
Les croquants
Jacques Brel:
Ne me quitte pas
Amsterdam
Le plat pays
Charles Aznavour:
La Mamma
Il faut savoir
Tu te laisses aller

Le grand public, lui, allait au «café-concert» ou au «music-hall». Dans les années 1930, la grande vedette° était **Joséphine Baker**, une danseuse noire américaine que tout le monde applaudissait quand elle chantait «J'ai deux amours: mon pays et Paris». Peu après, les Français ont découvert **Édith Piaf**, célèbre pour ses robes noires et sa voix terriblement poignante. Dans les années 1960, avec le développement de l'amplificateur et le succès de la guitare électrique, une nouvelle forme de chanson est apparue en France. C'était la chanson «yé-yé». Ce qui comptait,° ce n'était plus° le texte de la chanson, mais son rythme et surtout les contorsions du chanteur ou de la chanteuse sur scène° . . . La vedette de l'époque était **Johnny Hallyday** qui en quelques mois est devenue l'idole des jeunes Français. La chanson personnelle n'a cependant pas disparu. Elle est restée vivante° et variée avec **Georges Brassens**, l'anarchiste sympa, **Yves Montand**, le gentleman romantique, **Jacques Brel**, le poète venu du pays des brumes,° et **Charles Aznavour**, le petit bonhomme° à la voix grêle.°

Yves Montand   *Georges Brassens*   *Jacques Brel*   *Charles Aznavour*

■ *Les vedettes d'hier . . .*

Édith Piaf (1915-1963)

Édith Piaf a disparu il y a plus de quarante ans, mais sa voix est restée immortelle. Pour les millions de gens qui ont écouté cette voix vibrante d'émotion, elle est toujours la plus grande des chanteuses françaises. Édith Piaf a eu une enfance° misérable. Elle est née dans la rue et c'est dans la rue qu'elle a commencé à chanter pour gagner quelques pièces d'argent.° Un jour, alors° qu'elle chantait au coin° du boulevard MacMahon à Paris, le directeur d'un cabaret célèbre l'a entendue. Ému° par sa voix poignante, il l'a immédiatement engagée.° La phénoménale carrière de Piaf venait de commencer.

Le succès de ses chansons est facile à expliquer. Édith Piaf a chanté passionnément sa vie passionnée. Cette vie a été faite de moments heureux et surtout de moments tragiques. C'est donc avec une extraordinaire sincérité qu'Édith Piaf pouvait chanter le bonheur et le malheur, la fatalité et l'espoir,° l'amour merveilleux et l'amour désespéré. Quand Édith Piaf était sur scène, le public ne pouvait pas faire la différence entre sa vie et ses chansons.

---

vedette *star*   **ce qui comptait** *what counted*   **plus** *no longer*   **sur scène** *on the stage*   **vivante** *alive*   **brumes** *fog, mist*
bonhomme = *homme*   **grêle** *frail*   **enfance** *childhood*   **pièces d'argent** *coins*   **alors que** *while*   **au coin** *on the corner*
ému *moved*   **embauchée** *hired*   **espoir** *hope*

Joséphine Baker (1906–1975)

Joséphine Baker sur scène

Joséphine Baker était une artiste de music-hall. Pour des millions de Français, elle a aussi été une grande héroïne nationale. Pourtant Joséphine Baker n'était pas d'origine française, mais américaine. Elle est née dans une famille pauvre de la ville de Saint Louis dans le Missouri. À seize ans, elle est partie à New York pour faire une carrière dans le théâtre. Mais là, victime de la discrimination et du chômage,° elle n'a pas trouvé de travail.

Heureusement, un jour, la chance° lui a souri.° Un imprésario français l'a embauchée° pour faire une tournée° en France avec un groupe d'artistes noirs américains. Joséphine a fait ses débuts au Théâtre des Champs-Élysées en octobre 1925. Chacune° de ses entrées en scène était un triomphe. Pendant cette tournée, Joséphine Baker est tombée amoureuse° de Paris et Paris est tombé amoureux de «l'oiseau des îles». Joséphine Baker était la grande star du spectacle. Tous les soirs, elle donnait aux Français des leçons de danse. Bientôt, toute la France s'est mise° à danser le charleston. En quelques semaines, Joséphine Baker est devenue la reine° de Paris. Elle avait tout juste vingt ans.

Joséphine Baker a fait de nombreuses tournées à travers° l'Europe, mais c'est en France qu'elle se sentait chez elle.° En 1937, elle a décidé d'adopter la nationalité française. Pendant la guerre, fidèle° à son nouveau pays, elle a travaillé dans la Résistance. Pour ses services, elle a reçu les deux plus hautes décorations françaises: la Légion d'honneur et la Médaille de la Résistance. Pour la cérémonie, Joséphine Baker portait son uniforme de lieutenant de l'Armée de l'Air Française.

Après la guerre, Joséphine Baker a voyagé aux États-Unis. En butte° à nouveau à la discrimination, elle a décidé de se fixer° définitivement en France et de consacrer sa vie et sa fortune aux oeuvres° de charité. Elle a acheté un château pour accueillir° une douzaine d'orphelins de différentes races qu'elle avait adoptés et sauvés de la faim° et de la misère. C'était sa «tribu arc-en-ciel».° Ses ressources financières n'étant plus° suffisantes, elle est remontée sur scène à l'âge de 69 ans pour subvenir aux besoins° de sa famille d'adoption. À nouveau elle a connu le succès et c'est en plein triomphe qu'elle est morte en 1975.

Le jour de son enterrement,° la France entière a pris le deuil.° À Paris, une foule° immense a suivi le cortège funèbre.° Vingt et un coups de canon° ont été tirés° en son honneur: le plus grand adieu° français réservé à une femme américaine!

Joséphine Baker et sa «tribu arc-en-ciel»

---

chômage *unemployment* **chance** *luck* **souri** *smiled* **embauchée** *hired* **tournée** *tour* **chacune** *each one* **tombée amoureuse de** *fell in love with* **s'est mise à** *began to* **reine** *queen* **à travers** *across* **se sentait chez elle** *felt at home* **fidèle** = *loyale* **en butte à** *faced with* **se fixer** *to settle* **oeuvres** *works* **accueillir** *to provide shelter* **faim** *hunger* **arc-en-ciel** *rainbow* **n'étant plus** *no longer being* **subvenir aux besoins** *meet the needs* **enterrement** *funeral* **pris le deuil** *went into mourning* **foule** *crowd* **cortège funèbre** *funeral procession* **vingt et un coups de canon** *21-gun salute* **tirés** *fired* **adieu** *farewell*

■ . . . et vedettes d'aujourd'hui

Johnny Hallyday

Johnny Hallyday, le roi° du rock'n roll français, est entré en scène dans les années 1960. Comme° il avait un nom anglais, on pensait qu'il était américain. En réalité, il s'appelait Jean-Philippe Smet, était belge et ne parlait pas un mot d'anglais. Il portait un blouson de cuir, roulait° en grosse moto, jouait de la guitare et chantait «Je suis l'idole des jeunes».

Quarante ans plus tard, Johnny Hallyday n'a pas quitté la scène. Il est toujours° l'idole des jeunes . . . et des moins jeunes. Et quand il donne un grand concert public, 200 000 spectateurs viennent l'applaudir. Un record pour un chanteur français!

Jean-Jacques Goldman

Jean-Jacques Goldman est l'un des représentants du rock français moderne. Il compose lui-même ses chansons et les interprète à la guitare électrique. Il a commencé sa carrière avec un grand succès, «Quand la musique est bonne», et depuis vingt ans ses chansons sont généralement en tête du hit-parade français. Il a composé la musique du film **Astérix**.

Simple et généreux, Jean-Jacques Goldman participe souvent aux concerts organisés pour soutenir° les grandes causes humanitaires.

Lara Fabian

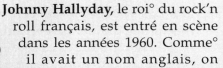

Lara Fabian a commencé sa carrière à quatorze ans, dans son pays natal, la Belgique. Elle est maintenant canadienne, et ses albums connaissent un vrai succès au Canada et en Europe. Elle interprète le personnage d'Esmeralda dans le film de Walt Disney, *Le Bossu° de Notre-Dame*.

Liane Foly

Liane Foly, lyonnaise, écrit elle-même beaucoup de ses chansons. Elle compose aussi une bonne partie des mélodies, et sa voix est à l'aise° dans une variété de styles: jazz, blues, music-hall. Elle incorpore aussi parfois le soul et le *rhythm 'n blues* à sa musique.

Pascal Obispo

Fils d'un joueur de football professionnel, Pascal Obispo préférait la musique et le sport à ses études quand il était au lycée. Devenu chanteur et compositeur, c'est aujourd'hui le grand représentant de la chanson romantique française moderne. En 2000, il a écrit une comédie musicale, *Les dix Commandements*, qui a connu un succès phénoménal.

---

roi *king* **comme** *since* **roulait** *drove* **toujours** *still* **soutenir** *to support* **lutte** *fight* **Le Bossu** *Hunchback*
à l'aise *comfortable*

▪ *La musique des jeunes* ▪

«De la musique avant toute chose» a dit un poète français.* Aujourd'hui, la musique fait partie de la vie de tout le monde, et en particulier des jeunes. À la maison, on peut écouter des CD sur sa chaîne hi-fi et télécharger de la musique sur son ordinateur. En voiture, on peut écouter la radio ou des cassettes. Quand on se promène dans la rue ou quand on fait du jogging, on peut écouter son baladeur.

Pour exprimer leur amour de la musique, les Français organisent chaque année une grande fête nationale appelée «la Fête de la Musique». Cette fête a lieu le vingt et un juin. Dans toutes les villes de France, il y a des concerts publics gratuits.° Ce jour-là, tous les Français sont dans la rue. Ils dansent, chantent, ou bien, ils écoutent la musique des orchestres° qui jouent un peu partout° dans les villes. Le slogan du jour est: «Pour la Fête de la Musique, faites de la musique.»

Quelle musique écoute-t-on en France quand on est jeune? En tête° du hit-parade, viennent les grandes vedettes de la chanson française: **Jean-Jacques Goldman, Lara Fabian, Liane Joly, Pascal Obispo**.... Mais à côté° de cette musique relativement traditionnelle existe une autre musique très populaire chez les jeunes. Cette musique reflète la réalité multiculturelle de la France d'aujourd'hui. La France est, en effet, une mosaïque de gens d'origines très différentes. À côté des Français de souche,° il y a aussi les immigrés venus d'autres pays européens, du Maghreb,** d'Afrique Noire, d'Asie...Chaque groupe a apporté sa culture et, en particulier, sa musique.

La musique française s'est enrichie de ces apports° et aussi des influences d'autres musiques populaires dans le monde: musiques américaine, anglaise, espagnole. . . . Elle est ainsi devenue une musique originale et variée.

▪ L'influence américaine: le rap

Le rap est né aux États-Unis dans les années 1980 et depuis il a fait le tour du monde. En France, il est représenté par **MC Solaar**. Ce «Monsieur Rap» est un Français d'origine tchadienne.*** Dans ses chansons, il exprime des messages sociaux positifs où il met en garde° les jeunes contre la violence et la délinquance.

MC Solaar, «Monsieur Rap»

▪ L'influence antillaise: le zouk

Le groupe Malavoi

Le zouk vient des **Antilles françaises** (**Martinique** et **Guadeloupe**). Pour les Antillais, «zouk» signifie «fête». Le zouk est donc une musique de fête où s'expriment la joie, l'humour et la fierté° d'être ce qu'on est.

La musique de zouk est typiquement antillaise. Expression de la culture martiniquaise et guadeloupéenne, elle représente la fusion d'éléments caraïbes, africains, français et espagnols. Dans un orchestre de zouk, le chanteur chante en créole. L'instrument principal est le tambour° ou la batterie° qui donne un rythme fort. Les autres instruments sont le synthétiseur, la basse, la guitare et parfois le piano.

Né il y a dix ans, le zouk est très populaire chez les jeunes Français. Il est représenté par des groupes comme *Kassav* (Martinique et Guadeloupe) et *Malavoi* (Martinique). Ces groupes ont fait connaître° le zouk en dehors° de la France et, en particulier, sur la côte est des États-Unis. Aujourd'hui, le zouk a un succès international.

---

* Paul Verlaine (1844-1896)

** Le Maghreb: l'Algérie, le Maroc, la Tunisie. Ces pays, en majorité arabes et musulmans, sont d'anciennes colonies ou protectorats français.

*** le Tchad: un pays d'Afrique

gratuits *free* **orchestres** *bands* **partout** *everywhere* **en tête** *on top* **à côté** *besides* **de souche** *native born* **les apports** *contributions* **met en garde** *warns* **la fierté** *pride* **le tambour** *drum* **la batterie** *drums* **fait connaître** *made known* **en dehors** *outside*

■ L'influence arabe: le raï

Le raï vient d'**Afrique du Nord** et plus particulièrement d'**Algérie**. Il exprime la mélancolie mais aussi la joie et l'espoir° des jeunes **Maghrébins**. C'est un peu leur «soul music». Le chanteur de raï chante en arabe et parfois en français ou même en anglais. Il est accompagné d'instruments traditionnels et aussi de guitare et de synthétiseur. Les grands représentants du Raï, **Khaled, Faudel** et **Cheb Mami,** sont Algériens ou d'origine algérienne.

Khaled

■ L'influence africaine: le rythme

Depuis une vingtaine d'années, **la musique africaine** a beaucoup de succès en France. Très variée, elle est représentée par un grand nombre de musiciens et de groupes qui viennent des différents pays de l'Afrique francophone.

1. **Touré Kunda** vient du **Sénégal** et chante en wolof,* sa langue maternelle,° et en français. Sa musique est traditionnelle et raffinée.

2. **Youssou N'Dour** vient aussi du **Sénégal**. Ses disques ont été produits aux États-Unis par le cinéaste américain, Spike Lee.

3. Le groupe **Soukous Stars** vient du **Zaïre** et joue de la musique africaine très rythmée avec beaucoup de tambour.

4. Les chanteuses du groupe **Zap Mama** sont d'origine européenne (belge) et africaine (zaïroise). Elles reprennent les chants traditionnels des peuples d'Afrique centrale. Dans d'autres chansons, elles mélangent° le français, l'espagnol, l'arabe et les langues africaines.

Manu Chao

■ MANU CHAO

Né en France de parents espagnols, Manu Chao a passé son enfance° dans la banlieue° parisienne. Influencé par le rock anglais, il a fondé° Mano Negra, un groupe de rock alternatif très populaire. Il a quitté ce groupe pour voyager en Espagne, en Amérique latine et en Afrique de l'Ouest. Là, il a enregistré les musiques locales sur un studio portable. Riche de ses expériences, il a décidé de chanter en solo.

Manu Chao écrit et chante en plusieurs langues (français, espagnol, anglais...). Ses chansons parlent de l'état du monde, des immigrants, de solidarité entre les peuples et de la lutte pour la vie°. Quelle que soit° la langue dans laquelle° il est exprimé°, ce message est universellement compris.

---

* la principale langue du Sénégal

espoir *hope* **la langue maternelle** *native language* **mélangent** *mix* **enfance** *childhood* **banlieue** *suburbs* **a fondé** *founded* **la lutte pour la vie** *struggle for survival* **quelle que soit** *whatever* **laquelle** *which* **exprimé** *expressed*

■ *La musique francophone en Amérique* ■

■ La chanson québécoise

Au Québec, chanter c'est affirmer son identité et sa culture, c'est exprimer sa fierté° d'être différent, c'est manifester° sa joie de vivre. Les interprètes de la chanson québécoise sont nombreux: **Gilles Vigneault**, le «poète de la chanson» qui chante son pays, **Isabelle Boulay**, **Garou** (de son vrai nom, **Pierre Garand**) et **Céline Dion**, qui est devenue une grande vedette° aux États-Unis.

Il faut également° mentionner les chanteurs acadiens du Nouveau Brunswick comme **Roch Voisine**, devenu une «idole» en France.

Céline Dion

■ La musique cajun

En pays cajun, on travaille dur,° mais on aime aussi la nourriture, la fête, la musique et la danse. Il n'est donc pas surprenant° que le grand événement de l'année soit le festival de musique cajun qui a lieu au mois de septembre à Lafayette.

Un orchestre joue du zydéco au festival

On vient de toute la région pour écouter la musique et danser aux sons° des orchestres de musique cajun et de zydéco.

La musique cajun est une musique de fête, très rythmée, où les musiciens utilisent des instruments traditionnels comme le violon, l'accordéon et la guitare, et où le chanteur mélange° l'anglais, le vieux français et le français moderne. Cette musique descend directement de la musique acadienne d'autrefois, mais au cours° des siècles et au contact de groupes ethniques différents, elle s'est enrichie d'éléments anglais, espagnols, indiens et africains. Aujourd'hui, grâce° à ses interprètes comme **Zachary Richard** et le groupe **Beausoleil**, la musique cajun connaît un regain° de popularité non seulement en Louisiane, mais dans tout le monde francophone.

Le zydéco ───────────

Le **zydéco** tire son nom du mot français «les haricots» et plus précisément du titre d'une chanson célèbre «Les haricots sont pas salés» composée par le légendaire **Clifton Chénier** (1925-1987). Le zydéco est né en Louisiane dans la région de Lafayette. C'est la forme moderne du **la-la**, musique de danse traditionnelle des Louisianais francophones d'origine africaine.

Clifton Chénier

Le zydéco est une variété de musique cajun, encore plus rythmée avec des accents de rock et de blues. Le chanteur chante en français ou en anglais et s'accompagne toujours d'un accordéon qui est l'instrument caractéristique du zydéco.

---

la fierté *pride* **manifester** = montrer **vedette** *star* **également** = aussi **dur** *hard* **surprenant** *surprising* **les sons** *beat* **mélange** *mixes* **au cours** *across* **grâce à** *thanks to* **regain** *renewal*

Une chanson: Mon pays

Mon pays ce n'est pas un pays c'est l'hiver
Mon jardin ce n'est pas un jardin c'est la plaine
Mon chemin ce n'est pas un chemin c'est la neige°
Mon pays ce n'est pas un pays c'est l'hiver

Dans la blanche cérémonie
Où la neige au vent° se marie
Dans ce pays de poudrerie°
Mon père a fait bâtir° maison
Et je m'en vais être fidèle°
À sa manière à son modèle
La chambre d'amis sera telle°
Qu'on viendra des autres saisons
Pour se bâtir à côté° d'elle

Mon pays ce n'est pas un pays c'est l'hiver
Mon refrain ce n'est pas un refrain c'est rafale°
Ma maison ce n'est pas une maison c'est froidure°
Mon pays ce n'est pas un pays c'est l'hiver

De mon grand pays solitaire
Je crie° avant que de me taire
À tous les hommes de la terre
Ma maison c'est votre maison
Entre mes quatre murs de glace°
Je mets mon temps et mon espace
À préparer le feu° la place
Pour les humains de l'horizon
Et les humains sont de ma race

Mon pays ce n'est pas un pays c'est l'envers°
D'un pays qui n'était ni pays ni patrie°
Ma chanson ce n'est pas ma chanson c'est ma vie
C'est pour toi que je veux posséder mes hivers

Gilles Vigneault

Dans les chansons qu'il compose, Gilles Vigneault exprime l'amour, l'amitié, la joie, l'attachement à son pays. Voici l'une des ses chansons les plus connues: *Mon pays.*

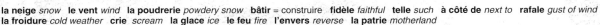

---

la neige *snow* **le vent** *wind* **la poudrerie** *powdery snow* **bâtir** = *construire* **fidèle** *faithful* **telle** *such* **à côté de** *next to* **rafale** *gust of wind*
la froidure *cold weather* **crie** *scream* **la glace** *ice* **le feu** *fire* **l'envers** *reverse* **la patrie** *motherland*

▪ *Et la musique classique?* ▪

Quand on pense à la musique classique, on pense généralement aux grands compositeurs allemands (Mozart, Beethoven . . .) ou italiens (Vivaldi, Verdi . . .). À tort,° on a tendance à oublier la musique classique française. Pourtant, au cours° des siècles, la France a produit de grands musiciens dont° les oeuvres° sont toujours au répertoire des plus grands orchestres du monde.

Aujourd'hui, la musique classique connaît un regain° de popularité chez les Français de tout âge et de toute condition sociale. Pour un quart d'entre° eux, c'est la musique qu'ils écoutent le plus souvent. Et, contrairement à ce qu'on peut penser, les jeunes ne lui sont pas hostiles. En fait, la musique classique vient au cinquième rang de leurs préférences musicales, après le rock et les chansons bien sûr, mais avant le jazz et la musique populaire.

Lully et le ballet

Le ballet est né en Italie, mais c'est en France qu'il s'est développé à l'époque de **Louis XIV** (1638-1715). Ce roi était un grand patron des arts et il aimait particulièrement la musique et la danse. Pour mettre en musique les comédies-ballets dans lesquelles° il jouait parfois lui-même, il a fait appel° à **Jean-Baptiste Lully** (1632-1687), un musicien d'origine italienne. Celui-ci a composé un grand nombre de ballets et d'opéras. C'est sous son influence que le ballet s'est codifié et a acquis sa technique classique. Le ballet était alors un spectacle à la fois grandiose et formel où les danseurs entraient en scène masqués et habillés des magnifiques costumes de l'époque.

Un ballet de Lully présenté à la cour de Louis XIV

Chopin: le poète du piano

T. Kwiatkouski *«La polonaise de Chopin»*

Frédéric Chopin (1810-1849) est né en Pologne° d'un père français et d'une mère polonaise. Enfant prodige, il compose et donne son premier concert à l'âge de neuf ans. À vingt ans, il quitte son pays, emportant dans une urne un peu de la terre° natale qu'il ne reverra° jamais.

Chopin s'établit° à Paris où il rencontre les artistes et les écrivains les plus célèbres de son époque. Parmi ceux-ci, il y a une jeune femme, **George Sand**, pour qui il va éprouver° une grande passion. Inspiré par l'amour et plus tard par la tristesse de la séparation, il compose pour le piano des oeuvres d'une grande intensité émotionnelle: études, ballades, nocturnes, fantaisies, préludes, impromptus, sonates et aussi polonaises et mazurkas en l'honneur de son pays natal. De santé° délicate et miné° par la tuberculose, il meurt à Paris à l'âge de 39 ans.

À tort *wrongly* au cours *across* dont *whose* les oeuvres *works* un regain *renewal* d'entre *of* lesquelles *which* a fait appel *asked*
Pologne *Poland* la terre *soil* ne reverra jamais *will never see* s'établit *settles* éprouver *feel* la santé *health* miné *weakened*

«Carmen» présenté à New York (Metropolitan Opera)

Bizet et l'opéra romantique

Tous les amateurs d'opéra connaissent l'air° célèbre «Toréador, en garde, Toréador! Toréador!» Cet air est tiré° de l'opéra *Carmen*, oeuvre du compositeur **Georges Bizet**.

Bizet (1838-1875) était un prodige musical. Il est entré au Conservatoire de Paris à l'âge de neuf ans et il en est sorti à dix-huit ans avec le premier Grand Prix de Rome, distinction réservée aux meilleurs jeunes musiciens de l'époque. De ses nombreuses compositions, la plus connue reste *Carmen*, opéra romantique plein° de passion, d'émotions intenses et d'action dramatique. Jugé immoral, cet opéra n'a pas eu de succès à l'époque de sa création. Très affecté par cet échec,° Bizet est mort trois mois après la première représentation° de son chef-d'oeuvre.°

Aujourd'hui, *Carmen* est le plus populaire des opéras français. Modernisé, il a été adapté pour le cinéma dans plusieurs versions.

Une affiche: «Carmen» vers 1900

L'action se passe à Séville dans l'Espagne romantique du dix-neuvième siècle. L'héroïne est Carmen, une gitane° belle, fière, passionnée, mais d'humeur changeante . . . Carmen travaille dans une manufacture de tabac. Un jour, elle blesse° une de ses collègues d'un coup de couteau à la joue. Le brigadier Don José vient l'arrêter. Pendant qu'elle est sous sa garde, Don José tombe éperdument amoureux de la belle gitane et il la laisse s'échapper. Il déserte lui-même et s'enfuit avec Carmen dans les montagnes où ils rejoignent une bande de contrebandiers.° Don José devient alors contrebandier.

Un jour, Micaela, une jeune fille du village où il habitait vient annoncer à Don José que sa mère est sur le point° de mourir. Celui-ci retourne dans son village pour voir sa mère. Pendant ce temps, Carmen va à Séville avec ses amies pour assister à une corrida. Là, elle n'a d'yeux que pour le héros de la corrida, le toréador Escamillo, qui est son nouvel amour. Don José revient pour chercher Carmen. Il la trouve à la corrida et il la tue° dans une crise° de jalousie. Puis, il se livre° à la police.

Debussy et la musique impressionniste

On considère **Claude Debussy** (1862-1918) comme l'un des fondateurs de la musique moderne. Élève au Conservatoire de Paris, il étudie les oeuvres des grands compositeurs, mais il refuse absolument d'imiter leur style ou leur technique. Il se révolte en particulier contre la musique romantique dominée par l'intensité dramatique et l'émotion.

Claude Debussy (1862-1918)

Comme l'ont fait les peintres impressionnistes pour la peinture, Debussy veut libérer la musique de tout principe, de toute convention, de toute tradition. En rejetant, par exemple, la règle des accords° progressifs et en utilisant les dissonances et les silences, il donne à la musique des sonorités nouvelles qui ont pu sembler étranges aux gens de son époque. La musique de Debussy, exemplifiée par son célèbre poème symphonique «La Mer», est une musique fluide, délicate, toute en nuances, où l'impression produite remplace l'émotion.

---

l'air *aria* **tiré de** = vient **plein** *full* **un échec** *failure* **la représentation** *performance* **le chef-d'oeuvre** *masterpiece* **gitane** *gypsy* **blesse** *wounds* **contrebandiers** *smugglers* **sur le point** *is going* **tue** *kills* **une crise** *fit* **il se livre** *gives himself up* **accords** *chords*

Bon voyage!

Thème et Objectifs

Culture
In this unit, you will discover . . .
- what French young people do when they travel abroad and where they go
- why the train is the most popular means of transportation in France
- how the Eurotunnel has linked Great Britain to France and the rest of Europe

Communication
You will learn how . . .
- to make travel plans and purchase tickets
- to go through passport control and customs
- to travel by plane and by train

Langue
You will learn how . . .
- to discuss future plans
- to talk about future events
- to describe what you would do under certain conditions

La *Passion des Voyages*

Pour les jeunes Français, le terme «vacances» est synonyme de «voyage.» Ceux qui restent en France vont bronzer sur les plages de l'Atlantique et de la Méditerranée ou faire de la marche à pied dans les Alpes et les Pyrénées. Mais aujourd'hui, ceux qui vont à l'étranger sont de plus en plus nombreux. Aller dans un pays où la langue, les gens, et les coutumes sont différents, ça, c'est l'aventure!

Suivant° leurs objectifs, on peut classer ces jeunes voyageurs en différentes catégories.

■ Pour ces jeunes voyageurs, «vacances» est synonyme de «voyage»!

Les «linguistes»

Les «séjours linguistiques» représentent la majorité des voyages à l'étranger. La formule classique consiste à passer deux ou trois semaines dans une famille en Angleterre (l'anglais étant° la langue la plus étudiée dans les lycées français).

Aujourd'hui, avec le développement des transports aériens et la diminution° du prix des voyages, les jeunes Français vont de plus en plus loin pour perfectionner° leur anglais. Patrick, par exemple, a passé le mois d'août dans une famille de Denver. Le haut point de son voyage a été la dernière semaine où la famille est allée faire du rafting dans le Colorado. Charlotte, elle, est allée en Australie dans une famille de ranchers. Là, elle a participé à toutes les activités, y compris la tonte des moutons.°

Les «actifs»

Ce sont ceux qui ont un projet particulier. Certains font un «stage» payé ou non payé dans une entreprise. Catherine a ainsi passé un mois en Allemagne à mélanger des colorants° dans une compagnie de produits chimiques. Là, elle a appris les dangers de la pollution et les moyens° de contrôler celle-ci.

Pour d'autres, leur projet a un objectif humanitaire. Jean-Baptiste, un lycéen de 17 ans, est allé au Sénégal avec une bande de copains de son lycée. Il explique: «Notre but° n'était pas de faire du tourisme, mais d'accomplir quelque chose d'utile. Nous avons participé à la construction d'un système d'irrigation dans un petit village. Pendant notre séjour, nous avons travaillé très dur, mais aussi nous avons découvert un mode° de vie tout à fait° différent et nous avons fait connaissance de gens absolument extraordinaires. Pendant ces trois semaines, nous avons appris plus que pendant un an au lycée!»

---

suivant *according to* **étant** *being* **diminution** *decrease* **perfectionner** *improve* **tonte des moutons** *sheep shearing*
mélanger des colorants *to mix dyes* **moyens** *means* **but** = *objectif* **mode** *way* **tout à fait** *quite*

Leurs destinations préférées

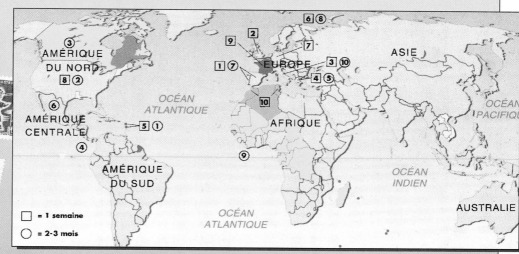

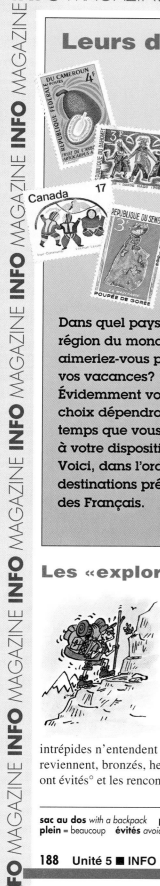

Dans quel pays ou région du monde aimeriez-vous passer vos vacances? Évidemment votre choix dépendra du temps que vous aurez à votre disposition. Voici, dans l'ordre, les destinations préférées des Français.

VACANCES D'UNE SEMAINE

1. l'Espagne, le Portugal
2. l'Angleterre
3. l'Italie
4. la Grèce
5. la Martinique, la Guadeloupe
6. les pays scandinaves*
7. l'Allemagne
8. les États-Unis
9. la France
10. l'Algérie, le Maroc, la Tunisie

VACANCES D'UN OU DEUX MOIS

1. la Martinique, la Guadeloupe
2. les États-Unis
3. le Canada
4. les pays d'Amérique latine**
5. la Grèce
6. le Mexique
7. l'Espagne, le Portugal
8. les pays scandinaves*
9. les pays d'Afrique noire***
10. l'Italie

* le Danemark, la Suède, la Norvège
** le Pérou, l'Argentine, le Brésil, l'Equateur, le Costa Rica, etc.
*** le Sénégal, la Côte d'Ivoire, le Cameroun, etc.

Les «explorateurs»

Ceux-là renouvellent la tradition des explorateurs français d'autrefois. Ils partent à l'aventure, sac au dos,° sans but précis pour des destinations mystérieuses. Julien, un étudiant en médecine, a parcouru° les hauts plateaux du Pérou en bus et en autostop. Marthe et Véronique, deux étudiantes d'une école de commerce, ont fait du trekking dans l'Himalaya. Elles sont parties du Népal et sont allées à pied par des sentiers° de haute montagne jusqu'au Tibet.

Pendant des semaines, les parents de ces voyageurs intrépides n'entendent pas parler° d'eux et s'inquiètent.° Mais finalement, ils reviennent, bronzés, heureux et avec plein° d'anecdotes sur les dangers qu'ils ont évités° et les rencontres qu'ils ont faites pendant leur fabuleux voyage. ■

DISCUSSION
Avec votre partenaire, imaginez que vous allez visiter la France (ou un autre pays francophone) cet été. Est-ce que vous voyagerez plutôt comme «linguiste,» comme «actif,» ou comme «explorateur»? Expliquez vos projets.

COMPOSITION
Décrivez des vacances «actives» que vous avez passées.

sac au dos with a backpack   **parcourir** ✻ to travel through   **sentiers** trails   **n'entendent pas parler** do not hear   **s'inquiètent** worry
plein = beaucoup   **évités** avoided

Impressions d'Amérique

Les États-Unis ont toujours fasciné les jeunes Français. Chaque été, ils sont toujours plus nombreux à réaliser leur rêve:° faire un voyage aux «States.»

Nous sommes à Roissy, l'aéroport international de Paris. Un groupe de jeunes Français de 15 à 18 ans vient de débarquer° d'un vol° Air France qui arrive de New York. Ils ont passé six semaines dans des familles américaines avec un programme d'échange. Voici quelques-unes de leurs impressions.

■ Émilie, Jean-Pascal, Sibylle, Christophe, Sonia et Arnaud à Roissy

Jean-Pascal «Les États-Unis sont un pays vraiment gigantesque. Là-bas, tout est grand: les gens, les maisons, les voitures, les distances. C'est aussi un pays magnifique. J'ai eu la chance d'aller dans une famille qui habite au Nouveau Mexique. Les villages indiens, les canyons, le désert, c'est fabuleusement beau!»

Émilie «Moi, ce qui m'a frappée,° c'est la variété ethnique des Américains. Ce qui est formidable,° c'est que toutes les races de la terre° y sont représentées. À Boston, par exemple, la ville où je suis restée, j'ai pu parler français avec des Haïtiens, et espagnol avec des Portoricains. Ça, c'est super.»

Christophe «Les Américains sont des gens vraiment sympas et hospitaliers. Ils sont beaucoup plus ouverts et plus décontractés° que nous. Aux États-Unis, par exemple, il est tout à fait facile de lier conversation° avec des gens qu'on ne connaît pas. En France, c'est quasi-impossible. Les Américains sont honnêtes. Ils disent toujours ce qu'ils pensent... Pendant mon séjour, il y a une seule chose que je n'ai pas aimée: la bouffe.»°

Sibylle «Je ne suis pas d'accord avec Christophe. La bouffe américaine n'est pas si mauvaise que ça, et puis, elle est très bon marché. Et il ne faut pas manger tout le temps des hamburgers ou des hot-dogs. Il y a des tas° de restaurants italiens, chinois, mexicains, thaïlandais, où on peut manger des choses absolument délicieuses. On n'est pas obligé de prendre ses repas que dans les fast-foods!»

Arnaud «Les Américains sont des gens dynamiques et superactifs. Malheureusement, ils sont obsédés° par l'argent. Et ils sont stressés parce qu'ils travaillent trop. Dans la famille où j'étais, la mère retournait à son bureau le samedi pour finir ce qu'elle n'avait pas terminé pendant la semaine. Et le fils travaillait dans un supermarché. La détente,° ça n'existe pas. Et puis, la vie de famille est limitée. Le soir, par exemple, les parents et les enfants faisaient réchauffer° des portions de pizza qu'ils mangeaient séparément. Il n'y avait jamais de repas commun.»

Sonia «Les États-Unis sont un pays très intéressant. Ce serait° un pays presque° parfait s'il n'y avait pas autant° de violence. Dans les journaux et à la télévision, on ne parle que° de crime. Et le soir, dans la ville où j'étais, il n'est pas recommandé de sortir seule. J'ai aimé mon voyage, mais je suis bien contente de rentrer en France.» ■

et vous?

SUJET DE DISCUSSION

Avec votre partenaire, choisissez deux des jeunes Français qui ont visité les États-Unis et analysez leurs impressions. Dites si vous êtes entièrement, partiellement ou pas du tout d'accord avec eux. Expliquez.

COMPOSITION: UNE LETTRE

Un copain français va venir passer un mois dans votre région. Vous voulez lui donner une bonne impression de cette région. Écrivez-lui une lettre où vous allez parler des sujets suivants:

- le pays
- la nourriture
- les gens
- les activités

---

rêve *dream* **débarquer** *to land* **vol** *flight* **frappée** *struck* **formidable** = *super* **terre** *earth* **décontractés** *relaxed* **lier conversation** = *parler*
bouffe *food (slang)* **des tas** = *beaucoup* **obsédés:** *obsessed* **détente** *relaxation* **faisaient réchauffer** *would reheat* **serait** *would be*
presque *almost* **(s'il n'y avait pas) autant** *not that much* **ne...que** *only*

LE FRANÇAIS PRATIQUE

Les voyages

Où vas-tu aller cet été?

Je vais voyager à l'étranger.

Ah bon? Dans quel pays?

Je vais visiter le Portugal.

Les voyages

— Où vas-tu aller cet été?

Je vais | **voyager**
faire un voyage
faire un séjour | **à l'étranger** *(abroad)*.

| **faire un séjour** | *to spend some time* |

— Ah bon? Dans quels **pays** *(countries)*?

Je vais visiter . . .
le Portugal.
la Grèce.
les Canaries.

Je vais aller . . .
au Mexique.
en Russie.
aux États-Unis.

Les pays

Révision ▶ pp. R14-R15

---

1 **Voyages à l'étranger**

Faites une liste de dix (10) pays que vous aimeriez visiter. Classez les pays par ordre de préférence. Comparez votre liste avec celle de votre partenaire.

Ma Liste
1.
2.
3.

- Quels sont les pays qui sont sur les deux listes?
- Quels sont les pays qui sont seulement *(only)* sur votre liste?

Maintenant expliquez pourquoi vous aimeriez aller dans les trois premiers pays de votre liste.

▶ **J'aimerais visiter le Sénégal parce que je voudrais mieux connaître l'Afrique . . .**

SÉNÉGAL

SOMMAIRE

Tunisie

PARIS-DAKAR ALLER SA...

ALPES et SUISSE

ISLE DE LA MARTINIQUE

Billet combiné

SNCF

LA SUISSE

Au coeur de l'Europe

Uri Schwyz Obwalden

St. Gallen Grischun Aargau Thurgau

Martinique

Évadez vous . . .

ITALIE

GRANDE-BRETAGNE

BELGIQUE

CIRCUITS

Vous avez une pièce d'identité?

Oui, j'ai un passeport.

Au contrôle des passeports

— Vous avez **une pièce d'identité** *(ID document)*?

Oui, j'ai | **un passeport.**
          | **une carte d'identité.**
          | **un permis de conduire** *(driver's license)*.

À la douane *(customs)*

— Vous avez des **bagages** *(luggage)*?

Oui, j'ai | **une valise** *(suitcase).*   **un bagage à main** *(carry-on bag)*.
          | **un sac.**   **un sac à dos** *(backpack)*.

— Est-ce que vous avez **quelque chose à déclarer?**

Non, je n'ai **rien à déclarer.**

NOTE CULTURELLE

Les Américains qui vont en France ont besoin d'un passeport
(et aussi d'un visa, s'ils veulent faire un long séjour).
   Les citoyens *(citizens)* des pays de l'Union Européenne
ont besoin seulement d'une pièce d'identité.

---

2 **Arrivée en France**

Cet été, vous faites un grand voyage autour du monde *(around the world)*. Vous arrivez en France,
après avoir visité plusieurs pays. Vous passez au contrôle des passeports et à la douane.
Composez et jouez le dialogue avec votre partenaire.

— Bonjour, monsieur/mademoiselle. Avez-vous une pièce d'identité?
— *(Present an ID document.)*
— Quels pays avez-vous visités avant de venir en France?
— *(Name a few countries.)*
— Avez-vous des bagages?
— *(Indicate the luggage that you are carrying.)*
— Avez-vous quelque chose à déclarer?
— *(Answer negatively.)*
— Où avez-vous acheté . . . ? *(customs officer names two or three things in your luggage,
   such as items of clothing, perfume, souvenirs)*
— *(For each item, mention a different country where you purchased it.)*
— Merci, monsieur/mademoiselle, et bon séjour en France.

A. Les expressions négatives

Note the following negative expressions and their use in the present and the passé composé.

AFFIRMATIVE	NEGATIVE	
quelqu'un *(someone, somebody)*	**ne . . . personne** *(no one, nobody)*	Je **ne** connais **personne** ici. Je **n**'ai rencontré **personne**.
quelque chose *(something)*	**ne . . . rien** *(nothing)*	Je **n**'ai **rien** à déclarer. Je **n**'ai **rien** acheté.
quelque part *(somewhere)*	**ne . . . nulle part** *(nowhere)*	Je **ne** me promène **nulle part**. Je **ne** suis allé **nulle part**.
quelque(s) *(some)*	**ne . . . aucun(e)** *(no, not any)*	Je **n**'ai **aucune** idée. Je **n**'ai acheté **aucun** cadeau.
et / ou *(and/or)*	**ne . . . ni . . . ni** *(neither . . . nor)*	Je **ne** vais **ni** au ciné **ni** au théâtre. Je **n**'ai visité **ni** Paris **ni** Québec.

➡ In the passé composé, negative expressions come AFTER the past participle,
except **rien** which comes before.

Nous **n**'avons vu **personne**.   BUT: Nous **n**'avons **rien** vu.

➡ **Personne** and **rien** can be used as subjects.

Personne n'a téléphoné.   **Rien n**'est impossible.

> **ALLONS PLUS LOIN**
>
> Note the following constructions:
>
> quelqu'un, quelque chose
personne, rien } + **de** + masculine adjective   J'ai rencontré **quelqu'un d'intéressant.**
>
> quelqu'un, quelque chose
personne, rien } + **à** + infinitive   Nous **n**'avons **rien à déclarer.**

B. L'expression ne . . . que

The expression **ne . . . que** is not a negative expression. It is a limiting expression that means *only*.
Its equivalent is **seulement**. Note its use in the following sentences.

Je parle français.

Je **ne** parle **que** français.   *I speak **only** French.*

Je **ne** parle français **qu**'en France.   *I speak French **only** in France.*

Je **ne** parle français en France   *I speak French in France*
  qu'avec mes amis.   ***only** with my friends.*

➡ Note the word order with **ne . . . que:**
- **ne** comes before the verb
- **que** comes before the word or phrase to which the restriction applies.

➡ Since **ne . . . que** is not a negative expression, the indefinite and partitive articles
do not change after the verb.

Je mange **des légumes.**   Je **ne** mange **que des légumes**.

1 C'est évident!

Informez-vous sur les personnes suivantes et dites ce qu'elles ne font pas. Utilisez les verbes entre parenthèses et une expression négative: **ne . . . personne, ne . . . rien, ne . . . nulle part.**

▶ Jean-Pierre est timide. (parler à)
   Il ne parle à personne.

1. Carole se repose. (faire)
2. Pauline est très malade. (manger)
3. Marc n'est pas sociable. (inviter)
4. Thomas reste chez lui. (aller)
5. Antoine n'a pas soif. (boire)
6. Philippe ne voyage pas cet été. (partir)
7. Bernard est un nouvel élève. (connaître)
8. Catherine n'a pas d'argent. (acheter)

2 Une mauvaise surprise

Quand Brigitte est rentrée du concert, elle a trouvé la porte et les fenêtres de son appartement grandes ouvertes *(wide open)* et les lumières allumées *(turned on)*. Elle appelle un inspecteur de police qui lui pose les questions suivantes. Brigitte répond négativement. Jouez le rôle de Brigitte.

▶ L'inspecteur: Avez-vous entendu quelque chose?
   Brigitte: **Non, je n'ai rien entendu.**

1. Avez-vous vu quelqu'un quand vous êtes rentrée?
2. Avez-vous observé quelque chose d'anormal?
3. Avez-vous remarqué quelqu'un de suspect?
4. Est-ce que vous avez donné votre adresse à quelqu'un récemment?
5. Est-ce que vous avez fait quelque chose de spécial hier soir?
6. Est-ce que vous avez invité quelqu'un chez vous la semaine dernière?
7. Est-ce que quelqu'un vous a téléphoné dans l'après-midi?
8. Est-ce que quelque chose d'important a disparu *(disappeared)*?
9. Est-ce que quelqu'un est venu réparer l'électricité récemment?
10. Est-ce qu'il y avait quelque chose de grande valeur *(value)* dans votre appartement?

3 À la douane

Vous arrivez à l'aéroport de Dorval à Montréal. Le douanier (joué par votre partenaire) vous pose certaines questions. Répondez-lui en choisissant une expression entre parenthèses.

> **Vous avez des bagages?**

> **Je n'ai qu'un bagage à main.**

(Je n'ai que deux valises.)

QUESTIONS	RÉPONSES
Vous avez des bagages?	(deux valises / un sac à dos / un bagage à main)
Vous avez une pièce d'identité?	(mon passeport / mon permis de conduire / une carte d'étudiant)
Vous avez des cadeaux?	(du parfum / des chocolats / des t-shirts)
Vous avez de l'argent?	(des dollars / des travellers chèques / une carte de crédit)
À part l'anglais, vous parlez d'autres langues?	(espagnol / allemand / français)
Vous allez rester longtemps?	(3 jours / 2 semaines / un mois)
Vous allez visiter plusieurs villes?	(Québec / Montréal / Toronto)

La France en train

■ Le train: c'est plus rapide, plus pratique, et plus sûr!

Pour les vacances de Mardi Gras, Marie-Hélène, une étudiante parisienne, est allée chez sa grand-mère qui habite à Marseille. Elle aurait pu° prendre l'avion ou conduire° sa voiture, mais elle a choisi d'y aller en train. Pourquoi? Parce que c'est plus rapide, plus pratique, et plus sûr. Avec le TGV (Train à Grande Vitesse), on peut aller de Paris à Marseille (750 kilomètres) en 3 heures. Il n'y a pas d'embouteillage,° pas de péage° à payer, et on arrive à sa destination frais et dispos.°

Le TGV, produit de la technologie française, est ce train super rapide qui circule sur un système spécial de rails et peut rouler° à une vitesse de 300 kilomètres à l'heure. La première ligne (Paris-Lyon) a été inaugurée en 1981, mais aujourd'hui le TGV dessert° presque° toutes les grandes villes françaises. Il y a un TGV Sud-est (orange), un TGV Atlantique (bleu) et un TGV Nord... En fait, 50% du service voyageurs est assuré par le TGV. Les autres trains sont peut-être un peu moins rapides, mais ils sont aussi confortables et aussi pratiques.

Les Français sont très fiers° de leurs trains et ceci pour de bonnes raisons:

■ Les trains français sont toujours à l'heure. Ils partent à l'heure indiquée et arrivent à l'heure indiquée. Avec le train, on n'est jamais en retard.

■ Les trains sont propres et confortables. Si on a faim, on peut prendre un repas au wagon-restaurant.° Sur les grandes distances, on peut voyager en wagon-lit.°

■ Le train est bon marché et très flexible. Il y a des réductions de prix pour les jeunes, pour les familles, pour les personnes âgées, pour les personnes qui voyagent souvent. Pour toutes ces personnes, les prix des billets varient selon l'époque où on voyage. Ils sont plus élevés° en période rouge (vacances) ou blanche (week-ends), et moins élevés en période bleue (le reste du temps).

Pour les touristes, il y a d'autres services intéressants. Avec «train + vélo» et «train + auto,» on peut voyager en train et louer un vélo ou une voiture quand on arrive à sa destination. Avec «train + hôtel,» on trouve toujours une chambre d'hôtel.

Les jeunes Américains peuvent acheter un Eurailpass. Cette carte leur permet de sillonner° l'Europe pendant plusieurs semaines pour un prix relativement modique°. Pour beaucoup de jeunes qui utilisent ce système, le train est non seulement un moyen° de transport mais c'est aussi un hôtel, un restaurant, une cafétéria et un lieu où ils peuvent rencontrer d'autres jeunes qui, comme eux, viennent découvrir le vieux continent. ■

Paris à Marseille

✈	(≈480 km l'heure)	640 km aériens	1h20
SNCF 🚄	(≈250 km l'heure)	750 km	3h00
🚗	(≈100 km l'heure)	773 km	7h35

et vous?

DISCUSSION
Vous allez visiter la France avec votre partenaire. Il/Elle voudrait voyager en avion, mais vous préférez voyager en train. Expliquez-lui les avantages du train. Votre partenaire va poser des questions.

COMPOSITION: UNE LETTRE
Alice, une copine française, va visiter les États-Unis cet été. Elle ne sait pas si elle va voyager en train ou en bus, et elle vous demande votre avis (opinion). Dites-lui quel système vous préférez et expliquez-lui les avantages et les inconvénients de ce système.

aurait pu *could have* **conduire** ✳ *to drive* **embouteillage** *traffic jam* **péage** *toll* **frais et dispos** *fresh and rested* **rouler** = *aller* **dessert** *services* **presque** *almost* **fiers** *proud* **wagon-restaurant** *dining car* **wagon-lit** *sleeping car* **élevés** *higher* **sillonner** = *voyager à travers* **modique** *low* **moyen** *means*

L'EUROTUNNEL

EURO TUNNEL

Aujourd'hui, l'Angleterre n'est plus une île. Avec l'Eurotunnel, on peut maintenant franchir° les 50 kilomètres qui séparent Coquelles (France) et Cheriton (Angleterre) sans quitter la terre ferme.° L'idée d'un tunnel sous la Manche est très ancienne. Le premier projet remonte° à Napoléon et date de 1802. Malheureusement, la rivalité franco-britannique, les guerres européennes, les difficultés techniques, et l'énorme coût financier ont pendant longtemps empêché° la réalisation de ce projet. Finalement, les travaux ont commencé en 1988 et depuis 1994, l'Eurotunnel est une réalité.

L'ANGLETERRE

Londres ✪
Douvres
Cheriton   Calais
Coquelles

LA MANCHE

LA FRANCE

Paris ✪

■ Chaque année, dix millions de voyageurs passent sous la mer pour aller de France en Angleterre, ou vice versa, en moins de 20 minutes.

Chaque année, dix millions de voyageurs passent sous la mer pour aller de France en Angleterre, ou vice versa, en moins de 20 minutes. Il y a en réalité deux tunnels, un tunnel nord et un tunnel sud, permettant le trafic dans les deux sens.° Ces deux tunnels sont exclusivement réservés au trafic ferroviaire,° mais les automobilistes peuvent tout de même° utiliser l'Eurotunnel en chargeant° leurs voitures sur des trains spéciaux.

Imaginez, par exemple, que vous habitez à Paris et que vous voulez déjeuner avec votre copain qui habite à Londres. C'est simple. Si vous préférez le train, vous prendrez l'Eurostar à 10 heures et vous arriverez à Londres à midi. Si, au contraire, vous préférez conduire, vous devez partir à sept heures. Vous prendrez l'autoroute° qui va de Paris jusqu'à l'accès de l'Eurotunnel. Là, vous monterez avec votre voiture sur une navette° spéciale qui vous amènera jusqu'au° terminal britannique. De là vous continuerez votre route. S'il n'y a pas trop d'embouteillages° dans Londres, vous serez à votre rendez-vous pour le déjeuner.

L'Eurotunnel est beaucoup plus qu'un grand exploit technique. Autrefois, la Manche représentait une formidable barrière qui protégeait l'Angleterre contre les invasions, mais qui la maintenait aussi dans son «splendide isolement». Aujourd'hui l'Eurotunnel joint l'Angleterre à la France et, par la France, à l'Allemagne, à la Belgique, à la Hollande et à tout le continent européen. C'est le symbole de la Nouvelle Europe, unie et en paix° avec elle-même. ■

QUESTIONS

1. Comment peut-on aller de Paris à Londres par la terre ferme?
2. Quels ont été les obstacles à la construction de l'Eurotunnel?
3. Pourquoi l'Eurotunnel est-il un grand exploit technique?
4. Quel est le symbole politique de l'Eurotunnel?

---

franchir = traverser   **terre ferme** *ground*   **remonte** *goes back*   **empêché** *prevented*   **sens** = directions   **ferroviaire** *railroad*   **tout de même** *nevertheless*
chargeant *loading*   **l'autoroute** *turnpike*   **navette** *shuttle train*   **jusqu'au** *up to*   **embouteillages** *traffic jams*   **paix** *peace*

LE FRANÇAIS PRATIQUE

Partons en voyage

Quelle sorte de billet désirez-vous?

Je voudrais acheter un billet.

En quelle classe?

Un aller et retour.

En classe économie.

À l'agence de voyages

—Je voudrais | **acheter un billet** (ticket).
réserver une place (seat).
confirmer ma réservation.
annuler ma réservation.
louer une voiture.

> **annuler** to cancel
> **louer** to rent

POUR ACHETER UN BILLET DE TRAIN OU D'AVION

— **Quelle sorte de** billet désirez-vous?
Un aller simple (one way).   **Un aller et retour** (round trip).

—En quelle classe?
En **première classe.**   En **deuxième classe** [en train].
En **classe affaires** (business)   En **classe économie** [en avion].

—En quelle section?
En section **fumeur.**   En section **non-fumeur.**

— **Quel siège** (seat)
— **Quelle place** | préférez-vous?
Un siège | près de la fenêtre.
Une place | près du **couloir** (aisle).

—Voici | votre billet.
| votre **carte d'embarquement** (boarding pass).

POUR OBTENIR DES RENSEIGNEMENTS (information)

—Est-ce que | **le vol** (flight) pour Nice | est **direct**?
| le train pour Marseille

Non, il y a | **une escale** (stop, stopover [of the plane]) | à Lyon.
| **une correspondance** (change of plane, train)

—Est-ce que le vol/le train est **à l'heure** (on time)?
Non, il est | **en avance** (early).   Il a **dix minutes d'avance.**
| **en retard** (late).   Il a **une heure de retard.**

Le vol numéro 23 à destination de Londres est **annulé.**

—Est-ce que le vol/le train est **complet** (full)?
Non, il y a **de la place** (room).

—Est-ce que ce siège/cette place est **libre** (free)?
Non, il/elle est **occupé(e).**

À l'aéroport

DÉPARTS

les horaires

le comptoir

la salle d'attente

le contrôle de sécurité

la porte

PORTE 32

le steward

le pilote

l'hôtesse de l'air

ARRIVÉES

DOUANE

un douanier

la livraison des bagages

Les passagers doivent . . .

AU DÉPART	**présenter** leur billet.
	obtenir leur carte d'embarquement.
	enregistrer leurs bagages.
	se présenter à la porte de départ.
	embarquer.
PENDANT LE VOL	mettre leur bagage à main sous le siège.
	attacher leur **ceinture de sécurité** (seat belt).
À L'ARRIVÉE	**débarquer.**
	chercher leurs bagages.
	passer par la douane.

L'avion va | **décoller** / **atterrir** | dans 10 minutes.

obtenir to get
enregistrer to check [luggage]
embarquer to board [a plane]

attacher to fasten

débarquer to deplane
passer par to go through

décoller to take off
atterrir to land

Mesdames et messieurs, bonjour.
Le capitaine Pascal et son équipage vous souhaitent la bienvenue à bord du vol Air France numéro 346 à destination de Montréal.
La durée du vol sera approximativement de 7 heures et 25 minutes et notre arrivée à Montréal est prévue pour 17h45 heure locale.
En prévision du départ, veuillez attacher votre ceinture de sécurité.

Départs

Arrivée

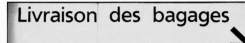

Livraison des bagages

Métro Orlyval porte E - F
et autres moyens de transport

À la gare

la sortie · le guichet · la consigne · le tableau d'affichage · un wagon · un train · le composteur · le quai

Les passagers doivent . . .

> acheter un billet.
> **composter** le billet.
> **monter dans** leur train.
> **descendre de** leur train à l'arrivée.

composter	to punch [a ticket]
monter (dans)	to get on [a train]
descendre (de)	to get off [a train]

Mais attention, il ne faut pas **rater** le train.
Si on rate le train, il faut | **prendre** | **le prochain train.**
                             | **attendre** | **le train suivant.**

rater	to miss

NOTE CULTURELLE

Avant de monter dans le train, les voyageurs doivent composter
leurs billets. Le composteur indique l'heure et la date à laquelle
le billet a été composté. Pendant le voyage, le contrôleur
(conductor) passe dans les wagons pour contrôler les billets.
Si on n'a pas composté son billet, on reçoit une amende (fine).

Attention, attention!
Quai numéro 12.
Le train à destination
de Lille va partir.
Attention au départ.

Un voyage en avion

Vous êtes à Genève avec votre partenaire. Demain, vous avez l'intention d'aller à Nice en avion. Décrivez toutes les étapes *(steps, stages)* de ce voyage en avion en mettant les activités suivantes dans l'ordre chronologique.

- attacher nos ceintures de sécurité
- aller à l'aéroport
- débarquer
- embarquer
- dormir un peu
- passer par la douane
- aller à la porte 18
- chercher nos places dans l'avion
- passer le contrôle de sécurité
- aller au comptoir d'Air France
- montrer notre carte d'embarquement à l'hôtesse
- enregistrer nos bagages
- réserver deux places pour Nice
- sortir de l'aéroport
- téléphoner à l'agence de voyages
- chercher nos valises à la livraison des bagages

▶ **D'abord, nous allons téléphoner à l'agence de voyages. Nous allons . . .**

Un voyage en train

Maintenant vous allez de Nice à Cannes en train. Avec votre partenaire, décrivez ce que vous allez faire pendant ce voyage, dans l'ordre chronologique.

À l'Agence Tours-Soleil

L'Agence Tours-Soleil organise des voyages très bon marché. Choisissez un voyage et une date de départ. Avec votre partenaire, complétez le dialogue correspondant et jouez-le en classe. (Votre partenaire va jouer le rôle de l'agent de voyages.)

L'AGENT: Où désirez-vous aller, monsieur/ mademoiselle?
VOUS: – – –
L'AGENT: Quel jour désirez-vous partir?
VOUS: – – –
L'AGENT: Désirez-vous un aller simple?
VOUS: – – –
L'AGENT: En quelle classe?
VOUS: – – –
L'AGENT: Quelle place préférez-vous?
VOUS: – – –
L'AGENT: Désirez-vous louer une voiture? (Quelle voiture?)
VOUS: – – –

VOYAGES TOURS-SOLEIL

DESTINATIONS	DÉPARTS	
Dakar	3 juin	4 juillet
Casablanca	10 avril	5 septembre
Tahiti	8 juillet	2 août
Hong Kong	1er août	3 septembre
Moscou	6 mai	4 juin
Tel Aviv	12 juin	10 août
Fort-de-France	1er juillet	10 septembre

HONG KONG

MOSCOU

HONG KONG
Prenez le temps . . .

MARTINIQUE
LE NORD : SAINT-PIERRE · MORNE-ROUGE · GRAND-RIVIÈRE

4 Pas de chance

Il y a des voyageurs qui n'ont pas de chance. Avec votre partenaire, complétez les échanges suivants.

1. «Est-ce que cette place est libre?»
   «Non, – – – .»

2. «Est-ce que le train est à l'heure?»
   «Non, – – – .»

3. «Est-ce que le vol à destination de Toronto a été confirmé?»
   «Non, – – – .»

4. «Est-ce que le vol est direct?»
   «Non, – – – à Genève.»

5. «Est-ce que le train pour Tours est direct?»
   «Non, – – – à Saint-Pierre.»

6. «Est-ce qu'il y a de la place sur le prochain vol?»
   «Non, – – – .»

5 Train ou avion?

Vous voulez visiter l'Europe avec votre partenaire. Vous n'êtes pas d'accord sur le mode de transport que vous allez utiliser pendant le voyage: train ou avion?

Chacun va choisir un mode de transport (train ou avion) et essayer de convaincre *(to convince)* son partenaire. Présentez vos arguments par ordre de préférence. Qui va gagner le débat? Voici quelques idées:

TRAIN

- C'est moins cher.
- On peut mieux voir le paysage.
- On peut faire connaissance de plus de personnes.
- On peut se déplacer *(to get around)* plus facilement.
- ??

AVION

- C'est plus rapide.
- C'est plus confortable.
- On est moins fatigué.
- On a plus de temps pour visiter le pays.
- ??

6 *Conversations libres*

Avec votre partenaire, choisissez l'une des situations suivantes. Composez le dialogue correspondant et jouez-le en classe.

1 Un voyage à Genève

Madame D'Argent est une femme d'affaires très occupée. Demain matin, elle a un rendez-vous à Genève. Elle téléphone à son agence de voyage qui lui annonce que malheureusement il n'y a plus de place sur l'avion Paris-Genève. L'employé(e) propose d'autres solutions, par exemple, le train, le vol Paris-Zurich/Zurich-Genève, etc.

Rôles: Madame D'Argent / l'employé(e)

2 Un voyage en avion

Caroline va aller à la Martinique avec son petit frère Julien, 8 ans. C'est la première fois que Julien prend l'avion. Il pose beaucoup de questions à sa soeur qui lui explique comment va se passer le voyage.

Rôles: Caroline / Julien

3 Trop tard!

Aujourd'hui vous partez en France. Malheureusement vous arrivez à l'aéroport avec cinq minutes de retard. Votre avion vient juste de partir. Allez au comptoir d'Air France et expliquez la situation à l'employé(e). (Donnez des précisions sur le vol que vous avez raté.) Demandez-lui de vous trouver une place sur le vol suivant.

Rôles: vous / l'employé(e) d'Air France

4 Contrôle de billets

Vous êtes dans le train Paris-Strasbourg. Vous avez acheté un billet de 2e classe. Vous n'avez pas fait attention et vous êtes allé(e) dans un wagon de 1re classe. Le contrôleur *(conductor)* arrive. Il vous demande de payer un supplément. Vous n'avez pas assez d'argent. Expliquez-lui la situation.

Rôles: vous / le contrôleur

A. Le futur

The FUTURE tense is used to describe what people WILL DO, what WILL HAPPEN.
The verbs in the following sentences are in the future tense.

L'avion **partira** dans dix minutes.	*The plane **will leave** in ten minutes.*
Nous **irons** en France cet été.	*We **will go** to France this summer.*

The future tense is a SIMPLE tense. It is formed as follows:

> FUTURE STEM + FUTURE ENDINGS

INFINITIVE	parler	finir	vendre	FUTURE
FUTURE STEM	parler-	finir-	vendr-	**ENDINGS**
FUTURE	je **parlerai** tu **parleras** il/elle/on **parlera** nous **parlerons** vous **parlerez** ils/elles **parleront**	finirai finiras finira finirons finirez finiront	vendrai vendras vendra vendrons vendrez vendront	-ai -as -a -ons -ez -ont
NEGATIVE	je **ne parlerai pas**			
INTERROGATIVE	est-ce que tu **parleras?** **parleras-tu?**			

The stem of the future always ends in **-r.**

➡ For most verbs,

> FUTURE STEM = INFINITIVE (*minus* **-e**, *if any*)

partir → je **partir**ai   **écrire** → j'**écrir**ai

La prochaine fois, je partirai à temps, je ne m'arrêterai pas en route, et j'arriverai le premier.

➡ Some verbs have irregular future stems.

INFINITIVE	FUTURE STEM	
acheter	**achèter-**	j'**achèterai**
appeler	**appeller-**	j'**appellerai**
payer	**paier-**	je **paierai**
avoir	**aur-**	j'**aurai**
être	**ser-**	je **serai**
aller	**ir-**	j'**irai**
faire	**fer-**	je **ferai**
venir	**viendr-**	je **viendrai**

INFINITIVE	FUTURE STEM	
devoir	**devr-**	je **devrai**
pouvoir	**pourr-**	je **pourrai**
vouloir	**voudr-**	je **voudrai**
envoyer	**enverr-**	j'**enverrai**
recevoir	**recevr-**	je **recevrai**
savoir	**saur-**	je **saurai**
voir	**verr-**	je **verrai**

Also: il y a → **il y aura**   il pleut → **il pleuvra**

> **Le futur**
>
> *Pratique* ▶ p. 57

1 Cet été

Demandez à votre partenaire s'il/si elle fera les choses suivantes cet été.
Si votre partenaire répond affirmativement, essayez de continuer la conversation.

▶ travailler?

Tu travailleras cet été?

Oui, je travaillerai.

Ah bon, qu'est-ce que tu feras?

Je serai serveur/serveuse dans un restaurant.

(Non, je ne travaillerai pas.)

- gagner de l'argent?
- rester chez toi?
- écrire à tes copains?
- être chez toi en août?
- avoir un job?
- faire du sport?

- faire du camping?
- aller à la mer?
- avoir l'occasion de voyager?
- aller à l'étranger?
- voir tes grands-parents?
- rendre visite à tes cousins?

2 Des vacances différentes

Cet été vous allez faire les choses de la colonne A. Votre partenaire a des projets différents
(des projets de la colonne B ou d'autres projets). Chacun expliquera ses projets à l'autre.

A	B
aller à la Martinique	aller au Canada
prendre l'avion	prendre le train
louer une voiture	louer un vélo
aller à l'hôtel	faire du camping
manger des plats épicés	manger du homard *(lobster)*
faire de la planche à voile	visiter les Parcs Nationaux
assister aux spectacles folkloriques	voir les matchs de baseball
voir mes copains	rendre visite à mon oncle
se reposer	être très actif/active
??	??

— **Moi, j'irai à la Martinique. Je prendrai l'avion.**
— **Eh bien, moi, je n'irai pas à la Martinique. J'irai au Canada. Je . . .**

3 Procrastination

Vous faites un voyage avec un(e) camarade qui ne fait jamais immédiatement ce qu'il/elle doit faire.
Votre partenaire va répondre à vos questions en utilisant un pronom complément.

▶ visiter le musée (samedi)
— **Quand est-ce que tu visiteras le musée?**
— **Je le visiterai samedi.**

1. écrire à tes parents (demain)
2. téléphoner à ta copine (samedi)
3. envoyer ces lettres (ce soir)
4. acheter ton billet (la semaine prochaine)
5. confirmer ta réservation (dans une semaine)
6. acheter des cadeaux (le jour du départ)
7. prendre des photos (pendant le weekend)
8. voir ce monument (dimanche)

ALLONS PLUS LOIN

Note the different uses of **quitter** and **partir**:

quitter + NOUN	*to leave (a place)*	Nous **quitterons** l'hôtel à 6 heures.
	to take leave of, to leave (a person)	J'**ai quitté** mon cousin à la gare.
partir	*to leave*	Je **partirai** demain matin.
partir de	*to leave from (a place)*	Nous **partirons de** New York.
partir à (en, pour)	*to leave for (a destination)*	Nous **partons en** France.

4 **Un voyage à Québec**

Vous allez visiter Québec avec un voyage organisé. Demandez à votre guide (votre partenaire) des détails sur ce voyage. Il/elle va vous répondre sur la base du programme.

Voyage à Québec...

vendredi 4 mai

10h25 arrivée à Québec
Air Canada, vol 208

14h00 tour de la ville en calèche

15h30 visite de la Citadelle et des plaines d'Abraham

19h30 dîner dans un restaurant québécois typique

samedi 5 mai

9h30 promenade en bateau sur le Saint-Laurent
après-midi libre

20h30 concert de chansons québécoises

dimanche 6 mai

8h45 excursion à Sainte Anne de Beaupré en autocar

16h38 départ de Québec
Air Canada, vol 209

▶ comment / aller à Québec?

— **Comment est-ce qu'on ira à Québec?**
— **On ira en avion.**

- quel jour / arriver à Québec?
- combien de jours / rester?
- comment / faire un tour de la ville?
- quel monument / voir vendredi après-midi?
- où / dîner vendredi soir?
- quand / faire une promenade en bateau?
- quoi / faire dimanche matin?
- comment / aller là-bas?
- quel jour / pouvoir faire du shopping?
- quel jour / revenir aux États-Unis?
- à quelle heure / partir?

SITE HISTORIQUE MAISON ST-HUBERT 1 km

VILLE DE QUÉBEC

Sainte Anne de Beaupré

5 **Une lettre**

Maintenant écrivez une lettre à votre cousin Patrick. Dans cette lettre, décrivez le voyage que vous allez faire.

Mon Cher Patrick,
Voici le programme de notre voyage organisé à Québec. Nous partirons le 4 mai. Nous voyagerons en avion...

B. L'usage du futur dans les phrases avec si

Note the use of the future in the following sentences.

Si le bus **n'arrive pas,**   *If the bus **does not come,***
   nous **prendrons** le train.   *we **will take** the train.*

Si je **passe** par l'agence de voyages,   ***If** I **go** by the travel agency,*
   j'**achèterai** les billets.   *I **will** buy the tickets.*

The above sentences express what WILL HAPPEN *if* a certain condition is met.
They consist of two parts:
- the **si** *(if)* clause, which expresses the condition
- the result clause, which tells what WILL HAPPEN

In French, as in English, the pattern of tenses is:

si-clause: PRESENT	result clause: FUTURE
Si j'**ai** de l'argent,	je **voyagerai**.

C. L'usage du futur après quand

Compare the use of tenses in French and English in the following sentences.

J'attacherai ma ceinture   *I **will fasten** my seat belt*
   quand l'avion **partira.**   ***when** the plane **leaves.***

Quand nous **arriverons** à Paris,   ***When** we **arrive** in Paris,*
   nous **passerons** par la douane.   *we **will go** through customs.*

When referring to future events, the French use the future tense in <u>both</u> the **quand** *(when)* clause and the main clause. The pattern is:

quand-clause: FUTURE	result clause: FUTURE
Quand j'**aurai** de l'argent,	je **voyagerai**.

➡ The future is also used after **quand** when the main clause is in the IMPERATIVE and a future event is implied.

Écris-moi quand tu **seras** à Nice.   *Write me when you **are** in Nice.*

Vocabulaire: Quelques conjonctions de temps

lorsque	*when*	**Lorsque** j'aurai mon passeport, je partirai.
dès que	*as soon as*	J'écrirai à Sylvie **dès que** j'aurai son adresse.
aussitôt que	*as soon as*	Nous vous téléphonerons **aussitôt que** nous serons à Nice.

➡ The future is used after these conjunctions, as it is after **quand.**

6 Attention!

Quand on voyage, il faut faire certaines choses sinon on aura un problème.
Exprimez cela pour les personnes suivantes.

PERSONNES	CHOSES À FAIRE	PROBLÈMES
vous	arriver à l'heure	rater la correspondance
nous	se dépêcher	rater le train
Béatrice	réserver à l'avance	ne pas trouver de place
les touristes	confirmer la réservation	payer un supplément
M. Duval	composter le billet	avoir une amende (fine)
	avoir un passeport	ne pas pouvoir voyager
	présenter la carte	monter dans l'avion
	d'embarquement	devoir les mettre sous le siège
	enregistrer les bagages	

▶ **Si M. Duval ne se dépêche pas, il ratera la correspondance.**

7 Une question de circonstances

Ce que nous faisons dépend des circonstances. Choisissez une question et dites ce que
vous ferez suivant les circonstances. Comparez vos réponses avec celles de votre partenaire.

1. Qu'est-ce que tu feras ce week-end . . .
   - s'il pleut?
   - s'il fait beau?
   - si tu restes chez toi?

3. Qu'est-ce que tu feras après l'école secondaire . . .
   - si tu vas à l'université?
   - si tu veux gagner ta vie?
   - si tu ne trouves pas de travail?

2. Qu'est-ce que tu feras cet été . . .
   - si tu travailles?
   - si tu as assez d'argent?
   - si tu vas à la mer?

4. Qu'est-ce que tu feras plus tard . . .
   - si tu es marié(e)?
   - si tu gagnes beaucoup d'argent?
   - si tu n'aimes pas ton travail?

8 Projets de voyage

Choisissez une personne et dites ce qu'elle fera quand elle sera dans un certain endroit.

nous	aller	(l') Égypte	assister à (une corrida, ??)
vous	être	(la) France	voir (les pyramides, ??)
Pauline	visiter	(le) Canada	aller à (un match de hockey, ??)
mes cousins		(les) États-Unis	visiter (le Grand Canyon, ??)
		(l') Espagne	parler (français, ??)
		(le) Mexique	acheter (du parfum, ??)
		(la) Chine	manger (du poulet frit, ??)

▶ **Quand Pauline sera en Espagne, elle parlera espagnol. Elle mangera . . .**

S'il te plaît! ────────────────────────────

Votre partenaire vous dit ce qu'il/elle va faire. Demandez-lui de faire les choses suggérées (ou d'autres choses de votre choix).

Je vais aller à la poste.

Eh bien, quand tu iras à la poste, envoie cette lettre, s'il te plaît.

D'accord, j'enverrai cette lettre.

1. partir
   (fermer la porte)
2. faire les courses
   (acheter du fromage)
3. passer à la bibliothèque
   (rendre ce livre)
4. aller à la gare
   (prendre les billets)
5. aller à l'agence de voyages
   (réserver les places)
6. voir Patrick
   (l'inviter à la boum)

10 **Une visite à Genève** ──────────────────────────────

Jean-Philippe, un étudiant belge, va aller à Genève. Il écrit à sa copine Nathalie qui habite dans cette ville. Complétez sa lettre avec le présent ou le futur des verbes indiqués.

Ma chère Nathalie,

Je _____ le vol Swissair 804 qui _____ à Genève le 2 juin à 10h35. Je te _____ dès que je _____ à mon hôtel. Si tu _____ libre, on _____ déjeuner ensemble. Sinon, je _____ un peu, et s'il _____ beau, je _____ un tour en ville.

De toute façon (anyway), on _____ ensemble le soir. Si tu _____, on _____ dans un restaurant qu'un copain m'a recommandé. Quand je te _____, je te _____ les photos que j'ai prises l'année dernière.

Écris-moi lorsque tu _____ cette lettre.

À bientôt,
Jean-Philippe

(prendre / arriver)

(téléphoner / être)

(être / pouvoir / se reposer)

(faire / faire)

(sortir)

(vouloir / aller)

(voir / montrer)

(recevoir)

11 **Bienvenue chez nous!** ──────────────────────────────

Votre amie française Frédérique va passer le week-end dans votre ville. Préparez un programme d'activités que vous ferez ensemble et écrivez une lettre à Frédérique où vous expliquez ce programme. Utilisez des verbes comme **aller, voir, visiter, faire, dîner, déjeuner, prendre, se promener, s'arrêter.**

Ma chère Frédérique,
Je suis très content(e) que tu passes le week-end dans ma ville. J'irai te chercher à l'aéroport [à la gare / à la station de bus] vendredi soir. Voici ce que nous ferons lorsque tu seras ici.
Samedi matin, nous ...

D. Le conditionnel

In the sentences below, the verbs in heavy print are in the CONDITIONAL.

Si c'était les vacances, . . .   *If it were summer vacation, . . .*
- je **voyagerais**   - *I **would travel***
- nous **irions** au Sénégal   - *we **would go** to Senegal*
- vous **n'étudieriez pas**   - *you **would not study***

The CONDITIONAL is used to describe what people WOULD DO, what WOULD HAPPEN if a certain condition were to be met.

The CONDITIONAL is a simple tense which is formed as follows:

> FUTURE STEM + IMPERFECT ENDINGS

INFINITIVE	**parler**	**finir**	**vendre**	**aller**	IMPERFECT ENDINGS
FUTURE	je **parler**ai	**finir**ai	**vendr**ai	**ir**ai	
CONDITIONAL	je **parler**ais	**finir**ais	**vendr**ais	**ir**ais	-ais
	tu **parler**ais	**finir**ais	**vendr**ais	**ir**ais	-ais
	il/elle/on **parler**ait	**finir**ait	**vendr**ait	**ir**ait	-ait
	nous **parler**ions	**finir**ions	**vendr**ions	**ir**ions	-ions
	vous **parler**iez	**finir**iez	**vendr**iez	**ir**iez	-iez
	ils/elles **parler**aient	**finir**aient	**vendr**aient	**ir**aient	-aient
NEGATIVE	je ne **parler**ais pas				
INTERROGATIVE	est-ce que tu **parler**ais? **parler**ais-tu?				

➡ Verbs that have an irregular future stem keep the same stem in the conditional.
  avoir **aur-** j'**aur**ais   être **ser-** je **ser**ais

---

12 **Vivement les vacances!** *(Waiting for summer vacation)*

Les personnes suivantes rêvent des vacances. Dites ce qu'elles feraient et ce qu'elles ne feraient pas. Soyez logique!

▶ Mme Leduc (travailler? se reposer?)
  Mme Leduc ne travaillerait pas. Elle se reposerait.

1. nous (préparer l'examen? voyager?)
2. les élèves (aller à la plage? étudier?)
3. vous (rester chez vous? faire du camping?)
4. Marc (être tout le temps à la plage? regarder la télé?)
5. toi (te lever tôt? dormir jusqu'à dix heures?)
6. moi (faire mes devoirs? sortir avec mes copains?)

Le conditionnel

Pratique ▶ p. 60

LECTURE

Le mystérieux homme en bleu

AVANT DE LIRE

Quand on lit une histoire illustrée, il est important de regarder les illustrations pour comprendre le sens général. Si on peut deviner° plus ou moins ce qui va arriver, il est beaucoup plus facile de comprendre les détails.

Le mystérieux homme en bleu est une histoire policière illustrée. Avec votre partenaire, regardez bien les illustrations pour avoir une idée générale de ce qui se passe. Avant de commencer la lecture de l'histoire à la page suivante, essayez de répondre aux questions suivantes.

1. Qui est le mystérieux homme en bleu?
   - un détective privé
   - un inspecteur de police
   - un espion international

2. Qui est Caroline?
   - une jeune touriste
   - la complice de l'homme en bleu
   - la cousine de l'homme à la mallette jaune

3. Pourquoi est-ce que la chambre de Caroline est en désordre?
   - Des voleurs sont entrés pour voler ses chèques de voyage.
   - La police est venue chercher des documents volés.
   - L'homme à la mallette est venu chercher son passeport.

Maintenant lisez l'histoire et voyez si vous aviez raison.

deviner *to guess*

Mots utiles

LES PERSONNAGES

un détective privé	*private eye*
un inspecteur de police	*police detective*
un(e) espion(ne)	*spy*
un voleur (une voleuse)	*thief*
un(e) complice	*accomplice*
une bande	*gang*

QUELQUES OBJETS

une loupe	*magnifying glass*
une mallette	*briefcase*
une plaque d'immatriculation	*license plate*

LES ACTIONS

récupérer	*to get back, recuperate*
arrêter	*to arrest*
cacher	*to hide*
voler	*to steal*
sauver	*to save*
disparaître *	*to disappear, to go away*

Le mystérieux homme en bleu

Première partie

Caroline a fait ses valises. Puis elle a pris son passeport et son billet d'avion et elle a appelé un taxi pour aller à Mirabel, l'aéroport international de Montréal. Dans le taxi, Caroline pense au voyage qu'elle va faire. 5
C'est la première fois qu'elle va en France. Elle passera trois semaines là-bas, avec l'argent qu'elle a économisé pendant l'année. Elle espère faire un excellent voyage. Ce sera peut-être un voyage plein d'aventures 10
extraordinaires. Qui sait?

Caroline est arrivée à l'aéroport une heure avant le départ de l'avion Montréal-Paris. Elle est allée au comptoir d'Air Canada où elle a présenté son billet 15
et son passeport et elle a enregistré ses bagages.
Puis, elle est allée dans la salle d'embarquement. Là, elle a immédiatement remarqué un mystérieux homme vêtu de 20
bleu:° pantalon bleu, pull bleu, blouson bleu, casquette bleue et lunettes de soleil. «Quel homme étrange!» a pensé Caroline.

Bientôt° on a annoncé le départ pour Paris. Caroline et les autres passagers sont montés dans l'avion. L'homme en bleu aussi. 25

Caroline est allée à sa place. Le mystérieux homme en bleu est venu s'asseoir derrière elle. Pendant le voyage, Caroline a regardé quelques magazines, puis elle a dîné et elle a vu le film. Après le film, elle a dormi un peu. 30
Quand elle s'est réveillée, Caroline a regardé derrière elle. L'homme en bleu n'était plus là… il avait changé de place.
Finalement, après six heures de vol, l'avion est arrivé à Roissy, l'aéroport de Paris. 35

vêtu de bleu = qui portait des vêtements bleus   **bientôt** = dans peu de temps

Caroline a pris son sac à main et elle est sortie de l'avion. Puis elle est allée chercher ses deux valises. Malheureusement, celles-ci sont très lourdes et Caroline n'est pas très forte. Voyant° l'embarras° de Caroline, un grand jeune homme blond avec une mallette de cuir jaune s'est approché d'elle.

40

– Est-ce que je peux vous aider avec vos valises?

– Ah oui, s'il vous plaît.

– Tenez, prenez ma mallette et moi, je vais porter vos valises.

45

Caroline a pris la mallette du jeune homme et le jeune homme a pris les valises de Caroline. Ils sont passés ensemble par la douane, sans problème.

De l'autre côté de° la douane, il y avait l'homme en bleu. Il a regardé longuement Caroline, puis il a disparu. «Ce type° est vraiment bizarre,» a pensé Caroline.

50

Caroline et son compagnon sont sortis de l'aéroport. Une femme très élégante, dans une petite voiture de sport rouge, attendait le jeune homme. Elle avait l'air un peu irritée de voir Caroline. Le jeune homme a posé les valises de Caroline par terre° et il a appelé un taxi pour elle. Caroline a remercié le jeune homme et elle lui a demandé un petit service.

55

– J'ai promis à mes amies de leur envoyer des photos de moi à Paris. Voici mon appareil. Est-ce que vous pouvez prendre une ou deux photos?

60

– Mais, bien sûr! Avec plaisir!

Caroline s'est mise° à côté de la voiture de sport et le jeune homme a pris plusieurs photos.

– Merci beaucoup.

– Bon séjour en France!

65

Le jeune homme est monté dans la voiture de sport qui est partie très vite. Caroline est montée dans le taxi et elle est allée directement à son hôtel.

voyant = quand il a vu   **l'embarras** = la difficulté   **de l'autre côté de** = après   **ce type** = cette personne
a posé = a mis   **par terre** = sur le trottoir (sidewalk)   **s'est mise** = est allé se placer

Avez-vous compris?

1. À quelle occasion est-ce que Caroline a rencontré l'homme en bleu pour la première fois? Décrivez-le.
2. Qu'est-ce que Caroline a fait dans l'avion Montréal-Paris?
3. À l'arrivée à l'aéroport, que fait le jeune homme blond pour aider Caroline? Qu'est-ce qu'elle fait en échange?
4. Quel service est-ce que Caroline demande au jeune homme à la sortie de l'aéroport?

À votre avis

Pourquoi la femme élégante était-elle irritée de voir Caroline?
- Elle était jalouse de Caroline.
- Elle était très pressée *(in a hurry)* de partir.
- Elle avait une autre raison. Laquelle?

Deuxième Partie

À l'hôtel, Caroline a défait ses valises. Elle a changé de vêtements et elle est sortie. Elle est allée d'abord dans un café où elle a commandé un café et des croissants. Quelques minutes après, l'homme en bleu est, lui aussi, entré dans le café. 70 75

«Encore lui!° Mais qu'est-ce qu'il fait ici?» a pensé Caroline.

Elle a fini son café et ses croissants, et elle est sortie du café en vitesse.°

Caroline est allée au jardin du Luxembourg où elle a fait une promenade. Derrière, il y avait l'homme en bleu. Elle a pris un taxi et elle est allée au musée du Louvre. L'homme en bleu est sorti d'un autre taxi et il est entré au Louvre. 80

«Zut, zut et zut! Pourquoi est-ce que ce type me suit partout?» Caroline est sortie

du musée et elle a pris un bus pour aller aux Champs-Elysées. Elle a regardé derrière elle. Cette fois-ci, l'homme en bleu ne la suivait pas. «Je l'ai finalement perdu… Je suis sauvée!» a-t-elle pensé. 85

À sept heures, Caroline a décidé de dîner sur un bateau-mouche.* Quelle façon magnifique de passer une première soirée à Paris! Finalement, à onze heures, elle est rentrée à son hôtel. Pas de trace de l'homme en bleu! 90

Quand Caroline a ouvert la porte de sa chambre, elle a tout de suite° vu que celle-ci° était dans le désordre le plus complet. Et debout,° au milieu de la chambre, était l'homme en bleu accompagné de deux hommes en imperméable beige.

«Qu'est-ce que vous faites dans ma chambre? a crié Caroline. Si vous ne sortez pas immédiatement, j'appellerai la police.» 95

«Mais, mademoiselle, a répondu l'homme en bleu, nous sommes de la police.» Et il a montré sa carte de police à Caroline.

– Qu'est-ce que vous voulez?

– Nous voulons savoir où est la mallette. 100

– Quelle mallette?

– La mallette de cuir jaune que votre complice vous a donnée.

– Je ne comprends pas. De quel complice parlez-vous?

– Allons, mademoiselle, ne faites pas l'innocente.°

– Mais je suis innocente! 105

– Alors, qui est ce jeune homme blond qui est sorti de l'aéroport avec vous ce matin?

– Mais, je ne sais pas! Je ne le connais pas!

* Les bateaux-mouches sont des bateaux touristiques qui traversent Paris. Le soir, on peut y dîner.

encore lui = toujours la même personne   **en vitesse** = rapidement
tout de suite = immédiatement   **celle-ci** *the latter* [= sa chambre]   **debout** *standing*   **ne faites pas l'innocente** *don't act innocent*

L'homme en bleu a compris que Caroline disait la vérité. Alors, il a expliqué: 110

«Je suis l'inspecteur de police Louis Legrand. Il y a un mois, des documents secrets très importants ont été volés au Ministère des Transports. Ces documents concernent la construction de la station 115 spatiale franco-canadienne. La semaine dernière, un de nos agents a signalé la présence à Montréal du chef de la bande responsable de ce vol. Cette personne, c'est le jeune homme blond avec qui vous étiez ce 120 matin. Samedi dernier, je suis allé à Montréal pour prendre contact avec notre agent. Grâce aux renseignements,° j'ai pu retrouver la trace du jeune homme en question. Je l'ai suivi quand il a pris l'avion Montréal-Paris.

«À Roissy, il vous a donné la mallette dans laquelle sont les documents. J'ai pensé 125 que vous étiez sa complice. En réalité, il a profité de vous pour passer la mallette par la douane sans problème. Je vous ai suivie parce que je pensais que vous aviez toujours° la mallette. J'ai fait erreur et je m'excuse. Évidemment, le problème pour nous, c'est que nous avons perdu la trace de ce dangereux bandit et de la mallette.»

«Je crois que je peux vous aider,» a répondu Caroline. 130

— Mais comment?

— Attendez demain, et donnez-moi votre adresse.

L'inspecteur Legrand a donné sa carte à Caroline et il a quitté l'hôtel, accompagné de ses deux assistants.

grâce aux renseignements = avec l'information qu'il m'a donnée   **toujours** *still*

Avez-vous compris?

1. Où est-ce que Caroline a revu l'homme après être sortie de l'hôtel? Où est-ce qu'elle l'a perdu?
2. Quelle surprise Caroline a-t-elle eue quand elle est rentrée chez elle?
3. Comment est-ce que l'homme en bleu et ses assistants ont justifié leur présence dans la chambre de Caroline?
4. D'après l'homme en bleu, qui est le jeune homme blond? Pourquoi a-t-il pensé que Caroline était sa complice?

Anticipons un peu!

Comment est-ce que Caroline va aider les policiers à retrouver le jeune homme blond?
- Elle a sa photo.
- Elle a son adresse.
- Elle a un autre renseignement. Lequel?

Troisième Partie

Le lendemain à deux heures 135
de l'après-midi, Caroline est allée voir
l'inspecteur Legrand au quartier général
de la police.

— Bonjour, Inspecteur, j'ai une très
bonne nouvelle pour vous. 140

— Ah bon? Quoi?

— Vous allez pouvoir retrouver
la trace de vos voleurs de documents.

— Vraiment? Comment?

Caroline a ouvert son sac d'où 145
elle a tiré° les photos prises hier à l'aéroport.

— Regardez bien ces deux photos. Je les ai fait développer ce matin.

— Mais ce sont des photos de vous!

— Oui, bien sûr, mais regardez de plus près la voiture de sport rouge.

— Je vois bien. C'est une Alfa-Roméo. 150

— C'est aussi la voiture qu'ont prise le jeune homme et sa véritable° complice
à l'aéroport. Prenez votre loupe. Vous pourrez lire très nettement son numéro
d'immatriculation.

L'inspecteur Legrand a pris sa loupe.

— Vous avez raison, mademoiselle. Je vais alerter immédiatement tous les postes 155
de gendarmerie pour qu'on retrouve cette voiture et ses occupants.

Une semaine après, la police a arrêté
le chef de bande et sa complice et les
documents secrets ont été récupérés.

L'histoire de Caroline a été 160
publiée en première page de tous
les journaux. Caroline a donné
plusieurs interviews à la radio et à
la télévision. Un studio de cinéma lui
a proposé un rôle dans un prochain 165
film et une maison d'édition a pris
contact avec elle pour publier le
récit° de ses aventures.

a tiré = a sorti   **véritable** = réelle   **le récit** = l'histoire

---

Avez-vous compris?

1. Qu'est-ce que Caroline a apporté le lendemain?
2. En quoi est-ce que cela a aidé l'inspecteur?
3. Comment s'est terminée l'histoire pour le jeune homme blond? pour Caroline?

Et vous?

Imaginez que vous êtes Caroline. Qu'est-ce que vous allez faire?
- Accepter l'offre du studio de cinéma?
- Écrire le récit de vos aventures?

Pourquoi avez-vous choisi cette option?

EXPRESSION ORALE

■ Dramatisation
Avec un groupe de camarades, transformez cette histoire en petite pièce de théâtre et jouez-la.

■ Situations
Avec votre partenaire, choisissez l'une des situations suivantes. Composez le dialogue correspondant et jouez-le en classe.

1 Un coup de téléphone
Caroline téléphone à un(e) ami(e) québécois(e) pour lui raconter ses aventures. L'ami(e) interrompt souvent et lui pose beaucoup de questions sur ce qui est arrivé.
(Utilisez la forme **tu**.)

Rôles: Caroline, son ami(e)

2 Une interview
Un(e) journaliste pour Radio-Québec a obtenu une interview avec Caroline et lui pose beaucoup de questions. Il/Elle voudrait savoir ce que Caroline fera si elle accepte la proposition du studio de cinéma ou de la maison d'édition. Caroline est très contente de répondre. (Utilisez la forme vous.)

Rôles: le/la journaliste, Caroline

EXPRESSION ÉCRITE

L'histoire de «l'homme en bleu» est écrite objectivement, et cependant vous avez pu remarquer que l'auteur décrit les événements du point de vue de Caroline. Utilisez votre imagination pour raconter la même histoire d'un autre point de vue. Voici trois options:

■ Le rapport de l'inspecteur de police
L'inspecteur Louis Legrand, qui vient de recevoir les photos de Caroline, écrit un rapport à son chef. Dans ce rapport, il décrit ce qui est arrivé et aussi comment il arrêtera les voleurs.

■ Journal d'un prisonnier
L'homme à la mallette jaune (vous pouvez lui donner un nom) est maintenant en prison. Dans son journal intime, il décrit les événements qui ont mené à son arrestation.

■ Article de journal
Un(e) journaliste écrit un article où il décrit comment la police a récupéré les documents volés. Il utilise un style très direct.

■ Les dates

- 1715

*Règne de
Louis XV*

- 1774

*Règne de
Louis XVI*

- **1789**: Prise
de la Bastille

**Révolution
française**

- 1804

***Premier Empire:
Napoléon Ier***

- 1814

- 1830 *Révolution*

- 1852

*Second Empire:
Napoléon III*

- 1870

■ Les événements

La Révolution française (1789-1799)

La Révolution française est peut-être la période la plus importante de l'histoire de France. Cette révolution a été inspirée par la Révolution américaine. Le 14 juillet 1789, les Français ont pris **la Bastille**, une prison qui était le symbole de l'autorité royale. Le 26 août de la même année, ils ont voté la **Déclaration des Droits de l'Homme et du Citoyen** qui proclamait un principe nouveau: l'égalité et la liberté pour tous les hommes.

Trois ans plus tard, les Français ont aboli la monarchie et ont institué la République. C'est la Révolution qui a donné à la France sa devise:° «**Liberté, Égalité, Fraternité**».

La Révolution a aussi divisé la France en «départements» et a institué le système métrique.

L'épopée napoléonienne (1799-1815)

Napoléon Bonaparte (1769-1821) était le plus brillant général de la Révolution française. En 1799, à l'âge de 30 ans, il a pris le pouvoir° absolu. Cinq ans plus tard, en 1804, il s'est proclamé empereur des Français sous le nom de **Napoléon Ier**.

À cette époque, la France avait beaucoup d'ennemis: tous les pays d'Europe étaient coalisés° contre elle. Allant de victoire en victoire, «l'Aigle» (c'était le nom que les soldats avaient donné à Napoléon) a battu ses adversaires les uns après les autres. Au passage, Napoléon annexait les pays qu'il venait de conquérir. En dix ans, il a conquis presque toute l'Europe. Mais finalement la chance a tourné et l'armée de Napoléon a été défaite en Russie. Prisonnier des Anglais, Napoléon est mort en exil sur une petite île loin de la France.

Génie militaire, Napoléon a été aussi un grand administrateur. Il a développé l'industrie. Il a encouragé les sciences. Il a ouvert de nombreuses écoles d'ingénieurs. Il a établi une solide administration. Il a institué le **Code Napoléon** qui reste la base du système de justice en France.

devise *motto*   **pouvoir** *power*   **coalisés** = alliés   **chance** *luck*

■ *Les personnes*

Marie-Antoinette, Reine de France

Marie-Antoinette (1755-1793) est peut-être la figure la plus tragique de l'histoire de France. C'était une princesse autrichienne,° mais elle avait autant de sang° français que son mari, **Louis XVI**. Elle a épousé° celui-ci à l'âge de 15 ans et est devenue reine° à 19 ans.

Idéaliste et généreuse, elle a pris parti pour la cause des insurgés américains. C'est en partie grâce à° son influence que Louis XVI a envoyé sa marine et ses meilleures troupes aider les Américains pendant la Guerre d'Indépendance.

Romantique, très belle et pleine° de vie, elle aimait les fêtes. Pendant la Révolution, la famille royale a tenté, sans succès, de s'échapper de France. Arrêtée, Marie-Antoinette a été accusée d'avoir aidé les ennemis de la patrie. Elle a été emprisonnée, jugée, condamnée à mort et guillotinée.

Marie-Antoinette (1755-1793)

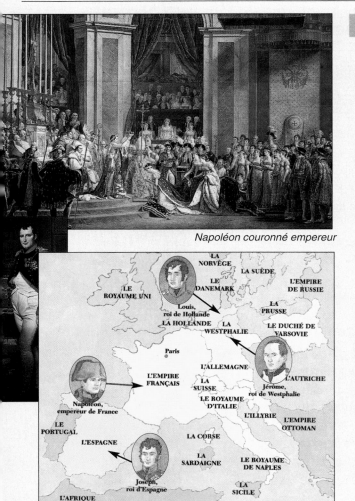

Napoléon couronné empereur

L'Empereur Napoléon et sa famille

Napoléon (1769-1821) est né en Corse,° une petite île au sud de la France. À l'âge de dix ans, il est allé en France faire ses études dans une école militaire. Ses camarades se moquaient° de lui parce qu'il parlait français avec l'accent corse. Napoléon, lui, pensait à sa famille à laquelle il était très attaché.

Vingt-cinq ans plus tard, quand il a été couronné empereur, toute sa famille était présente. Napoléon avait trois frères: **Joseph**, **Louis**, **Jérôme**. Quand il a conquis l'Europe, il a donné à chacun un royaume.° C'est ainsi que Joseph est devenu roi d'Espagne, Louis, roi de Hollande, et Jérôme, roi de Westphalie.

Napoléon avait une famille encore plus grande qui était son armée, la «**Grande Armée**». Il a couvert d'honneurs ses généraux victorieux, et il leur a donné des titres rappelant° leurs victoires ou leurs campagnes. Son meilleur général, **Murat**, était aussi son meilleur ami et le mari de sa soeur, Caroline. Napoléon l'a nommé maréchal, grand amiral, prince d'Empire, grand duc de Berg et finalement roi de Naples.

Napoléon avait un fils, qu'il a nommé Roi de Rome à sa naissance, mais qui n'a pas régné. Son neveu, **Charles Louis Napoléon**, est devenu empereur des Français en 1852, sous le nom de **Napoléon III**.

---

autrichienne *Austrian* **sang** *blood* **a épousé** *married* **reine** *queen* **grâce à** *thanks to* **pleine** *full*
Corse *Corsica* se moquaient de *were laughing at* royaume *kingdom* rappelant *recalling*

■ L'héritage ■ de la Révolution

La prise de la Bastille

La **Révolution** est probablement la période la plus importante de l'histoire de France. Elle met fin° à l'**Ancien Régime*** et à ses abus. Elle établit les bases d'un gouvernement démocratique en affirmant l'égalité de tous les citoyens.° Ce fut pendant la Révolution que furent proclamés la République, l'abolition de l'esclavage° et les droits° de l'homme et du citoyen. La Révolution française fut aussi marquée par un énorme effort de centralisation qui unifia la France en donnant un certain nombre d'institutions communes au pays. La plupart de ces institutions subsistent aujourd'hui. Voici quelques institutions françaises qui remontent° à la Révolution.

Documents: Déclaration des Droits de l'Homme

Déclaration des Droits de l'Homme

Article I

« Les hommes naissent et demeurent libres et égaux en droits. »

Article IV

« La liberté consiste à pouvoir faire tout ce qui ne nuit pas à autrui. »

Article IX

« La libre communication des pensées et des opinions est un des droits les plus précieux de l'homme. »

■ La devise de la France: Liberté, égalité, fraternité

Cette devise° rappelle les objectifs politiques et sociaux de la Révolution. Elle fut adoptée en juin 1793. Malgré plusieurs interruptions, la fameuse trilogie est restée la devise officielle de la France. Aujourd'hui elle figure° sur les documents officiels et sur les pièces de monnaie.

COURS CONSTITUTIONNELLES EUROPÉENNES
Protection des Droits de l'Homme
LA POSTE 1993
2,50   *RÉPUBLIQUE FRANÇAISE*

* L'Ancien Régime: entre le 15ᵉ siècle et 1789, la France était une monarchie et la société française était divisée en trois ordres: le clergé, la noblesse (*nobility*) et le Tiers État (*third estate*).

met fin à *puts an end to*   **citoyen** *citizen*   **esclavage** *slavery*   **droits** *rights*
remontent *go back*   **devise** *motto*   **figure** *is on*

■ La fête nationale du 14 juillet

La **fête nationale** commémore la prise° de la Bastille par les Parisiens le 14 juillet 1789. Par ce geste symbolique, la population mettait en question° le pouvoir° royal. La Bastille fut démolie et ses pierres servirent à la construction de nombreuses maisons parisiennes. Ce n'est qu'en 1880 que la date du 14 juillet a été adoptée comme fête nationale.

La première fête du 14 juillet en 1790

La «Fête nationale» aujourd'hui

■ Le drapeau bleu, blanc, rouge

Avant la Révolution, il n'existait pas de drapeau national mais uniquement des drapeaux militaires dont les couleurs et les motifs variaient de régiment à régiment. (Le seul symbole national était alors la personne du roi.) L'origine du drapeau français remonte à la prise de la Bastille le 14 juillet 1789. Les révolutionnaires qui participèrent à cet événement portaient au chapeau une cocarde bleue et rouge, aux couleurs de la ville de Paris. Quelques jours plus tard, le roi Louis XVI ajouta° cette cocarde° bleue et rouge à la cocarde blanche royale (le blanc était alors le symbole de la monarchie française), créant ainsi la cocarde tricolore.

Ces trois couleurs — bleu, blanc, rouge — firent leur apparition sur les drapeaux et les étendards° des armées révolutionnaires. En 1830, le drapeau tricolore à bandes verticales égales devint de façon définitive l'emblème national.

■ Marianne: symbole de la République

Marianne

Cette femme coiffée du bonnet révolutionnaire est le symbole de la République française. (On attribue le nom «Marianne» à une citoyenne de Colmar, Marie-Anne Reubell.) Cette figure allégorique apparut d'abord sur les pièces de monnaie de la Révolution. Elle réapparut brandissant un drapeau dans le fameux tableau de Delacroix, *La Liberté guidant le peuple*. Depuis 1880, les bustes de Marianne ornent° toutes les mairies de France et son portrait est représenté sur les timbres et les pièces de monnaie.

Delacroix *«La Liberté guidant le peuple»*

---

prise *taking* **mettait en question** *was questioning* **pouvoir** *power* **ajouta** *added* **cocarde** *cockade* **étendards** *military banners*
ornent = *décorent*

■ Le musée du Louvre

Situé dans l'ancien palais royal du **Louvre**, le musée du Louvre est une création de la Révolution. Construit au 12e siècle, le Louvre était à l'origine une forteresse. Embelli et maintes° fois transformé, il a été pendant longtemps la résidence des rois de France. Quand Louis XIV a installé sa cour à Versailles, le Louvre est laissé plus ou moins à l'abandon. En 1793, le gouvernement de la Révolution a décidé d'en faire un grand musée national où le peuple pouvait admirer les collections confisquées aux rois de France.

    Sous l'Empire, le Louvre est devenu le Musée Napoléon. Napoléon y apportait les trésors d'art qu'il avait saisis° au cours de ses campagnes à travers° l'Europe. Plus tard, le Louvre s'est enrichi

Le Louvre et la pyramide du Louvre

d'antiquités romaines, grecques, égyptiennes et orientales. Aujourd'hui, c'est l'un des plus grands musées du monde.

■ Les départements français

Les **départements** ont remplacé les «généralités» de l'Ancien Régime. Leur création est le résultat d'une réforme proposée peu avant la Révolution et mise en place en 1790. Le découpage° de la France en départements permettait une administration plus facile du pays. (Il était possible à un homme à cheval de parcourir° un département en une journée.) À l'origine, il y avait 83 départements. Aujourd'hui, il y a 96 départements métropolitains.

maintes = beaucoup de   **saisis** = pris par force   **à travers** *across*
le découpage = la division   **parcourir** *to travel across*

■ Le franc et la monnaie française

Avant la Révolution, la monnaie consistait en une multitude de pièces d'or, d'argent et de bronze (écus, louis, sous, deniers, liards**) dont la valeur et le poids° pouvaient varier. La Révolution française uniformisa le système monétaire en adoptant une unité décimale, le **franc**, divisible en décimes et centimes. Le franc est resté la monnaie nationale jusqu'° en 2001.

* **Écus, louis, sous, deniers, liards**: ce sont les noms de ces diverses pièces de monnaie.

■ Le système métrique

Avant la Révolution, on utilisait des unités de distance, de poids et de volume qui variaient de région en région. Ainsi, suivant les provinces, le pied pouvait représenter 10 ou 12 pouces°. Suivant les villes, la livre° pouvait représenter 12, 14 ou 15 onces. . . Le gouvernement révolutionnaire décida de créer un système simple et uniforme. C'est ainsi que fut créé en 1793 le système métrique décimal.

■ L'armée nationale

Avant la Révolution, l'armée était un privilège de la noblesse. Pour être officier, il fallait être noble ou acheter sa charge.° Les soldats étaient des engagés° et des mercenaires étrangers. Les armées de la Révolution incorporèrent les Français de toute condition sociale. À la bataille de Valmy (20 septembre 1792), l'armée française crie pour la première fois: «Vive la Nation!»

La bataille de Valmy, 1792

---

jusqu' *until*   **poids** *weight*   **pouces** *inches*   **la livre** *pound*   **charge** *rank*   **engagés** = volontaires

■ L'histoire de la «Marseillaise»

La **«Marseillaise»** est l'hymne national de la France. Elle a été composée pendant la Révolution, mais, malgré° son nom, elle n'est pas d'origine marseillaise. Où donc est née cette célèbre chanson et dans quelles circonstances? Voici son histoire.

LA FRANCE

Avril 1792. Nous sommes en pleine effervescence révolutionnaire. La France vient de déclarer la guerre à l'Autriche.° Pour protéger la frontière,° une armée, l'armée du Rhin, a été cantonnée° à Strasbourg. Il y a des soldats partout° dans les rues. Le 24 avril, le maire° de Strasbourg offre un grand banquet aux officiers de la garnison. On mange, on boit, on chante, et on crie des slogans: «Vive la patrie!», «À bas° la tyrannie!», «À bas les ennemis de la France!» La ferveur patriotique et révolutionnaire est à son comble.°

Parmi° les officiers, il y a un jeune capitaine. Il s'appelle **Rouget de Lisle**. Militaire, il aime aussi la poésie et il joue du violon. Le maire de Strasbourg s'adresse à lui: «Dites donc, Rouget, vous êtes bien poète et musicien. Alors, pourquoi est-ce que vous ne composez pas quelque chose pour ces braves soldats qui vont défendre la patrie?»°

Rouget de Lisle ne dit rien, mais, rentré chez lui, il prend son violon et joue quelques notes. Puis il prend une plume° et écrit ces mots sur une feuille de papier: **«Allons, enfants de la patrie. . . Le jour de gloire est arrivé. . .»** Toute la nuit, il travaille et retravaille les paroles et la musique d'un puissant° chant de guerre. Au petit matin, il a fini.

À dix heures, il se présente chez le maire. «Monsieur le maire, j'ai votre chanson.» Il se met° au piano et commence: «Allons, enfants de la patrie. . .» Chez le maire, c'est l'enthousiasme général. Rouget joue et rejoue l'air qu'il a intitulé «Chant de guerre pour l'armée du Rhin».

Le lendemain, le texte de cette chanson est imprimé° et distribué. Quelques jours plus tard, la musique de la Garde Nationale joue cet hymne révolutionnaire sur la place d'Armes° de Strasbourg. Dans la foule,° c'est le délire. Tout le monde reprend en chœur «Marchons, marchons. . .»

Bientôt° le «Chant de guerre pour l'armée du Rhin» est dans la bouche de tous les soldats. Il passe de garnison en garnison. Partout il enflamme les esprits. En juin 1792, la chanson arrive à Marseille. Là, un régiment de volontaires l'adopte comme son chant de marche. Ces soldats marseillais montent à Paris en chantant la redoutable chanson. Le chant de l'armée du Rhin devient le «Chant des Marseillais», puis, plus simplement, la «Marseillaise».

Le 14 juillet 1795, jour anniversaire de la Prise de la Bastille, la Marseillaise devient officiellement l'hymne national, mais pour quelques années seulement. En 1799, la Révolution est terminée. Un peu plus tard, Napoléon devient empereur. Général issu de la Révolution, il se méfie° maintenant de la révolution en général et des chants révolutionnaires en particulier. Il interdit° de jouer la Marseillaise.

La Marseillaise n'est plus l'hymne national français, mais elle devient un hymne révolutionnaire universel. C'est aux accents° de la Marseillaise que se font les révolutions du 19e siècle, en Allemagne, en Italie, dans le monde entier. . . Finalement, la République est rétablie en France et la Marseillaise redevient l'hymne national, mais seulement en 1879.

Depuis 1792, de nouvelles strophes° ont été ajoutées° au texte de la Marseillaise. Aujourd'hui, ce texte est l'objet de controverse. La Marseillaise est, en effet, un hymne terriblement guerrier° qui incite à la lutte° sans merci contre les ennemis de la patrie. À l'heure actuelle, la France n'a plus d'ennemis et elle veut la paix dans le monde. Pourquoi ne pas transformer la Marseillaise en un hymne pour la paix en changeant le texte? Beaucoup de Français seraient d'accord, mais beaucoup d'autres préfèrent garder ce texte traditionnel.

---

malgré in spite of **Autriche** Austria **frontière** border **cantonnée** stationed **partout** everywhere **maire** mayor **à bas** down with **à son comble** at its height **parmi** among **patrie** homeland **plume** (quill) pen **puissant** powerful **se met** = s'assied **imprimé** printed **place d'Armes** parade ground **foule** crowd **bientôt** soon thereafter **se méfie** is distrustful **interdit** prohibits **accents** tune **strophes** verses **ajoutées** added **guerrier** warlike **lutte** fight

MARCHE DES MARSEILLOIS
CHANTÉE SUR DIFERANS THEATRES
Chez Frère Passage du Saumon

La Marseillaise

Allons, Enfants de la Patrie,
Le jour de gloire est arrivé!
Contre nous de la tyrannie,
L'étendard sanglant° est levé,
L'étendard sanglant est levé.
Entendez-vous dans les campagnes
Mugir° ces féroces soldats?
Ils viennent jusque dans nos bras
Égorger° nos fils, nos compagnes.
refrain:
Aux armes, Citoyens!
Formez vos bataillons!
Marchons, marchons!
Qu'un sang impur abreuve nos sillons°!

Claude Joseph Rouget de Lisle (1760-1836)

Dans sa vie, le compositeur de la Marseillaise n'a pas eu de chance. Rouget de Lisle était d'origine noble. Quelque temps après avoir composé le célèbre hymne révolutionnaire, il est accusé d'être royaliste et, paradoxalement, d'être un ennemi de la Révolution. Condamné à mort, il échappe in extremis à la guillotine. (C'est la mort du dictateur Robespierre qui le sauve!)

Rouget de Lisle reprend l'uniforme et il est blessé° au combat. Il quitte l'armée et retourne à sa véritable vocation: la poésie et la musique. Il compose des chansons et écrit des pièces de théâtre, mais celles-ci n'ont pas beaucoup de succès. Vers° la fin de la vie, il n'a plus d'argent, mais beaucoup de dettes. Il meurt dans la misère.

blessé *wounded* **vers** *towards* **étendard sanglant** *blood-stained battle flag* **mugir** *roar* **égorger** *to slit the throats of*
qu'un sang impur abreuve nos sillons *may the impure blood [of our enemies] soak the furrows [of our fields].*

Chef-d'oeuvre° de la littérature française, *Les Misérables* a été adapté plus de 30 fois au cinéma. Plus récemment, une comédie musicale, tirée° du roman, a connu un succès retentissant° en France, en Angleterre et aux États-Unis.

L'action des *Misérables* se passe en France et se déroule° sur une période d'une vingtaine d'années au début du 19e siècle. Le personnage principal s'appelle **Jean Valjean**. Dans sa jeunesse, il a été arrêté pour avoir volé° un pain, un jour d'hiver. Arrêté pour ce menu° larcin,° il a été condamné au bagne* où il passe dix-neuf ans. Après plusieurs tentatives d'évasion,° il est finalement relâché,° mais il sera poursuivi toute sa vie par un policier implacable nommé **Javert**.

Sans argent, Jean Valjean va demander l'aumône° à la porte d'un évêque.° Celui-ci est un homme bon qui non seulement reçoit Jean Valjean, mais le traite comme un égal, l'invite à sa table et lui offre l'hospitalité. La nuit, Jean Valjean quitte la maison de l'évêque en emportant° des plats d'argent. Il est arrêté par la police et reconduit chez l'évêque. Au lieu de l'accuser, ce personnage charitable explique aux policiers qu'il a donné les plats d'argent à Jean Valjean et qu'il n'y a par conséquent aucune raison de l'arrêter.

* **Le bagne:** Lieu où on envoyait les hommes condamnés à des travaux forcés. On appelait ces prisonniers des «bagnards» ou des «forçats».

Victor Hugo, écrivain et homme politique

Victor Hugo (1802-1885), l'auteur des *Misérables*, est l'un des géants de la littérature française. C'est peut-être le plus grand écrivain du 19ᵉ siècle. Chef de l'école romantique, il a écrit un grand nombre de poésies, de romans et de pièces de théâtre qui ont fait scandale à l'époque pour leur audacité et leur caractère révolutionnaire.

Victor Hugo a aussi joué un rôle politique important. C'était le fils d'un général de Napoléon. S'il admirait beaucoup cet empereur, il détestait profondément son neveu, Louis-Napoléon, qui avait lui-même pris le pouvoir° par un coup d'état et était devenu empereur sous le nom de Napoléon III. Condamné pour ses idées républicaines, Victor Hugo a été obligé de s'enfuir° en Angleterre où il a passé plusieurs années d'exil.

Victor Hugo est rentré en France après l'abdication de Napoléon, acclamé comme un héros. Devenu sénateur, il a pris le parti des opprimés°, des déshérités, des gens sans protection et sans ressources et il s'est battu° pour la liberté, l'égalité et la justice. C'est cet esprit de compassion pour les petits gens qu'il manifeste dans sa grande oeuvre° *Les Misérables*.

Victor Hugo (1802-1885)

chef-d'oeuvre *masterpiece* **tirée de** = *basée sur* **retentissant** = *très grand* **se déroule** *takes place* **volé** *stolen* **menu** = *petit* **larcin** *theft* **tentatives d'évasion** *escape attempts* **relâché** *released* **l'aumône** = *la charité* **évêque** *bishop* **emportant** = *prenant avec lui* **pouvoir** *power* **s'enfuir** *to flee* **opprimés** *oppressed* **s'est battu** *fought* **oeuvre** *work*

Cet acte généreux va transformer Jean Valjean. Il prend le nom de **Monsieur Madeleine** et sous ce nom devient un personnage riche et respecté de tous. Élu° maire° de sa ville, il mène° une vie simple et exemplaire. À son tour, il est charitable et généreux avec tout le monde.

Un jour, il apprend qu'un homme vient d'être arrêté pour un vol° que lui, Jean Valjean, a commis autrefois. Pris° de remords, il va se dénoncer à la police. Condamné cette fois à la prison à vie, il arrive° à s'évader,° toujours poursuivi par Javert.

Les années ont passé. Jean Valjean habite maintenant à Paris. Il a recueilli° **Cosette**, une petite orpheline dont il a connu la mère autrefois. Cosette est fiancée à **Marius**, un étudiant aux idées révolutionnaires. Un jour la révolution éclate.° Marius prend la tête d'une barricade. Javert est fait prisonnier par les insurgés, mais Jean Valjean intervient en sa faveur et lui sauve la vie.

Marius est blessé lors d'une contre-attaque des forces gouvernementales. Averti° par **Gavroche**, un gamin° de Paris, Jean Valjean arrive. Il prend Marius dans ses bras et le transporte pendant des kilomètres à travers les égouts° de Paris. Javert l'attend. Il reconnaît l'ancien bagnard évadé. Les deux hommes se font face. Javert n'ose° pas arrêter l'homme qui lui a sauvé la vie. Il se suicide. . . Peu après, Marius et Cosette se marient, et Jean Valjean meurt, heureux d'avoir contribué à leur bonheur.

Gavroche, gamin de Paris

Immortalisé par Victor Hugo dans *Les Misérables*, Gavroche est l'éternel «gamin° de Paris». Il a une douzaine d'années. On ne sait où il vit, ni de quoi il vit. Sa vraie famille, c'est le petit peuple du quartier où il passe ses jours et ses nuits. C'est un rebelle, mais il n'est pas révolté. Il siffle,° il chante. . . Il est libre, insouciant,° joyeux. . . Il n'a peur de rien. Quand la révolution éclate, il monte sur les barricades. Frappé° par une balle,° il meurt héroïquement, en chantant une chanson.

élu *elected* **maire** *mayor* **mène** *leads* **vol** *theft* **pris par** *seized by* **arrive à** *manages to* **s'évader** *to escape* **recueilli** = *adopté*
éclate *breaks out* **averti** *notified* **gamin** *kid* **égouts** *sewers* **ose** *dares* **siffle** *whistles* **insouciant** *carefree*
frappé *hit* **balle** *bullet*

UNITÉ 6

Séjour en France

Thème et Objectifs

Culture

In this unit, you will discover . . .

- the different places where you can stay while visiting France
- how to use a French guidebook to find a hotel

Communication

You will learn how . . .

- to reserve a hotel room
- to ask for services in a hotel

Langue

You will learn how . . .

- to compare people or things
- to express who or what is the best
- to indicate what belongs to you and what belongs to other people
- to point out specific people or things and ask questions about them

Les jeunes touristes en France

Chaque année, soixante-quinze millions de touristes étrangers visitent la France. Ces touristes viennent principalement d'Allemagne, d'Angleterre, de Belgique, de Hollande et d'Italie, mais il y a aussi beaucoup de touristes américains, canadiens, japonais …. Pour accueillir° ces millions de touristes, la France dispose° d'un grand nombre d'hôtels de toutes catégories. Il y a des hôtels très simples et des hôtels très luxueux. Le sommet du luxe consiste à passer quelques jours dans un château historique datant du seizième ou du dix-septième siècle. Là, vous serez vraiment traité comme un prince — ou une princesse! Évidemment, tout le monde n'a pas les moyens° financiers de se payer «la vie de château.» Heureusement, pour les jeunes qui préfèrent l'aventure au confort et au luxe, il y a d'autres solutions moins chères et aussi intéressantes. En voici quelques-unes.

Le séjour à la ferme

Si on aime le grand air et si on n'a pas besoin de grand confort, on peut faire un séjour dans une ferme. Pendant les vacances, beaucoup de fermiers louent des «chambres d'hôte»° pour des prix très raisonnables. Le petit déjeuner est généralement compris° dans le prix de la chambre. Si on veut, on peut prendre les autres repas à la ferme aussi. L'ambiance est familiale et les produits de la ferme (souvent des spécialités régionales) sont absolument délicieux!

En été, il y a beaucoup de travail à faire dans les champs. Les fermiers ont souvent besoin de main d'oeuvre.° Ils recrutent parfois des étudiants pour participer à ces travaux. Dans ce cas le logement et la nourriture sont gratuits° et, en plus,° on reçoit° un peu d'argent.

Les auberges de jeunesse

Ce sont des hôtels très bon marché réservés aux jeunes touristes qui sont de passage dans une ville. Certaines auberges ont des chambres individuelles, mais généralement on dort dans un dortoir pour 6 à 10 personnes. L'atmosphère des auberges est sympathique et communale: on rencontre d'autres jeunes venus de tous les pays du monde, on fait la cuisine et on mange ensemble. On parle de ses voyages, on raconte des histoires et on rit° beaucoup. Si le confort est élémentaire,° la bonne humeur est toujours présente.

Pour aller dans les auberges de jeunesse, il faut être âgé de 18 ans et posséder une carte de la FUAJ (Fédération Unie des Auberges de Jeunesse) qu'on peut acheter pour 10 euros.

Le camping

Il y a différentes façons de faire du camping. On peut aller dans un terrain de camping aménagé.° En France il existe des milliers° de terrains de camping équipés d'eau courante, de WC et de douches. Si on préfère la nature ou la solitude, on peut aussi faire du «camping sauvage.» Dans ce cas, on plante sa tente là où on veut: dans une prairie, dans une forêt, près d'une rivière…. Mais attention! Si on est sur une propriété privée, il faut demander et obtenir° l'autorisation du propriétaire.°

et vous?

DISCUSSION
Avec votre partenaire, discutez le sujet suivant:
• Vous allez faire un voyage en France cet été, mais vous n'avez pas beaucoup d'argent. Quelle solution allez-vous choisir pour votre logement? (faire du camping? aller dans les auberges de jeunesse? prendre une chambre dans une ferme? trouver une autre solution?) Expliquez les avantages et les inconvénients de la solution que vous avez choisie.

accueillir ✻ to welcome dispose = a moyens = les ressources rire ✻ to laugh élémentaire = rudimentaire aménagé = équipé milliers thousands obtenir ✻ to get, obtain propriétaire owner chambres d'hôte guest rooms compris = inclus main d'oeuvre = travailleurs gratuits free en plus in addition reçoit = gagner

Le Guide MICHELIN

Quand on voyage, il est utile d'avoir des renseignements° pratiques sur les villes qu'on va visiter. Par exemple: Quelles sont les choses les plus intéressantes à voir? Quel est l'hôtel le plus confortable, ou le moins cher? Où sont les meilleurs restaurants? Pour obtenir ces renseignements, on peut téléphoner au bureau de Tourisme de la ville ou on peut suivre° les recommandations d'un ami, mais le plus simple est d'acheter un guide. Le plus célèbre guide français est *Le Guide Michelin.*

Pour chaque ville, *Le Guide Michelin Rouge* présente une sélection d'hôtels et de restaurants (et, si la ville est assez grande, un plan de la ville). Pour chaque hôtel et chaque restaurant de cette liste, tous les renseignements nécessaires sont donnés: adresse, qualité, prix, etc.... Les touristes peuvent facilement choisir les hôtels et les restaurants qui correspondent à leurs goûts... et à leurs ressources financières.

Le Guide Michelin est publié chaque année. Pour s'assurer de la qualité d'un restaurant ou du confort d'un hôtel, les inspecteurs Michelin visitent régulièrement, mais à l'improviste,° ces établissements. Suivant° les résultats de l'enquête, un restaurant ou un hôtel peut monter ou descendre de catégorie. Pour les grands restaurants, la classification dans *Le Guide Michelin* est extrêmement importante. Une étoile signifie le succès, deux étoiles l'honneur, trois étoiles la gloire. Dans toute la France, il y a seulement 22 restaurants «trois étoiles.»

une étoile   **deux étoiles**   **trois étoiles**

La société Michelin

Michelin est l'une des plus grandes entreprises françaises. Son activité principale n'est pas la publication de guides touristiques, mais la fabrication des pneus.° Aujourd'hui Michelin est le deuxième producteur de pneus du monde avec 18% de la production mondiale.

Le succès de cette firme remonte° à l'invention en 1891 du pneumatique démontable° avec chambre à air° par deux frères, André et Édouard Michelin. Cette invention a d'abord été appliquée à la bicyclette, puis à la voiture à cheval et finalement à l'automobile. Premier succès: en 1895, une voiture équipée de

pneus Michelin a terminé la course Paris-Bordeaux-Paris, faisant ainsi la preuve° qu'on pouvait rouler° sur de l'air. En 1899, grâce° au pneu, une autre automobile, la «Jamais Contente» a atteint° pour la première fois la vitesse° alors inimaginable de 100 kilomètres à l'heure.

Pour encourager la vente des pneus, il fallait encourager le tourisme. Pour cela, les frères Michelin ont eu l'idée géniale de publier des cartes et des guides touristiques (les Cartes et les Guides Michelin). Le Guide Michelin a été créé en 1900. Jusqu'en 1920, il était distribué gratuitement° à tous les automobilistes. Aujourd'hui, c'est le «best seller» français: 1.500.000 exemplaires° du fameux guide rouge sont vendus chaque année dans le monde!

---

renseignements = informations   **suivre** ✶ *to follow*   **l'improviste** *unannounced*   **suivant** *according to*   **pneus** *tires*   **remonte** *goes back*
démontable *which can be removed*   **chambre à air** *innertube*   **preuve** = *prouvant*   **rouler** *drive*   **grâce à** *thanks to*   **atteindre** ✶ *to reach*
vitesse *speed*   **gratuitement** *free of charge*   **exemplaires** *copies*

Comment lire le Guide Michelin

Les catégories

 Grand luxe et tradition

Grand confort

Très confortable

De bon confort

 Assez confortable

Simple mais convenable

L'installation

Repas au jardin ou en terrasse

Salle de remise en forme - Tennis

Piscine en plein air / couverte

Jardin

Ascenseur - Air conditionné

Chambres pour non-fumeurs

Prise Modem dans la chambre

P **P** *Parking - Parking clos - Garage*

Chambres accessibles aux handicapés physiques

TV *Télévision dans la chambre*

Petit déjeuner

GB *Carte Bancaire*

Imaginez que vous allez visiter le château d'Amboise, près de Tours. Vous avez réservé une chambre à l'hôtel Belle Vue. Voici la description de cet hôtel:

Un hôtel à Amboise

Amboise est une petite ville très touristique, à cause de son impressionnant château royal. Voici la description d'un hôtel à Amboise, l'Hôtel Belle Vue, dans le *Guide Michelin.*

```
      ┌─1─┐ ┌─2─┐                    ┌────3────┐        ┌4┐┌5┐
  🏠   Belle Vue sans rest, 12 quai Ch. Guinot ℰ 02 47 57 02 26, Fax 02 47 30 51 23 – |≋| TV. GB.
      ┌──6──┐    ┌7┐ ┌─8─┐
  15 mars-15 nov. – ☕ 6 – 32 ch 46/57.
     ◆ Hôtel simple en bordure de Loire. Les chambres, assez grandes, sont de bon confort.
  Sur l'arrière, elles sont plus calmes et offrent une jolie vue sur le château.
```

1 **la catégorie**
L'hôtel Belle Vue est un hôtel confortable. (C'est un hôtel de bon confort.)

2 **le restaurant**
Cet hôtel n'a pas de restaurant. (Il est sans restaurant.)

3 **l'adresse**
Cet hôtel est situé 12, quai Charles Guinot. Le numéro de téléphone est le 02 47 57 02 26. Le numéro de fax est le 02 47 30 51 23.

4 **l'installation**
Il y a un ascenseur. Les chambres ont la télévision.

5 **mode de paiement**
On accepte les cartes bancaires.

6 **période d'ouverture**
L'hôtel est ouvert du 15 mars au 15 novembre.

7 **le petit déjeuner**
Le petit déjeuner coûte 6 euros.

8 **le nombre et le prix des chambres**
Il y a 32 chambres. Le prix des chambres est de 46 à 57 euros par jour.

et vous?

1. Selon vous, quels sont les trois éléments les plus importants de l'installation d'un hôtel? Pourquoi?

2. Imaginez que vous allez visiter Amboise (ou une autre ville française.) Avec un(e) camarade, consultez le «Michelin Guide Rouge» sur l'Internet et choisissez un hôtel. Expliquez votre choix.

© Michelin Le Guide Rouge France 2002, Permission No. 02-US-001.

À l'hôtel

> **Je voudrais une chambre.**

> **J'aimerais une chambre pour une personne.**

> **Bonjour, monsieur. Vous désirez?**

> **Quel genre de chambre désirez-vous?**

Où loger?

| On peut | aller
loger
séjourner
passer la nuit | dans | un hôtel de luxe.
un hôtel bon marché mais confortable.
une auberge *(inn)* à la campagne.
une auberge de jeunesse *(youth hostel).* |

> **loger** *to stay*
> **séjourner** *to stay*

À la réception *(reception desk)*

— Bonjour, mademoiselle/monsieur. Vous désirez?

| Je voudrais
Je voudrais **réserver** | une chambre. |

— **Quel genre** *(type)* de chambre désirez-vous?

J'aimerais une chambre . . .

| **pour une personne** | **pour deux personnes** |
| **à un lit** | **à deux lits** |

| avec | **douche**
salle de bains | **la climatisation** *(air conditioning)*
l'air conditionné |
| | **téléphone**
télévision | **un balcon**
une belle vue *(view)* |

— **Combien de temps** | **comptez**-vous rester?
Jusqu'à *(until)* **quand**

Je compte rester . . .

deux nuits	jusqu'à mardi
une semaine	jusqu'au 12 juillet
	du 2 au 15 juin

— Comment allez-vous payer?

Je vais payer . . .

| **en espèces** *(cash)* | **avec des chèques de voyage** |
| **par chèque** | **avec une carte de crédit** |

— Vous avez la chambre 315.
Voici votre **clé** *(key)*.

RENSEIGNEMENTS SUPPLÉMENTAIRES

— Est-ce que l'hôtel a . . .

une piscine
une salle d'exercices
le service dans les chambres *(room service)*
un ascenseur
un accès pour personnes handicapées

— Est-ce que je pourrais avoir une chambre . . .

plus grande	**plus claire**
plus spacieuse	**mieux située**
plus confortable	**moins chère**
plus calme	**moins bruyante**

— Combien coûte . . .

| la chambre | **la pension complète** *(full room and board)* |
| le petit déjeuner | **la demi-pension** *(room, breakfast and dinner)* |

> **compter** *to plan, to count on*

EUROCARD
LA CARTE MAÎTRESSE

> **spacieux** *roomy*
> **clair** *sunny*
> **bien situé** *well located*
> **bruyant** *noisy*

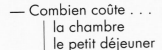
PETIT DÉJEUNER

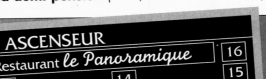

ASCENSEUR

Restaurant *le Panoramique*

Étages			
	13	14	16
	10	11	15
	7	8	12
	4	5	9
	1	2	6
			3

| Rez-de-chaussée | R | Réception | Coiffeur |
| | | Boutiques | Restaurant |

| Sous-sol | SS | Piscine | Garage |
| | | Salle d'exercices | |

1 La chose la plus importante

Quand on voyage, il est toujours agréable de séjourner dans des hôtels confortables. Voici certains éléments de confort symbolisés par des illustrations.

Liste

1.
2.
3.
4.
5.
6.

Quels sont les six éléments que vous considérez être les plus importants pour vous?

- Établissez votre liste en écrivant le nom de ces éléments par ordre d'importance.
- Comparez votre liste avec celle de votre partenaire.
- Quels sont les éléments que vous avez en commun avec votre partenaire?

2 Créa-dialogue: À l'hôtel Saint-François

Les touristes suivants veulent réserver une chambre à l'hôtel Saint-François. Choisissez l'un(e) de ces touristes. Avec votre partenaire, composez et jouez le dialogue entre ce/cette touriste (T) et le/la réceptionniste (R) de l'hôtel.

R: Allô, ici Hôtel Saint-François, bonjour!
T: *Say hello and say that you would like to reserve a room.*
R: *Ask what type of room the client would like.*
T: *Describe the room you would like to have, giving as many details as you wish.*
R: *Ask how long the client wants to stay.*
T: *Answer by giving the length of your stay.*
R: Je peux vous réserver une chambre *(give a price between 50 and 200 dollars).*
T: *Say whether you are going to take the room or not. If not, say thank you and good-bye.*
R: *If the client accepts, ask how he/she is going to pay.*
T: *Indicate your mode of payment.*
R: Parfait! Je vous réserve votre chambre.

TOURISTES

- un(e) étudiant(e) qui n'a pas beaucoup d'argent
- un professeur de français en vacances
- un(e) représentant(e) de commerce *(travelling salesperson)* en voyage d'affaires *(business trip)*
- un(e) journaliste
- un(e) millionnaire avec sa femme/son mari
- un couple de jeunes mariés *(newlyweds)*
- un couple de retraités *(retired couple)*

AMBOI...
...berge de la ramberge

3 Une lettre de réservation

Vous voulez passer plusieurs jours cet
été dans la ville d'Amboise avec votre
cousin(e). Écrivez une lettre de
réservation à l'Hôtel Belle Vue en
consultant le Guide Michelin à la page
229. Suivez le modèle proposé.

Annuelle 30/10-31/3 - Heb. rest. lundi sa...

Auberge Saint-Christophe
Cacve Médiévale~Diners aux Chandelles
2, rue de l' Englise
9551 Vétheuil
téléphone 01 34 78 11 50   fermé le mercredi

---

938 Grant Place
Boulder, CO 80302 USA
le 10 avril 200__

Novotel
Route de Chenonceaux
37400 Amboise, France

Monsieur, Madame,
   Je voudrais réserver une chambre non-
fumeur pour une personne. Je préférerais
une chambre avec une vue sur le château.
J'arriverai à Amboise le 21 juillet et je
partirai le 23.
   Dans l'attente de votre confirmation, je
vous prie d'agréer, Monsieur, Madame,
l'expression de mes sentiments distingués.

Patricia McDougall

        Patricia McDougall

Conversations libres

Avec votre partenaire, choisissez l'une des situations suivantes.
Composez le dialogue correspondant et jouez-le en classe.

1 Un touriste difficile

Vous êtes réceptionniste dans un
hôtel à Québec. Un(e) touriste très
difficile veut une chambre. Vous lui
montrez plusieurs chambres, mais
le/la touriste difficile veut toujours
quelque chose de différent. Il/elle
n'est jamais satisfait(e).

Rôles: le/la réceptionniste, le/la touriste

2 Une auberge de campagne

Vous voyagez en France avec toute
votre famille — 5 personnes au
total. Un soir vous arrivez dans une
petite auberge de campagne. Vous
n'avez pas réservé. L'hôtelier
(innkeeper) vous informe qu'il y a
seulement deux possibilités: une très
petite chambre sans confort et un
grand appartement très confortable
mais très cher. Négociez avec lui.

Rôles: le/la touriste, l'hôtelier

3 Une erreur

Vous avez réservé une chambre
bon marché dans un grand
hôtel à la Martinique. Quand
vous arrivez, on vous donne un
magnifique appartement avec
plage privée. Vous vous
installez. Dix minutes après,
la réceptionniste vous
téléphone pour vous dire qu'il
y a erreur et que vous devez
changer de chambre. Négociez
avec la réceptionniste pour
garder votre appartement.

*Rôles: la réceptionniste,
le/la touriste*

4 Déception

Vous allez passer deux semaines en
Normandie avec votre famille. Avant
votre départ, votre agence de voyages
vous a réservé des chambres dans
«une auberge de campagne très
pittoresque». En réalité, c'est un vieil
hôtel sans confort situé près d'une
gare où passent des trains toute
la nuit. À votre retour, vous passez
chez votre agent de voyages pour vous
plaindre *(to complain)*.

Rôles: le/la touriste, l'agent de voyages

5 La note

Vous venez de passer une semaine
dans une petite auberge en
Touraine. Au moment de payer,
vous présentez votre carte de
crédit américaine. La propriétaire
vous dit que l'hôtel accepte
seulement l'argent français.
Expliquez la situation et négociez
une solution.

Rôles: le/la touriste, la propriétaire

A. Le comparatif

Comparative constructions are used to compare people or things.

Cet hôtel est **aussi moderne que** l'autre.   *This hotel is **as modern as** the other one.*
J'ai **moins d'argent que** vous.   *I have **less money than** you.*

ADJECTIVES AND ADVERBS			
+ plus **– moins** **= aussi** } ADJECTIVE (or ADVERB) **(+ que)**	**plus** moderne **(que)** **moins** moderne **(que)** **aussi** moderne **(que)**	*more* modern *(than)* *less* modern *(than)* *as* modern *(as)*	

➡ STRESS PRONOUNS are used after **que**.

Je suis aussi intelligent **que toi.**

➡ The comparative of the ADJECTIVE **bon/bonne** is **meilleur/meilleure**.
The comparative of the ADVERB **bien** is **mieux**.
Compare:

Je suis **meilleur** en tennis **que** toi.   *I am **better** at tennis **than** you.*
Je joue **mieux.**   *I play **better**.*

NOUNS		
+ plus de **– moins de** } NOUN **(+ que)** **= autant de**	**plus d**'argent **(que)** **moins d**'argent **(que)** **autant d**'argent **(que)**	*more* money *(than)* *less* money *(than)* *as much* money *(as)*

1   Ah, le bon vieux temps!

Monsieur Ladoux a passé toute sa vie dans le même village. Il se souvient du bon temps de sa jeunesse où tout était meilleur qu'aujourd'hui. Jouez le rôle de Monsieur Ladoux. Soyez logique!

▶ air / pur?

Autrefois, l'air était plus pur.

1. les rivières / polluées?
2. les produits / artificiels?
3. la nourriture / bonne?
4. les jeunes / sérieux?
5. les gens / préoccupés par l'argent?

6. les relations entre les gens / bonnes?
7. la société / matérialiste?
8. les problèmes de l'existence / compliqués?
9. la vie / simple?

2 Où loger?

Vos amis et vous, vous voyagez en Touraine. Où allez-vous loger? Dans une auberge de campagne *(country inn)* ou dans un grand hôtel à Tours? Avec votre partenaire (ou votre groupe), faites une liste des avantages que vous désirez et classez-les par ordre d'importance. Faites votre choix sur la base de cette liste.

Auberge de campagne	**Grand hôtel en ville**
• C'est moins cher.	• C'est plus luxueux.
• C'est plus calme.	• C'est plus confortable.
• On s'y repose mieux.	• Les chambres sont mieux équipées.
• La nourriture est meilleure.	• La piscine est plus grande.
• On mange plus de produits naturels.	• Le service est mieux organisé.
• L'air est plus pur.	• On est servi plus rapidement.
• Les chambres sont moins bruyantes.	• On visite plus facilement la ville.
• Le service est plus personnalisé.	• Il y a plus de choses à faire.
• On dort mieux.	• Il y a plus de choses intéressantes à faire.
• ??	• ??

3 Décisions, décisions

Avec votre partenaire, discutez les choix suivants. Chacun va expliquer son choix et essayer de convaincre l'autre personne. Utilisez les suggestions suivantes ou votre imagination.

▶ Visiter le Canada ou le Mexique?
C'est un pays (intéressant? pittoresque? accueillant [*welcoming*]?. . .)

> **Tu vas visiter le Canada ou le Mexique?**
>
> **Je vais visiter le Mexique.**
>
> **Ah bon? Pourquoi?**
>
> **C'est un pays plus accueillant!**
>
> **D'accord, mais le Canada est un pays aussi accueillant et plus pittoresque. . . .**

1. Visiter San Francisco ou New York? C'est une ville (jolie? grande? intéressante? polluée? . . .)
2. Prendre l'avion ou le train? C'est un transport (cher? rapide? dangereux? polluant? . . .)
3. Étudier le japonais ou l'espagnol? C'est une langue (facile? difficile? utile? . . .)
4. Dîner dans un restaurant italien ou chinois? La nourriture est (bonne? légère? riche en calories? chère? naturelle? . . .)
5. Manger du poulet frit ou de la sole? C'est un plat (bon? naturel? léger? riche en calories? . . .)
6. Apprendre à faire du parapente ou de la voile? C'est un sport (facile? dangereux? spectaculaire? . . .)

4 C'est évident!

Comparez les choses ou les personnes suivantes en utilisant l'adjectif entre parenthèses. Faites une autre comparaison en utilisant la phrase qui suit. Soyez logique!

▶ Jacques (+ pauvre) Annie / Il a de l'argent.
Jacques est plus pauvre qu'Annie. Il a moins d'argent.

1. Nathalie (+ sportive) Philippe / Elle fait du sport.
2. Roger (+ économe) Antoine / Il dépense de l'argent.
3. Albert (= brillant) Thérèse / Il a des idées originales.
4. Sandrine (– heureuse) Sophie / Elle a des problèmes.
5. les voitures américaines (= économiques) les voitures japonaises / Elles consomment de l'essence *(gas)*.
6. l'hôtel Méridien (+ grand) l'hôtel Ibis / Il a des chambres.

B. Le superlatif

Superlative constructions are used to compare people or things with the rest of a group.

Voici l'hôtel **le plus moderne de** la ville.   *Here is **the most modern** hotel **in** the city.*
Et voilà **le plus petit** hôtel.   *And here is **the smallest** hotel.*

ADJECTIVES		
le/la/les { plus / moins } + ADJECTIVE (+ de)	**le/la/les plus** moderne(s) **(de)**	***the most*** modern ***(in)***
	le/la/les moins moderne(s) **(de)**	***the least*** modern ***(in)***

➡ After a superlative construction, **de** is used to introduce the reference group.

➡ The superlative of **bon / bonne** is **le meilleur / la meilleure** *(the best)*.
    Voici **le meilleur** restaurant du quartier.

➡ In a superlative construction, the position of the adjective (<u>before</u> or <u>after</u> the noun) is usually the same as in the regular construction. Note that when the adjective comes AFTER the noun, the article (**le, la, les**) is used twice.
    le plus grand musée   le musée **le plus** intéressant

➡ A superlative construction may be introduced by a possessive adjective.
    Compare: **ma plus belle** veste   **mon** livre **le plus intéressant**

ADVERBS	
le plus / **le moins** } + ADVERB	Qui voyage **le plus souvent?**
	Qui voyage **le moins vite?**

➡ The superlative of **bien** is **le mieux**.
    C'est moi qui joue **le mieux** au volley.

NOUNS	
le plus de / **le moins de** } + NOUN	C'est moi qui ai **le plus d'idées** mais **le moins d'argent.**

VOICI LA CHAMBRE LA MOINS CHÈRE DE L'HÔTEL.

C'EST AUSSI LA PLUS BRUYANTE!

5 **Compliments**

Faites un compliment à votre partenaire.
Il/elle va vous faire un compliment aussi.

- amusant
- sympa
- gentil
- drôle
- intéressant
- sportif
- intelligent
- patient
- étonnant *(amazing)*
- mignon
- dynamique
- ??

Alice, tu es la fille la plus intelligente de mes amies.

Et toi, David, tu es le garçon le plus drôle de mes amis.

6 Au Bureau de Tourisme

Vous travaillez au Bureau de Tourisme. Des touristes (vos partenaires) cherchent
des hôtels avec l'une des caractéristiques suivantes. Renseignez-les.

▶ — **Je cherche un hôtel.**
— **Quelle sorte d'hôtel cherchez-vous?**
— **Un hôtel <u>calme.</u>**
— **L'hôtel le plus calme de la ville est l'hôtel Bellevue.**

- calme
- grand
- cher
- confortable
- bon marché
- petit

Bureau de Tourisme				
HÔTEL	NOMBRE DE CHAMBRES	CONFORT	CALME	PRIX DES CHAMBRES
Hôtel Ibis	45	✳ ✳	🛌	60€
Hôtel Napoléon	150	✳ ✳ ✳	🛌 🛌	120€
Hôtel d'Isly	18	✳	🛌	85€
Hotel Bellevue	30	✳ ✳ ✳ ✳	🛌 🛌 🛌	125€

7 Le meilleur choix

Vous voyagez avec votre partenaire.
Expliquez-lui pourquoi vous faites certains choix.

▶ aller dans cet hôtel (moderne / la ville)

— **Allons dans cet hôtel!**
— **Pourquoi cet hôtel?**
— **C'est l'hôtel le plus moderne de la ville.**
— **Alors, d'accord!**

1. visiter ce musée (intéressant / la région)
2. prendre ce train (rapide / la journée)
3. acheter ces souvenirs
    (bon marché / le magasin)
4. dîner dans ce restaurant (bon / le quartier)
5. choisir ce plat (typique / le menu)

8 Les Oscars

Dites qui à votre avis est le/la meilleur(e)
dans les catégories suivantes.

- un bon acteur
- une bonne actrice
- un athlète sympathique
- une comédienne amusante
- un bon film de l'année
- une comédie drôle
- une émission (*TV program*) intéressante
- un sport intéressant
- une classe facile
- une bonne équipe de basket

▶ **Quel est le sport le plus intéressant?**
  À mon avis, c'est le football.
  (C'est le sport le plus spectaculaire.)

9 Au Syndicat d'Initiative

(At the Chamber of Commerce)

Vous travaillez pour
le Syndicat d'Initiative de
votre ville. Votre bureau
vient de recevoir la lettre
suivante d'un(e) touriste
français(e). Répondez à
sa lettre.

Monsieur, Madame,

Nous pensons visiter votre ville
le mois prochain. Pourriez-vous
nous indiquer:

> un hôtel moderne
> un bon restaurant
> des boutiques intéressantes
> des endroits pittoresques.

En vous remerciant de votre
attention, je vous prie de croire,
Monsieur, Madame, à l'expression
de mes sentiments distingués.

Jacques Delavigne
Jacques Delavigne

 **OFFICE DE TOURISME
SYNDICAT D'INITIATIVE**

Monsieur,

Nous vous remercions de
l'intérêt que vous portez à
notre ville. Permettez-moi de
répondre à vos questions.
L'hôtel le plus moderne
est . . .

En espérant que les
renseignements vous seront
utiles, nous vous prions
de croire, Monsieur, à
l'expression de nos
sentiments distingués.

Bendeville

À l'Hôtel de la Plage

Après une année de dur° travail, finalement arrive l'époque heureuse des vacances. Quand on décide de partir, on peut faire du camping ou louer une villa, mais l'idéal est d'aller à l'hôtel. Là, il n'y a pas de travaux domestiques à faire, pas de repas à préparer, pas de problèmes à résoudre.° Comme tout est fait pour vous, vous pouvez profiter° complètement et totalement d'un repos bien mérité.

Parfois, l'hôtel réserve quelques surprises aux touristes inexpérimentés.° Prenons, par exemple, le cas de Monsieur et Madame Lagarde. Les Lagarde ont réservé une chambre pour deux semaines à l'Hôtel de la Plage, réputé, d'après la brochure, pour le bon air marin qu'on y respire.° Mais quand ils arrivent à leur destination, ils ont la mauvaise surprise de découvrir que l'Hôtel de la Plage est situé près d'une voie de chemin de fer.° Quant à° la plage …

Florida et gab...
10 Rue Joliot...
29138 Lesco...
(Finistère)
Tél. 02.98.87...

* À l'hôtel, le meilleur accueil est réservé aux heureux voyageurs.
* À l'hôtel, vous profiterez du calme et de la tranquillité absolus.
* Les hôtels de qualité offrent à leurs clients tout le confort de la vie moderne
* Le grand air de la c... vous permettra de... comme si vou... enfant.
* La nuit pers... troubler votr...
* Les hôtels... complet à... raisonnables.

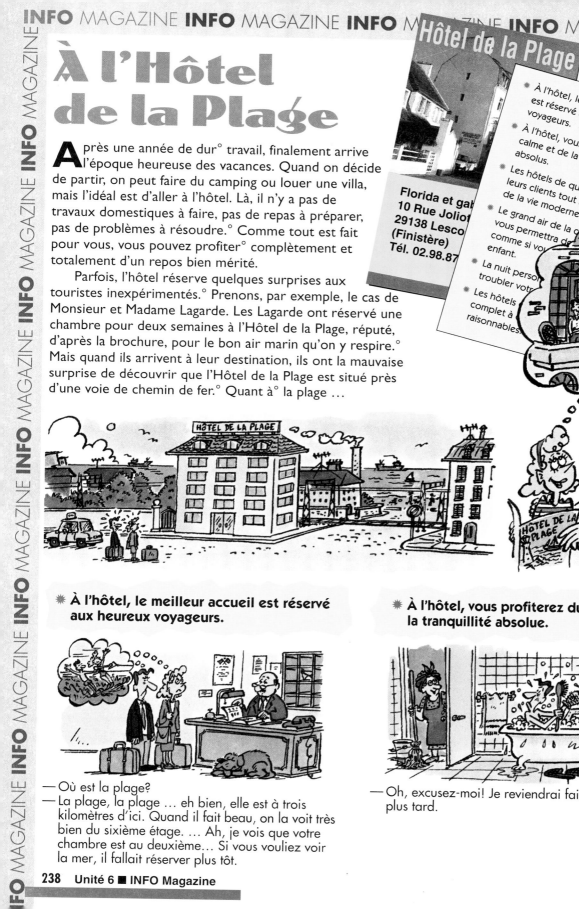

* **À l'hôtel, le meilleur accueil est réservé aux heureux voyageurs.**

—Où est la plage?
—La plage, la plage … eh bien, elle est à trois kilomètres d'ici. Quand il fait beau, on la voit très bien du sixième étage. … Ah, je vois que votre chambre est au deuxième… Si vous vouliez voir la mer, il fallait réserver plus tôt.

* **À l'hôtel, vous profiterez du calme et de la tranquillité absolue.**

—Oh, excusez-moi! Je reviendrai faire la chambre plus tard.

✳ **Les hôtels de qualité offrent à leurs clients tout le confort de la vie moderne.**

—Oh là là, chéri!° Quelle chaleur!° Peux-tu vérifier si le climatiseur° fonctionne?
—Oui, il fonctionne, mais c'est de l'air chaud qui sort!

✳ **Le grand air de la campagne vous permettra de dormir comme si vous étiez un enfant.**

—Je n'arrive pas° à dormir. Qu'est-ce que c'est que ce bruit? Est-ce qu'il y a des souris° ici?
—Mais non, ce sont les voisins d'à côté° qui mangent des chips.

✳ **La nuit personne ne viendra troubler votre sommeil.°**

—Bonjour, Monsieur Martin. Vous m'avez demandé de vous réveiller à cinq heures et demie. Bonne journée!
—Alllô! Quoi! Qu'est-ce que vous dites? Martin? Vous faites erreur! Je suis Monsieur Lagarde!

✳ **Les hôtels offrent un service complet à des prix très raisonnables.**

—Comment? vingt euros pour le petit déjeuner? Je croyais que tout était compris dans le prix! Et cette taxe locale de 5%! Qu'est-ce que c'est?

et vous?

EXPRESSION ORALE

Vous êtes Monsieur ou Madame Lagarde. Pour chaque épisode, vous téléphonez au directeur de l'hôtel (joué par votre partenaire) pour expliquer le problème. Le directeur essaie de trouver une solution.

EXPRESSION ÉCRITE

• Vous êtes Monsieur ou Madame Lagarde et vous écrivez à un(e) ami(e). Dans votre lettre, vous parlez des problèmes que vous avez eus pendant votre séjour.

• Décrivez un problème (réel ou imaginaire) que vous avez eu pendant un voyage et comment vous avez résolu ce problème.

---

dur *hard* **résoudre** ✳ *to solve* **inexperimentés** = *sans expérience* **respire** *breathes* **profiter** *to enjoy* **chemin de fer** *railroad track* **Quant à** *As for* **accueil** *welcome* **chéri** *darling* **chaleur** *heat* **climatiseur** *air conditioner* **Je n'arrive pas** = *je ne peux pas* **souris** *mice* **d'à côté** *next door* **sommeil** *sleep*

LE FRANÇAIS PRATIQUE

Services à l'hôtel

Bien sûr, monsieur, tout de suite.

Pouvez-vous m'apporter une couverture?

COMMENT DEMANDER UN SERVICE

Au garçon *(bellboy)*

Pouvez-vous | **monter** / **descendre** | mes bagages?

> **monter** *to bring up, carry up*
> **descendre** *to bring down, carry down*

À la femme de chambre *(chambermaid)*

Pouvez-vous m'apporter
- **une couverture** *(blanket)?*
- **un drap** *(sheet)?*
- **un oreiller** *(pillow)?*
- **une serviette** *(towel)?*
- **un portemanteau** *(hanger)?*
- **un cintre** *(hanger)?*

Pouvez-vous | **mettre** / **augmenter** / **baisser** | **le chauffage** *(heat)?* / **la climatisation**? / **l'air conditionné**?

> **mettre** *to turn on*
> **augmenter** *to turn up, raise*
> **baisser** *to turn down, lower*

Au (à la) réceptionniste

Pouvez-vous | me **servir** le petit déjeuner dans la chambre? / m'**appeler** un taxi?

> **servir** *to serve*
> **appeler** *to call*

Au standard *(operator)*

Pouvez-vous me **réveiller** à six heures et demie?

> **réveiller** *to wake*

Au (à la) gérant(e) *(manager)*

Pouvez-vous préparer ma **note** *(bill)?*

relais-hôtel de Montmirat
MONTMIRAT — 48 - St-Étienne-du-Valdonnez

1 Que dire?

Vous voyagez en France et vous êtes à l'hôtel. Qu'est-ce que vous allez demander dans les circonstances suivantes? (Votre partenaire va jouer le rôle du personnel de l'hôtel.)

▶ Vous arrivez à l'hôtel avec deux grosses valises.
— **Est-ce que vous pouvez monter mes bagages, s'il vous plaît?**
— **Oui, mademoiselle (monsieur). Tout de suite.**
— **Merci bien.**

- Vous voulez payer.
- Vous avez un train à 6h30 demain matin.
- Il fait très, très chaud dans votre chambre.
- Vous avez froid.
- Vous voulez rester au lit tard, mais vous voulez prendre votre petit déjeuner.
- Vous avez payé votre note et vous voulez aller à l'aéroport.
- Il va faire froid cette nuit.
- Vous devez quitter l'hôtel mais les bagages dans votre chambre sont très lourds.
- Vous avez beaucoup de vêtements que vous voulez pendre *(to hang up)*.

A. Le pronom interrogatif **lequel?**

The interrogative pronoun **lequel?** *(which one?)* replaces **quel?** + NOUN.

Quel hôtel préfères-tu?   **Lequel** préfères-tu?

Lequel? has the following forms:

	MASCULINE	FEMININE
SINGULAR	lequel?	laquelle?
PLURAL	lesquels?	lesquelles?

➡ The pronoun **lequel** consists of two parts, both of which agree with the noun it replaces:

$$\text{lequel} = \text{le} + \text{quel}$$

➡ Note how **à** and **de** contract with **lequel** to give the following forms:

à + lequel	→	**auquel**	de + lequel	→	**duquel**	
à + lesquels	→	**auxquels**	de + lesquels	→	**desquels**	
à + lesquelles	→	**auxquelles**	de + lesquelles	→	**desquelles**	

Il y a deux concerts.   **Auquel** veux-tu aller?   (= **à quel concert**?)
J'ai plusieurs cartes de la région.   **Desquelles** as-tu besoin?   (= **de quelles cartes**?)

B. Le pronom démonstratif **celui**

The demonstrative pronoun **celui** *(this one, the one)* replaces **ce** or **le** + NOUN.

Celui has the following forms:

	MASCULINE	FEMININE
SINGULAR	celui	celle
PLURAL	ceux	celles

Celui is never used alone. It occurs in the following combinations:

- **celui-ci, celui-là** *(this one, that one)*
  — Ta valise, c'est **celle-ci**?   *Your suitcase, is it **this one**?*
  — Non, c'est **celle-là**.   *No, it's **that one**.*

- **celui de** *(that of, the one belonging to)*
  Ce n'est pas mon passeport.
  C'est **celui de Valérie**.   *It's **Valérie's**. (= **that of Valérie**)*

  J'ai raté le train de 10 heures.
  Je prendrai **celui de 11 heures**.   *I will take **the 11 o'clock**.*
          *(= **the one of 11 o'clock**)*

- **celui qui, celui que** *(the one who(m), the one that)*

J'aime les hôtels confortables,
mais je préfère **ceux qui** ont
une belle vue.

*I prefer **those (the ones) that**
have a nice view.*

1 Préférences

Vous faites du shopping avec votre partenaire.
Vous discutez des choses que vous voyez.

1. ces chaussures / plus élégantes
2. ce vélo / plus solide
3. ces livres / plus intéressants
4. cette voiture / plus rapide
5. cet ordinateur / plus moderne
6. ces tee-shirts / plus à la mode

▶ Tu aimes <u>cette veste</u>?

Alors, laquelle préfères-tu?

Pourquoi?

Non, pas vraiment.

Celle-ci!

Elle est <u>plus jolie</u>.

2 Comparaisons

Lisez les descriptions suivantes et comparez
ces choses à celles qui sont indiquées entre
parenthèses.

▶ Ma maison est grande.
  (mon meilleur ami?)

  **Ma maison est plus (moins / aussi)
  grande que celle de mon meilleur
  ami.**

1. Notre voiture est grande.
   (les voisins?)
2. Ma chambre est spacieuse.
   (mes parents?)
3. Mes progrès en français sont rapides.
   (les autres étudiants?)
4. La cuisine de ma mère est bonne.
   (la cafétéria?)
5. L'air de la campagne est pollué.
   (la ville?)
6. Le climat de la Nouvelle-Angleterre
   est agréable.
   (la Floride?)
7. Les monuments de Paris sont beaux.
   (New York?)

3 Au choix

Vous voyagez à Paris avec votre partenaire. Vous
avez le choix entre deux possibilités. Demandez
à votre partenaire de choisir.

▶ deux hôtels (l'un a une grande piscine /
  l'autre, des chambres confortables)
  — **Il y a deux hôtels. Auquel veux-tu aller?**
  — **Je préfère aller à celui qui a
     des chambres confortables.**
     **(Je préfère aller à celui qui a
     une grande piscine.)**

1. deux restaurants
   (l'un sert des spécialités françaises /
   l'autre, des spécialités vietnamiennes)
2. deux musées
   (l'un a une exposition de photos /
   l'autre, une exposition d'art moderne)
3. deux piscines
   (l'une est au centre-ville /
   l'autre, dans la banlieue)
4. deux cinémas
   (l'un joue une comédie /
   l'autre, un western)
5. deux boutiques
   (l'une vend des jeans /
   l'autre, des chaussures)

C. Le pronom possessif le mien

POSSESSIVE PRONOUNS replace nouns introduced by a possessive adjective. Note the forms of the French possessive adjectives in the following sentences.

Ce n'est pas ta guitare.	C'est **la mienne**.	*It's **mine**.*
Marc écoute ses CD.	Anne écoute **les siens**.	*Anne is listening to **hers**.*
Votre chambre est grande.	**La nôtre** est confortable.	***Ours** is comfortable.*

	SINGULAR		PLURAL	
	MASCULINE	FEMININE	MASCULINE	FEMININE
mine	**le mien**	**la mienne**	**les miens**	**les miennes**
yours	**le tien**	**la tienne**	**les tiens**	**les tiennes**
his, hers, its	**le sien**	**la sienne**	**les siens**	**les siennes**
ours	**le nôtre**	**la nôtre**	**les nôtres**	
yours	**le vôtre**	**la vôtre**	**les vôtres**	
theirs	**le leur**	**la leur**	**les leurs**	

➡ Possessive pronouns consist of two parts, both of which agree with the noun they replace:

> **le** + POSSESSIVE WORD

➡ Note how **à** and **de** contract with the possessive pronoun:

à + le mien	→	**au mien**	de + le mien	→	**du mien**
à + les miens	→	**aux miens**	de + les miens	→	**des miens**
à + les miennes	→	**aux miennes**	de + les miennes	→	**des miennes**

Pronoms possessifs

Pratique ▶ p. 67

4 Possessions

Insistez sur la propriété des choses suivantes.

▶ Ce sont mes clés.
  Ce sont les miennes!

▶ C'est la voiture de mes parents.
  C'est la leur!

1. C'est ma serviette.
2. Ce sont tes lunettes de soleil.
3. C'est sa valise.
4. Ce sont ses CD.

5. Ce sont vos bagages.
6. C'est notre sac.
7. C'est l'ordinateur de Paul.
8. C'est le vélo d'Alice.

9. C'est le portable de Jérôme.
10. C'est la maison de tes cousins.
11. Ce sont les valises de Pierre et d'Isabelle.
12. C'est la tondeuse de nos voisins.

5 Camping

Vous faites du camping avec votre partenaire.
Vous avez oublié certaines choses. Demandez
à votre partenaire si vous pouvez prendre
les siennes.

▶ mon couteau

— **Dis, Daniel, j'ai oublié mon couteau.
   Est-ce que je peux prendre le tien?**
— **Le mien? Oui, d'accord!
   (Le mien? Ça non, pas question!)**

1. ma lampe de poche
2. mon sac de couchage
3. mes jumelles *(f. binoculars)*
4. ma serviette
5. mon savon
6. mon dentifrice
7. ma guitare
8. mes vitamines *(f)*

6 À qui est-ce?

Vous faites un voyage au Canada avec votre école. Vous avez trouvé certains objets mais
vous ne savez pas à qui ils sont. Votre partenaire va vous aider à identifier le propriétaire.

▶ — **C'est ta serviette?**
— **Non!**
— **Tu es sûr(e)?**
— **Absolument! La mienne est
   plus grande.**
— **Alors, c'est celle de François.**
— **Oui, c'est probablement la sienne.**

1. • ton sac
   • moins grand
   • Philippe

2. • ton appareil-photo
   • plus petit
   • Isabelle

3. • tes lunettes de soleil
   • noires
   • Claire

4. • ta veste
   • verte
   • David

5. • ta caméra
   • moins chère
   • Éric et Thomas

6. • tes valises
   • jaunes
   • Alice et Pauline

7 À l'aéroport

Vous êtes à l'aéroport avec votre partenaire.
Il/elle vous dit ce qu'il/elle va faire. Dites-lui
que vous allez faire les mêmes choses.

1. Je vais téléphoner à mes cousins.
2. Je vais dire au revoir à ma mère.
3. Je vais prendre une photo de ma soeur.
4. Je vais m'occuper de mon billet.
5. Je vais m'occuper de mes valises.
6. Je vais écrire une carte postale à mon professeur.

▶ **Je vais téléphoner
à mon copain.**

**Eh bien, moi, je vais
aussi téléphoner
au mien.**

LECTURE

Une étrange aventure

Le titre d'une histoire donne parfois aux lecteurs une idée générale du contenu et du ton de l'histoire.
Elle leur permet ainsi d'anticiper ce qui va arriver. C'est le cas, par exemple, du titre «Une étrange aventure».

- Vous savez que vous allez lire une **aventure**, c'est-à-dire un récit où l'<u>action</u> joue un rôle important.
- Vous savez aussi qu'au cours du récit quelque chose d'**étrange** va arriver.

En général, les histoires de ce genre commencent de façon très normale, très ordinaire. Puis, un petit problème survient et le mystère commence.

Au début (Partie I)
Déterminez le cadre général de l'histoire.

- Qui sont les protagonistes?
- Qu'est-ce qu'ils vont faire? Où vont-ils?
- Quel problème rencontrent-ils?

Au milieu (Partie II)
À mesure que l'histoire se développe, essayez de déterminer . . .

- les éléments qui vous semblent réels, vrais, ordinaires
- les éléments qui vous semblent étranges, mystérieux, irréels, bizarres

À la fin (Partie III)
Essayez . . .

- d'anticiper ce qui va se passer ensuite
- de trouver une solution au mystère de l'histoire

NOTE CULTURELLE

Les villages en France

Autrefois, la France était un pays rural. La majorité des Français habitaient dans des petits villages de moins de 2 000 habitants. Construits généralement autour d'une église, ces villages étaient reliés° entre eux par des petites routes le long desquelles° se trouvaient des fermes isolées. Les cafés, les boutiques, les petits commerces de toutes sortes, les nombreux ateliers d'artisan° donnaient beaucoup de vie et d'animation aux villages d'autrefois.

Avec l'exode rural et le développement des grandes villes, ces villages ont perdu de leur importance et surtout de leur animation. Aujourd'hui, la vie y est calme et monotone. La nuit, leurs rues sont complètement désertes.

reliés *linked* **le long desquelles** *along which* **ateliers d'artisan** *workshops*

UNE ÉTRANGE AVENTURE

I

John et Bob, deux étudiants américains, sont
arrivés à Paris à la fin de juin. Là, ils ont acheté
un scooter d'occasion avec l'intention de visiter
la France pendant l'été. Ils sont partis de Paris le
5 premier juillet dans la matinée°. Ils espèrent être à
Clermont-Ferrand dans la soirée. Ils ont un copain
là-bas qui les a invités.

Hélas, John et Bob ne savent pas que le
premier juillet, c'est le jour des grands départs.* Il
10 y a beaucoup de circulation sur les autoroutes et
même sur les routes nationales. Alors, John et Bob
décident de prendre des petites routes. Là, il y a
moins de circulation, mais le scooter n'avance
pas vite.

15 Il est neuf heures du soir maintenant. La nuit
commence à tomber et les deux garçons sont
encore loin de leur destination. C'est John qui
conduit le scooter. Il demande à Bob: « Tu sais où
nous sommes?»

20 Bob regarde la carte.

— Non, pas exactement. Dis, est-ce que tu as
encore de l'essence?

— Euh non! Pas beaucoup.

— Alors, il faut s'arrêter au prochain village.
J'espère qu'il y a une station-service. 25

— . . . Ou un hôtel!

Au prochain village, il y a bien une station-
service, mais elle est fermée . . . et il n'y a pas
d'hôtel. John demande:

— On continue? 30

— Oui, on continue . . . on n'a pas le choix.

Il fait maintenant nuit noire.° Pas une voiture
sur la route. John aperçoit une toute petite
lumière au loin.

— Regarde la lumière là-bas! 35

— C'est probablement une ferme. Nous
avons de la chance!

Les deux garçons arrivent à la ferme. Ils
frappent à la porte. Toc, toc, toc . . . Une voix
d'homme répond: 40

— Qui êtes-vous? Et qu'est-ce que vous
voulez?

— Nous sommes Américains. Nous sommes
perdus.

— Américains? Attendez! Je vous ouvre. 45

---

* **Le jour des grands départs:** Le jour où des millions de Français partent
en vacances.

la matinée = le matin   **il fait . . . nuit noire** *it is pitch black*

Avez-vous compris?

1. Qui sont John et Bob?
2. Comment vont-ils voyager en France?
3. Pourquoi est-ce qu'ils décident de prendre des petites routes?
4. Qu'est-ce qu'ils doivent trouver avant la nuit?
5. Qu'est-ce qu'ils font quand ils ne trouvent pas d'hôtel?

Mots utiles

une autoroute	*superhighway*
la circulation	*traffic*
l'essence	*gas*
une ferme	*farm*
une lumière	*light*
apercevoir *	*to notice*
conduire *	*to drive*
au loin	*in the distance*
d'occasion	*second-hand, used*

II

La porte de la ferme s'ouvre.

— Entrez vite . . . La nuit, cette route est très dangereuse, surtout pour vous!

John et Bob entrent dans la ferme. À l'intérieur, il y a un homme et une femme, le fermier et la fermière. Ils sont habillés en noir, comme les paysans d'autrefois. C'est la femme qui parle:

— Vous avez certainement faim. Hélas, nous n'avons pas grand-chose.° Je vais vous préparer des pommes de terre avec du lard.° Mon mari va vous chercher une bouteille de cidre à la cave.

John et Bob examinent la salle où ils sont. Les meubles sont rustiques et très anciens. Dans la cheminée, il y a un feu et sur la table il y a des chandelles.

L'homme revient avec la bouteille de cidre. La femme apporte le plat de pommes de terre. John et Bob mangent avec grand appétit.

— Merci, c'est délicieux!

L'homme parle: «Pourquoi merci? Nous sommes tellement heureux de vous recevoir! Mais vous êtes probablement très fatigués . . . Je vais vous montrer votre chambre.»

L'homme prend une chandelle et accompagne les deux garçons jusqu'à leur chambre.

— Excusez-nous, mais nous n'avons plus d'électricité. Je vous laisse la chandelle . . . Bonne nuit!

Puis l'homme descend les escaliers.

Bob dit à John:

— C'est rustique ici!

— Oui, c'est vraiment la campagne. Nous avons de la chance d'avoir trouvé cette ferme.

— Ces gens sont pauvres, mais ils sont vraiment généreux!

Quand Bob et John se réveillent le lendemain, il fait grand jour.°

— Quel jour sommes-nous?

— Nous sommes le deux juillet!

la cheminée

un feu

une chandelle

des meubles rustiques

— Au fait, tu as entendu les voitures qui se sont arrêtées devant la ferme pendant la nuit?

— Oh là là, oui! Quel bruit!

— Qu'est-ce que disaient les passagers?

— Je ne sais pas. Ils ne parlaient pas français. Je n'ai pas compris. Mais vraiment ils avaient l'air furieux!

— Je me demande bien qui c'était.

— Dis, il faut partir maintenant.

— C'est vrai! Il est dix heures déjà!

Bob et John descendent dans la salle où ils étaient hier. Mais il n'y a personne.

— Où sont nos hôtes?

— Je ne sais pas. Appelons-les.

— Monsieur? Madame?

Silence. Ils crient plus fort: «Monsieur! Madame!» Personne ne répond.

— Ils sont peut-être partis travailler dans les champs.

Bob et John sortent de la ferme, mais il n'y a personne dans les champs.

— Qu'est-ce qu'on fait?

— Il faut partir. On va laisser un mot sur la table et quand on reviendra à la fin de juillet, on s'arrêtera pour remercier ces gens de leur hospitalité.

— Bonne idée!

grand-chose = beaucoup
du lard salt pork
il fait grand jour the sun is up and shining

Mots utiles	
un bruit	*noise*
les champs	*fields*
un paysan	*peasant, farmer*
apporter	*to bring*
remercier	= dire merci
le lendemain	= le jour suivant
fort	*loudly*

Avez-vous compris?

1. Qui sont les habitants de la ferme? Décrivez-les.
2. Quelle est l'atmosphère générale de la ferme? Décrivez-la.
3. Quelle est l'attitude du fermier et de la fermière envers (*toward*) les jeunes Américains?

4. En quoi consiste le repas?
5. Que font John et Bob après le dîner?
6. Qu'est-ce qu'ils entendent pendant la nuit?
7. Quelle surprise les attend le lendemain?

III

Bob et John sont partis vers onze heures. Ils ont trouvé une station d'essence au prochain village et ils ont continué leur route . . .

20 Pendant quatre semaines ils ont parcouru la France en scooter. C'est maintenant la fin des vacances et le retour vers Paris. Bob et John pensent à leur aventure du premier juillet . . . Ils ont acheté des cadeaux pour leurs hôtes: une 25 bouteille de cognac pour le fermier et un joli vase de cristal pour sa femme.

John regarde la carte. Dans dix minutes, ils seront à la ferme. Ils pourront finalement remercier leurs hôtes de leur hospitalité . . .

30 — Je reconnais bien la route maintenant.
— Moi, aussi.
— Regarde les grands arbres là-bas. La ferme est juste en face.

Le scooter s'est arrêté devant les grands arbres, mais il n'y a pas de ferme.   135
— Tu es sûr que c'est ici?
— Absolument certain!

À la place de la ferme, il y a une haie d'arbustes et devant cette haie, une stèle avec une inscription.   140
— Dis, Bob, va voir ce qui est écrit.
Bob descend du scooter et va regarder l'inscription. Il revient vite, très, très pâle.
— Mon Dieu, c'est impossible!
— Qu'est-ce qu'il y a?   145
— Va voir toi-même!

une haie d'arbustes

une stèle

Mots utiles

un mot	= une note
un cadeau	gift, present
parcourir *	to travel across
en face	opposite

Anticipons un peu!

Avant de tourner la page, essayez de deviner ce que Bob a vu sur la stèle.

John descend à son tour du scooter. Il lit l'inscription suivante:

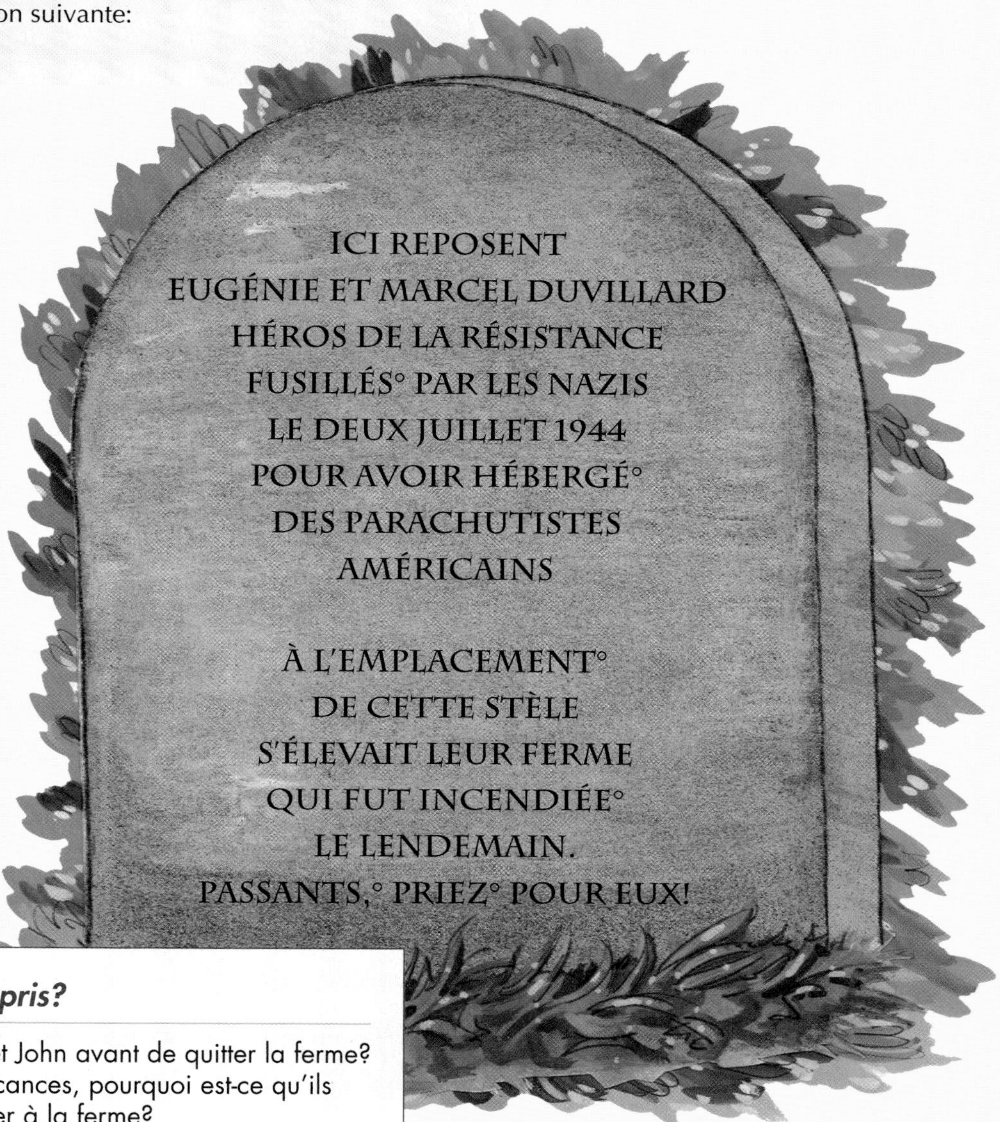

ICI REPOSENT
EUGÉNIE ET MARCEL DUVILLARD
HÉROS DE LA RÉSISTANCE
FUSILLÉS° PAR LES NAZIS
LE DEUX JUILLET 1944
POUR AVOIR HÉBERGÉ°
DES PARACHUTISTES
AMÉRICAINS

À L'EMPLACEMENT°
DE CETTE STÈLE
S'ÉLEVAIT LEUR FERME
QUI FUT INCENDIÉE°
LE LENDEMAIN.
PASSANTS,° PRIEZ° POUR EUX!

Avez-vous compris?

1. Que font Bob et John avant de quitter la ferme?
2. À la fin des vacances, pourquoi est-ce qu'ils veulent retourner à la ferme?
3. Quelle surprise les attend?
4. Qu'est-ce qui s'est passé à la ferme au début de juillet 1944?

fusillés *shot and killed* **pour avoir hébergé** *for having sheltered*
emplacement = endroit **s'élevait** *stood* **incendiée** *burned to the ground* **passants** = vous qui passez par ici **priez** *to pray*

LECTURE SUPPLÉMENTAIRE

L'histoire que vous avez lue évoque une époque très tourmentée de l'histoire de France: l'**Occupation** par les Allemands (1940-1944), puis la **Libération** par les Alliés (principalement des soldats américains et anglais), et par la **Résistance française**. Voir Interlude 6, pp. 252-255.

Pour découvrir un autre récit concernant cette période, lisez le texte *Au Revoir, les Enfants* (pp.256-259).

EXPRESSION ORALE

■ Discussion
Selon vous, est-ce que l'histoire que vous avez lue est possible ou impossible? Discutez votre opinion avec un(e) partenaire qui n'a pas la même opinion que vous.

■ Débat
Dans beaucoup de cultures, on peut trouver des «histoires de fantômes» *(ghost stories)* semblables à l'histoire racontée dans **Une étrange aventure**.
Vous-même, croyez-vous aux fantômes ou non? Exprimez votre opinion sur ce sujet et débattez la question avec un(e) partenaire qui n'a pas la même opinion que vous. Si possible, donnez des exemples en support de votre opinion.

■ Situations
Avec votre partenaire, choisissez l'une des situations suivantes. Composez le dialogue correspondant et jouez-le en classe.

1 Devant la stèle.
Bob et John sont devant la stèle. Ils viennent de lire l'inscription et maintenant ils essaient d'interpréter ce qui est arrivé lors de leur passage la nuit du premier juillet, en fonction des événements qui ont eu lieu les 1er et 2 juillet 1944. Par exemple:
• pourquoi le fermier a dit que la route était dangereuse
• selon les fermiers, qui étaient Bob et John et pourquoi ils étaient heureux de les recevoir
• qui étaient les gens qui étaient venus dans la nuit et qu'est-ce qu'ils cherchaient
• pourquoi le fermier et sa femme n'étaient pas là le lendemain matin

Rôles: Bob, John

2 Aux États-Unis.
En rentrant aux États-Unis, John a une conversation avec son grand-père qui lui aussi a été parachuté en France lors de l'invasion en 1944. Au cours de cette conversation, l'ancien soldat raconte ses aventures de guerre, par exemple, comment il a été recueilli *(picked up)* par les Résistants français.

Rôles: John, son grand-père

EXPRESSION ÉCRITE

■ Un peu d'histoire
Écrivez un petit rapport sur l'histoire de France entre 1940 et 1944. Dans ce rapport, expliquez en particulier le rôle ...
• des Allemands
• des Américains
• de la Résistance française
(Source: Encyclopédies, Manuels d'histoire)

■ Une étrange aventure
Écrivez votre propre «étrange aventure». Commencez par une situation très réaliste. Ensuite, ajoutez un élément mystérieux ou bizarre. Utilisez votre imagination.

INTERLUDE CULTUREL

■ Les dates   ■ Les événements

- **1870** *La France devient une république*

La Belle Époque

La Belle Époque (1870-1914)

Paris à la Belle Époque, représenté par le peintre Jean Béraud

C'est une époque de prospérité économique et d'intense création artistique, littéraire et scientifique. D'importants mouvements artistiques (**impressionnisme, fauvisme, cubisme, surréalisme**) naissent en France. Paris devient la capitale mondiale des lettres et des arts.

À l'extérieur, la France s'engage dans des expéditions coloniales et se construit un empire en Afrique occidentale et en Asie (Indochine).

- **1914** ***Première Guerre Mondiale***
- **1918**

Les guerres mondiales (1914-1918 et 1939-1945)

Soldats américains défilant sur les Champs-Élysées

- **1939** ***Deuxième Guerre Mondiale***

Ces deux terribles guerres opposent la France et l'Allemagne impériale (Première Guerre Mondiale) puis l'Allemagne nazie (Deuxième Guerre Mondiale). Dans ces deux guerres, l'intervention américaine est décisive.

En 1940, la France est occupée par les Allemands. Le 6 juin 1944, les troupes alliées commandées par le Général Eisenhower, débarquent sur les plages de Normandie: Utah Beach, Omaha Beach . . . La Libération de la France commence.

- **1945**

La France moderne (1945 - présent)

Le Louvre et sa pyramide, symboles du passé et de l'avenir.

- **1957** *Marché Commun*
- **1960** *Fin de l'ère coloniale*
- **1979** *Premier Parlement Européen*
- **1993** *Formation de l'Union Européenne*
- **2002** *Adoption de l'euro*

Ruinée par la guerre, la France reconstruit son économie. La construction de la France moderne passe par deux étapes° importantes.

- La décolonisation (1945-1962). Les anciennes colonies françaises d'Afrique du Nord, d'Afrique occidentale, et d'Asie deviennent des républiques indépendantes.
- L'intégration à l'Europe (1957 - présent). En 1957, la France devient membre de la **Communauté Économique Européenne** ou «**Marché Commun**». La création de cette grande zone de libre-échange permet l'expansion commerciale et industrielle de la France. Intégrée à l'Europe, la France est aujourd'hui un pays moderne avec l'un des niveaux de vie° les plus élevés du monde.

étapes *steps, stages*   **niveau de vie** *standard of living*

■ *Les personnes*

Marie Curie (1867-1934)

Marie Curie, née Sklodowska, est l'un des grands génies scientifiques des temps modernes. D'origine polonaise, elle vient à Paris en 1891 pour continuer ses études scientifiques. En 1895, elle épouse son professeur, **Pierre Curie**. Ensemble, ils découvrent le radium et le polonium, auquel elle donne le nom de son pays d'origine. En accord avec l'esprit scientifique, les Curie refusent de prendre une patente sur leur découverte et d'en tirer° tout° bénéfice commercial.

En 1898, Pierre et Marie Curie reçoivent le Prix Nobel de Physique pour leurs travaux sur la radioactivité. Après la mort accidentelle de son mari en 1905, Marie Curie continue ses travaux, isole le radium et reçoit le Prix Nobel de Chimie en 1911.

Marie Curie dans son laboratoire.

Jean Moulin (1899-1943)

Jean Moulin, héros de la Résistance

Jean Moulin est le héros de **la Résistance** française pendant la Deuxième Guerre Mondiale. En 1940, il se rallie au gouvernement de la France Libre, dirigé à Londres par le **Général de Gaulle**. Parachuté en France, il organise la Résistance contre les Allemands. Il est arrêté et torturé par la Gestapo.* Après sa mort, la Résistance continue. Les résistants, organisés en «maquis»° harcèlent les troupes d'occupation et préparent la **Libération**.

Simone Veil (1927-)

Simone Veil est une championne de l'Europe unie et des droits de la femme. Pendant la Deuxième Guerre Mondiale, elle est déportée dans un camp de concentration nazi. Après la guerre, elle fait de brillantes études de droit et de sciences politiques. À l'âge de 20 ans, elle devient attachée auprès du Ministre de la Justice. De 1974 à 1979, elle est nommée Ministre de la Santé. En 1979, elle est élue Député au Parlement européen et elle en est la première présidente.

Simone Veil et le drapeau européen

---

* La Gestapo (Geheime Staats Polizei = police secrète d'état) était l'instrument le plus dangereux du régime policier nazi.

tirer *to derive* **tout** *any* **maquis** *guerrilla groups*

■ *Charles de Gaulle, homme d'action*

Charles de Gaulle est peut-être l'homme qui a eu la plus grande influence sur l'histoire de la France du vingtième siècle. Jeune officier, il est fait prisonnier par les Allemands pendant la première guerre mondiale. Plus tard, il préconise°

une stratégie militaire basée sur l'utilisation massive des tanks, mais on ne l'écoute pas.

En 1940, la France capitule et est occupée par l'armée allemande. De Gaulle refuse d'accepter la défaite et part pour l'Angleterre. Le 18 juin 1940, il lance° à la radio de Londres son célèbre appel où il demande à tous les Français de continuer le combat contre l'Allemagne nazie. Pour cet acte de rébellion contre l'autorité officielle, il est condamné à mort par le gouvernement français d'alors. Il organise la Résistance et crée un gouvernement de la «**France Libre**».

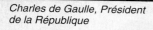

Charles de Gaulle, Président de la République

Le Général de Gaulle passe en revue les volontaires féminines de la France Libre.

Documents: Appel du 18 juin 1940

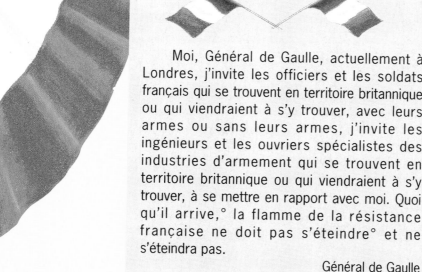

Appel du 18 juin 1940

Moi, Général de Gaulle, actuellement à Londres, j'invite les officiers et les soldats français qui se trouvent en territoire britannique ou qui viendraient à s'y trouver, avec leurs armes ou sans leurs armes, j'invite les ingénieurs et les ouvriers spécialistes des industries d'armement qui se trouvent en territoire britannique ou qui viendraient à s'y trouver, à se mettre en rapport avec moi. Quoi qu'il arrive,° la flamme de la résistance française ne doit pas s'éteindre° et ne s'éteindra pas.

Général de Gaulle

---

préconise *advocates* **lance** *sends out* **quoi qu'il arrive** *whatever happens* **s'éteindre** *to go out, to be extinguished*

En août 1944, le Général de Gaulle rentre dans Paris libéré par les troupes alliées. En 1945, il est élu président provisoire de la République française, mais il démissionne° parce qu'il n'a pas les pouvoirs° de gouverner.

Peu après, la France connaît deux longues et tragiques guerres coloniales, d'abord la guerre d'Indochine, puis la guerre d'Algérie. L'Algérie est alors un territoire français avec une population en majorité musulmane.° Les Algériens musulmans veulent leur indépendance et décident de prendre les armes contre la France. Le gouvernement français ne sait pas comment arrêter cette guerre impopulaire. La France est au bord° de la guerre civile.

Les Français font appel à de Gaulle qui devient Président de la République en 1959. De Gaulle comprend que l'ère coloniale est finie. Il négocie l'indépendance avec l'Algérie, puis avec les colonies françaises d'Afrique Noire qui deviennent des républiques amies de la France.

De Gaulle veut restaurer la grandeur de la France. Il comprend que l'avenir° de la France dépend de son intégration dans une Europe forte et indépendante. Il mène° alors une politique marquée par la réconciliation avec l'Allemagne et une certaine distance vis-à-vis des États-Unis. De Gaulle veut aussi réformer les institutions françaises. Beaucoup de Français n'acceptent pas ses réformes et protestent en organisant de violentes manifestations en mai 1968. Peu après, de Gaulle se retire de la vie publique.

Le Général de Gaulle sur les Champs-Élysées à la Libération de Paris en 1944

Le Général de Gaulle avec un chef d'état africain

Les manifestations à Paris, mai 1968

démissionne *resigns* **pouvoirs** *powers* **musulmane** *Moslem*
au bord de *on the edge of* **l'avenir** = le futur **il mène** = il fait

■ *Liberté, liberté*

Pour l'humanité, la liberté est le bien° le plus précieux. C'est le principe fondamental de la démocratie. Dans la *Déclaration d'indépendance* américaine et dans la *Déclaration des droits de l'homme* de la Révolution française, la liberté est un droit inaliénable et imprescriptible.°

Pourtant,° tous les êtres humains ne sont pas libres. Les Français, par exemple, ont perdu leur liberté quand leur pays a été occupé par les troupes allemandes entre 1940 et 1944. Ils rêvaient° alors de cette liberté qu'il fallait reconquérir et beaucoup sont morts pour elle en combattant dans la Résistance.

Illustrations du poème par l'artiste Fernand Léger

Paul Éluard

Paul Éluard, auteur du poème *Liberté*, était un poète surréaliste et un membre très actif de la Résistance. Il a publié ce poème pendant l'occupation dans un livre intitulé *Poésie et vérité* 1942. Interdit° par la censure allemande, ce livre était distribué clandestinement et parachuté en milliers d'exemplaires° par l'aviation alliée.

un bien = une possession   **imprescriptible** *which cannot be legally taken away*
pourtant *however*   **rêvaient** *dreamed*   **interdit** *forbidden*   **exemplaires** *copies*

■ *Au Revoir, les Enfants*

Au Revoir, les Enfants est un film réalisé par le cinéaste français contemporain **Louis Malle**. C'est un film autobiographique dans lequel Louis Malle évoque un épisode dramatique de sa jeunesse.

Louis Malle, réalisateur du film, avec deux des acteurs principaux

Liberté

Paul Éluard

Sur mes cahiers d'écolier
Sur mon pupitre° et les arbres
Sur le sable° sur la neige
J'écris ton nom

Sur toutes les pages lues
Sur toutes les pages blanches
Pierre sang° papier ou cendre°
J'écris ton nom

Sur les images dorées°
Sur les armes des guerriers°
Sur la couronne° des rois
J'écris ton nom

Sur la jungle et le désert
Sur les nids° sur les genêts*
Sur l'écho de mon enfance
J'écris ton nom

Sur mes refuges détruits
Sur mes phares écroulés°
Sur les murs de mon ennui
J'écris ton nom

Sur l'absence sans désirs
Sur la solitude nue°
Sur les marches° de la mort
J'écris ton nom

Sur la santé revenue
Sur le risque disparu
Sur l'espoir° sans souvenirs
J'écris ton nom

Et par le pouvoir° d'un mot°
Je recommence ma vie
Je suis né pour te connaître
Pour te nommer *Liberté.*

***Genêt** or *broom* is a European shrub with bright yellow flowers that grows wild in the woods and uncultivated fields

pupitre *school desk* **sable** *sand* **sang** *blood* **cendre** *ashes* **dorées** *gilded* **guerriers** *warriors* **couronne** *crown* **nids** *nests*
phares écroulés *lighthouses that have collapsed* **nue** *naked* **marches** *steps, stairs* **espoir** *hope* **pouvoir** *power* **mot** *word*

Le film se passe au cours de° l'hiver 1944. À cette époque la France est occupée par les Allemands qui ont imposé la loi° hitlérienne partout. Les Juifs,° en particulier, sont traqués,° et quand ils sont pris, ils sont envoyés dans les camps d'extermination. Les Français qui les aident ou les abritent° sont, eux aussi, passibles de mort.

Parmi les Français, il y a ceux qui résistent aux Allemands, et ceux qui collaborent avec eux, mais la majorité attend passivement l'arrivée des Alliés et la fin de la guerre.

La vie est difficile. Comme la nourriture manque,° le marché noir s'installe partout. De plus en plus fréquemment, la population civile est soumise aux bombardements de l'aviation alliée . . .

au cours de = *pendant* **loi** *law* **Juifs** *Jews* **traqués** *hunted down* **abritent** *shelter* **manque** *is lacking*

L'action du film a lieu dans une école catholique de garçons dont le directeur, **le père Jean**, est un prêtre° d'une grande intégrité morale. Le héros du film est un jeune garçon d'une douzaine d'années, **Julien Quentin** (c'est, bien sûr, Louis Malle lui-même), qui est pensionnaire° avec son frère aîné François dans cette école.

1 Le film commence à la rentrée des classes après les vacances de Noël. Dans la première scène, Julien est à la gare. Il dit au revoir à sa mère, puis il prend son train. Quand il arrive au collège, il retrouve tous ses copains. Dans la classe, il y a un nouvel élève qui s'appelle
2 **Jean Bonnet**. C'est un garçon timide et réservé qui ne parle jamais de sa famille. C'est aussi un brillant élève, en maths, en français, en musique. Julien, qui était jusqu'alors° le meilleur élève de la classe, sent en lui un rival. Il questionne Jean sur son passé, mais celui-ci lui répond d'une façon évasive.

Louis Malle (1932-1995)

Louis Malle est l'un des grands réalisateurs° du cinéma français moderne. Il a d'abord fait des films documentaires, comme son premier film *Le monde du silence*, réalisé en coopération avec Jacques-Yves Cousteau, l'explorateur du monde marin.°

Dans ses films plus récents, Louis Malle a traité de thèmes personnels comme celui évoqué dans *Au revoir, les Enfants*.

Louis Malle était marié avec l'actrice américaine Candice Bergen et habitait à New York.

1
Julien dit au revoir à sa mère avant de prendre son train pour rentrer au collège.

2
Au collège, il y a un nouvel élève. Il s'appelle Jean Bonnet.

3
Les deux garçons deviennent amis.

réalisateur *director*   **marin** = de la mer   **prêtre** *priest*   **pensionnaire** *boarding student*   **jusqu'alors** *until then*

4

Le jeune employé est renvoyé pour avoir fait du marché noir.

5

Un soldat allemand entre dans la salle de classe pour arrêter Jean.

Un jour, Julien découvre la vérité: Jean Bonnet s'appelle en réalité Jean Keppelstein et il est juif. Les prêtres l'ont recueilli° avec deux autres enfants juifs pour le soustraire° à la police allemande. Au collège, il est en sécurité tant que° sa véritable identité reste cachée.° Depuis cette découverte, les relations entre les deux garçons **3** changent et ils deviennent amis.

Un samedi, au cours d'une sortie, ils se perdent dans la forêt. Julien arrête une voiture de patrouille allemande. Jean veut s'échapper, mais il est rattrapé.° Les soldats allemands ramènent les deux garçons à l'école. Cette fois-ci, il y a plus de peur° que de mal!° Un autre jour, la famille de Julien invite Jean à déjeuner dans un grand restaurant. Jean assiste à une scène pénible° où un client juif, décoré de la Légion d'Honneur,* est insulté par un Milicien, auxiliaire français de la police allemande.

Les jours passent . . . Un employé de l'école est **4** renvoyé° pour avoir fait du marché noir avec les élèves. Pour se venger, il dénonce la présence d'enfants juifs à l'école. La police allemande arrive et encercle l'école. Un soldat entre dans la salle de classe pour arrêter Jean. **5** D'autres soldats fouillent° l'école. Les deux autres élèves juifs sont découverts et arrêtés ainsi que° le père Jean qui était membre de la Résistance. Au moment de quitter l'école, escorté par des soldats allemands, le **6** père Jean dit un dernier au revoir à ses élèves: «Au revoir, les enfants! À bientôt!»

Personne ne reviendra. Jean et ses deux camarades juifs mourront à Auschwitz. Le père Jean mourra au camp de Mauthausen.

6

Le père Jean dit un dernier au revoir aux élèves de l'école.

* La Légion d'Honneur: haute distinction donnée aux gens qui ont servi la France.

recueilli *taken in* **soustraire à** *to protect from* **tant que** *as long as* **cachée** *hidden* **rattrapé** *caught*
peur *fright* **mal** *harm* **pénible** *painful* **renvoyé** *fired* **fouillent** *to search* **ainsi que** *as well as*

UNITÉ **7**

*La forme
et la santé*

Thème et Objectifs

Culture

In this unit, you will discover . . .
- how the French take care of their health
- why the French drink mineral water
- how the French help provide health care to less fortunate people around the world

Communication

You will learn how . . .
- to see a doctor or dentist and explain what is wrong
- to follow the doctor's instructions

Langue

You will learn how . . .
- to express your doubts and fears
- to affirm your beliefs
- to let people know how you feel about both present and past events

Les Français et leur santé

En France comme ailleurs,° la santé et la forme sont la préoccupation de tout le monde. Pour rester en forme, les jeunes Français pratiquent toutes sortes de sports: la natation en été, le ski en hiver, le foot, le basket, le vélo, le jogging, la marche à pied en toute saison. Il arrive° cependant que les personnes en excellente santé tombent malades. Il faut alors aller voir un médecin.

Pour les maladies ordinaires, on va voir un médecin généraliste. Pour les maladies spécifiques, on doit consulter un spécialiste: oculiste pour les yeux, cardiologue pour le coeur, dermatologue pour les maladies de peau,° stomatologue pour la bouche, gastro-entérologue pour l'estomac … Si on a besoin d'une radio,° on va chez un radiologue.

En cas d'urgence° ou d'accident sérieux, on peut téléphoner au SAMU (Service d'Aide Médicale Urgente). Il suffit de composer le numéro 15. Le SAMU est un service public rattaché à un hôpital. Suivant la gravité du problème, le SAMU envoie un médecin d'urgence, une ambulance de réanimation ou une ambulance ordinaire.

Le système médical français a le grand avantage d'être presque gratuit.° La majorité des Français sont inscrits° à la Sécurité Sociale. Avec la Sécurité Sociale, le gouvernement français prend en charge les dépenses médicales et la santé de ses citoyens.° Les gens qui vont chez le médecin ou chez le dentiste remplissent° une feuille° de Sécurité Sociale qui leur permet° d'être remboursés à 75%. Et quand ils vont chez le pharmacien, les médicaments° sont aussi remboursés.

Les Français aiment se soigner.° Ce sont les plus grands consommateurs de médicaments du monde. En général, les médicaments qu'ils prennent, comme l'aspirine ou les vitamines, sont fabriqués par les grandes compagnies pharmaceutiques. Ils prennent aussi toute une variété de médicaments à base de produits naturels (fruits, fleurs, plantes, herbes sauvages,° feuilles° ou écorce° d'arbre, etc.). Ce sont des infusions pour la digestion, l'insomnie ou la migraine, des pilules° pour le foie,° des pastilles° et des sirops pour la toux,° des crèmes et des pommades° pour la peau, etc.… En pratiquant cette médecine «écologique,» ils redécouvrent° les secrets des remèdes traditionnels.

Les femmes-médecins

Aujourd'hui, il y a beaucoup de femmes-médecins en France. Elles représentent 35% du corps médical. C'est seulement en 1870 que la première femme a reçu son diplôme de médecin de la Faculté de Médecine de Paris. Cette jeune femme n'était d'ailleurs pas française, mais anglaise!

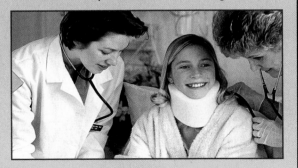

et vous?

DÉBATS

Choisissez un des sujets de débat et prenez une position pour ou contre. Débattez votre position avec votre partenaire. Si possible, utilisez des exemples pour établir votre position.
1. Les Américains consomment trop de médicaments.
2. Le sport est la meilleure prévention contre la maladie.
3. Quand on est malade, il est préférable d'utiliser des médicaments naturels.

ailleurs *elsewhere*　**il arrive** *it happens*　**peau** *skin*　**radio** *x-ray*　**cas d'urgence** *emergency*　**gratuit** *free of charge*
inscrire ✷ *to register*　**citoyens** *citizens*　**remplissent** *fill out*　**feuille** *form*　**permettre** ✷ *to allow*　**médicaments** *medicine, drugs*
se soigner *to take care of one's health*　**sauvages** *wild*　**feuilles** *leaves*　**écorce** *bark*　**pilules** *pills*　**le foie** *liver*　**des pastilles** *tablets*
la toux *cough*　**des pommades** *ointments*　**redécouvrir** ✷ *to rediscover*

L'eau, c'est la santé

Au café ou au restaurant, Stéphanie commande généralement de l'eau minérale. Sandrine en boit un grand verre le matin quand elle se lève, et le soir quand elle se couche. Quant à° Christophe, il ne va jamais au lycée sans emporter° une bouteille d'eau minérale dans son sac. L'eau minérale est la boisson favorite des Français. Ils en boivent en moyenne° 125 litres par personne (hommes, femmes, et enfants) et par an. Ce sont les champions du monde de la consommation d'eau minérale.

■ Au café, les jeunes commandent de l'eau minérale.

L'eau a de nombreux avantages. C'est le plus naturel des produits. Elle contient° zéro calorie. Elle facilite l'élimination des toxines et la régénération des cellules de notre corps. (N'oublions pas que le corps° humain est composé de deux tiers° d'eau!)

En outre,° les eaux minérales ont certaines propriétés thérapeutiques qui dépendent des minéraux qu'elles contiennent (magnésium, calcium, potassium, sodium, etc.) Certaines eaux sont bonnes pour la digestion, d'autres pour le foie° ou les reins.° Certaines sont recommandées pour les rhumatismes, d'autres pour les maladies de peau.° En France, il existe des centaines d'eaux minérales différentes. Ces eaux viennent de sources° thermales situées principalement dans les zones montagneuses: Massif Central (Vichy), Alpes (Évian), Vosges (Vittel, Contrexéville), Pyrénées (Amélie-les-Bains).

La façon la plus normale d'utiliser une eau minérale est d'en boire tous les jours. Une autre façon consiste à faire une «cure» dans la région qui produit° une eau particulière. Là, non seulement on boit de grandes quantités d'eau minérale, mais on utilise celle-ci pour prendre des bains et pour se faire faire des massages. Cette tradition remonte° aux Romains qui connaissaient bien les vertus de l'eau et qui ont découvert° un grand nombre de sources thermales en Gaule il y a 2000 ans. Aujourd'hui des centaines de milliers de Français vont chaque été faire une cure dans les stations thermales spécialisées.

D'autres personnes préfèrent aller à la mer et pratiquer la «thalassothérapie.» Cette méthode consiste à profiter des avantages combinés de l'eau de mer, de l'air et du climat marins. On peut prendre des bains de mer très chauds, des saunas ou des bains de boue.° La thalassothérapie est recommandée pour les personnes qui souffrent° de fatigue ou de stress, pour celles qui veulent se remettre° en forme, et aussi pour les athlètes professionnels.

La France des eaux

Il existe plus de 100 stations thermales en France. Chacune a sa spécialité.

- Si vous avez des problèmes de digestion, allez à Vichy, Vittel, Évian ou Contrexéville.
- Si vous avez de l'asthme, allez à Amélie-les-Bains.
- Si vous avez une peau délicate, allez à la Bourboule.
- Si vous avez des rhumatismes, allez à Aix-les-Bains, comme autrefois la reine Victoria, ou à Plombières, comme l'empereur Napoléon III.

PROJET

Allez dans un supermarché et faites une liste des eaux minérales qu'on y vend. Indiquez l'origine géographique de ces eaux minérales.

---

quant à *as for*   **emporter** *to take along*   **en moyenne** *on the average*   **contenir** ✻ *to contain*   **le corps** *body*   **deux tiers** *two-thirds*
en outre = en plus   **le foie** *liver*   **les reins** *kidneys*   **la peau** *skin*   **les sources** *springs*   **produire** ✻ *to produce*   **remonte** *dates back*
découvrir ✻ *to discover*   **boue** *mud*   **souffrir** ✻ *to suffer*   **se remettre** ✻ *to get back (into shape)*

Le savez-vous?

Que savez-vous de votre santé et de la santé en général? Faites le test suivant. Combien de phrases pouvez-vous compléter? [Pour connaître les réponses, allez au bas de la page.]

1. Le matin, notre température normale est de …
   a. 35 degrés
   b. 37 degrés
   c. 40,2 degrés

2. En moyenne, un adolescent de 16 ans a besoin de … par jour.
   a. 1.500 calories
   b. 2.800 calories
   c. 3.400 calories

3. Notre niveau d'adrénaline augmente quand …
   a. on a faim
   b. on a la grippe
   c. on se met en colère

4. La grippe est une maladie causée par …
   a. un virus
   b. le froid
   c. la mauvaise hygiène

5. Un dermatologue est un médecin qu'on peut consulter quand on a …
   a. de l'acné
   b. des rhumatismes
   c. mal à la tête

6. Le calcium est l'élément principal du squelette et des dents. Une excellente source de calcium est …
   a. le lait
   b. la viande
   c. le poisson

7. Il ne faut pas fumer parce que le tabac est un poison qui peut provoquer beaucoup de maladies sérieuses, en particulier …
   a. l'anémie
   b. la tuberculose
   c. le cancer du poumon

8. La pénicilline est un antibiotique. Son rôle est de …
   a. faciliter la digestion
   b. éliminer les produits toxiques
   c. détruire les bactéries qui provoquent les infections

9. Quand on est à la plage, il est prudent de se protéger contre le soleil. À long terme, l'exposition trop longue au soleil peut provoquer …
   a. l'insomnie
   b. la polio
   c. le cancer de la peau

10. Les personnes qui ont un problème avec leur cholestérol doivent éviter (avoid) de manger …
    a. des fruits
    b. des légumes
    c. des oeufs

11. La mononucléose est une maladie qui affecte …
    a. le sang
    b. les muscles
    c. l'estomac

12. Le jogging, le cyclisme, et la gymnastique sont des activités aérobiques. Le résultat principal d'une activité aérobique est …
    a. de développer nos muscles
    b. d'augmenter notre rythme cardiaque
    c. d'éliminer les toxines

13. En cas de transfusion sanguine, il est important de connaître son groupe sanguin. Le groupe sanguin le plus rare est …
    a. le groupe A
    b. le groupe B
    c. le groupe O

14. Quand on est diabétique, il est déconseillé de manger …
    a. du pain
    b. du sucre
    c. du fromage

RÉPONSES 1b, 2b, 3c, 4a, 5a, 6a, 7c, 8c, 9c, 10c, 11a, 12b, 13b, 14b

LE FRANÇAIS PRATIQUE

Une visite médicale

> Avez-vous un rendez-vous ?

> Oui, j'ai un rendez-vous avec le docteur Lavie à deux heures.

Dans la salle d'attente *(waiting room)*

— Avez-vous **un rendez-vous** *(appointment)*?

    Oui, j'ai un rendez-vous avec
le docteur Lavie à deux heures.

le médecin	**le/la chirurgien(ne)** *surgeon*
le/la dentiste	**l'infirmier(ère)** *nurse*
le spécialiste	**l'oculiste**

**FMP (FÉDÉRATION
MUTUALISTE PARISIENNE**

CENTRES OPTIQUE MÉDICALE

24 r St Victor 75005 P_____ 01 40 46 11 37
10-12 av Georges Clémenceau
93139 Noisy le Sec_____ 01 48 44 00 32

Dans le cabinet *(office)* **du médecin**

— Comment allez-vous?

  Comment vous sentez-vous?

Ça va,	**je me sens bien.**
	je me **porte** bien.
	je suis **en bonne santé** *(health)*.
	je suis **bien portant(e)** *(in good health)*.

se sentir *to feel*

se porter bien *to be in
good health*

Ça ne va pas.	**Je ne me sens pas bien.**
Je suis	**malade** *(sick)*.
Je me sens	

fatigué	**faible**	*weak*
nerveux	**déprimé**	*depressed*

— **Avez-vous de la fièvre?**

    Oui, j'ai de la fièvre.

    J'ai **39 degrés de température.**

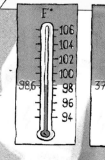

Médecins qualifiés:
chirurgie générale

• **Bougival**
NATHAN Georges
  2 rte Celle St Cloud_____ 01 39 12 28 84

• **Celle Saint Cloud(La)**
ROMANO Mauro
  22 av Jonchère_____ 01 30 82 23 48

• **Chambourcy**
MIRABEL André
  1 all résidence_____ 01 39 65 32 48

Comment vous SANTÉ vous ?

Qu'est-ce qui ne va pas?

Je tousse.

— Est-ce que **ça vous fait mal**?
  Aïe *(Ouch)*! Oui, ça fait mal.
  Non, ça ne fait pas mal.

faire mal *to hurt*

— Où **avez-vous mal?**
  J'ai mal | à la tête.
               | à la gorge *(throat).*
               | au ventre *(stomach).*
  J'ai mal au coeur *(I feel nauseous).*

Les parties du corps

Révision ▶ p. R12

— **Qu'est-ce qui ne va pas?** *(What's wrong?)*

  Je tousse.

tousser *to cough*	**éternuer** *to sneeze*
vomir *to throw up*	**saigner** *(to bleed)* **du nez**

  J'ai **un rhume** *(a cold).* Je suis **enrhumé(e)**.
  J'ai **une douleur** *(pain)* dans le dos.

des nausées	
de l'eczéma	
des vertiges	*dizzy spells*
des boutons	*a rash*

— Quelles **maladies** *(diseases)* **d'enfance** avez-vous eues?
  J'ai eu **la rougeole** *(measles).*

les oreillons	*mumps*
la varicelle	*chicken pox*
la rubéole	*German measles*
la coqueluche	*whooping cough*

Maux de tête

Le soulagement est possible.

VOTRE DOS VOUS FAIT MAL?

Association d'orthopédie du Québec

République Rwandaise
Ministère de la santé Publique
et des Affaires Sociales

Programme de Vaccination

Vaccination	Dose	Date
le tétanos		
la tuberculose		
la poliomyélite		
la diphtérie		
la coqueluche		
la rougeole		

—Est-ce que vous pouvez **ouvrir la bouche?**

avaler	*to swallow*
respirer	*to breathe, breathe in*
tousser	

—Je vais vous **examiner.**
prendre la température.
prendre la tension *(blood pressure).*
faire une analyse de sang *(blood test).*
faire une piqûre *(shot, injection).*
faire une radio *(x-ray).*

Obtenez la réponse
LE DIMANCHE 27 FÉVRIER
Prises de tension artérielle
GRATUITES
ENTRÉE 11 H ET 18 H
dans toutes les PJC Jean Coutu
JEAN COUTU

—Vous avez **une pneumonie.**

un rhume	**une angine** *strep throat*
de l'asthme	**une bronchite**
la grippe *flu*	**la mononucléose**

—Je vais vous **soigner** *(to treat).*
Voici **une ordonnance** *(prescription).*
Prenez **ce médicament** *(medicine)* . . .
le matin et le soir.
deux fois *(times)* **par jour.**
toutes les 4 heures.

une **de l'aspirine**	*un* **ces comprimés** *pills*
un **cet antibiotique**	*un* **ces cachets** *tablets*
une **ces vitamines**	*un* **ces gouttes** *drops*

—Vous devez **vous reposer.**
vous soigner.
rester au lit.
prendre rendez-vous
revenir | dans une semaine.

se reposer	*to rest*
se soigner	*to take care of oneself*

Voici une ordonnance. Vous devez prendre rendez-vous dans une semaine.

Merci, docteur.

Les faits sur la vitamine E

webber VITAMINE E
source naturelle
100%

Clinique de traitement de l'asthme
555, avenue University
Toronto (Ontario) M5G 1X8
HSC

200 COMPRIMÉS   325 CHACUN
ASPIRINE
Comprimés d'Acide Acétylsalicylique
ON PEUT S'Y FIER

1 Qu'est-ce qu'ils ont?

Choisissez l'option **a**, **b** ou **c** qui correspond logiquement à chaque situation.

1. Thomas va chez l'oculiste.
   a. Il va bien.
   b. Il a les oreillons.
   c. Il a mal aux yeux.

2. Roger a 39 degrés de température.
   a. Il est bien portant.
   b. Il a de la fièvre.
   c. Il a froid.

3. J'ai des difficultés à avaler.
   a. J'ai une angine.
   b. J'ai la rubéole.
   c. J'ai une crampe d'estomac.

4. Ma petite soeur tousse tout le temps.
   a. Elle a la varicelle.
   b. Elle a une bronchite.
   c. Elle est déprimée.

5. Thierry a envie de vomir.
   a. Il éternue.
   b. Il a de la tension.
   c. Il a mal au coeur.

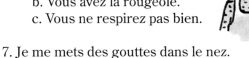

6. Vous avez des boutons.
   a. Vous avez la grippe.
   b. Vous avez la rougeole.
   c. Vous ne respirez pas bien.

7. Je me mets des gouttes dans le nez.
   a. J'ai un rhume.
   b. Je prends des cachets.
   c. J'ai besoin de vitamines.

8. L'infirmière m'a fait une radio.
   a. Je prends des comprimés.
   b. J'ai beaucoup de tension.
   c. Je me suis cassé le bras.

9. J'ai besoin de médicaments.
   a. Je vais à la pharmacie.
   b. Je vois le chirurgien.
   c. Je suis en bonne santé.

10. Je voudrais voir le médecin.
   a. Je me soigne.
   b. Je me sens bien.
   c. Je dois prendre rendez-vous.

2 Créa-dialogue

Aujourd'hui vous ne vous sentez pas bien du tout. Regardez la liste et choisissez une maladie ou un malaise. Décrivez vos symptômes à votre partenaire.

Ça va?

Qu'est-ce que tu as?

Tu es sûr(e)?

Non, je ne me sens pas bien.

Je crois que j'ai le rhume des foins.

Oui, j'éternue tout le temps et j'ai mal aux yeux.

la grippe	**la mononucléose**	**un rhume**	**une bronchite**
une angine	**une indigestion**	**de l'asthme**	**une pneumonie**
le rhume des foins (hay fever)		**une allergie**	**??**

3 À la clinique

Un(e) malade va dans une clinique où il/elle a rendez-vous.
Avant de voir le médecin, l'infirmier(ère) lui pose des questions.
Complétez le dialogue et jouez-le en classe avec votre partenaire.

Centre de Santé

Kirkland

"LE CENTRE DE SANTÉ"

POUR LE RESPECT GLOBAL
DES PRINCIPES DE
SOINS DE SANTÉ

17000 Hymus Blvd.
Kirkland, Québec
H9J 2W2

Infirmier(ère): Vous avez un rendez-vous?
  Malade: *Answer affirmatively and give the time.*
Infirmier(ère): Comment vous sentez-vous?
  Malade: *Say how you feel.*
Infirmier(ère): Avez-vous de la fièvre?
  Malade: *Give your temperature.*
Infirmier(ère): Où avez-vous mal?
  Malade: *Explain.*
Infirmier(ère): Avez-vous d'autres symptômes?
  Malade: *Give at least two symptoms.*
Infirmier(ère): Quelles maladies d'enfance avez-vous eues?
  Malade: *Mention two.*
Infirmier(ère): Est-ce que vous avez été malade cet hiver?
  Malade: *Answer affirmatively and explain.*
Infirmier(ère): Est-ce que vous prenez des médicaments?
  Malade: *Answer affirmatively and explain.*
Infirmier(ère): Merci. Le médecin va vous examiner.

Conseil de la santé et des services sociaux
de la région de Montréal métropolitain

Urgences santé
9 – 1 – 1

4 C'est vous le médecin!

Vous êtes médecin. Vos malades vous parlent de leurs problèmes. Dites-leur de ne pas
s'inquiéter et expliquez-leur ce que vous allez faire. Puis, donnez-leur une ordonnance.

- Je tousse tout le temps.
- J'ai de la fièvre.
- J'ai des boutons.
- J'ai des vertiges.
- J'ai des difficultés à respirer.
- J'ai des douleurs dans le dos.
- J'ai été mordu *(bitten)* par
  un chien.
- J'ai des palpitations
  (rapid pulse).

▶ **Je me sens très faible.**

**Ne vous inquiétez pas.
Je vais vous prendre la tension.
Si c'est nécessaire, je vais vous faire
une analyse de sang. Voici une ordonnance.
Prenez ces cachets deux fois par jour.**

Conversations libres

Avec votre partenaire, choisissez l'une des situations suivantes. Composez le dialogue correspondant et jouez-le en classe.

---

1   Zut alors!

Vous voyagez en France. Un jour vous vous réveillez avec un malaise généralisé et des boutons sur la figure. Vous téléphonez au médecin qui vous demande des détails.

Rôles: le/la touriste, le médecin

---

2   Un(e) malade imaginaire

Ce matin, il y a un examen de maths très important que vous n'avez pas préparé. Vous allez voir l'infirmier(ère) de l'école. Vous lui expliquez que vous êtes très malade. (Inventez des symptômes pour cette maladie imaginaire.) L'infirmier(ère) a des doutes sur votre maladie.

Rôles: l'élève, l'infirmier(ère)

---

3   Histoire médicale

Vous êtes infirmier(ère) dans une école française. Vous interviewez un(e) candidat(e) pour l'équipe de foot. Posez-lui des questions sur son état général, par exemple . . .

- s'il (si elle) a des problèmes de santé
- s'il (si elle) a mal quelque part
- quelles maladies d'enfance il(elle) a eues
- s'il (si elle) a été malade cet hiver
- s'il (si elle) prend des médicaments, etc.

Rôles: l'infirmier(ère), l'athlète

---

4   Une cure miracle

Un charlatan prétend avoir inventé une cure miracle pour toutes sortes de maladies. Un journaliste très incrédule lui pose des questions.

Rôles: le charlatan, le journaliste

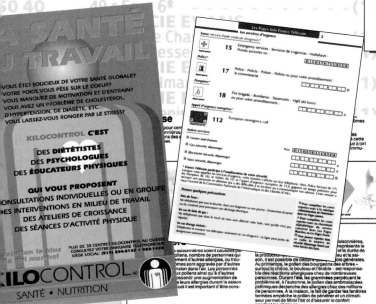

A. Le concept du subjonctif: temps et modes

When we use verbs, we use them in a certain TENSE and a certain MOOD.

- The TENSE of a verb indicates *when* the action takes place.
  The PRESENT, the PASSÉ COMPOSÉ, the IMPERFECT and the FUTURE are tenses.

- The MOOD reflects the attitude of the speaker or the subject toward the action.
  The INDICATIVE and the SUBJUNCTIVE are moods.

The INDICATIVE MOOD is *objective.*
  It is used to describe *facts.* It states what is considered to be *certain.*
  It is the mood of *what is.*

The SUBJUNCTIVE MOOD is *subjective.*
  It is used to express *feelings, judgments,* and *emotions* relating to an action.
  It states what is considered to be *desirable, possible, doubtful,* or *uncertain.*
  It is the mood of *what may or might be.*

➡ Although the subjunctive is rarely used in English, it is a mood frequently used in French.
  Compare the moods in the following sentences:

(fact)	Je sais que tu **es** généreux.	*I know that you **are** generous.*
(wish)	Je souhaite que tu **sois** plus patient avec moi.	*I wish that you **were** more patient with me.*

Both the indicative and the subjunctive may occur in a dependent clause introduced by **que**.
The choice between the indicative and the subjunctive depends on what the subject or speaker expresses in the main clause.

MAIN CLAUSE (the subject expresses . . .)	DEPENDENT CLAUSE
• a **fact**, a **belief**	→ INDICATIVE
• a **wish**, a **necessity**, an **obligation** • an **emotion** or **feeling** • a **doubt** or **possibility**	→ SUBJUNCTIVE

Le subjonctif:
  formation régulière
  formation irrégulière
_____

Révision ▶ 📖 pp. R19, R21; R23-31

Je sais que tu as une belle moto.

J'aimerais mieux que tu aies une voiture de sport!

BROM BROM

1 Chez le médecin

Vous êtes médecin. Choisissez un patient et dites ce qu'il doit faire et ne pas faire.

il faut que
il ne faut pas que

PATIENTS	ACTIVITÉS	
tu	faire du sport	manger trop
vous	aller à la piscine	manger des produits
M. Marcoux	être déprimé(e)	naturels
Mme Lenoir	être nerveux(se)	boire de l'eau minérale
ces enfants	être optimiste	prendre ces médicaments
ces malades	avoir trop de	se coucher tard
	tension	se reposer
	avoir peur de la	se soigner
	piqûre	

B. Les verbes croire et craindre

	croire *(to believe)*		craindre *(to fear, to be afraid of)*	
PRÉSENT	je **crois**	nous **croyons**	je **crains**	nous **craignons**
	tu **crois**	vous **croyez**	tu **crains**	vous **craignez**
	il/elle/on **croit**	ils/elles **croient**	il/elle/on **craint**	ils/elles **craignent**
PASSÉ COMPOSÉ	j'**ai cru**		j'**ai craint**	

Verbes conjugués comme **craindre:**
    plaindre *(to be sorry for)*
    se plaindre de *(to complain about)*
    peindre *(to paint)*
    éteindre *(to turn off, to extinguish)*

2 Vive la différence!

Chacun fait des choses différentes. Exprimez cela en faisant les substitutions suggérées.

1. Jérôme se plaint de sa copine.
   (les élèves - le professeur / le professeur - l'administration / toi - tout)

2. Isabelle croit à son horoscope.
   (moi - l'avenir [*future*] / vous - l'amitié / Roméo et Juliette - l'amour éternel)

3. Marc peint un tableau *(picture)*.
   (vous - la cuisine / moi - mon bureau / ces artistes - des portraits)

4. J'ai peint ma chambre en bleu.
   (mes cousins - en jaune / vous - en gris / nous - en rouge)

C. L'usage du subjonctif: émotions et sentiments

Note the use of the subjunctive in the following sentences.

Je suis content **que tu sois** en bonne santé.	*I am happy **that you are** in good health.*
Nous sommes tristes **que vous partiez.**	*We are sad **that you are leaving.***
Le médecin craint **que j'aie** les oreillons.	*The doctor fears **that I have** mumps.*

The SUBJUNCTIVE is used after a verb or expression of EMOTION (happiness, sadness, fear, surprise, anger, regret, . . .), when the emotion concerns someone or something *other than the subject.*

➡ When the emotion concerns the subject itself, an infinitive construction is used. Compare:

INFINITIVE	SUBJUNCTIVE
Je suis content d'**aller** en France.	Je suis content **que tu ailles** en France.
Alice a peur d'**être** malade.	Le médecin a peur **qu'Alice soit** malade.

Vocabulaire: Verbes et expressions d'émotion

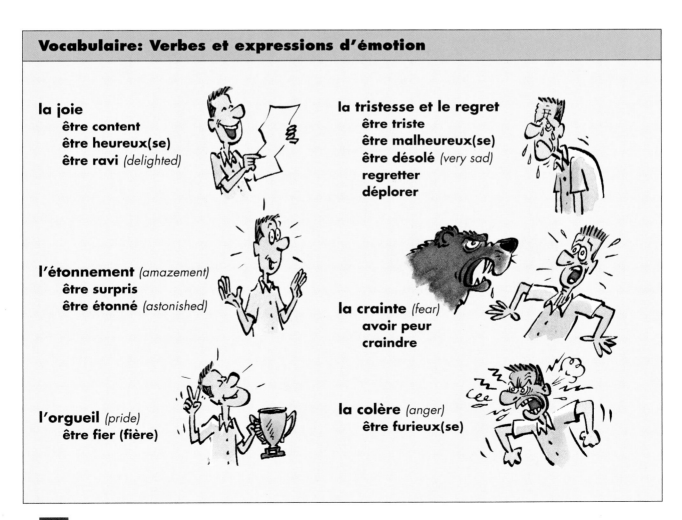

la joie
  être content
  être heureux(se)
  être ravi *(delighted)*

la tristesse et le regret
  être triste
  être malheureux(se)
  être désolé *(very sad)*
  regretter
  déplorer

l'étonnement *(amazement)*
  être surpris
  être étonné *(astonished)*

la crainte *(fear)*
  avoir peur
  craindre

l'orgueil *(pride)*
  être fier (fière)

la colère *(anger)*
  être furieux(se)

Speech bubbles in image: "JE SUIS TRISTE DE PARTIR." — "JE SUIS SI TRISTE QUE TU PARTES !" — "EH BIEN, MOI, JE SUIS CONTENT QU'IL PARTE !"

3 Consultations

Vous êtes médecin. Votre partenaire
va décrire un symptôme.
Vous allez exprimer votre diagnostic.

▶ — Je tousse tout le temps.
— J'ai peur que vous ayez une bronchite.

SYMPTÔMES	DIAGNOSTIC
• éternuer	• une allergie
• avoir mal au ventre	• une indigestion
• avoir très mal à la gorge	• une angine
• tousser tout le temps	• une bronchite
• avoir des boutons	• la grippe
• se sentir très faible	• la mononucléose
• avoir de la fièvre	• le rhume des foins *(hay fever)*
	• ??

4 Mes sentiments

Décrivez vos sentiments dans les circonstances suivantes.
Choisissez une des options entre parenthèses ou une option de votre choix.

▶ (heureux ou triste?) Mes copains vont en France cet été.
Je suis heureux/heureuse que mes copains aillent en France cet été.

1. content ou jaloux? (Mes cousins ont une voiture de sport.)
2. désolé ou surpris? (Mon frère ne dit pas la vérité.)
3. triste ou content? (Le professeur est malade aujourd'hui.)
4. furieux ou étonné? (Ma copine/mon copain ne vient pas au rendez-vous.)
5. content ou désolé? (L'examen de français est annulé.)
6. surpris ou fier? (L'équipe de baseball de l'école gagne le championnat.)

5 Leurs réactions

Décrivez les réactions des personnes suivantes aux situations entre parenthèses.
Utilisez une expression d'émotion du Vocabulaire.

▶ Alice (Son copain sort avec une autre fille.)
Alice est triste (furieuse) que son copain sorte avec une autre fille.

1. Thomas (Sa copine française écrit toutes les semaines.)
2. Le médecin (Monsieur Larose fait des exercices.)
3. Stéphanie (Marc vient à sa boum.)
4. Monsieur Dupont (Sa fille a le premier prix du conservatoire.)
5. Le professeur (Le mauvais élève réussit à l'examen.)
6. Nathalie (Jean-Pierre est en retard au rendez-vous.)
7. Catherine (Sa cousine oublie la date de son anniversaire.)
8. Les supporteurs *(fans)* (Leur équipe perd le match.)
9. Les écologistes (On fait des économies d'énergie.)

D. Le subjonctif après les expressions de doute

Compare the use of the INDICATIVE and the SUBJUNCTIVE in the sentences below.

CERTAINTY OR BELIEF (INDICATIVE)	DOUBT, DISBELIEF OR UNCERTAINTY (SUBJUNCTIVE)
Je crois que tu **es** fatigué.	Je doute que tu **sois** malade.
Le médecin pense que j'**ai** la grippe.	Il ne pense pas que j'**aie** la mononucléose.
Il est sûr qu'Alice **est** trop pâle.	Il n'est pas sûr qu'elle **soit** déprimée.
Tu crois que tu **es** très intelligent!	Crois-tu que tu **sois** sympathique?

The INDICATIVE is used after verbs and expressions of CERTAINTY or BELIEF.
The SUBJUNCTIVE is used after verbs and expressions of DOUBT and UNCERTAINTY.

➡ Verbs like **croire, penser, être sûr, être certain**,
and expressions like **il est sûr, il est certain**,
are used to convey <u>belief</u>, <u>knowledge</u>, or <u>conviction</u> of certain facts.

- When used in the AFFIRMATIVE, they are followed by the INDICATIVE.
- When used in the INTERROGATIVE or the NEGATIVE, however, these verbs and expressions may convey an element of doubt or uncertainty. In this case they are followed by the SUBJUNCTIVE.

ALLONS PLUS LOIN

Depending on the level of certainty or doubt that the speaker wants to convey, certain expressions may be followed by the indicative OR the subjunctive. Compare:

Il semble que tu **as** raison.	*It seems that you are right.* (This is pretty sure.)
Il semble que tu **aies** raison.	*It would seem that you are right.* (It is much less sure.)

Vocabulaire: Verbes et expressions de certitude et de doute

EXPRESSIONS DE CERTITUDE (+ INDICATIF)	EXPRESSIONS DE DOUTE (+ SUBJONCTIF)
je sais que . . .	**je doute que . . .**
je dis que . . .	
je crois que . . .	**je ne crois pas que . . .**
	crois-tu que . . . ?
je pense que . . .	**je ne pense pas que . . .**
	penses-tu que . . . ?
je suis sûr(e) que . . .	**je ne suis pas sûr(e) que . . .**
	es-tu sûr(e) que . . . ?
il est sûr / vrai / certain que . . .	**il n'est pas sûr / vrai / certain que . . .**
	est-il sûr / vrai / certain que . . . ?
il est clair que . . .	**il est douteux que . . .**
il est probable que . . .	**il est possible que . . .**
il est évident que . . .	**il est impossible que . . .**

6 **L'optimiste et le pessimiste**

L'optimiste voit l'existence sous un aspect positif. Le pessimiste voit l'existence sous un aspect négatif. Avec votre partenaire, jouez le rôle de l'optimiste et du pessimiste.

> **Je crois que la vie est belle.**
>
> **Je doute que la vie soit belle.**

▶ la vie / être belle

1. les gens / être généreux
2. les jeunes / avoir un idéal
3. les parents / faire le maximum pour aider leurs enfants
4. la situation économique / être excellente
5. on / faire des progrès dans tous les domaines

6. les journalistes / dire la vérité
7. le président / être honnête avec le public
8. le monde / être moins dangereux qu'avant
9. on / découvrir prochainement *(soon)* une cure contre le SIDA *(AIDS)*

7 **Êtes-vous d'accord?**

Voici quelques propositions. Choisissez une proposition et exprimez votre opinion sur ce sujet. Pour cela, utilisez l'une des expressions du vocabulaire. Si possible, illustrez votre opinion en formulant une réflexion personnelle.

▶ la majorité des gens / être superstitieux?
> **Je ne pense pas que la majorité des gens soient superstitieux.**
> **Moi, par exemple, je n'hésite pas à voyager le vendredi 13.**

1. l'argent / faire le bonheur?
2. les gens / être fondamentalement honnêtes?
3. les gens idéalistes / être naïfs?
4. la liberté / être un mythe?
5. les femmes / avoir les mêmes responsabilités que les hommes?

6. les extra-terrestres / exister?
7. il / être facile de changer son destin?
8. il / être possible d'éliminer la violence dans la société?
9. tout le monde / avoir les mêmes choses?

Les médecins et l'action humanitaire

Nathalie, 27 ans, vient d'obtenir° son diplôme de médecin. Dans quelques semaines elle va partir pour l'Afghanistan. Hélène, une infirmière de 35 ans, rentre de Thaïlande où elle a passé dix mois dans les camps de réfugiés. Emmanuel, 25 ans, n'a pas de spécialité médicale, mais il a passé deux ans au Bangladesh avec «Médecins sans frontières.»° Nathalie, Hélène, Emmanuel: trois exemples parmi° des milliers de Français qui ont décidé de faire quelque chose pour les oubliés° de la terre.°

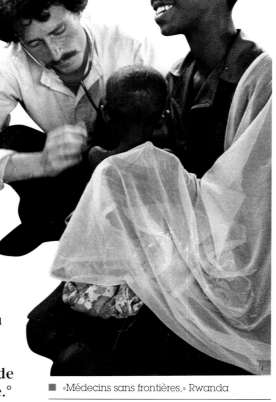

■ «Médecins sans frontières,» Rwanda

Nathalie explique: «Comme médecins, notre premier rôle est d'aider les gens qui sont dans la détresse. Aujourd'hui, la détresse humaine existe

■ Les organisations comme «Médecins du monde,» «Les Médecins aux pieds nus,» et «Médecins sans frontières» envoient des volontaires dans les régions où il y a une urgence médicale.

partout° dans le monde, et spécialement dans les pays du tiers-monde° où des centaines de milliers de gens souffrent° de la misère, de la faim et de la maladie. Dans ces pays, les catastrophes naturelles, les épidémies, la guerre° civile font des millions de victimes chaque année. Nous autres° citoyens° des pays dits *civilisés,* nous ne pouvons pas rester insensibles° au sort° de ces êtres° humains qui sont nos frères et nos soeurs. Nous devons agir°. Malheureusement, les besoins sont immenses et nos ressources très limitées. Nous sommes là non seulement pour soigner les gens, mais pour leur redonner° l'envie° de vivre.»°

Plusieurs organisations ont été créées en France pour répondre aux besoins de santé des pays du tiers-monde. Ces organisations envoient des volontaires dans des régions où il y a une urgence médicale, et plus spécialement dans des pays d'Afrique et d'Asie: en Éthiopie, en Somalie et au Libéria, au Pakistan, au Cambodge, par exemple.

---

obtenir ✳ *to get, obtain* **frontières** *borders* **parmi** *among* **les oubliés** *forgotten people* **la terre** *earth* **partout** *everywhere* **tiers-monde** *third world* **souffrir** ✳ *to suffer* **la guerre** *war* **autres** *others* **citoyens** *citizens* **insensibles** *insensitive* **au sort** *fate* **êtres** *beings* **agir** *to act* **pour leur redonner** *to give back* **l'envie** *desire* **vivre** ✳ *to live*

Pour être volontaire, il n'est pas nécessaire d'être médecin ou infirmier. Il suffit° d'être une personne de bonne volonté° et de croire à la solidarité des peuples de la terre. Les organisations les plus connues sont «Médecins sans frontières» qui intervient° dans plus de 80 pays, «Médecins du monde» qui a 6000 volontaires dans 40 pays, et «Les Médecins aux pieds nus.»° L'originalité de cette dernière organisation est d'utiliser des médicaments d'origine végétale ou animale et les techniques traditionnelles des pays d'intervention, comme par exemple, l'acupuncture dans les pays d'Asie.

et vous?

DÉFINITIONS

Définissez les mots ou expressions suivants. (Quand c'est possible, donnez des exemples.)

- un(e) volontaire
- la bonne volonté
- une épidémie
- la solidarité
- un réfugié

- l'action humanitaire
- les pays du tiers-monde
- une catastrophe naturelle
- la guerre civile

EXPRESSION ÉCRITE

1. Imaginez que vous voulez être volontaire pour l'une des organisations mentionnées dans le texte. Écrivez une courte lettre où vous expliquez ...
   - pourquoi l'action humanitaire vous intéresse
   - dans quel pays vous voudriez aller et pourquoi
   - ce que vous voulez faire pour aider les gens de ce pays
2. Imaginez que vous collectez des fonds pour "Médecins Sans Frontières." Dans une lettre à un ami, vous décrivez cette organisation.

"Médecins Sans Frontières" — une organisation humanitaire mondiale

Malgré° le progrès scientifique, le monde moderne n'échappe° pas aux catastrophes humaines et naturelles de toutes sortes: guerres,° révolutions, tremblements de terre,° inondations,° famines, épidémies... Ces catastrophes n'ont pas de frontières, mais elle affectent généralement les pays les plus pauvres et créent des urgences médicales pour les populations les plus vulnérables: enfants, femmes et personnes âgées. Pour répondre à ces urgences, il faut agir° rapidement et indépendamment de toute considération politique.

Dans ce but,° un groupe de médecins français a créé en 1971 une organisation qui a pour mission d'envoyer des volontaires partout° où les populations sont en danger. Cette organisation, appelée "Médecins Sans Frontières," est maintenant une organisation internationale. Chaque année, 2500 volontaires—médecins, chirurgiens, infirmières—partent en mission à travers° le monde. Leur but est non seulement d'apporter une aide médicale à ceux qui en ont besoin, mais aussi de faire respecter la dignité humaine. Présents sur tous les continents, les "Médecins Sans Frontières" sont intervenus en Somalie, en Éthiopie, au Kosovo, au Congo, en Afghanistan, en Palestine... Pour son travail humanitaire, cette organisation a reçu le prix° Nobel de la Paix° en 1999.

---

il suffit = il est suffisant   **volonté** will   **intervenir** ✳ to intervene   **pieds nus** bare feet   **malgré** in spite of   **échappe (à)** escapes (from)   **guerres** wars
tremblements de terre earthquakes   **inondations** floods   **agir** to act   **dans ce but** to this end   **partout** everywhere   **à travers** across   **prix** prize   **paix** peace

PARTIE 2

HOPITAL FRANCO BRITANNIQUE

LE FRANÇAIS PRATIQUE

Accidents et soins dentaires

À l'hôpital

Cette personne est **blessée** *(injured, hurt)*.
Elle vient de **se blesser** *(to get hurt)*.
Elle s'est cassé le bras.

se blesser à la tête	**se casser** *(to break)* **la jambe**
se couper *(to cut)* **à la main**	**se fracturer l'épaule**
se brûler *to get burned*	**se fouler** *(to twist)* **la cheville** *ankle*

L'infirmier(ère) va lui **faire une radio** *(x-ray)*.

faire un plâtre *cast*	**faire un pansement** *bandage*
donner des béquilles *crutches*	**mettre des sutures** *stitches*

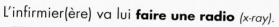

Aïeee!

Cette personne est blessée.

On va lui faire une radio.

---

1 Créa-dialogue: Qu'est-ce qui est arrivé?

Vous rencontrez les personnes suivantes. Avec votre partenaire, choisissez l'une des illustrations. Composez le dialogue correspondant et jouez-le en classe. Utilisez votre imagination pour expliquer l'accident!

— Eh Antoine, ça va?
— Hm, comme ci comme ça.
— Pourquoi est-ce que tu as un plâtre?
— Je me suis cassé le bras.
— Comment est-ce que c'est arrivé?
— Eh bien, voilà. Je faisais de l'alpinisme samedi dernier et je suis tombé.

1. Juliette
2. Thomas
3. Jean-Pierre
4. Véronique
5. Grégoire
6. Vanessa

Speech bubbles: "Oh là là, j'ai mal aux dents." / "Vous avez une carie."

Chez le dentiste

—Oh là là, j'ai **mal aux dents**.
  Vous avez **une carie** *(cavity)*.
  Je vais vous | faire **un plombage** *(filling)*.
            | faire **une piqûre de novocaïne**.
            | **enlever** *(to remove)* | cette dent.
            | | **cette dent de sagesse** *(wisdom tooth)*.

Bonnes dents, belles dents. C'est promis!

EMOFORM

2 Chez le dentiste

Avec votre partenaire, composez le dialogue suivant entre le/la dentiste et le/la patient(e).

Dentiste: *Ask the patient what's wrong.*
  Patient: *Say that you have a toothache.*
Dentiste: *Ask patient to open his/her mouth.*
          Say that the patient has a cavity and explain what you are going to do.
  Patient: *Ask if it is going to hurt.*
Dentiste: *Say no, and tell your patient that you will give him/her a shot*
          of novocain.
  Patient: *Say that you are not feeling well . . . and then faint.*

Conversations libres

Avec votre partenaire, choisissez l'une des situations suivantes.
Composez le dialogue correspondant et jouez-le en classe.

1 Accident de moto

Xavier a eu un accident de moto. Le lendemain,
son amie Florence lui rend visite à l'hôpital et lui
pose des questions. Xavier explique ce qui est
arrivé et ce que le médecin a fait.

Rôles: Xavier, Florence

2 Visite chez le dentiste

Le petit Pierre (6 ans) a mal aux dents. Sa mère
pense qu'il a probablement une carie et veut
l'amener chez le dentiste. Pierre a peur, et
sa mère essaie de le rassurer en expliquant ce que
le dentiste va faire. Pierre n'est pas du tout rassuré.

Rôles: la mère, Pierre

A. Le passé du subjonctif

FORMS

The past subjunctive is a compound tense formed according to the pattern:

> present subjunctive of **avoir** or **être** + past participle

parler	aller	s'amuser
que j'**aie parlé**	que je **sois allé(e)**	que je me **sois amusé(e)**
que tu **aies parlé**	que tu **sois allé(e)**	que tu te **sois amusé(e)**
qu'il **ait parlé**	qu'il **soit allé**	qu'il se **soit amusé**
qu'elle **ait parlé**	qu'elle **soit allée**	qu'elle se **soit amusée**
que nous **ayons parlé**	que nous **soyons allé(e)s**	que nous nous **soyons amusé(e)s**
que vous **ayez parlé**	que vous **soyez allé(e)(s)**	que vous vous **soyez amusé(e)(s)**
qu'ils **aient parlé**	qu'ils **soient allés**	qu'ils se **soient amusés**
qu'elles **aient parlé**	qu'elles **soient allées**	qu'elles se **soient amusées**

➡ The agreement of the past participle in compound tenses also applies to the past subjunctive.

Je suis content que tu **aies téléphoné** à ces filles.

Je suis heureux que tu **les aies invité es** à la boum.

USES

Compare the use of the present and the past subjunctive.

Je doute que Paul **téléphone** ce soir.	*I doubt that Paul **will call** tonight.*
Je doute qu'il **ait téléphoné** hier.	*I doubt that he **called** yesterday.*
Je regrette que vous **ne veniez pas** cet après-midi.	*I am sorry that you **are not coming** this afternoon.*
Je regrette que vous **ne soyez pas venu** samedi.	*I am sorry that you **did not come** on Saturday.*

❚ The past subjunctive is used instead of the present subjunctive to refer to past events or situations.

1 Drôles d'excuses!

Votre partenaire n'est pas venu(e) à une répétition *(rehearsal)* de la chorale samedi dernier. Il/elle va choisir une (mauvaise!) excuse. Vous êtes le directeur/la directrice et vous avez des doutes.

▶ — **Je ne suis pas venu(e) à la répétition parce que j'ai raté le bus.**
— **Ah oui? Écoute, Christophe, je doute que tu aies raté le bus.**

EXCUSES
- J'ai eu la grippe.
- Je me suis foulé la cheville.
- Je suis tombé(e) dans les escaliers.
- Je suis allé(e) chez le dentiste.
- J'ai raté *(missed)* le bus.
- Le bus a eu un accident.
- Mon réveil *(alarm clock)* n'a pas sonné.
- Ma cousine s'est mariée.
- Mon arrière-grand-mère est morte.

2 Réactions!

Votre partenaire va décrire un événement (imaginaire) qui lui est arrivé.
Exprimez votre réaction. Pour cela, choisissez une expression de la page 272.

ÉVÉNEMENTS

- mon oncle / avoir un accident
- ma cousine / se marier
- mon copain / voir un OVNI *(UFO)*
- ma grande soeur / gagner une bourse *(scholarship)* pour l'université
- ma grand-mère / se casser le bras

- ma copine / oublier la date de mon anniversaire
- mes parents / rencontrer le président des États-Unis
- ma tante / m'acheter une voiture de sport

RÉACTIONS

joie?
tristesse?
surprise?
doute?

> Ma tante m'a acheté une voiture de sport!

> Ah oui? Écoute, je doute qu'elle t'ait acheté une voiture de sport.

(Eh bien, bravo! Je suis ravi(e) qu'elle t'ait acheté une voiture de sport.)

3 Ce qu'ils pensent

Décrivez ce que pensent les personnes suivantes.

▶ l'infirmière / craindre / tu / te fouler la cheville.
L'infirmière craint que tu te sois foulé la cheville.

1. le médecin / ne pas croire / je / me casser la jambe.
2. je / être content / tu / venir à la boum
3. Pauline / être heureuse / Jérôme / lui écrire une lettre
4. vous / être surpris / l'équipe / gagner le match
5. le guide / avoir peur / les alpinistes *(mountain climbers)* / se perdre dans la montagne
6. le professeur / douter / vous / faire vos devoirs
7. Madame Dumont / être fière / sa fille / réussir à l'examen d'ingénieur

4 Les mystères de l'univers

Beaucoup de mystères n'ont pas été élucidés *(cleared up)*. Avec votre partenaire, choisissez un des sujets suivants et discutez-le. Exprimez votre opinion en utilisant une expression de doute ou de certitude, et le passé du subjonctif ou le passé composé de l'indicatif.

▶ les Vikings / découvrir l'Amérique?
Je doute (je ne crois pas / il est douteux) que les Vikings aient découvert l'Amérique.
ou: **Je suis sûr(e) (il est probable) que les Vikings ont découvert l'Amérique.**

1. les Égyptiens / utiliser l'électricité?
2. Dracula / exister?
3. un écrivain inconnu *(unknown)* / écrire les pièces de Shakespeare?
4. des navigateurs romains / explorer l'Amérique du Sud?
5. des extra-terrestres / venir sur la Terre?
6. des ingénieurs russes / inventer la bombe atomique?
7. un agent soviétique / assassiner le président Kennedy?

LECTURE

En voyage

d'après Guy de Maupassant

L'histoire que vous allez lire est racontée par un médecin au cours d'un voyage en train. Les autres passagers du compartiment où il se trouve ont déjà fait le récit d'aventures plus ou moins rocambolesques° dont ils sont évidemment les héros. Ces histoires ont un point commun: elles se passent toutes dans un train.

C'est maintenant le tour du médecin. L'histoire qu'il choisit de raconter est une histoire d'amour, l'amour simple et purement spirituel unissant un homme et une femme qui se sont rencontrés dans un train.

rocambolesques = avec beaucoup d'incidents extraordinaires

NOTE CULTURELLE

Guy de Maupassant (1850-1893) a écrit des romans et des pièces de théâtre, mais il est surtout célèbre pour les centaines de contes et nouvelles qu'il a publiés. Maupassant utilise un style clair, objectif et impersonnel. Il décrit avec précision les faits, laissant au lecteur le souci° de découvrir les sentiments qui animent les personnages de ses contes.

souci *care*

Le contexte historique

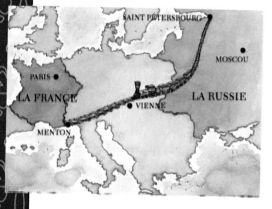

Pour comprendre une histoire, il faut la situer dans son contexte historique. L'action de l'histoire racontée par le médecin se passe à la fin du 19e siècle dans un train qui va de Russie jusqu'à la Côte d'Azur en France. Les voyages de ce genre étaient très longs. Ils étaient relativement sûrs,° mais de temps en temps les trains étaient attaqués par des bandits ou par des révolutionnaires, alors particulièrement actifs dans les pays de l'Europe de l'Est et surtout en Russie.

Parmi° les passagers du train, il y a une jeune femme mariée à un aristocrate russe. Très malade, elle va en France pour se soigner. Comme les gens riches de l'époque, elle est accompagnée de ses serviteurs et elle a réservé un wagon pour elle seule.

sûrs *safe*   **parmi** *among*

Anticipons un peu!

Imaginez que vous êtes la jeune femme russe. Au cours du voyage, un homme fait irruption dans le compartiment où vous êtes seule. Il est très pâle, paraît confus et vous remarquez qu'il est blessé. Cet homme vous demande de l'aider.

Qu'est-ce que vous allez faire?
- tirer la sonnette d'alarme
- appeler vos serviteurs
- aider l'homme

À supposer que vous avez décidé d'aider cet homme, qu'est-ce que vous allez demander à cet homme de faire?
- se livrer à la police
- aller à l'hôpital
- ne jamais plus vous parler

EN VOYAGE

1

Le médecin commença ainsi son histoire:

«Moi, je n'ai pas d'aventure extraordinaire à vous raconter.
Je vais seulement vous parler d'une jeune femme que j'ai connue,
une de mes clientes, à qui il arriva la chose la plus singulière°
5 du monde, et aussi la plus mystérieuse et la plus attendrissante.°

C'était une Russe, la comtesse Marie Baranow, une très grande
dame, d'une exquise beauté. Vous savez comme les Russes peuvent
être belles, avec leur nez fin, leur bouche délicate, leurs yeux d'une
indéfinissable couleur, d'un bleu gris, et leur charme à la fois tendre
10 et sévère, que les Français trouvent tellement séduisant.

La comtesse Marie souffrait depuis plusieurs années de tuberculose.
Pour la soigner, son médecin, qui la savait très malade, voulait l'envoyer
dans le sud de la France, mais elle refusait obstinément de quitter Saint
Pétersbourg. Finalement, l'automne dernier, le docteur, réalisant la gravité
15 de l'état° de sa patiente, parla à son mari qui ordonna à sa femme de partir
pour Menton.

Résignée, elle prit le train. Elle était seule dans son wagon, ses gens de
service° occupant un autre compartiment. Elle restait contre la portière, un
peu triste, regardant passer les campagnes et les villages de la Russie. Elle
20 se sentait bien isolée dans la vie, sans enfants, sans parents et avec un mari
qui ne l'aimait plus et qui avait décidé de l'exiler à des milliers de
kilomètres de son pays.

À chaque station, son serviteur Ivan venait voir si elle avait besoin de
quelque chose. C'était un vieux domestique, totalement dévoué, à qui elle
25 pouvait demander n'importe quoi.

singulière = étrange   **attendrissante** *touching*   **l'état** = la condition   **gens de services** = domestiques

Mots utiles

la comtesse	*countess*
la portière	= la porte d'un train
souffrir *	*to suffer*
dévoué	*devoted*
exquis	*exquisite*
séduisant	*attractive*
à la fois	*at the same time*
n'importe quoi	*anything*

NOTES CULTURELLES

La tuberculose. La tuberculose est une maladie très grave qui
attaque les poumons.° Au 19e siècle, c'était une maladie très
commune et, comme il n'y avait pas de vaccin et pas
d'antibiotiques, elle était généralement mortelle. Pour se soigner,
les gens riches allaient dans les régions où l'air était pur et le
climat sain°: dans les Alpes, par exemple, ou sur la Côte d'Azur.

Saint Pétersbourg. Saint Pétersbourg, ou Pétersbourg, était la
capitale de la Russie impériale. C'était là que les tsars et les
aristocrates russes avaient leurs palais.°

Menton et la Côte d'Azur. Menton est une petite ville très
pittoresque située sur la Côte d'Azur ou Riviera française.
Aujourd'hui, cette région attire° des millions de touristes chaque
année. Au siècle dernier, les seuls visiteurs étaient des familles
anglaises et des aristocrates russes qui venaient là à cause du
climat. Dans le cimetière de Menton, on peut voir encore
aujourd'hui de nombreuses tombes aux inscriptions russes.

poumons *lungs*   **sain** *healthy*   **palais** *palaces*   **attire** *attracts*

Avez-vous compris?

1. Qu'est-ce que le médecin pense des femmes russes?
2. Quelle était la maladie de la comtesse?
3. Qu'est-ce que son docteur en Russie voulait qu'elle fasse?
4. Avec qui a-t-elle fait le voyage?
5. Quels étaient les sentiments de la comtesse quand elle était dans le train?
6. Est-ce qu'elle avait une vie familiale intéressante? Expliquez.

Anticipons un peu!

Quelque chose de dramatique va arriver dans la scène suivante. Selon vous, qu'est-ce qui va se passer?

2

La nuit commençait à tomber. Le train allait maintenant très vite. Très énervée,° la comtesse ne pouvait pas dormir. Elle eut alors l'idée de compter l'argent que son mari lui avait donné avant son départ. Elle ouvrit son sac, en vida le contenu sur ses genoux et commença à compter les pièces d'or.

Tout d'un coup, la comtesse Marie sentit un vent froid sur son visage. Elle leva la tête et elle vit un homme qui venait d'entrer dans son wagon. Il était grand, bien habillé, et il était blessé à la main. Il referma la porte, s'assit en face de la comtesse et la regarda de ses grands yeux noirs. Puis, il prit un mouchoir dans sa poche et en enveloppa son poignet pour arrêter le sang qui coulait. 30

La jeune femme eut très peur. Cet homme certainement l'avait vue compter son or. Il était venu pour la voler, ou, pire encore, pour la tuer. Il la regardait fixement, essoufflé,° le visage convulsé, prêt, sans doute, à l'attaquer. 35

Il dit brusquement:

— Madame, n'ayez pas peur. 40

Elle ne répondit rien, incapable d'ouvrir la bouche. Son coeur battait et ses oreilles bourdonnaient.°

L'homme continua:

— Je ne suis pas un malfaiteur°, madame. 45

Elle ne disait toujours rien, mais ses genoux tremblaient tellement que tout l'or tomba sur le sol° du wagon.

Surpris, l'homme regarda ce flot° de métal, puis il se baissa pour ramasser les pièces.

Prise de panique, la comtesse se leva. Elle courut vers la portière pour sauter du train. L'homme comprit ce qu'elle voulait faire. Il l'attrapa, la saisit dans ses bras, et l'obligea à s'asseoir. 50

— Écoutez-moi, madame, dit-il. Je ne suis pas un malfaiteur. La preuve° c'est que je vais ramasser cet argent et vous le rendre. Je suis moi-même en grand danger. Si vous ne m'aidez pas à passer la frontière, je suis un homme mort. Dans une heure, nous serons à la dernière station russe. Dans une heure dix, nous serons dans un autre pays. Si vous ne me secourez° pas, je suis condamné. Je ne peux pas vous expliquer pourquoi, mais croyez-moi. Je n'ai pas tué, je n'ai pas volé, et je n'ai rien fait de mal. Je vous jure que je suis un homme d'honneur, mais je ne peux pas vous en dire plus. 55 60

Mots utiles

un coin	corner
une frontière	border
le genou;	
les genoux	knee; lap
un mouchoir	handkerchief
une pièce d'or	gold coin
le poignet	wrist
se baisser	to stoop, bend down
battre *	to beat
compter	to count
couler	to flow
envelopper	to wrap
jurer	to swear
ralentir	to slow down
ramasser	to pick up
remplir	to fill
rouler	to roll (along); to travel
sauter	to jump
siffler	to whistle
tuer	to kill
vider	to empty
voler	to steal
muet (muette)	silent
pire	worse

énervée = nerveuse **essoufflé** out of breath **bourdonnaient** were buzzing **malfaiteur** = criminel
sol floor **flot** stream, cascade **preuve** proof **secourez** = aidez

L'homme se mit à genoux. Comme il l'avait dit, il ramassa toutes les pièces d'or, et en remplit le sac qu'il donna à la comtesse. Puis il alla s'asseoir à l'autre coin du wagon.

La comtesse Marie ne bougeait° pas. Immobile et muette, elle retrouva   65
peu à peu son calme. L'homme ne faisait pas un geste pas un mouvement. Il restait droit,° les yeux fixés devant lui. De temps en temps, elle le regardait rapidement. C'était un homme de trente ans environ.° Il était très beau, avec l'apparence d'un gentilhomme.

Le train continuait à rouler très vite dans la nuit. Puis, il siffla plusieurs   70
fois, ralentit et finalement s'arrêta.

bougeait = changeait de position   **droit** *sitting upright*   **environ** = approximativement

---

Avez-vous compris?

1. Qu'est-ce que la comtesse faisait quand l'homme est entré dans le wagon?
2. Quelle était l'apparence physique de cet homme? Décrivez-le.
3. Quelle a été la réaction de la comtesse quand elle a vu cet homme? Pourquoi?
4. Qu'est-ce que l'homme a fait quand l'argent a roulé sur le sol?
5. Qu'est-ce que la comtesse a voulu faire ensuite?
6. Quel service est-ce que l'homme a demandé à la comtesse?

Anticipons un peu!

À votre avis, est-ce que la comtesse va protéger l'inconnu?
- Si oui, comment?
- Si non, qu'est-ce qu'elle va faire?

3

Ivan, le vieux serviteur, parut à la portière du wagon pour prendre les ordres de la comtesse. Celle-ci regarda son étrange compagnon, puis elle dit à son serviteur d'une voix brusque:

— Ivan, je n'ai plus besoin de toi. Tu vas retourner à Saint Pétersbourg.   75

Le serviteur, très surpris, ouvrit des yeux énormes. Tremblant d'émotion, il put à peine dire:

— Mais, madame . . . Je pensais que . . .

D'un ton très assuré, la comtesse répondit: 80

— J'ai changé d'avis. Tu ne viendras pas avec moi à Menton. Je veux que tu restes en Russie… Tiens, prends cet argent pour payer ton billet de retour. Et donne-moi ton manteau, ta casquette et ton passeport.

Ivan enleva sa casquette et son manteau qu'il lui donna, sans   85
comprendre, à la comtesse. Il lui tendit son passeport et, puis, les larmes aux yeux, descendit du train.

Le train repartit vers la frontière. Alors, la comtesse dit à son voisin:

— Mettez ce manteau et cette casquette. Vous êtes maintenant Ivan, mon serviteur. Je mets une seule condition à ce que je fais pour vous: 90
vous ne me parlerez jamais. Je ne veux pas que vous me disiez un seul mot, même pour me remercier.

L'inconnu s'inclina,° sans prononcer un mot. Bientôt le train s'arrêta de nouveau. Des policiers en uniforme entrèrent dans le wagon. Ils regardaient partout comme s'ils cherchaient quelqu'un. La comtesse leur dit d'un ton   95
impérieux:

— Je suis la comtesse Baranow de Saint Pétersbourg, et voici mon domestique Ivan.

s'inclina *bowed*

Mots utiles	
une casquette	*cap*
un inconnu	*stranger*
une larme	*tear*
changer d'avis	*to change one's mind*
enlever	*to take off*
paraître *	*to appear*
rompre	*to break*
tendre	*to hand, give*
à cause de	*because of*
à peine	*hardly, scarcely*
debout	*standing*

Puis elle tendit les passeports à un officier qui les lui rendit en saluant. Les hommes sortirent du wagon et continuèrent leur ronde d'inspection. Après une heure d'arrêt, le train se remit en route. 100

Pendant toute la nuit, l'homme et la femme restèrent en tête-à-tête,° muets tous les deux. Le matin, le train s'arrêta dans une gare allemande. L'inconnu descendit du wagon. Debout, sur le quai, il dit à la comtesse:

— Pardonnez-moi, madame, de rompre ma promesse, mais à cause 105
de moi, vous avez perdu votre domestique. Il est juste que je
le remplace. Avez-vous besoin de quelque chose?

Elle répondit froidement:

— Allez chercher ma femme de chambre.

Il y alla, puis il monta dans un autre wagon. 110

Quand elle descendait à quelque buffet° de gare, elle le voyait de loin qui la regardait . . . Le train arriva finalement à Menton.

en tête-à-tête *face to face*   **buffet** *food wagon*

Avez-vous compris?

1. Qu'est-ce que la comtesse demande à Ivan, son vieux serviteur?
2. Comment est-ce que l'inconnu échappe *(escapes)* au contrôle des policiers?
3. Quelle promesse est-ce que la comtesse exige de l'inconnu?
4. Que fait l'inconnu quand le train s'arrête à la gare allemande?

Anticipons un peu!

• D'après vous, est-ce que l'inconnu va tenir *(keep)* sa promesse?
• Comment va se terminer cette histoire?

4

Le docteur toussa, puis il continua son histoire:

Un jour que je recevais mes clients dans mon cabinet, j'eus la visite
d'un grand garçon que je n'avais jamais vu. Il me dit: 115

— Docteur, je viens vous demander des nouvelles de la comtesse
Marie Baranow. Elle ne me connaît pas. Je suis un ami de son mari.
C'est lui qui m'envoie.

Je répondis:

— La comtesse est très, très malade. Je doute qu'elle rentre un jour   120
en Russie.

À ces mots, cet homme se mit à pleurer comme un enfant. Il se leva
et sortit brusquement de mon cabinet.

Ce soir-là, comme d'habitude, je rendis visite à la comtesse dans
son hôtel. Je lui dis qu'un étranger était venu m'interroger° sur sa santé.   125
Elle parut émue et me raconta toute l'histoire que je viens de vous dire.
Puis elle ajouta:

— Cet homme que je ne connais pas me suit maintenant comme
mon ombre. Je le rencontre chaque fois que je sors. Il me regarde
d'une étrange façon, mais il ne m'a jamais parlé.   130

Elle réfléchit, puis ajouta:

— Je parie qu'il est sous mes fenêtres.

interroger = poser des questions

Mots utiles

un baiser	*kiss*
un être	*human being*
un fou	*crazy person*
une ombre	*shadow*
un sourire	*smile*
ajouter	*to add*
deviner	*to guess*
gâter	*to spoil*
parier	*to bet*
pleurer	*to cry*
se retourner	*to turn back*
réfléchir	*to think, reflect on*
suivre *	*to follow*
bouleversé	*overwhelmed*
douloureux	*painful*
ému	*moved, touched*
jusqu'au bout	*to the end*

Elle quitta sa chaise longue, alla à la fenêtre et me montra, en effet, l'homme qui était venu dans mon cabinet. Il était assis sur un banc et regardait dans la direction de l'hôtel. Quand il nous vit, il se leva et partit sans se retourner.

J'assistai ainsi à une chose surprenante et douloureuse, à l'amour muet de ces deux êtres qui ne se connaissaient pas.

Il l'aimait passionnément, avec la reconnaissance° et la dévotion d'un animal sauvé de la mort. Chaque jour, il venait me demander «Comment va-t-elle?», comprenant que j'avais deviné leur amour. Et il pleurait affreusement quand il apprenait qu'elle était chaque jour plus faible et plus pâle.

Elle me disait: «Je ne lui ai parlé qu'une seule fois, mais il me semble que je le connais depuis toujours.»

Et quand ils se croisaient° dans la rue, elle lui rendait son salut avec un sourire grave et charmant. Je sentais qu'elle était heureuse, elle qui savait qu'elle était perdue. Oui, je la sentais heureuse d'être aimée ainsi, avec ce respect et cette constance, avec cette poésie exagérée, avec cette dévotion totale et absolue. Et pourtant, elle refusait désespérément de le rencontrer, de connaître son nom, de lui parler . . .

Elle disait: «Non, non, cela me gâterait cette étrange amitié. Il faut que nous restions étrangers l'un à l'autre.»

Lui aussi continua à garder ses distances. Il voulait respecter jusqu'au bout l'absurde promesse de ne jamais lui parler, promesse qu'il avait faite dans le wagon.

Souvent, pendant ses longues heures de faiblesse, elle se levait de sa chaise longue et allait à sa fenêtre pour voir s'il était là. Et quand elle l'avait vu, toujours immobile sur son banc, elle revenait se coucher avec un sourire aux lèvres.

Elle est morte un matin vers dix heures. Comme je sortais de l'hôtel, il vint vers moi, le visage bouleversé. Il savait déjà la nouvelle.

— Je voudrais la voir une seconde seulement, en votre présence, dit-il.

Je lui pris le bras et rentrai dans la maison. Quand il fut devant le lit de la morte, il lui prit la main et l'embrassa d'un interminable baiser. Puis il se sauva° comme un fou. Je ne l'ai jamais revu.

❧ ❧ ❧

la reconnaissance = la gratitude   **se croisaient** = se rencontraient   **se sauva** = partit

Le docteur toussa de nouveau, et il dit:

— Voilà certainement la plus singulière aventure de train que
je connaisse. Il est vrai que les hommes sont un peu fous.

175   Une femme dit à mi-voix.°

— Ces deux êtres-là étaient moins fous que vous ne croyez . . .
Ils étaient . . . ils étaient . . .

Et elle se mit à pleurer, sans terminer sa phrase. On changea de
conversation pour la calmer. Personne n'a su ce qu'elle voulait dire.

à mi-voix *in a low voice*

Avez-vous compris?

1. Sous quel prétexte l'inconnu va-t-il voir le médecin? Quelle est sa réaction quand il apprend la vérité?
2. Qu'est-ce que la comtesse explique au médecin ce soir-là? Où était l'inconnu à ce moment-là?
3. Quel sentiment est-ce que la comtesse éprouve *(feel)* pour l'inconnu? Comment explique-t-elle son refus de lui parler?
4. À votre avis, comment est-ce que l'inconnu a appris la mort de la comtesse? Qu'est-ce qu'il demande au médecin?
5. À votre avis, est-ce que l'inconnu était un fou ou un héros? Expliquez pourquoi?

EXPRESSION ORALE

■ Dramatisation

Avec un(e) partenaire, jouez la scène du train (partie 3 de l'histoire).

■ Sujets de discussion

A. L'inconnu du train

Avec votre partenaire, créez une identité et une personnalité à l'inconnu du train. Imaginez, par exemple:

- qui il est
- d'où il vient
- comment, pourquoi, et dans quelles circonstances il a été blessé?
- comment et pourquoi il est entré dans le wagon où était la comtesse?
- pourquoi il a demandé sa protection?

Rappelez-vous: L'inconnu a dit qu'il était un homme d'honneur, qu'il n'avait pas tué, qu'il n'avait pas volé, et qu'il n'avait rien fait de mal.

B. L'amour platonique

Un amour platonique est un amour purement spirituel, comme l'amour qui unit l'inconnu et la comtesse russe.

- Pensez-vous que cet amour soit réel?
- Pensez-vous qu'un tel amour puisse exister aujourd'hui?

Prenez une position pour ou contre et illustrez-la avec des exemples.

■ Situations

Avec votre partenaire, choisissez l'une des situations suivantes. Composez le dialogue correspondant et jouez-le en classe.

1. Une visite

La comtesse sait qu'elle va mourir. Quelques jours avant sa mort, elle accorde (grants) une visite à l'inconnu du train en lui demandant d'expliquer ses actions.

Rôles: la comtesse, l'inconnu

2. Explications

La comtesse vient de mourir. Rentré chez lui, le docteur raconte à sa femme les faits de la journée. La femme du docteur demande des explications.

Rôles: le docteur, sa femme

3. Il y a trente ans . . .

Trente ans ont passé. Au lieu de retourner en Russie, l'inconnu est resté en France. Un jour, il raconte l'histoire à un(e) ami(e) qui demande des détails.

Rôles: l'inconnu, son ami(e)

EXPRESSION ÉCRITE

■ Notice nécrologique *(Obituary)*

Vous êtes journaliste. Écrivez une brève notice nécrologique sur la comtesse Marie Baranow. (Inventez-lui une biographie.)

■ Journal intime

Dans son journal intime, la comtesse décrit la scène du train. Écrivez cette page de journal.

■ Lettre d'adieu

Sachant que la comtesse va mourir, l'inconnu lui écrit une lettre où il avoue ses sentiments. (Évidemment il ne la lui enverra pas, parce qu'il respecte la promesse qu'il a faite.) Écrivez cette lettre d'adieu.

■ *Français et Européens* ■

Pour les Français d'aujourd'hui, l'Europe est une réalité bien concrète. Ils portent des chemises italiennes et des imperméables anglais. Ils mangent des oranges espagnoles et du fromage hollandais. Au café, ils commandent de la bière belge ou irlandaise. Ils conduisent des voitures allemandes. Ils vont passer les vacances en Grèce ou au Portugal, et ils voyagent, bien sûr, avec un passeport européen. Dans leur mode de vie et aussi dans leurs attitudes, les Français se sentent à la fois français et européens.

La construction de l'Europe a commencé après la Deuxième Guerre Mondiale, avec la création du **Marché Commun**. Aujourd'hui, la **Communauté Européenne** est un grand ensemble de douze pays. Elle a son Parlement, sa cour° de Justice, son unité monétaire et son drapeau.

L'existence d'un grand marché européen a permis le développement économique de la France. La France actuelle° est un pays moderne, riche et prospère. C'est l'un des leaders mondiaux dans beaucoup de domaines industriels et scientifiques: automobile, électronique, transports, communications, construction aéronautique et aérospatiale, produits pharmaceutiques, recherche° médicale et scientifique . . . Grâce° au développement économique de leur pays, les Français ont un niveau de vie° élevé et bénéficient de beaucoup d'avantages sociaux. Cela ne signifie pas, cependant, que la France soit un pays parfait.° Comme dans la plupart° des pays, il y a beaucoup de problèmes importants à résoudre.°

L'unification de l'Europe

L'Union Européenne est un groupe de quinze pays qui forment une union économique. Ces pays sont la France, l'Allemagne, l'Italie, la Belgique, les Pays-Bas, le Luxembourg, la Grande-Bretagne, l'Irlande, le Danemark, la Grèce, le Portugal, l'Espagne, l'Autriche, la Finlande, la Suède. Voici quelques étapes de cette unification européenne.

1944	Trois pays, **la Belgique, les Pays-Bas** et **le Luxembourg** décident de former une zone de libre-échange:°le Bénélux.
1957	Le Traité° de Rome crée la CEE (Communauté Économique Européenne) ou «Marché Commun» entre six pays: **la France, l'Allemagne, l'Italie** et les trois pays du Bénélux.
1973	**Le Danemark, l'Irlande** et **la Grande-Bretagne** entrent dans la CEE.
1979	Élections d'un parlement européen au suffrage universel. Une Française, Simone Veil, est la première présidente de ce parlement.
1981-1994	Six autres pays (**l'Autriche, l'Espagne, la Finlande. la Grèce, le Portugal** et **la Suède**) se joignent à la **CEE** qui devient **Union européenne** en 1993.
1999	L'**euro** est adopté comme monnaie commune par onze pays de l'Union européenne.
2002	Les anciennes monnaies nationales disparaissent dans les pays qui ont.

---

cour *court* **actuelle** = d'aujourd'hui **recherche** *research* **grâce à** *thanks to* **niveau de vie** *standard of living* **parfait** *perfect*
la plupart *the majority* **résoudre** *to solve, resolve* **libre-échange** *free trade* **traité** *treaty* **désormais** *henceforth*
prévoit *plans ahead for* **étapes** *steps, stages*

■ *Oui à l'Europe!*

Les Français sont généralement très favorables à l'Europe. Nous avons demandé à quatre Français d'âges différents d'expliquer pourquoi.

Un lycéen (14 ans)

Pendant les vacances de printemps, je suis allé passer dix jours en Hollande avec les élèves de ma classe. Je ne me suis pas senti dépaysé° du tout. Évidemment, les Hollandais parlent une autre langue, et leur nourriture est différente, mais en général nous avons beaucoup de points communs avec eux. Et je suis sûr que c'est la même chose avec les Allemands, les Anglais et les Italiens. Nous sommes tous européens!

Une étudiante (21 ans)

Je suis étudiante à l'IEP (Institut d'Études politiques) de Strasbourg. Dans ma classe, il y a 25 pourcent d'étudiants étrangers, surtout allemands, anglais et belges. Moi-même, je vais passer l'année prochaine à l'université de Fribourg en Allemagne. Tout ça, grâce au programme *Erasmus*, qui facilite les échanges entre les universités européennes. Avec *Erasmus*, l'Europe est une réalité bien concrète pour nous, étudiants.

Une jeune cadre° (28 ans)

Je suis diplômée d'une école de commerce française, mais maintenant je travaille en Allemagne pour une compagnie anglaise. J'ai un job intéressant et je gagne très bien ma vie. Si un jour je décide de changer d'entreprise, avec mon expérience internationale je n'aurais pas de problèmes à trouver quelque chose d'autre. Si l'Europe n'existait pas, je n'aurais pas ces possibilités!

Un retraité (80 ans)

Autrefois l'histoire européenne, c'était l'histoire des conflits permanents entre la France et l'Allemagne ou l'Angleterre. Je parle en connaissance de cause° parce que j'ai fait la guerre de 40* et que j'ai passé quatre ans en Allemagne dans un camp de prisonniers. Maintenant, avec la nouvelle Europe, la guerre est devenue impossible. Je suis pour l'intégration politique de l'Europe parce que cela signifie paix° et prospérité pour mes petits-enfants . . . et leurs enfants.

* La guerre de 40, c'est la Deuxième Guerre Mondiale (1940-1944). Voir à la page 252.

dépaysé *lost (in a strange place)* **cadre** *executive* **en connaissance de cause** *knowingly* **paix** *peace*
fond *background* **suffit** = *est suffisant*

Les symboles de l'Europe

Le drapeau européen

Le drapeau européen représente un cercle de 12 étoiles jaunes sur un fond° bleu. Les douze étoiles représentent les douze pays de la Communauté européenne.

Le passeport européen

Les citoyens des pays de l'**Union européenne** ont un passeport de format unique, le passeport européen. Cependant, ce passeport n'est pas nécessaire pour aller dans les autres pays de la CE: une simple pièce d'identité suffit.°

■ *Nous, c'est les autres!* ■

La France d'aujourd'hui est un pays riche et prospère. Ses habitants ont l'un des niveaux de vie les plus élevés du monde. Pourtant, comme toute société moderne, la société française a ses problèmes et ses victimes.° Il y a les chômeurs,° les sans-abri,° les gens qui ont faim. Que fait-on pour ces déshérités de la société? Certains Français ont répondu à cette question par leurs actions.

EMMAÜS FRANCE
FONDATEUR ABBE PIERRE

L'abbé Pierre et les «Chiffonniers d'Emmaüs»

L'abbé* **Pierre** a 90 ans ou un peu plus. C'est un homme simple qui, depuis 40 ans, porte le même béret et la même pèlerine° noire. C'est aussi l'un des hommes les plus admirés de France. Issu d'une famille riche, l'abbé Pierre a décidé de mettre sa religion en pratique et de devenir l'apôtre° des pauvres.

En réalité, l'abbé Pierre s'appelle Henri Grouès. C'est pendant la Guerre de 1940, quand il travaillait dans la Résistance, qu'il a pris le nom d'Abbé Pierre. Cette guerre, qui a duré° quatre ans, a causé la destruction d'un très grand nombre de maisons et d'immeubles dans toute la France. À la fin de la guerre, il y avait des milliers de «sans-abri». L'abbé Pierre est devenu leur porte-parole° lorsqu'il a été élu° député° à l'Assemblé Nationale** en 1945.

Mais pour l'abbé Pierre, l'activité politique n'était pas suffisante. Devant l'inaction du gouvernement, il a décidé de passer à l'action tout court.° C'est ainsi qu'il a créé les «Chiffonniers° d'Emmaüs», une organisation qui donnait du travail, un logement, et surtout une raison de vivre° à ceux que personne ne voulait employer: les alcooliques, les anciens repris de justice,° et tous les déshérités de la terre. Pour rappeler° aux Français l'existence des sans-abri, l'abbé Pierre a décidé de «squatériser», d'une manière illégale mais non injuste, les immeubles vides° ou abandonnés. Plus récemment, en 1991, il a créé des «boutiques-solidarité» pour aider les gens qui n'ont pas les moyens° de vivre comme tout le monde.

L'abbé Pierre et deux de ses protégés

L'abbé Pierre aujourd'hui

La misère n'a évidemment pas de frontière° et l'action de l'abbé Pierre est devenue internationale. Il y a aujourd'hui plus de 250 centres Emmaüs en France et 600 dans le monde.

* **L'abbé**: un titre religieux donné à certains prêtres catholiques.
** **L'Assemblée Nationale**: Avec le Sénat, chambre parlementaire qui vote les lois *(laws)*. C'est l'équivalent du «House of Representatives» du congrès américain.

victimes *casualties* **chômeurs** *unemployed* **sans-abri** *homeless* **pèlerine** *cape* **apôtre** *apostle, defender* **duré** *lasted* **porte-parole** *spokesperson* **élu** *elected* **député** *congressman* **tout court** = *directement* **chiffonniers** *ragpickers* **raison de vivre** *aim in life* **anciens repris de justice** *former prison inmates* **rappeler** *remind* **vides** *empty* **moyens** *means* **frontière** *border*

Coluche et les «Restos du Coeur»

À son époque, **Coluche**, de son vrai nom Michel Colucci, était le comédien le plus célèbre de France. Son visage bonhomme,° ses manières rustres,° sa salopette° étaient universellement connus. Mais pour Coluche, faire des films, se produire° à la télévision et gagner de l'argent, ne suffisait pas. Coluche était un homme généreux, courageux et juste qui ne pouvait pas tolérer la misère ou les inégalités sociales. Alors, un jour il est passé à l'action et il a créé les «**Restaurants du coeur**». Cette organisation prépare des repas chauds pour les sans-abri, pour les personnes sans ressources, et généralement pour tous ceux qui ont faim et qui n'ont pas d'argent.

En 1986, Coluche s'est tué dans un accident de moto, mais son oeuvre° continue. Aujourd'hui, les 1500 «Restos° du coeur», animés par des milliers de bénévoles,° servent 60 millions de repas gratuits par an.

Coluche, le comédien au grand coeur

Jeunes Français, bénévoles qui servent des repas gratuits au «Restos du Coeur»

---

bonhomme *good-natured*   **rustres** *boorish, lacking good manners*   **salopette** *overalls*   **se produire** = se montrer   **oeuvre** *charitable works*
restos = restaurants   **bénévoles** = volontaires

■ *La France, une mosaïque* ■

Les Français d'aujourd'hui ne s'appellent pas seulement Dupont, Moreau, Petit ou Normand. Ils s'appellent aussi Belkacem, Lopez, Nguyen et Meyer. Ils sont blancs, noirs, bruns et jaunes. Ils vont à l'église, à la mosquée, au temple et à la synagogue*. . . Loin d'être un pays homogène, la France est en réalité une mosaïque marquée par l'intégration, la fusion et la cohabitation de cultures différentes.

Historiquement, la France a d'abord été une terre d'invasion. Au cours° des dix premiers siècles,° elle a été occupée par les Romains, les Germains, les Scandinaves . . . Au 19ᵉ siècle, elle est devenue une terre d'asile° pour des milliers de réfugiés politiques venus d'Allemagne, de Pologne, de Hongrie et de Russie.

Au 20ᵉ siècle, La France est devenue une terre d'immigration pour des millions de travailleurs étrangers. Le développement économique et industriel a en effet créé un énorme besoin de main d'oeuvre.° Pour répondre à ce besoin, le gouvernement français a invité des étrangers à venir travailler en France. Dans les années 20, ces travailleurs venaient principalement d'Italie et de Pologne. Dans les années 50, ils venaient surtout du Portugal et d'Espagne.

Depuis les années 60, la majorité des travailleurs étrangers qui viennent en France ne sont pas européens. Ce sont principalement des Maghrébins (Algériens, Marocains et Tunisiens) venus des pays d'Afrique du Nord. D'autres, moins nombreux, viennent d'Afrique occidentale° (Mali, Sénégal, Cameroun . . .) et d'Asie (Viêt-nam, Laos, Cambodge).

Après les États-Unis, la France est le pays du monde qui a le plus grand nombre d'immigrants. Les 4,5 millions d'étrangers qui habitent en France représentent 8% de la population du pays. Ces étrangers, d'origine européenne, africaine ou asiatique, donnent à la France d'aujourd'hui un visage véritablement multi-culturel et multi-ethnique.

* En France, les **Catholiques** vont **à l'église**, les **Musulmans** *(Moslems)* vont **à la mosquée**, les **Protestants** vont **au temple**, les **Juifs** vont **à la synagogue**.

---

au cours de = pendant   **un siècle** = 100 ans   **terre d'asile** *land of asylum*   **main d'oeuvre** *labor, manpower*   **occidentale** *Western*

Le Maghreb et les Maghrébins

Maghreb est un mot arabe qui signifie *le pays où le soleil se couche.*° Autrefois, le Maghreb représentait l'extrémité occidentale du monde musulman. Le Maghreb désigne les trois pays d'Afrique du Nord: l'**Algérie**, le **Maroc** et la **Tunisie**. Les Maghrébins sont les habitants de ces pays.

La majorité des Maghrébins sont arabes et musulmans. Leur religion est l'**Islam**. Un grand nombre de Maghrébins (environ deux millions) ont émigré en France où ils représentent le groupe le plus important d'étrangers.

LES ÉTRANGERS EN FRANCE

Algériens	1 250 000	Espagnols	350 000
Marocains	700 000	Tunisiens	350 000
Portugais	600 000	Vietnamiens	250 000
Italiens	400 000	Turcs	180 000

---

se couche *sets*

■ *Djamila ou le dilemme de l'intégration*

Djamila, 17 ans, est une jeune «beur». Cela signifie qu'elle est fille d'immigrés maghrébins. Ses parents sont venus d'Algérie il y a vingt ans, et elle, elle est née à Marseille. Elle a la nationalité française, parle français, va dans un lycée français où presque tous ses copains sont d'origine française. Après le bac, elle compte aller à l'université et un jour devenir vétérinaire. Est-ce qu'elle se sent vraiment française? Ou bien, est-elle restée algérienne?

Djamila explique son dilemme.

«Fondamentalement, je suis française, mais je suis différente parce que ma famille est différente. Mes parents sont arabes et musulmans pratiquants.° Cela ne signifie pas seulement qu'ils célèbrent l'aïd* et qu'ils ne mangent pas de porc et ne boivent pas d'alcool. Cela signifie aussi qu'ils ont une conception différente de la vie. Mon père, par exemple, ne veut pas que je sorte seule avec un garçon, alors que mes copines françaises n'ont pas besoin de demander la permission. C'est parfois une situation difficile, mais j'obéis parce que j'ai beaucoup de respect et d'admiration pour mon père. C'est un homme honnête qui a travaillé très dur pour donner un minimum de confort à sa famille.

* **L'aïd:** Cette fête musulmane, aussi appelée «fête du mouton», rappelle le sacrifice d'Abraham et d'Isaac.

■ *L'influence maghrébine en France*

La présence de plus de deux millions de Maghrébins en France a modifié et enrichi la culture française dans beaucoup de domaines. Par exemple:

■ Religion

Aujourd'hui, l'**Islam** est la deuxième religion pratiquée en France, après la religion catholique et avant les religions protestantes et juives. Il y a 6000 mosquées en France et 5 millions de Musulmans.

■ Cuisine

Le **couscous**, plat traditionnel d'Afrique du Nord, est devenu un plat très populaire en France. C'est un plat de semoule° cuit à la vapeur° et servi avec des légumes, de la viande et une sauce très pimentée.° Pour manger un bon couscous, on peut aller dans les restaurants marocains, algériens ou tunisiens. Si on veut manger un couscous chez soi, il suffit d'acheter une boîte de couscous au supermarché.

D'autres spécialités maghrébines sont les gâteaux au miel,° les gâteaux aux amandes° appelés «cornes° de gazelle» et le thé à la menthe.°

■ Vocabulaire

La langue française d'aujourd'hui contient un certain nombre de mots d'origine arabe, comme:

un toubib	*un médecin*
un bled	*un petit village, généralement isolé et sans intérêt*
un méchouï	*une grande fête où on mange généralement du mouton rôti*
avoir la baraka	*avoir de la chance*
c'est kif-kif	*c'est la même chose*

COUSCOUS REGIA MOYEN

500 g

---

pratiquants = qui observent les préceptes de leur religion **semoule** *semolina* **cuit à la vapeur** *steamed*
pimentée *hot, spicy* **miel** *honey* **amandes** *almonds* **cornes** *horns* **menthe** *mint*

«Mes parents ont la nostalgie de leur pays. Parfois, ils parlent de rentrer en Algérie et ils voudraient que je vienne avec eux. Je suis allée plusieurs fois en Algérie où nous avons de la famille, mais là-bas, je ne me sens pas chez moi. Chez moi, c'est en France. C'est là où j'habite et c'est là où je vais faire ma vie. Parce que je suis intégrée, je sais que je n'aurai pas de difficulté à trouver un bon emploi. Pourtant, il y a des problèmes. Par exemple, quand je sors avec mes copines beurs et que nous parlons arabe entre nous, j'ai parfois l'impression qu'on nous regarde de travers.° À ce moment-là, je me sens alors algérienne, et fière° d'être différente.»

Quelques prénoms arabes

FILLES

Aïcha	Ourida
Djamila	Sakinna
Farida	Soraya
Leïla	Yasmina
Malika	Zeïna
Nacera	Zohra

GARÇONS

Ahmed	Latif	Omar
Ali	Malek	Rachid
Farid	Malik	Saïd
Hacine	Mohamed	Toufik
Ismaïl	Mouloud	Youssef
Kateb	Mustapha	

La grande mosquée de Paris

Les cinq principes de la religion musulmane

La religion musulmane est l'une des religions les plus importantes du monde. Elle est pratiquée par plus d'un milliard° de personnes, principalement au Moyen Orient, au Pakistan, en Indonésie, en Afrique du Nord et en Afrique occidentale.

La religion musulmane a cinq principes fondamentaux. Ces principes sont assez simples.

- Il y a un seul Dieu,° **Allah.**
- Chaque jour, le Musulman doit faire ses prières° cinq fois, tourné dans la direction de la **Mecque,**° ville natale du prophète Mahomet, et ville sainte° de l'islam.
- Le Musulman doit être charitable. Chaque année, il doit donner un pourcentage de sa fortune aux pauvres.
- Chaque année, le Musulman doit faire le jeûne° du **Ramadan.** Pendant les 30 jours du Ramadan, il doit s'abstenir totalement de manger et de boire du matin jusqu'au soir.
- Durant sa vie, le Musulman doit aller une fois en pèlerinage° à la Mecque. Ce pèlerinage s'appelle le **hadj.**

Horaire des prières

Al-Fajr	4 h 27
Ach-Chrouq	5 h 58
Ad-Dohr	12 h 36
Al-Asr	16 h 10
Al-Maghrib	19 h 08
Al-Ichaa	20 h 37

de travers = d'une manière étrange   **fière** *proud*   **un milliard** *one billion*   **Dieu** *God*   **prières** *prayers*
Mecque *Mecca (today in Saudi Arabia)* **sainte** *holy* **jeûne** *fast* **pèlerinage** *pilgrimage*

■ *SOS Racisme*

Les travailleurs immigrés qui viennent en France apportent avec eux une culture spécifique. Ils ont leurs coutumes, leurs traditions, leur religion, leur langue, leur musique, leur cuisine, leur façon de s'habiller . . . Ces immigrés sont généralement heureux d'habiter en France, même si les conditions de travail et de logement sont souvent difficiles.

De leur côté,° la majorité des Français, les jeunes en particulier, acceptent assez bien les immigrés même si leur culture est différente de la culture traditionnelle française. D'autres, au contraire, ont beaucoup de difficultés à accepter la réalité multi-culturelle de la France d'aujourd'hui. Ils ne comprennent pas que cette réalité est irréversible. Certains pensent que les immigrés sont responsables des problèmes comme le chômage,° la délinquance, ou la drogue.° Des extrémistes voudraient même renvoyer° les immigrés dans leur pays d'origine. En France, comme dans d'autres pays européens, le racisme et la discrimination contre les immigrés sont devenus des problèmes importants à résoudre.°

Comment combattre le racisme? Un jour, il y a dix ans, des copains d'origine diverse discutaient justement° de leurs différences. «Nous sommes blancs, noirs, marron, bronzés!° Nous sommes copains depuis des années et nous le resterons, parce que nous disons oui à la solidarité et non au racisme.» Ce jour-là, un grand mouvement, **SOS Racisme**, était né.

De père martiniquais et de mère alsacienne, **Harlem Désir**, le fondateur et premier président de **SOS Racisme**, est bien le symbole même de la France multi-ethnique. «Chez nous, dit-il, on respecte l'individu et on écoute les autres.»

Les activités de **SOS Racisme** sont très nombreuses: aider les immigrés, trouver des avocats pour les victimes de la discrimination, combattre le racisme sous toutes ses formes, et, plus généralement, changer les attitudes et faire accepter le droit° à la différence. Pour mobiliser l'opinion, **SOS Racisme** organise des campagnes, des marches, et surtout de grands concerts publics où les jeunes viennent manifester leur solidarité au mouvement.

L'emblème° de **SOS Racisme** est une main ouverte, bleue, rouge ou orange, avec un slogan «Touche pas à mon pote!»° Ce slogan signifie «Nous sommes différents, mais nous sommes frères et soeurs. Si tu attaques l'un de nous, nous sommes là pour le défendre et le protéger.» Cette petite main symbolique a eu un succès extraordinaire, non seulement en France, mais aussi en Suisse et en Belgique. Des dizaines de milliers de jeunes, surtout des lycéens, portent cet emblème sur leurs vêtements. C'est une façon de dire à tout le monde: «Je suis pour la justice, pour l'intégration et contre le racisme et la discrimination.»

Une manifestation, SOS Racisme

---

de leur côté *as far as they are concerned* **chômage** *unemployment* **drogue** *drug addiction* **renvoyer** *to send back* **résoudre** *to solve* **justement** *as a matter of fact* **bronzés** *light brown* **droit** *right* **emblème** = *logo* **pote** = *copain* (slang)

♦♦♦ Éthiopie ♦♦♦

La chanson *Éthiopie** est chantée sur la musique universellement connue de *We are the world*. Cette chanson exprime la solidarité du peuple français avec les peuples les moins favorisés de la terre° et en particulier avec le peuple éthiopien, victime de la famine et de la guerre civile. Les chanteurs français les plus célèbres l'ont chantée dans de grands concerts publics organisés pour aider les enfants d'Éthiopie.

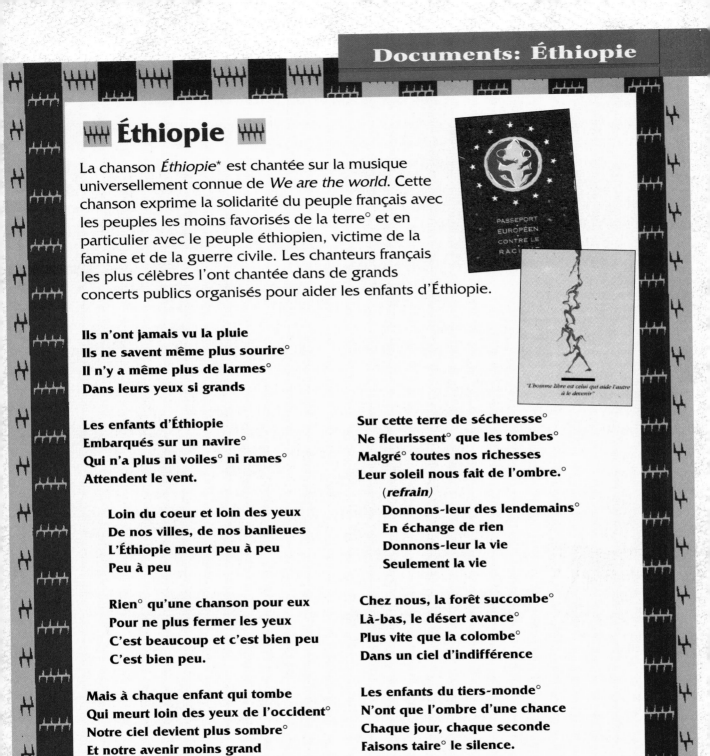

PASSEPORT
EUROPÉEN
CONTRE LE
RAC...

"L'homme libre est celui qui aide l'autre
à le devenir"

Ils n'ont jamais vu la pluie
Ils ne savent même plus sourire°
Il n'y a même plus de larmes°
Dans leurs yeux si grands

Les enfants d'Éthiopie
Embarqués sur un navire°
Qui n'a plus ni voiles° ni rames°
Attendent le vent.

   Loin du coeur et loin des yeux
   De nos villes, de nos banlieues
   L'Éthiopie meurt peu à peu
   Peu à peu

   Rien° qu'une chanson pour eux
   Pour ne plus fermer les yeux
   C'est beaucoup et c'est bien peu
   C'est bien peu.

Mais à chaque enfant qui tombe
Qui meurt loin des yeux de l'occident°
Notre ciel devient plus sombre°
Et notre avenir moins grand

Sur cette terre de sécheresse°
Ne fleurissent° que les tombes°
Malgré° toutes nos richesses
Leur soleil nous fait de l'ombre.°
   (*refrain*)
   Donnons-leur des lendemains°
   En échange de rien
   Donnons-leur la vie
   Seulement la vie

Chez nous, la forêt succombe°
Là-bas, le désert avance°
Plus vite que la colombe°
Dans un ciel d'indifférence

Les enfants du tiers-monde°
N'ont que l'ombre d'une chance
Chaque jour, chaque seconde
Faisons taire° le silence.

* L'Éthiopie est un pays d'Afrique, voisin de la Somalie.

terre *earth* **sourire** *to smile* **larmes** *tears* **navire** = bateau **voiles** *sails* **rames** *oars* **rien que** = seulement **l'occident** *Western world* **sombre** = noir
sécheresse *drought* **fleurissent** *blossom* **tombes** *tombstones* **malgré** *in spite of* **nous fait de l'ombre** *casts a shadow on us* **lendemains** *tomorrows*
succombe = meurt **avance** = progresse **colombe** *dove* **tiers-monde** *Third World* **faisons taire** = mettons fin à

En ville

Thème et Objectifs

Culture
In this unit, you will discover . . .
- how French cities developed historically and what they look like
- the advantages and disadvantages of urban life
- what types of street artists you might see in Paris or other large cities

Communication
You will learn how . . .
- to arrange to meet friends
- to explain where people live
- to describe your neighborhood

Langue
You will learn how . . .
- to make wishes or suggestions
- to formulate polite requests
- to narrate past actions in sequence
- to indicate what you would do in certain circumstances

◆ LES VILLES FRANÇAISES ◆

Les Français sont des citadins°. Aujourd'hui, 90% de la population habite en zone urbaine et presque° la moitié° dans des villes de plus de 100.000 habitants. L'urbanisme est peut-être un phénomène relativement récent, mais les grandes villes françaises sont très anciennes. Marseille et Nice ont été fondées au sixième siècle avant Jésus-Christ par des marins° grecs. Paris, Lyon, Bordeaux, Toulouse, Strasbourg, Rouen, et Tours étaient déjà des centres urbains à l'époque romaine, il y a 2000 ans.

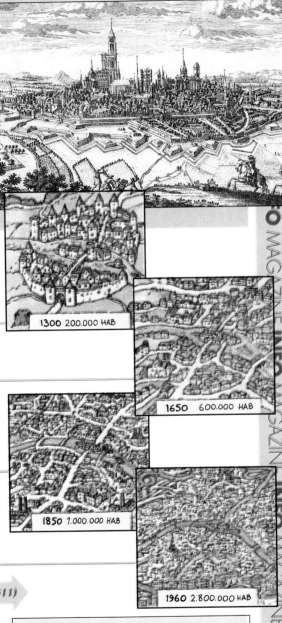

1300 200.000 HAB

1650 600.000 HAB

1850 1.000.000 HAB

1960 2.800.000 HAB

À l'origine, les villes ont été créées autour d'un point stratégique important: un port naturel, le croisement° de deux routes, le passage d'une rivière . . .

◆ Au Moyen Age, on a construit° un château et des remparts pour protéger ces villes.

◆ Quand les villes ont grandi° à partir° du XVIIe siècle, les remparts ont été détruits°. Les villes se sont alors développées autour d'un nouveau centre, ou le long° de larges avenues, suivant° un plan d'urbanisme bien établi.

◆ Avec la révolution industrielle au XIXe siècle, de vastes banlieues industrielles se sont développées concentriquement autour des villes.

◆ Au XXe siècle et particulièrement après 1960, les possibilités de travail ont attiré° des millions d'habitants de la campagne vers les grandes villes. Cet exode rural a nécessité la construction d'énormes quartiers résidentiels dans la banlieue de ces villes.

L'histoire des villes françaises explique leur géographie. (Suite à la page 310-311)

et vous?

Faites un bref historique de la ville où vous habitez ou d'une grande ville des États-Unis. Vous pouvez mentionner . . .
- quand cette ville a été fondée: par qui? et pourquoi?
- comment elle s'est développée
- combien d'habitants elle a aujourd'hui et quelles sont ses activités principales

NOM FRANÇAIS	NOM LATIN
Paris	LUTETIA
Lyon	LUGDUNUM
Marseille	MASSILIA
Bordeaux	BURDIGALA
Toulouse	TOLOSA
Nice	NICAEA
Strasbourg	ARGENTORATUM
Rouen	ROTOMAGUS
Tours	CAESARODUNUM

citadins *city people* **presque** *almost* **moitié** *half* **marins** *sailors*
croisement *crossing* ✳ **construire** *to build* **grandi** *grew in size*
à partir *beginning in* ✳ **détruire** *to destroy* **le long de** *along*
suivant *according to* **attiré** *attracted*

VILLE OU CAMPAGNE?

Êtes-vous un citadin ou un villageois?
Êtes-vous plutôt fait(e) pour la vie en ville ou pour
la vie à la campagne?
Pour déterminer cela, évaluez les avantages et les inconvénients
des villes. Donnez une note positive de 0 (pas important) à
+5 (très important) à chacun des avantages.
Donnez une note négative de 0 (pas important) à -5 (très important)
à chacun des inconvénients.°

AVANTAGES

INCONVÉNIENTS

- **Il y a beaucoup d'endroits où on peut aller.**
  On peut aller au ciné, dans les magasins, aux restaurants . . .

- **Il y a beaucoup de choses intéressantes à faire.**
  On peut voir des expositions, assister à des événements culturels . . .

- **On peut faire la connaissance de beaucoup de gens d'origines° différentes.**
  Dans les villes, il y a une grande diversité ethnique, culturelle et sociale.

- **Les villes sont généralement animées.**
  On ne s'ennuie° jamais parce qu'il y a toujours de la vie et du mouvement.

- **Il y a trop de voitures et, par conséquent, trop de bruit et trop de pollution.**
  On ne peut pas se promener tranquillement.°

- **On perd le contact avec la nature.**
  Il n'y a pas assez d'arbres, pas assez de plantes, pas assez de fleurs.

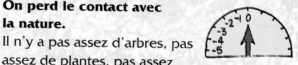

- **Pour beaucoup de gens, la vie est difficile.**
  Pour cela, les gens des villes sont souvent stressés et irritables.

- **Il y a beaucoup d'inégalités sociales.**
  Il y a trop de gens pauvres et sans-abri.°

---

inconvénients *drawbacks*   **origines** *backgrounds*   **s'ennuie** *gets bored*   **tranquillement** *safely*   **sans-abri** *homeless people*

INTERPRÉTATION

Faites le total des points positifs et négatifs.
Quel total obtenez-vous?

de 15 à 20 points

Vous êtes certainement un(e) citadin(e), mais vous
ignorez les charmes de la campagne. Un jour, vous
devriez y faire un tour.

de 5 à 14 points

Vous êtes une personne optimiste et vous aimez la
proximité des gens. Vous appréciez les avantages de la vie
en ville. Pour cela, vous en minimisez les inconvénients.

de 4 à -4 points

Vous êtes une personne réaliste. Vous êtes conscient(e)
des problèmes des grandes villes, mais vous les tolérez.

de -5 à -14 points

Vous n'aimez pas vivre là où il y a trop de gens. Vous
préférez le calme et la tranquillité.

de -15 à -20 points

La ville n'est évidemment pas faite pour vous. Mais
ne soyez pas trop idéaliste! La campagne aussi a
ses problèmes.

INTERVIEW DANS LA RUE

Nous sommes place de Jaude à
Clermont-Ferrand, un samedi après-midi.

Une journaliste de «La Montagne»,
le journal local, interviewe les
gens qui passent. Elle parle
maintenant à un homme d'une
cinquantaine d'années qui porte
un sac à provisions.°

— Bonjour, Monsieur. Vous êtes
  d'ici?
— Non, je suis de la campagne.
— Qu'est-ce qui vous attire° à
  Clermont? Le cinéma?
  les restaurants? les cafés?
— Non, je n'y vais jamais.
— Pouvez-vous me dire alors pourquoi vous venez ici?
— Ben, vous voyez, je viens pour faire mes courses.
— Il n'y a pas de supermarché chez vous?
— Si, mais en ville il y a un plus grand choix.
— Vous venez souvent à Clermont-Ferrand?
— Oui, toutes les semaines.
— Vous aimez cette ville?
— Pas tellement.°
— Pourquoi donc?
— Ben, il y a trop de circulation,° trop de bruit. . .
  Et puis, les gens sont pressés° et malpolis.°
— Alors, pourquoi est-ce que vous ne restez pas
  chez vous?
— Parce que chez moi, c'est trop calme. Alors,
  je viens en ville pour trouver un peu d'animation.

sac à provisions *shopping bag*   **attire** *attracts*   **pas tellement** *not that much*   **circulation** *traffic*   **pressés** *in a hurry*   **malpolis** = *impolis*

LE FRANÇAIS PRATIQUE

Un rendez-vous en ville

> Qu'est-ce que tu fais samedi?

> Je suis libre.

> Est-ce que tu veux voir une exposition avec moi?

> Bonne idée! À quelle heure est-ce qu'on va se retrouver?

> À deux heures et demie.

COMMENT SE DONNER RENDEZ-VOUS

— Qu'est-ce que tu fais samedi?
   Je suis libre.

— Est-ce que tu veux | aller au ciné | avec moi?
   voir une exposition
   prendre un pot
   faire un tour en ville

> **prendre un pot** *to have something to drink in a café*

— Où est-ce qu'on va **se donner rendez-vous?**
   Chez moi.   **Devant** *(in front of)* le ciné.
   Au café «Le Bistro».   **À côté de** *(next to)* la poste.
                                En face de *(across from)* la librairie.

— À quelle heure est-ce qu'on va | **se retrouver?**
                                  | **se rencontrer?**

   À deux heures et demie.

— Alors, | d'accord! | **À samedi,** deux heures et demie devant le ciné.
         | **entendu** *(agreed).* | *(See you on Saturday . . .)*

1 Créa-dialogue: Une invitation

Il y a un(e) nouvel(le) élève français(e) dans
votre classe. Invitez le/la. Composez le dialogue
avec votre partenaire qui va jouer le rôle
de l'élève.

— *Ask your friend what he/she is doing on a date of your choice..*	⇄	*(He/she is free.)*
— *Propose something interesting to do.*	⇄	*(He/she accepts.)*
— *Ask where you can meet.*	⇄	*(He/she selects a place close to the activity you proposed.)*
— *Ask at what time you are going to meet.*	⇄	*(He/she chooses a time.)*
— *Say that you will see him/her at the time and place you have agreed on.*	→	

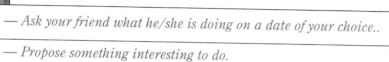

LES RENCONTRES ET LES RENDEZ-VOUS

| On peut | **rencontrer**
(meet by chance, run into)
faire la connaissance de
(meet for the first time) | **quelqu'un.** |

| On peut | **sortir avec**
avoir un rendez-vous avec
donner rendez-vous à
(make a date) | **quelqu'un.** |

| On peut | **se donner rendez-vous**
(agree to meet)
se rencontrer
(meet each other)
se retrouver
(meet each other) | **quelque part** *(somewhere).* |

Conversations libres

Avec votre partenaire, choisissez l'une des situations suivantes. Composez ensemble un dialogue correspondant à cette situation et jouez ce dialogue en classe.

1   Une jeune fille amoureuse

Jérôme veut téléphoner à sa camarade de classe Véronique. C'est Sylvie, la soeur de Véronique, qui répond. Sylvie, qui est secrètement amoureuse de *(in love with)* Jérôme, essaie d'obtenir un rendez-vous avec lui.

Rôles: Jérôme / Sylvie

2   Au Jardin du Luxembourg

Une étudiante américaine est au Jardin du Luxembourg (un parc public à Paris). Un étudiant français engage la conversation. Il veut inviter la jeune Américaine à un concert de rock à la Villette. D'abord la jeune fille refuse poliment. L'étudiant français insiste. Elle finit par accepter l'invitation.

Rôles: l'étudiant français / l'étudiante américaine

3   Rendez-vous

Philippe téléphone à Juliette pour voir une exposition. Juliette a déjà vu cette exposition et propose autre chose.

Rôles: Philippe / Juliette

4   Une amie de passage *(A visiting friend)*

Marc téléphone souvent à sa cousine. Aujourd'hui, elle n'est pas chez elle et c'est une amie de passage qui répond. Marc s'excuse, puis il continue la conversation. Dans cette conversation il essaie de savoir ce que cette jeune fille aime faire. Finalement, il propose un rendez-vous. La jeune fille accepte, puis refuse.

Rôles: Marc / la jeune fille

A. La construction si + imparfait

Formation de l'imparfait

Révision ▶ p. R5

Note the use of the IMPERFECT in the following sentences:

Ah, si j'**étais** riche . . .   *Oh, if only I **were** rich . . .*

Ah, si mon frère me **prêtait**   *Oh, if only my brother **would lend me***
  sa voiture . . .   *his car . . .*

Dis, Alain, **si on allait** en ville?   *Hey, Alain, **what about going** downtown?*

Dis, Sophie, **si tu m'aidais?**   *Hey, Sophie, **what about helping me?***

To express a WISH or to make a SUGGESTION, the French often use the construction:

si + IMPERFECT

B. Le plus-que-parfait

As in English, the PLUPERFECT **(le plus-que-parfait)** is used to describe what people HAD DONE or WHAT HAD HAPPENED before another past action or event.

Cet été, j'ai visité Québec.   *This summer I visited Quebec City.*

L'année d'avant, **j'avais visité** Montréal.   *The year before, **I had visited** Montreal.*

Quand nous sommes arrivés à la gare,   *When we arrived at the station,*
le train **était parti.**   *the train **had left.***

The PLUPERFECT is formed as follows:

IMPERFECT of **avoir** or **être** + PAST PARTICIPLE

INFINITIVE	voyager	aller	s'amuser
PLUPERFECT	j' **avais voyagé** tu **avais voyagé** il/elle **avait voyagé** nous **avions voyagé** vous **aviez voyagé** ils/elles **avaient voyagé**	j' **étais allé(e)** tu **étais allé(e)** il/elle **était allé(e)** nous **étions allé(e)s** vous **étiez allé(e)(s)** ils/elles **étaient allé(e)s**	je **m'étais amusé(e)** tu **t'étais amusé(e)** il/elle **s'était amusé(e)** nous **nous étions amusé(e)s** vous **vous étiez amusé(e)(s)** ils/elles **s'étaient amusé(e)s**
NEGATIVE	je **n'avais pas voyagé**	je **n'étais pas allé(e)**	je **ne m'étais pas amusé(e)**
INTERROGATIVE	est-ce que tu **avais voyagé?** **avais-tu voyagé?**	tu **étais allé(e)?** **étais-tu allé(e)?**	tu **t'étais amusé(e)?** **t'étais-tu amusé(e)?**

➡ In the pluperfect, the agreement rules for the past participle are the same as in the passé composé.

J'ai vu Pauline ce matin.   Je l'avais vue hier aussi.

J'ai développé les photos que j'avais prises cet été.

1 En ville

Vous rencontrez votre partenaire en ville. Suggérez-lui de faire quelque chose avec vous (colonne A).
Votre partenaire va refuser et expliquer pourquoi. Il/elle va aussi proposer autre chose (colonne B).
Acceptez ou refusez. Continuez le dialogue jusqu'à ce que vous trouviez une chose d'intérêt commun.

Dis, Corinne, si on prenait un pot?

Bonne idée! Allons au ciné.

Hm, je n'ai pas soif. on allait plutôt au ciné?

(Écoutez, j'ai vu tous les films de la semaine. Et si on . . .)

A : VOUS	B: VOTRE PARTENAIRE
• aller dans une pizzeria	• aller dans un restaurant chinois
• prendre un pot	• aller au ciné
• faire un tour dans le centre	• se promener dans le parc
• voir une exposition	• jouer aux jeux vidéo
• aller dans les magasins	• téléphoner à des copains
• ??	• ??

2 Et avant?

Lisez ce que ces personnes ont fait et dites ce qu'elles avaient fait avant.

▶ Le week-end dernier, Philippe est sorti avec Alice. (le week-end d'avant / avec Karine)
   Le week-end d'avant, il était sorti avec Karine.

1. Dimanche, nous sommes allés au ciné. (samedi soir / à un concert)
2. Hier, j'ai pris un pot au Balto. (avant-hier / au Saint Victor)
3. Cet après-midi, tu t'es promené en ville. (ce matin / dans le parc)
4. Hier, tu as donné rendez-vous à Catherine dans un café. (jeudi / devant le musée)
5. Ce week-end, les touristes ont visité le château d'Amboise. (le week-end dernier / le château de Chenonceaux)
6. Cet été, nous sommes allés au Canada. (l'été d'avant / au Mexique)

3 Trop tard!

On fait parfois les choses trop tard. Décrivez
ce qui est arrivé aux personnes suivantes.

▶ Jean-Claude arrive à l'aéroport.
   L'avion est parti.
   **Quand Jean-Claude est arrivé
   à l'aéroport, l'avion était parti.**

1. Nous arrivons au théâtre.
   La pièce *(play)* a commencé.
2. Olivier téléphone à Catherine.
   Elle est sortie avec Jean-Paul.
3. La serveuse apporte l'addition.
   Les clients sont partis.
4. Monsieur Renaud entre dans la cuisine.
   Le chien a mangé le bifteck.
5. Vous arrivez à la pâtisserie.
   Le pâtissier a vendu le dernier gâteau.
6. Le lièvre *(hare)* arrive.
   La tortue *(tortoise)* a gagné la course.

4 Pourquoi?

Expliquez pourquoi les choses suivantes sont
arrivées. Attention: le verbe peut être affirmatif
ou négatif.

▶ Les touristes n'ont pas trouvé
   de chambre d'hôtel. (réserver?)
   Ils n'avaient pas réservé.

1. Monsieur Dupont a raté son avion.
   (se dépêcher?)
2. Tu n'as pas vu l'éclipse de lune *(moon)*.
   (se coucher trop tôt?)
3. Vous n'êtes pas allés au concert.
   (acheter les billets?)
4. Thomas n'a pas vu le film à la télé.
   (rentrer trop tard chez lui?)
5. Nous avons eu une indigestion. (manger trop?)
6. Les élèves ont eu une mauvaise note
   à l'examen. (étudier?)

La géographie des villes françaises

L'histoire des villes françaises, décrite brièvement à la page 303, explique leur aspect et leur structure si différents des villes américaines. Une ville française typique comprend° les quartiers suivants.

LA VILLE MÊME

La «vieille ville»

C'est le quartier historique, aujourd'hui très touristique, où l'on trouve les vestiges du passé: la cathédrale, des rues étroites,° des maisons anciennes très pittoresques, parfois un château, des vestiges de remparts et même des ruines romaines. Les maisons anciennes ont souvent été restaurées. Ce sont des résidences très recherchées° par les habitants des villes qui y trouvent à la fois° le confort du présent et le charme du passé.

Le «centre-ville»

C'est l'endroit le plus dynamique, le plus animé et, pour beaucoup de gens, le plus intéressant de la ville. Situé généralement autour d'une place monumentale, on y trouve les bâtiments administratifs (la mairie, le palais de justice, la poste. . .), les grands magasins, les boutiques de luxe, les cinémas, le théâtre municipal, les cafés et les meilleurs restaurants de la ville. Il y a parfois un jardin public avec des fontaines, des parterres de fleurs° et des bancs.° Le week-end les gens viennent au centre-ville pour faire leur shopping et pour se distraire.° Quand il fait beau, ils s'asseyent° à la terrasse des cafés pour voir le spectacle de la rue et aussi pour être vus.

Les quartiers résidentiels

Ils sont situés autour du centre-ville et le long d'avenues transversales. C'est là que les gens habitent. Les immeubles ont un maximum de six étages. Leur rez-de-chaussée est généralement occupé par des boutiques. Le reste est divisé en appartements.

comprend *includes*   **étroites** *narrow*   **recherchées** *sought after*   **à la fois** *at the same time*
parterres de fleurs *flower beds*   **bancs** *benches*   **se distraire** *to have fun*
✶s'asseoir *to sit down*

LA BANLIEUE

Les banlieues qui s'étendent° autour des villes sont modernes, mais la vie y est généralement monotone, banale, même ennuyeuse°. Il y a différentes sortes de banlieues. Dans les banlieues «chic», les gens habitent dans des maisons individuelles entourées° de jardins. Dans les banlieues ouvrières°, les gens habitent dans des «grands ensembles°». Ce sont des immeubles de 10, 20 ou 30 étages, à l'architecture simple mais souvent sans grand intérêt. Dans les banlieues les plus défavorisées, les gens habitent dans des logements précaires sans confort et sans hygiène. Pour aider les habitants des banlieues pauvres, le gouvernement français a financé la construction d'HLM (habitation à loyer modéré°) où les gens pourraient avoir l'occasion de louer ou acheter leur appartement à des conditions avantageuses.

Les «villes nouvelles»

Toutes les grandes villes du monde ont un problème commun: la qualité de la vie y est menacée par une expansion trop rapide et souvent anarchique. Pour limiter l'expansion de Paris et de sa banlieue, le gouvernement français a décidé de créer cinq villes entièrement nouvelles dans la région parisienne: Cergy-Pontoise, Saint-Quentin-en-Yvelines, Évry, Melun-Sénart, Marne-la-Vallée. Ces «villes nouvelles» sont de dimension moyenne°. Elles ont de 80 000 à 250 000 habitants. Tout a été planifié° pour assurer à ceux-ci un bon équilibre entre le travail et les loisirs. Ces villes offrent° à leur population non seulement des logements et des emplois, mais aussi des centres commerciaux, des équipements culturels et sportifs, des parcs de loisirs. Et, pour maintenir le contact avec la nature, des espaces verts et des plans d'eau° y ont été aménagés.°

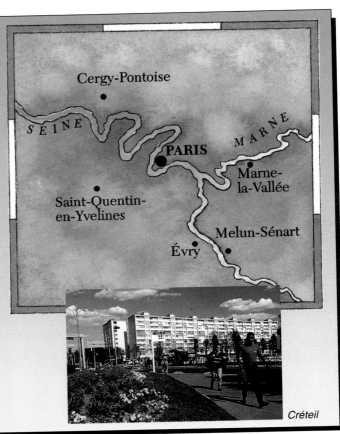

Créteil

et vous?

Imaginez que vous allez passer une année dans une grande ville française. Où préféreriez-vous habiter? dans la vieille ville? au centre-ville? dans un quartier résidentiel? dans la banlieue? dans une «ville nouvelle»? Expliquez pourquoi.

s'étendent *extend*   **ennuyeuse** *boring*   **entourées** *surrounded*   **ouvrières** *working class*   **grands ensembles** *housing projects*
loyer modéré *low rent*   **moyenne** *average*   **planifié** *planned*   ***offrir** *to offer*   **plans d'eau=** lacs artificiels
aménagés = développés

LE FRANÇAIS PRATIQUE

Comment expliquer où on habite

> Où habites-tu?

> J'habite 18, place Voltaire.

Les nombres

Révision ▶ p. R10

— Où habites-tu?

J'habite | 10, rue de la République.
| 25, avenue Victor Hugo.
| 120, boulevard Raspail.
| 18, place Voltaire.

dans la 35e rue.
dans la 6e avenue.

— Où est-ce exactement?

C'est | dans **le centre-ville.**
| dans **la banlieue** (suburbs).
| dans **le quartier** (district, area, neighborhood) Saint-Pierre.

— Dans quel genre de résidence habites-tu?

J'habite dans | **une maison individuelle.**   **un immeuble** (apartment building)
| **un appartement.**   **un HLM*** (low-income housing project)
| **une tour** (high rise).

— C'est près d'ici?

Oui, c'est | **tout près** (nearby).   Non, c'est | **loin.**
| **à 100 mètres.** | **à 3 kilomètres.**
| **à dix minutes à pied.** | **à 20 minutes en bus.**

— Comment est-ce qu'on peut aller là-bas?

On peut y aller | à pied.   On peut prendre | un bus.
| à vélo. | un taxi.
                                   | le métro.

* HLM = Habitation à Loyer Modéré (low-rent housing)

---

1 ### Une invitation à dîner

Vous avez invité votre camarade français(e) à dîner chez vous.
Votre camarade accepte, mais il/elle a besoin de renseignements
pour aller chez vous. Il/elle veut savoir . . .

- votre adresse
- dans quelle partie de la ville vous habitez
- si c'est loin de l'école
- comment aller chez vous

Vous lui expliquez. Composez le dialogue correspondant avec
votre partenaire et jouez-le en classe.

Dans mon quartier, il y a . . .

des boutiques

des commerces
(small businesses)

un grand centre
commercial *(mall)*

une station-service

un centre sportif

un centre de loisirs
(recreation center)

une Maison des Jeunes
(Youth center)

une bibliothèque

un musée

un parc

un jardin public

une mairie *(city hall)*

une poste *(post office)*

un poste de police
une gendarmerie } *(police station)*

une caserne de pompiers

FLASH d'information

La police nationale et la gendarmerie sont deux corps
de police distincts. Certaines de leurs fonctions sont
semblables, mais d'autres sont différentes. L'un des rôles
de la gendarmerie est d'assurer la police° des routes.
C'est à eux qu'on a affaire° quand on ne respecte pas
le code de la route.°

la police *law enforcement*
avoir affaire à *to have to deal with*   **code de la route** *traffic regulations*

2 Créa-dialogue: En ville

Votre partenaire, qui est français(e), visite votre ville. Il/elle veut faire l'une des choses suivantes.
Dites-lui à quel endroit aller et si c'est loin d'ici.

▶ Je voudrais envoyer
des lettres.

Est-ce que c'est
loin d'ici?

Comment est-ce que
je peux aller là-bas?

Va à la poste.

Non,
c'est à 500 mètres.

Vas-y à pied.

(Prends le bus.)

- faire réparer ma voiture
- faire une promenade à pied
- jouer au volley
- rencontrer de jeunes Américains

- emprunter un livre
- faire des achats
- déclarer la perte *(loss)*
  de mon passeport

- interviewer un membre du conseil
  municipal *(city council)*
- envoyer des lettres
- voir une exposition de photos

LANGUE ET COMMUNICATION

A. Révision: le conditionnel

The CONDITIONAL is used to express what WOULD HAPPEN, what people WOULD DO in certain circumstances.

Review the formation of the conditional:

FUTURE STEM + IMPERFECT ENDINGS

Formation du conditionnel

Révision ▶ 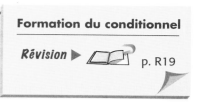 p. R19

INFINITIVE	parler		ENDINGS
FUTURE	je	**parler**ai	
CONDITIONAL	je	**parler**ais	-ais
	tu	**parler**ais	-ais
	il/elle/on	**parler**ait	-ait
	nous	**parler**ions	-ions
	vous	**parler**iez	-iez
	ils/elles	**parler**aient	-aient

Verbs with irregular stems:

payer	je **paier**ais	devoir	je **devr**ais
acheter	j'**achèter**ais	pouvoir	je **pourr**ais
		vouloir	je **voudr**ais
appeler	j'**appeller**ais		
être	je **ser**ais		
avoir	j'**aur**ais	envoyer	j'**enverr**ais
aller	j'**ir**ais	recevoir	je **recevr**ais
faire	je **fer**ais	savoir	je **saur**ais
venir	je **viendr**ais	voir	je **verr**ais

1 Au choix

Supposez que vous ayez le choix entre les possibilités suivantes. Que choisiriez-vous? (Si vous voulez, expliquez votre choix.)

▶ habiter en ville ou à la campagne?
   J'habiterais à la campagne (parce que j'aime la nature).

1. habiter dans le centre-ville ou en banlieue?
2. travailler dans un restaurant ou dans un supermarché?
3. assister à un concert ou à un match de foot?
4. passer les vacances à la mer ou à la campagne?
5. aller au ciné ou au restaurant?
6. voir une comédie ou un film d'aventures?
7. avoir une moto ou une voiture de sport?
8. faire du ski nautique ou du parapente?
9. être acteur (actrice) de cinéma ou
      athlète professionnel(le)?

2 Les élections municipales

Vous êtes journaliste pour le journal de votre ville.
Vous interviewez votre partenaire qui est
candidat(e) à la mairie.

- ▶ construire des HLM?
  - — **Est-ce que vous construiriez des HLM?**
  - — **Oui, je construirais des HLM.**
    - **(Non, je ne construirais pas de HLM.)**

- développer les transports publics
- fermer le jardin public la nuit
- contrôler la pollution
- taxer les commerces
- créer un centre de loisirs pour
  les personnes âgées
- construire une nouvelle caserne de pompiers
- fermer la bibliothèque le dimanche
- interdire la circulation dans le centre-ville

3 La meilleure solution

Imaginez que vous êtes dans les situations suivantes. Qu'est-ce que vous feriez?
Comparez votre solution avec celle de votre partenaire.

SITUATION A

Vous habitez la banlieue. Vous êtes allé(e) au
cinéma dans le centre-ville. Vous voulez rentrer
chez vous, mais vous n'avez pas assez d'argent
pour prendre le bus et vos parents ne sont pas
à la maison.
Que feriez-vous?

- rentrer à pied?
- demander de l'argent à un passant *(passerby)*?
- faire de l'auto-stop *(hitchhiking)*?
- ??

SITUATION B

Pour son anniversaire, vous avez invité votre meilleur(e)
ami(e) à dîner chez vous. Au moment de préparer le repas,
vous vous apercevez *(realize)* que la cuisinière *(stove)* ne
marche pas. Que feriez-vous?

- téléphoner à votre ami(e) et annuler le repas?
- acheter une pizza?
- inviter votre ami(e) au restaurant?
- ??

SITUATION C

Votre frère a une copine. Un jour vous découvrez que
cette copine sort avec un autre garçon. Que feriez-vous?

- dire la vérité à votre frère?
- parler à la copine de votre frère?
- envoyer une lettre d'insultes à l'autre garçon?
- ??

SITUATION D

Vous êtes dans un ascenseur quand une
panne d'électricité *(power failure)* paralyse
tout l'immeuble. Que feriez-vous?

- attendre calmement l'arrivée
  des pompiers?
- forcer la porte?
- monter sur le toit de l'ascenseur?
- ??

4 Les vacances idéales

Avec votre partenaire, discutez des vacances idéales. Posez-vous
les questions suivantes (en français, bien sûr!)

- *where would you go?*
- *how would you travel?*
- *how long would you stay?*
- *in what type of hotel would you stay?*
- *at what time would you get up?*

- *what would you do in the morning?*
- *what would you do in the afternoon?*
- *what would you do to meet people?*
- *what would you do to stay in shape* **(en forme)?**
- *what would you do in the evenings?*

Puis, mettez-vous d'accord et écrivez un petit paragraphe
où vous décrivez ce que vous feriez.

Pour nos vacances idéales, nous irions...

B. Le conditionnel dans les phrases avec si

Note the use of the conditional in the following sentences.

Si j'avais une voiture,
  j'**irais** à la campagne.

If I had a car (but I don't),
  *I **would go** to the country.*

Si nous habitions à Paris,
  nous **voyagerions** en métro.

If we were living in Paris (but we aren't),
  *we **would travel** by subway.*

The CONDITIONAL is used to express what WOULD HAPPEN,
if certain conditions contrary to reality <u>were</u> met.

In such sentences, the construction is usually:

si-clause: IMPERFECT	result clause: CONDITIONAL
Si je **gagnais** à la loterie,	j'**achèterais** une moto.

➡ In French, the CONDITIONAL is <u>never</u> used in the **si**-clause.

---

5 **Si j'habitais . . .**

Pour chaque endroit, décrivez 2 ou 3 choses que vous feriez si vous habitiez là.

▶ à Paris

**Si j'habitais à Paris, je parlerais français
  tout le temps.
Je voyagerais en métro.
Je visiterais de temps en temps
  le musée d'Orsay.
J'irais parfois écouter des concerts
  à la Villette . . . .**

1. à San Francisco
2. en Floride
3. à la Martinique
4. dans le centre-ville
5. dans un petit village à la campagne
6. dans la banlieue d'une grande ville

---

6 **Rêves** *(Dreams)*

Rêver ne coûte rien. Expliquez les rêves des personnes suivantes en utilisant
les éléments des colonnes A et B. Soyez logique!

	A	**B**
nous	• invisible	• savoir tout
vous	• multi-millionnaire	• protéger les innocents
Sandrine	• extra-lucide	• voyager dans l'espace
Philippe	• Superman/Wonder Woman	• habiter dans un château
mes copains	• Robin des Bois *(Robin Hood)*	• avoir une Rolls-Royce
		• aider les pauvres
		• voler comme des oiseaux
		• passer à travers les murs
		• connaître le passé, le présent et l'avenir

▶ **Si Philippe était Robin des Bois,
  il aiderait les pauvres.**

7 Problèmes et solutions

Votre partenaire va choisir l'un des problèmes suivants.
Dites-lui ce que vous feriez à sa place. Donnez-lui
2 ou 3 suggestions (affirmatives ou négatives).

Je grossis.
> **Si je grossissais, je mangerais moins.
> J'irais au centre sportif et je ferais
> de la gymnastique tous les jours.
> Je ne prendrais pas le bus pour
> aller à l'école. J'irais à pied.**

- Je n'ai pas d'appétit.
- Je dors trop.
- Je ne me sens pas très bien.
- Je perds mon temps.
- Je ne réussis pas à mes examens.
- J'ai besoin d'argent.
- Je suis déprimé(e) *(depressed)*.
- J'ai un problème avec mon copain (ma copine).
- J'ai des difficultés avec mes parents.
- Mon frère (ma soeur) m'embête tout le temps.

8 Que feriez-vous?

Choisissez l'une des situations suivantes et composez un petit paragraphe où vous décrivez
ce que vous feriez (ou ce que vous ne feriez pas) si vous étiez dans cette situation.
Utilisez le conditionnel . . . et votre imagination!

1. Pour impressionner Stéphanie, sa nouvelle copine, Raphaël l'a invitée dans un grand restaurant. Au moment de payer, Raphaël s'aperçoit *(realizes)* qu'il a perdu son portefeuille.
   > **Si j'étais Raphaël, . . .**

2. Depuis plusieurs semaines, Caroline reçoit des lettres d'un admirateur inconnu. Elle veut savoir qui est ce mystérieux correspondant.
   > **Si j'étais Caroline, . . .**

3. Jérôme a emprunté la voiture de Cécile. Au moment de rendre la voiture à son amie, il remarque une éraflure *(dent, scratch)* fraîche. Il n'est pas sûr que cette éraflure était là quand il a emprunté la voiture.
   > **Si j'étais Jérôme, . . .**

4. Jean-Claude a passé la soirée dans une petite salle de la bibliothèque municipale. Il est maintenant onze heures. Au moment de sortir, Jean-Claude s'aperçoit qu'il est seul et que toutes les portes sont fermées à clé.
   > **Si j'étais Jean-Claude, . . .**

5. Madame Lescot a invité ses amis à dîner. Au moment de préparer le repas, elle s'aperçoit que sa cuisinière *(stove)* ne marche pas.
   > **Si j'étais Madame Lescot, . . .**

6. Monsieur Rimbaud voyage souvent en avion. Un jour, il prend par erreur une valise qui n'est pas à lui. Chez lui, il ouvre la valise et découvre un million de dollars . . . et l'adresse d'une bande de terroristes.
   > **Si j'étais Monsieur Rimbaud, . . .**

9 Qu'est-ce que vous feriez à leur place?

Avec votre partenaire, choisissez une des situations suivantes et dites ce que vous feriez
dans ces situations.

A

B

C

C. Le conditionnel: autres usages

POLITE REQUESTS

The conditional of verbs such as **vouloir, pouvoir, devoir** is used instead of the present to express a WISH or REQUEST in a MORE POLITE manner. Compare:

Je veux regarder tes photos.	*I want to look at your pictures.*
Je voudrais regarder tes photos.	*I would like to look at your pictures.*
Peux-tu me prêter ton vélo?	*Can you loan me your bike?*
Pourrais-tu me prêter ton vélo?	*Could you loan me your bike?*
Vous devez être à l'heure.	*You must be on time.*
Vous devriez être à l'heure.	*You should be on time.*

INDIRECT SPEECH

The conditional is used to report what people mentioned IN THE PAST about a FUTURE EVENT. It describes what they said they WOULD DO or what WOULD HAPPEN later. Compare the use of tenses in the following sentences:

Maintenant, Éric **dit** qu'il **ira** au ciné.	*Now Eric **says** that he **will go** to the movies.*
Hier, il **a dit** qu'il **irait** au concert.	*Yesterday he **said** that he **would go** to the concert.*

After a declarative verb (such as **dire** or **écrire**), future events are expressed according to the following tense sequence:

DECLARATIVE VERB	FUTURE EVENT
present	future
past (imperfect, passé composé, pluperfect)	conditional

10 Soyons polis!

Montrez que vous êtes poli(e). Pour cela, reformulez les phrases suivantes en utilisant le conditionnel.

▶ Est-ce que tu veux un dessert?
Est-ce que tu voudrais un dessert?

1. Je veux te parler.
2. Nous voulons sortir avec vous.
3. Peux-tu m'inviter à ta boum?
4. Pouvons-nous amener nos amis?

5. Pouvez-vous être à l'heure?
6. Tu dois m'aider.
7. Vous devez être plus généreux.
8. Vous ne devez pas mentir *(tell lies)*.

11 Messages téléphoniques

Votre partenaire a écouté votre répondeur *(answering machine)* et il/elle a noté les messages suivants. Demandez-lui qui a téléphoné et ce que chaque personne a dit.

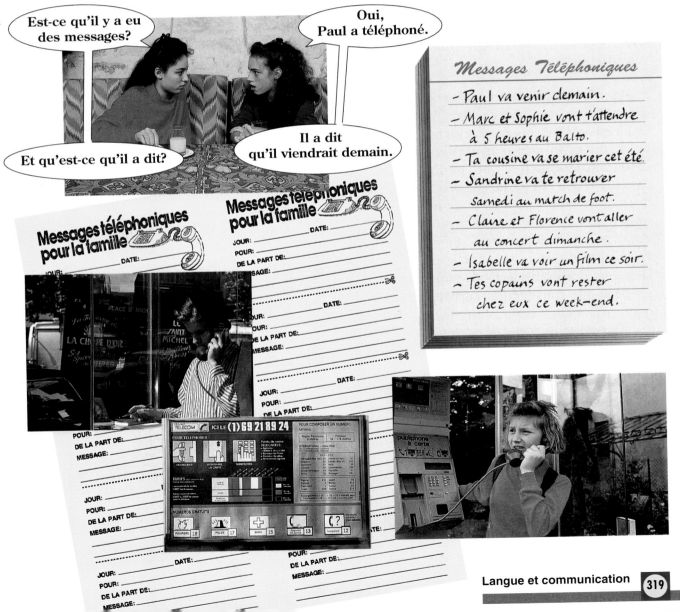

Est-ce qu'il y a eu des messages?

Oui, Paul a téléphoné.

Et qu'est-ce qu'il a dit?

Il a dit qu'il viendrait demain.

Messages Téléphoniques

- Paul va venir demain.
- Marc et Sophie vont t'attendre à 5 heures au Balto.
- Ta cousine va se marier cet été.
- Sandrine va te retrouver samedi au match de foot.
- Claire et Florence vont aller au concert dimanche.
- Isabelle va voir un film ce soir.
- Tes copains vont rester chez eux ce week-end.

Le spectacle
EST DANS
LA RUE

Pour les Français, la rue n'est pas seulement un endroit où l'on passe pour aller au travail, à l'école, ou dans des magasins. C'est aussi un endroit où l'on vit.° On y rencontre ses amis. On s'y repose (à la terrasse des cafés). On y dîne (à la terrasse des restaurants). Et surtout, on s'y distrait.°

La rue est en effet un théâtre permanent qui offre toutes sortes de spectacles aux «badauds».° Certains spectacles sont spontanés et gratuits: un accident, une querelle entre deux automobilistes, une manifestation,° le passage d'une personne célèbre,° le tournage° d'un film, etc. Les autres spectacles sont organisés par des «artistes» et laissés° à l'appréciation personnelle des passants. Si vous jugez° que le spectacle est bon, vous laisserez° quelques pièces de monnaie° dans le chapeau que vous tendra° l'artiste. Sinon, vous quitterez les lieux avant la fin° du spectacle.

Autrefois, les «artistes des rues» étaient des jongleurs,° des chanteurs, des montreurs° d'animaux (ours,° singes,° chiens savants,° etc. . .). Les artistes d'aujourd'hui ne sont pas tellement° différents des artistes d'autrefois et leur principe est le même: l'artiste s'installe dans un endroit fréquenté; les «badauds» arrivent; l'artiste commence son spectacle; à la fin du spectacle, il fait la quête.° Il y a plusieurs catégories d'artistes de rue:

◇ LES MUSICIENS

Ce sont les plus nombreux.° Suivant° la clientèle ou le quartier, ils jouent du jazz, du rock, de la musique folklorique, de la musique indienne, des rythmes africains, ou même de la musique classique. L'important° est que la musique soit bonne et que le musicien soit sympathique ou ait l'air exotique. Parce que leur musique plaît,° les jeunes musiciens américains qui jouent en France ont généralement beaucoup de succès!

◇ LES MIMES

Ils opèrent° généralement devant la terrasse d'un café. Leur costume est classique: pantalon noir, gilet° rayé,° chapeau noir. La technique du mime consiste à suivre° un passant et à imiter tous ses gestes avec la plus grande exactitude possible. Le passant ne s'aperçoit° de rien, mais les spectateurs qui sont à la terrasse du café rient° . . . et contribuent!

---

*vivre to live   ***se distraire** to have fun   **badauds** onlookers   **manifestation** demonstration   **célèbre** famous   **tournage** making
laissés left   **jugez** = pensez   **laisserez** = mettrez   **monnaie** coins   **tendra** = présentera   **fin** end   **jongleurs** jugglers
montreurs exhibitor   **ours** bears   **singes** monkeys   **savants** trained   **tellement** that (much)   **fait la quête** passes the hat   **nombreux**
numerous   **suivant** according to   **L'important** = la chose importante   ***plaire** to please   **opèrent** = travaillent   **gilet** vest   **rayé** striped
*suivre to follow   ***s'apercevoir** to notice   ***rire** to laugh

LES AUTOMATES

◆ Ils sont déguisés en personnages d'autrefois. Leur visage couvert de poudre° ne manifeste° aucune expression. Leurs gestes sont complètement mécaniques. Ils tournent la tête à droite, à gauche, ils lèvent° le bras comme des marionnettes. On ne sait vraiment pas s'ils sont réels . . . jusqu'au° moment où ils descendent de leur piédestal et passent le chapeau.

L'automate

C'est une «automate». Nous l'avons rencontrée un jour d'été à Strasbourg devant la cathédrale. Il était sept heures du soir. Elle avait le visage encore° tout blanc, et elle portait un grand chapeau de paille,° à la mode de 1900. Le spectacle était terminé et elle allait partir sur sa grosse moto. Nous lui avons parlé.

— Vous êtes d'ici?
— Non, je suis de la banlieue. Je viens ici parce que ça marche bien.
— Ça a marché aujourd'hui?
— Pas trop mal. J'ai fait 150 euros!
— Quel est votre endroit préféré?
— Ici devant la cathédrale. . . Il y a toujours des cars° pleins° de touristes étrangers.
— Quels sont vos meilleurs clients?
— En général, tout le monde donne quelque chose, mais j'aime beaucoup les Allemands. Ils comprennent l'effort et la qualité du travail.
— Est-ce que votre métier° est dur?°
— Très dur! Il faut se concentrer. . . C'est difficile quand il y a tant° de gens qui passent, le bruit, le vent. . . Et puis il y a la préparation, le maquillage.° Ça prend du temps! Enfin, l'essentiel, c'est que les gens s'amusent. Quand ils s'amusent, comme aujourd'hui, je sais que j'ai bien fait mon travail.
— Merci, et bonne chance.

et vous?

DÉFINITIONS
Définissez les mots suivants.
- un badaud
- une manifestation
- un animal savant
- un jongleur
- un mime
- un automate
- une marionnette
- faire la quête

EXPRESSION ÉCRITE
Vous êtes en vacances à Paris. Écrivez une lettre à un(e) ami(e) où vous décrivez un spectacle de rue auquel vous avez assisté. Mentionnez, par exemple:
- le genre de spectacle
- ce que «l'artiste» a fait (donnez des détails)
- comment vous avez trouvé le spectacle
- si vous avez donné de l'argent (pourquoi ou pourquoi pas)

---

poudre *powder* **manifeste** = *montre* **lèvent** *raise* **jusqu'au** *until* **encore** *still* **paille** *straw* **cars** *buses* **pleins** *full*
métier = *profession* **dur** = *difficile* **tant** *so many* **maquillage** *make-up*

LANGUE ET COMMUNICATION

A. Le conditionnel passé

The PAST CONDITIONAL is used to express what WOULD HAVE HAPPENED under certain circumstances. Note the forms of the verbs in heavy print:

À ta place,
    je **n'aurais pas pris** ma voiture.
Je **serais allé(e)** en ville en bus.

In your place (If I had been you),
    *I **would not have taken** my car.*
*I **would have gone** downtown by bus.*

FORMS

The PAST CONDITIONAL is formed as follows:

> CONDITIONAL of **avoir** or **être** + PAST PARTICIPLE

> In the past conditional, the agreement rules for the past participle are the same as in the passé composé.
>
> Tu n'as pas invité **ta copine.** À ta place, je l'aurais invité**e**.

INFINITIVE	**voyager**	**aller**	**s'amuser**
PAST CONDITIONAL	j' **aurais voyagé** tu **aurais voyagé** il/elle/on **aurait voyagé** nous **aurions voyagé** vous **auriez voyagé** ils/elles **auraient voyagé**	je **serais allé(e)** tu **serais allé(e)** il/elle/on **serait allé(e)** nous **serions allé(e)s** vous **seriez allé(e)(s)** ils/elles **seraient allé(e)s**	je **me serais amusé(e)** tu **te serais amusé(e)** il/elle/on **se serait amusé(e)** nous **nous serions amusé(e)s** vous **vous seriez amusé(e)(s)** ils/elles **se seraient amusé(e)s**
NEGATIVE	je **n'aurais pas voyagé**	je **ne serais pas allé(e)**	je **ne me serais pas amusé(e)**
INTERRROGATIVE	est-ce que tu **aurais voyagé?** **aurais-tu voyagé?**	tu **serais allé(e)?** **serais-tu allé(e)?**	tu **te serais amusé(e)?** **te serais-tu amusé(e)?**

USES

The following sentences express what WOULD HAVE HAPPENED **if** certain past conditions HAD BEEN MET.

Note the use of tenses in the sentences below.

Si j'**avais étudié,**
    j'**aurais réussi** à l'examen.
Si vous **étiez allés** à la boum,
    vous **vous seriez amusés.**

*If I **had studied,***
    *I **would have passed** the exam.*
*If you **had gone** to the party,*
    *you **would have had fun.***

Hypothetical sentences that refer to the past are usually formed according to the pattern:

si-clause	MAIN or RESULT clause
pluperfect	past conditional

ALLONS PLUS LOIN

Note the English equivalents of the past conditional of **vouloir, pouvoir** and **devoir**.

J'**aurais voulu voir** ce film.	*I **wish** I **had seen** that movie.*
	*(I **would have liked to see** that movie.)*
Tu **aurais pu me téléphoner.**	*You **could have called** me.*
Vous **auriez dû attendre.**	*You **should have waited.***

1 L'incendie

Sébastien habite au deuxième étage d'un immeuble. Hier, il y a eu un commencement *(beginning)* d'incendie *(fire)* dans cet immeuble. Voici ce qu'il a fait. Dites si oui ou non vous auriez fait les mêmes choses.

▶ Sébastien est resté calme.
Moi aussi, je serais resté(e) calme.
(Moi, je ne serais pas resté(e) calme.)

1. Il a téléphoné aux pompiers.
2. Il a téléphoné à sa copine.
3. Il a fermé la porte de l'appartement à clé.
4. Il a pris sa mini-chaîne.
5. Il a laissé son argent dans un tiroir *(drawer)*.
6. Il est allé dans la salle de bains.
7. Il a mis une serviette mouillée *(wet)* sous la porte.
8. Il a ouvert la fenêtre.
9. Il a attendu dix minutes.
10. Il s'est impatienté.
11. Il a sauté *(jumped)* par la fenêtre.
12. Il s'est cassé la jambe.

2 Vive la différence!

Votre partenaire est allé(e) en ville. Il/elle explique ce qu'il/elle a fait. Dites lui que vous auriez fait quelque chose de différent. (Utilisez le même verbe, mais avec une expression de votre choix.)

▶ aller au musée
— **Je suis allé(e) au musée.**
— **Eh bien moi, à ta place, je ne serais pas allé(e) au musée.**
Je serais allé(e) au ciné (au café, dans les magasins, . . .).

1. voir une exposition
2. déjeuner au café
3. manger un sandwich
4. se promener dans le parc
5. passer à la Maison des Jeunes
6. aller au centre commercial
7. acheter des CD
8. rentrer à pied

3 Tant pis pour toi!

Votre partenaire vous décrit certains problèmes qu'il/elle a eus. Dites-lui que c'est de sa faute et expliquez pourquoi.

▶ rater l'examen / étudier

1. se perdre en ville / prendre ton plan *(map)*?
2. attendre une heure au restaurant / réserver une table?
3. arriver en retard au rendez-vous / regarder ta montre?
4. attraper un coup de soleil / mettre de la crème solaire?

J'ai raté l'examen.

Est-ce que tu avais étudié?

Non, je n'avais pas étudié.

Tant pis pour toi! Si tu avais étudié, tu n'aurais pas raté l'examen.

4 Dommage!

Les personnes suivantes n'ont pas fait certaines choses. Décrivez ce qui serait arrivé si elles avaient fait ces choses. Attention: le verbe entre parenthèses peut être affirmatif ou négatif.

▶ Jérôme n'a pas fait attention. (tomber dans les escaliers?)
Si Jérôme avait fait attention, il ne serait pas tombé dans les escaliers.

1. Nous ne nous sommes pas dépêchés. (rater le train?)
2. Patrick n'a pas lu les annonces. (trouver un job cet été?)
3. Mes copains n'ont pas acheté de billets. (aller au concert?)
4. Je n'ai pas utilisé ma calculatrice. (se tromper dans le problème?)
5. Les joueurs ne se sont pas entraînés. (gagner le match?)
6. Vous n'avez pas attendu. (voir l'éclipse?)
7. Tu n'as pas mis ton manteau. (attraper une pneumonie?)
8. Les élèves ne se sont pas reposés. (dormir pendant la classe?)
9. Le Petit Chaperon Rouge *(Little Red Riding Hood)* n'a pas écouté sa mère. (rencontrer le loup *[wolf]*?)

B. Résumé: l'usage des temps avec si

Review the sequence of tenses with **si**.

To describe...	**si**–clause	main or result clause	
• a possibility (concerning a future event)	PRESENT	FUTURE IMPERATIVE	**Si** je **vais** en ville, j'**achèterai** le journal. **Si** tu **vas** au supermarché, **achète** du pain.
• a hypothetical situation (usually contrary to reality)	IMPERFECT	CONDITIONAL	**Si** j'**avais** un billet, j'**irais** au concert.
• a hypothetical situation in the past	PLUPERFECT	PAST CONDITIONAL	**Si** j'**avais étudié**, je **n'aurais pas raté** l'examen.

5 Vive la différence!

Vous et votre partenaire, vous n'êtes pas d'accord. Votre partenaire vous dit ce qu'il/elle fera. Dites-lui ce que vous feriez si vous étiez dans les mêmes circonstances. (Choisissez une option différente.)

▶ avoir faim / manger quoi?
— **Si j'ai faim, je mangerai un sandwich.**
— **Eh bien, moi, si j'avais faim, je mangerais une pizza.**

1. avoir soif / boire quoi?
2. avoir de l'argent / acheter quoi?
3. sortir samedi / aller où ?
4. aller au cinéma / voir quoi?
5. aller à Paris / visiter quoi?
6. aller en Europe / voyager comment?

6 Et si cela arrivait . . . ?

Avec votre partenaire, choisissez une des situations suivantes et discutez de ce que vous feriez et de ce que vous ne feriez pas si vous étiez dans cette situation. Puis, écrivez un paragraphe d'au moins 5 lignes où vous décrirez les résultats de votre discussion.

1. Vous êtes témoins d'un cambriolage.
2. Vous êtes prisonniers/prisonnières de dangereux bandits.
3. Vous êtes perdu(e)s dans la jungle tropicale.
4. Vous êtes invité(e)s à la Maison Blanche.
5. Vous assistez au mariage d'un copain français.
6. Un réalisateur *(movie producer)* vous offre un rôle dans son prochain film.
7. Vous découvrez un trésor *(treasure)* dans une maison abandonnée.

7 Achats

Complétez les phrases suivantes avec la forme du verbe **acheter** qui convient.

1. Si je vais à la poste, j'___ des timbres.
2. Si nous ___ des billets, nous aurions pu aller au concert samedi soir.
3. S'il avait de l'argent, mon oncle ___ un appartement dans le centre-ville.
4. Qu'est-ce que tu ___ si tu gagnes de l'argent l'été prochain?
5. Si j'étais passé à la boulangerie, j'___ des croissants.
6. Si tu ___ des CD dans ce magasin, tu paieras moins cher.
7. Est-ce que tu ___ cette veste si elle était en solde?
8. Si Paul ___ une moto, il vendrait son vélo.

8 Un discours électoral

À chaque élection, Monsieur Duroc est candidat à la mairie de Clocheville. Cette année, il se présente à nouveau. Vous êtes son/sa secrétaire. Complétez son discours *(speech)* avec la forme correcte du verbe entre parenthèses.

Messieurs et Mesdames,

J'ai le plaisir d'annoncer pour la sixième fois ma candidature à la mairie de Clocheville. Si vous (voter) pour moi aux dernières élections, vous (voir) les nombreuses améliorations que j'(apporter) à notre bonne ville. Je/j' (construire) une nouvelle gendarmerie, une nouvelle poste et, bien sûr, une nouvelle mairie. J'(éliminer) la pollution et la criminalité. Aujourd'hui, votre ville (être) belle, propre et sans danger.

Malheureusement, aux dernières élections, vous avez voté pour mon adversaire qui est un incapable. Si je/j' (être) à sa place, je/j' (avoir) honte de me présenter à nouveau. Heureusement, vous êtes intelligents. Quand vous (voter) pour moi dimanche prochain, vous (voter) pour quelqu'un de responsable et d'honnête. Si je/j' (être) élu, vous (pouvoir) être fiers à nouveau de votre ville!

Merci!

LECTURE

Les pêches

d'après André Theuriet

André Theuriet (1833-1907)
Comme beaucoup d'écrivains français, André Theuriet s'est exprimé dans des genres littéraires différents: le roman, le conte, la poésie, le théâtre. Dans ses contes, Theuriet décrit la société de son époque. Pour son oeuvre, il a été élu membre de l'Académie Française.

AVANT DE LIRE

Le contexte historique

Pour bien comprendre une histoire, il faut la placer dans son contexte historique. L'histoire suivante se passe à la «Belle Époque», il y a environ° cent ans. La vie était alors assez différente d'aujourd'hui et deux aspects sont particulièrement importants pour l'histoire que vous allez lire.

• À cette époque, les gens riches organisaient de temps en temps de grandes réceptions° chez eux. Ces fêtes, généralement très formelles, étaient des événements importants de la vie mondaine.° Il était donc essentiel pour son standing social d'y être invité.

• Un autre aspect important pour l'histoire concerne l'alimentation d'alors. Comme les transports étaient très limités (l'automobile et l'avion n'existaient pas encore!), la distribution des produits frais,° et particulièrement des fruits, était très localisée et très saisonnière. Si on voulait manger des fruits frais, il fallait attendre l'été, ou bien, si on avait beaucoup d'argent, il fallait faire venir° spécialement ces produits de Provence, d'Italie ou d'Espagne.

environ = approximativement **réception** = soirée de gala **mondaine** = sociale **frais** *fresh*
faire venir *to have shipped*

Imaginez que vous êtes invité(e) à un très grand mariage. Votre meilleur(e) ami(e), qui est malade, ne peut pas vous accompagner. Vous lui avez promis de lui rapporter un morceau° du gâteau nuptial.

Le gâteau a été servi, mais comme vous êtes un peu timide, vous n'avez pas osé° en demander un second morceau à l'hôtesse. Vous n'avez cependant pas oublié votre promesse.

Vous allez au buffet et, quand personne ne regarde, vous prenez un morceau de gâteau pour votre ami(e). Comment feriez-vous pour le ramener° sans être vu(e)?

- Je le mettrais dans ma poche de pantalon ou de jupe.
- Je le cacherais sous ma veste.
- Je le mettrais dans mon sac.
- Je l'envelopperais dans une serviette.°

morceau *piece*   **osé** *dared*   **ramener** *to bring back*   **serviette** *napkin*

LES PÊCHES

1

C'est au cours d'un dîner organisé par les anciens élèves du lycée de province où j'avais fait mes études que j'ai revu mon copain d'enfance Vital Herbelot. C'est lui qui est venu me saluer° après le café. À vrai dire, je ne l'avais pas reconnu. Vêtu d'un costume de velours côtelé°
5 et d'une chemise à carreaux,° les cheveux en brosse et le visage bronzé, il respirait° la santé et la bonne humeur. Certes, ce n'était pas le grand garçon élégant, distingué, mais un peu timide, que j'avais connu vingt-cinq ans
10 avant. Élève très doué, il était promis à l'avenir le plus brillant. Après le bac, il avait tout de suite trouvé un poste dans la plus grande banque de la ville.

Un peu surpris de le revoir, je lui ai
15 demandé:

— Alors, tu es° toujours dans la banque?

— Oh non, il y a bien longtemps que je l'ai quittée. . . J'habite à la campagne maintenant…
20 Je suis cultivateur!

— Cultivateur, toi?! Mais je croyais que tu t'intéressais à la finance.

— C'est vrai… Et si j'avais continué, j'aurais certainement fait une «brillante carrière», comme on dit . . .Aujourd'hui je serais peut-être le président d'une grande banque nationale ou internationale… Qui sait? Mais
25 tu vois, il m'est arrivé quelque chose°, il y a vingt ans de cela.

— Quoi? Qu'est-ce qui t'est arrivé?

— Oh, une histoire de pêches . . . mais une histoire qui a changé mon existence. Pour le meilleur!

— Tu as dit «une histoire de pêches»?
30 — Oui, une absurde histoire de pêches.

Voulant satisfaire ma curiosité évidente, Vital Herbelot a commencé à me raconter son histoire.

Mots utiles	
un ancien élève	*alumnus*
un cultivateur	*farmer*
une pêche	*peach*
doué	*gifted*
vêtu de	*dressed in*
au cours de	*during, in the course of*
à vrai dire	*to tell the truth*

saluer = *dire bonjour*   **velours côtelé** *corduroy*   **à carreaux** *plaid*   **respirait** = *était l'expression de*
tu es = *tu travailles*   **il m'est arrivé quelque chose** *something happened to me*

Tu sais que j'étais fils et petit-fils d'employés relativement modestes.°
C'est ma mère qui a insisté pour que je fasse des études et que
j'obtienne mon bac. Tu te souviens, sans doute, que j'aimais les études
et que j'ai obtenu mon bac avec mention.° Aussi, je n'ai pas eu de   35
difficulté à trouver du travail.

Après le bac, j'ai été immédiatement embauché dans une grande
banque d'affaires.° Tous mes camarades de classe convoitaient°
le poste que je venais d'obtenir. Rappelle-toi comme vous étiez tous
un peu jaloux de moi! Comme j'étais très travailleur et très discipliné   40
et que je réussissais bien dans les affaires que je traitais, j'ai vite
obtenu plusieurs promotions, et avec celles-ci des augmentations
de salaire importantes.

Au bout de trois ans, j'étais devenu l'un des adjoints° principaux
du patron de la banque. Je t'assure que je gagnais bien ma vie, mais en   45
contrepartie,° je devais sacrifier tout mon temps aux affaires de
la banque. C'est à ce moment-là que je me suis marié avec une jeune
fille qui avait toutes les qualités et qui, de plus, était très jolie.

Mots utiles

embaucher	*to hire*
obtenir *	*to get, obtain*
au bout de	*after, at the end of*

Anticipons un peu!

Vital Herbelot avait une
situation brillante. Maintenant,
il est cultivateur.
À votre avis, qu'est-ce qui s'est
passé?

- Il a eu un grave accident.
- Il a commis une faute
  (mistake) professionnelle.
- Sa femme est tombée
  malade.
- Quelque chose d'autre
  s'est passé. Imaginez quoi!

Avez-vous compris?

1. À quelle occasion est-ce que le narrateur rencontre Vital Herbelot?
2. Pourquoi est-ce qu'il ne le reconnaît pas?
3. Quelle est la profession de Vital Herbelot maintenant?
4. Quelle était sa profession autrefois?

2

Mon patron était un homme très riche et très mondain.° De
temps en temps il organisait de grandes réceptions où il invitait tous   50
les notables° de la ville et quelques-uns de ses employés supérieurs.°
Il y avait généralement un repas suivi d'un bal.

Peu de temps après mon mariage, j'ai reçu ma première invitation
à l'une de ces réceptions. Malheureusement, quelques jours avant
l'événement, ma femme est tombée malade. Je pensais envoyer mes   55
excuses, mais ma femme a insisté pour que j'aille à cette réception.
— Ton patron est un homme généreux, mais très autoritaire. S'il ne te
voyait pas à la première réception à laquelle il t'invite, il serait
certainement très vexé, et cela nuirait° à ta carrière.

modestes = assez pauvres   **avec mention** with honors
une banque d'affaires investment bank   **convoitaient** = désiraient secrètement
adjoints = assistants   **en contrepartie** in exchange   **mondain** of fashionable society
notables = personnes importantes   **employés supérieurs** top executives   **nuirait à** = ruinerait

60   Bien sûr, j'aurais préféré rester avec ma femme, mais, convaincu
par ses arguments, j'ai finalement accepté l'invitation.
       Ce soir-là, je me suis donc habillé pour l'occasion. Alors qu'elle
m'aidait à ajuster ma cravate, ma femme m'a dit:
—Je regrette vraiment de ne pas pouvoir t'accompagner.

65 Il y aura un très beau buffet … et j'ai entendu dire que la femme de
ton patron a fait venir° spécialement des primeurs* du Midi. Il paraît
même qu'il y aura des pêches… Tu sais comme je les aime.
Et pourtant, c'est absolument impossible d'en trouver dans les
magasins en cette saison… Oh, ces pêches! Est-ce que tu pourrais

70 m'en rapporter une … Une seule … S'il te plaît!
       Surpris de cette requête inattendue, j'ai essayé d'expliquer à ma
femme que c'était difficile. Comment un monsieur en habit noir°
pourrait-il prendre une pêche et la mettre dans sa poche sans être vu?
       Mais ma femme a insisté: «Rien de plus facile, au contraire …

75 Tu profiteras d'un moment où tout le monde sera en train
de danser. Tu t'approcheras du buffet et tu prendras une pêche
comme si c'était pour toi et tu la dissimuleras° adroitement.°
Personne ne te verra… Oh, je sais bien, c'est un caprice,° mais ça me
ferait tellement plaisir! Allez, promets-moi …»

80   Comment refuser quelque chose à la femme qu'on aime?
J'ai fini par promettre, puis j'ai pris mon manteau et mon chapeau.
Au moment où j'allais partir, ma femme m'a regardé de ses grands
yeux bleus et m'a dit: «N'oublie pas!»

Mots utiles	
un bal	*dance*
un caprice	*whim*
une pêche	*peach*
une requête	*request*
s'approcher de	*to approach*
convaincre *	*to convince*
entendre dire	*to hear (it said)*
faire plaisir à	*to please*
profiter de	*to take advantage of*
inattendu	*unexpected*
alors que	*while*

Avez-vous compris?

1. Pourquoi Madame Herbelot ne va-t-elle pas à la réception?
2. Pourquoi conseille-t-elle à son mari d'y aller?
3. Qu'est-ce qu'elle lui demande de faire?
4. Pourquoi est-ce que son mari hésite?

3

85   Ce soir-là, toute la société° de la ville était réunie° chez mon
patron. Il y avait le maire, le président du tribunal, le général
commandant la garnison et ses officiers supérieurs, et toutes les
grandes familles de la ville.
       Mon patron avait bien fait les choses. Le dîner était exquis. Après

90 le dîner, les invités passèrent au grand salon et le bal commença. Vers

Anticipons un peu!

À votre avis, comment est-ce
que Vital Herbelot va satisfaire
la requête de sa femme?

- Il va demander à l'hôtesse
  de la réception
  la permission de prendre
  une pêche.
- Il va prendre une pêche
  sans demander
  la permission.
- Il va acheter des pêches
  chez un marchand.
- Il va rentrer chez lui sans
  pêche.
- Il va faire autre chose.
  Imaginez quoi!

---

* **Les primeurs du Midi.** À cause de son climat, le Midi (dans le sud de la France) produit des
  primeurs, c'est-à-dire, des fruits et légumes consommables avant la saison normale.

a fait venir = a commandé   **habit noir** *formal evening dress*   **dissimuleras** = cacheras
adroitement *skillfully*   **caprice** *whim*   **la société** = la haute société   **était réunie** = se trouvait

minuit, il y eut un temps de repos pendant lequel un buffet fut servi dans une petite pièce à côté du salon. Au milieu de la table trônaient° les fameuses pêches venues° spécialement du Midi. Disposées° en pyramide sur un plateau de faïence,° elles provoquaient l'admiration générale. Oui vraiment, elles étaient superbes! Je pensais alors à la promesse que j'avais faite à ma femme et me demandais comment j'allais la réaliser. Ce n'était pas facile!

95

Les domestiques préposés° au service montaient une garde vigilante° autour de ces magnifiques et coûteux fruits. De temps en temps, sur un signe de mon patron, le maître d'hôtel prenait délicatement une pêche, la découpait avec un couteau d'argent, et en présentait les deux moitiés à un invité de marque.° Il en restait encore une demi-douzaine quand l'orchestre se remit° à jouer. Les invités se précipitèrent au salon et on recommença à danser.

100

C'est alors que j'exécutai mon projet. Je pris mon chapeau et mon manteau, comme si j'allais partir. Puis, sous un prétexte quelconque,° je passai dans la petite salle où était dressé° le buffet. Heureusement les domestiques étaient partis. Je me trouvais donc seul. M'assurant que personne ne me regardait, je ne pris non pas une mais deux de ces magnifiques pêches et je les mis discrètement dans mon chapeau. Pressant celui-ci très fort° contre ma poitrine, j'allai saluer° mon hôte et mon hôtesse. Je les remerciai de leur aimable invitation, puis je me dirigeai, digne et fier de moi, vers la sortie.

105

110

Mon projet avait parfaitement réussi. Que ma femme serait heureuse quand elle verrait le produit de mon larcin inoffensif! C'est alors que se produisit l'incident ...

115

trônaient = occupaient la place d'honneur   **venues** *brought*   **disposées** = arrangées
faïence *glazed pottery*   **préposés** *assigned*   **montaient une garde vigilante** *kept watchful guard*
de marque = important   **se remit à** = recommença à   **un prétexte quelconque** *some pretext or other*   **dressé** = *placé*   **fort** *tightly*   **saluer** = dire au revoir à

Mots utiles

un larcin	*small theft*
la moitié	*half*
la poitrine	*chest*
s'assurer	*to make sure*
découper	*to cut (into pieces)*
se demander	*to wonder*
se diriger vers	*to move toward*
se précipiter	*to dash*
se produire	*to happen*
digne	*dignified*
inoffensif	*harmless*
comme si	*as if*
reste . . .	*there is/ are . . . left*

Avez-vous compris?

1. À quel moment de la réception sont servies les pêches? Par qui? À qui? Comment?
2. Comment Vital Herbelot réussit-il à prendre deux pêches?
3. Qu'est-ce qu'il fait pour passer inaperçu *(unnoticed)*?

Anticipons un peu!

À votre avis, qu'est-ce qui va se passer ensuite?
- Vital Herbelot va apporter les pêches à sa femme qui sera très contente.
- Il sera dénoncé par un domestique qui l'a vu et il sera arrêté par la police.
- Après être sorti, il fera tomber *(will drop)* les pêches dans la rue et il ne pourra pas les rapporter à sa femme.
- Quelque chose d'autre arrivera. Imaginez quoi.

120   Avant de sortir, il fallait que je traverse le salon où les jeunes gens et
les jeunes filles continuaient à valser.° On organisait justement une
nouvelle figure: une danseuse est placée au centre des danseurs qui
exécutent une ronde° autour d'elle. Elle doit tenir un chapeau à la main et
en coiffer° le jeune homme avec qui elle veut danser. C'était justement
125 la fille de mon patron qui devait se placer au centre du groupe. Me voyant
avec mon chapeau pressé contre la poitrine, elle s'écria:

    — Monsieur Herbelot! Monsieur Herbelot! Nous avons besoin de votre
chapeau! S'il vous plaît, prêtez-le-nous pour quelques minutes seulement.

    Et sans attendre ma réponse, elle me prit le chapeau des mains d'un
130 mouvement brusque. Les pêches tombèrent et roulèrent sur le sol devant
les invités ébahis.°

    La musique s'arrêta. Tout le monde riait maintenant, sauf mon patron
qui avait l'air absolument furieux. Même les domestiques semblaient
se moquer de moi… Alors la fille du patron me donna mon chapeau en
135 me disant d'une voix ironique:

    — Eh bien, monsieur Herbelot, ramassez donc vos pêches!

    J'aurais voulu être cent pieds sous terre.° Rouge de confusion, je pris
mon chapeau, balbutiai° quelques mots d'excuses, et partis comme un fou. Je
rentrai chez moi et, la mort dans le coeur, je racontai le désastre à ma femme.

140   Le lendemain, l'histoire courait° la ville. Quand je suis entré
à mon bureau ce matin-là, mes collègues savaient ce qui s'était
passé. Les plus malicieux° murmuraient° à mon passage: «Hé,
Monsieur Herbelot, ramassez donc vos pêches.» Dans la rue,
j'entendais les enfants des écoles dire en me montrant du doigt:
145 «Regardez! C'est le monsieur aux pêches!»

    Huit jours après, j'ai quitté la banque et la ville. Ma femme
et moi, nous nous sommes installés à la campagne, chez
un vieil oncle qui avait une grande ferme. Je ne connaissais rien
aux travaux des champs,° mais avec l'aide de mon oncle,
150 j'ai vite appris. Quand celui-ci est mort, j'ai hérité de la ferme.
C'est comme ça que je suis devenu cultivateur!

    Tiens, si tu es libre dimanche prochain, viens donc
me rendre visite. Nous déjeunerons ensemble.

Mots utiles	
hériter de	to inherit
s'installer	to settle
montrer du doigt	to point at
se moquer de	to laugh at, to make fun of
ramasser	to pick up
traverser	to go across, to cross
justement	precisely at that moment

valser = danser la valse *(waltz)* **exécutent une ronde** = dansent dans un
cercle **coiffer** = mettre sur la tête **ébahis** *open-mouthed*
sous terre *underground* **balbutiai** *mumbled* **courait** = circulait dans
malicieux *inclined to tease* **murmuraient** *would say in a low voice*
travaux des champs *farm work*

Avez-vous compris?

1. De quelle façon le larcin de Vital Herbelot a-t-il
été découvert?
2. Quelle a été la réaction des autres invités?
3. Quelle a été la réaction de ses collègues
le lendemain?
4. Qu'est-ce qu'il a décidé de faire à la suite
de l'incident?

Et vous?

Qu'est-ce que vous auriez fait si vous aviez été à
la place de Vital Herbelot? Expliquez pourquoi.

- J'aurais présenté mes excuses à mon patron
et j'aurais gardé mon poste.
- J'aurais fait un procès *(filed a suit)* à mes
collègues de bureau pour harcèlement
professionnel.
- J'aurais quitté la ville et j'aurais cherché un
travail similaire dans une autre ville.
- J'aurais fait comme Vital Herbelot.
- J'aurais fait quelque chose d'autre.
Expliquez quoi.

Mots utiles

un verger	orchard
un pêcher	peach tree
cueillir *	to pick
sourire *	to smile
d'ailleurs	besides
en souvenir de	in memory of

5

Intrigué par l'histoire de mon ancien camarade de lycée, j'ai accepté son invitation. Le dimanche suivant, je suis donc allé chez lui. Là, j'ai fait la connaissance de sa femme, toujours jolie à quarante-cinq ans, et de leurs magnifiques enfants. Nous avons fait un excellent déjeuner, accompagné d'un agréable vin blanc que mon ami faisait lui-même.

Après le déjeuner, il m'a proposé de faire un tour de la ferme. Il était particulièrement fier de son verger. Alors que j'admirais particulièrement un pêcher chargé de fruits splendides, il m'a dit:

— Celui-là, je l'ai planté en souvenir de l'histoire que je t'ai racontée! J'ai eu de la chance. Sans cette histoire absurde, je serais resté un bureaucrate toute ma vie. D'accord, j'aurais peut-être plus d'argent, mais je ne serais pas plus heureux. D'ailleurs, comment être plus heureux? J'ai tout pour moi.

Puis, il a cueilli deux énormes pêches et il me les donna en souriant:

— Tu verras! Ce sera les meilleures pêches que tu aies jamais mangées!

chargé de *laden with*   **travaux des champs** *farm work*

Avez-vous compris?

1. Quelle est l'atmosphère générale à la ferme de Vital Herbelot?
2. Qu'est-ce que Vital Herbelot pense de son sort *(fate)*?

À votre avis

Est-ce que Vital Herbelot a pris la meilleure décision possible? Expliquez pourquoi.

APRÈS LA LECTURE

EXPRESSION ORALE

■ La morale de l'histoire

L'histoire des pêches peut avoir plusieurs morales. Choisissez l'une des morales suivantes (ou bien, créez votre propre morale) et expliquez pourquoi elle correspond le mieux à l'histoire.

• L'argent ne fait pas le bonheur.

• Les petits incidents peuvent avoir des conséquences importantes.
• Il vaut mieux être pauvre que ridicule.
• Le crime ne paie pas.
• Il ne faut jamais écouter les mauvais conseils.
• Le ridicule tue.
• Les gens trop ambitieux sont toujours punis.

■ Débat

Avec votre partenaire, débattez les avantages et les inconvénients de la vie en ville et à la campagne, en fonction de l'histoire que vous avez lue. Chacun va choisir une opinion différente.

■ Situations

Avec votre partenaire, choisissez l'une des situations suivantes. Composez le dialogue correspondant et jouez-le en classe.

1 Détails

Quand elle voit rentrer son mari le soir de la réception, Madame Herbelot comprend que quelque chose d'extraordinaire s'est passé. Elle veut avoir des détails.

Rôles: Monsieur et Madame Herbelot

2 À la fête

Une personne qui a assisté à la fête raconte l'histoire des pêches à un(e) voisin(e). Ce(tte) voisin(e) pose beaucoup de questions. La personne qui a été à la fête a tendance à exagérer un peu pour faire plus d'effet.

Rôles: la personne qui a été à la réception et son(sa) voisin(e)

3 Une décision

Le jour après l'incident, Vital Herbelot explique à sa femme ce qui s'est passé au bureau et dans la rue. Ils discutent de ce qu'ils doivent faire pour éviter *(to avoid)* ces problèmes. Ils prennent une décision.

Rôles: Monsieur et Madame Herbelot

4 Vingt ans après

Vingt ans après l'incident, l'un des enfants de Vital Herbelot apprend que son père a été cadre *(executive)* dans une banque. Il veut connaître le passé de son père.

Rôles: Monsieur Herbelot et son fils (sa fille)

5 Ville ou campagne ?

Après la promenade dans la ferme, le camarade de lycée de Vital Herbelot explique à son ami que la vie en ville a beaucoup d'avantages aussi. Vital Herbelot n'est pas d'accord.

Rôles: Vital Herbelot et son camarade de lycée

EXPRESSION ECRITE

■ «La Belle époque»

Relisez le texte et faites une liste des détails qui indiquent que cette histoire se passe il y a cent ans.

■ Lettre à un(e) ami(e)

Imaginez que vous êtes dans la situation de Vital Herbelot. Après avoir terminé vos études, vous avez trouvé un bon poste dans une banque (ou une autre sorte de travail). Vous avez reçu plusieurs promotions et vous gagnez très bien votre vie. Un jour, cependant, vous réalisez que cette existence ne correspond pas à ce que vous voulez vraiment faire.

Écrivez une lettre à un(e) ami(e). Dans cette lettre, informez-le(la) de votre décision de quitter votre travail, expliquez pourquoi et dites ce que vous allez faire.

■ Sujets de composition

1. Une situation embarrassante.
Décrivez une situation embarrassante, réelle ou imaginaire, dans laquelle une personne que vous connaissez s'est trouvée.

2. Un incident
Décrivez une situation, réelle ou imaginaire, dans laquelle un petit incident a eu des conséquences très importantes pour vous ou pour une personne que vous connaissez.

LES ANTILLES FRANCOPHONES

■*Un peu d'histoire*■

■ Les dates

■ Les événements

-1492-1502

Christophe Colomb fait plusieurs voyages en Amérique. Au cours de° ces voyages, il «découvre» plusieurs îles qui seront plus tard occupées par les Français: Hispaniola (1492), la Guadeloupe (1493), la Martinique (1502). À l'époque de Christophe Colomb, ces îles étaient habitées depuis des siècles par différents groupes d'«Indiens» — nom donné par Christophe Colomb aux populations caraïbes. Ces Indiens sont rapidement décimés° par les maladies et les mauvais traitements des Européens.

-1635

Les premiers colons° français arrivent à la Martinique et à la Guadeloupe. Peu après, ils font venir° de force des Africains pour travailler comme esclaves° dans leurs plantations.

-vers 1640

L'île de la Tortue,° au nord-ouest d'Hispaniola, sert de base à des pirates de toutes nationalités. Des colons français s'installent à Saint-Domingue, la partie ouest d'Hispaniola.

-1697

Saint-Domingue (Haïti) devient officiellement une colonie française.

-1763

La France perd ses colonies continentales d'Amérique (le Canada, la Louisiane), mais elle garde ses îles des Antilles.

-1791

Les Africains de Saint-Domingue se révoltent contre les Français. Toussaint Louverture devient l'un des chefs de cette révolte.

-1794

La Révolution française déclare l'abolition de l'esclavage dans toutes ses colonies.

-1802

L'esclavage est rétabli par Napoléon, ce qui provoque une nouvelle insurrection en Haïti. Napoléon envoie ses troupes pour mater° cette insurrection.

-1804

Après la victoire des Africains révoltés sur les troupes françaises, Saint-Domingue devient un pays indépendant et prend le nom d'Haïti. Les Français quittent Haïti, mais le français reste la langue officielle du pays.

-1848

L'esclavage est définitivement aboli dans les colonies françaises. Les habitants de la Martinique et de la Guadeloupe deviennent des citoyens° français à part entière.°

-1902

L'éruption de la montagne Pelée à la Martinique fait plus de 30 000 morts.

-1946

La Martinique et la Guadeloupe deviennent des départements d'outre-mer.°

-1990

Jean-Bertrand Aristide est élu démocratiquement Président de la République haïtienne. Quelques mois après, un coup d'État militaire l'oblige à s'exiler aux États-Unis.

-1994

La démocratie est rétablie avec l'aide du gouvernement américain.

-2002

L'euro devient la monnaie officielle en Martinique et Guadeloupe.

au cours de = pendant **décimés** *killed* **colons** *settlers* **ils font venir** = ils amènent **esclaves** *slaves* **tortue** *turtle* **mater** *to put down*
citoyens *citizens* **à part entière** = 100% **outre-mer** *overseas*

La malédiction caraïbe

Nous sommes à la Martinique en 1900. À cette époque, Saint-Pierre est la capitale de l'île. Avec ses distilleries, ses docks, ses magasins, ses banques, c'est un centre économique et commercial très actif. Dans le port, on peut voir des bateaux français, mais aussi des bateaux anglais, des bateaux américains, des bateaux italiens, des bateaux japonais, des bateaux chiliens . . . Sur ces bateaux, les marins chargent° le sucre, le rhum et les produits tropicaux de l'île.

Saint-Pierre est aussi une ville artistique et culturelle. Le dimanche, les gens vont au concert ou au théâtre. Il y a, en effet, un théâtre, le seul théâtre de toutes les Antilles. Saint-Pierre mérite bien son nom de «Paris des Antilles».

En réalité, Saint-Pierre est une ville en danger. La ville est située au pied d'un volcan, la montagne Pelée. Le 8 mai 1902, à sept heures cinquante du matin, la montagne Pelée explose! À huit heures, la ville est totalement dévastée. La cathédrale, le théâtre, le jardin botanique, les monuments, les maisons sont maintenant un immense désert de ruines. En moins de cinq minutes, toute la population de Saint-Pierre a péri.° Il y a 30 000 victimes . . . et un survivant. Ce survivant est un prisonnier. Ironiquement, les murs de la prison l'ont protégé contre la violence de l'explosion.

L'explosion de la montagne Pelée est une des grandes catastrophes dans l'histoire de l'humanité. Cette catastrophe a été annoncée dans une vieille légende caraïbe. Les Indiens caraïbes sont les premiers habitants de la Martinique. Quand les Français arrivent en 1635, ils veulent faire des Caraïbes leurs esclaves. Les Caraïbes résistent, mais ils sont finalement battus.° Courageusement, ils préfèrent la mort à l'esclavage.

Avant de mourir, le dernier chef caraïbe donne sa malédiction° aux Français:

> «*Aujourd'hui, vous êtes les plus forts,*
> *mais demain*
> *la montagne de feu va nous venger.*»°

La «montagne de feu», c'est bien sûr la montagne Pelée. Le 8 mai 1902, la malédiction caraïbe s'est réalisée!

---

chargent *load* **péri** *perished, died* **battus** *beaten* **malédiction** *curse* **venger** *to avenge*

▪ *Deux Martiniquais célèbres* ▪

■ L'impératrice Joséphine (1763-1814)

Joséphine Tascher de la Pagerie est née à la Martinique dans la plantation de ses parents. Un jour, quand elle était petite, sa gouvernante° noire lui dit: «Un jour, tu gouverneras la France.» Joséphine évidemment ne croit pas cette prédiction extraordinaire. Elle grandit° et devient une jeune fille très belle et très élégante. À seize ans, elle épouse un jeune officier noble, Alexandre de Beauharnais, mais celui-ci est guillotiné pendant la Révolution. Joséphine elle-même est emprisonnée et échappe de peu° à la mort.

L'impératrice Joséphine

Peu de temps après, Joséphine rencontre Napoléon qui tombe éperdument° amoureux d'elle. Ils se marient en 1796. Quand Napoléon devient empereur en 1804, Joséphine devient impératrice,° réalisant ainsi la prédiction de sa gouvernante. Joséphine et Napoléon n'ont pas d'enfant. Napoléon veut avoir un fils pour assurer la succession de son trône. Il divorce et se remarie avec une princesse autrichienne.° Cependant, Napoléon reste très ami avec Joséphine qui, pour les Français, continue d'être la véritable° impératrice.

Aimé Césaire, poète et homme politique

■ Aimé Césaire (1913-   ): Poète et homme politique

Originaire de la Martinique, **Aimé Césaire** va à Paris pour faire ses études universitaires. Là, il rencontre d'autres étudiants noirs avec qui il fonde un journal intitulé *L'Étudiant noir*. C'est dans ce journal qu'il définit la notion de **négritude**. Pour exprimer la valeur de la personnalité noire, Césaire choisit la poésie. En 1939, il écrit un livre de poèmes intitulé *Cahier d'un retour au pays natal*. Césaire est aussi un homme d'action et, pour lui, l'action, c'est la politique. Il rentre à la Martinique où il fonde un parti, *le Parti Progressiste Martiniquais*. Il devient maire° de Fort-de-France. Élu° député° de la Martinique, il défend les intérêts des habitants de son île.

■ Qu'est-ce que la négritude?

La négritude est un mouvement littéraire, philosophique et politique, né à Paris dans les années 1930. Les fondateurs de ce mouvement étaient des étudiants noirs, venus de différentes colonies françaises: Aimé Césaire (Martinique), Léon Damas (Guyane française), Léopold Senghor (Sénégal).

En quête de° leur identité, ces écrivains redécouvrent leurs racines° africaines qu'ils veulent valoriser.° La négritude est la reconnaissance d'une identité noire spécifique. Les Noirs ont leur personnalité, leur culture, leur système de valeurs, leur façon de percevoir et de comprendre l'univers. Ils doivent préserver et être fiers de cette identité spécifique liée° à l'Afrique, terre° de leurs ancêtres communs.

> *«La négritude est la conscience d'être noir, simple reconnaissance d'un fait, qui implique acceptation, prise en charge de son destin de noir, de son histoire et de sa culture.»*
>
> — *Aimé Césaire*

---

gouvernante *governess*   **grandit** = devient grande   **échappe de peu** *narrowly escapes*   **éperdument** = passionnément
impératrice = la femme de l'empereur   **autrichienne** *Austrian*   **véritable** = réelle   **maire** *mayor*   **élu** *elected*   **député** *congressman*
en quête de *in search of*   **racines** *roots*   **valoriser** *to emphasize the value of*   **liée** *linked*   **terre** *land*

Pour saluer le Tiers-Monde

Dans ce poème, écrit en 1960, Aimé Césaire, de son île de la Martinique, salue les pays d'Afrique qui viennent de gagner leur indépendance. Ce poème est dédié à son ami, Léopold Senghor, président du Sénégal.

La Guinée

Madagascar

Le Cameroun

>   Ah!
> mon demi-sommeil d'île si trouble
> sur la mer!
>
> Et voici de tous les points du péril
> l'histoire qui me fait le signe° que
> j'attendais.
>
> Je vois pousser° des nations.
> Vertes et rouges*, je vous salue,
> bannières, gorges° du vent ancien,
> Mali, Guinée, Ghana
> et je vous vois, hommes,
> point maladroits° sous ce soleil nouveau!
>
> Écoutez:
>   de mon île lointaine°
>   de mon île veilleuse°
> je vous dis Hoo!
>   Et vos voix me répondent
>   et ce qu'elles disent signifie:
> «Il y fait clair.» Et c'est vrai:
> même à travers orage et nuit
> pour nous, il y fait clair.

> Vois:
>   l'Afrique n'est plus
>   au diamant du malheur
>   un noir coeur qui se strie;°
>
> notre Afrique est une main hors du ceste,°
> c'est une main droite, la paume° devant
> et les doigts bien serrés;°
>
> c'est une main tuméfiée°,
> une blessée-main-ouverte,
> tendue°,
>   brunes, jaunes, blanches,
> à toutes mains, à toutes les mains blessées
> du monde.

* Les drapeaux des pays africains de Mali, de Guinée et de Ghana ont les couleurs vertes, rouges et jaunes

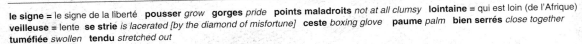

le signe = le signe de la liberté **pousser** *grow* **gorges** *pride* **points maladroits** *not at all clumsy* **lointaine** = qui est loin (de l'Afrique)
veilleuse = lente **se strie** *is lacerated [by the diamond of misfortune]* **ceste** *boxing glove* **paume** *palm* **bien serrés** *close together*
tuméfiée *swollen* **tendu** *stretched out*

▪ *Haïti* ▪

■ *Un champion de la liberté: Toussaint Louverture (1743-1803)*

Haïti est une nation indépendante depuis près de 200 ans.
Le héros de l'indépendance haïtienne s'appelle Toussaint Louverture.
Voici l'histoire de ce grand champion de la liberté.

Cette histoire commence à la fin du 18e siècle. La partie occidentale° d'Haïti s'appelait alors Saint-Domingue. C'était une colonie française où il y avait 20 000 Français et 500 000 Africains qui travaillaient très dur comme esclaves dans les plantations des Français.

En 1789, ces esclaves ont eu un grand espoir.°Une révolution libérale venait d'éclater en France. Est-ce que cette révolution allait émanciper les Noirs? En principe, oui. Les révolutionnaires français ont décidé d'abolir l'esclavage dans les colonies. Malheureusement, Saint-Domingue était loin de Paris et les Français de l'île ont refusé de libérer leurs esclaves. Pour les Africains, il y avait une seule° solution: la révolte. En 1791, les Africains de Saint-Domingue sont entrés en rébellion contre leurs maîtres.

Trois ans plus tard, en 1794, les Anglais, qui étaient en guerre contre la France, ont voulu occuper Saint-Domingue. Pour les Français, la situation était extrêmement grave. Le gouverneur de Saint-Domingue a décidé alors de rencontrer le chef des esclaves révoltés. Ce chef était Toussaint Louverture. Il avait 4 000 hommes sous ses ordres. Il a proposé au gouverneur un marché:° «Garantissez la liberté des Noirs et mes troupes vont combattre avec vous contre les Anglais.» Le gouverneur n'avait pas le choix. Il a accepté.

Quelques semaines après, Toussaint Louverture, l'ancien esclave, a été nommé commandant. C'était un brillant stratège. Ses troupes ont chassé les Anglais de Saint-Domingue. En juillet 1795, Toussaint Louverture a été nommé général de brigade et vice-gouverneur de Saint-Domingue. En réalité, c'était maintenant lui le chef de l'île.

Avec l'émancipation des esclaves, Toussaint Louverture avait réalisé sa première ambition. Cependant, il avait une autre ambition: obtenir l'indépendance de Saint-Domingue. Oui, mais comment? Il fallait d'abord organiser le pays. Toussaint Louverture a créé une administration moderne. Il a ouvert des écoles. Il a développé le commerce. S'il a réussi dans ses projets, c'est parce que c'était un homme juste. Il ne faisait pas de distinction entre les anciens maîtres blancs et les anciens esclaves noirs. Ainsi, il a pu mobiliser tous les talents. Les résultats de cette politique ont été immédiats. En 1800, Saint-Domingue était un pays riche et prospère. Économiquement, c'était un pays indépendant.

Toussaint Louverture, un champion de la liberté.

Administrativement, cependant, Saint-Domingue était toujours une colonie française. La France, à ce moment-là, était gouvernée par Napoléon Bonaparte. Napoléon était un général brillant mais très autoritaire. Il n'aimait pas l'indépendance de Toussaint Louverture. Pire,° il a décidé de rétablir l'esclavage à Saint-Domingue. Pour cela, il a préparé une formidable expédition. Le premier février 1802, 22 000 soldats français sont arrivés dans l'île. C'était la guerre! La guerre d'indépendance a mal commencé pour les Noirs. Leur chef, Toussaint Louverture a été capturé par traîtrise.° Déporté en France, il est mort après dix mois de captivité.

La mort de Toussaint Louverture a encouragé la résistance des Noirs. Ceux-ci ont finalement battu l'armée française. Le premier janvier 1804, Saint-Domingue est devenue une nation indépendante et a pris le nom d'Haïti.

---

occidentale *western* **espoir** *hope* **une seule** *only one* **un marché** *a deal* **pire** *worse* **traîtrise** *treachery*

Pour Haïti

René Depestre est né en Haïti en 1926. À l'âge de vingt ans, il a été exilé de son pays à cause de ses activités politiques. Il habite actuellement° à Paris. Depestre est un poète engagé° qui dénonce l'oppression et l'injustice. Dans ce poème, il évoque sa terre° natale qu'il a quittée il y a longtemps, mais à laquelle il pense sans cesse.°

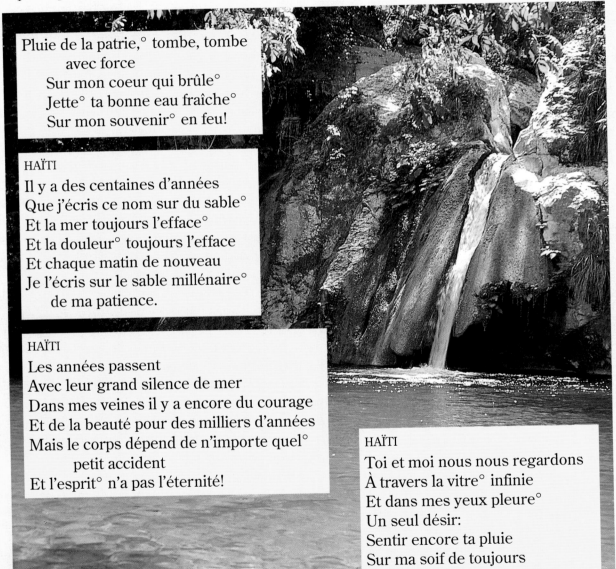

Pluie de la patrie,° tombe, tombe
    avec force
  Sur mon coeur qui brûle°
  Jette° ta bonne eau fraîche°
  Sur mon souvenir° en feu!

HAÏTI

Il y a des centaines d'années
Que j'écris ce nom sur du sable°
Et la mer toujours l'efface°
Et la douleur° toujours l'efface
Et chaque matin de nouveau
Je l'écris sur le sable millénaire°
    de ma patience.

HAÏTI

Les années passent
Avec leur grand silence de mer
Dans mes veines il y a encore du courage
Et de la beauté pour des milliers d'années
Mais le corps dépend de n'importe quel°
    petit accident
Et l'esprit° n'a pas l'éternité!

HAÏTI

Toi et moi nous nous regardons
À travers la vitre° infinie
Et dans mes yeux pleure°
Un seul désir:
Sentir encore ta pluie
Sur ma soif de toujours
Sur ma peine de toujours!

René Depestre, *Journal d'un animal marin* (Paris, Seghers, 1964)

---

actuellement = à présent **engagé** *politically active* **terre** *land* **sans cesse** *unceasingly* **patrie** *native land (= Haïti)* **brûle** *is burning* **jette** *throw*
fraîche *cool* **souvenir** *memory* **sable** *sand* **efface** *erases* **douleur** *pain, suffering* **millénaire** = qui a mille ans **n'importe quel** *any* **esprit** *soul, spirit*
vitre *glass* **pleure** *is crying*

■ *En Haïti, l'art, c'est la vie*

Tous les Haïtiens, ou presque, ont une âme° d'artiste. En Haïti,
l'art est partout:° sur les murs, sur les devantures des magasins,° sur les volets° des
maisons, dans les églises, sur les autobus, sur les camions° ou sur les voitures. Et
maintenant, il se trouve aussi dans les collections privées et dans les musées.

L'art haïtien est avant tout un art populaire: il est issu du peuple et il est fait pour le peuple. À la différence des artistes européens ou américains, les artistes haïtiens n'ont généralement pas reçu de formation technique dans des écoles d'art spécialisées. Ils ont appris eux-mêmes à peindre.° Leur style, souvent appelé «style naïf», est caractérisé par un dessin° relativement simple, l'absence de perspective et l'usage d'une palette aux couleurs chaudes et vibrantes.

Les sources de l'art haïtien sont intérieures et personnelles: c'est l'environnement immédiat de l'artiste, la nature, la culture, la religion et les croyances° d'un peuple aux profondes racines° africaines. Les sujets représentés expriment la vie et l'âme de ce peuple. Ce sont souvent des scènes de la vie quotidienne, la ville avec ses gens aux vêtements multicolores ou la campagne haïtienne avec sa végétation luxuriante, parfois des cérémonies ou des sujets religieux, ou des scènes historiques.

C'est un Américain, DeWitt Peters, qui a fait découvrir au monde les merveilles de l'art haïtien. Peters était venu en Haïti au début° des années 1940 pour enseigner° l'anglais. Lui-même peintre, il a tout de suite° été séduit° par l'art simple et coloré des peintres haïtiens. Avec l'aide des gouvernements haïtien et américain, il a ouvert un Centre d'Art où étaient exposées les oeuvres° des meilleurs peintres haïtiens. L'existence de ce centre a encouragé de nombreuses vocations d'artistes. Autrefois méconnu,° l'art haïtien est aujourd'hui apprécié par un nombre croissant° d'amateurs° un peu partout dans le monde.

J.M. Obin «*La Bataille de Vertières*»

Salnave Philippe-Auguste «*Les crocodiles*»

J.M. Obin est spécialiste de scènes historiques. Ce tableau représente la dernière bataille de la guerre d'indépendance haïtienne qui a eu lieu le 13 novembre 1803 à Vertières. Au cours de cette bataille décisive, l'armée des anciens esclaves, commandée par le général Dessalines (au centre), met en fuite l'armée française (à droite). Quelques jours plus tard, l'armistice est déclaré. Le premier janvier 1804, Haïti devient une nation indépendante.

Avocat de profession, **Salnave Philippe-Auguste** s'est consacré à plein temps à la peinture à l'âge de 51 ans. Dans un style délicat et symbolique, il peint des scènes exotiques remplies d'animaux sauvages. Ici il a choisi comme sujet des crocodiles qu'on trouve encore dans les régions marécageuses° et reculées° d'Haïti. Ces crocodiles semblent protéger des fleurs aquatiques, symboles de la liberté chèrement acquise par les Haïtiens en 1804.

âme *soul* **partout** *everywhere* **devantures des magasins** *storefronts* **volets** *shutters* **camions** *trucks* **peindre** *to paint* **dessin** *design* **croyances** *beliefs* **racines** *roots* **début** *beginning* **enseigner** *to teach* **tout de suite** = *immédiatement* **séduit** *attracted, seduced* **oeuvres** *works* **méconnu** = *peu connu* **croissant** *increasing* **amateurs** *art-lovers* **marécageuses** *swampy* **reculées** *remote*

Préfète Duffaut *«Village magique»*

Préfète Duffaut est l'un des peintres haïtiens les plus célèbres. Il n'avait jamais vu d'oeuvres artistiques quand il a commencé à peindre vers l'âge de 20 ans. Dans un style tout à fait personnel, il aime peindre des villages imaginaires, mais très détaillés, avec des rues en zigzag qui s'accrochent aux flancs des montagnes. La présence de montagnes caractérise les tableaux de Duffaut et rappelle l'origine du nom d'Haïti qui, en langue arawak, signifie «pays de montagnes».

Hector Hyppolite, *«Agoué et son consort»*

Hector Hyppolite, l'un des premiers peintres exposés au Centre d'Art, était aussi un *houngan*, c'est-à-dire un prêtre vaudou. Dans ce tableau, Hyppolite a peint Agoué, loa de la mer, symbolisée ici par une ancre marine, et son consort.

* Pour une définition de l'animisme, voir page 375.

Dans ce tableau, **Dieuseul Paul** représente des *loas*, esprits bénéfiques° ou maléfiques° de la religion vaudou. Cette religion populaire d'Haïti a inspiré beaucoup d'autres artistes haïtiens. Originaire du Bénin en Afrique, le vaudou intègre les croyances et rituels des religions animistes* africaines avec certains éléments de la religion catholique. Les pratiquants du vaudou vénèrent un grand nombre de dieux et

Dieuseul Paul *«Loas»*

de loas représentant les forces visibles et invisibles du monde qui nous entoure. Chaque pratiquant a son propre° loa.

Pauleus Vital *«Paysage de Sables-Cabaret»*

Comme son demi-frère Préfète Duffaut, **Pauleus Vital** aime peindre les paysages de montagnes, mais d'une façon réaliste et précise. Dans ce tableau, l'artiste représente le travail quotidien des gens de la campagne. On peut remarquer la régularité des champs et la luxuriance de la végétation haïtienne, rendue encore plus intense par les couleurs brillantes utilisées par l'artiste.

---

bénéfiques = qui font du bien   **maléfiques** = qui font du mal   **propre** *own*

Rue Cases-nègres est un film entièrement martiniquais. Réalisé par **Euzhan Palcy**, une cinéaste martiniquaise, d'après l'oeuvre° de l'écrivain martiniquais **Joseph Zobe**l, il est joué par des acteurs martiniquais, sur une musique de biguine martiniquaise.

L'action du film se passe en 1930 dans une Martinique bien différente de la Martinique d'aujourd'hui. Les différentes scènes sont reliées° entre elles par la présence d'un jeune garçon d'une douzaine d'années, **José Hassam**, un orphelin° élevé° par sa grand-mère, **M'man-Tine** (Grand-maman Amantine). Tous deux habitent rue Cases-Nègres, une rue pauvre d'un petit village de Martinique.

Les conditions de vie sont difficiles. Tout le monde doit travailler très dur° dans les champs de canne à sucre pour ne gagner presque rien. Pour échapper° à cette misère, il n'y a qu'une solution: l'instruction.°

Le jeune José a plusieurs mentors. D'abord, M'man-Tine, la vieille grand-mère pieuse,° qui va tout faire pour que son petit-fils aille à l'école. Il y a aussi le vieux **Médouze**, en quelque sorte le père spirituel de José. Médouze a passé toute sa vie au travail et maintenant son corps est usé° et brisé°. Il rêve° de l'Afrique lointaine, pays des ancêtres où il voudrait un jour retourner. Il raconte à José l'histoire du peuple: le départ forcé d'Afrique, l'esclavage dans les plantations des «Békés»*, l'émancipation qui en réalité n'a pas changé grand-chose, et le travail, le travail, toujours le travail . . . Émerveillé° et attentif, le jeune José écoute le vieillard° évoquer les éléments de la sagesse° africaine: respect de la nature, respect de la vie . . .

Il y a aussi les professeurs de José. Ils ont remarqué l'intelligence du jeune garçon et en sont d'abord surpris. L'un d'eux accuse même José d'avoir triché° à une composition. José est reçu au certificat d'études** et reçoit une bourse° partielle pour aller étudier à Fort-de-France. Malheureusement, la bourse n'est pas suffisante. M'man-Tine est une femme fière et déterminée. Elle a décidé que son petit-fils continuerait ses études, quoi qu'il lui en coûte° à elle. Malgré° son âge, la vieille femme va s'établir° à Fort-de-France où elle travaille comme lingère° pour gagner l'argent des études. L'administration comprend finalement la situation et accorde° une bourse complète à José.

*Pour son film **Rue Cases-Nègres**, la réalisatrice° Euzhan Palcy a reçu le César (Oscar français) du meilleur premier film.*

M'man-Tine peut retourner à son village où elle meurt heureuse d'avoir accompli son rêve.

Cette histoire simple sert de trame° générale au film où se succèdent° une série de petites scènes souvent réalistes, parfois comiques (les rapports entre José et sa tante Madame Léonce), parfois pénibles° (les rapports entre son copain Léopold et le père de celui-ci). Par son décor, le monde qu'Euzhan Palcy nous présente dans son film peut paraître archaïque et lointain.° Les gens qui vivent dans ce monde sont pauvres et simples, mais ils sont honnêtes, droits,° généreux, fiers et avant tout ils sont humains!

---

* «Békés» est un mot créole qui désigne les descendants des anciens colons blancs venus de France pour établir des plantations dans les Antilles.

** Le certificat d'études = un diplôme de fin des études primaires.

---

l'oeuvre = le livre   **reliées** linked   **orphelin** = enfant qui a perdu son père et sa mère   **élevé** raised   **dur** hard   **échapper à** to escape from
l'instruction education   **pieuse** pious   **usé** worn out   **brisé** broken   **rêve** dreams   **émerveillé** amazed   **vieillard** = vieil homme   **sagesse** wisdom
triché cheated   **bourse** scholarship   **quoi qu'il lui en coûte** whatever it may cost her   **malgré** in spite of   **s'établir** to settle   **accorde** = donne
lingère laundry woman   **trame** plot   **se succèdent** follow one another   **pénibles** painful   **lointain** distant   **droits** straightforward   **réalistisatrice** director

■ Quelques scènes du film

Sur cette photo, on peut voir les personnages principaux du film. Au premier plan, le jeune José Hassam en costume et chapeau blancs. Derrière lui, sa grand-mère M'Man Tine. Derrière M'man Tine, on peut remarquer Euzhan Palcy, la réalisatrice du film.

Dans les champs de canne à sucre, les habitants du village travaillent très dur sous l'oeil vigilant d'un contremaître (foreman) à cheval.

José habite avec M'man Tine dans une case très simple. Pendant que sa grand-mère reprise (darns) les vêtements, José s'adonne (devotes himself) à son passe-temps favori: la lecture.

Tous les jours, José va à l'école avec les enfants du village.

José est l'élève le plus brillant de sa classe. Il répond avec intelligence et imagination aux questions de l'instituteur (teacher), Monsieur Roc.

José vient d'être reçu au certificat d'études. Monsieur Roc est très fier de son élève.

José a reçu une bourse partielle pour continuer ses études au lycée. M'man Tine part avec lui pour Fort-de-France.

Les relations personnelles

Thème et Objectifs

Culture
In this unit, you will discover . . .
- what friendship and family life mean to the French
- what young people in France do to help the disadvantaged
- what is involved in planning a wedding in France

Communication
You will learn how . . .
- to talk about friends and acquaintances
- to explain how people get along with one another
- how to congratulate people on their success or comfort them when they are feeling down
- to describe the various phases of the life cycle

Langue
You will learn how . . .
- to talk about how people interact with each other
- to describe people and things in a clear and complete manner

Les amis et la famille

Pour les Français, les rapports humains ont énormément d'importance. L'amitié, par exemple, est considérée comme la valeur la plus importante de l'existence. Elle passe avant le travail, l'argent et même l'amour. Un ami, évidemment, n'est pas n'importe qui.° Ce n'est pas une personne qu'on rencontre un jour et qu'on oublie le lendemain. C'est généralement quelqu'un qu'on connaît depuis très longtemps, souvent depuis l'enfance et avec qui on a beaucoup d'expériences communes.° C'est la personne spéciale à qui on dit tout, avec qui on partage° ses joies et ses peines° et sur qui on peut compter dans les moments les plus difficiles de l'existence. Les vrais amis sont peu nombreux, mais ces amis-là, c'est pour la vie.

Un autre aspect de la vie en France est la solidité des relations familiales. Autrefois, le milieu familial était très vaste et la vie familiale très active. La famille comprenait° non seulement enfants, parents, grands-parents, cousins, tantes et oncles, mais aussi toutes les autres personnes qui avaient une ascendance° commune ou qui étaient alliées par le mariage. On se réunissait assez régulièrement le dimanche, autour d'un grand repas familial, ou plus occasionnellement pour les fêtes de famille: anniversaires, mariages, cérémonies religieuses, etc.

Aujourd'hui, la famille proche se limite au couple, à leurs enfants et aux parents qu'on voit régulièrement. Cette famille est généralement très unie. Parents et enfants s'entendent° bien, même au moment difficile de l'adolescence. D'après une enquête, 77% des adolescents

français considèrent que leurs relations avec leurs parents sont excellentes ou très bonnes. De même, 88% des jeunes de 18 à 24 ans déclarent s'entendre bien avec leurs parents.

Si la vie de famille est moins active qu'autrefois, «l'esprit de famille» est resté intact. La solidarité familiale joue beaucoup dans les différentes phases de l'existence. Les parents font énormément d'efforts et de sacrifices pour assurer une bonne éducation à leurs enfants. Après leurs études, ils continuent à les aider moralement et matériellement. À leur tour, les enfants s'occupent de leurs parents au moment de leur vieillesse.

Pour les Français, la famille, c'est sacré!

---

n'importe qui *just anyone* **communes** *shared, in common* **partage** *shares* **peines** *sorrows* **comprenait** *included* **ascendance** *ancestry*
s'entendent *get along*

Les qualités d'un(e) ami(e)

Nous choisissons nos amis parce qu'ils ont beaucoup de qualités.
Évidemment, certaines qualités sont plus importantes que d'autres.
Parmi les qualités suivantes, choisissez les cinq qui comptent le plus pour vous
et classez-les par ordre d'importance.

- l'intelligence
- l'humour
- le courage

- la patience
- la loyauté
- l'apparence physique
- la bonne humeur

- la franchise
- la sincérité
- l'honnêteté
- ??

- la générosité
- la sensibilité
- la discrétion

et vous?

Comparez votre liste de qualités avec celles de vos camarades de classe.
Vous pouvez aussi établir une liste des préférences de toute la classe.

NOUS ET LES AUTRES

La vie moderne a beaucoup d'avantages. La majorité des gens habitent dans des maisons confortables et modernes, gagnent bien leur vie, et ont des loisirs intéressants. Mais en France, comme ailleurs, il y a aussi beaucoup de gens qui ne profitent pas de ces avantages. Il y a des jeunes qui n'ont pas de travail, des familles qui n'ont pas d'argent et parfois pas d'abri, des personnes âgées qui sont malades et qui n'ont pas de famille pour s'occuper d'elles. Ces personnes aussi font partie de la société, mais la société a tendance à les oublier.

ACCUEIL TRAVAIL

Nous accueillons des personnes en difficulté, à la recherche d'un hébergement, et qui acceptent par leur travail de participer à la vie de la communauté.

Seule source de revenus, il permet de faire face aux besoins de la communauté. Chaque compagnon est appelé à travailler selon ses capacités et ses moyens. Il est ainsi reconnu et revalorisé.

NE JETEZ PAS VOTRE CŒUR
À LA POUBELLE

IL PEUT ENCORE SERVIR.
EMMAÜS

abri shelter

Heureusement, tout le monde n'est pas égoïste. Voici le cas de trois jeunes Français qui ont décidé de «faire quelque chose» pour les autres.

Patrick Esquivel

(15 ans, lycéen)

Dans l'immeuble où j'habite, il y a une vieille dame qui a perdu son mari l'année dernière et qui maintenant vit° toute seule dans son appartement au cinquième étage sans ascenseur. Je fais les courses pour elle une ou deux fois par semaine. Ça l'aide un peu, mais le plus important, c'est quand je passe une heure ou deux à bavarder° avec elle. Je lui parle de ce que je fais au lycée et elle me raconte sa vie. J'apprends des choses fascinantes, et elle ne se sent plus seule.°

Claire Delamotte

(19 ans, étudiante)

Je travaille deux jours par mois aux «Restos° du coeur». C'est une organisation bénévole° qui prépare des repas chauds pour les sans-abri°, les personnes sans ressources et, plus généralement, pour tous ceux qui ont faim. Mon travail varie. Parfois je travaille à la collecte de la nourriture. D'autres fois, je travaille à la cuisine ou bien je sers les repas.

Dans une société qui glorifie l'argent et la réussite, il est important de préserver les vraies valeurs qui n'ont rien à voir° avec celles que nous proposent les médias. Quand je travaille aux «Restos», je suis en contact avec la réalité de la misère humaine et je peux faire quelque chose d'utile. Le problème, c'est que nous avons de plus en plus de clients!

Steevy Gustave

(23 ans, musicien professionnel)

Je suis d'origine martiniquaise, mais maintenant j'habite dans la région parisienne. Dans ma banlieue, il y a beaucoup de problèmes de délinquance juvénile et de drogue. Heureusement, il y a une «Maison des Jeunes» qui attire° pas mal° de monde. J'y travaille souvent comme animateur. Mon but°, c'est de récupérer les jeunes drogués en les intéressant à la musique. Ce n'est pas toujours facile, mais avec de la persévérance et beaucoup d'encouragement, on y arrive.°

- Selon vous, lequel de ces jeunes Français fait la chose la plus utile? Expliquez pourquoi.
- Avez-vous déjà travaillé comme «volontaire»? Décrivez votre expérience.

---

vit / vivre *to live*   **bavarder** *to chat*   **seule** *lonely, alone*   **Restos** = *restaurants*   **bénévole** *charitable*   **sans-abri** *homeless*
rien à voir = *rien à faire*   **attire** *attracts*   **pas mal** = *beaucoup*   **but** = *objectif*
on y arrive *one can do it*

Les amis, les copains et les relations personnelles

— Tiens, voilà Catherine.
— Qui est-ce?
— C'est une copine.
— Tu la connais depuis longtemps?
— Oui, depuis deux ans.
— Est-ce que tu peux me la présenter?
— Oui, volontiers!

Tiens, voilà Catherine.

Qui est-ce?

C'est une copine.

LES PERSONNES QU'ON CONNAÎT

un ami **une amie**	est quelqu'un	qu'on connaît depuis longtemps pour qui on a beaucoup d'affection en qui on a **une confiance** *(trust)* absolue
un copain **une copine**	est quelqu'un	qu'on connaît bien qu'on voit souvent avec qui on fait beaucoup de choses
un camarade **une camarade**	est quelqu'un	avec qui on va en classe
une connaissance	est quelqu'un	qu'on connaît assez bien qu'on voit de temps en temps

1 **Un(e) ami(e) n'est pas n'importe qui** *(A friend is not just anybody)* ————

Quelle est votre définition d'un ami?

- Considérez la liste suivante et faites une liste des cinq caractéristiques les plus importantes. Vous pouvez aussi mentionner d'autres caractéristiques.
- Comparez votre liste avec celle de votre partenaire.

Faites la même chose pour la définition d'une amie.

Un ami Une amie	est quelqu'un . . .

- ■ qui est toujours d'accord avec moi
- ■ qui me comprend
- ■ à qui je peux parler de tout
- ■ qui me dit toujours la vérité
- ■ qui m'aide quand j'ai un problème
- ■ en qui j'ai complète confiance
- ■ pour qui j'ai beaucoup d'admiration
- ■ qui ne me critique jamais

- ■ qui me donne des conseils
- ■ qui me prête de l'argent quand j'en ai besoin
- ■ qui est toujours loyal(e)
- ■ que je respecte
- ■ qui me respecte
- ■ qui me pardonne *(forgives)* toujours
- ■ ??

LES SENTIMENTS

On éprouve . . .   ou au contraire . . .

| **éprouver** to feel |

de l'amitié *(friendship)*
de l'affection
de la sympathie *(instinctive liking)*
de l'admiration
du respect

de l'envie
de la jalousie *(jealousy)*
de l'antipathie
de l'animosité
de l'aversion

L'amitié et l'amour

On | **aime bien** quelqu'un.
    | **a de l'amitié pour** quelqu'un.

On | **tombe amoureux/amoureuse de** quelqu'un.
    | **aime** quelqu'un.
    | **a le coup de foudre pour** quelqu'un.

| **aimer bien** to like |
| **aimer** to love |
| **tomber amoureux de** to fall in love with |
| **avoir le coup de foudre pour** to fall in love with at first sight |

---

2 **Mes sentiments**

Choisissez deux des personnes suivantes et décrivez quel(s) sentiment(s) vous éprouvez pour chaque personne. Comparez vos sentiments avec ceux de votre partenaire.

Frankenstein   Monsieur Richard   Juliette   Jérôme

Patricia   Claire   Le comte Dracula   Pierre

LES RELATIONS PERSONNELLES

— Qu'est-ce que tu fais samedi?
— Je sors avec une copine.
— Tu t'entends bien avec elle?
— Oui, en général je m'entends bien avec elle.
   Parfois on se dispute, mais après on se réconcilie.

Qu'est-ce que tu fais samedi?

Je sors avec une copine.

Les rapports / Les relations

On peut . . .

avoir | de **bons rapports** avec | quelqu'un.
       | de **bonnes relations** avec

avoir | de **mauvais rapports** avec | quelqu'un.
       | de **mauvaises relations** avec

s'entendre bien avec (to get along with)
être d'accord avec (to agree with)

se réconcilier avec (to make up with)

avoir confiance en (to trust)

s'entendre mal avec
ne pas s'entendre avec

se disputer (to have an argument)
avoir une dispute avec
se quereller (to have a fight)
se fâcher avec (to be upset at)
rompre avec (to break up with)

COMMENT FÉLICITER QUELQU'UN

Bravo!
Quelle bonne nouvelle!

Je suis content(e) | pour toi.
Je me réjouis

féliciter to congratulate
se réjouir to be happy

Félicitations! (Congratulations!)
Je te félicite.

COMMENT PLAINDRE ET CONSOLER QUELQU'UN

plaindre* to feel sorry for

Mon pauvre! Ma pauvre!
Quel dommage!
Quelle malchance (bad luck)!
Tu n'as pas de chance.

Je te plains.
Je suis désolé(e) pour toi.
Ne t'en fais pas! (Don't worry! Don't feel bad!)
Ça s'arrangera! (Things will be okay!
   Everything will work out all right!)

3 Mon copain et moi

Décrivez vos relations avec votre copain (copine).
Comparez vos réponses avec celles de votre partenaire.

1. J'ai une confiance – – – en lui/elle.
   - complète
   - presque totale
   - assez limitée
   - ??

2. En général, je m'entends – – –
   avec lui/elle.
   - parfaitement
   - très bien
   - relativement bien
   - ??

3. Quand nous nous querellons, c'est
   d'habitude (*usually*) moi qui . . .
   - ai raison
   - gagne
   - cède (*gives in*) le premier/la
     première
   - ??

4. Quand nous avons une dispute
   sérieuse, nous nous réconcilions . . .
   - immédiatement
   - au bout (*after*) d'une heure
   - au bout d'une semaine
   - ??

5. Quand nous nous disputons,
   c'est à cause de . . .
   - ses copains
   - sa famille
   - mes copains
   - ??

6. En ce moment, nos rapports sont . . .
   - excellents
   - relativement bons
   - tendus (*tense*)
   - ??

4 Mes rapports personnels

Choisissez l'une des personnes suivantes et décrivez vos rapports avec cette personne.

mon meilleur ami	mon petit/grand frère	mes voisins
ma meilleure amie	ma petite/grande soeur	mon prof de maths
un(e) autre ami(e)	mes cousins	mon prof d'anglais
	un(e) autre membre de ma famille	un autre adulte

▶ **En général je m'entends bien avec ma cousine, mais je ne suis pas tout le temps
d'accord avec elle. De temps en temps je me dispute avec elle. . . .**

5 Ça va?

Choisissez d'être l'une des personnes
suivantes. Votre partenaire va vous demander
si ça va et pourquoi. Décrivez un événement
heureux ou malheureux. Il/elle va vous
féliciter ou exprimer sa sympathie.

▶ — **Ça va?**
— **Non, ça ne va pas.**
— **Qu'est-ce qui t'est arrivé?**
— **Je viens de me fâcher avec ma copine.**
— **Ne t'en fais pas. Ça s'arrangera.**

A. Les verbes réfléchis: sens réciproque

Reflexive verbs may be used to express a RECIPROCAL ACTION. In this case, the reflexive pronouns often correspond to the English expression *each other.* In the examples below, note the form of the verbs in heavy print.

Alain connaît Sophie. Sophie connaît Alain. }	Ils **se connaissent.**	*They **know each other.***
J'écris à ma copine. Ma copine m'écrit. }	Nous **nous écrivons**.	*We **write each other.***
Tu téléphones à Claire. Claire te téléphone. }	Vous **vous téléphonez.**	*You **phone each other**.*

Since a reciprocal action involves two or more people, the subject of a reciprocal verb is always plural: **nous, vous, ils, elles.**

➡ The subject may also be **on** used in the plural sense of **nous**.

> **On se verra** demain. *We **will see each other** tomorrow.*

Ils s'entendent bien.

Oui, mais hier, ils se sont disputés.

❶ Entre amis

Les personnes suivantes sont des amis. Décrivez leurs relations.

▶ Jérôme et moi / se voir souvent
  Nous nous voyons souvent.

1. Marc et Pauline / se téléphoner tous les jours
2. toi et tes amis / s'écrire pendant les vacances
3. Philippe et Cécile / se donner souvent rendez-vous
4. moi et mes copains / se retrouver après les classes
5. toi et François / se rendre visite tous les week-ends
6. toi et tes voisins / s'entendre bien
7. moi et mes cousins / se disputer rarement
8. Caroline et Charlotte / se réconcilier après chaque dispute

Relations personnelles

Informez-vous sur les personnes suivantes et décrivez leurs relations en utilisant les verbes entre parenthèses dans des phrases affirmatives ou négatives.

▶ Jérôme et Alice sont fiancés. (s'aimer?)
   Ils s'aiment.

1. Marc et François sont de bons copains.
   (s'aider? se disputer? se fâcher souvent?)
2. Mes voisins et moi, nous avons de bons rapports.
   (s'entendre? s'inviter? se téléphoner?)
3. Jean-Paul et toi, vous êtes amis mais vous n'habitez pas dans la même ville.
   (se voir souvent? se téléphoner? s'écrire?)
4. Claire et sa cousine ne sont jamais d'accord.
   (se disputer? s'entendre bien? se réconcilier facilement?)
5. Delphine et moi, nous sommes fâchés.
   (se parler? s'entendre mal? se quereller?)

Courrier du coeur

Complétez les lettres à Zoé avec les formes appropriées des verbes suggérés.

(1) s'entendre *(présent)*
(2) se fâcher *(passé composé)*
(3) ne plus se parler *(présent)*
(4) se disputer *(imparfait)*
(5) ne pas se revoir *(passé composé)*

Chère Zoé,

Je sors avec une fille depuis trois mois. En général, nous —— (1) très bien, mais la semaine dernière, il y a eu un drame.

Nous —— (2) parce que je suis arrivé à un rendez-vous avec vingt minutes de retard. Depuis, nous —- (3). Je ne veux pas rompre, mais j'ai peur de faire le premier pas!

Désolé

Cher désolé,

C'est toi qui étais en retard. Alors, si tu veux te réconcilier avec ta copine, c'est à toi de faire le premier pas.

Zoé

Chère Zoé,

L'été dernier, j'ai fait la connaissance d'un garçon avec qui je suis sortie pendant quelques temps. Un jour, j'ai rompu avec lui parce que nous —— (4) tout le temps. Depuis, nous —— (5).

Samedi dernier, j'ai appris, par hasard, qu'il sortait avec ma cousine. Maintenant, je ne peux plus dormir. Je pense sans cesse à lui et je crois que je l'aime toujours!

Nostalgique

Chère Nostalgique,

Tu n'es pas amoureuse, seulement jalouse! Oublie ton copain et cherche quelqu'un de plus compatible avec toi.

Zoé

À votre tour

Maintenant écrivez une lettre à Zoé. Dans cette lettre, vous décrivez un problème que vous avez avec un(e) ami(e) imaginaire. Votre partenaire jouera le rôle de Zoé et vous donnera un conseil.

B. Révision: Les pronoms relatifs **qui** et **que**

When we want to describe people or things, we often use adjectives. We can also use CLAUSES which refer back or relate to the people and things being described (the ANTECEDENTS). Such clauses are called RELATIVE CLAUSES and are introduced by RELATIVE PRONOUNS. Note how the French relative pronouns **qui** and **que** are used to convert two clauses into a single sentence.

J'ai un ami. **Il** habite à Paris.

→ J'ai un ami **qui** habite à Paris.   *I have a friend **who** lives in Paris.*

J'ai un ami. Je **l'**invite souvent.

→ J'ai un ami **que** j'invite souvent.   *I have a friend **whom (that)** I often invite.*

J'ai lu le livre. **Il** était sur la table.

→ J'ai lu le livre **qui** était sur la table.   *I read the book **that** was on the table.*

J'ai lu le livre. Tu **l'**as apporté.

→ J'ai lu le livre **que** tu as apporté.   *I read the book **that** you brought.*

Both **qui** and **que** may refer to people, things, or ideas.
The choice between **qui** and **que** is determined by their function in the sentence.

- **Qui** (*who, that, which*) is the SUBJECT of the verb of the relative clause.
- **Que** (*whom, that, which*) is the DIRECT OBJECT of the verb of the relative clause.

➡ The verb that follows **qui** always agrees with the ANTECEDENT of **qui**.

Est-ce que c'est **vous** **qui** **avez pris** ces photos?

➡ Although the object pronoun *whom, that, which* may be omitted in English, **que** is always expressed in French.

➡ When the verb that follows **que** is in the passé composé, its past participle agrees with the ANTECEDENT of **que**.

J'ai aimé **le film** **que** j'ai **vu** hier.   J'ai téléphoné **aux filles** **que** j'ai **vues** au cinéma.

5 Mes amis

Ces personnes sont vos amis. Présentez-les à vos copains, d'après le modèle.

▶ Juliette (Elle habite à Québec.)
   Je vous présente Juliette. C'est une fille qui habite à Québec.
▶ Marc (Je l'invite souvent.)
   Je vous présente Marc. C'est un garçon que j'invite souvent.

1. Thomas (Je le connais depuis cinq ans.)
2. Nathalie (Elle habite près de chez moi.)
3. Sandrine (Elle va à mon école.)
4. Philippe (Je le vois tous les week-ends.)
5. Claire (Elle est dans ma classe de maths.)
6. Antoine (Il est venu chez moi le week-end dernier.)
7. Bruno (Je l'ai rencontré pendant les vacances.)
8. Delphine (Je l'ai invitée à la boum.)

6 Pauvre Corinne!

Corinne n'a pas de chance. Expliquez pourquoi en complétant
les phrases suivantes avec **qui** ou **que (qu')**.

1. Elle a voulu aller dans un magasin _____ était fermé aujourd'hui.
2. Elle a pris un bus _____ est tombé en panne *(broke down)*.
3. Elle a acheté une montre _____ ne marche pas.
4. Elle n'a pas compris les exercices _____ le professeur a donnés.
5. Elle a vu un film _____ elle a trouvé stupide.
6. Elle a invité à dîner une copine _____ n'est pas venue.
7. Elle a perdu le numéro de téléphone d'un garçon _____ elle
   a rencontré à une boum.
8. Elle a perdu le bracelet _____ son père lui a donné pour son
   anniversaire.

7 Compliments . . . et insultes

Votre ami(e) français(e) — votre partenaire — veut avoir votre opinion sur certaines
choses qu'il/elle a faites. Faites-lui un compliment . . . ou une insulte.

▶ la veste / acheter
   très belle . . . ou moche?
 — **Qu'est-ce que tu penses de la
    veste que j'ai achetée?**
 — **Elle est très belle!
    (Elle est moche!)**

1. les copines / inviter
   sympathiques . . . ou snobs?
2. l'ami / rencontrer
   intelligent . . . ou stupide?
3. le repas / préparer
   délicieux . . . ou infect *(disgusting)*?

4. les photos / prendre
   jolies . . . ou ratées?
5. le poème / écrire
   sublime . . . ou ridicule?
6. l'histoire / raconter
   amusante . . . ou idiote?

C. La construction préposition + pronom relatif

In the examples below, the relative clause is introduced by a preposition **(avec).**
Note the forms of the relative pronouns as they refer to people or things.

Philippe a une copine. Il va souvent au cinéma **avec cette copine.**

→ Philippe a une copine **avec qui** il va souvent au cinéma.
   *Philippe has a friend **with whom** he often goes to the movies.*

Tu as des idées. Je ne suis pas d'accord **avec ces idées.**

→ Tu as des idées **avec lesquelles** je ne suis pas d'accord.
   *You have ideas **with which** I do not agree.*

When relative pronouns are used with prepositions (**avec, pour, sur,** etc.), the constructions are:

PREPOSITION + **qui**	to refer to <u>people</u>
PREPOSITION + **lequel**	to refer to <u>things</u>

➡ **Leque**l agrees with the noun it represents. It has the same forms
   as the corresponding interrogative pronoun:

   lequel   laquelle   lesquels   lesquelles

➡ In French, the preposition (**avec, pour,** etc.) always comes <u>before</u> the relative pronoun.
   (In English, the preposition may come at the end of the sentence.) Compare:

   Tu as des idées **avec lesquelles** je ne suis pas d'accord.
      *You have ideas **with which** I do not agree.*
      *You have ideas **that** I do not agree **with.***

ALLONS PLUS LOIN

The relative pronoun **lequel,** like the interrogative **lequel?,** contracts with **à** and **de.**

Tu as assisté **à ce concert**?   Oui, c'est le concert **auquel** j'ai assisté.

Tu habites **près de ce parc**?   Oui, c'est le parc **près duquel** j'habite.

8 Qu'est-ce qu'on fait avec?

Définissez les choses suivantes en expliquant ce qu'on fait avec.

un ordinateur	• un objet	tondre la pelouse
un sécateur	• une chose	se brosser les dents
une raquette	• un appareil	repasser les chemises
une tondeuse	• une machine	surfer sur l'Internet
un fer	• un produit	couper des fleurs
le dentifrice	• un instrument	jouer au tennis

▶ **Une tondeuse est une machine avec laquelle on tond la pelouse.**

9 Relations personnelles

Décrivez vos relations avec trois personnes de votre choix en utilisant les suggestions suivantes.

quelqu'un	aller souvent chez . . .
un(e) ami(e)	téléphoner souvent à . . .
une personne	avoir beaucoup d'admiration pour . . .
un(e) adulte	pouvoir compter sur . . .
une personne de ma famille	éprouver du respect pour . . .
un professeur	éprouver de l'amitié pour . . .
des gens	avoir confiance en . . .
??	s'entendre bien avec . . .
	s'entendre mal avec . . .
	??

??

▶ **Mon oncle George est une personne de ma famille sur qui je peux compter.**

10 Le job d'Alice

Alice a trouvé un job dans une entreprise d'électronique. Un jour elle montre à un ami l'endroit où elle travaille. Complétez ses phrases.

▶ Voici la compagnie pour **laquelle je travaille.**

1. Voici le laboratoire dans _____.
2. Voici les collègues avec _____.
3. Voici le projet sur _____.
4. Voici l'ordinateur avec _____.
5. Voici les nouvelles machines avec _____.
6. Voici l'ingénieur pour _____.

D. Le pronom relatif **dont**

Note how in the examples below, the relative pronoun **dont** replaces a noun introduced by **de**.

Je ne connais pas la fille. Tu parles **de cette fille**.
→ Je ne connais pas la fille **dont** tu parles.
   *I don't know the girl **(whom, that)** you are talking **about**.*

Je connais le restaurant. Tu parles **de ce restaurant**.
→ Je connais le restaurant **dont** tu parles.
   *I know the restaurant **(that)** you are talking **about**.*

Marc a trouvé le livre. Il avait besoin **de ce livre**.
→ Marc a trouvé le livre **dont** il avait besoin.
   *Marc found the book **(that)** he needed.*

The relative pronoun **dont** replaces

> **de** + NOUN or NOUN PHRASE

Dont is, therefore, often used with verbs and verbal expressions that are followed by **de**:

avoir besoin de	parler de
se souvenir de	faire la connaissance de
avoir envie de	discuter de
s'occuper de	être amoureux de

➡ **Dont** may refer to PEOPLE or THINGS.

➡ Note the word order with **dont**:

> (antecedent) + **dont** + subject + verb . . .

ALLONS PLUS LOIN

Dont is also used to replace **de** + NOUN in sentences where **de** indicates possession or relationship. In this type of construction, **dont** is the equivalent of *whose*.

Voici l'ami.
   La soeur **de cet ami** habite à Paris.

Voici l'ami **dont** la soeur habite à Paris.
*This is the friend **whose** sister lives in Paris.*

Voici l'ami.
   Je t'ai donné l'adresse **de cet ami**.

Voici l'ami **dont** je t'ai donné l'adresse.
*This is the friend **whose** address I gave you.*

---

11 **Tant mieux!**

Décrivez ce que les personnes suivantes ont fait.

▶ Christophe / trouver les livres (Il avait besoin de ces livres.)
   Christophe a trouvé les livres dont il avait besoin.

1. Pauline / acheter les chaussures (Elle avait envie de ces chaussures.)
2. Marc / trouver le magazine (Il avait besoin de ce magazine.)
3. Madame Lavoie / acheter la voiture (Elle avait envie de cette voiture.)
4. Thomas / voir le film (Sa copine lui a parlé de ce film.)
5. Véronique / visiter l'exposition (On a parlé de cette exposition dans le journal.)
6. Bruno / sortir avec la fille (Il a fait la connaissance de cette fille chez Sophie.)
7. Christine / avoir des nouvelles des enfants (Elle s'était occupée de ces enfants pendant les vacances.)
8. Caroline / se marier avec le garçon (Elle était amoureuse de ce garçon.)

12 **Et vous?**

Mentionnez un exemple d'une chose ou d'une personne correspondant aux définitions suivantes. Comparez vos réponses avec celles de votre partenaire.

▶ un objet dont vous avez besoin tous les jours   **Mon stylo (mon peigne, ma brosse à dents, . . .) est un objet dont j'ai besoin tous les jours.**

1. un objet dont vous n'avez pas besoin en ce moment
2. une chose dont vous avez envie
3. un sujet dont vous parlez avec vos amis
4. un sujet dont vous discutez avec vos parents.

5. un événement important dont vous vous souvenez bien
6. une personne dont vous avez fait la connaissance récemment
7. une personne dont vous avez fait la connaissance pendant les vacances

Le mariage
EN FRANCE

*U*n jour, un jeune homme et une jeune fille qui s'aiment, décident de se marier. Ils annoncent la bonne nouvelle° à leurs familles respectives et à leurs amis proches.° Pour célébrer cet événement, il y a parfois une cérémonie assez simple, les fiançailles,° où le jeune homme et la jeune fille promettent° de se marier. Comme symbole de cette promesse, le fiancé offre° une bague — la bague de fiançailles — à sa fiancée.

Le mariage a lieu six mois ou un an plus tard. C'est un événement qui demande beaucoup de préparation. Il faut fixer la date du mariage, organiser la cérémonie, établir la liste des invités, envoyer les invitations, etc.

En principe, pour se marier, un jeune homme doit être âgé de 18 ans minimum et une jeune fille doit avoir 15 ans. En réalité, les Français attendent beaucoup plus longtemps avant de se marier. En moyenne,° les hommes se marient à 28 ans et les femmes à 26 ans. Avant le mariage, les fiancés doivent accomplir un certain nombre de formalités administratives: examen médical, publication des bans° de mariage, etc... S'ils le désirent, ils peuvent aussi établir officiellement un «contrat de mariage» qui détermine la disposition de leurs biens.° Quand ces formalités sont faites, ils peuvent se marier. En général, les gens choisissent de se marier le week-end et en été. (80% des mariages français sont célébrés le samedi. 60% ont lieu de juin à septembre.)

La majorité des Français ont deux mariages: un mariage civil et un mariage religieux. Le mariage civil est obligatoire. Il a lieu à la mairie de la ville où l'on habite. C'est d'habitude une cérémonie assez simple à laquelle assistent seulement le jeune couple, leurs familles proches, leurs témoins° et quelques amis intimes. Pour cette occasion, le maire° porte une écharpe°tricolore,° signe de sa fonction officielle. Il marie les époux,° les félicite° et leur délivre° un document officiel, le «livret° de famille» où seront inscrits° les événements importants de leur vie commune (naissance des enfants, décès°...). Le jeune homme et la jeune fille sont maintenant légalement mariés.

Cinquante-deux pour cent des Français décident d'avoir aussi un mariage religieux. Le mariage religieux a toujours lieu *après* le mariage civil. Il est célébré à l'église (pour les catholiques), au temple (pour les protestants) ou à la synagogue (pour les juifs).

---

nouvelle *news*   **proches** *close*   **fiançailles** *engagement*   **promettent / promettre** *to promise*   **offre / offrir** *to give*   **moyenne** *on the average*
bans = annonce officielle   **biens** *assets*   **témoins** *witnesses*   **maire** *mayor*   **écharpe** *sash*   **tricolore** = bleu-blanc-rouge   **époux** *spouses*
félicite *congratulate*   **délivre** = donne   **livret** *booklet*   **inscrits / inscrire** *to inscribe*   **décès** *death*

C'est généralement une grande cérémonie à laquelle assistent toute la famille et un grand nombre d'invités: amis, voisins, relations, etc. Traditionnellement la mariée porte une longue robe blanche. À la main elle tient° un bouquet de fleurs d'oranger. Sur la tête, elle porte une couronne.° Un voile de dentelle° lui couvre° le visage. Accompagnée de son père, elle avance vers l'autel° où l'attend son fiancé. Pendant la cérémonie, le jeune homme et la jeune fille échangent leurs alliances° en présence de leurs témoins. Après la cérémonie, les jeunes mariés sortent de l'église accompagnés des garçons d'honneur° et des demoiselles d'honneur.° On prend beaucoup de photos. Puis tout le monde va au repas de noces.°

Comme les Français aiment se marier à la campagne, le repas de noces a souvent lieu dans une petite auberge ou dans la maison de campagne des parents de la mariée. C'est un repas très joyeux. On fait des discours.° On porte

des toasts au bonheur des jeunes mariés. On raconte des histoires. On chante des chansons. Et surtout, on mange bien. Au dessert, il y a une «pièce montée», c'est-à-dire un gâteau à l'architecture compliquée, que découpent° les mariés. Après le repas, on danse. Les jeunes mariés restent quelque temps avec les invités, puis ils partent en voyage de noces dans leur voiture décorée de rubans° blancs.

Comment se sont-ils rencontrés?

Autrefois les gens qui se mariaient avaient beaucoup de choses en commun. Ils étaient issus du même milieu social et avaient la même religion. Généralement, ils habitaient dans la même ville ou le même village et souvent ils se connaissaient depuis leur enfance.

Aujourd'hui, le mariage unit de plus en plus de gens qui se sont rencontrés par hasard.° Voici comment les futurs couples se forment:

Sur 100 jeunes mariés, se sont rencontrés ...

- au bal — 18%
- dans un lieu public — 14%
- au travail — 13%
- chez des particuliers° — 10%
- pendant leurs études — 9%
- dans un club ou une association — 8%
- au cours° d'une fête chez des amis — 7%
- à l'occasion d'une sortie ou au spectacle (cinéma, concert, théâtre,. . .) — 5%
- pendant les vacances — 5%
- dans une discothèque — 4%
- par relations de voisinage — 3%
- dans une fête publique — 3%
- par annonces°, agence matrimoniale, Internet — 1%

---

et vous?

DÉFINITIONS

Définissez les mots et les expressions suivants.

- les fiançailles
- les bans
- un contrat de mariage
- une alliance
- un mariage civil
- le livret de famille
- le mariage religieux
- la famille proche
- les témoins
- une écharpe tricolore
- les garçons d'honneur
- les demoiselles d'honneur
- le repas de noces
- une «pièce montée»
- un voyage de noces

DISCUSSION

Avec votre partenaire, faites une liste des similarités et des différences entre un mariage français et un mariage américain.

EXPRESSION ORALE

Imaginez que vous allez vous marier. Préférez-vous avoir un mariage simple ou un mariage formel? Expliquez pourquoi.

EXPRESSION ÉCRITE

Décrivez un mariage (réel ou imaginaire) auquel vous avez assisté.

(Qui étaient les mariés? Où a eu lieu la cérémonie? Combien y avait-il d'invités? Comment était habillés le marié et la mariée? les demoiselles et les garçons d'honneur? Comment s'est déroulé la cérémonie? . . .)

---

tient / tenir *to hold* **couronne** *crown, tiara* **voile de dentelle** *lace veil* **couvre / couvrir** *to cover* **autel** *altar*
alliances *wedding rings* **garçons d'honneur** *ushers* **demoiselles d'honneur** *bridesmaids* **noces** = *mariage* **discours** *speeches*
découpent = *coupent* **rubans** *ribbons* **par hasard** *by chance* **chez des particuliers** *at the home of friends or acquaintances*
au cours de = *pendant* **annonces** *personal ads*

LE FRANÇAIS PRATIQUE

Les phases de la vie

L'ENFANCE · on **naît**
· on **grandit**

naître*	*to be born*
grandir	*to grow up*
développer	*to develop*

LA JEUNESSE
L'ADOLESCENCE · on **développe** sa personnalité
(la vie scolaire) · on **fait des études** | élémentaires
secondaires
universitaires

(la vie sociale) · on **fait connaissance** | d'autres personnes
· on **rencontre**
· on **se fait** des amis

se faire des amis	*to make friends*

L'ÂGE ADULTE
(la vie familiale) · on **rencontre** quelqu'un de spécial
· on **tombe amoureux** de cette personne
· on décide de | **vivre** ensemble
se fiancer
se marier
ou de rester **célibataire** *(single)*

tomber amoureux de	*to fall in love with*
vivre	*to live*
se fiancer	*to get engaged*
se marier	*to get married*

· on **élève** une famille

parfois on | **se sépare**
divorce
et on **se remarie**

élever	*to raise*
se séparer	*to separate*
divorcer	*to get divorced*
se remarier	*to remarry*

(la vie active) · on **choisit** un métier ou une profession
· on **trouve** un job
· on **travaille** dur
· on **gagne** sa vie
· on **obtient** une promotion

gagner sa vie	*to earn a living*
obtenir*	*to get*

LA VIEILLESSE · on **prend** sa retraite
· on **s'occupe** de façons diverses
· on **vieillit**
  parfois on **tombe malade**
· on **meurt**

prendre sa retraite	*to retire*
s'occuper	*to keep busy*
vieillir	*to grow old*
tomber malade	*to get sick*
mourir*	*to die*

RAPPEL!

naître: il/elle est né(e)
mourir: il/elle est mort(e)

1 Mon avenir

Faites une liste de 5 choses que vous voulez accomplir dans votre vie. Classez-les par ordre d'importance. Comparez votre liste avec celle de votre partenaire.

Cinq choses que je voudrais faire dans ma vie
1.
2.
3.
4.
5.

2 Débat

Vous avez décidé de vous marier. Votre partenaire a décidé de rester célibataire (ou vice versa). Chacun va expliquer les raisons et les avantages (et désavantages) de sa décision.

3 Une vie

Catherine parle de son grand-père. Complétez cette description avec le passé composé des verbes de la liste. Soyez logique!

élever	naître
faire la connaissance	prendre sa retraite
faire ses études	tomber amoureux
ne pas gagner	tomber malade
grandir	travailler dur
se marier	trouver un job
mourir	ne pas vieillir

Mon grand-père _____ dans un petit village de la province de Québec où il _____ et où il _____ secondaires. À l'âge de 17 ans, il a immigré aux États-Unis et il _____ dans une usine de textile.

Un jour, il _____ d'une jeune fille, ma grand-mère dont il _____. Ils _____ peu de temps après et ensemble ils _____ une famille de six enfants.

Durant sa vie, mon grand-père _____ beaucoup d'argent. Il _____ après 50 ans de travail dans la même usine. Malheureusement, mon grand-père et ma grand-mère _____ ensemble. Ma grand-mère, en effet, _____ et elle _____ en 1975. Mon grand-père _____ dix ans après, à l'âge de 85 ans.

4 À votre tour

Composez la biographie d'une personne de votre famille (votre grand-père ou votre grand-mère) ou d'une personne âgée imaginaire.

A. Résumé: les pronoms relatifs

Review the use of the relative pronouns in the chart below.

The relative pronoun functions as . . .	The relative pronoun refers to: PEOPLE	THINGS
SUBJECT	**QUI** l'ami **qui** est arrivé	**QUI** la lettre **qui** est arrivée
DIRECT OBJECT	**QUE** la fille **que** tu connais	**QUE** le café **que** tu connais
OBJECT OF A PREPOSITION (other than **de**)	**QUI** la personne **avec qui** je travaille	**LEQUEL** la machine **avec laquelle** je travaille
OBJECT OF THE PREPOSITION **de**	**DONT** le garçon **dont** je te parle	**DONT** le livre **dont** je te parle

1 Photos de vacances

Catherine montre ses photos de vacances à son frère Marc. Jouez les deux rôles en faisant les substitutions suggérées. (Utilisez les pronoms qui conviennent.)

▶ Mélanie / Nous avons rencontré cette fille à la plage.

Tu te souviens de Mélanie?

Non, pas vraiment.

Mais si! C'est la fille que nous avons rencontrée à la plage!

Ah, oui. Je me souviens maintenant.

1. Jean-Paul / Tu jouais au tennis avec ce garçon.
2. Pierre et Jérôme / Ces garçons nous ont invités à une boum.
3. Alice / J'ai dîné chez cette fille un jour.
4. Véronique / Tu as fait la connaissance de cette fille dans un café.
5. La Tulipe noire / Nous passions nos soirées dans cette discothèque.

2 Quel pronom?

Complétez les phrases avec le pronom qui convient.

1. Je n'ai pas trouvé le livre . . .
   ___ j'avais besoin.
   ___ était sur la table.
   dans ___ il y a des photos de Paris.
   ___ j'ai acheté ce matin.

2. Ma cousine va se marier avec un jeune homme . . .
   avec ___ elle est fiancée depuis un an.
   ___ elle connaît depuis deux ans.
   ___ elle a fait la connaissance à la Martinique.
   ___ travaille pour une agence de voyage.

3. Nous allons dîner dans le restaurant . . .
   ___ mon frère m'a recommandé.
   ___ sert des spécialités régionales.
   ___ tout le monde parle.
   devant ___ nous sommes passés ce matin.

4. Je suis sorti avec les amis . . .
   ___ je t'ai parlé.
   ___ m'ont téléphoné ce matin.
   avec ___ je suis allé en vacances.
   ___ j'ai vus le week-end dernier.

3 La légende de Tristan et Yseult

Complétez le texte suivant avec les formes appropriées des pronoms qui conviennent.

Tristan et Yseult est une très vieille légende _(1)_ date du Moyen Âge et _(2)_ on retrouve dans les littératures anglaise, française et allemande de l'époque.

Cette légende relate la tragique histoire de deux jeunes gens, unis par un amour _(3)_ ils ne peuvent pas contrôler. Dans cette légende, le roi Marc va épouser une jeune fille _(4)_ il ne connaît pas mais _(5)_ ses conseillers lui ont parlé. Il envoie Tristan, son neveu en _(6)_ il a toute confiance, chercher cette jeune fille _(7)_ s'appelle Yseult et _(8)_ habite en Irlande. Tristan trouve Yseult et la ramène en Cornouailles°, le pays du roi Marc. Sur le bateau _(9)_ les transporte, Tristan et Yseult boivent par mégarde° une potion _(10)_ un magicien avait préparée pour assurer l'amour éternel entre Marc et Yseult. Sous l'influence de la potion _(11)_ ils ont bue, Tristan et Yseult tombent éperdument° amoureux l'un de l'autre.

À leur retour, le roi Marc, _(12)_ a découvert la vérité, chasse le pauvre Tristan. Des années passent. Tristan a épousé une autre jeune fille _(13)_ il a fait la connaissance dans son exil. En réalité, il ne cesse de penser à la belle Yseult _(14)_ il est resté amoureux. Un jour, il participe à une bataille au cours de _(15)_ il est très grièvement° blessé! Yseult à _(16)_ on a annoncé la nouvelle veut revoir l'homme _(17)_ elle aime toujours. Malheureusement, quand elle arrive chez Tristan, celui-ci est déjà mort. À son tour, Yseult meurt de désespoir. Les deux amants _(18)_ la vie a séparés sont finalement unis par la mort.

Cornouailles *Cornwall (in southwestern England)* **par mégarde** = par accident **éperdument** *madly* **grièvement** = très sérieusement

4 Descriptions

Choisissez l'une des situations suivantes et décrivez la chose ou la personne dont il est question. Pour cela, utilisez la construction relative dans au moins trois phrases différentes.

▶ Vous avez perdu votre cahier d'exercices. Décrivez ce cahier.

C'est un cahier qui est assez grand.
C'est le cahier que j'avais avec moi ce matin.
C'est le cahier dans lequel j'ai pris beaucoup de notes.
C'est un cahier dont j'ai absolument besoin.

1. Vous avez perdu la montre que votre oncle vous a donnée pour votre anniversaire. Décrivez cette montre.
2. Vous avez dîné dans un restaurant qu'un ami vous a recommandé. Décrivez ce restaurant.
3. Vous avez trouvé un job pour l'été. Décrivez ce job.
4. Vous avez inventé une machine. Décrivez cette machine.
5. Vos parents ont acheté une nouvelle voiture. Décrivez cette voiture.
6. Vous avez fait la connaissance d'un(e) étudiant(e) francophone très sympathique à la dernière réunion du club français. Décrivez cet(te) étudiant(e).
7. L'été dernier, vous avez rencontré une personne très intéressante. Décrivez cette personne.

B. Ce qui, ce que et ce dont

Note the use of **ce qui, ce que** and **ce dont** in the following sentences.

Je voudrais savoir **ce qui** t'intéresse.	*I would like to know **what** interests you.*
Dis-moi **ce qui** est arrivé.	*Tell me **what** happened.*
Je ne sais pas **ce que** tu fais.	*I don't know **what** you are doing.*
Montre-moi **ce que** tu as acheté.	*Show me **what** you bought.*
Dis-moi **ce dont** tu as envie.	*Tell me **what** you want.*
Je ne comprends pas **ce dont** tu parles.	*I don't understand **what** you are talking about.*

Ce qui, **ce que**, and **ce dont** correspond to *what*.

- **Ce qui** is equivalent to **la chose/les choses qui . . . .**
  It functions as the SUBJECT of the verb that follows.

- **Ce que** is equivalent to **la chose/les choses que . . . .**
  It functions as the DIRECT OBJECT of the verb that follows.

- **Ce dont** is equivalent to **la chose/les choses dont . . . .**
  It replaces a phrase with **de**.

Je voudrais savoir
ce qui t'intéresse.

Dis-moi ce qui
est arrivé!

Montre-moi ce qu
tu as acheté.

Je ne comprends pas
ce dont tu parles.

5 **Précisions**

Votre partenaire vous explique certaines choses sans préciser. Demandez-lui de préciser
en utilisant les expressions entre parenthèses avec **ce qui, ce que** ou **ce dont**.

▶ Quelque chose m'amuse. (Dis-moi . . .)
  Dis-moi ce qui t'amuse.
▶ J'ai besoin de quelque chose. (Je voudrais savoir . . .)
  Je voudrais savoir ce dont tu as besoin.

1. Quelque chose m'intéresse. (Explique-moi . . .)
2. Je fais quelque chose. (Je voudrais savoir . . .)
3. J'ai envie de quelque chose. (Dis-moi . . .)
4. Quelque chose m'est arrivé. (Raconte-moi . . .)
5. J'ai acheté quelque chose. (Montre-moi . . .)
6. Mon copain m'a parlé de quelque chose. (Dis-moi . . .)

6 **Qu'est-ce qu'ils font?**

Complétez les phrases avec **ce qui, ce que (ce qu')** ou **ce dont**.

1. Je suis au supermarché. J'achète . . .

   ___ est sur ma liste
   ___ j'ai besoin
   ___ j'ai oublié hier

2. Marc veut faire un cadeau d'anniversaire à
   Sylvie. Il lui demande . . .

   ___ l'intéresse
   ___ elle a envie
   ___ elle aimerait avoir

3. Christine et Françoise font du shopping. Elles
   regardent . . .

   ___ est en solde
   ___ elles ont envie
   ___ elles voudraient acheter si
       elles avaient de l'argent

4. Le professeur aide les élèves. Il explique . . .

   ___ il a parlé la semaine dernière
   ___ est difficile
   ___ ils ne comprennent pas

5. Monsieur Dumont nettoie son appartement.
   Il range . . .

   ___ est en désordre
   ___ il veut garder
   ___ il n'a pas besoin

6. Madame Moreau a été témoin d'un accident.
   Elle explique à la police . . .

   ___ elle a vu
   ___ elle se souvient
   ___ est arrivé

LECTURE

Le bracelet

Michelle Maurois

Michelle Maurois (1914 – 1994) vient d'une famille d'écrivains et d'intellectuels. Son père, André Maurois, était membre de l'Académie française. Connue pour ses contes, Michelle Maurois a aussi écrit des essais et des romans.

AVANT DE LIRE

Lisez le titre de cette histoire et puis regardez l'illustration. Décrivez avec le maximum de détails:
- la jeune fille
- la marchande d'antiquités
- le magasin
- le bracelet qui est à la vitrine

Anticipons un peu!

Répondez aux questions suivantes, en expliquant votre opinion.
- Quel genre d'histoire est-ce? une histoire drôle? une histoire policière? une histoire sentimentale?
  Maintenant lisez l'histoire pour voir si vous avez raison.
- Quel est le sujet de cette histoire?
- Est-ce que la marchande vendra le bracelet à la jeune fille? Pourquoi ou pourquoi pas?
Maintenant lisez l'histoire pour voir si vous avez raison.

Le bracelet

I

—Bonjour Madame, dit Denise, entrant dans le magasin de bric-à-brac.°

    —Mademoiselle ... Je ne suis pas encore Madame.

    —Excusez-moi, dit la jeune fille déconcertée. Bonjour Mademoiselle.

    —Entrez ma belle, dit la marchande sans lâcher° son tricot.

5   Denise se dirige vers la très vieille femme, vêtue d'une longue robe rouge, assise sur une chaise basse. Son visage est usé,° ses cheveux d'un blanc de neige, mais son regard° reste jeune et souriant.°

    —S'il vous plaît, Mademoiselle, quel est le prix du bracelet qui se trouve au milieu de la vitrine?

10   —Il n'est pas à vendre, dit la vieille, souriant toujours.

    —Comment cela?

    —Tout est à vendre, sauf le bracelet.

    —Mais ... vous l'exposez.

    —Oui, mais pas pour qu'on l'achète.

15   —Ah! dit Denise étonnée.° C'est dommage. Il me plaît. J'aime beaucoup les bijoux anciens.

    La marchande se lève. Elle est toute voûtée° et avance à petits pas.° La jeune fille regarde autour d'elle avec curiosité; ces vieux objets excitent son imagination, rappellent des époques disparues, des familles éteintes°.

20 Ici sont mêlés° tasses chinoises, assiettes romantiques,° boîtes marquées du «N» napoléonien,* vases de Venise° plus ou moins cassés, verres de Bohême.°

    La marchande prend dans la vitrine le bracelet et revient vers la jeune fille. Ce bracelet est en or, recouvert° de pierres de toutes les couleurs.

25 Chaque pierre a la forme d'un cœur.

    —Il est fermé par un saphir de la couleur de mes yeux, dit la vieille femme. Il est joli, n'est-ce pas, mon bracelet?

    —Très joli, dit Denise en le prenant dans ses mains.

    Quand elle le voit de près, la jeune fille est encore plus tentée. Le travail°

30 est fin, délicat. C'est un charmant bijou qui vient d'être nettoyé et qui brille de mille feux. On le remarque d'autant plus que tout ce que contient le magasin° est recouvert de poussière.

Mots utiles	
un bracelet	*bracelet*
des bijoux	*(pieces of) jewelry*
la marchande d'antiquités	*antique dealer*
une pierre	*stone, gem*
la poussière	*dust*
le tricot	*knitting*
une vitrine	*store window*
briller	*to shine*
se diriger vers	*to go toward*
exposer	*to exhibit*
plaire *	*to please*
tenter	*to tempt*
d'autant plus que	*all the more that*
autour de	*around*
sauf	*except*

* **Boîtes marquées du «N» napoléonien.** As presents to his courtiers, Napoleon used to give small boxes decorated with the imperial «N».

bric-à-brac = antiquités bon marché   **lâcher** = laisser   **usé** = vieux   **son regard** = les yeux   **souriant** *smiling*   **étonnée** *astonished*
voûtée *bent over*   **pas** *steps*   **éteintes** = qui n'existent plus   **mêlés** *mixed together*   **romantiques** = décorées de sujets romantiques
vases de Venise *Venitian glass vases*   **verres de Bohême** *[red] Bohemian glasses*   **recouvert de** *covered with*   **travail** *workmanship*
ce que contient le magasin = ce qu'il y a dans le magasin

Avez-vous compris?

1. Pourquoi est-ce que Denise entre dans le magasin?
2. À votre avis, quel âge a la marchande (approximativement)? Expliquez pourquoi vous pensez cela.
3. À votre avis, est-ce qu'elle est mariée? Expliquez comment vous savez cela.
4. En quoi le bracelet est-il différent des autres objets? Décrivez ce bracelet.

Anticipons un peu

À votre avis, pourquoi est-ce que la marchande ne veut pas vendre le bracelet? Expliquez pourquoi vous pensez cela.

- Le bracelet n'est pas à elle.
- C'est un souvenir personnel.
- Elle l'a promis à une personne de sa famille.
- Il coûte trop cher.
- Une autre raison. Imaginez laquelle.

II

Denise adore les bijoux, elle en possède plusieurs, mais elle n'a pas de bracelet. Elle vient de recevoir son salaire du mois et elle a envie de faire une folie.°

—Mais pourquoi, demande-t-elle, pourquoi ne voulez-vous pas me le céder?° 35

—Parce qu'il est à moi et parce que j'y tiens plus qu'à tout au monde.

—Mais tout, ici, n'est-il pas à vous?

—Non. Les autres objets, je les ai achetés, tandis que ce bracelet m'a été donné. 40

—Alors, pourquoi l'exposer?

—C'est un cadeau de mon fiancé.

Denise regarde la marchande et se tait. Le mot «fiancé» dans la bouche de la vieille femme est surprenant. 45

—Frédéric avait vingt ans ... Frédéric Cottet, c'est le nom de mon fiancé. Un jour il m'a apporté ce bracelet pour me tenir compagnie pendant son absence. Il partait pour un très long voyage ... Il n'est pas revenu.

—Excusez-moi, j'ai été indiscrète. Comme c'est triste!

—Oh non! Je l'attends.

—Vous ... vous l'attendez ...? dit la jeune fille. 50

—Tous les jours, à toutes les heures. Et comme il ne sait sans doute pas où me trouver, je laisse le bracelet au milieu de la vitrine pour qu'il le reconnaisse: voilà pourquoi il n'est pas à vendre.

—Je comprends, dit Denise lentement. 55

—Je vais d'ailleurs vite le remettre. Si Frédéric passait juste maintenant ...

«La vieille femme est sûrement folle, se dit Denise en la suivant des yeux, mais touchante, mystérieuse. Peut-être ne finit-on jamais de rêver?»

La marchande prend un verre sur lequel on peut lire en lettres dorées,° un peu effacées,° «souvenir» et le tend° à la jeune fille. 60

—Je vous le donne parce que vous êtes si jolie.

—Oh! C'est trop gentil,° mais je ne peux pas l'accepter...

—Cela me fait plaisir. Et revenez me voir.

Denise part, le verre serré° dans sa main, le cœur un peu lourd. Cette nuit-là, dans son lit, elle ne réussit pas à s'endormir. Son esprit° ne peut pas se détacher° de la vieille marchande, attendant toute sa vie sans se décourager. 65

Mots utiles

faire plaisir à	to please
posséder	to own, possess
remettre *	to put back
rêver	to dream
suivre *	to follow
surprendre *	to surprise
tenir * à	to hold dear, to cherish
tenir	
* compagnie	to keep company
fou (folle)	crazy

une folie = quelque chose d'extravagant   **me le céder** = to let me have it   **doré** = d'or   **effacer** to erase
tend = donne   **gentil** = généreux   **serré** held tightly   **esprit** mind   **se détacher** = oublier

Avez-vous compris?

1. Qui est Frédéric Cottet?
2. Pourquoi est-ce que la marchande ne veut pas vendre le bracelet?
3. Pourquoi est-ce qu'elle continue à l'exposer dans la vitrine?
4. Qu'est-ce que Denise pense de la marchande?

À votre avis

Exprimez votre opinion sur les sujets suivants et expliquez pourquoi vous avez cette opinion.

- Est-ce que la vieille femme est bizarre, complètement folle ou simplement sentimentale?
- Est-ce que Frédéric Cottet est une personne réelle ou bien est-ce qu'il existe seulement dans l'imagination de la vieille femme?
- Est-ce que Frédéric Cottet va revenir un jour? Si oui, dans quelles circonstances?

III

Quelques mois plus tard, l'été est venu. Denise en sortant du bureau, rentre un soir par la rue où se trouve le magasin de bric-à-brac. Brillant de tous
70 ses feux, le bracelet est toujours là. La vieille femme est assise sur le trottoir devant la porte, travaillant au même tricot. Elle reconnaît la jeune fille et lui fait un grand sourire.

—Venez vous asseoir avec moi, ma belle,
75 prenez une chaise à l'intérieur.°

La jeune fille s'installe contre le mur de la maison à côté de la marchande.

—Vous avez eu beaucoup de clients aujourd'hui? demande Denise.
80 —Oh non! Je n'ai eu personne. J'ai été plus tranquille pour penser. Moi, je ne suis jamais seule ... Frédéric est près de moi ... Et vous? Avez-vous un fiancé?

—Non, dit la jeune fille en rougissant.
85 —Pourquoi?

—Je connais peu de jeunes gens ...

—Quand Frédéric viendra, je lui demanderai de vous présenter un de ses amis.

Denise frissonne; elle est saisie par une sorte d'anxiété.°
90 —Je dois rentrer, dit-elle. Ma mère m'attend. Il va être l'heure du dîner.

—Je laisse ouvert° le plus longtemps possible. Frédéric termine peut-être tard son travail. Mais je vais fermer dans quelques minutes.

La marchande se dirige vers la vitrine, sort le bracelet que Denise regarde une fois de plus avec admiration et l'attache à son bras.
95 —Je le mets tous les soirs pour dormir, dit-elle.

—Je reviendrai vous voir, dit la jeune fille.

—Adieu, ma belle. À bientôt.

Mais quelques jours plus tard, Denise tombe malade et reste couchée° près d'un mois. Elle est obligée d'aller se reposer à la montagne. Les soucis causés
100 par sa maladie lui ont fait un peu oublier la vieille dame et son éternellement jeune fiancé.

à l'intérieur = à l'intérieur du magasin anxiété = peur je laisse ouvert = je garde le magasin ouvert
couchée = au lit

Mots utiles	
un souci	concern, worry
un sourire	smile
un trottoir	sidewalk
frissonner	to shiver, shudder
saisir	to seize, take

Avez-vous compris?

1. Selon vous, est-ce que les choses ont changé quand Denise revient plus tard?
2. Qu'est-ce que la marchande propose à Denise quand elle apprend que celle-ci n'est pas mariée?
3. Quelle est la réaction de Denise?
4. Pourquoi est-ce que Denise ne revient pas voir la marchande?

Anticipons un peu

Selon vous, comment va se terminer l'histoire? Expliquez votre réponse.

• Frédéric Cottet reviendra et il se mariera avec la marchande.
• La marchande apprendra la mort de Frédéric Cottet et finalement vendra le bracelet à Denise.
• Un jour Denise fera la connaissance du petit-fils de Frédéric Cottet et se mariera avec lui.
• Quelque chose d'autre arrivera. Imaginez quoi.

IV

À son retour, Denise passe par hasard, un jour, devant le magasin qui lui plaisait tant. De très loin, elle voit
105 que le bracelet n'est plus dans la vitrine. Elle s'aperçoit aussi que quelque chose a changé. Il y a plus d'ordre, tout paraît plus propre qu'autrefois. Surprise, elle ouvre
110 la porte du magasin et voit une femme brune de cinquante ans environ, installée derrière un bureau.

—La vieille dame n'est plus là? demande la jeune fille.
115 —Non ... elle est morte depuis un mois ...

—Oh! Cela me fait de la peine,° dit Denise. Elle était si charmante.

—Elle est morte brusquement. On
120 l'a trouvée un matin ici, par terre. Vous savez, elle était un peu bizarre ...

—Oui, dit Denise, un peu bizarre ...

—Je ne sais pas ce que je vais faire du magasin ...

—Oh! J'espère que vous le garderez, il a tant de charme.
125 —Est-ce que vous désirez quelque chose?

—Il y avait dans la vitrine, dit la jeune fille, un bracelet avec des pierres de couleur en forme de cœurs: il me plaisait beaucoup.

—En effet, il était très joli. Ma tante l'avait déjà quand j'étais toute petite° ... Je l'ai vendu quelques jours après sa mort. Un
130 matin, un vieux monsieur, tout voûté, est resté longtemps dans la rue à regarder la vitrine. Puis il est entré. Il était complètement sourd° et nous avons eu beaucoup de mal° à nous comprendre. Je crois qu'il trouvait le bracelet trop cher mais il en avait très envie et, à la fin il l'a acheté.
135 —Vous ne savez pas comment il s'appelait?

—Je ne me souviens pas, mais il m'a payée par chèque. Cela vous intéresse de savoir son nom?

—Oui. J'attendais d'avoir assez d'argent pour acheter ce bracelet. Je vais essayer de joindre le vieux monsieur et lui
140 demander de me le céder.°

La femme brune ouvre un secrétaire,° cherche dans des papiers.

—Ah voilà le nom: Frédéric Cottet.

Mots utiles	
s'apercevoir *	notice
joindre *	to contact (someone)
paraître *	to look, appear, seem
environ	about, approximately
par hasard	by chance
par terre	on the ground
tant de	so much

me fait de la peine = me rend triste   **toute petite** = très jeune
sourd *deaf*   **beaucoup de mal** = beaucoup de difficultés
me le céder = me le vendre
un secrétaire = un petit bureau

Avez-vous compris?

1. Qu'est-ce qui a changé quand Denise retourne au magasin?
2. Qui est la nouvelle marchande par rapport à l'ancienne?
3. Qui a finalement acheté le bracelet?

EXPRESSION ORALE

■ Débat: L'amour éternel

Selon vous, est-ce que l'amour éternel, tel qu'il est décrit dans l'histoire, est possible? Prenez une position pour ou contre et débattez le sujet avec votre partenaire. Si possible, donnez des exemples.

■ Situations

Avec votre partenaire, choisissez l'une des situations suivantes. Composez le dialogue correspondant et jouez-le en classe.

1 Coups de téléphone

Après chaque visite au magasin, Denise téléphone à un(e) ami(e) pour raconter ce qui s'est passé. L'ami(e) demande des détails.

Rôles: Denise, l'ami(e)

2 Conversation

Denise a réussi à retrouver Frédéric Cottet. Celui-ci lui pose des questions sur sa fiancée d'autrefois.

Rôles: Denise, Frédéric Cottet

EXPRESSION ÉCRITE

■ Frédéric Cottet

Écrivez l'histoire de Frédéric Cottet en inventant des détails. Par exemple:

• Où, quand et comment Frédéric a-t-il rencontré la dame de la boutique?
• À quelle occasion est-ce qu'il lui a offert le bracelet?
• Pourquoi est-il parti à l'âge de vingt ans?
• Où est-il allé et qu'est-ce qu'il a fait là-bas?
• Pourquoi a-t-il mis si longtemps à revenir?
• Pourquoi est-ce qu'il est finalement revenu?
• Quelles étaient ses pensées en revoyant le bracelet dans la vitrine? etc.

■ Une lettre

La vieille dame, avant de mourir, décide d'écrire une lettre à Frédéric Cottet. Dans cette lettre, elle explique ce qu'elle a fait pendant son absence, pourquoi elle l'a attendu si fidèlement *(faithfully)* et comment elle espérait le revoir.

■ Une autre conclusion

Imaginez une autre conclusion moins triste et plus romantique à l'histoire que vous avez lue. Pour cela, réécrivez complètement le quatrième épisode.

L'AFRIQUE DANS LA COMMUNAUTÉ

▪ *Un peu d'histoire* ▪

■ *Les dates* ## ■ *Les événements*

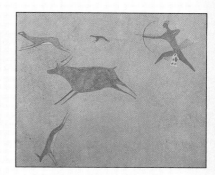

- **6000** *av. J.-C.*	
- *Tassili*	
- **0**	
- **670** *arrivée des Arabes*	
- **700** *Empire du Ghana (700-1200)*	
-	
-	
-	
- **1200** *Empire du Mali (1200-1500)*	
- **1300** *Empire de Songhaï (1350-1600) Royaume du Bénin (1350-1900)*	
-	
- **1500**	
- **1600**	
- **1860**	
- **1900**	
- **1960** *Indépendance*	
- **2000**	

Empires africains

Colonisation

Indépendance

La préhistoire en Afrique occidentale

Pendant six mille ans avant Jésus-Christ, le Sahara était une savane habitée par un peuple qui a laissé de remarquables peintures rupestres° dans la région de Tassili.

7e - 8e siècles: Conquête de l'Afrique du Nord par les Arabes

En 670, les Arabes arrivent en Afrique du Nord où ils imposent la religion musulmane. Ils établissent progressivement des relations commerciales avec les populations d'Afrique occidentale. Au contact des Arabes, beaucoup d'Africains adoptent la religion musulmane.

10e - 16e siècles: Période de prospérité et de grande civilisation

De puissants et vastes empires se succèdent en Afrique occidentale: empire du **Ghāna**, empire du **Mali**, empire de **Songhaï**. La prospérité de ces empires est basée sur le commerce avec l'Afrique du Nord. Les caravanes chargées de° sel traversent le Sahara. Elles arrivent à Tombouctou, capitale de l'empire du Mali, et repartent avec de l'or et des pierres précieuses. Une civilisation brillante se développe dans toute la région.

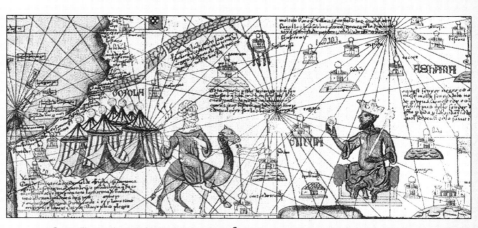

Cette illustration, tirée d'un atlas du 14ᵉ siècle, montre un marchand arabe rendant visite au Roi du Mali. Celui-ci tient dans sa main une pépite° d'or.

rupestres *on rock walls* **chargées de** *loaded with* **pépite** *nugget*

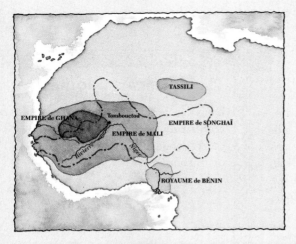

14e - 19e siècles: Le royaume de Bénin

Indépendamment des empires d'Afrique occidentale, le royaume du Bénin se développe dans la région tropicale près du Golfe de Guinée. Le génie de cette civilisation est préservé dans de splendides sculptures de bronze.

17e et 19e siècles: Arrivée des Européens — esclavage et colonisation

À partir du 17ᵉ siècle, l'arrivée des Européens provoque le déclin progressif de cette grande civilisation africaine. Les Européens viennent en Afrique chercher des esclaves pour travailler dans leurs plantations des Antilles, de Louisiane, du Brésil . . . Des centaines de milliers d'Africains sont arrachés° de leur terre° ancestrale et déportés en Amérique dans des conditions épouvantables°. Cet odieux trafic d'êtres° humains dure jusqu'au début du 19ᵉ siècle.

Dans la seconde moitié du 19ᵉ siècle, les Européens, qui ont déjà établi des comptoirs° sur le littoral°, décident de coloniser l'intérieur du continent. C'est ainsi que l'Afrique occidentale et équatoriale est découpée° en colonies anglaises, françaises et belges. Les Européens imposent des structures administratives et économiques qui ne correspondent pas à la culture africaine traditionnelle.

20e siècle: De l'exploitation à l'indépendance

Les pays européens exploitent leurs colonies africaines. Un grand nombre de soldats africains sont recrutés par l'armée française et combattent courageusement en Europe pendant les deux guerres mondiales (1914-1918 et 1939-1945).

Après la deuxième guerre mondiale, les leaders politiques africains réclament l'indépendance des colonies avec de plus en plus d'insistance. À partir de 1960, ces colonies deviennent des pays indépendants, membres des Nations Unies.

*Cette plaque de bronze représente l'**oba** ou roi du Bénin avec sa famille. Ses serviteurs le protègent du soleil.*

---

arrachés *torn away* **terre** *land* **épouvantables** *ghastly* **êtres** *beings* **comptoirs** *trading posts* **littoral** *coast* **découpée** *cut up*

■ L'Afrique francophone et sa culture

■ Qu'est-ce que c'est que l'Afrique francophone?

C'est un groupe d'une douzaine de pays d'Afrique occidentale et équatoriale où le français est la langue officielle. Parmi ces pays, les plus importants sont **le Sénégal, la Côte-d'Ivoire, le Mali, la République démocratique du Congo, le Bénin, le Cameroun** . . . Autrefois ces pays étaient des colonies françaises ou belges. Indépendants depuis 1960, ils ont décidé de garder le français comme langue administrative et commerciale. En général, les jeunes apprennent le français à l'école secondaire et parfois dès° l'école primaire.

■ Quelles langues parle-t-on en Afrique?

Il y a un très grand nombre de langues africaines. Au Sénégal, par exemple, on parle **wolof**. En Côte-d'Ivoire, on parle **baoulé** et **dioula**. Au Mali, il y a dix langues régionales. Ces langues reflètent la grande diversité ethnique des peuples d'Afrique. En Côte-d'Ivoire, par exemple, on compte au moins soixante groupes ethniques différents.

Les noms baoulés

Dans les familles baoulés, les noms traditionnels donnés aux enfants correspondent aux jours de la semaine où ils sont nés.

	GARÇONS	FILLES
lundi	**Kouassi**	**Akissi**
mardi	**Kouadio**	**Adjoua**
mercredi	**Konan**	**Amelan**
jeudi	**Koffi**	**Affoué**
vendredi	**Yao**	**Aya**
samedi	**Kouakou**	**Ahou**
dimanche	**Kouamé**	**Amoin**

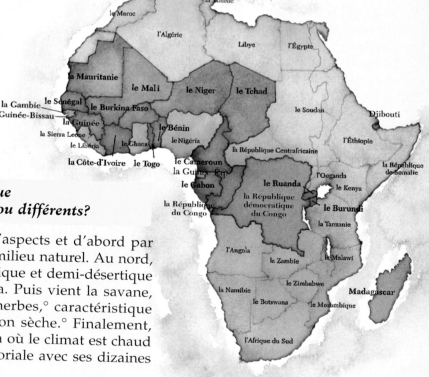

■ Est-ce que les pays de l'Afrique francophone sont semblables ou différents?

Ils sont différents par beaucoup d'aspects et d'abord par leur climat, leur végétation et leur milieu naturel. Au nord, par exemple, il y a une zone désertique et demi-désertique qui est le prolongement° du Sahara. Puis vient la savane, c'est-à-dire une région de hautes herbes,° caractéristique des régions chaudes à longue saison sèche.° Finalement, plus au sud et le long du littoral,° là où le climat est chaud et humide, on trouve la forêt équatoriale avec ses dizaines d'espèces d'arbres différents.

---

dès *as of*   **prolongement** = extension   **herbes** *grass*   **sèche** *dry*   **littoral** *coast*

■ Quelles sont les religions de l'Afrique francophone?

Cela dépend des pays. La religion musulmane est très importante dans les régions de l'ouest et du nord où il y a eu beaucoup de contacts avec les Arabes. C'est le cas, par exemple, au Mali, au Sénégal, et au Niger, où la grande majorité des gens sont musulmans. Au sud et au centre, au contraire, ce sont les religions animistes qui prédominent, par exemple, en Côte d'Ivoire, au Bénin, et au Burkina-Faso. Dans tous ces pays, il y a aussi des minorités catholiques. N'oublions pas, par exemple, que la plus grande

Mosquée de Djemé, Mali

basilique catholique du monde, la Basilique de Notre Dame de la Paix, se trouve à Yamoussoukro, en Côte d'Ivoire, et qu'elle a été inaugurée en 1989 par le pape Jean-Paul II.

La Basilique de Notre Dame de la Paix à Yamoussoukro

Une mosquée au Niger

■ Qu'est-ce que l'animisme?

C'est la religion traditionnelle de l'Afrique noire. L'animisme attribue une âme° aux plantes, aux animaux, aux phénomènes naturels, et plus généralement à toutes les forces de la nature. Les animistes pratiquent ainsi le culte des ancêtres avec qui on peut communiquer et qui peuvent avoir une influence positive ou négative sur les événements de la vie quotidienne.° L'animisme explique l'importance de la nature, des animaux et des génies dans la littérature africaine.

âme *soul* **quotidienne** *daily*

■ *Quel est le rôle de la famille dans la société africaine?*

Pour les Africains, la famille représente une structure très importante. Tous les membres de la famille s'aident et doivent s'entraider.° La famille africaine est très vaste. Elle comprend° non seulement les grands-parents, les parents et les enfants, mais aussi tous les oncles, tantes, cousins et cousines unis par les liens de sang° et de mariage.

Dans les villages où la polygamie existe, la famille est encore plus grande puisqu'elle comprend aussi les demi-frères et les demi-sœurs. Le père est le chef de famille. Il est respecté et son autorité n'est pas contestée. S'il a plusieurs femmes, chacune a sa propre case ou maison où elle élève° ses enfants.

À côté de la famille visible, il y a aussi la famille invisible, celle des ancêtres qui restent très présents dans la mémoire des Africains. On peut communiquer avec l'esprit de ses ancêtres et, inversement, ils peuvent communiquer avec nous et influencer les événements de notre vie quotidienne.

En Mauritanie, la décoration des maisons est traditionnellement réservée aux femmes. À cause des conditions climatiques, ces maisons doivent souvent être repeintes. Ici, les femmes utilisent des éléments géométriques pour décorer leurs maisons.

---

s'entraider *help each other*   **comprend** *includes*   **liens de sang** *blood ties*   **élève** *raises*

■ Quelles sont les caractéristiques de la littérature africaine traditionnelle?

La littérature africaine traditionnelle est très différente de la littérature européenne. C'est avant tout une littérature orale. Son but° principal est d'expliquer et de transmettre de génération en génération les coutumes, les traditions et les valeurs du groupe. Ses thèmes sont variés: la création du monde, l'origine de l'humanité, l'histoire des ancêtres et de la tribu, les relations entre les gens. Ses formes d'expression sont la poésie, la fable, la légende, et surtout le conte.° Il y a toutes sortes de contes: contes moraux, contes humoristiques, contes d'aventures, contes d'amour, contes du merveilleux . . . Dans ces contes, les personnages sont souvent des animaux qui représentent en réalité les humains avec leurs qualités et leurs défauts.

Les conteurs° africains s'appellent des «griots». Dans les villages de l'Afrique traditionnelle, le griot joue un rôle très important. C'est lui qui transmet l'histoire et les traditions de chaque famille du village.

Aujourd'hui, il y a aussi une littérature écrite très abondante. Cette littérature reprend les thèmes de la littérature orale (contes, fables) ou traite les thèmes plus personnels (poésie, romans, récits autobiographiques). L'un des représentants les plus connus de la littérature africaine moderne est l'écrivain sénégalais Léopold Sédar Senghor. Ce poète s'exprime en français sur des thèmes africains ou des thèmes universels, comme la liberté. Considéré comme l'un des plus grands écrivains d'expression française, il a été élu en 1980 membre de l'Académie française.

Léopold Sédar Senghor: Poète et homme d'action

Homme de lettres et brillant intellectuel, Léopold Senghor (1906 - 2001) a aussi joué un rôle politique très important dans l'histoire de l'Afrique francophone. Après la deuxième guerre mondiale, il a milité pour l'indépendance de son pays, le Sénégal. Quand le Sénégal est devenu une république indépendante en 1958, il en est devenu le premier président (1958-1980).

Documents: Une fable africaine

La gélinotte et la tortue

Un jour, une gélinotte° rencontra une tortue qui avançait lentement à travers la plaine. «Pourquoi est-ce que tu ne vas pas plus vite?» demanda-t-elle à la tortue. «Parce que je suis une tortue» répondit la tortue. «Eh bien, moi, je te suis supérieure non seulement parce que je vais plus vite que toi, mais aussi parce que je peux voler.»°

À ce moment des chasseurs passèrent par là. Ils mirent le feu aux herbes de la plaine pour déloger des gazelles qui s'y étaient cachées.° Le cercle de feu se rapprocha des deux animaux exposés à un péril certain. La tortue se cacha dans le trou° laissé par le pied d'un éléphant, et elle survécut. La gélinotte voulait s'envoler, mais elle fut étouffée° par la fumée° et mourut.

N'est pas supérieur celui qui se vante°

---

but = objectif   **conte** *short story*   **conteurs** *storytellers*   **gélinotte** *grouse*   **voler** *to fly*
cachées *hidden*   **trou** *hole*   **étouffée** *suffocated*   **fumée** *smoke*   **se vante** *boasts*

Afrique

Afrique mon Afrique
Afrique des fiers guerriers° dans les savanes ancestrales
Afrique que chante ma grand-Mère
Au bord° de son fleuve° lointain°
Je ne t'ai jamais connue

Mais mon regard est plein de ton sang
Ton beau sang noir à travers les champs répandu°
Le sang de ta sueur°
La sueur de ton travail
Le travail de l'esclavage
L'esclavage de tes enfants

Afrique dis-moi Afrique
Est-ce donc toi ce dos qui se courbe°
Et se couche° sous le poids° de l'humilité
Ce dos tremblant à zébrures° rouges
Qui dit oui au fouet° sur les routes de midi

Alors gravement une voix me répondit
Fils impétueux cet arbre robuste et jeune
Cet arbre là-bas
Splendidement seul au milieu de fleurs blanches et fanées°
C'est l'Afrique ton Afrique qui repousse°
Qui repousse patiemment obstinément
Et dont les fruits ont peu à peu
L'amère° saveur° de la liberté.

David Diop (1927-1960)

Né en France d'un père sénégalais et d'une mère camerounaise*, David Diop est l'un des écrivains les plus militants de la littérature africaine. Dans ce poème, publié en 1956, il dénonce le colonialisme et entrevoit° l'indépendance de l'Afrique. Diop est mort dans un accident d'avion alors° qu'il venait s'établir° définitivement au Sénégal, devenu° depuis peu° un état indépendant.

* **Le Cameroun** = un pays de l'Afrique francophone

Baobab dans la savane africaine

---

guerriers *warriors* au bord *on the shore* fleuve = rivière lointain = distant répandu *spilled* sueur *sweat* se courbe *is bent over*
se couche *is doubled over* poids *weight* zébrures *stripes (caused by lashing)* fouet *whip* fanées *withered* repoussse *grows back*
amère *bitter* saveur *taste* entrevoit = anticipe alors que *when* s'établir *to settle* devenu = qui était devenu depuis peu = récemment

---

▪ L'art africain ▪
et
son influence sur l'art européen

Parmi les arts africains traditionnels, la forme la plus développée est la sculpture. Les principaux objets sculptés sont des statues et des masques. Pour les Africains, ces objets ne sont pas considérés comme des objets artistiques, mais comme des objets religieux. Dans les cérémonies rituelles, par exemple, les masques sont portés par des danseurs pour honorer l'esprit des ancêtres et demander leur protection.

La majorité des masques africains sont en bois. Ils représentent généralement des figures humaines sous des formes stylisées. On peut noter l'importance des formes géométriques: lignes droites° ou courbes, cercles, ovales, triangles, etc. Cette stylisation transforme le corps et le visage humains et permet l'expression d'émotions très intenses.

Au début du 20e siècle, les Européens ont pris connaissance° de l'art africain grâce à plusieurs expositions coloniales où figuraient masques et statues de l'Afrique noire. L'originalité de cet art a d'abord choqué le public peu habitué° à la représentation non-conventionnelle de l'être humain. Les grands artistes de l'époque, au contraire, ont été très impressionnés par la simplification stylistique de l'art africain. Matisse, Modigliani et surtout Picasso ont incorporé cette simplification dans leurs propres oeuvres.° En particulier, l'usage des formes géométriques, directement inspiré par la sculpture africaine, est à la base du cubisme qui allait révolutionner l'art européen du 20e siècle.

Ce masque africain a appartenu au peintre Vlaminck qui l'a montré à ses amis artistes. On peut noter les ressemblances entre ce masque et la sculpture de Modigliani.

Modigliani, *Tête de femme*

À remarquer l'influence des masques africains sur le célèbre tableau de Picasso, *Les Demoiselles d'Avignon.*

Picasso, *Étude pour les Demoiselles d'Avignon*

---

droites *straight* ont pris connaissance *became aware* habitué *accustomed* oeuvres *works*

Bernard Dadié

Bernard Dadié, né en 1916, est originaire de la Côte d'Ivoire. C'est l'un des écrivains les plus féconds° de la littérature africaine d'expression française. Il a écrit des contes, des poèmes, des romans et des pièces de théâtre. Militant nationaliste, Dadié a été arrêté en 1949 et a passé seize mois en prison pour ses activités politiques. Après l'indépendance de la Côte d'Ivoire, il a été nommé Ministre de la Culture de son pays.

La légende baoulé est extraite du livre **Légendes africaines**. Dans ce récit, Dadié explique comment son peuple, les Baoulés, ont reçu leur nom grâce au sacrifice de leur reine, la reine Pokou.

Il y a longtemps, très longtemps, vivait au bord d'une lagune calme, une tribu paisible° de nos frères. Ses jeunes hommes étaient nombreux, nobles et courageux, ses femmes étaient belles et joyeuses. Et leur reine, la reine Pokou, était la plus belle parmi les plus belles.

Depuis longtemps, très longtemps, la paix était sur eux et les esclaves mêmes, fils des captifs des temps révolus,° étaient heureux auprès de leurs heureux maîtres.

Un jour, les ennemis vinrent nombreux comme des magnans.° Il fallut quitter les paillotes,° les plantations, la lagune poissonneuse,° laisser les filets,° tout abandonner pour fuir.°

Ils partirent dans la forêt. Ils laissèrent aux épines° leurs pagnes,* puis leur chair.° Il fallait fuir toujours, sans repos, sans trêve,° talonné° par l'ennemi féroce.

Et leur reine, la reine Pokou, marchait la dernière, portant au dos son enfant.

---

* **Pagne**: a rectangular strip of cloth made of vegetal fibers which is worn as a loincloth or wrapped around the hips to form a short skirt.

féconds *prolific* **paisible** *peaceful* **révolus** *long past* **magnans** *red ants* **paillotes** *straw huts* **poissonneuse** = avec beaucoup de poissons
filets *nets* **fuir** *to flee* **épines** *thorns* **chair** *flesh* **sans trêve** *unceasingly* **talonné** *followed close on their heels*

À leur passage l'hyène ricanait,° l'éléphant et le sanglier° fuyaient, le chimpanzé grognait° et le lion étonné° s'écartait du chemin.°

Enfin, les broussailles° apparurent, puis la savane et les rôniers° et, encore une fois, la horde entonna° son chant d'exil:

Mi houn Ano, Mi houn Ano, blâ ô
Ebolo nigué, mo ba gnan min —

> Mon mari Ano, mon mari Ano, viens,
> Les génies de la brousse° m'emportent.

Harassés, exténués,° amaigris,° ils arrivèrent sur le soir au bord d'un grand fleuve dont la course° se brisait° sur d'énormes rochers.

Et le fleuve mugissait,° les flots° montaient jusqu'aux cimes° des arbres et retombaient et les fugitifs étaient glacés d'effroi.°

Consternés,° ils se regardaient. Était-ce là l'Eau qui les faisait vivre naguère,° l'Eau, leur grande amie? Il avait fallu qu'un mauvais génie l'excitât contre eux.

Et les conquérants devenaient plus proches.°

Et, pour la première fois, le sorcier° parla: «L'eau est devenue mauvaise, dit-il, et elle ne s'apaisera° que quand nous lui aurons donné ce que nous avons de plus cher.»° Et le chant d'espoir° retentit:°

Ebe nin flê nin bâ
Ebe nin flâ nin nan
Ebe nin flê nin dja
Yapen'sè ni djà wali

> Quelqu'un appelle son fils
> Quelqu'un appelle sa mère
> Quelqu'un appelle son père
> Les belles filles se marieront.

Et chacun donna ses bracelets d'or et d'ivoire, et tout ce qu'il avait pu sauver.

Mais le sorcier les repoussa du pied° et montra le jeune prince, le bébé de six mois: «Voilà, dit-il, ce que nous avons de plus précieux.»

Et la mère, effrayée,° serra° son enfant sur son coeur. Mais la mère était aussi la reine et, droite° au bord de l'abîme, elle leva l'enfant souriant° au-dessus de sa tête et le lança dans l'eau mugissante.

Alors des hippopotames, d'énormes hippopotames émergèrent et, se plaçant les uns à la suite° des autres, formèrent un pont° et sur ce pont miraculeux le peuple en fuite° passa en chantant:

Ebe nin flê nin bâ
Ebe nin flâ nin nan
Ebe nin flê nin dja
Yapen'sè ni djà wali

> Quelqu'un appelle son fils
> Quelqu'un appelle sa mère
> Quelqu'un appelle son père
> Les belles filles se marieront.

Et la reine Pokou passa la dernière et trouva sur la rive° son peuple prosterné.°

Mais la reine était aussi la mère et elle put dire seulement «baouli», ce qui veut dire: l'enfant est mort.

Et c'était la reine Pokou et le peuple garda le nom de Baoulé.

ricanait *was laughing* **sanglier** *wild boar* **grognait** *grunted* **étonné** *astonished* **s'écartait** *moved aside* **broussailles** *brush* **rôniers** *palm trees*
entonna = *commença à chanter* **la brousse** *the bush* **exténués** = *très fatigués* **amaigris** *very thin* **la course** = *l'eau* **se brisait** *was breaking*
mugissait *was roaring* **flots** *waves* **cimes** = *sommets* **glacés d'effroi** *frozen with fright* **consternés** *in alarm* **naguère** = *dans le passé*
plus proches *closer* **sorcier** *witch doctor* **s'apaisera** = *deviendra calme* **cher** = *précieux* **espoir** *hope* **retentit** *resounded*
repoussa du pied *kicked away* **effrayée** *scared* **serra** *clutched* **droite** *standing tall* **souriant** *smiling* **à la suite de** *right behind* **pont** *bridge*
en fuite *fleeing* **rive** *shore* **prosterné** *prostrate, face to the ground*

UNITÉ 10

Vers la vie active

Thème et Objectifs

Culture
In this unit, you will discover . . .
- what the **bac** is all about and why it is so important for French young people
- which are the most popular professions in France
- how to prepare for an interview with a French company

Communication
You will learn how . . .
- to talk about what you plan to study in the future
- to indicate what type of job or profession you would like to have
- to describe your personal qualifications
- to prepare a résumé in French

Langue
You will learn how . . .
- to describe simultaneous actions
- to indicate why you do certain things
- to explain under which conditions or constraints you do certain things
- to express how your actions may depend on what others do
- to describe how your actions have an effect on other people

CE FAMEUX BAC!

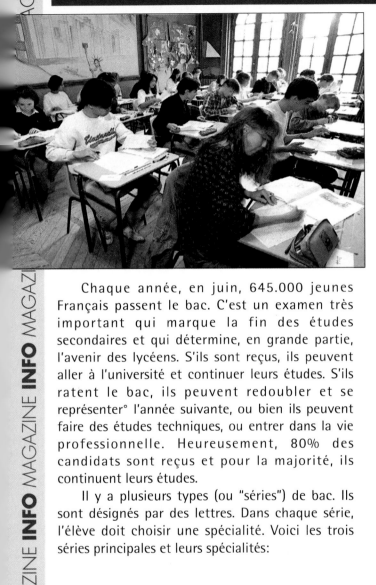

Corinne, 17 ans, et Guillaume, 18 ans, sont en «terminale», c'est-à-dire, en dernière année de leurs études secondaires. Dans quelques semaines, ils vont passer le bac. Corinne est une excellente élève et pourtant elle a le trac.° «J'ai beaucoup étudié, mais on ne sait jamais. Qu'est-ce que je vais faire si je ne suis pas reçue?° Je n'ai vraiment pas envie de redoubler.»° Guillaume, lui, redouble. Il est plus philosophe et plus décontracté° que Corinne. «Si je n'ai pas mon bac cette fois, je vais m'engager dans l'armée. Après, on verra!»

Chaque année, en juin, 645.000 jeunes Français passent le bac. C'est un examen très important qui marque la fin des études secondaires et qui détermine, en grande partie, l'avenir des lycéens. S'ils sont reçus, ils peuvent aller à l'université et continuer leurs études. S'ils ratent le bac, ils peuvent redoubler et se représenter° l'année suivante, ou bien ils peuvent faire des études techniques, ou entrer dans la vie professionnelle. Heureusement, 80% des candidats sont reçus et pour la majorité, ils continuent leurs études.

Il y a plusieurs types (ou "séries") de bac. Ils sont désignés par des lettres. Dans chaque série, l'élève doit choisir une spécialité. Voici les trois séries principales et leurs spécialités:

Ces spécialités sont importantes parce qu'elles déterminent le genre d'études universitaires qu'on peut faire et, par conséquent, sa profession future. Par exemple, si on veut être médecin ou pharmacien, il est conseillé° de faire un bac S, spécialité sciences de la vie et de la terre. Si on pense faire des études de droit° et devenir avocat, il est préférable de faire un bac ES, spécialité sciences économiques et sociales.

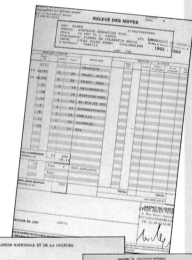

Série littéraire, bac L:
- langues vivantes
- philosophie
- art
- mathématiques

Série économique et sociale, bac ES:
- sciences économiques et sociales
- mathématiques
- langues vivantes

Série scientifique, bac S:
- mathématiques
- physique chimie
- sciences de la vie et de la terre
- technologie industrielle

a le trac is scared, nervous   **si je ne suis pas reçue** = si je ne réussis pas   **redoubler** to repeat a grade
décontracté relaxed   **se représenter** retake (the exam)   **conseillé** = recommandé   **droit** law

Les études universitaires durent au moins deux ans. Aussi, certains jeunes qui ont le bac préfèrent étudier en I.U.T. (Institut Supérieur de Technologie) où ils peuvent obtenir un diplôme universitaire de technologie après deux années d'études. Les "grandes écoles" sont une autre option. Ce sont des écoles spécialisées dans certains domaines: commerce, administration publique, professions d'ingénieur, etc. Pour entrer° dans ces écoles prestigieuses, il faut passer un concours° extrêmement difficile, auquel la plupart des candidats échouent.° Cependant, si on est reçu, et si on obtient° le diplôme d'une de ces écoles, on a toutes les chances de faire une brillante carrière dans le commerce, la finance, l'industrie et même la politique.

Comme on peut le voir, les diplômes ont beaucoup d'importance en France. Un diplôme représente une carte d'entrée dans la vie professionnelle. Voilà pourquoi les parents insistent pour que leurs enfants étudient. Les enfants sont générale- ment d'accord pour faire l'effort nécessaire. En France, les études, c'est sérieux!

Petite histoire du bac

◆ Au Moyen-Âge, un bachelier* était un jeune gentilhomme qui voulait être chevalier.° Vers 1500, c'était un étudiant qui avait écrit une thèse° de philosophie.

◆ Le bac moderne date de Napoléon qui l'a institué° en 1808. La première année, il y avait 32 candidats. En 1900, il y en avait 4 000. Aujourd'hui, il y en a 645 000.

◆ Le bac a d'abord été un examen exclusivement masculin. La première «candidate» se présenta en 1861. (C'était une institutrice° de 37 ans!) Aujourd'hui, 57% des candidats sont en réalité . . . des candidates.

◆ À l'origine, l'examinateur interrogeait° le candidat sur une liste de questions préparées à l'avance et tirées au sort.° En un an, le candidat devait apprendre la réponse à 500 questions différentes. Ce système donna lieu° à la pratique de «bachotage», selon laquelle l'élève apprend par coeur un grand nombre d'informations sans en connaître nécessairement le sens.°

◆ Le bac se démocratise.° En 1900, seulement un jeune Français sur cent passait le bac. Aujourd'hui, cette proportion est de 80%.

* De nos jours, un «bachelier» est une personne qui a son baccalauréat.

DÉFINITIONS
Définissez les mots ou expressions suivants:
- le «bac»
- le «terminale»
- redoubler
- être reçu à un examen
- l'université
- être prioritaire
- une «grande école»
- un concours

ET VOUS?
Quel genre d'étudiant(e) êtes-vous? Êtes-vous plutôt comme Corinne ou comme Guillaume? Expliquez.

EXPRESSION ORALE
- Avec votre partenaire, discutez les avantages et les inconvénients d'aller à l'université.
- Expliquez à un(e) ami(e) français(e) (votre partenaire) le système d'enseignement aux États-Unis (par exemple, quels sujets on peut choisir à l'école secondaire, comment on obtient son diplôme, ce qu'on doit faire pour aller à l'université, etc.)

EXPRESSION ÉCRITE
Écrivez une lettre à un copain français où vous dites ce que vous allez faire si vous avez votre diplôme d'études secondaires et si vous ne l'avez pas.

entrer = être accepté   **concours** competitive exam   **échouent** = ne réussissent pas   **obtient / obtenir** to obtain, get   **chevalier** knight   **thèse** = essai   **institué** = créé   **institutrice** = professeur d'école primaire   **interrogeait** = posait des questions   **tirées au sort** chosen at random   **donna lieu** gave rise   **sens** meaning   **se démocratise** = devient démocratique

Il a raté le bac

Mathieu gagne très bien sa vie. Il a une voiture de sport, voyage en première classe et, surtout, il fait ce qu'il aime. Pourtant, il a raté le fameux bac. Il raconte:

" Je ne suis pas fait° pour les études. Au lycée, ça n'allait vraiment pas. J'étais nul° en maths et en sciences, médiocre° dans les autres disciplines. La seule activité que j'aimais, c'était le sport. Là, j'étais vraiment «top», mais évidemment, ça ne suffisait° pas. J'ai raté mon bac une première fois, j'ai redoublé et je l'ai raté à nouveau. Alors, j'ai abandonné mes études. J'ai cherché un job. Tous les jours, je lisais les petites annonces dans les journaux et je téléphonais, mais sans bac je n'avais aucune chance. Alors, j'ai décidé de m'engager° dans l'armée.° J'ai opté pour un engagement° de trois ans. Pendant ce temps, j'ai continué à faire du sport et, surtout, j'ai fait un stage° de parachutisme.

Malheureusement, après mon service, ma situation n'avait pas changé! J'avais pensé être professeur d'éducation physique, mais sans diplôme, ce n'était pas possible. Alors, j'ai fait des petits boulots.° J'ai été chauffeur de taxi. J'ai travaillé dans un fast-food. J'ai été garde du corps° d'un banquier. Tout cela n'était pas ma vocation, et je cherchais désespérément à faire autre chose.

Un jour, finalement, la chance° m'a souri.° On tournait° un film dans le quartier où j'habitais. Je suis allé là pour regarder. Il y avait une scène où l'acteur principal devait sauter° du troisième étage d'une maison en flamme. Ce jour-là, le cascadeur° qui devait le remplacer n'est pas venu. Le metteur en scène° avait l'air désespéré. Alors, j'ai offert mes services. Ça a si bien marché° qu'on m'a embauché° pour le reste du film.

Depuis, je suis cascadeur professionnel. J'ai déjà une vingtaine de films à mon actif.° Évidemment, je ne suis pas la grande vedette,° mais je suis bien payé. Je voyage dans tous les pays du monde. Je connais des tas° d'acteurs et d'actrices et de temps en temps on me demande mon autographe... Et surtout, j'ai trouvé ma voie!° "

Les jeunes Français et l'armée

Le service militaire a été longtemps une tradition nationale en France. Symbole de démocratie et d'égalité, il était obligatoire° pour les garçons et volontaire° pour les filles. A 18 ans, les jeunes gens faisaient un service militaire de dix mois. Ce service militaire, aussi appelé «service national,» a été supprimé° en 2002.

Le système traditionnel a été remplacé par un système plus simple. À l'âge de 16 ans, tous les jeunes Français, garçons et filles, doivent être recensés° à la mairie.° Avant l'âge de 18 ans, ils doivent suivre une journée° de «Préparation à la défense,» pour laquelle ils reçoivent un certificat de préparation.

Les volontaires° peuvent faire une courte «préparation militaire» ou s'engager° dans l'armée, la police ou chez les pompiers° pour une période plus longue.

Service National
Vous et nous, un service à se rendre.

et vous?

- Selon vous, quelle est la «morale» de l'histoire de Mathieu?
- Aimeriez-vous être cascadeur / cascadeuse? Expliquez pourquoi ou pourquoi pas.

EXPRESSION ORALE

- Vous êtes journaliste. Interviewez Mathieu (joué par votre partenaire).
- Connaissez-vous des personnes qui n'étaient pas faites pour les études mais qui ont trouvé un job intéressant? Donnez un ou plusieurs exemples.

---

ne suis pas fait cut out nul = zéro médiocre below average suffisait = c'était suffisant m'engager enlist L'armée the army engagement service
stage training session petits boulots = jobs garde de corps bodyguard chance luck souri / sourire to smile tournait = filmait sauter to jump
cascadeur stuntman metteur en scène director si bien marché went so well embauché hired à mon actif behind me vedette = star tas = beaucoup
voie way obligatoire compulsory volontaire optional supprimé abolished recensé registered mairie town hall journée day volontaires volunteers
s'engager enlist pompiers firefighters

LE FRANÇAIS PRATIQUE

Études ou travail?

Qu'est-ce que tu vas fair après le lycée?

Je vais continuer mes études.

— Qu'est-ce que tu vas faire après le lycée?

Je vais | continuer mes études
        | aller à l'université

chercher | **du travail**
         | **un emploi** *job*

gagner ma vie

> **gagner sa vie** *to earn a living*

— Qu'est-ce que tu vas étudier?

Je vais | **étudier** les sciences
        | **faire des études de** biologie
        | **me spécialiser en** chimie

> **se spécialiser en** *to major in*

— Qu'est-ce que tu veux faire plus tard?

Je voudrais être médecin.

LES ÉTUDES

Les études scientifiques et techniques
- la **chimie**
- la **physique**
- les **maths**
- l'**informatique**
- les **études d'ingénieur**

Les études médicales
- la **biologie**
- la **médecine**
- la **pharmacie**
- les **études vétérinaires**

Les sciences humaines
- l'**histoire**
- la **psychologie**
- les **sciences économiques**
- les **sciences politiques**

Les études commerciales
- le **commerce** *business*
- la **gestion** *management*
- le **marketing**
- la **publicité** *advertising*
- la **comptabilité** *accounting*

Les études juridiques
- le **droit** *law*

Les études littéraires et artistiques
- la **philosophie**
- la **littérature**
- les **langues étrangères**
- le **journalisme**
- la **musique**
- le **dessin** *art, design*

1 À l'université

Imaginez que vous avez décidé d'aller à l'université. Choisissez . . .
- une spécialité principale *(major)*
- deux spécialités secondaires *(minors)*

Comparez votre choix de spécialité principale avec le reste de la classe.
Quelle est la spécialité favorite?

QUELQUES PROFESSIONS

La médecine
un **médecin**
un(e) **chirurgien(ne)** *surgeon*
un(e) **dentiste**
un(e) **pharmacien(ne)**
un(e) **vétérinaire**
un(e) **infirmier (-ère)**

Le commerce, les affaires *business*
un(e) **vendeur (-euse)** *salesperson*
un(e) **représentant(e)** de commerce
un(e) **spécialiste de marketing**
un(e) **homme (femme) d'affaires**

La finance
un(e) **banquier (-ière)**
un(e) **agent de change** *stockbroker*

Le droit *law*
un(e) **avocat(e)** *lawyer*
un(e) **juge**

La fonction publique *civil service*
un(e) **fonctionnaire** *civil servant*
un(e) **diplomate**
un(e) **assistant(e) social(e)** *social worker*

La technique et les sciences
un(e) **scientifique**
un **ingénieur**
un(e) **chercheur (-euse)** *researcher*
un(e) **technicien(ne)**
un(e) **informaticien(ne)**
un(e) **spécialiste de logiciel** *software*
un(e) **spécialiste de données** *data*

L'administration
un(e) **cadre** *executive*
un(e) **patron(ne)** *boss*
un(e) **chef** *(head)* **de personnel**
un(e) **directeur (-trice)** *manager*

Les emplois de bureau *office*
un(e) **employé(e)** *clerk*
un(e) **secrétaire**
un(e) **comptable** *accountant*

Les services
un **agent immobilier** *real estate agent*
un **agent d'assurances** *insurance agent*

FLASH d'information

Les professions préférées des Français

Ce qui compte le plus dans le choix d'une profession, ce n'est pas nécessairement la possibilité de gagner beaucoup d'argent, c'est avant tout de faire quelque chose d'intéressant. Voici la liste des dix professions préférées des Francais, par ordre d'intérêt.

1.	Chercheur scientifique	16%	6.	Acteur	10%
2.	Pilote	14%	7.	Chef de publicité	7%
3.	Médecin	14%	8.	Professeur d'université	5%
4.	Journaliste	14%	9.	Avocat	5%
5.	Chef d'entreprise	11%	10.	Banquier	4%

2 Choix professionnels

Faites une liste des cinq professions qui sont les plus intéressantes pour vous et des cinq professions qui sont les moins intéressantes. Comparez votre liste avec celle de votre partenaire et expliquez votre choix.

Ma Liste
☺ ☹
1.
2.
3.
4.
5.

3 Après le lycée

Vous avez décidé de continuer vos études, mais votre partenaire a décidé de chercher du travail (ou vice versa). Expliquez votre décision respective en donnant des arguments. Considérez, par exemple, les aspects suivants . . .

- gagner sa vie
- se perfectionner en . . . *(to increase one's skills in)*
- être indépendant(e)
- avoir plus d'options plus tard

LANGUE ET COMMUNICATION

A. La construction préposition + infinitif

Note the use of the infinitive in the following sentences.

Je voudrais aller à l'université
pour me spécialiser en informatique.

Tu ne réussiras pas à ton examen
sans étudier.

Donne-moi ton adresse
avant de partir en vacances.

I would like to go to college
(in order) to major in computer science.

You will not pass your exam
without studying.

Give me your address
before leaving on vacation.

In French, the INFINITIVE is used
after prepositions such as
pour *(in order to)*
avant de *(before)*
sans *(without)*

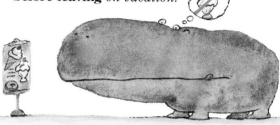

Il faut manger pour vivre, et non pas vivre pour manger.

1 À l'université

Chacun a ses raisons pour aller à l'université. Expliquez les
raisons des étudiants suivants.

▶ Christine étudie la physique.
Christine va à l'université pour étudier la physique.

1. Nous étudions la biologie.
2. Vous apprenez la comptabilité.
3. Je fais des études de droit.
4. Jean-Paul se spécialise en chimie.
5. Tu continues tes études de musique.
6. Hélène et Alice retrouvent leurs copains de lycée.
7. Marc est avec sa copine.
8. Philippe et Antoine jouent dans l'équipe de football.

2 Ne t'en fais pas! *(Don't worry!)*

Dites à votre partenaire ce qu'il/elle doit faire. Il/elle va suivre vos conseils.

▶ sortir / prendre la clé

1. aller chez tes copains / téléphoner
2. organiser une boum / demander la permission à tes parents
3. répondre à cette question / réfléchir *(think)*
4. quitter le restaurant / payer l'addition
5. prendre la voiture / faire le plein d'essence
6. partir en vacances / réserver une chambre d'hôtel
7. aller à l'entrevue / préparer ton curriculum vitae

▶ **Ne sors pas sans prendre la clé!**

Ne t'en fais pas! Je prendrai la clé avant de sortir.

3 Conseils

Votre partenaire va choisir un objectif de la liste ou un objectif de son choix.
Expliquez-lui ce qu'il faut faire pour atteindre *(to reach)* cet objectif.

OBJECTIFS		
• être interprète	• gagner de l'argent	• devenir professeur
• être avocat	• aller à l'université	• devenir vétérinaire
• être ingénieur	• être millionnaire	• ??

▶ **Pour être ingénieur,
il faut faire des
études d'ingénieur
(être bon en maths,
aller dans une université
spécialisée, . . .)**

B. L'infinitif passé

The verbs in heavy print are in the PAST INFINITIVE. Note the forms of the past infinitive in the following sentences.

Je suis content d'**avoir trouvé** un emploi.
Nous ne regrettons pas d'**être allés** à l'université.
Alice a étudié après **s'être reposée**.

*I am happy to **have found** a job.*
*We do not regret **to have gone** (having gone) to college.*
*Alice studied after **having rested**.*

FORMS

The PAST INFINITIVE is formed as follows:

> **avoir** or **être** + PAST PARTICIPLE

➡ When the past infinitive is a reflexive verb, the reflexive pronoun represents the same person as the subject of the sentence.

> **Je** ne me souviens pas de **m'**être promené dans ce parc.

USES

The PAST INFINITIVE is used instead of the present infinitive to describe an action that takes place <u>before</u> the action of the main verb. It is <u>always</u> used after **après.**

Qu'est-ce que tu vas faire
après avoir fini tes études?

What are you going to do
***after having finished (after finishing)** your studies?*

4 Leurs sentiments

Expliquez les sentiments des personnes suivantes en fonction de ce qu'elles ont fait.

▶ Patrick / être content / trouver un bon job
  Patrick est content d'avoir trouvé un bon job.

1. Alice / être heureuse / aller au Canada l'été dernier
2. Thomas / être enchanté / faire la connaissance de ta cousine
3. nous / avoir peur / rater l'examen
4. Bruno / être furieux / se tromper dans le problème de maths
5. vous / s'excuser / arriver en retard au rendez-vous
6. Madame Simon / être fière / créer sa propre *(own)* entreprise.

5 Hier

Demandez à votre partenaire à quelle heure il/elle a fait les choses suivantes hier et ce qu'il/elle a fait après.

▶ te coucher

1. te lever
2. prendre le petit déjeuner
3. arriver à l'école
4. déjeuner
5. rentrer chez toi
6. dîner
7. finir tes devoirs

À quelle heure est-ce que tu t'es couché?

Et qu'est-ce que tu as fait après t'être couché?

À dix heures et demie.

J'ai lu un livre.

(Je me suis endormi. J'ai regardé la télé . . .)

C. Le participe présent

FORMS

Note the forms of the PRESENT PARTICIPLE in the following sentences.

Parlant français et anglais,
je voudrais travailler pour une firme internationale.

Speaking French and English,
I would like to work for an international compa

J'ai rencontré mes copains
en **allant** au cinéma.

I met my friends
while **going** to the movies.

The PRESENT PARTICIPLE always ends in **-ant.** It is formed as follows:

STEM	+	ENDING
nous-form of the present	+	**-ant**

parler:	nous **parl**ons	→ **parlant**	aller:	nous **all**ons	→ **allant**
finir:	nous **finiss**ons	→ **finissant**	faire:	nous **fais**ons	→ **faisant**
attendre:	nous **attend**ons	→ **attendant**	sortir:	nous **sort**ons	→ **sortant**
acheter:	nous **achet**ons	→ **achetant**	voir:	nous **voy**ons	→ **voyant**
commencer:	nous **commenç**ons	→ **commençant**	lire:	nous **lis**ons	→ **lisant**
manger:	nous **mange**ons	→ **mangeant**	prendre:	nous **pren**ons	→ **prenant**

➡ There are three irregular present participles:

être → **étant**   avoir → **ayant**   savoir → **sachant**

➡ With reflexive verbs, the reflexive pronoun represents the same
person as the subject.

En **me** promenant, **j'**ai rencontré mon professeur d'histoire.

USES

The construction **en** + PRESENT PARTICIPLE is used to express:

- SIMULTANEOUS ACTION (*while, on, upon* doing something)

Éric écoute la radio
en **lavant** sa voiture.

Éric is listening to the radio
while **washing** his car.

- CAUSE AND EFFECT (*by* doing something)

Il gagne de l'argent
en **lavant** des voitures.

He earns money
by **washing** cars.

C'est en forgeant qu'on devient forgeron.

6 Études de langues

Pour chaque personne, choisissez une langue et dites comment elle apprend cette langue.

moi	l'espagnol
vous	le français
mon copain	l'anglais
Alice et Catherine	

- écouter Radio-France
- étudier à l'Alliance Française
- regarder des westerns à la télé
- écouter des chansons mexicaines
- passer les vacances en Argentine
- surfer sur l'Internet
- sortir avec des amis québécois
- lire des romans d'Hemingway

▶ **Mon copain apprend l'espagnol en
écoutant des chansons mexicaines
(en passant les vacances en Argentine).**

7 C'est simple!

Cet été Céline a travaillé pour gagner de l'argent. Marc lui pose des questions sur son job.
Céline lui répond. Avec votre partenaire, jouez les deux rôles.

▶ gagner de l'argent cet été
   travailler dans un restaurant

> **Comment as-tu gagné de l'argent cet été?**

> **C'est simple! J'ai gagné de l'argent en travaillant dans un restaurant.**

1. trouver ce job
   lire les annonces

2. contacter le restaurant
   téléphoner à la propriétaire *(owner)*

3. réussir à l'entrevue
   avoir une bonne attitude

4. apprendre ton travail
   regarder les autres employés

5. recevoir tes pourboires *(tips)*
   être attentive et polie avec les clients

8 Zut alors!

Les personnes suivantes ont eu des problèmes. Expliquez quand ou comment c'est arrivé.

▶ Monsieur Lasalle s'est coupé. (Il se rasait.)
   Monsieur Lasalle s'est coupé en se rasant.

1. Stéphanie s'est blessée. (Elle faisait de l'alpinisme.)
2. Je suis tombé. (Je descendais les escaliers.)
3. Tu t'es cassé une dent. (Tu mangeais du homard [*lobster*].)
4. Vincent a perdu son portefeuille. (Il allait au cinéma.)
5. Nous nous sommes perdus. (Nous nous promenions à la montagne.)
6. Vous avez eu un accident. (Vous faisiez du parapente.)

9 Comment?

Dites comment les personnes suivantes font certaines choses.

▶ Philippe célèbre son anniversaire. Il organise une boum.
   Philippe célèbre son anniversaire en organisant une boum.

1. Catherine reste en forme. Elle nage tous les jours.
2. Isabelle se repose. Elle écoute de la musique classique.
3. Jérôme amuse ses amis. Il imite Jim Carrey.
4. Alice gagne de l'argent. Elle fait du baby-sitting.
5. Thomas aide ses parents. Il passe l'aspirateur.
6. Stéphanie s'informe. Elle lit des magazines.
7. Carole reste en contact avec ses amis. Elle leur écrit pour leur anniversaire.
8. Marc soigne sa grippe. Il boit du thé chaud.
9. Édouard contribue à la protection de l'environnement. Il ramasse *(picks up)* les vieux papiers.
10. Hélène fait des bonnes actions *(deeds)*. Elle aide une famille d'immigrés.

10 Et vous?

Avec votre partenaire, dites comment vous faites les mêmes choses que celles de l'activité 9.

▶ **Moi, je célèbre mon anniversaire en faisant du bowling avec mes copains.**

COMMENT SE PRÉSENTER À UNE ENTREVUE

Vous avez surfé sur l'Internet pour trouver un job. Vous avez trouvé une petite annonce qui vous a intéressé(e). Vous avez téléphoné. On vous a demandé d'envoyer votre curriculum vitae. Quelques jours plus tard, on vous a convoqué(e)° pour une entrevue. Finalement le grand jour est arrivé. Ne le ratez pas! Voici quelques conseils.

Pour l'entrevue

◆ Habillez-vous correctement.

La présentation a beaucoup d'importance. Soignez-la!° Pour les garçons, mettez un costume et une cravate. Pour les filles, mettez une robe classique. Si vous avez le temps, passez chez le coiffeur quelques jours avant l'entrevue. Laissez vos lunettes de soleil chez vous, même s'il fait beau. Évitez les couleurs criardes° et les parfums excessifs. Et pas de coiffure extravagante.

◆ Arrivez à l'heure ou même un peu avant.

Soyez poli avec la réceptionniste. Attendez patiemment votre tour, même si la personne avec qui vous avez rendez-vous est en retard.

◆ Ne soyez pas intimidé.

Même si vous avez le trac° intérieurement°, ayez l'air décontracté. (Ce n'est pas le dernier jour de votre vie, mais peut-être le premier jour de votre vie professionnelle.) Ne mâchez° pas de chewing-gum pour masquer votre nervosité.

Pendant l'entrevue

◆ Répondez clairement et distinctement aux questions de l'interviewer.

Mettez en valeur° vos talents et vos qualifications, mais sans les exagérer. Surtout, ne vous inventez pas un curriculum vitae extraordinaire. (À votre âge, il est normal que votre expérience professionnelle soit limitée.)

◆ Soyez attentif et respectueux.

Ayez l'air intéressé par ce qu'on vous dit. N'interrompez pas l'interviewer quand il vous parle. Posez des questions, mais seulement au bon° moment. À l'occasion, prenez des notes. (Pour cela, n'oubliez pas d'apporter un carnet et un stylo à l'entrevue. Cela fera bonne impression.) Ne regardez jamais votre montre pendant l'entrevue.

◆ Ne soyez pas trop personnel.

Parlez de votre vie personnelle seulement si cela a un rapport° avec vos qualifications pour le job. Ne soyez pas familier avec votre interviewer. (Par exemple, n'essayez pas de savoir qui sont les personnes sur les photos qui peuvent être sur son bureau!)

---

convoqué(e) *called* **Soignez-la!** *pay careful attention to it* **criardes** *loud* **trac** *are scared, nervous* **intérieurement** *inside* **mâchez** *chew* **mettez en valeur** *emphasize* **interrompez / interrompre** *to interrupt* **bon** *right* **rapport** *connection*

Ne parlez jamais de salaire.

Si vous êtes accepté pour le job, il sera temps d'en discuter à ce moment-là.

Après l'entrevue

◆ **Soyez persévérant sans être trop insistant.**

Si possible, écrivez une lettre assez courte dans laquelle vous remerciez l'interviewer de l'entretien qu'il vous a donné. Cela l'aidera à se souvenir de vous. Ne téléphonez pas tous les jours à la compagnie pour connaître les résultats de l'entrevue. En fait, attendez au moins 15 jours avant de vous informer sur votre sort.°

◆ **Restez optimiste.**

Même en cas de réponse négative, vous avez acquis° l'expérience de l'entrevue. Cela vous sera utile pour la prochaine fois.

et vous?

Avec votre partenaire, déterminez quels sont les trois (3) conseils les plus utiles et dites pourquoi.

EXPRESSION ÉCRITE

Décrivez une entrevue personnelle que vous avez eue. Mentionnez, par exemple:

- comment vous étiez habillé(e)
- quand vous êtes arrivé(e) à l'entrevue
- comment vous vous sentiez
- qui était l'interviewer
- quelles questions il/elle vous a posées
- comment vous avez répondu
- quels problèmes vous avez eus pendant l'entrevue
- qu'est-ce que vous avez fait après l'entrevue
- quel a été le résultat de cette entrevue

CURRICULUM VITAE

et vous?

Vous voulez travailler pour une compagnie française. Préparez votre propre curriculum vitae sur le modèle indiqué.

sort *fate*
acquis / acquérir* *to acquire*
courant *fluent*
sur demande *on request*

CURRICULUM VITAE

Karine PERRAUDIN
125, rue de l'Ermitage
37100 Tours
tél. 02-47-31-22-51
19 ans

ÉTUDES	1 année de préparation, École Supérieure de Commerce Bac S, mention assez bien
LANGUES	Anglais (courant°) Allemand Notions d'espagnol
EXPÉRIENCE	été 2003 Stage d'un mois à CANAL-PLUS (service marketing)
	été 2002 Réceptionniste dans un hôtel 3 étoiles
	été 2001 Animatrice dans une colonie de vacances pour enfants handicapés
POSTE SOUHAITÉ	Stage de 4 à 6 semaines, si possible rémunéré, dans un service de publicité ou de marketing. Préférence pour compagnie internationale.
SPORTS ET LOISIRS	Tennis, Natation, Escalade, Musique (violon), Photo
RÉFÉRENCES	Sur demande.°

LE FRANÇAIS PRATIQUE

La vie professionnelle

— Où voudrais-tu travailler?
  Je voudrais travailler **dans/pour une banque.**

> **Où voudrais-tu travailler?**
>
> Je voudrais travailler pour une banque.

un bureau	**une compagnie internationale**
une usine *factory*	**un cabinet** *(office)* **d'avocat**
une agence de voyages	**un laboratoire de recherches**

— **Dans quelle branche d'activité** voudrais-tu | travailler?
  faire carrière?

  J'aimerais travailler dans **la finance.**

le commerce *trade*	**l'informatique**
l'industrie	**la recherche** *(research)* **scientifique**
la communication	**la fonction publique** *civil service*
la publicité *advertising*	**les relations publiques**
les assurances *insurance*	**l'immobilier** *real estate*
les affaires *business*	**l'électronique**

— **Pour quel genre d'entreprise** voudrais-tu travailler?

  Je voudrais travailler **pour une** | **petite** | **entreprise.**
  | **grande** |

une compagnie	**moyenne** *average size*
une firme	**multinationale**
une société	

  Je voudrais | travailler **à mon propre compte** *(for myself)*.
  | **créer ma propre** *(own)* **entreprise**.

— **Qu'est-ce que tu recherches**
  Qu'est-ce qui t'intéresse | dans ce travail?
  Qu'est-ce qui compte le plus |

  | **rechercher** *to look for, search* |

  Je recherche **un bon salaire.**

une bonne ambiance *atmosphere*
de bonnes conditions de travail
la possibilité de promotion
des responsabilités importantes
des avantages sociaux *fringe benefits*

1 Un sondage

Conduisez un sondage dans la classe pour déterminer . . .

- le lieu de travail préféré
- le type d'entreprise préféré
- la branche d'activité préférée
- l'aspect le plus important d'un travail

2 Choix professionnel

Votre partenaire et vous, vous allez choisir une profession qui vous intéresse.
(Chacun va choisir une profession différente.) Comparez les avantages
de chaque profession sur la base des éléments suivants.

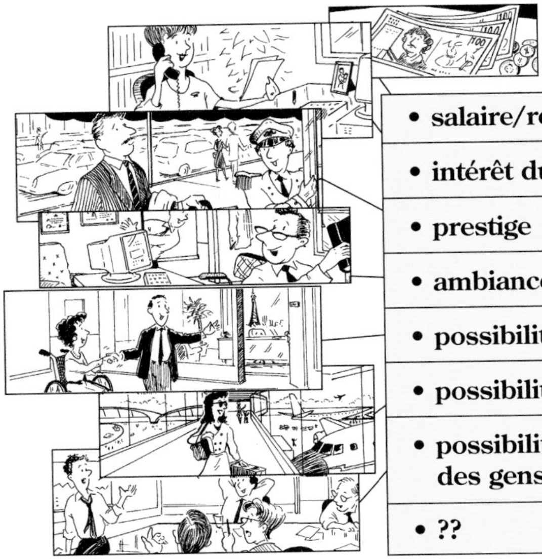

	faible	moyen(ne)	assez bon(ne)	bon(ne)	excellent(e)
• salaire/rémunération					
• intérêt du travail					
• prestige					
• ambiance de travail					
• possibilité de promotion					
• possibilité de voyager					
• possibilité de rencontrer des gens intéressants					
• ??					

3 La meilleure solution

Préféreriez-vous travailler pour une compagnie ou créer votre propre entreprise?
Chaque solution a ses avantages, mais aussi ses désavantages. Avec votre partenaire, évaluez
ces avantages et ces désavantages.

- Quelle est la meilleure solution pour vous?
- Quelle est la meilleure solution pour votre partenaire?

AVANTAGES		
peu important	important	très important

DÉSAVANTAGES		

Créer sa propre entreprise

- Satisfaction personnelle
- Indépendance
- Heures flexibles
- Possibilité de devenir riche
- ??

- Possibilité d'échec (failure)
- Risques financiers
- Travail très dur
- Trop de responsabilités
- ??

Travailler pour une compagnie

- Horaire régulier
- Salaire régulier
- Avantages sociaux
- Responsabilités limitées
- ??

- Salaire limité
- Hiérarchie pesante (heavy)
- Travail monotone
- Pas assez de responsabilités
- ??

À la recherche d'un emploi

POUR TROUVER DU TRAVAIL

Qu'est-ce que tu vas faire pour trouver du travail?

— Qu'est-ce que tu vas faire pour trouver du travail?

Je vais | **lire les annonces** *classified ads.*
répondre à l'annonce.
téléphoner au chef du personnel.
prendre rendez-vous *to make an appointment.*
envoyer mon curriculum vitae *resume.*
solliciter *to ask for* | **une entrevue** *interview.*
une interview.
un entretien.

aller à l'entretien.

Je vais lire les annonces.

PENDANT L'INTERVIEW

— Quel emploi cherchez-vous?

Je cherche **un emploi temporaire.**

un job d'été	**un emploi à mi-temps** *half time*
un stage *internship*	**un emploi à temps partiel** *part time*
	un emploi à plein temps *full time*

— Avez-vous déjà travaillé?

Oui, j'ai travaillé dans | un hôpital.
une boutique.
un supermarché.

Non, je n'ai **pas d'expérience professionnelle.**

— Qu'est-ce que vous savez faire?

Je sais **parler anglais.**

parler français, espagnol, chinois . . .
conduire une voiture
utiliser / **me servir d'**	**un ordinateur**
classer des documents

conduire *to drive*
se servir de *to use*
classer *to file*

— Quelles sont vos qualifications personnelles?

J'ai **l'esprit d'initiative.**

de l'ambition
le sens des contacts humains
le goût (*liking*) **des responsabilités**
une bonne formation (*education*) **générale**
des connaissances (*knowledge*) **techniques**

— Quels documents avez-vous apportés?
   J'ai **mon curriculum vitae**.

> **des lettres de recommandation**
> **mes références**
> **mes diplômes**

Quels documents avez-vous apportés?

J'ai mon curriculum vitae.

— Merci! **Vous faites l'affaire!** *(You are qualified.)*
   Nous allons vous | **offrir** un emploi.
                    | **embaucher.**

> **offrir** *to offer*
> **embaucher** *to hire*

   Je suis désolé(e), mais **vous ne faites pas l'affaire**.

Conversations libres

Avec votre partenaire, choisissez l'un des sujets suivants.
Composez et jouez le dialogue correspondant à ce sujet.
Votre partenaire va jouer l'autre personne.

1   Jobs d'été

Votre camarade et vous, vous habitez
en France. Discutez de ce que vous
allez faire pour trouver un job cet été.
Rôles: deux étudiants français.

2   Télémarketing

Dans le journal, vous avez lu une annonce dans
laquelle une firme française de produits
cosmétiques cherche des étudiants américains
pour vendre ses produits par téléphone.
Téléphonez à cette firme pour expliquer vos
qualifications.

*Rôles: un(e) étudiant(e) américain(e) /
  le représentant de la firme*

3   Agence de voyages

Une agence de voyages française cherche
un(e) assistant(e). Vous avez obtenu une
entrevue avec le chef du personnel.
C'est le jour de l'entrevue.

Rôles: un(e) candidat(e) / le chef du personnel

4   Compagnie internationale

Vous venez d'obtenir votre diplôme universitaire avec
une spécialité en littérature française. Vous répondez
à l'annonce d'une compagnie internationale qui
recrute des étudiants pour son département de
marketing. Vous n'avez pas fait d'études de marketing.
Expliquez à l'interviewer pourquoi vous voulez le job
et pourquoi vous êtes tout de même *(nevertheless)*
qualifié(e).

Rôles: un(e) candidat(e) / l'interviewer

5   Office de Tourisme

Vous habitez en France. L'Office de Tourisme
de votre ville recrute des étudiants parlant
anglais pour développer le tourisme dans
la région. Vous avez une entrevue avec
la directrice de l'Office du Tourisme.

Rôles: un(e) candidat(e) / la directrice

A. La construction conjonction + subjonctif

Note the use of the subjunctive in the following sentences.

Je te prête le journal
pour que tu lises les petites annonces.

I am lending you the paper
***so that you read** the ads.*

Téléphone au chef du personnel
avant qu'il parte en vacances.

Call the head of personnel
***before he leaves** on vacation.*

Nous vous engagerons
à condition que vous ayez
de bonnes recommandations.

We will hire you
provided that you have
good recommendations.

The SUBJUNCTIVE is used after certain conjunctions which express:

- PURPOSE or INTENT

pour que	so that	Le professeur explique **pour que** vous **compreniez**.

- CONDITION or RESTRICTION

à condition que	provided, on condition that	Nous ferons une promenade à vélo **à condition qu'**il **fasse** beau.
à moins que	unless	J'irai à la plage **à moins qu'**il **fasse** mauvais.
sans que	without	Philippe est parti **sans que** tu lui **dises** au revoir.

- TIME LIMITATION

avant que	before	Je vous téléphonerai **avant que** vous **partiez.**
jusqu'à ce que	until	Nous attendrons **jusqu'à ce que** vous **veniez.**

➡ The INFINITIVE is used after **avant de, pour,** and **sans** when the subject of the main clause and the dependent clause are the same.

Victor est venu . . .
pour parler de ses projets.
avant d'aller en France.
sans avoir rendez-vous.

Victor est venu . . .
pour que vous parliez de vos projets.
avant que vous alliez en vacances.
sans que vous ayez rendez-vous.

➡ Remember that the INDICATIVE is used after conjunctions, such as
parce que, pendant que, depuis que, lorsque.

Je cherche du travail **parce que** j'ai besoin d'argent.

1 Prêts

Vous êtes une personne généreuse qui prête ce qu'elle a. Choisissez une chose
et dites à qui vous allez la prêter et pourquoi.

▶ **Je vais prêter dix dollars à mon cousin Christophe (à ma soeur**
   Michelle) pour qu'il/elle aille au cinéma.

QUOI?	POURQUOI?
mon vélo	s'acheter un livre
mon gant de baseball	faire un tour à la campagne
ma radiocassette	aller au ciné
ma mini-chaîne	prendre des photos
dix dollars	organiser une boum
vingt dollars	écouter ce nouveau CD
??	??

2 Il y a toujours une raison

Expliquez pourquoi les personnes suivantes font certaines choses pour d'autres personnes.

▶ Madame Bertrand / donner de l'argent à sa nièce / s'acheter une mini-chaîne
   Madame Bertrand donne de l'argent à sa nièce pour qu'elle s'achète une mini-chaîne.

1. Thomas / prêter son vélo à son copain / faire une promenade à la campagne
2. Monsieur Thibault / payer les études à sa fille / être avocate
3. Madame Rémi / envoyer un chèque à son fils / payer sa scolarité *(tuition)*
4. le professeur / écrire des lettres de recommandation aux élèves / trouver du travail
5. Marc / inviter sa copine à dîner / faire la connaissance de ses parents
6. Madame Lombard / envoyer ses enfants en Angleterre / apprendre l'anglais

3 Dépêchez-vous!

Dites à votre partenaire de se dépêcher de faire certaines choses.

> **Va à la bibliothèque avant qu'elle ferme.**

▶ aller à la bibliothèque (elle va fermer)

1. téléphoner à ta copine (elle va sortir)
2. ranger ta chambre (tes copains vont venir)
3. finir tes devoirs (on va aller au ciné)
4. promener le chien (il va faire noir)
5. acheter cette mini-chaîne (les prix vont augmenter)
6. chercher un job (les vacances vont commencer)
7. demander des lettres de recommandation (tes profs
   vont partir en vacances)
8. répondre à cette annonce (la compagnie va
   embaucher quelqu'un d'autre)

4 Conditions

François demande à sa mère s'il peut faire certaines choses. Sa mère accepte mais à certaines conditions. Avec votre partenaire, jouez les deux rôles.

▶ aller à la boum / rentrer avant minuit

    FRANÇOIS: **Dis, est-ce que je peux <u>aller</u> <u>à la soirée</u>?**

    SA MÈRE: **Je veux bien, mais à condition que tu rentres avant minuit.**

    FRANÇOIS: **Bon, d'accord! Je rentrerai avant minuit.**

1. regarder mon nouveau DVD / finir tes devoirs avan
2. écouter mes CD / ne pas faire de bruit
3. inviter un copain à dîner / mettre la table
4. organiser un pique-nique / faire les courses
5. prendre la voiture / être prudent
6. voyager cet été / réussir à tes examens

5 Négociation

Votre partenaire va vous demander de faire une des choses suivantes pour lui/elle. Négociez un échange.

- prêter ton VTT
- prêter ton portable
- prêter dix dollars
- inviter au café

- inviter à ta boum
- présenter à tes copains
- aider avec le devoir
- aider à ranger ma chambre

▶ — **Dis, est-ce que tu peux me prêter ton VTT?**
   — **D'accord, mais à condition que tu me prêtes ton appareil-photo (que tu m'aides avec le problème de maths, . . .)**

6 Une promenade à vélo

Vous êtes en Touraine avec votre partenaire.
Vous organisez une promenade à vélo.
Expliquez vos projets à votre partenaire.

▶ Nous ferons une promenade samedi.
    (à condition que / il fait beau)
    Nous ferons une promenade samedi à condition qu'il fasse beau.

1. Le matin, nous visiterons le château d'Amboise.
    (à moins que / il est fermé)
2. Je te prêterai mon appareil-photo.
    (pour que / tu prends des photos)
3. Après, nous ferons un pique-nique.
    (à moins que / nous trouvons une petite auberge sympathique)
4. Nous irons dans cette auberge.
    (à condition que / elle a des spécialités régionales)
5. Ensuite nous continuerons notre promenade.
    (jusqu'à ce que / nous sommes fatigués)
6. Nous rentrerons.
    (avant que / il fait nuit)

le château d'Amboise

7 Double effet

En général, nos actions nous concernent nous-mêmes. Elles peuvent aussi concerner d'autres personnes. Exprimez cela d'après le modèle.

▶ J'achète le journal pour lire les petites annonces. (tu)
J'achète le journal pour que tu lises les petites annonces.

1. Madame Gustave passe un an au Brésil pour apprendre le portugais. (ses enfants)
2. Monsieur Guyon commande un taxi pour être à l'heure au rendez-vous. (son patron)
3. Nous allons dans ce magasin pour regarder les ordinateurs. (vous)
4. Je rendrai visite à mes cousins avant de partir en vacances. (ils)
5. Nous te téléphonerons avant d'aller en France. (tu)
6. Monsieur Durand ne partira pas sans avoir son passeport. (sa femme)
7. Nous ne quitterons pas Paris sans voir Notre Dame. (nos enfants)
8. Monsieur Thomas achète un nouveau logiciel *(software)* pour faire sa comptabilité *(accounting)*. (sa secrétaire)
9. Je téléphone à la directrice pour avoir une entrevue. (tu)
10. Madame Rimbaud relit la lettre avant de signer. (son patron)
11. Le chef du personnel n'engagera pas ces candidats sans parler au président de la compagnie. (ils)

8 C'est vous le président!

C'est vous le président de votre propre entreprise. Tous les mois, vous réunissez votre personnel. Faites votre présentation en complétant les phrases suivantes.

1. Je vous ai demandé de venir pour que . . .
   (vous / discuter des progrès de l'entreprise)
2. Nos ventes *(sale)* ont progressé depuis que . . .
   (je / vous avoir parlé le mois dernier)
3. En particulier, nos exportations vers le Japon ont augmenté depuis que . . .
   (le franc / avoir été dévalué)
4. J'ai contacté notre agence de Tokyo pour que . . .
   (elle / faire de la publicité à la télévision)
5. Nous devons développer de nouveaux produits sans que . . .
   (nos concurrents / le savoir)
6. Pour financer ces produits, je vais emprunter de l'argent à la Banque Nationale de Paris pendant que . . . (les taux [*rates*] d'intérêt / être favorables)
7. Nous allons réussir à moins que . . .
   (la situation économique / devenir mauvaise)
8. J'augmenterai vos salaires à condition que . . .
   (vous / continuer dans vos efforts)
9. Pour ma part, je vais continuer à travailler jusqu'à ce que . . .
   (cette compagnie / être la première compagnie dans sa spécialité)
10. C'est possible parce que . . .
    (nos produits / être les meilleurs produits du monde)

LECTURE

Le portrait

Yves Thériault

AVANT DE LIRE

Le but d'un conte est de distraire.° Pour cela, un conte doit contenir un élément qui attirera et maintiendra l'attention du lecteur: humour, intrigue, développement psychologique, etc.

Dans le conte que vous allez lire, Hélène, une jeune fille canadienne, découvre un portrait dans le grenier de la ferme où elle habite avec sa famille. Elle apprend que c'est le portrait d'un oncle mort il y a longtemps et dont personne ne veut parler.

D'après cette courte introduction, quel est, selon vous, l'élément que l'auteur utilisera pour retenir l'attention des lecteurs?

- l'humour?
- le mystère?
- l'intrigue?
- le récit d'aventures?
- le développement psychologique?
- autre élément?

distraire *to entertain*

Yves Thériault (1915-1983) est un auteur québécois. Avant de se consacrer à la littérature, il a fait un peu tous les métiers: conducteur de camion, marchand de fromages, présentateur à la radio, traducteur... Écrivain très prolifique, il a écrit des essais, des contes sur des thèmes canadiens, aussi bien qu'une série de romans policiers.

LE PORTRAIT

1

   J'ai trouvé le portrait dans le grenier, un matin de juin. J'y étais allée chercher des pots° pour les confitures de fraises, puisque nous étions au temps de l'année pour ces choses.

   Le portrait était derrière un bahut.° J'ai vu la dorure° du cadre. J'ai tiré à moi,
5 et voilà que c'était le portrait.

   Celui d'un homme jeune, aux cheveux bruns, à la bouche agréable, et des yeux qui me regardaient. De grands yeux noirs, vivants . . .

   J'ai descendu le portrait dans la cuisine.

   — Voilà, mère, c'était au grenier.
10 Elle regarda le portrait d'un air surpris.

   — Nous avions donc ça ici, ma fille? Tiens, tiens . . .

   J'ai demandé:

   — Qui est l'homme? Parce que c'est un bel homme. Il est vêtu° à la mode ancienne, mais c'est un magnifique gaillard . . .°
15 — Ton oncle, dit-elle, le frère de ton père. Le portrait a été peint alors qu'il était jeune.

   — Quel oncle?

   Je ne connaissais qu'une vague tante, pâle, anémique, qui vivait à la ville et venait chez nous une fois l'an. C'était, à ma connaissance, la seule parente de mon
20 père.

   Je l'ai dit à ma mère.

   — Je ne me connais pas d'oncle . . .

   — C'était le plus jeune frère de ton père. Ils étaient quatre. Trois garçons,
25 une fille. Il ne reste que ton père et ta tante Valérienne.

   — Les autres sont morts?

   Elle fit° oui de la tête.

   — Même celui-là? dis-je, même ce bel oncle-là?

   — Oui.

<table>
<tr><td colspan="2">Mots utiles</td></tr>
<tr><td>le cadre</td><td>frame</td></tr>
<tr><td>la colère</td><td>anger</td></tr>
<tr><td>le grenier</td><td>attic</td></tr>
<tr><td>chercher à</td><td>= essayer de</td></tr>
<tr><td>descendre</td><td>to bring down</td></tr>
<tr><td>pendre</td><td>to hang</td></tr>
<tr><td>secouer</td><td>to shake</td></tr>
<tr><td>tirer</td><td>to pull, draw</td></tr>
<tr><td>ça n'a pas
  d'importance</td><td>that doesn't matter</td></tr>
<tr><td>il ne reste que…</td><td>there is/are
  only . . . left</td></tr>
<tr><td>mieux vaut</td><td>= il vaut mieux</td></tr>
</table>

pot *jar* **bahut** *cupboard* **dorure** *gilt* **vêtu** *dressed* **gaillard** *guy* **fit** = dit

— Ce n'est pas juste de mourir quand on est si jeune et si beau . . . Non, ce n'est pas juste . . . Eh bien, oui, j'avais un bel oncle. Dommage qu'il soit mort . . . 30

Ma mère me regardait curieusement.

—Hélène, tu dis de drôles de choses . . .

Mais je n'écoutais pas ma mère. Je regardais le portrait. Maintenant, à la lumière plus crue° de la cuisine, le portrait me paraissait encore plus beau, encore mieux fait . . . Et j'aimais bien les couleurs. 35

— Je le pends dans ma chambre, dis-je . . .

— Comme tu voudras, dit ma mère, aujourd'hui, ça n'a plus d'importance.

La remarque n'était pas bien claire, et j'ai voulu savoir.

— Vous ne trouvez pas que c'est d'en dire beaucoup, et bien peu, mère? 40

— Peut-être. De celui-là, mieux vaut en dire le moins possible . . .

— Comment se nommait-il?°

— Tout simplement Jean . . .

— Et qu'est-ce qu'il faisait, demandai-je, qu'est-ce qu'il faisait dans la vie?

Mais ma mère secoua la tête. 45

— Pends, dit-elle, ce portrait où tu voudras . . . Ça n'a plus d'importance, mais si tu veux un bon conseil, ne dis rien, ne cherche à rien savoir. Et surtout, ne parle de rien à ton père.

Au fond,° ça n'avait pas d'importance. J'aimais le coup de pinceau° de l'artiste. J'aimais sa façon de tracer, de poser° la couleur, j'aimais les teintes° chaudes . . . 50

crue *direct* **se nommait-il** = s'appelait-il **au fond** *deep down* **coup de pinceau** *brush stroke*
poser = mettre **teintes** = couleurs

Je trouvais l'oncle bien beau, et bien jeune. Mais ça n'était pas si important que je doive encourir° d'inutiles colères. Et quelque chose me disait, quelque chose dans le ton de la voix de ma mère, dans la détermination de son visage,
55   que mon père n'aimerait pas du tout que j'aborde° le sujet de son frère Jean.

encourir *to incur* **aborde** = approche

Avez-vous compris?

1. Comment Hélène a-t-elle découvert le portrait?
2. Qu'est-ce que sa mère lui explique? Qu'est-ce qu'elle ne lui explique pas?
3. Qu'est-ce qu'Hélène pense de son oncle?
4. Qu'est-ce qu'elle veut faire du portrait?

Anticipons un peu!

Hélène a décidé de mettre le portrait dans sa chambre. D'après vous, qu'est-ce qui va se passer dans l'épisode suivant?

- Le portrait va disparaître.
- Le portrait va vouloir communiquer quelque chose à Hélène.
- Hélène va tomber malade et mourir mystérieusement.
- L'oncle Jean va réapparaître dans la maison familiale bien vivant *(alive)*.
- Autre possibilité?

Expliquez votre choix.

2

J'ai pendu le portrait au mur de ma chambre.

Je l'ai regardé chaque matin en m'éveillant, et chaque soir avant de souffler la lampe.

Et puis, au bout de deux semaines, une nuit, j'ai senti que quelqu'un me touchait l'épaule.

Je me suis éveillée en sursaut,° j'ai allumé ma lampe de chevet.° J'avais des sueurs froides le long du corps . . . Mais il n'y avait personne dans ma chambre.

Machinalement,° j'ai regardé le portrait, et en le voyant j'ai crié, je crois, pas fort,° mais assez tout de même, et je me suis enfoui° la tête sous l'oreiller.°

Dans le portrait, l'oncle Jean, très habilement° rendu,° regardait droit devant lui... Mais lorsque je me suis éveillée, j'ai vu qu'à cette heure-là de la nuit, il regardait ailleurs. En fait il regardait vers la fenêtre. Il regardait dehors . . .

Le matin, je n'ai rien dit. Je n'ai rien dit non plus les jours suivants, même si, chaque nuit, quelqu'un . . . ou quelque chose m'éveillait en me touchant l'épaule. Et même si chaque nuit, l'oncle Jean regardait par la fenêtre . . .

Naturellement, je me demandais bien ce que ça voulait dire. Plusieurs fois je me suis pincée, très fort,° pour être bien sûre que je ne dormais pas.

Chose certaine, j'étais bien éveillée.

Et quelque chose se passait . . . Mais quoi?

Au sixième matin . . . vous voyez comme je suis patiente . . . j'ai voulu tout savoir de maman.

— L'oncle Jean, qui est-il? Qu'est-ce qu'il faisait? Pourquoi ne faut-il pas en parler devant papa, de cet oncle?

— Tu as toujours le portrait dans ta chambre? dit ma mère.

— Oui.

Elle continua ses occupations pendant quelques minutes, puis elle vint s'asseoir devant moi, à la table.

— Ma fille, me dit-elle, il y a des choses qui sont difficiles à dire. Moi, ton oncle Jean, je l'aimais bien, je le trouvais charmant. Et ça mettait ton père dans tous les états° quand j'osais dire de telles choses.

Je lui ai demandé:

— Mais pourquoi, mère?

— Parce que ton oncle Jean, c'était une sorte de mouton noir dans la famille . . . il a eu des aventures, je t'épargne° les détails. Surtout, il avait la bougeotte.° Il s'est enfui jeune de la maison, on ne l'a revu que plus tard . . . . Puis il est reparti. Un jour, ton père a reçu une lettre. Ton oncle Jean s'était fait tuer,° stupidement, dans un accident aux États-Unis. On a fait transporter son corps ici, pour être enterré dans le lot° familial au cimetière. Il n'aurait pas dû . . . mais . . .

en sursaut *with a start* **de chevet** *bedside* **machinalement** *unconsciously* **pas fort** *not very loud* **enfoui** *buried* **oreiller** *pillow* **habilement** *skillfully* **rendu** = *peint* **pincée très fort** *pinched hard* **dans tous les états** = *en colère* **épargne** *spare* **bougeotte** *travelling urge* **s'était fait tuer** *was killed* **lot** *plot*

Mots utiles	
l'épaule	shoulder
la sueur	sweat
un testament	will
allumer	to light
crier	to scream
se demander	to wonder
s'enfuir *	to run away
éveiller	to wake up
oser	to dare
souffler	to blow out
vouloir dire	to mean
ailleurs	elsewhere
au bout de	= après
tel (telle)	such

— Pourquoi? ai-je demandé, pourquoi n'aurait-il pas dû?

— Parce que, dans un testament découvert par la suite dans les effets de Jean, celui-ci exigeait d'être enterré n'importe où, mais pas dans le lot° familial . . .

Il disait dans cet écrit qu'il n'avait aucunement° le désir de reposer aux côtés de la paisible° et sédentaire famille. Il avait un autre mot pour eux . . . pas très gentil.

Moi je croyais comprendre, maintenant.

— Est-ce que papa l'a fait transporter ailleurs?

— Euh . . . non . . . question° des dépenses que ça signifiait° . . . Jean n'a rien laissé, il est mort pauvre.

100

lot *plot* **aucunement** = pas du tout **paisible** *quiet* **question des** = à cause des **signifiait** = représentait

| *Avez-vous compris?* | *Anticipons un peu!* |

Avez-vous compris?

1. Pourquoi est-ce qu'Hélène s'est éveillée en sursaut?
2. En quoi le portrait de son oncle était-il différent à ce moment-là?
3. Que pensait la mère d'Hélène de l'oncle Jean?
4. Quelles étaient les rapports entre le père d'Hélène et son frère Jean?
5. Comment est mort l'oncle Jean?
6. Qu'est-ce que son testament stipulait? Est-ce qu'il a été respecté?

Anticipons un peu!

D'après vous, qu'est-ce que l'oncle Jean voulait communiquer à Hélène?

- Qu'elle ouvre la fenêtre.
- Qu'elle sorte *(take out)* le portrait de la maison.
- Qu'elle prie *(pray)* pour lui.
- Qu'elle quitte elle-même la maison familiale et parte à l'aventure.

Expliquez votre choix.

3

Ce soir-là, j'ai mieux dormi. J'ai été éveillée vers quatre heures, et toute la scène d'habitude s'est répétée.

— Soit,° ai-je déclaré au portrait de l'oncle Jean . . . Demain, je vais faire quelque chose.

Et le lendemain matin, j'ai pris le portrait, et je l'ai porté dehors, derrière la remise.° Je l'ai appuyé là, face au soleil levant.°

Plusieurs fois dans la journée, je suis allée voir. L'oncle Jean regardait en face, mais j'ai cru voir comme une lueur° amusée dans ses yeux. Je me suis dit que je n'avais pas remarqué ce sourire auparavant.°

Au crépuscule,° le portrait était encore là . . .

Durant la nuit, je fus éveillée de nouveau. Seulement, au lieu d'une main discrète sur mon épaule, ce fut un très gentil baiser sur la joue qui m'éveilla.

Et je vous jure que pendant les quatre ou cinq secondes entre le sommeil profond et l'éveil complet, j'ai bien senti des lèvres tièdes° sur ma joue.

Je me suis rendormie paisiblement. J'avais comme une sensation de bien-être.

Au matin, le portrait n'était plus à sa place.

J'ai demandé à papa s'il l'avait pris, et il m'a dit que non. Maman n'y avait pas touché. Mes petits frères non plus.

Le portrait avait disparu. Et moi j'étais convaincue que sa disparition° coïncidait avec le baiser de reconnaissance si bien donné au cours de la nuit.

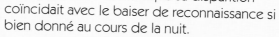

Vous voulez une explication? Je n'en ai pas. La chose est arrivée. Elle s'est passée comme ça peut être une suite° de rêves. Freud aurait une explication, je suppose . . . N'empêche° que les faits sont là. Un portrait est disparu, et l'oncle Jean regardait. Pour un homme qui avait toujours eu la bougeotte, c'était tout de même assez significatif . . .

105

110

115

120

125

130

soit *all right, so be it* **remise** *shed* **levant** *rising* **lueur** *gleam* **auparavant =** *avant*
crépuscule *dusk* **tièdes** *warm* **disparition** *disappearance*
suite *series, sequence* **n'empêche que** *nevertheless*

Mots utiles

un baiser	*kiss*
le bien-être	*well-being*
l'éveil	*wakefulness*
la reconnaissance	= la *gratitude*
un rêve	*dream*
le sommeil	*sleep*
appuyer	*to lean*
jurer	*to swear*
se rendormir *	*to go back to sleep*

Avez-vous compris?

1. Qu'est-ce qu'Hélène fait avec le portrait? Pourquoi?
2. Quelle semble être la réaction du portrait? Pourquoi?
3. Qu'est-ce qui se passe cette nuit-là? Pourquoi?
4. Que devient le portrait?
5. Quelle est l'explication d'Hélène?

Et vous?

D'après vous, qu'est-ce qui est arrivé au portrait?

EXPRESSION ORALE

■ Situations

Avec votre partenaire, choisissez l'une des situations suivantes. Composez le dialogue correspondant et jouez-le en classe.

1 L'histoire du portrait

Hélène raconte l'histoire du portrait à un(e) copain (copine). Incrédule, celui-ci (celle-ci) veut connaître les détails.

Rôles: Hélène, le copain (la copine)

2 La rupture

Quelques années après, Hélène demande à son père les raisons de la rupture avec son jeune frère Jean. Le père hésite et finalement répond à Hélène qui veut des détails. (Imaginez les raisons de cette rupture.)

Rôles: Hélène, le père

EXPRESSION ÉCRITE

■ Le journal d'Hélène

Vous êtes Hélène. Dans votre journal, décrivez les événements suivants.
- la découverte du portrait
- ce qui s'est passé la première nuit
- ce qui s'est passé la dernière nuit

■ La biographie de l'oncle Jean

Un jour Hélène a trouvé dans le grenier le journal de l'oncle Jean dans lequel il décrit sa vie. Avec votre partenaire, imaginez la biographie de l'oncle Jean. Décrivez, par exemple . . .
- où il a passé sa jeunesse
- quelles étaient ses relations avec sa famille (Pourquoi s'est-il disputé avec sa famille?)
- quels problèmes il a eus
- pourquoi il s'est enfui une première fois
- où il est allé et qu'est-ce qu'il a fait
- pourquoi il est revenu
- pourquoi il est reparti une seconde fois
- où il est allé cette fois-là et qu'est-ce qu'il a fait
- comment il est mort

■ L'histoire franco-américaine ■ en dix questions

Depuis cinq siècles, l'histoire de la France et celle de l'Amérique du Nord sont étroitement liées.° Voici quelques pages d'histoire franco-américaine.

1. *Combien est-ce qu'il y a d'Américains d'origine française?*

Aux États-Unis, il y a plus de trois millions et demi de personnes qui se considèrent d'origine française. En outre,° il y a aussi dix millions de personnes qui ont au moins un ancêtre d'origine française. Ces personnes habitent principalement dans les états de la Nouvelle Angleterre et en Louisiane.

Festival en Louisiane
La Nouvelle-Orléans
Une fête française à Boston

2. *Quand est-ce que les premiers Français sont venus sur le continent américain?*

L'arrivée de Jacques Cartier à Gaspé (1534).

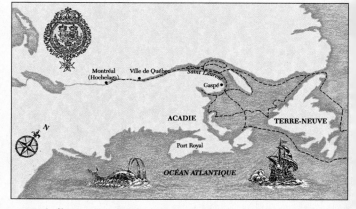

Jacques Cartier, un explorateur français, est arrivé au Canada en 1534. Sa mission était de trouver des mines d'or et de diamants pour le roi de France. Au lieu de découvrir des richesses fabuleuses, il a découvert un immense pays inconnu des Européens: le Canada. Il a débarqué° à Gaspé le 24 juillet 1534. Là, il a planté une croix° dans le sol,° et il a pris possession de la région au nom du roi de France. Au cours d'une seconde expédition l'année suivante, il a découvert l'estuaire d'un grand fleuve° qu'il a appelé le Saint-Laurent (parce que c'était le 10 août, fête de Saint Laurent). Puis il a remonté° ce fleuve jusqu'à un petit village indien appelé Hochelaga, site de la future ville de Montréal.

Les premiers colons français sont arrivés au Canada seulement 70 ans plus tard. Ils se sont d'abord installés° en Acadie (aujourd'hui la Nouvelle Écosse°) où ils ont fondé Port Royal (aujourd'hui Annapolis Royal) en 1605. En 1608, **Samuel de Champlain** a fondé la ville de **Québec**.

---

liées *interwoven* **en outre** *in addition* **a débarqué** *landed* **croix** *cross* **sol** *ground* **fleuve** = *rivière* **a remonté** *sailed up* **se sont installés** *settled* **Nouvelle Écosse** *Nova Scotia*

3. Quand a été fondé Montréal?

En 1642, une petite expédition de 50 Français sous le commandement de Paul Chomedey de **Maisonneuve** est arrivée sur le site du village indien d'**Hochelaga**. Le but° de cette expédition était de créer une communauté religieuse pour soigner les malades et convertir les Iroquois. C'est ainsi qu'est née la ville de **Montréal**, appelée alors Ville Marie de Montréal. Parmi les membres de l'expédition, il y avait une jeune femme, **Jeanne Mance**, co-fondatrice de Montréal avec Maisonneuve. En 1644, elle a fondé l'Hôtel-Dieu*, un hôpital qui existe toujours aujourd'hui.

Peu à peu, Montréal a grandi.° C'est devenu un important centre du commerce de la fourrure° et le point de départ d'importantes expéditions vers la région des Grands Lacs et le Mississippi. Avec une population de 3 300 000 d'habitants, en majorité francophones, Montréal est aujourd'hui la seconde ville d'expression française du monde.

Jeanne Mance et Paul Chomedey de Maisonneuve, fondateurs de Montréal

Les «Filles du Roy»

Après la fondation de Québec (1608) et de Montréal (1642), des familles françaises se sont installées au Canada, mais ces familles n'étaient pas nombreuses: quelques dizaines seulement. Le roi Louis XIV, qui voulait établir une grande colonie, a encouragé le départ de centaines de colons. C'étaient des «habitants» qui travaillaient la terre,° des «coureurs des bois»° qui faisaient le commerce de la fourrure° avec les Indiens, et des soldats qui défendaient la colonie contre les attaques des Anglais et de leurs alliés iroquois.

Évidemment, pour assurer la survie° et le développement de cette petite colonie, il fallait que ces hommes se marient et aient des enfants. Oui, mais où trouver des épouses? L'administration royale a eu l'idée de recruter des jeunes filles françaises, volontaires pour partir dans un pays totalement inconnu et y fonder une famille. Pour les encourager, le roi leur donnait une dot° et leur assurait une éducation.

Les «filles du Roy» arrivent au Canada (1665-1675)

C'est ainsi qu'entre 1665 et 1675, plus de mille jeunes Françaises, les «Filles du Roy», ont quitté leur pays pour la grande aventure. Arrivées au Canada, elles étaient accueillies° dans des centres d'apprentissage° fondés par une autre Française, **Marguerite Bourgeoys**. Là, elles apprenaient ce qui était nécessaire pour survivre dans un pays rude° et parfois hostile. Puis, elles se mariaient . . .

Un très grand nombre de familles québécoises d'aujourd'hui descendent directement de ces courageuses pionnières, arrivées au Canada il y a plus de 300 ans.

---

* **Hôtel-Dieu**: nom donné autrefois à l'hôpital public de la ville.

but = objectif **a grandi** = s'est développé **fourrure** *fur* **terre** *earth* **coureurs des bois** *fur trappers* **survie** *survival* **dot** *dowry*
accueillies *welcomed* **centres d'apprentissage** = écoles **rude** *rough*

4. Qu'est-ce qu'on appelle les «guerres françaises et indiennes» (1689-1763)?

Les Français ont créé une vaste colonie qu'ils ont appelée **la Nouvelle France**. Ce n'était pas les seuls occupants de cette partie de l'Amérique du Nord. Il y avait aussi les Anglais qui s'étaient établis en Nouvelle Angleterre. La rivalité entre ces deux groupes était intense. Chacun avait des alliés indiens. Les alliés des Français étaient les Hurons et les Algonquins. Les alliés des Anglais étaient les Iroquois. De temps en temps, chaque groupe faisait des raids sur le territoire de l'autre.

Finalement en 1756, une guerre générale a éclaté° entre la France et l'Angleterre. Au début, les Français ont été victorieux. Mais l'armée anglaise était bien supérieure en nombre et les forts français sont tombés les uns après les autres. Les Anglais ont pris Québec en 1759 et Montréal

Les «guerres françaises et indiennes»

en 1760. Au traité de Paris de 1763, la France a dû abandonner toutes ses colonies d'Amérique du Nord. Le Canada et toute la rive est du Mississippi sont passés sous contrôle anglais.

5. Quand la Louisiane était-elle française?

LaSalle prend possession de la Louisiane au nom de la France

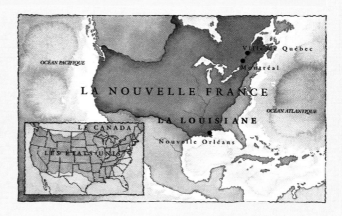

Vers le milieu du 17ᵉ siècle, des expéditions françaises, parties de Montréal, avaient exploré la région des Grands Lacs. En 1673, le père **Marquette** avait découvert le Mississippi, mais personne ne savait jusqu'où allait ce long fleuve. **Cavelier de La Salle** décida d'entreprendre° cette exploration. En 1681, il organisa une petite expédition et il partit à l'aventure. Après un voyage très difficile, il arriva à l'estuaire du Mississippi le 9 avril 1682.

Au passage, La Salle prit possession des territoires qu'il traversait° au nom de la France. Il nomma cette région **Louisiane** en l'honneur du roi Louis XIV. Plus tard, d'autres Français

arrivèrent dans la région. Ils fondèrent **la Nouvelle Orléans** en 1718 et construisirent des forts le long du Mississippi. À cette époque, la Louisiane était un immense territoire puisqu'elle représentait toute la vallée du Mississippi et ses affluents.°

À la suite° de traités, la France dut abandonner la Louisiane. La rive° ouest du Mississippi devint espagnole en 1762 et la rive est devint anglaise en 1763.

En 1800, la France acquit° par traité la partie espagnole. En 1803, Napoléon, qui avait besoin d'argent pour financer ses guerres, la revendit aux États-Unis pour la somme de 15 millions de dollars.

---

a éclaté *broke out* **entreprendre** *undertake* **traversait** *crossed* **affluents** *tributaries* **à la suite** *as a result* **rive** *shore, bank* **acquit** *acquired*

6. *Qui sont les Huguenots français?*

«Huguenot» était le nom que les Français donnaient aux Protestants au 16e siècle. À cette époque, il y avait des guerres de religion entre Protestants et Catholiques. Les Protestants, très inférieurs en nombre, ont été persécutés et chassés° de France. Beaucoup sont allés en Hollande et en Allemagne. Certains ont immigré en Amérique. Des Huguenots français venus de La Rochelle, France, ont fondé la ville de New Rochelle, New York, en 1688.

Parmi les Américains d'origine huguenote: Peter Minuit qui a acheté Manhattan pour 24 dollars, Paul Revere, patriote et héros de la Révolution américaine, John Jay, premier juge de la Cour Suprême, Louis Tiffany, joaillier de réputation internationale.

Peter Minuit, arrivant à la Nouvelle Amsterdam, aujourd'hui New York.

Paul Revere, patriote américain d'origine française

7. *Comment les Français ont-ils aidé les Américains pendant la guerre d'Indépendance?*

Quand ils ont déclaré leur indépendance en 1776, les Américains avaient besoin d'aide. Pour obtenir cette aide, ils ont envoyé Benjamin Franklin comme ambassadeur en France. Franklin, qui était très admiré et très respecté des Français, a pleinement réussi dans cette mission. Conseillé par sa femme Marie-Antoinette, le roi de France, Louis XVI, a reconnu° la jeune république des États-Unis en 1778. Mieux, il a décidé d'envoyer sa flotte° et ses meilleures troupes au secours° des «insurgés» américains.

La bataille de Yorktown

La bataille décisive de la guerre d'Indépendance a eu lieu à Yorktown en octobre 1781. D'un côté° il y avait une armée anglaise commandée par Cornwallis. De l'autre côté, il y avait une armée américaine commandée par Washington et une armée française commandée par **Rochambeau.** Pendant que la bataille faisait rage,° la flotte française empêchait° les renforts° anglais d'arriver. Encerclées, les troupes anglaises ont capitulé. Cette victoire franco-américaine a mis fin aux hostilités. Deux ans plus tard, l'Angleterre reconnaissait l'indépendance des États-Unis.

---

chassés *expelled* **reconnu** *recognized* **flotte** *fleet* **au secours** = *pour aider* **côté** *side* **faisait rage** *was raging*
empêchait *prevented* **renforts** *reinforcements*

8. Qui était La Fayette?

Une université, de nombreuses écoles, plusieurs villes portent le nom de ce héros de la guerre d'Indépendance américaine. Qui était exactement **La Fayette**?

La Fayette (1757-1834) était un aristocrate français qui appartenait° à l'une des familles les plus illustres du pays. En 1777, il avait seulement vingt ans et il était immensément riche. Un jour, il a entendu parler° de la Révolution américaine. Il a pris contact avec Benjamin Franklin qui était alors l'ambassadeur des États-Unis en France. Après cette entrevue, il a décidé de rejoindre les «insurgés» américains comme volontaire. Malheureusement, le roi de France était tout à fait opposé à cette idée et lui a interdit de partir. Que faire? La Fayette était un jeune homme déterminé avec beaucoup d'imagination … et beaucoup d'argent. Il a quitté la France en secret. Il est allé en Espagne où il a acheté un bateau qu'il a appelé *La Victoire* et il est parti pour les États-Unis.

Après avoir débarqué° en Caroline du Sud, La Fayette est allé à Philadelphie pour offrir ses services au Congrès américain. Le Congrès, impressionné par ses qualités et son enthousiasme, l'a nommé général auprès° de George Washington. Les deux hommes sont immédiatement devenus de grands amis.* En Octobre 1777, La Fayette a pris part à sa première bataille et il a été blessé à la jambe. Peu de temps après, le Congrès, reconnaissant son courage et ses talents militaires, lui a donné le commandement de la division de Virginie.

En 1779, La Fayette est retourné brièvement en France. Sa mission était de plaider la cause américaine et d'obtenir l'aide de la France. Il est allé voir le roi qui cette fois-ci l'a écouté. Quelques temps après, l'armée française est arrivée aux États-Unis. De retour aux États-Unis, La Fayette a rejoint son poste de commandement. À la bataille décisive de Yorktown, en 1781, il était à la tête d'une division américaine dans l'armée de Washington.

Après la guerre d'Indépendance, La Fayette est rentré en France où il a continué à combattre pour la justice et pour les idées nouvelles de liberté et d'égalité. Quand la Révolution française a éclaté en 1789, c'était l'homme le plus populaire de France. C'est lui qui a proposé la déclaration européenne des *Droits de l'homme et du citoyen* et qui a fait accepter le drapeau tricolore comme drapeau national. La Fayette était aussi un membre très actif du Club des Amis des Noirs, un club politique qui voulait l'abolition de l'esclavage° dans les colonies françaises. À cause du rôle important qu'il a joué aux États-Unis d'abord et en France ensuite, on appelle souvent La Fayette «le héros des deux mondes».

La Fayette, héros de la guerre d'Indépendance américaine.

---

* Plus tard, La Fayette a nommé son fils George Washington La Fayette.

appartenait *belonged to* **a entendu parler de** *heard about* **débarqué** *landed* **auprès de** *on the staff of* **esclavage** *slavery*

Une lettre du Marquis de La Fayette à Madame de La Fayette

La Fayette est arrivé aux États-Unis le 13 juin 1777. Quelques jours plus tard, il était à Charleston où il a écrit la lettre suivante à sa jeune femme. Dans cette lettre, il décrit ses premières impressions sur le pays et ses habitants.

Adrienne de Noailles de La Fayette

1777, à Charlestown

... Je vais à présent vous parler du pays, mon cher cœur, et de ses habitants. Ils sont aussi aimables que mon enthousiasme avait pu se le figurer.° La simplicité des manières, le désir d'obliger,° l'amour de la patrie° et de la liberté, une douce° égalité, règnent ici parmi tout le monde. L'homme le plus riche et le plus pauvre sont de niveau,° et quoiqu'il y ait° des fortunes immenses dans ce pays, je défie° de trouver la moindre° différence entre leurs manières respectives les uns pour les autres.

J'ai commencé par la vie de campagne, chez le major Huger; à présent, me voici à la ville. Tout y ressemble assez à la façon anglaise, excepté qu'il y a plus de simplicité chez eux qu'en Angleterre. La ville de Charlestown est une des plus jolies, des mieux bâties° et des plus agréablement peuplées que j'aie jamais vues. Les femmes américaines sont fort jolies, fort simples et d'une propreté° charmante...

Ce qui m'enchante ici, c'est que tous les citoyens sont frères. Il n'y a en Amérique ni pauvres, ni même ce qu'on appelle paysans.° Tous les citoyens ont un bien honnête,° et tous, les mêmes droits° que le plus puissant° propriétaire du pays.

Les auberges sont bien plus différentes d'Europe; le maître et la maîtresse se mettent à table avec vous, font les honneurs d'un bon repas, et en partant vous payez sans marchander.° Quand on ne veut pas aller dans une auberge, on trouve des maisons de campagne où il suffit d'être bon Américain pour être reçu avec les attentions qu'on aurait en Europe pour un ami.

... Il est fort avant° dans la nuit, il fait une chaleur affreuse, et suis dévoré de moucherons° qui vous couvrent de grosses ampoules,° mais les meilleurs pays ont, comme vous voyez, leurs inconvénients.

Adieu mon cœur, adieu.

Lafayette

---

figurer = imaginer   **obliger** = rendre service   **patrie** *fatherland*   **douce** *gentle*   **de niveau** *at the same level*   **quoiqu'il y ait** *although they are*
défie *challenge*   **la moindre** = la plus petite   **bâties** *built*   **propreté** *cleanliness, hygiene*   **paysans** *peasants*   **un bien honnête** *a property of their own*
droits *rights*   **puissant** *powerful*   **marchander** *to bicker over the price*   **fort avant** = très tard   **moucherons** *gnats*   **ampoules** *swellings*

9. Qui a dit «La Fayette, nous voilà!» et à quelle occasion?

On attribue cette phrase au général américain John Pershing à son arrivée en France en 1917. En rendant hommage à La Fayette, héros français de la guerre d'Indépendance, il voulait réaffirmer l'amitié et la solidarité qui unissaient le peuple français et le peuple américain. Le général Pershing était le commandant du corps expéditionnaire américain en France pendant la Première Guerre Mondiale (1914-1918).

En réalité, les premiers Américains qui sont venus aider la France pendant cette guerre étaient des volontaires incorporés dans l'armée française. Parmi ceux-ci, il y avait les pilotes de la fameuse «Escadrille Lafayette». Il y avait aussi les ambulanciers de l'«American Field Service Ambulance Corps». C'était des lycéens de 17 ans, des étudiants de Yale et de Harvard, ou de simples citoyens venus par idéalisme.

Les États-Unis sont officiellement entrés en guerre aux côtés° de la France et de l'Angleterre en avril 1917. Cette année-là, des centaines de milliers de soldats américains sont venus combattre sur le sol° français. Parmi ces soldats, il y avait un jeune capitaine d'artillerie venu du Missouri, Harry Truman, futur président des États-Unis. C'est grâce à l'intervention des troupes américaines que les Alliés ont finalement pu gagner la guerre en 1918.

Pilotes de l'Escadrille Lafayette. *(Remarquez que ces pilotes américains portent des uniformes français.)*

10. Où se trouve Omaha Beach?

Omaha Beach se trouve en Normandie. C'est sur cette plage et d'autres plages normandes que le plus grand débarquement° de l'histoire a eu lieu le 6 juin 1944. Ce jour-là, 100 000 soldats américains, anglais, canadiens, français, polonais° ont débarqué sur le sol de France occupé par l'Allemagne nazie. Peu après, les armées alliées commandées par le général Eisenhower ont libéré le reste de la France. Près de Omaha Beach il y a un grand cimetière où se trouvent les tombes de 9 385 soldats américains, héros de la libération de la France.

Le 6 juin 1944 les troupes alliées débarquent sur la plage d'Omaha Beach en Normandie

Un GI réconforte un enfant français

---

aux côtés de *on the side of* **sol** *soil* **débarquement** *landing* **polonais** *Polish*

Villes américaines — noms français

U n certain nombre de villes américaines portent des noms français. Ces noms rappellent quelques épisodes de la longue histoire franco-américaine.

Duluth (Minnesota)
Cette ville porte le nom d'un Français, Daniel **du Luth** (1636-1710), explorateur du Lac Supérieur et ami des Indiens de la région.

Fond du Lac (Wisconsin)
Cette ville est appelée ainsi à cause de sa position à l'extrémité sud du lac Winnebago. Au 18e siècle, c'était un centre où les Français faisaient le commerce de la fourrure avec les Indiens.

Détroit (Michigan)
Cette ville a été fondée en 1701 par un explorateur français, Antoine **de la Mothe Cadillac**, futur gouverneur de la Louisiane. À l'origine, la ville s'appelait Fort Pontchartrain du Détroit, en l'honneur du ministre français de la Marine.

Marietta (Ohio)
En 1788, d'anciens° soldats de la guerre d'Indépendance ont fondé une petite colonie qu'ils ont appelée Mariette, en l'honneur de la reine de France, **Marie-Antoinette**. Dix ans plus tôt, Marie-Antoinette avait convaincu° son mari d'envoyer ses troupes à l'aide des patriotes américains.

Laramie (Wyoming)
Cette ville porte le nom de Jacques **La Ramie**, un trappeur canadien qui est arrivé dans la région vers 1820. Il a construit une cabane pour stocker ses fourrures. Plus tard, Fort Laramie, bâti sur ce site, a joué un rôle important dans la conquête de l'ouest.

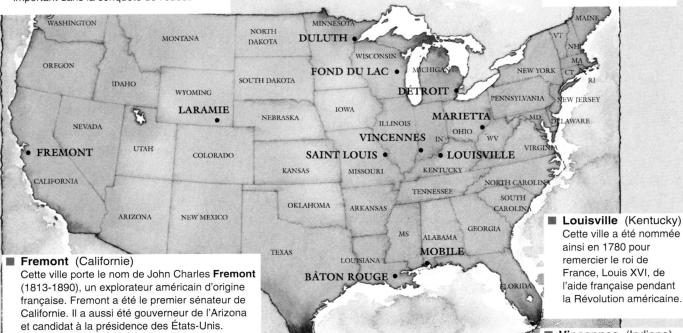

Fremont (Californie)
Cette ville porte le nom de John Charles **Fremont** (1813-1890), un explorateur américain d'origine française. Fremont a été le premier sénateur de Californie. Il a aussi été gouverneur de l'Arizona et candidat à la présidence des États-Unis.

Louisville (Kentucky)
Cette ville a été nommée ainsi en 1780 pour remercier le roi de France, Louis XVI, de l'aide française pendant la Révolution américaine.

Vincennes (Indiana)
Cette ville porte le nom de son fondateur, l'explorateur canadien Jean-Baptiste **Vincennes** (1668-1719). Elle est restée pendant longtemps une ville française. Pendant la guerre d'Indépendance, ses habitants ont aidé les Américains contre les Anglais.

Bâton Rouge (Louisiane)
En 1699, une expédition française découvre le site de la ville actuelle.° Les Indiens de la région appellent ce site «Istrouma» expression qui signifie «bâton° rouge». Les Français donnent ce nom au fort qu'ils construisent là quelques années plus tard.

Saint Louis (Missouri)
René Chouteau, un jeune homme de la Nouvelle Orléans, avait seulement 15 ans quand il a fondé Saint Louis en 1764. Il a nommé la ville en l'honneur de deux rois de France: **Louis XV** et son patron, **Saint Louis**.

Mobile (Alabama)
Vers 1700, des explorateurs français sont arrivés dans la région. Ils ont construit un fort qu'ils ont appelé Fort Louis de la Mobile: Fort Louis, en l'honneur du roi de France, Louis XIV; de la Mobile, du nom de Mauvile, une tribu indienne de la région.

---

actuelle *present* **bâton** *stick, pole* **anciens** *former* **convaincu** *convinced*

■ *Les héritiers de la Louisiane française* ■

Des gens d'origine française, venus surtout du Canada, ont été les premiers blancs à occuper la partie centrale de ce qui allait devenir les États-Unis. C'était pour la plupart des soldats, des missionnaires, des trappeurs. Ils construisirent des comptoirs° et des forts dans la vallée du Mississippi. Après la fondation de la Nouvelle Orléans en 1718, une colonie française s'établit en Louisiane. Au cours des années qui suivirent, cette colonie s'enrichit d'éléments nouveaux: d'abord Acadiens venus du Canada, puis Créoles venus des Antilles françaises. Les descendants de ces deux groupes représentent aujourd'hui la quasi-totalité de la population de la Louisiane d'origine française.

La Mothe-Cadillac, explorateur français

Des musiciens cajuns

■ Les Acadiens ou «Cajuns»

Les Acadiens doivent leur nom à leur région d'origine, l'Acadie, ce territoire du Nord-Est canadien représenté aujourd'hui par les provinces du Nouveau Brunswick et de la Nouvelle Écosse.° C'est dans cette région que s'établirent des colons français dès° 1640. Devenus sujets britanniques à la suite° d'un traité° (1713) qui donnait l'Acadie à l'Angleterre, les Acadiens refusèrent de prêter serment° à leur nouveau gouvernement. Pour cet acte de rébellion, toute la population française fut expulsée d'Acadie par l'armée anglaise. Un grand nombre d'Acadiens retournèrent en France. D'autres s'éparpillèrent° dans les territoires français d'Amérique. Un premier contingent de 231 réfugiés arriva en Louisiane en 1765, suivi d'autres groupes de plusieurs milliers de personnes. Leurs descendants et leurs alliés par mariage (Espagnols, Allemands, Indiens) constituent la population «cajun» actuelle. Aujourd'hui cette population habite principalement dans la région des bayous. Les centres cajuns se reconnaissent facilement à leurs noms français: Lafayette, Abbeville, Saint Martinville, Ville Platte, Thibodaux.

■ Les Créoles

Il existe plusieurs définitions du terme *créole*. La définition généralement acceptée s'applique aux descendants des habitants de Saint Domingue (aujourd'hui Haïti), blancs et noirs, venus en Louisiane pendant la Révolution française (1789-1799) et, plus tard, après l'indépendance d'Haïti (1804). Ces créoles s'établirent à la Nouvelle Orléans et dans les plantations à proximité du Mississippi et des bayous. Beaucoup de créoles de la Nouvelle Orléans habitaient le quartier du Vieux Carré° qu'ils quittèrent vers 1910.

---

comptoirs *trading posts* **Nouvelle Écosse** *Nova Scotia* **dès** *beginning in* **à la suite de** *as the result of* **traité** *treaty*
prêter serment *to pledge allegiance* **s'éparpillèrent** *were scattered* **Carré** *Square*

RÉVEILLE

Réveille,° réveille! . . .
C'est les goddams* qui viennent
brûler° la récolte.°
Réveille, réveille, hommes acadiens
pour sauver le village.

Mon grand-grand-grand-grand-père
est venu de la Bretagne;
le sang de ma famille est mouillé° l'Acadie
et là les maudits* viennent
nous chasser comme des bêtes,
détruire les saintes familles**
nous jeter° tous au vent.
      Réveille, réveille! . . .

J'ai entendu parler
de monter avec Beausoleil***
pour prendre le fusil,°
battre les sacrés° maudits.
J'ai entendu parler°
d'aller en la Louisiane
pour trouver de la bonne paix
là-bas dans la Louisiane.
      Réveille, réveille! . . .

Zachary Richard

Zachary Richard est un poète et chanteur cajun. Dans cette chanson célèbre, il évoque un événement historique important: l'attaque des Acadiens par les Anglais et leur expulsion. La sonnerie de clairon° «Réveille, réveille» alerte la population que les soldats anglais arrivent.

J'ai vu mon pauvre père
qui était fait prisonnier
pendant que ma mère,
ma belle mère braillait.°
J'ai vu ma belle maison
qui était mise aux flammes.
Et moi j'suis resté orphelin.°
Orphelin de l'Acadie.
      Réveille, réveille! . . .

Réveille, réveille! . . .
C'est les goddams* qui viennent
voler° les enfants.
Réveille, réveille, hommes acadiens
pour sauver l'héritage.

   * **les goddams; les maudits** (*cursed ones):* Terme qui désigne les soldats anglais.
  ** **Les saintes familles:** Les familles acadiennes françaises étaient catholiques.
          Massacrées par les soldats protestants anglais, elles sont devenues martyres.
*** **Beausoleil:** Capitaine, héros de la Résistance acadienne contre les Anglais.

sonnerie de clairon *bugle call*   **réveille** *wake up*   **brûler** *to burn*   **récolte** *crops*   **mouillé** *soaked (in)*   **jeter** *to throw*   **fusil** *rifle*   **sacrés** *«cursed»*
entendu parler *heard about*   **braillait** *was crying and screaming*   **orphelin** *orphan*   **voler** *to steal*

▪ *Le drapeau acadien* ▪

Les différents éléments du drapeau des Acadiens de Louisiane rappellent l'histoire du peuple cajun.

 Les fleurs de lys sur fond bleu étaient l'emblème des rois de France. Elles représentent l'héritage français des cajuns et leur langue.

 La tour jaune sur fond rouge était l'emblème des rois d'Espagne. Quand les premiers Acadiens sont arrivés en Louisiane, celle-ci était devenue espagnole. Cette partie du drapeau rappelle l'hospitalité du gouverneur espagnol.

Le blanc était la couleur de l'ancienne Acadie. Le triangle de cette couleur rappelle l'origine canadienne des Cajuns. L'étoile jaune est un double symbole. Elle représente la dévotion des Acadiens à la Vierge Marie, leur sainte patronne. Elle symbolise aussi le patriotisme des premiers Acadiens et leur participation comme volontaires à la Guerre d'indépendance (1775-1783). À peine arrivés en Louisiane, ils se sont ralliés à la cause américaine. Organisés en milices, ils ont combattu victorieusement contre les Anglais.

Tête à tête Pair Activities

CONTENTS

M. Mercier

Mme Dubois

Élève B

La rentrée

Partie 1

Il y a deux nouveaux professeurs à l'école: Madame Dubois et Monsieur Mercier. Prenez une feuille de papier. Écoutez bien la description physique de ces personnes faite par votre partenaire. Dessinez leurs portraits sur la base des informations qu'il/elle vous donne.

M. Moreau

Mlle Bertin

Partie 2

Maintenant c'est à votre tour de faire la description de deux autres professeurs: Madame Dubois et Monsieur Mercier.

▶ Faites une description détaillée de chaque personne:

- le visage
- le nez
- les cheveux
- la bouche
- les yeux
- le(s) signe(s) particulier(s)

Votre partenaire va dessiner un portrait de ces deux personnes sur la base de vos informations.

La rentrée

Élève A

Partie 1

Il y a deux nouveaux professeurs à l'école:
Mademoiselle Bertin et Monsieur Moreau.

▶ Faites une description détaillée de chaque personne:

- le visage
- le nez
- les cheveux
- la bouche
- les yeux
- le(s) signe(s) particulier(s)

Votre partenaire va dessiner un portrait de ces deux personnes sur la base de vos informations.

Mlle Bertin

M. Moreau

Partie 2

Maintenant c'est à votre tour de dessiner. Prenez une feuille de papier. Écoutez bien la description physique de deux autres professeurs, Madame Dubois et Monsieur Mercier. Dessinez leurs portraits sur la base des informations données par votre partenaire.

Mme Dubois

M. Mercier

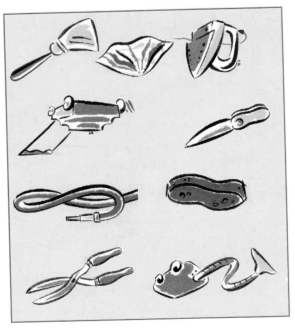

(texte imprimé à l'envers — Élève B)

Élève A: Je crois que l'éponge est dans
la cuisine (sous l'évier, ...)

Élève B: D'accord! (Volontiers!)
Où est l'éponge?

Élève A: Est-ce que tu peux essuyer
la table?

Il/elle vous va vous dire où trouver l'objet.

▶ Acceptez et demandez-lui où est l'objet
nécessaire pour accomplir chaque tâche *(task)*.

Votre partenaire vous demande de l'aider dans
certains petits travaux domestiques.

Travaux domestiques

Élève B

Travaux domestiques — **Élève A**

Vous travaillez à la maison et dans le jardin.

▶ Choisissez six petits travaux domestiques et
demandez à votre partenaire de vous aider
avec chaque tâche *(task)*.

Il/elle accepte et vous demande où trouver
l'objet nécessaire à chaque tâche. Répondez-lui.

Élève A: **Est-ce que tu peux essuyer
la table?**

Élève B: **D'accord! (Volontiers!)
Où est l'éponge?**

Élève A: **Je crois que l'éponge est dans
la cuisine (sous l'évier, ...)**

☐	**essuyer la table**
☐	**couper le pain**
☐	**éplucher les pommes**
☐	**repasser la nappe** *(tablecloth)*
☐	**passer l'aspirateur dans le salon**
☐	**laver la voiture**
☐	**tailler les arbustes**
☐	**arroser les plantes**
☐	**tondre la pelouse**
☐	**balayer le garage**
☐	**nettoyer la salle à manger**

Cambriolage -------- **Élève B**

Vous avez été témoin d'un cambriolage *(burglary)* avec votre partenaire, mais vos souvenirs *(memories)* de l'accident sont différents. Chacun à son tour va décrire six (6) détails de l'événement d'après l'illustration qu'il a. Si vous n'êtes pas d'accord avec votre partenaire, rectifiez sa description.

Élève A: Il y avait deux voitures dans la rue.

Élève B: C'est vrai.

Élève B: La première voiture était jaune.

Élève A: C'est faux! Elle était bleue.

Cambriolage -------- **Élève A**

Vous avez été témoin d'un cambriolage *(burglary)* avec votre partenaire, mais vos souvenirs *(memories)* de l'accident sont différents. Chacun à son tour va décrire six (6) détails de l'événement d'après l'illustration qu'il a. Si vous n'êtes pas d'accord avec votre partenaire, rectifiez sa description.

Élève A: Il y avait deux voitures dans la rue.

Élève B: C'est vrai.

Élève B: La première voiture était jaune.

Élève A: C'est faux! Elle était bleue.

Les courses — Élève B

Cet après-midi, vous allez faire les courses dans les magasins sur votre liste des courses.

Partie 1

Dites à votre partenaire dans quels magasins vous allez aller. Pour chaque magasin, demandez-lui si vous pouvez acheter quelque chose pour lui/elle. Écoutez bien sa réponse. Puis, inscrivez sa requête dans une liste des courses comme celle à droite. (Utilisez une autre feuille de papier.)

> Élève B: Je vais passer à la pharmacie. Qu'est-ce que je peux acheter pour toi?
>
> Élève A: Achète-moi deux boîtes de coton-tiges, s'il te plaît.

Partie 2

Maintenant vérifiez votre liste.

> Élève B: À la pharmacie je vais acheter deux boîtes de coton-tiges.
>
> Élève A: Oui, c'est ça. (Non, je voulais…)

Liste Des Courses

- à la pharmacie
  deux boîte de coton-tiges
- à la supérette
- à la papeterie
- chez le photographe

Les courses — Élève A

Vous avez besoin des produits suivants. Pour chaque produit, déterminez une certaine quantité (par exemple, deux boîtes de coton-tiges). Indiquez ces quantités sur une autre feuille de papier.

Partie 1

Votre partenaire va faire les courses cet après-midi et vous dit dans quels magasins il/elle va passer. Demandez-lui d'acheter les produits qui figurent sur votre liste.

> Élève B: Je vais passer à la pharmacie. Qu'est-ce que je peux acheter pour toi?
>
> Élève A: Achète-moi deux boîtes de coton-tiges, s'il te plaît.

Partie 2

Maintenant votre partenaire va vérifier sa liste.

> Élève B: À la pharmacie je vais acheter deux boîtes de coton-tiges
>
> Élève A: Oui, c'est ça. (Non, je voulais…)

À l'agence de voyage — Élève B

Partie 1

Vous êtes agent de voyage. Voici l'horaire du train TGV Paris - Côte d'Azur. Répondez aux questions d'un voyageur (votre partenaire) qui veut aller de Paris à Nice.

Partie 2

Vous êtes à Nice et vous voulez aller à Paris en train TGV. Demandez les renseignements suivants à l'agent de voyage (votre partenaire).

- nombre de trains pour Paris?
- heure de départ et d'arrivée du premier train?
- heure de départ du dernier train?
- train le plus rapide?

Paris / Ile de France › Côte d'Azur

PARIS-GARE-DE-LYON	Départ	11.12	13.49	22.30
Marseille	Arrivée			
Toulon	Arrivée			5.00
Les Arcs-Draguignan	Arrivée		19.21	
ST-RAPHAEL	Arrivée	16.47	19.39	5.48
Cannes	Arrivée	17.13	20.04	6.14
Antibes	Arrivée	17.26	20.17	6.25
NICE	Arrivée	17.43	20.33	6.44

À l'agence de voyage — Élève A

Partie 1

Vous êtes à Paris et vous voulez aller à Nice en train TGV. Demandez les renseignements suivants à l'agent de voyage (votre partenaire).

- nombre de trains pour Nice?
- heure de départ et d'arrivée du premier train?
- heure de départ du dernier train?
- train le plus rapide?

Partie 2

Vous êtes agent de voyage. Voici l'horaire du train TGV Côte d'Azur - Paris. Répondez aux questions d'un voyageur (votre partenaire) qui veut aller de Nice à Paris.

Côte d'Azur › Paris / Ile de France

NICE	Départ	8.57	9.45	12.16	21.58
Antibes	Départ	9.13	10.01	12.36	22.12
Cannes	Départ	9.25	10.14	12.49	22.24
ST-RAPHAEL	Départ	9.51	10.39	13.14	22.50
Les Arcs-Draguignan	Départ	10.10		13.32	
Toulon	Départ	10.47			23.46
Marseille	Départ	10.40			
PARIS-GARE-DE-LYON	Départ		16.25	19.22	6.46

Élève B

Partie 2

Vous voulez passer une semaine dans un petit hôtel: "L'auberge du moulin". Avant de faire votre réservation, vous téléphonez au (à la) réceptionniste — votre partenaire — pour obtenir les renseignements (*information*) suivants.

- **Nombre de chambres?**
- **Prix des chambres?**
- **Prix du petit déjeuner?**
- **Téléphone et télévision?**
- **Piscine et salle d'exercice?**
- **Ascenseur et air conditionné?**

Élève A: **Quel est le prix des chambres?**
Élève B: Les prix vont de 110 € à 180 € par jour.

Vacances

Partie 1

Vous êtes le/la réceptionniste à l'hôtel "Relais Soleil". Répondez à votre client(e) — votre partenaire — qui voudrait quelques renseignements.

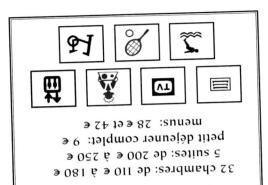

Relais Soleil

32 chambres: de 110 € à 180 €
5 suites: de 200 € à 250 €
petit déjeuner complet: 9 €
menus: 28 € et 42 €

Élève A

Vacances

Partie 1

Vous voulez passer une semaine à l'hôtel de luxe "Relais Soleil". Avant de faire votre réservation, vous téléphonez au (à la) réceptionniste — votre partenaire — pour obtenir les renseignements (*information*) suivants.

- **Prix des chambres?**
- **Prix du petit déjeuner?**
- **Prix des repas?**
- **Service en chambre?**
- **Éléments de confort?**
- **Possibilités de faire du sport?**

Élève A: **Quel est le prix des chambres?**
Élève B: Les prix vont de 110 € à 180 € par jour.

Partie 2

Vous êtes le/la réceptionniste à "L'auberge du Moulin." Répondez à votre client(e) — votre partenaire — qui voudrait quelques renseignements.

AUBERGE DU MOULIN

12 chambres: de 50 à 100 €
petit déjeuner: 6,50 €
menus: 20 et 30 €

Élève B

(texte à l'envers)

- enlever une dent
- faire un plombage

****

- faire un plâtre
- faire un pansement
- donner un antibiotique
- donner des médicaments
- faire une piqûre
- faire une radio
- prendre la température

- Ask how your patient feels.
- Ask where it hurts.
- Ask what happened to him/her.
- Tell him/her what you are going to do.

Faites un diagnostic en complétant la conversation suivante. Puis, proposez un traitement, en vous inspirant des suggestions à droite.

Vous examinez un(e) patient(e) — votre partenaire.

Vous êtes médecin (ou dentiste).

Chez le médecin

Chez le médecin — **Élève A**

Vous allez chez le médecin (ou le dentiste). Choisissez l'un des problèmes suggérés par les illustrations. Écoutez le médecin — votre partenaire — et répondez à ses questions.

- Tell the doctor how you feel.
  Je me sens ...
  (Je ne me sens pas ...)

- Tell the doctor where it hurts.
  J'ai mal ...

- Tell the doctor what happened.
  (Use your imagination.)
  Je suis tombé(e) d'un arbre et je me suis fracturé ...

Élève B

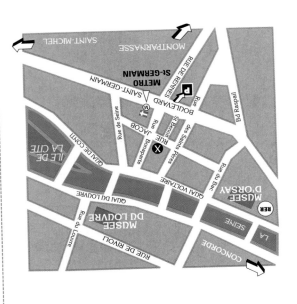

Rendez-vous parisien

Vous êtes à Paris à l'hôtel d'Angleterre situé rue Jacob — "X" sur le plan *(street map)* à droite. Votre partenaire vous donne rendez-vous dans un café.

- Demandez-lui comment y aller.
- Suivez ses instructions sur le plan.

Voici le début du dialogue:

Élève A: **Est-ce que tu veux prendre un pot avec moi dans mon café préféré?**

Élève B: Oui, bien sûr, comment est-ce que je vais là-bas?

Élève A: **Tu sors de l'hôtel et tu tournes à droite dans la rue Jacob.**

Élève B: D'accord, je tourne à droite dans la rue Jacob. Et après?

Élève A: ...

Avez-vous trouvé le café de votre partenaire? Confirmez votre rendez-vous avec lui.

Élève B: Est-ce que c'est le café qui se trouve en face de (à côté de, sur) ...?

Rendez-vous parisien

Élève A

Votre partenaire visite Paris. Il/elle loge à l'hôtel d'Angleterre situé rue Jacob — "X" sur le plan *(street map)* à droite.

- Choisissez un des cafés marqués 1, 2 ou 3.
- Donnez-lui rendez-vous dans ce café et expliquez-lui en détail comment y aller à pied.

Voici le début du dialogue:

Élève A: **Est-ce que tu veux prendre un pot avec moi dans mon café préféré?**

Élève B: Oui, bien sûr, comment est-ce que je vais là-bas?

Élève A: **Tu sors de l'hôtel et tu tournes à droite dans la rue Jacob.**

Élève B: D'accord, je tourne à droite dans la rue Jacob. Et après?

Élève A: ...

À la fin, votre partenaire va confirmer votre rendez-vous.

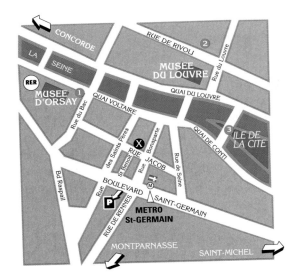

Élève B

Partie 2

Voici la continuation de la biographie de Marie Curie. Lisez le texte deux fois: d'abord en silence, ensuite à haute voix pour votre partenaire.

> Dans leur laboratoire, Pierre et Marie Curie ont travaillé sur les phénomènes de la radioactivité. Dans leurs recherches, ils ont découvert deux éléments nouveaux: le polonium et le radium. Pour ces travaux, ils ont reçu le Prix Nobel de Physique en 1903.
>
> Malheureusement Pierre Curie est mort dans un accident. Marie a continué ses travaux. En 1911, elle a reçu le Prix Nobel de Chimie. Les recherches de Marie Curie sur les rayons-X ont permis les progrès de la médecine moderne. Marie Curie est morte en 1934.

Puis, répondez à ses questions.

Élève B: Quand est née Marie Curie?
Élève A: Elle est née en 1867.

Partie 1

Votre partenaire va vous lire la biographie de Marie Curie, génie scientifique du 20ᵉ siècle. Écoutez bien et prenez des notes sur les sujets suivants:

- date de naissance
- nationalité d'origine
- date de son arrivée à Paris
- nom du mari
- nom de leur fille

Si c'est nécessaire, posez des questions à votre partenaire. Puis écrivez un paragraphe basé sur vos notes.

Marie Curie

Partie 1

Voici une courte biographie de Marie Curie, génie scientifique du 20ᵉ siècle. Lisez le texte deux fois: d'abord en silence, ensuite à haute voix pour votre partenaire.

> Marie Curie était d'origine polonaise. Elle est née à Varsovie en 1867. Au lycée, c'était une élève brillante. À l'âge de 16 ans, elle a obtenu son diplôme. Puis elle a travaillé dans un laboratoire de physique expérimentale.
>
> Après quelques années, elle a décidé de continuer ses études scientifiques en France. En 1891, elle a quitté la Pologne, son pays natal. Elle est arrivée à Paris et elle s'est inscrite à l'université.
>
> Là, elle a rencontré un jeune professeur de physique et de chimie. Il s'appelait Pierre Curie. Ils se sont mariés en 1895 et ils ont eu une petite fille, nommée Irène.

Puis, répondez à ses questions.

Élève B: Quand est née Marie Curie?
Élève A: Elle est née en 1867.

Élève A

Partie 2

Maintenant votre partenaire va continuer la biographie. Écoutez bien et prenez des notes sur les sujets suivants:

- découvertes scientifiques
- première distinction
- événement tragique
- deuxième distinction
- date de la mort

Si c'est nécessaire, posez des questions à votre partenaire. Puis écrivez un paragraphe basé sur vos notes.

Élève B

Choix professionnels

Vous êtes conseiller(conseillère) professionnel(le).

- Votre client — votre partenaire — va vous indiquer quatre de ses préférences personnelles.
- Pour chaque option, suggérez deux (2) professions qui correspondent à cette préférence.

Élève A: **Moi, je préfère [travailler seul(e)].**

Élève B: Alors, vous pouvez être [écrivain ou chercheur (chercheuse).]

Élève A: **Mais j'aime aussi …**

Élève B: Dans ce cas, vous pouvez devenir …

- acteur (actrice)
- assistant(e) social(e)
- banquier (banquière)
- chercheur (chercheuse)
- scientifique
- chimiste
- cinéaste
- dessinateur (dessinatrice)
- diplomate
- écrivain
- fonctionnaire
- homme (femme) d'affaires
- infirmier (infirmière)
- journaliste
- médecin
- photographe
- professeur
- représentant(e) de commerce
- secrétaire
- steward (hôtesse de l'air)
- vendeur (vendeuse)

Choix professionnels ——————————— **Élève A**

Vous voulez avoir une profession qui corresponde à vos préférences personnelles.

- Choisissez une option dans quatre (4) des catégories suivantes.
- Indiquez votre première préférence à votre conseiller(conseillère) professionnel(le) — votre partenaire — et demandez-lui quelle profession vous convient.
- Il/elle vous donnera deux possibilités.
- Continuez, en lui indiquant les trois autres préférences.

D'après vous, quelle est la meilleure suggestion?

1 ☐ voyager	ou	☐ rester à la maison
2 ☐ gagner beaucoup d'argent	ou	☐ avoir une vie de famille
3 ☐ avoir beaucoup de responsabilités	ou	☐ être indépendant(e)
4 ☐ avoir une profession artistique	ou	☐ avoir une profession scientifique
5 ☐ travailler beaucoup	ou	☐ avoir des vacances
6 ☐ travailler seul(e)	ou	☐ travailler avec d'autres

Élève A: **Moi, je préfère [travailler seul(e)].**

Élève B: Alors, vous pouvez être [écrivain ou chercheur (chercheuse).]

Élève A: **Mais j'aime aussi …**

Élève B: Dans ce cas, vous pouvez devenir …

REFERENCE SECTION

APPENDIX A: *Reprise*

1 VERBES

A. Le présent

Révision
present tense of stem-changing verbs
Appendix C pp. R20-21

Verbes réguliers

	parler	**-er**	finir	**-ir**	vendre	**-re**
STEM	**parl-**		**fini-**		**vend-**	
je	**parle**	**-e**	**finis**	**-is**	**vends**	**-s**
tu	**parles**	**-es**	**finis**	**-is**	**vends**	**-s**
il/elle/on	**parle**	**-e**	**finit**	**-it**	**vend**	**—**
nous	**parlons**	**-ons**	**finissons**	**-issons**	**vendons**	**-ons**
vous	**parlez**	**-ez**	**finissez**	**-issez**	**vendez**	**-ez**
ils/elles	**parlent**	**-ent**	**finissent**	**-issent**	**vendent**	**-ent**

NEGATIVE
je **ne parle pas**
je **ne finis pas**
je **ne vends pas**

INTERROGATIVE	
est-ce qu'il/elle **parle?**	**parle-t**-il/elle?
est-ce qu'il/elle **finit?**	**finit**-il/elle?
est-ce qu'il/elle **vend?**	**vend**-il/elle?

Le verbe **sortir** (to go out)

STEM	**sor-**		**sort-**	
	je **sors**	nous **sortons**		
	tu **sors**	vous **sortez**		
	il/elle/on **sort**	ils/elles **sortent**		

Verbes comme sortir

partir	to leave	je **pars**	nous **partons**
dormir	to sleep	je **dors**	nous **dormons**
servir	to serve	je **sers**	nous **servons**

Les verbes **vouloir** (want, wish), **pouvoir** (can, be able) et **devoir** (must, have to)

	vouloir	pouvoir	devoir
je	**veux**	**peux**	**dois**
tu	**veux**	**peux**	**dois**
il/elle/on	**veut**	**peut**	**doit**
nous	**voulons**	**pouvons**	**devons**
vous	**voulez**	**pouvez**	**devez**
ils/elles	**veulent**	**peuvent**	**doivent**

Ils doivent travailler.

Les verbes **prendre** (to take), et **mettre** (to put, place)

	prendre	mettre
je	**prends**	**mets**
tu	**prends**	**mets**
il/elle/on	**prend**	**met**
nous	**prenons**	**mettons**
vous	**prenez**	**mettez**
ils/elles	**prennent**	**mettent**

Verbes comme prendre

apprendre	to learn
comprendre	to understand

Verbes comme mettre

promettre	to promise
permettre	to permit, allow

Les verbes être, avoir, aller, faire, venir

PRESENT	être (to be)	avoir (to have)	aller (to go)	faire (to do, make)	venir (to come)
je (j')	suis	ai	vais	fais	viens
tu	es	as	vas	fais	viens
il/elle/on	est	a	va	fait	vient
nous	sommes	avons	allons	faisons	venons
vous	êtes	avez	allez	faites	venez
ils/elles	sont	ont	vont	font	viennent

Quelques expressions avec **avoir**

avoir chaud/froid	to be warm, hot/cold
avoir faim/soif	to be hungry/thirsty
avoir raison/tort	to be right/wrong
avoir sommeil	to be sleepy
avoir peur (de)	to be afraid (of)
avoir de la chance	to be lucky
avoir . . . ans	to be . . . years old
avoir mal	to hurt
avoir besoin de	to need
avoir envie de	to feel like, to wish

Quelques expressions avec **faire**

faire $\begin{cases} \text{du (de l')} \\ \text{de la (de l')} \\ \text{des} \end{cases}$ + $\begin{array}{l} sport \\ subject\ (of\ study) \\ activity \end{array}$

faire du ski   **faire de la natation**
faire de l'algèbre   **faire des maths**
faire du camping   **faire du théâtre**

faire attention (à)	to pay attention (to), to be careful (with), to watch out (for)
faire les courses	to go shopping (for food)
faire des achats	to go shopping (for items other than food)
faire la cuisine	to cook
faire la vaisselle	to do the dishes
faire ses devoirs	to do one's homework
faire ses valises	to pack (one's suitcases)
faire une promenade (à pied)	to go for a walk
faire une promenade (en auto, à vélo)	to go for a ride (by car, by bicycle)
faire un tour	to take a walk, ride
faire une randonnée	to take a hike, a long drive
faire un voyage	to go on a trip, to take a trip
faire un séjour	to spend time (in a place away from home)

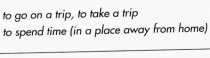

B. Le passé composé

Le passé composé avec **avoir**

PAST PARTICIPLE	parler → parlé	finir → fini	vendre → vendu
PASSÉ COMPOSÉ	j'**ai parlé** tu **as parlé** il/elle/on **a parlé** nous **avons parlé** vous **avez parlé** ils/elles **ont parlé**	j'**ai fini** tu **as fini** il/elle/on **a fini** nous **avons fini** vous **avez fini** ils/elles **ont fini**	j'**ai vendu** tu **as vendu** il/elle/on **a vendu** nous **avons vendu** vous **avez vendu** ils/elles **ont vendu**
NEGATIVE	je **n'ai pas parlé**		
INTERROGATIVE	**est-ce que** tu **as parlé?** **as**-tu **parlé?** **a-t**-il/elle **parlé?**		

PARTICIPES PASSÉS DE[S]
VERBES IRRÉGULIERS

-é	être	j'ai **été**
-ait	faire	j'ai **fait**
-ert	ouvrir	j'ai **ouvert**
	découvrir	j'ai **découve[rt]**
-i	suivre	j'ai **suivi**
	dormir	j'ai **dormi**
	sentir	j'ai **senti**
-is	mettre	j'ai **mis**
	prendre	j'ai **pris**
	apprendre	j'ai **appris**
-it	dire	j'ai **dit**
	écrire	j'ai **écrit**
-uit	conduire	j'ai **conduit**
	détruire	j'ai **détruit**
-u	avoir	j'ai **eu**
	boire	j'ai **bu**
	savoir	j'ai **su**
	voir	j'ai **vu**
	pouvoir	j'ai **pu**
	devoir	j'ai **dû**
	vouloir	j'ai **voulu**
	recevoir	j'ai **reçu**
	lire	j'ai **lu**
	courir	j'ai **couru**
	connaître	j'ai **connu**
	vivre	j'ai **vécu**
	il y a	il y a **eu**
	il faut	il a **fallu**

Le passé composé avec **être**

PASSÉ COMPOSÉ	je **suis allé** tu **es allé** il/on **est allé** nous **sommes allés** vous **êtes allé(s)** ils **sont allés**	je **suis allée** tu **es allée** elle **est allée** nous **sommes allées** vous **êtes allée(s)** elles **sont allées**
NEGATIVE	je **ne suis pas allé(e)**	
INTERROGATIVE	**est-ce que** tu **es allé(e)?** **es**-tu **allé(e)?** **est**-il/elle **allé(e)?**	

VERBES CONJUGUÉS AVEC **ÊTRE**

aller *(to go)*   je **suis allé(e)**
venir *(to come)*   je **suis venu(e)**

arriver *(to arrive, come)*   je **suis arrivé(e)**
partir *(to leave)*   je **suis parti(e)**

entrer *(to enter, come in)*   je **suis entré(e)**
sortir *(to go out)*   je **suis sorti(e)**

monter *(to go up)*   je **suis monté(e)**
descendre *(to go down)*   je **suis descendu(e)**
tomber *(to fall)*   je **suis tombé(e)**

passer *(to pass)*   je **suis passé(e)**
rester *(to stay)*   je **suis resté(e)**
rentrer *(to go back)*   je **suis rentré(e)**
retourner *(to return)*   je **suis retourné(e)**
revenir *(to come back)*   je **suis revenu(e)**

devenir *(to become)*   je **suis devenu(e)**

naître *(to be born)*   je **suis né(e)**
mourir *(to die)*   je **suis mort(e)**

C. L'imparfait

The imperfect tense is formed as follows:

> **nous**-form of the present minus **-ons** + endings

	parler	finir	vendre	faire	endings
(PRESENT) nous	**parl**ons	**finiss**ons	**vend**ons	**fais**ons	
IMPERFECT STEM	**parl-**	**finiss-**	**vend-**	**fais-**	
je	parlais	finissais	vendais	faisais	-ais
tu	parlais	finissais	vendais	faisais	-ais
il/elle/on	parlait	finissait	vendait	faisait	-ait
nous	parlions	finissions	vendions	faisions	-ions
vous	parliez	finissiez	vendiez	faisiez	-iez
ils/elles	parlaient	finissaient	vendaient	faisaient	-aient

NEGATIVE	je **ne parlais pas**
INTERROGATIVE	**est-ce que** tu **parlais**? **parlais**-tu?

IMPERFECT STEMS	
manger	je mangeais
commencer	je commençais
être	j'étais
avoir	j'avais
aller	j'allais
venir	je venais
sortir	je sortais
dormir	je dormais
mettre	je mettais
suivre	je suivais
devoir	je devais
pouvoir	je pouvais
vouloir	je voulais
savoir	je savais
connaître	je connaissais
prendre	je prenais
dire	je disais
lire	je lisais
écrire	j'écrivais
conduire	je conduisais
boire	je buvais
croire	je croyais
voir	je voyais

HIER APRÈS-MIDI, NOUS SOMMES ALLÉS EN VILLE. NOUS AVONS VU UN ACCIDENT.

PENDANT LES VACANCES, J'ALLAIS SOUVENT À LA PLAGE. IL Y AVAIT TOUJOURS BEAUCOUP DE MONDE.

D. Passé composé ou imparfait?

Use:	to describe:	
the PASSÉ COMPOSÉ	• what you did • what happened	Hier après-midi, nous **sommes allés** en ville. Nous **avons vu** un accident.
the IMPERFECT	• what you used to do • what used to be	Pendant les vacances, j'**allais** souvent à la plage. Il y **avait** toujours beaucoup de monde.
	• what you were doing • what was going on	Hier à neuf heures, je **regardais** la télé. Il y **avait** une comédie.
	• the circumstances of an event (time, weather)	Quelle heure **était**-il? Quel temps **faisait**-il?

A. Les articles

In French, nouns are frequently introduced by ARTICLES. The choice of article depends on the underlined context in which the noun is used.

These articles . . .		introduce . . .	
DEFINITE:	le (l') la (l')	a noun used in a GENERAL or COLLECTIVE sense	J'aime **le** fromage. **La** patience est une qualité.
	les	a SPECIFIC thing (or things)	Voici **le** fromage. *(the one I bought)* **La** patience du professeur est remarquable.
INDEFINITE:	un une	one (or several) WHOLE items	J'ai acheté **un** fromage. *(a whole cheese)*
	des	one of a kind	Ce boulanger *(baker)* fait **un** pain excellent. Vous avez **une** patience extraordinaire.
PARTITIVE:	du (de l') de la (de l') des	SOME, ANY, a PORTION an UNSPECIFIED AMOUNT of something	Nous mangeons **du** fromage. *(just a piece)* Vous avez **de la** patience. Veux-tu **des** spaghetti?

REMARKS:

➡ In underlined negative sentences, **un, une, du, de la, des → de (d').**

Marc mange **du** fromage.   Alice ne mange pas **de** fromage.
Philippe a **un** couteau.   Mélanie n'a pas **de** couteau.

➡ The DEFINITE article is generally used after the following verbs:

aimer   J'aime **le** gâteau.
préférer   Marc préfère **la** glace.

➡ The PARTITIVE article is often, but not always underlined, used after the following:

voici   **boire**   **acheter**
voilà   **manger**   **avoir**
il y a   **prendre**   **vouloir**

It is the context that determines which article is used. Compare:
Je mange **la** pizza.   *(= the pizza that I bought)*
Je mange **une** pizza.   *(= a whole pizza)*
Je mange **de la** pizza.   *(= a piece of pizza)*

➡ The PARTITIVE article is underlined not used to introduce a subject. Compare:
Le lait est dans le réfrigérateur.   Il y a **du lait** dans le réfrigérateur.

➡ The PARTITIVE article can be used with underlined abstract as well as underlined concrete nouns.
Vous avez **de l'argent.**   Moi, j'ai **du talent.**

Philippe préfère le gâteau.

Les boissons sont sur la table.

B. Les adjectifs irréguliers

Irregular feminine forms

MASCULINE	FEMININE		
-eux	-euse	curieux	curieuse
-f	-ve	actif	active
-en	-enne	canadien	canadienne
-on	-onne	mignon	mignonne
-el	-elle	ponctuel	ponctuelle
-er	-ère	régulier	régulière
-et	-ète	discret	discrète

Ils sont actifs!

Irregular masculine plural forms

SINGULAR	PLURAL		
-eux	-eux	curieux	curieux
-al	-aux	loyal	loyaux

Les adjectifs: **beau, nouveau, vieux**

SINGULAR			PLURAL	
MASCULINE		FEMININE	MASCULINE	FEMININE
beau	(bel)	belle	beaux	belles
nouveau	(nouvel)	nouvelle	nouveaux	nouvelles
vieux	(vieil)	vieille	vieux	vieilles

Est-ce que ces belles maisons à Annecy sont nouvelles?

REMARKS:

➡ In French, adjectives usually come <u>after</u> the noun.

J'aime la musique **classique**.   Anne porte une jupe **rouge** et **noire**.

➡ The following adjectives usually come <u>before</u> the noun:

> grand ≠ petit   jeune ≠ vieux   joli = beau
> bon ≠ mauvais   nouveau ≠ ancien

Nous avons une grande maison dans un **vieux** quartier de Tours.

NOTE: Often **des → de** before a plural adjective.

Il porte **des** sandales. Il porte **de vieilles** sandales.

Ce monsieur est-il jeune ou vieux?

C. Les noms irréguliers

SINGULAR	PLURAL		
-al	-aux	un animal	des animaux
-eau	-eaux	un chapeau	des chapeaux
-eu	-eux	un cheveu	des cheveux

➡ A few nouns in **-al** form their plural by adding **–s**:

   un festival   **des festivals**

Malice est un animal domestique.

D. Les pronoms compléments d'objet direct et indirect

FORMS AND USES

SUBJECT	DIRECT and INDIRECT
je (j')	me (m')
tu	te (t')
nous	nous
vous	vous

SUBJECT	DIRECT	INDIRECT
il	le (l')	lui
elle	la (l')	
ils	les	leur
elles		

A DIRECT OBJECT answers the questions:
qui? *(whom?)* or **quoi?** *(what?)*

qui?	Je vois **Pauline**.	Je **la** vois.
quoi?	Je vois **la voiture**.	Je **la** vois.

VERB + DIRECT OBJECT
(quelqu'un)

aider	inviter
aimer	regarder
chercher	rencontrer
connaître	retrouver
écouter	voir

VERB + INDIRECT OBJECT
(à quelqu'un)

dire à
écrire à
parler à
téléphoner à
rendre visite à
rendre service à

donner à *(to give)*
emprunter à *(to borrow)*
montrer à *(to show)*
prêter à *(to lend)*
rendre à *(to return, to give back)*

An INDIRECT OBJECT answers the question:
à qui? *(to whom?)*

à qui?	Je parle **à Pauline.**	Je **lui** parle.

E. Connaître ou savoir?

Connaître and **savoir** both mean *to know*, but they are used differently.

Connaître . . . is used with NOUNS (or pronouns) designating:

je	connais
tu	connais
il/elle/on	connaît
nous	connaissons
vous	connaissez
ils/elles	connaissent

- PEOPLE   **Je connais** Jean-Philippe.
- PLACES   **Je connais** bien Paris.
  Je connais un bon restaurant italien.
- INFORMATION   Je **ne connais pas** ton adresse.

POSITION

Object pronouns come **before** the verb EXCEPT in affirmative commands.

	AFFIRMATIVE	NEGATIVE
Present	Je **t'**invite. Je **le** connais. Je **lui** téléphone.	Je ne **t'**invite pas. Je ne **le** connais pas. Je ne **lui** téléphone pas.
Passé composé	Je **t'**ai vu. Je **l'**ai invité. Je **leur** ai parlé.	Je ne **t'**ai pas vu. Je ne **l'**ai pas invité. Je ne **leur** ai pas parlé.
Imperative (commands)	Écris-**moi**. Invite-**les**. Rends-**leur** visite.	Ne **m'**écris pas. Ne **les** invite pas. Ne **leur** rends pas visite.
Infinitive construction	Je vais **t'**inviter. Je vais **les** voir. Je vais **leur** écrire.	Je ne vais pas **t'**inviter. Je ne vais pas **les** voir. Je ne vais pas **leur** écrire.

Savoir . . .	is used (with):	Tu **sais**? Non, je ne **sais** pas.

je	**sais**
tu	**sais**
il/elle/on	**sait**
nous	**savons**
vous	**savez**
ils/elles	**savent**

Savoir . . . is used (with):

Tu **sais**? Non, je ne **sais** pas.

- ALONE
- a CLAUSE introduced by . . .
  - **que** *(that)* — Je **sais** que tu as une nouvelle moto.
  - **si** *(if, whether)* — Est-ce que tu **sais** si Éric va venir?
  - an INTERROGATIVE expression — Je ne **sais** pas où tu habites.
Sais-tu qui a téléphoné?
Je ne **sais** pas quand je vais aller à Nice.
- an INFINITIVE — **Savez**-vous utiliser un ordinateur?
- a NOUN designating something LEARNED — Les élèves ne **savent** pas la leçon.

3 VOCABULAIRE ....

A. Les nombres et les dates

LES NOMBRES CARDINAUX

To count, we use CARDINAL numbers: 1, 2, 3 . . .

0 à 99

0	zéro	10	dix	20	vingt	60	soixante
1	un	11	onze	21	vingt et un	61	soixante et un
2	deux	12	douze	22	vingt-deux	70	soixante-dix
3	trois	13	treize	23	vingt-trois	71	soixante et onze
4	quatre	14	quatorze	30	trente	72	soixante-douze
5	cinq	15	quinze	31	trente et un	80	quatre-vingts
6	six	16	seize	40	quarante	81	quatre-vingt-un
7	sept	17	dix-sept	48	quarante-huit	90	quatre-vingt-dix
8	huit	18	dix-huit	49	quarante-neuf	91	quatre-vingt-onze
9	neuf	19	dix-neuf	50	cinquante	99	quatre-vingt-dix-neuf

100 à 1 000 000

100	cent	400	quatre cents	1 000	mille
101	cent un	520	cinq cent vingt	1 210	mille deux cent dix
110	cent dix	675	six cent soixante-quinze	2 000	deux mille
200	deux cents	880	huit cent quatre-vingts	15 000	quinze mille
215	deux cent quinze	900	neuf cents	100 000	cent mille
371	trois cent soixante et onze			1 000 000	un million

LES NOMBRES ORDINAUX

To rank or put in sequence, we use ORDINAL numbers: 1st, 2nd, 3rd . . .

> ordinal number = cardinal number + **ième**
> (minus **-e**, if any)

deux	→ **deuxième**
douze	→ **douzième**
vingt et un	→ **vingt et unième**
cent huit	→ **cent huitième**

EXCEPTIONS:

un	→ **premier (première)**
cinq	→ **cinquième**
neuf	→ **neuvième**

LA DATE

When giving the date in French, use cardinal numbers:

> **le douze octobre**
> **le vingt juillet**

However, use the ordinal number (**premier**) for the first of the month:

> **le premier mai**

B. La nourriture et les boissons

Boulangerie Pâtisserie

le pain *bread*
un croissant
un gâteau *cake*
une tarte *pie*

Boucherie

la viande *meat*
le rosbif
le jambon *ham*
le porc
le veau *veal*

Alimentation générale

le ketchup
la mayonnaise
le sel *salt*
le poivre *pepper*
le sucre *sugar*
la confiture *jam*
le riz *rice*
les spaghetti
les céréales

Produits laitiers
(Dairy products)

le lait *milk*
le beurre *butter*
la margarine
le fromage *cheese*
la glace *ice cream*
le yaourt *yogurt*
un oeuf *egg*

Poissonnerie

le poisson *fish*
la sole
le thon *tuna*
le saumon *salmon*

Fruits

une orange
une banane
un melon
une pomme *apple*
une poire *pear*
une pamplemousse
  grapefruit
une fraise *strawberry*
une cerise *cherry*
du raisin *grapes*

Légumes

le céleri
une salade *lettuce*
une carotte
une tomate
une pomme de terre
  potato
des petits pois *peas*

Boissons

le thé
le café
l'eau *water*
l'eau minérale
le jus de fruits
le jus de pomme
le jus de raisin

C. Les parties du corps

le corps (body)

- la tête
- le nez
- la bouche
- l'épaule (f.)
- un doigt
- le bras
- le ventre
- l'estomac (m.)
- le genou
- la jambe
- la figure
- les cheveux
- l'oeil (les yeux)
- l'oreille
- le cou
- le dos
- le coeur
- la main
- le pied

Note the expression **avoir mal à:**

J'ai mal à la tête.	*I have a headache. (My head hurts.)*
J'ai mal au dos.	*I have a backache. (My back hurts.)*
J'ai mal aux dents.	*I have a toothache.*
J'ai mal au coeur.	*I have an upset stomach.*

E. Les pays

LES CONTINENTS ET LES PAYS DU MONDE

L' Amérique du Nord et l'Amérique du Sud

1. le Canada
2. les États-Unis
3. le Mexique
4. le Guatemala
5. le Venezuela
6. le Pérou
7. le Brésil
8. l'Argentine
9. le Chili

L' Afrique

10. le Maroc
11. l'Algérie
12. la Tunisie
13. l'Égypte
14. le Sénégal
15. la Côte d'Ivoire
16. la République démocratique du Congo
17. Madagascar

L' Europe

18. la France
19. l'Espagne
20. le Portugal
21. l'Angleterre
22. l'Irlande
23. l'Écosse
24. la Belgique
25. le Luxembourg
26. la Suisse
27. les Pays-Bas
28. l'Allemagne
29. l'Italie
30. la Grèce
31. le Danemark
32. la Norvège
33. la Suède
34. la Pologne
35. la Russie

Le Moyen-Orient

36. Israël
37. le Liban
38. l'Arabie Saoudite

L' Asie et l'Océanie

39. la Chine
40. le Japon
41. la Corée
42. le Viêt-nam
43. le Cambodge
44. l'Inde
45. les Philippines
46. l'Australie
47. la Nouvelle Zélande

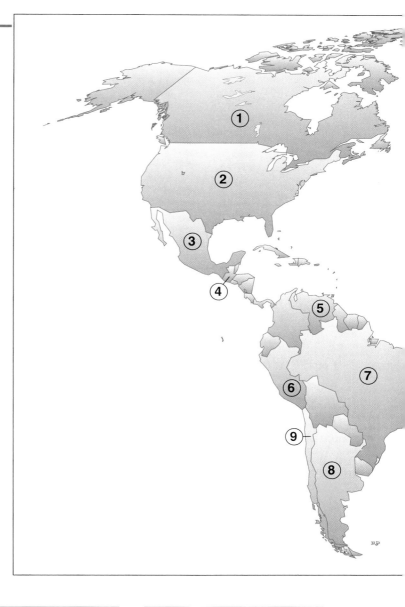

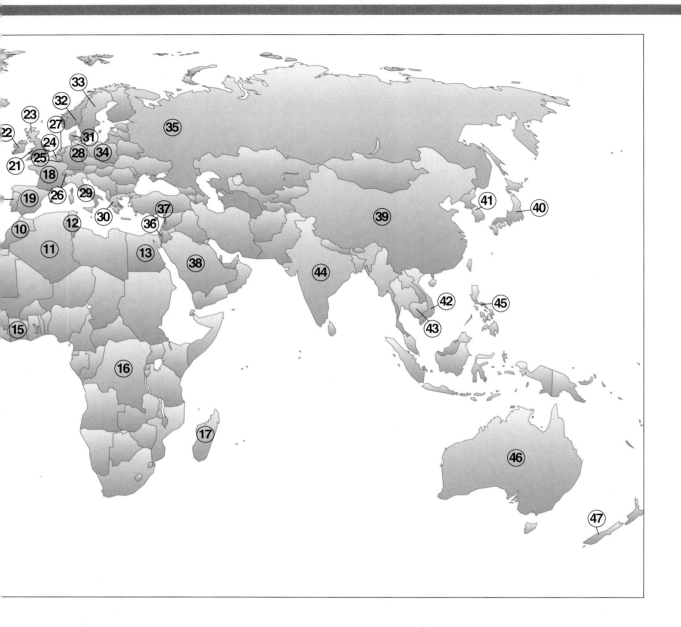

Les articles et les prépositions avec les noms de pays

	masculine country beginning with a consonant	feminine country or masculine country beginning with a vowel	plural country
Je visite . . .	**le** Canada	**la** France **l'**Iran	**les** États-Unis
Je vais . . . J'habite . . .	**au** Canada	**en** France **en** Iran	**aux** États-Unis
Je viens . . .	**du** Canada	**de** France **d'**Iran	**des** États-Unis

APPENDIX B: *Sound-Spelling Correspondence*

Vowels

SOUND	SPELLING	EXAMPLES
/a/	**a, à, â**	M<u>a</u>dame, l<u>à</u>-b<u>a</u>s, thé<u>â</u>tre
/i/	**i, î**	v<u>i</u>site, N<u>i</u>ce, d<u>î</u>ne
	y (initial, final, or between consonants)	<u>Y</u>ves, Gu<u>y</u>, st<u>y</u>le
/u/	**ou, où, oû**	T<u>ou</u>louse, <u>où</u>, a<u>oû</u>t
/y/	**u, û**	t<u>u</u>, L<u>u</u>c, s<u>û</u>r
/o/	**o** (final or before silent consonant)	pian<u>o</u>, idi<u>o</u>t, Marg<u>o</u>t
	au, eau	j<u>au</u>ne, Cl<u>au</u>de, b<u>eau</u>
	ô	h<u>ô</u>tel, dr<u>ô</u>le, C<u>ô</u>te-d'Ivoire
/ɔ/	**o**	M<u>o</u>nique, N<u>o</u>ël, j<u>o</u>lie
	au	P<u>au</u>l, rest<u>au</u>rant, L<u>au</u>re
/e/	**é**	D<u>é</u>d<u>é</u>, Qu<u>é</u>bec, t<u>é</u>l<u>é</u>
	e (before silent final **z, t, r**)	ch<u>e</u>z, <u>e</u>t, Rog<u>e</u>r
	ai (final or before final silent consonant)	j'<u>ai</u>, m<u>ai</u>, japon<u>ai</u>s
/ɛ/	**è**	Mich<u>è</u>le, <u>È</u>ve, p<u>è</u>re
	ei	s<u>ei</u>ze, n<u>ei</u>ge, Tour <u>Ei</u>ffel
	ê	t<u>ê</u>te, <u>ê</u>tre, Vi<u>ê</u>t-nam
	e (before two consonants)	<u>e</u>lle, Pi<u>e</u>rre, Ann<u>e</u>tte
	e (before pronounced final consonant)	Mich<u>e</u>l, av<u>e</u>c, ch<u>e</u>r
	ai (before pronounced final consonant)	franç<u>ai</u>se, <u>ai</u>me, M<u>ai</u>ne
/ə/	**e** (final or before single consonant)	j<u>e</u>, D<u>e</u>nise, v<u>e</u>nir
/ø/	**eu, oeu**	d<u>eu</u>x, Mathi<u>eu</u>, <u>eu</u>ro, <u>oeu</u>fs
	eu (before final **se**)	nerv<u>eu</u>se, génér<u>eu</u>se, séri<u>eu</u>se
/œ/	**eu, oeu** (before final pronounced consonant except /z/)	h<u>eu</u>re, n<u>eu</u>f, Lesi<u>eu</u>r, s<u>oeu</u>r, c<u>oeu</u>r, <u>oeu</u>f

Nasal vowels

SOUND	SPELLING	EXAMPLES
/ɑ̃/	**an, am**	Fr<u>an</u>ce, qu<u>an</u>d, l<u>am</u>pe
	en, em	H<u>en</u>ri, p<u>en</u>dant, déc<u>em</u>bre
/ɔ̃/	**on, om**	n<u>on</u>, Sim<u>on</u>, b<u>om</u>be
/ɛ̃/	**in, im**	Mart<u>in</u>, <u>in</u>vite, <u>im</u>possible
	yn, ym	s<u>yn</u>dicat, s<u>ym</u>pathique, Ol<u>ym</u>pique
	ain, aim	Al<u>ain</u>, améric<u>ain</u>, f<u>aim</u>
	(o) + in	l<u>oin</u>, m<u>oin</u>s, p<u>oin</u>t
	(i) + en	b<u>ien</u>, Juli<u>en</u>, vi<u>en</u>s
/œ̃/	**un, um**	<u>un</u>, Lebr<u>un</u>, parf<u>um</u>

Semi-vowels

SOUND	SPELLING	EXAMPLES
/j/	**i, y** (before vowel sound)	bien, piano, Lyon
	-il, -ill (after vowel sound)	oeil, travaille, Marseille
/ɥ/	**u** (before vowel sound)	lui, Suisse, juillet
/w/	**ou** (before vowel sound)	oui, Louis, jouer
/wa/	**oi, oî, oy** (before vowel)	voici, Benoît, voyage

Consonants

SOUND	SPELLING	EXAMPLES
/b/	**b**	Barbara, banane, Belgique
/k/	**c** (before **a, o, u,** or consonant)	Coca-Cola, cuisine, classe
	ch(r)	Christine, Christian, Christophe
	qu, q (final)	Québec, qu'est-ce que, cinq
	k	kilo, Kiki, ketchup
/ʃ/	**ch**	Charles, blanche, chez
/d/	**d**	Didier, dans, médecin
/f/	**f**	Félix, franc, neuf
	ph	Philippe, téléphone, photo
/g/	**g** (before **a, o, u,** or consonant)	Gabriel, gorge, légumes, gris
	gu (before **e, i, y**)	vague, Guillaume, Guy
/ɲ/	**gn**	mignon, champagne, Allemagne
/ʒ/	**j**	je, Jérôme, jaune
	g (before **e, i, y**)	rouge, Gigi, gymnastique
	ge (before **a, o, u**)	orangeade, Georges, nageur
/l/	**l**	Lise, elle, cheval
/m/	**m**	Maman, moi, tomate
/n/	**n**	banane, Nancy, nous
/p/	**p**	peu, Papa, Pierre
/r/	**r**	arrive, rentre, Paris
/s/	**c** (before **e, i, y**)	ce, Cécile, Nancy
	ç (before **a, o, u**)	ça, garçon, déçu
	s (initial or before consonant)	sac, Sophie, reste
	ss (between vowels)	boisson, dessert, Suisse
	t (before **i** + vowel)	attention, Nations Unies, natation
	x	dix, six, soixante
/t/	**t**	trop, télé, Tours
	th	Thérèse, thé, Marthe
/v/	**v**	Viviane, vous, nouveau
/gz/	**x**	examen, exemple, exact
/ks/	**x**	Max, Mexique, excellent
/z/	**s** (between vowels)	désert, télévision, Louise
	z	Suzanne, zut, zéro

APPENDIX C: *Verbes*

1 REGULAR VERBS

INFINITIF	parler *(to talk, speak)*	finir *(to finish)*	vendre *(to sell)*	se laver *(to wash oneself)*
PRÉSENT	je **parle** tu **parles** il **parle** nous **parlons** vous **parlez** ils **parlent**	je **finis** tu **finis** il **finit** nous **finissons** vous **finissez** ils **finissent**	je **vends** tu **vends** il **vend** nous **vendons** vous **vendez** ils **vendent**	je **me lave** tu **te laves** il **se lave** nous **nous lavons** vous **vous lavez** ils **se lavent**
IMPÉRATIF	**parle!** **parlons!** **parlez!**	**finis!** **finissons!** **finissez!**	**vends!** **vendons!** **vendez!**	**lave-toi!** **lavons-nous!** **lavez-vous!**
PASSÉ COMPOSÉ	j'**ai parlé** tu **as parlé** il **a parlé** nous **avons parlé** vous **avez parlé** ils **ont parlé**	j'**ai fini** tu **as fini** il **a fini** nous **avons fini** vous **avez fini** ils **ont fini**	j'**ai vendu** tu **as vendu** il **a vendu** nous **avons vendu** vous **avez vendu** ils **ont vendu**	je **me suis lavé(e)** tu **t'es lavé(e)** il/elle **s'est lavé(e)** nous **nous sommes lavé(e)s** vous **vous êtes lavé(e)(s)** ils/elles **se sont lavé(e)s**
IMPARFAIT	je **parlais** tu **parlais** il **parlait** nous **parlions** vous **parliez** ils **parlaient**	je **finissais** tu **finissais** il **finissait** nous **finissions** vous **finissiez** ils **finissaient**	je **vendais** tu **vendais** il **vendait** nous **vendions** vous **vendiez** ils **vendaient**	je **me lavais** tu **te lavais** il **se lavait** nous **nous lavions** vous **vous laviez** ils **se lavaient**
PLUS-QUE-PARFAIT	j'**avais parlé** tu **avais parlé** il **avait parlé** nous **avions parlé** vous **aviez parlé** ils **avaient parlé**	j'**avais fini** tu **avais fini** il **avait fini** nous **avions fini** vous **aviez fini** ils **avaient fini**	j'**avais vendu** tu **avais vendu** il **avait vendu** nous **avions vendu** vous **aviez vendu** ils **avaient vendu**	je **m'étais lavé(e)** tu **t'étais lavé(e)** il/elle **s'était lavé(e)** nous **nous étions lavé(e)s** vous **vous étiez lavé(e)(s)** ils/elles **s'étaient lavé(e)s**
PASSÉ SIMPLE	je **parlai** tu **parlas** il **parla** nous **parlâmes** vous **parlâtes** ils **parlèrent**	je **finis** tu **finis** il **finit** nous **finîmes** vous **finîtes** ils **finirent**	je **vendis** tu **vendis** il **vendit** nous **vendîmes** vous **vendîtes** ils **vendirent**	je **me lavai** tu **te lavas** il **se lava** nous **nous lavâmes** vous **vous lavâtes** ils **se lavèrent**

INFINITIF	parler *(to talk, speak)*	finir *(to finish)*	vendre *(to sell)*	se laver *(to wash oneself)*
FUTUR	je **parlerai** tu **parleras** il **parlera** nous **parlerons** vous **parlerez** ils **parleront**	je **finirai** tu **finiras** il **finira** nous **finirons** vous **finirez** ils **finiront**	je **vendrai** tu **vendras** il **vendra** nous **vendrons** vous **vendrez** ils **vendront**	je **me laverai** tu **te laveras** il **se lavera** nous **nous laverons** vous **vous laverez** ils **se laveront**
CONDITIONNEL	je **parlerais** tu **parlerais** il **parlerait** nous **parlerions** vous **parleriez** ils **parleraient**	je **finirais** tu **finirais** il **finirait** nous **finirions** vous **finiriez** ils **finiraient**	je **vendrais** tu **vendrais** il **vendrait** nous **vendrions** vous **vendriez** ils **vendraient**	je **me laverais** tu **te laverais** il **se laverait** nous **nous laverions** vous **vous laveriez** ils **se laveraient**
CONDITIONNEL PASSÉ	j'**aurais parlé** tu **aurais parlé** il **aurait parlé** nous **aurions parlé** vous **auriez parlé** ils **auraient parlé**	j'**aurais fini** tu **aurais fini** il **aurait fini** nous **aurions fini** vous **auriez fini** ils **auraient fini**	j'**aurais vendu** tu **aurais vendu** il **aurait vendu** nous **aurions vendu** vous **auriez vendu** ils **auraient vendu**	je **me serais lavé(e)** tu **te serais lavé(e)** il/elle **se serait lavé(e)** nous **nous serions lavé(e)s** vous **vous seriez lavé(e)(s)** ils/elles **se seraient lavé(e)s**
SUBJONCTIF	que je **parle** que tu **parles** qu'il **parle** que nous **parlions** que vous **parliez** qu'**ils parlent**	que je **finisse** que tu **finisses** qu'il **finisse** que nous **finissions** que vous **finissiez** qu'ils **finissent**	que je **vende** que tu **vendes** qu'il **vende** que nous **vendions** que vous **vendiez** qu'ils **vendent**	que je **me lave** que tu **te laves** qu'il **se lave** que nous **nous lavions** que vous **vous laviez** qu'ils **se lavent**
PASSÉ DU SUBJONCTIF	que j'**aie parlé** que tu **aies parlé** qu'il **ait parlé** que nous **ayons parlé** que vous **ayez parlé** qu'ils **aient parlé**	que j'**aie fini** que tu **aies fini** qu'il **ait fini** que nous **ayons fini** que vous **ayez fini** qu'ils **aient fini**	que j'**aie vendu** que tu **aies vendu** qu'il **ait vendu** que nous **ayons vendu** que vous **ayez vendu** qu'ils **aient vendu**	que je **me sois lavé(e)** que tu **te sois lavé(e)** qu'il/elle **se soit lavé(e)** que nous **nous soyons lavé(e)s** que vous **vous soyez lavé(e)(s)** qu'ils/elles **se soient lavé(e)s**
PARTICIPE PRÉSENT	**parlant**	**finissant**	**vendant**	**se lavant**
INFINITIF PASSÉ	**avoir parlé**	**avoir fini**	**avoir vendu**	**s'être lavé(e)**

2 VERBS WITH SPELLING CHANGES

Some -**er** verbs have spelling changes in certain tenses. These changes are highlighted in the chart below. All other forms of these verbs are similar to those of regular -**er** verbs.

The verbs listed below follow the pattern of the indicated model verbs. Note that reflexive verbs are conjugated with **être** in the compound tenses. (All others are conjugated with **avoir**.)

verbs like **acheter** (to buy)	verbs like **appeler** (to call)	verbs like **préférer** (to prefer)
amener (to take, bring along)	**s'appeler** (to be named, to be called)	**accélérer** (to accelerate)
élever (to educate, to raise)	**empaqueter** (to bag)	**célébrer** (to celebrate)
enlever (to take off)	**épousseter** (to dust)	**espérer** (to hope)
lever (to lift, raise)	**étinceler** (to twinkle)	**s'inquiéter** (to worry)
se lever (to get up)	**jeter** (to throw)	**posséder** (to possess, to own)
mener (to take, to lead)	**rappeler** (to call back)	**protéger** (to protect)
promener (to walk [a dog])	**se rappeler** (to remember)	**répéter** (to repeat)
se promener (to take a walk, take a ride)	**rejeter** (to reject)	**sécher** (to dry)
		se sécher (to dry oneself)
		suggérer (to suggest)

INFINITIF	PRÉSENT		IMPÉRATIF	PASSÉ COMPOSÉ	IMPARFAIT
acheter e → è	j'**achète** tu **achètes** il **achète**	nous **achetons** vous **achetez** ils **achètent**	**achète!** achetons! achetez!	j'**ai acheté**	j'**achetais** nous **achetions**
appeler l → ll (double consonant)	j'**appelle** tu **appelles** il **appelle**	nous **appelons** vous **appelez** ils **appellent**	**appelle!** appelons! appelez!	j'**ai appelé**	j'**appelais** nous **appelions**
préférer é → è	je **préfère** tu **préfères** il **préfère**	nous **préférons** vous **préférez** ils **préfèrent**	**préfère!** préférons! préférez!	j'**ai préféré**	je **préférais** nous **préférions**
payer y → i	je **paie** tu **paies** il **paie**	nous **payons** vous **payez** ils **paient**	**paie!** payons! payez!	j'**ai payé**	je **payais** nous **payions**
commencer c → ç (before a, o)	je **commence** tu **commences** il **commence**	nous **commençons** vous **commencez** ils **commencent**	commence! **commençons!** commencez!	j'**ai commencé**	je **commençais** nous **commencions**
manger g → ge (before a, o)	je **mange** tu **manges** il **mange**	nous **mangeons** vous **mangez** ils **mangent**	mange! **mangeons!** mangez!	j'**ai mangé**	je **mangeais** nous **mangions**

verbs like **payer** (to pay, pay for)

balayer (to sweep)
employer (to use, to employ)
s'ennuyer (to be bored)
essayer (to try)
essuyer (to wipe, to dry)
nettoyer (to clean)

verbs like **commencer** (to begin, start)

annoncer (to announce, proclaim)
divorcer (to divorce)
se fiancer (to get engaged)
menacer (to threaten)

verbs like **manger** (to eat)

arranger (to arrange, to fix)
changer (to change)
charger (to charge)
s'en charger (to take charge)
corriger (to correct)
dégager (to shorten)
déranger (to disturb)
diriger (to direct, to run)
exiger (to demand)
égorger (to slit the throat)
embaucher (to hire)
interroger (to interrogate)
juger (to judge)

mélanger (to mix)
nager (to swim)
négliger (to neglect)
neiger (to snow)
obliger (to oblige)
partager (to share)
plonger (to dive)
protéger (to protect)
ranger (to pick up, to put away)
venger (to avenge)
voyager (to travel)

PASSÉ SIMPLE	FUTUR	CONDITIONNEL	SUBJONCTIF	PARTICIPE PRÉSENT
j'achetai il acheta ils achetèrent	j'achèterai	j'achèterais	que j'achète que nous achetions	achetant
j'appelai il appela ils appelèrent	j'appellerai	j'appellerais	que j'appelle que nous appelions	appelant
je préférai il préféra ils préférèrent	je préférerai	je préférerais	que je préfère que nous préférions	préférant
je payai il paya ils payèrent	je paierai	je paierais	que je paie que nous payions	payant
je commençai il commença ils commencèrent	je commencerai	je commencerais	que je commence que nous commencions	commençant
je mangeai il mangea ils mangèrent	je mangerai	je mangerais	que je mange que nous mangions	mangeant

3 | AUXILIARY FORMS

INFINITIF	PRÉSENT		IMPARFAIT		FUTUR	
avoir	j'ai	nous avons	j'avais	nous avions	j'aurai	nous aurons
	tu as	vous avez	tu avais	vous aviez	tu auras	vous aurez
	il a	ils ont	il avait	ils avaient	il aura	ils auront
être	je suis	nous sommes	j'étais	nous étions	je serai	nous serons
	tu es	vous êtes	tu étais	vous étiez	tu seras	vous serez
	il est	ils sont	il était	ils étaient	il sera	ils seront

4 | IRREGULAR VERBS

For the conjugation of the irregular verbs listed below, follow the pattern of the indicated verbs. Verbs conjugated with **être** as an auxiliary verb in the compound tenses are noted with an asterisk (*). All others are conjugated with **avoir**.

accueillir	(see **cueillir**)	**craindre**	(see **peindre**)	**s'endormir**	(see **dormir**)
admettre	(see **mettre**)	**cuire**	(see **conduire**)	**s'enfuir**	(see **fuir**)
apercevoir	(see **recevoir**)	**débattre**	(see **battre**)	**entreprendre**	(see **prendre**)
apparaître	(see **connaître**)	**décevoir**	(see **recevoir**)	**entretenir**	(see **tenir**)
appartenir	(see **tenir**)	**découvrir**	(see **ouvrir**)	**éteindre**	(see **peindre**)
apprendre	(see **prendre**)	**décrire**	(see **écrire**)	**s'étendre**	(see **rendre**)
atteindre	(see **peindre**)	**se déplacer**	(see **placer**)	**inscrire**	(see **écrire**)
attendre	(see **rendre**)	**déplaire**	(see **plaire**)	**interdire**	(see **dire**)
combattre	(see **battre**)	**détruire**	(see **conduire**)	**interrompre**	(see **rompre**)
comprendre	(see **prendre**)	**descendre**	(see **rendre**)	**intervenir**	(see **venir**)
confier	(see **planifier**)	* **devenir**	(see **venir**)	**introduire**	(see **conduire**)
conquérir	(see **acquérir**)	**disparaître**	(see **connaître**)	**joindre**	(see **peindre**)
construire	(see **conduire**)	**effacer**	(see **placer**)	**lancer**	(see **placer**)
contenir	(see **tenir**)	**élire**	(see **lire**)	**maintenir**	(see **tenir**)
convaincre	(see **vaincre**)	**entendre**	(see **rendre**)	**se marier**	(see **planifier**)
couvrir	(see **ouvrir**)	**s'entendre**	(see **rendre**)	**se méfier**	(see **planifier**)

INFINITIF	PRÉSENT		IMPÉRATIF	PASSÉ COMPOSÉ	IMPARFAIT
acquérir (to acquire, get)	j'**acquiers** tu **acquiers** il **acquiert**	nous **acquérons** vous **acquérez** ils **acquièrent**	acquiers acquérons acquérez	j'ai acquis	j'acquérais
aller (to go)	je **vais** tu **vas** il **va**	nous **allons** vous **allez** ils **vont**	va allons allez	je suis allé(e)	j'allais

CONDITIONNEL		SUBJONCTIF	
j'aurais	nous aurions	que j'aie	que nous ayons
tu aurais	vous auriez	que tu aies	que vous ayez
il aurait	ils auraient	qu'il ait	qu'ils aient
je serais	nous serions	que je sois	que nous soyons
tu serais	vous seriez	que tu sois	que vous soyez
il serait	ils seraient	qu'il soit	qu'ils soient

mentir	(see sortir)	promettre	(see mettre)	*revenir	(see venir)
obtenir	(see tenir)	reconnaître	(see connaître)	sentir	(see sortir)
offrir	(see ouvrir)	réconcilier	(see planifier)	servir	(see sortir)
opérer	(see céder)	reconstruire	(see conduire)	souffrir	(see ouvrir)
paraître	(see connaître)	récupérer	(see céder)	sourire	(see rire)
parcourir	(see courir)	redécouvrir	(see ouvrir)	soutenir	(see tenir)
*partir	(see sortir)	réduire	(see conduire)	se souvenir	(see venir)
parvenir	(see venir)	remarier	(see planifier)	subvenir	(see venir)
pendre	(see rendre)	remercier	(see planifier)	succéder	(see céder)
se perdre	(see rendre)	remettre	(see mettre)	surprendre	(see prendre)
permettre	(see mettre)	se rendre à	(see rendre)	survenir	(see venir)
peser	(see acheter)	renoncer	(see placer)	survivre	(see vivre)
plaindre	(see peindre)	renvoyer	(see envoyer)	tondre	(see rendre)
poursuivre	(see suivre)	répandre	(see rendre)	se tordre	(see rendre)
prédire	(see dire)	répondre	(see rendre)	traduire	(see conduire)
prévoir	(see voir)	ressentir	(see sortir)		
produire	(see conduire)	retenir	(see tenir)		

PASSÉ SIMPLE	FUTUR	CONDITIONNEL	SUBJONCTIF	PARTICIPE PRÉSENT
j'acquis	j'acquerrai	j'acquerrais	que j'acquière que nous acquérions	acquérant
j'allai	j'irai	j'irais	que j'aille que nous allions	allant

INFINITIF	PRÉSENT		IMPÉRATIF	PASSÉ COMPOSÉ	IMPARFAIT
appuyer *(to push)*	j'**appuie** tu **appuies** il **appuie**	nous **appuyons** vous **appuyez** ils **appuient**	**appuie!** **appuyons!** **appuyez!**	j'ai **appuyé**	j'**appuyais**
s'asseoir *(to sit down)*	je m'**assieds** tu t'**assieds** il s'**assied**	nous nous **asseyons** vous vous **asseyez** ils s'**asseyent**	**assieds-toi!** **asseyons-nous!** **asseyez-vous!**	je me suis **assis(e)**	je m'**asseyais**
avoir *(to have)*	j'**ai** tu **as** il **a**	nous **avons** vous **avez** ils **ont**	**aie!** **ayons!** **ayez!**	j'ai **eu**	j'**avais**
il y a *(there is, are)*	il **y a**		– –	il **y a eu**	il **y avait**
battre *(to beat)*	je **bats** tu **bats** il **bat**	nous **battons** vous **battez** ils **battent**	**bats!** **battons!** **battez!**	j'ai **battu**	je **battais**
boire *(to drink)*	je **bois** tu **bois** il **boit**	nous **buvons** vous **buvez** ils **boivent**	**bois!** **buvons!** **buvez!**	j'ai **bu**	je **buvais**
céder *(to cede)*	je **cède** tu **cèdes** il **cède**	nous **cédons** vous **cédez** ils **cèdent**	**cède!** **cédons!** **cédez!**	j'ai **cédé**	je **cédais**
conduire *(to drive)*	je **conduis** tu **conduis** il **conduit**	nous **conduisons** vous **conduisez** ils **conduisent**	**conduis!** **conduisons!** **conduisez!**	j'ai **conduit**	je **conduisais**
connaître *(to know)*	je **connais** tu **connais** il **connaît**	nous **connaissons** vous **connaissez** ils **connaissent**	**connais!** **connaissons!** **connaissez!**	j'ai **connu**	je **connaissais**
courir *(to run)*	je **cours** tu **cours** il **court**	nous **courons** vous **courez** ils **courent**	**cours!** **courons!** **courez!**	j'ai **couru**	je **courais**
croire *(to believe, think)*	je **crois** tu **crois** il **croit**	nous **croyons** vous **croyez** ils **croient**	**crois!** **croyons!** **croyez!**	j'ai **cru**	je **croyais**
cueillir *(to gather, pick)*	je **cueille** tu **cueilles** il **cueille**	nous **cueillons** vous **cueillez** ils **cueillent**	**cueille!** **cueillons!** **cueillez!**	j'ai **cueilli**	je **cueillais**
devoir *(must, to have to, owe)*	je **dois** tu **dois** il **doit**	nous **devons** vous **devez** ils **doivent**	**dois!** **devons!** **devez!**	j'ai **dû**	je **devais**

PASSÉ SIMPLE	FUTUR	CONDITIONNEL	SUBJONCTIF		PARTICIPE PRÉSENT
j'appuyai	j'appuierai	j'appuierais	que j'**appuie** que nous **appuyions**		appuyant
je m'assis	je m'assiérai	je m'assiérais	que je m'**asseye** que nous **nous asseyions**		s'asseyant
j'eus	j'aurai	j'aurais	que j'**aie** que tu **aies** qu'il **ait**	que nous **ayons** que vous **ayez** qu'ils **aient**	ayant
il y eut	il y aura	il y aurait	qu'**il y ait**		– –
je battis	je battrai	je battrais	que je **batte** que nous **battions**		battant
je bus	je boirai	je boirais	que je **boive** que nous **buvions**		buvant
je cédai	je céderai	je céderais	que je **cède** que nous **cédions**		cédant
je conduisis	je conduirai	je conduirais	que je **conduise** que nous **conduisions**		conduisant
je connus	je connaîtrai	je connaîtrais	que je **connaisse** que nous **connaissions**		connaissant
je courus	je courrai	je courrais	que je **coure** que nous **courions**		courant
je crus	je croirai	je croirais	que je **croie** que nous **croyions**		croyant
je cueillis	je cueillerai	je cueillerais	que je **cueille** que nous **cueillions**		cueillant
je dus	je devrai	je devrais	que je **doive** que nous **devions**		devant

INFINITIF	PRÉSENT		IMPÉRATIF	PASSÉ COMPOSÉ	IMPARFAIT
dire (to say, tell)	je **dis** tu **dis** il **dit**	nous **disons** vous **dites** ils **disent**	**dis!** **disons!** **dites!**	j'**ai dit**	je **disais**
dormir (to sleep)	je **dors** tu **dors** il **dort**	nous **dormons** vous **dormez** ils **dorment**	**dors!** **dormons!** **dormez!**	j'**ai dormi**	je **dormais**
écrire (to write)	j'**écris** tu **écris** il **écrit**	nous **écrivons** vous **écrivez** ils **écrivent**	**écris!** **écrivons!** **écrivez!**	j'**ai écrit**	j'**écrivais**
envoyer (to send)	j'**envoie** tu **envoies** il **envoie**	nous **envoyons** vous **envoyez** ils **envoient**	**envoie!** **envoyons!** **envoyez!**	j'**ai envoyé**	j'**envoyais**
être (to be)	je **suis** tu **es** il **est**	nous **sommes** vous **êtes** ils **sont**	**sois!** **soyons!** **soyez!**	j'**ai été**	j'**étais**
faire (to make, do)	je **fais** tu **fais** il **fait**	nous **faisons** vous **faites** ils **font**	**fais!** **faisons!** **faites!**	j'**ai fait**	je **faisais**
falloir (to be necessary)	il **faut**	– –	– –	il **a fallu**	il **fallait**
fuir (to flee)	je **fuis** tu **fuis** il **fuit**	nous **fuyons** vous **fuyez** ils **fuient**	**fuis!** **fuyons!** **fuyez!**	j'**ai fui**	je **fuyais**
lire (to read)	je **lis** tu **lis** il **lit**	nous **lisons** vous **lisez** ils **lisent**	**lis!** **lisons!** **lisez!**	j'**ai lu**	je **lisais**
mettre (to put, place)	je **mets** tu **mets** il **met**	nous **mettons** vous **mettez** ils **mettent**	**mets!** **mettons!** **mettez!**	j'**ai mis**	je **mettais**
mourir (to die)	je **meurs** tu **meurs** il **meurt**	nous **mourons** vous **mourez** ils **meurent**	**meurs!** **mourons!** **mourez!**	je **suis mort(e)**	je **mourais**

PASSÉ SIMPLE	FUTUR	CONDITIONNEL	SUBJONCTIF	PARTICIPE PRÉSENT
je **dis**	je **dirai**	je **dirais**	que je **dise** que nous **disions**	**disant**
je **dormis**	je **dormirai**	je **dormirais**	que je **dorme** que nous **dormions**	**dormant**
j'**écrivis**	j'**écrirai**	j'**écrirais**	que j'**écrive** que nous **écrivions**	**écrivant**
j'**envoyai**	j'**enverrai**	j'**enverrais**	que j'**envoie** que nous **envoyions**	**envoyant**
je **fus**	je **serai**	je **serais**	que je **sois** que nous **soyons** que tu **sois** que vous **soyez** qu'il **soit** qu'ils **soient**	**étant**
je **fis**	je **ferai**	je **ferais**	que je **fasse** que nous **fassions**	**faisant**
il **fallut**	il **faudra**	il **faudrait**	qu'il **faille**	– –
je **fuis**	je **fuirai**	je **fuirais**	que je **fuie** que nous **fuyions**	**fuyant**
je **lus**	je **lirai**	je **lirais**	que je **lise** que nous **lisions**	**lisant**
je **mis**	je **mettrai**	je **mettrais**	que je **mette** que nous **mettions**	**mettant**
je **mourus**	je **mourrai**	je **mourrais**	que je **meure** que nous **mourions**	**mourant**

INFINITIF	PRÉSENT		IMPÉRATIF	PASSÉ COMPOSÉ	IMPARFAIT
naître *(to be born)*	je **nais** tu **nais** il **naît**	nous **naissons** vous **naissez** ils **naissent**	**nais!** **naissons!** **naissez!**	je **suis né(e)**	je **naissais**
ouvrir *(to open)*	j'**ouvre** tu **ouvres** il **ouvre**	nous **ouvrons** vous **ouvrez** ils **ouvrent**	**ouvre!** **ouvrons!** **ouvrez!**	j'**ai ouvert**	j'**ouvrais**
peindre *(to paint)*	je **peins** tu **peins** il **peint**	nous **peignons** vous **peignez** ils **peignent**	**peins!** **peignons!** **peignez!**	j'**ai peint**	je **peignais**
placer *(to place)*	je **place** tu **places** il **place**	nous **plaçons** vous **placez** ils **placent**	**place!** **plaçons!** **placez!**	j'**ai placé**	je **plaçais**
plaire *(to please)*	je **plais** tu **plais** il **plaît**	nous **plaisons** vous **plaisez** ils **plaisent**	**plais!** **plaisons!** **plaisez!**	j'**ai plu**	je **plaisais**
planifier *(to plan)*	je **planifie** tu **planifies** il **planifie**	nous **planifions** vous **planifiez** ils **planifient**	**planifie!** **planifions!** **planifiez!**	j'**ai planifié**	je **planifiais**
pleuvoir *(to rain)*	il **pleut**	– –	– –	il **a plu**	il **pleuvait**
pouvoir *(to be able, can)*	je **peux** tu **peux** il **peut**	nous **pouvons** vous **pouvez** ils **peuvent**	– –	j'**ai pu**	je **pouvais**
prendre *(to take, have)*	je **prends** tu **prends** il **prend**	nous **prenons** vous **prenez** ils **prennent**	**prends!** **prenons!** **prenez!**	j'**ai pris**	je **prenais**
recevoir *(to receive, get, obtain)*	je **reçois** tu **reçois** il **reçoit**	nous **recevons** vous **recevez** ils **reçoivent**	**reçois!** **recevons!** **recevez!**	j'**ai reçu**	je **recevais**
rendre *(to render)*	je **rends** tu **rends** il **rend**	nous **rendons** vous **rendez** ils **rendent**	**rends!** **rendons!** **rendez!**	j'**ai rendu**	je **rendais**
résoudre *(to resolve)*	je **résous** tu **résous** il **résout**	nous **résolvons** vous **résolvez** ils **résolvent**	**résous!** **résolvons!** **résolvez!**	j'**ai résolu**	je **résolvais**
rire *(to laugh)*	je **ris** tu **ris** il **rit**	nous **rions** vous **riez** ils **rient**	**ris!** **rions!** **riez!**	j'**ai ri**	je **riais**

PASSÉ SIMPLE	FUTUR	CONDITIONNEL	SUBJONCTIF	PARTICIPE PRÉSENT
je **naquis**	je **naîtrai**	je **naîtrais**	que je **naisse** que nous **naissions**	**naissant**
j'**ouvris**	j'**ouvrirai**	j'**ouvrirais**	que j'**ouvre** que nous **ouvrions**	**ouvrant**
je **peignis**	je **peindrai**	je **peindrais**	que je **peigne** que nous **peignions**	**peignant**
je **plaçai**	je **placerai**	je **placerais**	que je **place** que nous **placions**	**plaçant**
je **plus**	je **plairai**	je **plairais**	que je **plaise** que nous **plaisions**	**plaisant**
je **planifiai**	je **planifierai**	je **planifierais**	que je **planifie** que nous **planifiions**	**planifiant**
il **plut**	il **pleuvra**	il **pleuvrait**	qu'il **pleuve**	**pleuvant**
je **pus**	je **pourrai**	je **pourrais**	que je **puisse** que nous **puissions**	**pouvant**
je **pris**	je **prendrai**	je **prendrais**	que je **prenne** que nous **prenions**	**prenant**
je **reçus**	je **recevrai**	je **recevrais**	que je **reçoive** que nous **recevions**	**recevant**
je **rendis**	je **rendrai**	je **rendrais**	que je **rende** que nous **rendions**	**rendant**
je **résolus**	je **résoudrai**	je **résoudrais**	que je **résolve** que nous **résolvions**	**résolvant**
je **ris**	je **rirai**	je **rirais**	que je **rie** que nous **riions**	**riant**

INFINITIF	PRÉSENT		IMPÉRATIF	PASSÉ COMPOSÉ	IMPARFAIT
rompre *(to break)*	je **romps** tu **romps** il **rompt**	nous **rompons** vous **rompez** ils **rompent**	**romps!** **rompons!** **rompez!**	j'ai **rompu**	je **rompais**
savoir *(to know)*	je **sais** tu **sais** il **sait**	nous **savons** vous **savez** ils **savent**	**sache!** **sachons!** **sachez!**	j'ai **su**	je **savais**
sortir *(to go out)*	je **sors** tu **sors** il **sort**	nous **sortons** vous **sortez** ils **sortent**	**sors!** **sortons!** **sortez!**	je **suis sorti(e)**	je **sortais**
suivre *(to follow)*	je **suis** tu **suis** il **suit**	nous **suivons** vous **suivez** ils **suivent**	**suis!** **suivons!** **suivez!**	j'ai **suivi**	je **suivais**
se taire *(to be quiet)*	je **me tais** tu **te tais** il **se tait**	nous **nous taisons** vous **vous taisez** ils **se taisent**	**tais-toi!** **taisons-nous!** **taisez-vous!**	je **me suis tu(e)**	je **me taisais**
tenir *(to hold)*	je **tiens** tu **tiens** il **tient**	nous **tenons** vous **tenez** ils **tiennent**	**tiens!** **tenons!** **tenez!**	j'ai **tenu**	je **tenais**
vaincre *(to win,* *conquer)*	je **vaincs** tu **vaincs** il **vainc**	nous **vainquons** vous **vainquez** ils **vainquent**	**vaincs!** **vainquons!** **vainquez!**	j'ai **vaincu**	je **vainquais**
valoir *(to be worth,* *deserve, merit)*	je **vaux** tu **vaux** il **vaut**	nous **valons** vous **valez** ils **valent**	**vaux!** **valons!** **valez!**	j'ai **valu**	je **valais**
venir *(to come)*	je **viens** tu **viens** il **vient**	nous **venons** vous **venez** ils **viennent**	**viens!** **venons!** **venez!**	je **suis venu(e)**	je **venais**
vivre *(to live)*	je **vis** tu **vis** il **vit**	nous **vivons** vous **vivez** ils **vivent**	**vis!** **vivons!** **vivez!**	j'ai **vécu**	je **vivais**
voir *(to see)*	je **vois** tu **vois** il **voit**	nous **voyons** vous **voyez** ils **voient**	**vois!** **voyons!** **voyez!**	j'ai **vu**	je **voyais**
vouloir *(to want, wish)*	je **veux** tu **veux** il **veut**	nous **voulons** vous **voulez** ils **veulent**	**veuille!** **veuillons!** **veuillez!**	j'ai **voulu**	je **voulais**

PASSÉ SIMPLE	FUTUR	CONDITIONNEL	SUBJONCTIF	PARTICIPE PRÉSENT
je **rompis**	je **romprai**	je **romprais**	que je **rompe** que nous **rompions**	**rompant**
je **sus**	je **saurai**	je **saurais**	que je **sache** que nous **sachions**	**sachant**
je **sortis**	je **sortirai**	je **sortirais**	que je **sorte** que nous **sortions**	**sortant**
je **suivis**	je **suivrai**	je **suivrais**	que je **suive** que nous **suivions**	**suivant**
je **me tus**	je **me tairai**	je **me tairais**	que je **me taise** que nous **nous taisions**	**se taisant**
je **tins**	je **tiendrai**	je **tiendrais**	que je **tienne** que nous **tenions**	**tenant**
je **vainquis**	je **vaincrai**	je **vaincrais**	que je **vainque** que nous **vainquions**	**vainquant**
je **valus**	je **vaudrai**	je **vaudrais**	que je **vaille** que nous **valions**	**valant**
je **vins**	je **viendrai**	je **viendrais**	que je **vienne** que nous **venions**	**venant**
je **vécus**	je **vivrai**	je **vivrais**	que je **vive** que nous **vivions**	**vivant**
je **vis**	je **verrai**	je **verrais**	que je **voie** que nous **voyions**	**voyant**
je **voulus**	je **voudrai**	je **voudrais**	que je **veuille** que nous **voulions**	**voulant**

5 PASSÉ SIMPLE

The PASSÉ SIMPLE is a past tense which is used mainly in literary French. You may encounter the passé simple in newspaper and magazine articles, in short stories and novels. The passé simple is generally not used in conversational French, nor is it used in informal notes and letters.

FORMS

The PASSÉ SIMPLE is a simple tense.
For REGULAR VERBS, this tense is formed as follows:

PASSÉ SIMPLE = INFINITIVE STEM + PASSÉ SIMPLE ENDINGS

INFINITIVE	parler	
STEM	parl-	ENDINGS
je	parlai	-ai
tu	parlas	-as
il/elle/on	parla	-a
nous	parlâmes	-âmes
vous	parlâtes	-âtes
ils/elles	parlèrent	-èrent

INFINITIVE	finir	
STEM	fin-	ENDINGS
je	finis	-is
tu	finis	-is
il/elle/on	finit	-it
nous	finîmes	-îmes
vous	finîtes	-îtes
ils/elles	finirent	-irent

INFINITIVE	vendre	
STEM	vend-	ENDINGS
je	vendis	-is
tu	vendis	-is
il/elle/on	vendit	-it
nous	vendîmes	-îmes
vous	vendîtes	-îtes
ils/elles	vendirent	-irent

PASSÉ SIMPLE OF SELECTED IRREGULAR VERBS
(FOR RECOGNITION)

il alla	aller
il but	boire
il conduisit	conduire
il connut	connaître
il craignit	craindre
il crut	croire
il dit	dire
il dormit	dormir
il dut	devoir
il eut	avoir
il écrivit	écrire
il fallut	il faut
il fit	faire
il fut	être
il lut	lire
il mit	mettre
il mourut	mourir
il naquit	naître
il ouvrit	ouvrir
il plut	plaire
il plut	il pleut
il prit	prendre
il put	pouvoir
il reçut	recevoir
il rit	rire
il sortit	sortir
il suivit	suivre
il tint	tenir
il vécut	vivre
il vit	voir
il voulut	vouloir
il sut	savoir

Many IRREGULAR VERBS have irregular stems in the passé simple.
These are always given in the **je**-form in dictionaries and verb charts.

Irregular verbs fall into three groups, according to their endings:

	je-form in **-us** connaître		**je**-form in **-is** prendre		**je**-form in **-ins** venir	
je	**connus**	**-us**	**pris**	**-is**	**vins**	**-ins**
tu	**connus**	**-us**	**pris**	**-is**	**vins**	**-ins**
il/elle/on	**connut**	**-ut**	**prit**	**-it**	**vint**	**-int**
nous	**connûmes**	**-ûmes**	**prîmes**	**-îmes**	**vînmes**	**-înmes**
vous	**connûtes**	**-ûtes**	**prîtes**	**-îtes**	**vîntes**	**-întes**
ils/elles	**connurent**	**-urent**	**prirent**	**-irent**	**vinrent**	**-inrent**

➡ Note that **aller** follows the pattern of **-er** verbs: **j'allai, il alla, ils allèrent.**

USES

The passé simple corresponds to the simple past in English.

Champlain **fonda** Québec en 1608.   *Champlain **founded** Quebec in 1608.*

Contrast the use of the past tenses in French:

To express:	in LITERARY French:	in CONVERSATIONAL French:
• an on-going event or action (*what was happening*)	IMPERFECT **Il neigeait.** *(It was snowing.)*	IMPERFECT **Il neigeait.** *(It was snowing.)*
• a habitual past action (*what used to happen*)	IMPERFECT **En hiver, nous faisions du ski.** *(In winter, we used to go skiing.)*	IMPERFECT **En hiver, nous faisions du ski.** *(In winter, we used to go skiing.)*
• a specific event completed at a given moment in the past (*what happened*)	PASSÉ SIMPLE **Paul tomba et se cassa le bras.** *(Paul fell and broke his arm.)*	PASSÉ COMPOSÉ **Paul est tombé et il s'est cassé le bras.** *(Paul fell and broke his arm.)*
• an action that took place in the past at an indefinite time and has consequences in the present (*what has happened*)	PASSÉ COMPOSÉ **Personne ne l'a vu depuis l'accident.** *(Nobody has seen him since the accident.)*	PASSÉ COMPOSÉ **Personne ne l'a vu depuis l'accident.** *(Nobody has seen him since the accident.)*

La France

l'Angleterre

la Manche

Lille
NORD[2]

la Belgique

l'Allemagne

le Luxembourg

LES VOSGES

Le Havre
HAUTE-NORMANDIE

PICARDIE

Caen
Rouen

BASSE-NORMANDIE

Versailles
PARIS
RÉGION
PARISIENNE[1]

CHAMPAGNE-
ARDENNE

Meuse

LORRAINE

Nancy

Strasbourg

ALSACE

Rhin

Colmar

BRETAGNE

Rennes

PAYS DE LA LOIRE

Loire

Seine

FRANCHE-
COMTÉ

Nantes

Tours

CENTRE

Dijon

BOURGOGNE

Saône

la Suisse

OCÉAN
ATLANTIQUE

POITOU-
CHARENTES

LIMOUSIN

Vichy

AUVERGNE

Annecy

RHÔNE-ALPES

Lyon

Clermont-
Ferrand

Grenoble

LES ALPES

l'Italie

Bordeaux

Garonne

LE MASSIF
CENTRAL

Rhône

AQUITAINE

MIDI-PYRÉNÉES

Albi

Nîmes

Avignon

PROVENCE-
CÔTE D'AZUR[3]

Nice

Toulouse

Montpellier

Cannes

Monaco

l'Espagne

LANGUEDOC-
ROUSSILLON

Marseille

Toulon

Saint-
Tropez

LES PYRÉNÉES

Mer Méditerranée

LA CORSE

[1]Also known as Île-de-France
[2]Also known as Nord-Pas-de-Calais
[3]Also known as Provence-Alpes-Côte d'Azur (Bottin 1989)

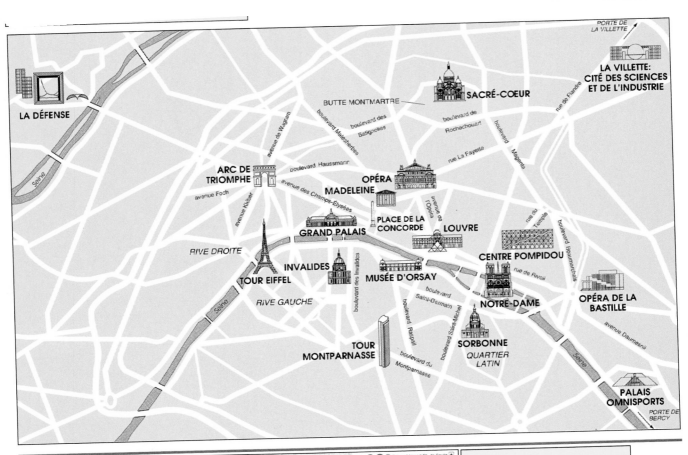

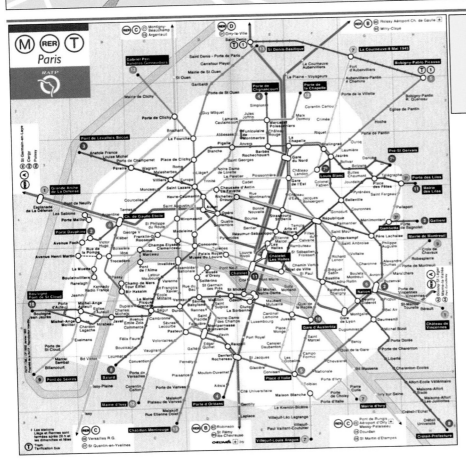

Paris
Métro Map

Le Monde francophone

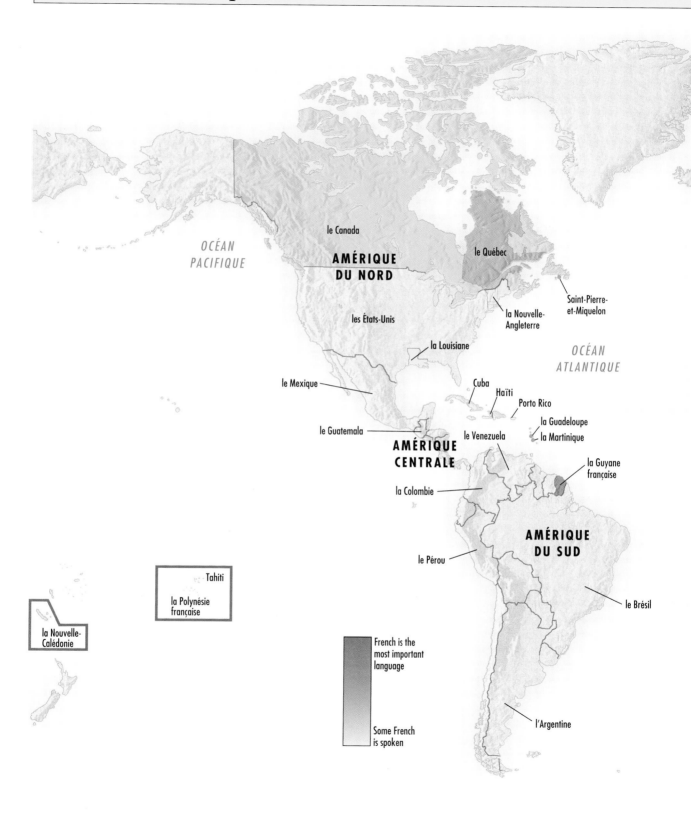

OCÉAN PACIFIQUE

le Canada

le Québec

AMÉRIQUE DU NORD

Saint-Pierre-et-Miquelon

la Nouvelle-Angleterre

les États-Unis

la Louisiane

OCÉAN ATLANTIQUE

le Mexique

Cuba

Haïti

Porto Rico

la Guadeloupe

le Guatemala

le Venezuela

la Martinique

AMÉRIQUE CENTRALE

la Guyane française

la Colombie

AMÉRIQUE DU SUD

le Pérou

le Brésil

Tahiti

la Polynésie française

la Nouvelle-Calédonie

French is the most important language

Some French is spoken

l'Argentine

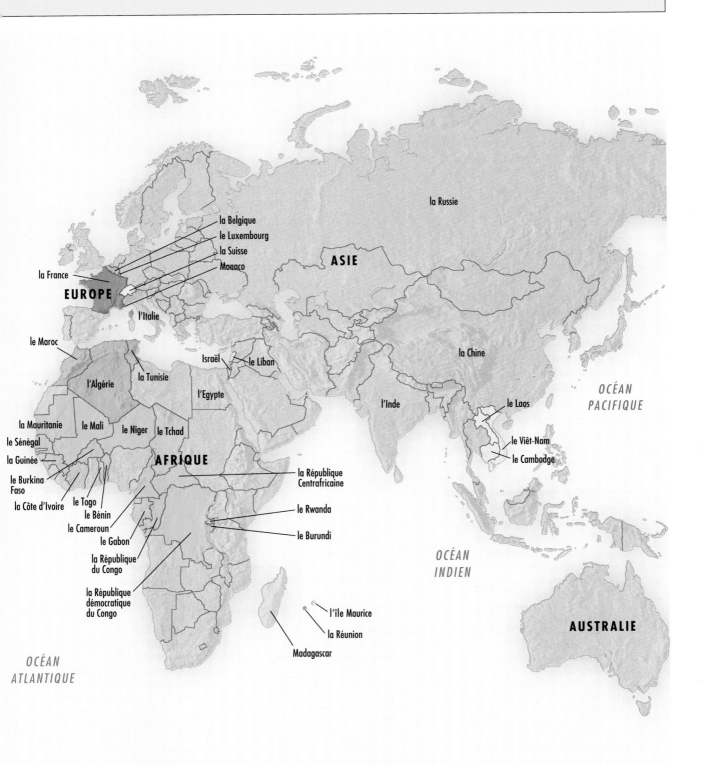

la Russie

la Belgique
le Luxembourg
la Suisse
Monaco

la France

EUROPE

l'Italie

ASIE

le Maroc

Israël   le Liban

la Chine

l'Algérie   la Tunisie

l'Egypte

**OCÉAN
PACIFIQUE**

la Mauritanie   le Mali   le Niger   le Tchad

l'Inde

le Laos

le Sénégal

la Guinée

AFRIQUE

la République
Centrafricaine

le Viêt-Nam

le Cambodge

le Burkina
Faso

le Togo

la Côte d'Ivoire

le Bénin

le Rwanda

le Cameroun

le Burundi

le Gabon

la République
du Congo

**OCÉAN
INDIEN**

la République
démocratique
du Congo

l'île Maurice

AUSTRALIE

la Réunion

Madagascar

**OCÉAN
ATLANTIQUE**

VOCABULAIRE: Français-Anglais

The French—English vocabulary contains active and passive words from the text, as well as the important words of the illustrations used within the units.

The numbers and letters following an entry indicate the first unit section in which the words or phrase is activated. The following abbreviations have been used:

R	Reprise
L	Lecture
IM	Info Magazine
IC	Interlude Culturel
FP	Français Pratique
TA	Teacher's Annotation
LC	Langue et Communication
A	Appendix

The number after the section abbreviation indicates the unit *Partie* in which the vocabulary word is introduced.

An asterisk (*) after the unit reference indicates that the word or phrase is presented in the *Mots Utiles* section of the reading.

Nouns: If the article of a noun does not indicate gender, the noun is followed by *m. (masculine)* or *f. (feminine)*. If the plural is irregular, it is given in parentheses.

Adjectives: Adjectives are listed in the masculine form. If the feminine form is irregular, it is given in parentheses. Irregular plural forms are also given in parentheses.

Verbs: Verbs are listed in the infinitive form. An asterisk (*) in front of an active verb means that it is irregular. (For forms, see the verb charts in the Appendix.) Irregular past participle *(p. p.)*, present participle *(pres. part.)*, future *(fut.)*, and subjunctive *(subj.)* forms are listed separately.

Words beginning with an **h** are preceded by a bullet (•) if the **h** is aspirate; that is, if the word is treated as if it begins with a consonant sound.

A

à to, at
  à + *length of time* (length of time) from . . . **8.FP2**
  à + *distance* (distance) from . . . **8.FP2**
  à + *date, time until,* see you at (date, time) **8.FP1**
  à + *mode of transport* by (mode of transport) . . .
abord: d'abord first, at first **3.FP2**
aborder to approach
l' **abri** *m.* shelter
abriter to shelter
un **accent** accent, tone
accès: un accès pour personnes handicapées handicap access **6.FP1**
un **accident** accident **3.FP2**
un **accord** chord
  d'accord OK **2.FP2**
accorder to grant

*accueillir** to provide shelter; to welcome
acheter to buy **5.FP2**
s' **acheter** to buy (oneself) **1.FP3**
l' **acier** *m.* steel **2.FP3**
*acquérir** to acquire
actif: à mon actif to my credit
actuel (actuelle) current, present
actuellement currently
adieu *(pl. adieux)* farewell
un **adjoint** assistant
un **adolescent** teenager
l' **admiration** *f.* admiration **9.FP1**
s' **adresser à** to speak to
adroitement skillfully
l' **aéroport** *m.* airport **5.FP2**
une **affaire** business, affair
  faire l'affaire to be qualified **10.FP3**
les **affaires** *f.* business **2.L***
l' **affection** *f.* affection **9.FP1**
affluent tributary

agence: une agence de voyages travel agency **5.FP2**
agent: un agent d'assurances insurance agent **10.FP1**
  un agent de change stockbroker **10.FP1**
  un agent de police policeman
  un agent immobilier real estate agent **10.FP1**
*agir** to act
*s' agir: il s'agit de** it is about
aider (à) to help **2.FP2**
aïe! ouch! **7.FP1**
ailleurs elsewhere **7.IM**
  d'ailleurs besides **8.L***
aimer to like **2.LC2**; to love **9.FP1**
  aimer bien to like **9.FP1**
l' **aîné** eldest **R.L***
ainsi que as well as
l' **air** *m.* aria
  l'air conditionné air conditioning **6.FP1**

aise: à l'aise   comfortable
ajouté   added
ajouter   to add
alléché   attracted, tempted
aller: un aller et retour   round-trip ticket 5.FP2
   un aller simple   one-way ticket 5.FP2
*aller   to go 6.FP1
   aller à l'entretien   to go on an interview 10.FP2
   aller à la pêche   to go fishing 3.FP1
   aller voir   to go look 1.L*
*s' en aller   to go away 1.LC4
une allergie   allergy 7.FP1
une alliance   wedding ring
   allumer   to light 10.L*
   allumer un feu   to light a fire 2.L*
une allumette   match 4.FP1
une allure   allure, impression
   alors que   whereas
les Alpes f.   the Alps 1.LC1
l' alpinisme m.   mountain climbing
   faire de l'alpinisme   to go mountain climbing 3.FP1
   altier (altière)   proud
l' aluminium m.   aluminum 2.FP3
   amaigri   very thin
une amande   almond
un amateur   amateur
une ambiance   atmosphere 10.FP2
l' ambition f.   ambition 10.FP3
l' âme f.   soul
   à l'âme tendre   with a soft heart
   aménagé   equipped, developed
   amer (amère)   bitter
un ami (une amie)   friend 9.FP1
l' amitié f.   friendship 9.FP1
l' amour m.   love
   amoureux (amoureuse) de   in love with
l' ampleur f.   extent 4.L*
un ampli   amplifier 4.FP3
l' ampoule f.   swelling
s' amuser   to have fun 1.FP3
   ancien (ancienne)   old, former 2.FP3
   un ancien élève   alumnus 8.L*
l' angine f.   strep throat 7.FP1
un animal (pl. animaux)   animal 2.FP1
une animateur (une animatrice)   counselor
l' animosité f.   animosity 9.FP1
une annonce   notice, ad 2.IM

   annulé   canceled 5.FP2
   annuler   to cancel 5.FP2
une antenne   antenna 4.FP3
un antibiotique   antibiotic 7.FP1
l' antipathie f.   antipathy 9.FP1
l' anxiété f.   anxiety
s' apaiser   to calm down
l' appareil-photo m.   camera 4.FP3
apercevoir   to notice 6.L
*s' apercevoir   to notice
un apôtre   apostle, defender
l' apparence f.   appearance 2.FP3
un appartement   apartment 8.FP2
appartenir à   to belong to 2.L
   appeler   to call 6.FP2
s' appeler   to be called, named 1.LC4
un apport   contribution
   apporter   to bring 6.L*
s' approcher (de)   to approach, come closer 1.LC4
   appuyer   to lean 10.L* to push
   après   after, afterwards 3.FP2
l' après-rasage m.   aftershave 1.FP2
l' aquarium m.   aquarium 2.FP1
un arbuste   shrub 2.FP1
l' arc-en-ciel m.   rainbow
   arche: l'Arche f. de Saint Louis   the Arch of St. Louis 2.FP3
l' argent m.   silver R.L*
l' armée f.   the army
une armoire   wardrobe, closet 1.L*
   arraché   torn away
   arracher   to pull out
   arranger   to fix 4.L*
   ça s'arrangera   things will be okay 9.FP1
   arrêter   to arrest 5.L*
s' arrêter   to stop (oneself) 1.FP3
l' arrière-garde f.   rear guard
   arriver   to happen 3.FP2
   arriver à   to manage to 4.L*
   il arrive   it happens
   il est arrivé quelque chose   something happened
   on y arrive   one can do it
   arroser   to water (plants, flowers)
l' arrosoir m.   watering can
un article   item 4.FP1
l' ascendance f.   ancestry
un ascenseur   elevator 6.FP1
l' aspirateur m.   vacuum
l' aspirine f.   aspirine 4.FP1
*s' asseoir   to sit down 1.LC4
   assez   enough 3.LC1

l' assistance f.   audience
un(e) assistant(e) sociale   social worker 10.FP1
   assister à   to be present at; to see 3.FP2
l' assurance f.   insurance
s' assurer   to make sure 8.L*
l' asthme m.   asthma 7.FP1
   astucieux (astucieuse)   smart
un atelier   studio
   un atelier d'artisan   craftsman workshop
   athlétique   athletic 1.FP1
   attacher   to attach 5.FP2
*atteindre   to reach
*attendre   to wait 5.FP2
*s' attendre à   to expect
   attendant: en attendant   in the meantime
   attendrissant   touching
*atterrir   to land 5.FP2
   attirant   attractive, alluring
   attiré   attracted
   attirer   to attract
   attraper   to catch, get 3.FP1
   attraper un coup de soleil   to get a sunburn 3.FP1
une auberge   inn 6.FP1
   une auberge de jeunesse   youth hostel 6.FP1
   aucun   no
   aucunement   not at all
   augmenter   to increase
l' aumône f.   charity
   auparavant   before
   auprès de   with; next to
   aussitôt que   as soon as 5.LC2
   autant   as much
   d'autant plus que   all the more that 9.L*
un autel   altar
l' autoroute f.   turnpike
   autour de   around 9.L*
   autre: un autre   another; another one 4.LC1
   autre chose?   is there something else? 4.FP1
   autre chose à faire   something else to do 2.FP2
   d'autres   other(s), some other(s); other ones 4.LC1
   les autres   the others
   autrefois   in the past
l' Autriche f.   Austria
   autrichien (autrichienne)   Austrian
   avaler   to swallow 7.FP1
une avance   advance, progress
   en avance   early 5.FP2
   dix minutes d'avance   ten

minutes early **5.FP2**

avant: avant de before
10.LC1

avant tout above all

l' **avant-bras** *m.* forearm

avant-hier the day before
yesterday **3.FP2**

avantage: un avantage
social fringe benefit
10.FP2

l' **avenir** *m.* future

l' **aversion** *f.* aversion **9.FP1**

averti notified

aveu *(pl. aveux)* admission

aveugle blind

avis: à votre avis in your
opinion **RA**

un **avocat (une avocate)** lawyer
10.FP1

*avoir to have

avoir affaire à to have to
deal with **8.FP2**

avoir beau essayer to try in
vain **4.L***

avoir confiance to trust
9.FP2

avoir de la chance to have
good luck **9.FP1**

avoir de la peine to be sad,
in pain **3.L***

avoir l'air décontracté to
look relaxed

avoir le coup de foudre
pour to fall in love with at
first sight **9.FP1**

avoir le mal de mer to be
seasick **3.FP1**

avoir le trac to be scared,
nervous

avoir lieu to take place **2.L***

avoir mal to hurt, have pain
7.FP1

avoir mal à l'estomac to
have an upset stomach **1.L***

avoir mal à la gorge to
have a sore throat **7.FP1**

avoir mal à la tête to have
a headache **1.L***

avoir mal au coeur to feel
nauseous **7.FP1**

avoir mal au ventre to
have a stomach ache **7.FP1**

avoir peur to be scared
7.LC1

avouer to admit, avow **2.L***

B ▬▬▬▬▬▬▬

un **badaud** onlooker

les **bagages** *m.* baggage, luggage
5.FP1

un **bagage à main** carry-on
luggage **5.FP1**

une **bague** ring **R.L***

un **bahut** cupboard

se **baigner** to go swimming **3.FP1**

un **bain** bath **1.FP3**

un **baiser** kiss **7.L***

baisser to turn down, lower
6.FP2

se **baisser** to stoop, bend down
7.L*

un **bal** dance **8.L***

un **balai** broom **2.FP1**

une **balance** scale

balayer to sweep **2.FP1**

balbutier to mumble

un **balcon** balcony **6.FP1**

une **balle** bullet

un **ballon** balloon **2.FP3**

un **banc** bench

une **bande** gang **5.L***

en bande in a group

la **banlieue** suburbs

la **banque** bank **10.FP2**

une **banque d'affaires**
investment bank

un **banquier (une banquière)**
bank teller **10.FP1**

des **bans** official announcements

une **barbe** beard **1.FP1**

barbu bearded **1.FP1**

bas (basse) low **2.FP3**

à bas down with

bâtiment: le bâtiment des
Nations Unies United
Nations building **2.FP3**

*bâtir to build

un **bâton** stick, pole

la **batterie** drums

*battre to beat **7.L***

*se **battre** to fight

battu beaten

bavarder to chat

beaucoup a lot; very **3.LC1**

beaucoup de mal a lot of
difficulty, pain

bénéfique beneficial

bénévole voluntary

une **béquille** crutch **7.FP2**

berger: un berger
allemand shepherd dog

une **bestiole** small animal

une **bête** animal **3.L***

une **bêtise** silliness, stupidity **3.L***

une **bibliothèque** library, bookcase
8.FP2

bien well, good **1.FP4**

bien portant in good health
7.FP1

bien serré close together
6.FP1

bien situé well located
6.FP1

bien sûr of course **2.FP2**

un **bien** possession; asset

un **bien honnête** a property
of one's own

les **biens** *m.* wealth **2.L***

les biens immobiliers
m. real estate

un **bien-aimé** beloved

le **bien-être** well-being **10.L***

un **bienfait** benefit, blessing

bientôt soon

un **bijou** *(pl. bijoux)* jewel,
jewelry **9.L***

un **billet** letter; ticket **5.FP2**

la **biologie** biology **10.FP1**

le **blé** wheat

blessé injured, wounded

blesser to hurt

se **blesser** to get hurt, injure
oneself **3.FP1**

bleu blue **1.FP1**

un **bloc** pad (of paper) **4.FP1**

blond blond **1.FP1**

un **bocal** glass jar **3.L***

le **bois** wood **2.FP3**

en bois wooden

un **bois** woods

une **boîte** club, nightspot; box
4.FP1

une boîte de
couleurs paintbox

le **bonheur** happiness

bon (bonne) right; good

il est bon que it is good
that **2.LC2**

bonhomme good-natured

un **bonhomme** fellow, man

la **bonté** goodness

le **bord** brim; edge **3.IM**

au bord de on the edge of

un **bossu** hunchback

la **bouche** mouth **1.FP1**

bouclé curly, wavy

la **boue** mud

la **bouffe** food, grub

la **bougeotte** travelling urge

bouger to move (around)

sans bouger without
moving

boule: la boule à zéro bald
head **4.L***

bouleversé overwhelmed **7.L***

un **boulot** job

bourdonner to buzz

bourguignon
(bourguignonne) people
native to Burgundy

une **bourse** scholarship

bout: au bout de after, at the

end of 8.L*
une **bouteille**   bottle 2.FP3
une **boutique**   shop 4.FP1
un **bouton**   button (on camera) 4.FP3
   des **boutons**   a rash 7.FP1
un **bracelet**   bracelet 9.L*
   brailler   to cry and scream
   branche: une branche d'activité   branch office 10.FP2
   brancher   to plug in
le **bras**   arm 7.FP2
   Bravo!   Bravo! 9.FP1
   bref   brief
les **bretelles** f.   suspenders
le **bric-à-brac**   odds-and-ends
le **bricolage**   fixing and building things
un **brigand**   bandit
   brillant   shiny 2.FP3
   briller   to shine 3.FP3
la **brique**   brick 2.FP3
   brisé   broken
   briser   to break
se **briser**   to break
la **bronchite**   bronchitis 7.FP1
   bronzé   light brown, tan
   bronzer   to tan oneself 3.FP1
   brosse: une brosse à cheveux   hairbrush 1.FP2
   une brosse à dents   toothbrush 1.FP2
se **brosser**   to brush (one's hair, one's teeth) 1.FP2
   se brosser les dents   to brush one's teeth 1.FP2
le **brouillard**   fog 3.FP3
la **brousse**   bush, undergrowth
la **broussaille**   brushwood
un **bruit**   noise
   brûlé   burned
   brûler   to burn
se **brûler**   to burn oneself 7.FP2
la **brume**   fog 3.FP3
   brun   brown 1.FP1
   bruyant   noisy 6.FP1
un **buffet**   sideboard 1.L*, food wagon
un **bureau** (pl. bureaux)   office
   un bureau de tabac   tobacco shop
le **but**   objective
   dans ce but   to this end
un **butin**   booty
   butte: en butte à   faced with

C

   ça: ça a eu lieu   this happened, took place 3.FP2
   ça fait combien?   how much does that come to? 4.FP1
   ça ira   things will go well
   ça n'a pas d'importance   that doesn't matter 10.L*
   ça s'est passé . . .   this happened . . . 3.FP2
   ça vous fait mal?   does it hurt you? 7.FP2
une **cabine**   booth
   cabinet: un cabinet d'avocat   lawyer's office 10.FP2
   un cabinet de médecin   doctor's office
   caché   hidden
   cacher   to hide 5.L*
se **cacher**   to hide (oneself) 7.FP1
un **cachet**   tablet (medicine) 7.FP1
un **cadeau** (pl. cadeaux)   gift 6.L*
un **cadre**   frame 10.L*
un(e) **cadre**   executive
la **cage**   cage 2.FP1
la **caisse**   check-out counter
   calme   calm 1.FP4
un(e) **camarade**   acquaintance, classmate 9.FP1
un **cambriolage**   burglary 3.FP2
un **camion**   truck
la **campagne**   country (side)
le **Canada**   Canada 1.LC1
un **canapé**   small sofa 1.L*
les **Canaries** f.   Canary Islands 5.FP1
   cantonné   quartered, stationed
une **carotte**   carrot 2.FP1
le **caoutchouc**   rubber 2.FP3
la **capacité**   capacity, volume 2.FP3
un **caprice**   whim 8.L*
un **car**   bus
une **carie**   cavity 7.FP2
un **carnet**   notebook 4.FP1
   carré   square 1.FP1
   carreaux: à carreaux   plaid
un **carrosse**   horse-drawn carriage
   carte: une carte d'embarquement   boarding pass 5.FP2
   une carte d'identité   identification card 5.FP1
   une carte de crédit   credit card 6.FP1
   une carte postale   postcard 4.FP1
un **carton**   cardboard 2.FP3
   cas: un cas d'urgence   emergency
un **cascadeur (une cascadeuse)**   stuntman
   caserne: une caserne de pompiers   fire station 8.FP2

une **casquette**   cap (hat)
   cassé   broken 4.FP3
   casser   to break 3.FP1
se **casser**   to break (body part) 3.FP1
   se casser la jambe   to break one's leg 3.FP1
une **casserole**   pot, pan 1.L*
   cause: à cause de   because of 7.L*
une **caution**   deposit
un **cavalier (une cavalière)**   horseman (horsewoman)
   ce: ce n'est pas croyable!   that's not for real! 3.FP2
   ce sera prêt   this will be ready 4.FP3
   c'est arrivé   it happened 3.FP2
   c'est incroyable!   that's unbelievable! 3.FP2
   c'est tout?   that's all? 4.FP1
   c'est votre tour   it's your turn 4.FP1
   c'est vous le patron (patronne)!   you're the boss! 2.LC2
   céder   to give up
   ceinture: une ceinture de sécurité   seat belt 5.FP2
   célèbre   famous
   célibataire   single
   celui (celle)   this one 6.LC2
   celui-ci (celle-ci)   this one 2.L*
   celui-là (celle-là)   that one
   celui (celle) de   that of, the one belonging to 6.LC2
   celui (celle) qui   the one who(m), the one that 6.LC2
la **cendre**   ash(es)
   centre: un centre d'apprentissage   training school
   un centre de loisirs   recreation center 8.FP2
   un centre sportif   gym, sports center 8.FP2
le **centre-ville**   town center, downtown 8.FP2
   certain(e)s   some; certain ones 4.LC1
la **chair**   flesh
la **chaleur**   warmth
   chambre: une chambre à air   inner tube
   une chambre d'hôte   guest room
   champêtre   rural
un **champ**   field 6.L*
   sur le champ   immediately

faire peur à   to scare **3.FP1**
un **phare**   lighthouse
la **pharmacie**   pharmacy **4.FP1**; pharmaceutics (practice of) **10.FP1**
un **pharmacien (une pharmacienne)**   pharmacist **10.FP1**
le **phénix**   phoenix
la **philosophie**   philosophy **10.FP1**
une **photocopie**   photocopy **4.FP1**
le **photographe**   photographer **4.FP1**
la **physique**   physics **10.FP1**
pièce: une pièce d'argent   coin
une pièce d'eau   pool
une pièce d'identité   identity card **5.FP1**
une pièce d'or   gold coin **7.L***
pied: à pied   on foot **8.FP2**
pieds nus   bare feet
une **pierre**   stone **2.FP3**
pieuse (pieux)   pious
une **pile**   battery **4.FP1**
un **pillard**   looter
un **pilote**   pilot **5.FP2**
une **pilule**   pill
pimenté   hot, spicy
le **pinceau (pl. pinceaux)**   brush
pincé   pinched
piquer   to sting **3.FP1**
être piqué par les moustiques   to be bitten by mosquitos **3.FP1**
piqûre: une piqûre de novocaïne   shot of novocaine **7.FP2**
faire une piqûre   to give a shot, injection **7.FP1**
pire   worse **7.L***
une **piscine**   swimming pool **6.FP1**
pitoyable   pitiful **4.L***
une **place**   seat **5.FP2**
de la place   room **5.FP2**
la place d'Armes   parade ground
***plaindre**   to feel sorry for **7.LC1**
***se plaindre de**   to complain about **7.LC1**
***plaire**   to please
plaisanter: tu plaisantes!   you're kidding! **3.FP2**
plaisir: avec plaisir!   with pleasure! **2.FP2**
faire plaisir à   to please **8.L***

planifier   to plan
une **plante**   plant **2.FP1**
plaque: une plaque d'immatriculation   license plate **5.L***
le **plastique**   plastic **2.FP3**
en plastique   plastic **2.FP3**
plat   flat **2.FP3**
plein   full
en plein air   outdoors
plein de   a lot of
pleurer   to cry **1.L***
plier   to fold (up) **3.L***
le **plomb**   lead **2.FP3**
un **plombage**   tooth filling **7.FP2**
plonger   to plunge
la **pluie**   rain **3.FP3**
une **plume**   (quill) pen
la **plupart**   most of them, the majority **4.LC1**
la plupart de   most of **4.LC1**
plus   more **6.FP1**
en plus   in addition
de plus en plus   more and more
plus d'allure
plusieurs   several **4.LC1**
un **pneu (pl. pneux)**   tire
une **pneumonie**   pneumonia **7.FP1**
une **poche**   pocket **1.L***
le **poids**   weight **1.FP1**
un **poignet**   wrist **7.L***
un **poing**   fist
point: sur le point de   on the verge
pointu   pointed **2.FP3**
poissonneux (poissonneuse)   full of fish
la **poitrine**   chest **8.L***
poli   polished **2.FP3**
la **police**   law enforcement **8.FP2**
la **Pologne**   Poland
polluer   to pollute **3.FP1**
la **pollution**   pollution **8.FP3**
polonais   Polish
une **pommade**   ointment
un **pompier**   firefighter
un **pont**   bridge
la **porte**   door; boarding gate **5.FP2**
un **portemanteau (pl. portemanteaux)**   hanger **6.FP2**
un **porte-parole**   spokesperson
porter: porter des lunettes   to wear eyeglasses **1.FP1**
se porter bien   to be in good health **7.FP1**
un **portier (une portière)**   doorman

une **portière**   train door **7.L***
le **Portugal**   Portugal **5.FP1**
poser   to put, to place
posséder   to own, possess **9.L***
possibilité: la possibilité de promotion   opportunity for promotion **10.FP2**
la **poste**   post office **4.FP1**
la poste restante   general delivery **4.FP1**
poste: le poste de police   police station **8.FP2**
un **pot**   jar
un **pote**   buddy
une **poubelle**   garbage can **1.L***
un **pouce**   inch
la **poudre**   powder
la **poudrerie**   powdery snow
les **poumons** *m.*   lungs
pour   in order to **10.LC1**
pour que   so that **10.LC2**
un **pourboire**   restaurant tip
pourtant   however
pousser   to grow
pousser des cris   to scream **3.L***
pousser un gros soupir   to let out a large sigh
la **poussière**   dust
***pouvoir**   to be able to
le **pouvoir**   power
un **pratiquant**   practitioner (religion)
se **précipiter**   to dash
préconiser   to advocate
***prédire**   to predict **3.FP3**
préférer   to prefer **2.LC2**
***prendre**   to take
on ne l'y prendrait plus   he wouldn't be taken in again
prendre connaissance   to become aware
prendre la température   to take one's temperature **7.FP1**
prendre la tension   to take one's blood pressure **7.FP1**
prendre le deuil   to be in mourning
prendre rendez-vous   to make an appointment, date **7.FP1**
prendre sa retraite   to retire **9.FP2**
prendre un bain de soleil   to sunbathe **3.FP1**
prendre un pot   to go for a drink **8.FP1**
pris   seized
préoccupé   worried **1.FP4**
se **préparer**   to get ready **1.FP3**

to get lost   se perdre **3.FP1**
to get married   se marier **9.FP2**
to get off (train)   *descendre **5.FP2**
to get on (train)   monter **5.FP2**
to get ready   se préparer **1.FP3**
to get rid of   se débarrasser **3.L***
to get sick   tomber malade **9.FP2**
to get undressed   se déshabiller **1.FP3**
to get upset   s'énerver **1.LC4**
to get   attraper **3.FP1**
give me ten (of them)   donnez-m'en dix **4.FP1**
to give a hand   donner un coup de main **2.FP2**
to give a shot, injection   faire une piqûre **7.FP1**
gift   un cadeau (pl. cadeaux) **6.L***
gifted   doué **8.L***
girlfriend   une copine **9.FP1**
glass   un verre **2.FP1**
glass jar   un bocal **3.L***
glue   la colle **4.FP1**
to go   aller **6.FP1**
to go away   s'en aller **1.LC4**
to go back to sleep   *se rendormir **10.L***
to go camping   faire du camping **3.FP1**
to go fishing   aller à la pêche **3.FP1**
to go for a drink   prendre un pot **8.FP1**
to go look   aller voir **1.L***
to go mountain climbing   faire de l'alpinisme **3.FP1**
to go on a trip   *faire un voyage **5.FP1**
to go on an interview   aller à un entretien **10.FP3**
to go on holiday, spend some time   faire un séjour **5.FP1**
to go out   *sortir **2.FP1**
to go scuba diving   faire de la plongée sous-marine **3.FP1**
to go swimming   se baigner **3.FP1**
to go through   passer par **5.FP2**
to go to bed   se coucher **1.FP3**
to go windsurfing   faire de la planche à voile **3.FP1**
God   Dieu *m.* **2.IC**
gold   l'or *m.* **R.L***
gold coin   une pièce d'or **7.L***
gold (hair)   châtain clair **1.FP1**

good working conditions   de bonnes conditions de travail **10.FP2**
grass   l'herbe *f.* **2.FP1**
Greece   la Grèce **5.FP1**
green   vert **1.FP1**
grey   gris **1.FP1**
to grow (in size) **3.L***
to grow old   *vieillir **9.FP2**
to grow up   grandir **9.FP3**
to guess   deviner **3.FP2**
gym, sports center   un centre sportif **8.FP2**

H

hair   les cheveux *m.* **1.FP1**
hair perm   une permanente **4.FP2**
hairbrush   une brosse à cheveux **1.FP2**
haircut   une coupe de cheveux **4.FP2**
haircut and a blow-dry   une coupe-brushing **4.FP2**
hairdresser   le coiffeur **4.FP2**
half   la moitié **2.L***
half-time employment   un emploi à mi-temps **10.FP3**
to hand, give   *tendre **7.L***
handicap access   un accès pour personnes handicapées **6.FP1**
handkerchief   un mouchoir **1.L***
to hang (up)   *pendre **10.L***
hanger   un portemanteau (pl. portemanteaux) **6.FP2**; un cintre **6.FP2**
to happen   se passer **3.FP2**; arriver **3.FP2**
happy   heureux (heureuse) **1.FP4**; content **1.FP4**
hard   dur **2.FP3**
harmless   inoffensif (inoffensive) **8.L***
to have pain, to hurt   avoir mal **7.FP1**
to have a career   faire carrière **10.FP2**
to have a cold   être enrhumé **7.FP1**
to have a headache   avoir mal à la tête **1.L***
to have a picnic   faire un pique-nique **3.FP1**
to have a soar throat   avoir mal à la gorge **7.FP1**
to have a stomach ache   avoir mal au ventre **7.FP1**
to have an argument   se disputer **9.FP1**

to have an upset stomach   avoir mal à l'estomac **1.L***
to have good luck   avoir de la chance **9.FP1**
to have fun   s'amuser **1.FP3**
to have to deal with   avoir affaire à **8.FP2**
hayfever   un rhume des foins **7.FP1**
head of personnel   un chef de personnel **10.FP1**
in good health   en bonne santé **7.FP1**
to hear (it said)   entendre dire **8.L***
hedge   une haie d'arbustes **6.L***
heel (of shoe)   un talon **4.FP3**
height, size (person)   la taille **1.FP1**
heir (heiress)   un héritier (une héritière) **R.L***
to help   aider à **2.FP2**
to hide   cacher **5.L***
high   haut **2.FP3**
history   l'histoire *f.* **10.FP1**
to hold   *tenir **3.L***
to hold dear, cherish   *tenir à **9.L***
hospital   l'hôpital *m.* **7.FP2**
hot/warm   chaud **2.FP3**
hotel   un hôtel **6.FP1**
housework   les travaux *m.* domestiques **2.FP1**
how much does that come to?   ça fait combien? **4.FP1**
how do you feel?   comment te sens-tu? **1.FP4**
how long?   combien de temps? **6.FP1**
how many would you like?   combien en voulez-vous? **4.FP1**
how much do I owe you?   combien est-ce que je vous dois? **4.FP1**
humid, wet   humide **2.FP3**
hurricane   un ouragan **3.FP3**
to hurry (oneself)   se dépêcher **1.FP3**
to hurt   faire du mal **3.L***
to hurt one's head   se blesser à la tête **7.FP2**

I

I need   il me faut **4.FP1**
ice   la glace **3.FP3**
identification card   une carte d'identité **5.FP1**
if   si **5.LC2**
important   important **10.FP2**
impossible!   pas possible! **3.FP2**

Text Credits

p. 4: source: *Bulletin Pacijou* volume 1, number 4, June 1992.
p. 56: Eugène Ionesco, "Deuxième conte pour enfants de moins de trois ans," *Présent passé, Passé présent* © 1968 Mercure de France.
p. 67: Robert Desnos, "La fourmi," from *Chantefables et chantefleurs* ©1944 Librairie Gründ. **p. 68:** Jacques Prévert, "Pour faire le portrait d'un oiseau" from *Paroles* © 1949 Éditions Gallimard Collections Folio. **p. 96:** "Le Partage de la couverture," in Louis Brandin, ed., *Lais et Fabliaux du Treizième siècle.* [Poèmes et récits de la vieille France, tome XVI] © 1932 Boccard. **pp. 100–101:** Excerpt from *Astérix le Gaulois* © 1961 Éditions Albert René/Goscinny–Uderzo. **p. 110:** source: *Journal Français d'Amérique,* May 3, 1993. **p. 111:** source: *Journal Français d'Amérique,* May 26 1992. **p. 123:** Jacques Prévert, "Soyez polis," from *Histoires* © 1963 Gallimard. **p. 134:** Sempé/Goscinny, "King" in *Les Aventures de Petit Nicolas* © 1966 Macmillan/Glencoe Publishing. **pp. 142–145:** *Cyrano de Bergerac,* © 1989. **p. 146:** La Fontaine, "Le corbeau et le renard," from *Fables Choisies,* Livre I. **p. 170:** "Une histoire de cheveux" adapted from "Une bonne coupe," by Christian Grenier, in Michel Barbier, ed., *Onze Nouvelles Inédites.* © Hachette. **p. 183:** Lyrics to "Mon pays" by Gilles Vigneault © Musicor. **p. 256:** Paul Éluard, "Liberté," from *Oeuvres complètes* © 1968 Gallimard: Bibliothèque de la Pléiade. Illustrations by Fernand Léger © 1953 Éditions Senghers. **pp. 256–259:** *Au*

revoir, les enfants © 1986. **p. 282:** Guy de Maupassant, "En voyage," *Le Gaulois,* May 10 1883. **p. 297:** source: *INSEE* 1999. **p. 301:** Lyrics to "Éthiopie" © 1985 EMI Records. **p. 326:** "Les pêches," by André Theuriet and adapted by D. C. Heath. **p. 336:** source: Interview with Aimé Césaire in *Les écrivains noirs de langue française: naissance d'une littérature,* Lilyan Kesteloot © 1964 Université de Bruxelles. **p. 337:** "Pour saluer le tiers-monde," from *Ferrements,* Aimé Cesaire © 1960 Éditions Le Seuil. **p. 339:** René Depestre, "Pour Haïti," from *Journal d'un animal marin,* © 1964 Éditions Senghers. **pp. 342–343:** *Rue Cases-nègres,* © 1983. **p. 345:** source: *Francoscopie,* 1993. **p. 359:** source: *Francoscopie,* 1993. **p. 366:** Michelle Maurois, "Le bracelet," *Contes de Michelle Maurois,* © 1966 Meiden, Boston: Houghton Mifflin. **p. 377:** Blaise Cendrars, "La gélinotte et la tortue," from *Anthologie nègre,* © 1921 Éditions la Sirène. **p. 378:** David Diop, "Afrique," from *Coups de Pilon* © 1964 Éditions Senghers. **pp. 380–381:** Bernard Dadié, "Légende baoulé," from *Légendes africaines* © 1966, 1973 Éditions Seghers. **p. 387:** source: *Francoscopie,* 1993. **p. 403:** Yves Thériault, "Le Portrait," *L'île introuvable* © 1968 Éditions du jour.
p. 415: excerpt from LaFayette *In the Age of the American Revolution: Selected Letters and Papers, 1777–1790,* Volume 1 © 1977 Cornell University Press. **p. 419:** Lyrics to "Réveille" by Zachary Richard © 1976–1986 Les Éditions du Marais Bouleur.

Acknowledgements

The editorial staff at D.C. Heath would like to extend special thanks to the following people for their help and support in the production of **Discovering French–*Rouge*:**

William Price, Day Junior High School

Arthur Greenspan, Colby College

Seldan Rodman

The staffs of the French Library and the French Consulate in Boston.

Realia Credits

pp. 33–34: compilation of realia from *La Redoute* spring/summer 1990, *Elle* September 10, 1984, *Madame Figaro* November 26, 1988, *Cosmopolitain* October 1988, *Marie Claire* number 394 June. **p. 72:** realia from *Astrapi* magazine July 1989 and *L'Ami des jardins* magazine April 1986. **pp. 109–110:** Le Ministère de l'environnement, France. **p. 111:** environmental ad campaign from Monoprix stores, June 1989. **p. 121:** environmental ad campaign from Monoprix stores, June 1989. **p. 123:** compilation of realia from *La Redoute* spring/summer 1990, and *Elle* September 10, 1984.
p. 127: weather map from *Le Figaro* January 27, 1994. **p. 159:** Le Ministère du tourisme, Quebec. **p. 161:** compilation of realia from France Telecom and Jean Louis David salons. **p. 163:** France Telecom. **p. 181:** compilation of CD and tape jackets from Youssou N'Dour, *The Lion,* Virgin Records © 1989; Souskous Stars, *"Gozando,"* Stern's Records © 1993; Touré Kunda *Dance of the Leaves (The Celluloid Recordings 1983–1987),* Metrotone Records © 1993; Zap Mama *Adventures in Afropea 1,* Warner Bros. Records © 1993. **p. 190:** Mix of realia from Embassy of Switzerland, Washington, DC; Brittours; Air Canada; International Travel Service Tunisia. **p. 194:** Eurail, USA. **p. 199:** compilation of realia from

Martinique Tourist Office/IGN Paris; British Airways; and Recta Folder Maps/Cartographia. **p. 203:** Greater Québec Area Tourism and Convention Bureau; Québec Minister of Tourism and International Relations. **p. 206:** Swiss Bank Corporation.
pp. 230–231: Office du tourisme et des congrès de la Communauté urbaine de Québec. **p. 233:** Syndicat d'Initiative d'Amboise. **pp. 240–241:** compilation of realia from French Office of Tourism and L'Hôtel Saint Germain. **pp. 264–266:** mix of realia from Ministère des Communications/Communication-Québec; France Telecom; Healthwest Consultants, May 1991; Health and Welfare, Canada; Canadian Psychiatric Association; République Rwandaise/Ministère de la santé publique et des affaires sociales; Clinique de traitement de l'asthme; Weber Vitamins; Uniprix; Jean Coutou. **pp. 268–269:** compilation of realia from Clinic Lac-saint-Louis, Pointe-Claire Québec; Centre de Santé, Kirkland, Québec; Clinique de traitement de l'asthme; KiloControl. **p. 277:** compilation of realia from Médecins aux pieds nus, Médecins sans frontières. **p. 279:** *Marie Claire* number 394 June. **p. 319:** France Telecom. **p. 383:** Ministère de l'éducation.

la **chance** luck

une **chandelle** candle **6.L***

changer: changer d'avis to change one's mind **7.L***

un **chantier** worksite

une **charge** burden **2.L***; rank

chargé loaded; responsible

chargé de laden with; loaded with

charger to load

se **charger** to take care of

un **chariot** shopping cart

chassé expelled

la **chasse** hunting

le **chat** cat **2.FP1**

châtain chestnut (hair) **1.FP1**

châtain clair gold (hair) **1.FP1**

châtain foncé brown (hair) **1.FP1**

chaud hot/warm **2.FP3**

le **chauffage** heating

une **chaussure** shoe

chauve bald **1.FP1**

chef: un chef de personnel head of personnel **10.FP1**

un **chef-d'oeuvre** masterpiece

chemin: un chemin de fer railroad

la **cheminée** fireplace

une **chemise** shirt **2.FP1**

un **chenil** kennel

chèque: un chèque de voyage traveler's check **6.FP1**

par chèque (paid) by check **6.FP1**

cher (chère) precious, dear

chercher to claim (luggage) **5.FP2**

chercher à to try to **10.L***

un **chercheur (une chercheuse)** researcher **10.FP1**

chéri darling

un **chevalier** knight

chevet: au chevet bedside

les **cheveux** m. hair **1.FP1**

les **cheveux en brosse** crew-cut **1.FP1**

la **cheville** ankle **7.FP2**

chez: chez des particuliers at private homes

chez soi at home

le **chien** dog **2.FP1**

un **chiffon** cloth rag **2.FP1**

chiffonné wrinkled

un **chiffonnier (une chiffonnière)** ragpicker

la **chimie** chemistry **10.FP1**

un **chirurgien (une chirurgienne)** surgeon **7.FP1**

***choisir** to choose **9.FP2**

le **chômage** unemployment

un **chômeur (une chômeuse)** unemployed person

chouette super **3.L***

la **chrétienté** Christendom

une **cicatrice** scar **1.FP1**

le **ciel** (pl. cieux) sky

une **cime** peak

un **cintre** hanger **6.FP2**

circulaire circular **2.FP3**

la **circulation** traffic **6.L***

les **ciseaux** m. scissors **1.FP2**

un **citadin** city dweller

un **citoyen (une citoyenne)** citizen

clair light; sunny **6.FP1**

classe: la classe affaires business class **5.FP2**

la **classe économie** tourist class **5.FP2**

la **deuxième classe** second class **5.FP2**

la **première classe** first class **5.FP2**

classer to file **10.FP3**

la **clé** key

la **climatisation** air conditioning **6.FP1**

le **climatiseur** air conditioner

le **clou** nail (metal) **2.FP3**

coalisé allied

une **cocarde** cockade

code: le code de la route traffic regulations **8.FP2**

un **coffre** safe **R.L***

coiffer to cover (head)

le **coiffeur** hairdresser **4.FP2**

une **coiffure** hairstyle

un **coin** corner

au coin on the corner

du coin from the neighborhood, area

la **colère** anger **7.LC1**

en colère angry **1.FP4**

un **colis** package **4.FP1**

la **colle** glue **4.FP1**

coller to stick, to glue

une **colombe** dove

un **colon** settler

combien: combien de temps? how long? **6.FP1**

combien en voulez-vous? how many would you like? **4.FP1**

combien est-ce que je vous dois? how much do I owe you? **4.FP1**

comble: à son comble at its height

une **commande** order

comme since

comme convenu as agreed

comme d'habitude as usual

comme si as if **8.L***

le **commerce** business, trade **10.FP1**

un **commerce** (small) business, shop **8.FP2**

commun in common, shared

la **communication** communication **10.FP2**

une **compagnie** company **10.FP2**

une compagnie internationale international company **10.FP2**

complet (complète) complete, full (sold out) **5.FP2**

un(e) **complice** accomplice **5.L***

composer to dial

composter to punch (ticket) **5.FP2**

le **composteur** ticket-punching machine **5.FP2**

***comprendre** to include

y compris including

un **comprimé** pill (medicine) **7.FP1**

la **comptabilité** accounting **10.FP1**

un(e) **comptable** accountant **10.FP1**

compte: à son propre compte on his own account **10.FP2**

compter to count on, to plan; to count **6.FP1**

le **comptoir** trading post; counter **5.FP2**

la **comtesse** countess **7.L***

un **concours** competitive exam

la **condition** condition **2.FP3**

à condition que provided, on condition that **10.LC2**

de bonnes conditions de travail good working conditions **10.FP2**

conduire** to lead **3.L; to drive

une **confiance** trust **9.FP1**

confiant trusting

confier entrust

confirmer to confirm **5.FP2**

la **confiture** jam

confortable comfortable **6.FP1**

confus upset

une **connaissance** acquaintance **9.FP1**

en connaissance de cause knowingly

faire la connaissance to meet (for the first time)

les connaissances
techniques technical
knowledge 10.FP3
connu known
un conseil advice
conseillé recommended
la consigne baggage-check
5.FP2
une consigne rule
la consistance consistency 2.FP3
consterné dismaying
*construire to build
un conte short story
*contenir to contain
content happy 1.FP4
conteur (conteuse) storyteller
continuer to continue
un contrebandier (une
contrebandière) smuggler
contrepartie: en
contrepartie in exchange
contrôle: un contrôle de
sécurité security check
5.FP2
un contrôle de passeports
passport check 5.FP1
*convaincre to convince
convaincu convinced
convaincant convincing
convoiter to desire secretly
convoquer to call in (for an
interview)
un copain (une copine)
boy/girlfriend 9.FP1
la coqueluche whooping cough
7.FP1
un cor horn
une corbeille wastepaper basket,
trash 2.FP1
un corbeau (pl. corbeaux) crow
le cordonnier shoe repairer
4.FP3
une corne horn
Cornouailles Cornwall (in
southwestern England)
le corps body
une correspondance connection
(plane) 5.FP2
la Corse Corsica
cortège: un cortège funèbre
funeral procession
costaud solid, well-built 1.FP1
côté: la Côte d'Azur French
Riviera (blue coast)
un côté side 4.L*
à côté (de) besides, next to
d'à côté next door
de l'autre côté de on the
other side of
de leur côté as far as they
are concerned

sur les côtés on the sides
4.FP2
un coton-tige cotton swab 4.FP1
le cou neck 1.FP1
couché in bed
se coucher to go to sleep 1.FP3;
to set (sun); to be doubled
over
couler to flow
un couloir aisle 5.FP2; corridor
coup: un coup de main a
helping hand, help
un coup de pinceaux
brush stroke
un coup de téléphone
phone call
une coupe (hair) cut
une coupe de cheveux
haircut 4.FP2
une coupe-brushing haircut and a
blow-dry 4.FP2
couper to cut 2.FP1
se couper to cut (oneself) 1.FP2
se couper à la main to cut
one's hand 7.FP2
se couper les cheveux to
cut one's hair 4.FP2
coupez-les-moi courts cut
my hair short 4.FP2
une cour courtyard; court
courant fluent
courbé rounded, arched 2.FP3
se courber to bend over
coureur: un coureur (une
coureuse) des bois fur
trapper
courir to run 1.L
une couronne crown
le courrier mail 4.FP1
cours: au cours (de) during,
in the course of
au cours de l'engagement
during battle
la course water
court short
un couteau (pl. couteaux) knife
2.FP1
couvert overcast 3.FP3
une couverture blanket 2.L*
*couvrir to cover
*craindre to fear, be afraid of
7.LC1
la crainte fear 7.LC1
le crâne skull 4.L*
un crayon pencil 4.FP1
créer: créer sa propre
entreprise start one's own
business 10.FP2
crème: la crème à
raser shaving cream
1.FP2

le crépuscule dusk
cri: un cri de
ralliement rallying cry
criard loud (color)
crier to yell, shout 1.L*
une crise fit
*croire to believe 7.LC1
un croisement crossing
se croiser to cross, meet
croissant increasing
une croix cross
la croyance belief
*cueillir to pick (flowers)
cuisiner to cook
cuit: cuit à la vapeur steamed
le cuivre copper 2.FP3
un cultivateur (une cultivatrice)
farmer 8.L*
un curriculum vitae résumé
10.FP3
cutané of the skin

D

dans: dans les approximately
dans tous ses états very
upset
dame: une dame de
compagnie lady-in-waiting
un débarquement landing
débarquer to disembark, land
5.FP2
débarrasser to clear 2.FP1
débarrasser la table to
clear the table 2.FP1
se débarrasser to get rid of 3.L*
se débloquer to unlock
débordant overflowing
debout standing
le début beginning
un débutant beginner
un décès death
des déchets m. trash
décimé killed
décoller to take off (plane)
5.FP2
un découpage division
découpé cut out
découper to cut (into pieces)
8.L*
*découvrir to discover
décrocher to pick up (phone)
déçu disappointed, deceived
1.FP4
un défaut fault, failing
défendu forbidden 3.L*
défier to challenge
dégager to shorten (hair) 4.FP2
des dégâts damage
dehors outside 3.FP2
en dehors outside

déjà already, yet; ever **3.LC1**
délivrer to give, deliver
demander to ask, necessitate
demande: sur demande on request
se demander to wonder **8.L***
démarche: les démarches *f.* **amoureuses** steps in courtship
démissionner to resign
se démocratiser to become democratic
demoiselle: une demoiselle d'honneur bridesmaid
démontable that can be dismantled
démonter to take apart
une **dent** tooth **7.FP2**
une dent de sagesse wisdom tooth **7.FP2**
le **dentifrice** toothpaste **1.FP2**
un **dentiste** dentist **7.FP1**
le **déodorant** deodorant **1.FP2**
dépaysé lost (in a strange place)
se dépêcher to hurry (oneself) **1.FP3**
dépens: aux dépens at the expense (of)
se déplacer to move (around)
déplorer to deplore **7.LC1**
déprimé depressed **7.FP1**
depuis peu recently
un **député** congressman
déranger to bother
la **dérision** mockery
dernier (dernière) last **3.FP2**
se dérouler to take place
derrière in back **4.FP2**
le **dérrière** behind, rear end
dès as of; beginning in
dès lors from then on
dès que as soon as **5.LC2**
un **désastre** catastrophe **4.L***
***descendre** to get off (train) **5.FP2**; to bring down **6.FP2**
descendre: avoir + descendu to have taken or carried something down **3.LC1**
descendre: être + descendu to have gone down **3.LC1**
se déshabiller to get undressed **1.FP3**
désirer to wish **2.LC2**
désolé sorry, sad **2.FP2**
le **désordre: en désordre** in disorder **2.FP1**
désormais henceforth

le **dessin** design, art
dessus: par-dessus on
sur le dessus on top **4.FP2**
se détacher to separate, break away
détective: un détective privé private eye **5.L***
une **détente** relaxation
***détruire** to destroy
devant in front (of) **8.FP1**
sur le devant in front **4.FP2**
une **devanture (de magasin)** storefront
développer to develop (photos, personnality) **4.FP3**
***devenir** to become
deviner to guess **3.FP2**
une **devise** motto
***devoir** must; to owe **4.FP1**
dévoué devoted **7.L***
une **diapo** picture slide **4.FP1**
un **dieu (une déesse; pl. dieux)** god, deity **2.IC**
Dieu *m.* God **2.IC**
Mon Dieu! My goodness **3.FP2**
digne dignified **8.L***
la **dimension** dimension, size **2.FP3**
la **diminution** decrease
dîner to dine, have dinner **3.LC1**
un(e) **diplomate** diplomat **10.FP1**
un **diplôme** diploma **10.FP3**
***dire: à vrai dire** to tell the truth
direct direct (flight) **5.FP2**
un **directeur (une directrice)** director **10.FP1**
se diriger vers to move toward **8.L***
un **discours** speech
disparaître** to disappear, go away **5.L
disparition disappearance
disposé arranged
disposer to have (at one's disposal)
une **dispute** an argument **9.FP1**
se disputer to have an argument **9.FP1**
dissimuler to hide
***distraire** to amuse
***se distraire** to have fun
divorcer to get a divorce **9.FP2**
un **docteur** doctor **1.LC1**
dommage: il est dommage que it is too bad that **2.LC2**

donner: donner à manger à to feed **2.FP1**
donner lieu to give rise
donner rendez-vous à to make an appointment/date with **8.FP1**
donner un coup de main to give a hand **2.FP2**
donnez-m'en dix give me ten (of them) **4.FP1**
se donner rendez-vous to agree to meet **8.FP1**
dont whose
doré gilded, golden
la **dorure** gilt
une **dot** dowry
la **douane** customs **5.FP1**
un **douanier (une douanière)** customs officer
doucement gently
la **douceur** kindness
une **douche** shower **1.FP3**
doué gifted **8.L***
une **douleur** pain, suffering **7.FP2**
douloureux (douloureuse) painful **7.L***
se douter bien to be sure
doux (douce) soft, gentle
un **drap** sheet (bedding) **6.FP2**
dressé placed, prepared
une **drogue** drug
droit straight, upright **2.FP3**; straightforward
le **droit** law; right
drôlement truly **4.L***
dur hard **2.FP3**; difficult
la **durée** duration, period
durer to last **2.L***

E

eau: l'eau *f.* **de toilette** perfume **1.FP2**
ébahi open-mouthed
s' écarter to move aside
échapper à to escape from
échapper de peu to escape narrowly
une **écharpe** sash
un **échec** failure
une **échelle** ladder
des échelles in steps (hair), uneven **4.L***
échouer to fail
un **éclair** (flash of) lightning **3.FP3**
éclatant very loud
éclater to break out
une **écorce** bark (tree)
écossais Scottish
l' **écran** *m.* screen

un **écrivain** writer
écroulé collapsed
l' **eczéma** *m.* rash (skin) **7.FP1**
effacer to erase
effrayé scared
également equally, also
égorger to slit the throat of
l' **égout** *m.* sewer
un **élastique** rubber band **4.FP1**
l' **électronique** *f.* electronics **10.FP2**
élémentaire elementary
élevé raised, high **2.FP3**
mal élevé impolite, poorly raised
élever to raise (children) **2.L***
s' **élever** to stand up
élu elected
l' **emballage** *m.* packaging
embarquer to board (plane) **5.FP2**
l' **embarras** *m.* difficulty
embaucher to hire
emblème *m.* emblem, logo
s' **embêter** to get bored **1.LC4**
l' **embouteillage** *m.* traffic jam
embrasser to kiss **1.L***
une **embuscade** ambush **2.IC**
émerveillé amazed
emmener (person) to bring **3.L***
empaqueter to bag (groceries)
empêcher de to prevent, keep from (doing) **1.L***
n'empêche que nevertheless
s' **empêcher (de)** to stop, prevent oneself from **4.L***
l' **emplacement** *m.* site, location
un **emploi** employment, job **10.FP1**
un emploi à mi-temps half-time job **10.FP3**
un emploi à plein temps full-time job **10.FP3**
un emploi à temps partiel part-time job **10.FP3**
un emploi temporaire temporary job **10.FP3**
un **employé (une employée)** employee, clerk **10.FP1**
emporter to take along; to carry off
ému moved, touched
encore still
encore lui! him again!
***encourir** to incur
*s' **endormir** to fall asleep
endroit: cet endroit précis this very spot
énervé nervous; upset,

bothered **1.FP4**
s' **énerver** to get upset **1.LC4**
l' **enfance** *f.* childhood
enfiler to put on (clothes)
enfin at last **3.FP2**
***enfouir** to bury
*s' **enfuir** to run away, flee
engagé politically active
un **engagé** volunteer
l' **engagement** *m.* military service
s' **engager** to enlist
enlever to take off, remove **4.FP3**
s' **ennuyer** to be bored
ennuyeux (ennuyeuse) boring
énorme enormous **2.FP3**
*s' **enquérir de** to inquire
une **enquête** survey
enregistrer to check (luggage) **5.FP2**
enseigner to teach
ensuite next **3.FP2**
entendre: entendre dire** to hear (it said) **8.L
entendre parler de to hear about
*s' **entendre** to get along with
entendu agreed **8.FP1**
enterré buried
l' **enterrement** *m.* funeral
enterrer to bury
entonner to begin to sing
entouré surrounded
s' **entraider** to help each other out
entre among
entre-temps meanwhile
***entreprendre** to undertake
une **entreprise** company **10.FP2**
entrer to be accepted (school)
***entretenir** to take care of
entretenu maintained
un **entretien** *m.* interview **10.FP3**
***entrevoir** to anticipate
une **entrevue** interview **10.FP3**
un **envahisseur** invader
une **enveloppe** envelope **4.FP1**
envelopper to wrap **7.L***
l' **envers** *m.* reverse
l' **envie** *f.* envy, desire
environ about, approximately
l' **environnement** *m.* environment **3.FP1**
un **envoyé** messenger
envoyer to send
épais (épaisse) thick **2.FP3**
épargne spare
s' **éparpiller** to scatter
l' **épaule** *f.* shoulder
une **épée** sword
éperdument madly

une **épine** thorn
une **épingle** pin **4.FP1**
une épingle de sûreté safety pin **4.FP1**
éplucher to peel **2.FP1**
une **éponge** sponge **2.FP1**
épouser to marry **2.L***
épouvantable ghastly
les **époux** *m.* spouses, husband and wife
épris enamored
éprouver to feel, experience
l' **escalade** *f.* rock climbing
faire de l'escalade to go rock climbing
une **escale** stopover, connection **5.FP2**
l' **esclavage** *m.* slavery
une **esclave** slave
espèces: en espèces in cash **6.FP1**
un **espion (une espionne)** spy **5.L***
l' **espoir** *m.* hope
l' **esprit** *m.* soul, spirit; mind
un esprit d'initiative enterprising mind **10.FP3**
essayer to try
l' **essence** *f.* gasoline **6.L***
essentiel: il est essentiel que it is essential that **2.LC2**
essoufflé out of breath
essuyer to wipe **2.FP1**
s' **essuyer** to wipe (oneself) dry **1.FP2**
s'essuyer les mains to dry one's hands **1.FP2**
et and **5.LC1**
s' **établir** to settle, establish
l' **étagère** *f.* shelf
un **étang** pond
une **étape** step, stage
l' **état** *m.* condition **2.FP3**
les **États-Unis** *m.* United States **1.LC1**
***éteindre** to turn off
*s' **éteindre** to go out, be extinguished
éteint out, off, extinct
un **étendard** military banner
***étendre** to extend
*s' **étendre** to extend
éternuer to sneeze **7.FP1**
l' **étoffe** *f.* fabric **2.FP3**
une **étoile** star
étonnant amazing **6.LC1**
étonné astonished **7.LC1**
l' **étonnement** *m.* amazement **7.LC1**
étouffé suffocated

étranger: à l'étranger abroad
  5.FP1
*être to be
  être accueilli to be
    welcomed, invited
  être d'accord to agree
    9.FP2
  être enrhumé to have a
    cold 7.FP1
  être reçu to be accepted
    (school)
  être témoin de to witness
    3.FP2
  être tranquille to be alone,
    undisturbed 1.L*
un être human being
étroit narrow, tight 2.FP3
une étude course of study 10.FP1
  faire des études (de) to
    study 9.FP3
  les études d'ingénieur
    engineering studies 10.FP1
  les études vétérinaires
    veterinary studies 10.FP1
  étudier to study 10.FP1
s' évader to escape
l' éveil m. wakefulness 10.L*
  éveiller to wake up 10.L*
un événement event 3.FP2
un évêque bishop
l' évier m. kitchen sink
  avoir plein l'évier to have a
    sink full (of pots)
  éviter to avoid 3.FP1
  examiner to examine 7.FP1
s' excuser to excuse oneself
    apologize 1.FP3
  exécuter: executer une
    ronde to dance in a circle
un exemplaire copy (books,
    magazines)
  exiger to insist 2.L*
  expérience: l' expérience f.
    professionnelle
    professional experience
    10.FP3
  expliquer to explain 2.L*
  exposer to exhibit 9.L*
  exprimé expressed
  exquis exquisite 7.L*
  exténué exhausted

F

  fabriquer to do, make 3.L*
  face: en face de opposite
    6.L*, across from 8.FP1
  fâché upset 3.L*
se fâcher to be upset 9.FP1
la façon manner
  faible weak 1.FP1

la faïence glazed pottery
la faim hunger
*faire to make, do
  faire appel to call; to ask
  faire bouillir to boil 4.LC3
  faire carrière to have a
    career 10.FP2
  faire connaître to make
    known
  faire couper les cheveux
    to get a haircut
  faire cuire to cook 4.LC3
  faire de la planche à voile
    to go windsurfing 3.FP1
  faire de la plongée
    sous-marine to go scuba
    diving 3.FP1
  faire du camping to go
    camping 3.FP1
  faire (du) mal à to hurt
    3.L*
  faire frire to fry 4.LC3
  faire l'innocent to act
    innocent
  faire la cour to court
    (somebody)
  faire la vaisselle to wash
    the dishes 2.FP1
  faire le ménage to do
    housework 2.FP1
  faire partie to be a part of
  faire rage to rage
  faire réchauffer to reheat
  faire taire to silence, stifle
  faire un pique-nique to
    have a picnic 3.FP1
  faire un plâtre to make a
    cast (broken bone) 7.FP2
  faire une analyse de sang
    to take a blood sample
    7.FP1
  faire une promenade en
    bateau to take a boat trip
    3.FP1
*se faire: se faire des amis to
    make friends 9.FP2
  se faire mal to get hurt
    3.FP1
  se faire nommer to name
    oneself
  se faire tuer to have oneself
    killed
s'en faire to worry 4.L
un fait fact 3.FP2
  un fait divers a minor news
    event 3.FP2
*falloir to be necessary
  il me faut I need 4.FP1
  fané withered
  fard: le fard à paupières
    eyeshadow 1.FP2

  fatigué tired 1.FP4
la faune wildlife
une fauve wild beast
  fécond prolific
  Félicitations! Congratulations!
    9.FP1
  féliciter to congratulate 9.FP1
  femme: la femme de
    chambre chambermaid
le fer (metal) iron 2.FP3
  un fer à repasser iron (for
    clothes) 2.FP1
une ferme farm 6.L*
  ferroviaire railroad
un feu (pl. feux) fire
une feuille form (paper); leaf (tree)
le feuillage leaves
les fiançailles f. engagement
se fiancer to get engaged 9.FP2
la ficelle string 4.FP1
  fichu ruined
  fidèle loyal, faithful
  fier (fière) proud 3.L*
la fierté pride
la fièvre fever 7.FP1
la figure face 1.FP1
  figurer to appear, figure; to
    imagine
un filet net
le filtre filter 4.FP3
  fin refined
la fin end
    à la fin towards the end
  finalement finally 3.FP2
la finance finance 10.FP2
*finir to finish 3.LC1
une firme firm (company) 10.FP2
se fixer to settle
le flash camera flash 4.FP3
une fleur flower 2.FP1
*fleurir to bloom
un fleuve river
  flexible flexible 2.FP3
la flore plant life
un flot stream, cascade; wave
une flotte fleet
le foie liver
  fois: une fois once 7.FP1
    à la fois at the same time
    deux fois par jour twice a
      day 7.FP1
une folie madness, lunacy
  fonction: la fonction
    publique civil service
    10.FP2
  fonctionner to function 4.FP3
un(e) fonctionnaire civil servant
    10.FP1
le fond background; depth
    au fond in the back; deep
      down

fonder   to found
*fondre: fondre en larmes   to break into tears
la force   strength
la forêt   forest 3.FP1
la formation   training
la forme   form 2.FP3
   en forme   in shape 1.FP4
   formidable   great, terrific
   fort   loud 6.L*; strong 1.FP1; tightly
   fort avant   very late
   fou (folle)   crazy 3.L*
un fou (une folle)   madman/madwoman 7.L*
un fouet   whip
   fougueux (fougueuse)   brave
   fouiller   to search
la foule   crowd
se fouler   to sprain 7.FP2
le four   oven 1.L*
la fourrure   fur
se fracturer   to fracture 7.FP2
   fragile   weak 2.FP3
la fraîcheur   coolness
   frais (fraîche)   fresh, cool
      frais et dispos   fresh and rested
le français   French (language) 1.LC1
      à la française   in the French manner
*franchir   to cross, to bridge
   frapper   to knock (on door) 1.L*; to strike
les freins m.   brakes 4.FP3
   fréquenter   to visit
les fringues f.   clothing
   frisé   curly, frizzy 1.FP1
   frissonner   to shiver, shudder 9.L*
   froid   cold 2.FP3
   froidure   cold weather
le front   forehead 1.FP1
la frontière   border
*fuir   to flee
      en fuite   in flight, fleeing
*s' enfuir   to flee
la fumée   smoke
   furieux (furieuse)   furious 1.FP4
un fusil   gun, rifle
   fusillé   shot and killed

G

   gagner: gagner sa vie   to earn one's living R.L*
un gaillard   guy
un gamin   kid
   gant: un gant de toilette   wash

cloth 1.FP2
un garçon   bellboy 6.FP2
   un garçon d'honneur   usher (wedding)
   garde: un garde du corps   bodyguard
   garder   to keep
la gare   train station 5.FP2
   gâter   to spoil 7.L*
le gazon   grass
   gelé   frozen 3.FP3
une gélinotte   grouse
   gênant   bothersome 3.L*
une gendarmerie   police station 8.FP2
un genou (pl. genoux)   knee, lap 7.L*
un genre   kind
   gens: les gens m. de service   servants
   gentil (gentille)   nice 2.FP2
le/la gérant(e)   manager 6.FP2
la gestion   management 10.FP1
un gilet   vest
   gitan   gypsy
un gîte   simple lodging
   glacé: glacé d'effroi   frozen with fear
la glace   ice 3.FP3; mirror 1.FP2
   glisser   to slip 3.FP1
le goût   taste
      le goût des responsabilités   the inclination for responsibility 10.FP3
une goutte   drop 7.FP1
une gouvernante   governess
   grâce à   thanks to
   grain: un grain de beauté   beauty mark 1.FP1
   grand   big 1.FP1
      un grand centre commercial   mall 8.FP2
      un grand ensemble   housing project
      une grande surface   shopping center
grandir   to grow (in size) 3.L; to grow up 9.FP3
   gratuit   free
   gratuitement   free of charge
la Grèce   Greece 5.FP1
   grêle   frail
le grenier   attic
une grenouille   frog 3.L*
   grièvement   seriously
la grippe   the flu 7.FP1
   gris   grey 1.FP1
   grogner   to grunt
   gronder   to scold
   gros (grosse)   fat, heavyset; big
la guerre   war

   guerrier (guerrière)   warlike
un guerrier (une guerrière)   warrior
le guichet   ticket window 5.FP2

H

   habilement   skillfully
s' habiller   to get dressed 1.FP3
   habit: habit m. noir   formal evening dress
   habitué à   accustomed to
   haie: une haie d'arbustes   hedge 6.L*
   hardiment   boldly
   hasard: par hasard   by chance
   haut   high 2.FP3
le•haut-parleur   loudspeaker 4.FP3
   héberger   to shelter
l' herbe f.   grass 2.FP1
   hériter (de)   to inherit 8.L*
un héritier (une héritière)   heir/heiress R.L*
   heure: à l'heure   on time 5.FP2
   heureux (heureuse)   happy 1.FP4
   hier   yesterday 3.FP2
      hier soir   last night 3.FP2
l' histoire f.   history 10.FP1
un HLM (Habitation à Loyer Modéré)   low-income housing 8.IM
   homme: un homme (une femme) d'affaires   business man, woman 10.FP1
   mi-homme   half man
   honteux (honteuse)   ashamed
l' hôpital m.   hospital 7.FP2
un horaire   schedule 5.FP2
un hôtel   hotel 6.FP1
      un hôtel bon marché   inexpensive hotel 6.FP1
      un hôtel de luxe   luxury hotel 6.FP1
   hôtesse: l'hôtesse f. de l'air   stewardess 5.FP2
l' humeur f.   mood 4.L*
      de bonne humeur   in a good mood 1.FP4
      de mauvaise humeur   in a bad mood 1.FP4
   humide   humid, wet 2.FP3

I

   ici: d'ici une semaine   one week from now 4.FP3
   il y a   ago 3.FP2
      il n'y a pas de quoi   you're welcome 2.FP2

il n'y aura pas there won't be

s' illuminer to brighten

un immeuble apartment building

l' immobilier *m.* real estate 10.FP2

s' impatienter to get impatient 1.LC4

une impératrice emperor's wife

important important 10.FP2

l' important *m.* the important thing 8.IM

il est important que it is important that 2.LC2

n'importe quel any

n'importe qui (just) anyone

n'importe quoi anything 7.L*

imprescriptible that which cannot be legally taken away

imprimé printed

imprimer to print

improviste: à l'improviste unannounced

imprudent careless, imprudent

inattendu unexpected 8.L*

incendié burned to the ground

un incendie fire

s' incliner to bow

un inconnu stranger 7.L*

un inconvénient inconvenience, drawback

l' indigestion *f.* indigestion 7.FP1

indispensable: il est indispensable que it is indispensable that 2.LC2

indisponible unavailable

l' industrie *f.* industry 10.FP2

inexpérimenté inexperienced

infirme crippled

un infirmier (une infirmière) nurse 7.FP1

un informaticien (une informaticienne) computer specialist 10.FP1

un ingénieur engineer 10.FP1

injuste unfair R.L*

inoffensif (inoffensive) harmless 8.L*

l' inondation *f.* flood

*inquiet (inquiète) worried

s' inquiéter to worry

*inscrire to enroll; to register to inscribe

insensible insensitive

insister: insister pour que to insist that 2.LC2

l' insolation *f.* sunstroke

insouciant carefree

inspecteur: un inspecteur de

police police detective 5.L*

s' installer to settle 8.L*

instituer to create, institute

institutrice (primary school) teacher

l' instruction *f.* education

insu: à l'insu de without the knowledge of

*interdire to prohibit

interdit forbidden

s' intéresser to be interested

intérieur: à l'interieur inside

intérieurement internally, inside

interrogé interviewed, asked

interroger to interrogate

*interrompre to interrupt

*intervenir to intervene

une interview interview 10.FP3

*introduire to introduce; to lead

un invité guest

J

la jalousie jealousy 9.FP1

jardin: un jardin public public garden 8.FP2

le jardinage gardening

jeter to throw 3.FP1

se jeter to throw oneself

jeûne fast

job: un job d'été summer job 10.FP3

la joie joy 7.LC1

joindre to contact (someone) 9.L

un jongleur (une jongleuse) juggler

la joue cheek

jour: dans deux jours in two days' time 4.FP3

un jour de congé day off 4.L*

il fait grand jour the sun is up and shining

le journalisme journalism 10.FP1

la journée day

un(e) juge judge 10.FP1

juger to judge, think

un Juif (une Juive) Jew

jurer to swear

jusqu'à up to, until

jusqu'à quand until when 6.FP1

jusqu'alors until then

jusqu'au bout to the end 7.L*

jusqu'ici until now 4.L*

juste fair R.L*

il est juste que it is fair that 2.LC2

justement precisely at that moment 8.L*; as a matter of fact

L

laboratoire: un laboratoire de recherche research laboratory 10.FP2

lâcher to loosen, let go

laid ugly

la laine wool

laisser to leave R.L*

laisser ouvert to leave open

laisser tomber to drop

laissez-les-moi longs leave my hair long (haircut) 4.FP3

lancer to launch 4.L*; to send out

lancer un défi to challenge

la langue tongue

une langue étrangère foreign language 10. FP1

la langue maternelle native language

un lapin rabbit 2.FP1

un larcin small theft

le lard salt pork

large wide 2.FP3

une larme tear 7.L*

le lavabo bathroom sink 2.FP1

laver to wash 2.FP1

laver le linge to do laundry 2.FP1

se laver to wash (oneself) 1.FP3

se laver la figure to wash one's face 1.FP2

léger (légère) light 2.FP3

les légumes *m.* vegetables 2.FP1

le lendemain the day after 6.L*

la lenteur slowness

la lentille (camera) lens 4.FP3

les lentilles *f.* **de contact** contact lenses 1.FP1

lequel (laquelle) which

lesquels (lesquelles) which

la lessive detergent 4.FP1

une lettre letter 4.FP1

une lettre de recommandation letter of recommendation 10.FP3

levant rising

lever to raise

se lever to get up

libre free 2.FP2

le libre-échange free trade

librement freely

lié   interwoven, linked
lien: les liens *m.* de sang
      blood ties
lier: lier conversation   to talk,
      initiate conversation
un lieu (pl. lieux)   location
      au lieu de   instead of
le linge   laundry
une lingère   laundry woman
la lingerie   laundry room 2.FP1
*lire   to read
lisse   straight (hair) 1.FP1;
      smooth 2.FP3
lit: à un lit   with one bed 6.FP1
      faire le lit   to make the bed
      2.FP1
un litre   liter 1.LC1
la littérature   literature 10.FP1
le littoral (pl. littoraux)   coast
livraison: la livraison des
      bagages   baggage claim
      5.FP2
une livre   pound
se livrer   to give oneself up
un livret   booklet
une locataire   tenant
loger   to live, lodge 2.L*
la loi   law
loin   far, far away 8.FP2
au loin   in the distance 6.L*
lointain   distant
long (longue)   long 1.FP1
      à la longue   in the long run
      le long de   along
lorsque   when 3.LC2
un lot   plot
louer   to rent
une loupe   magnifying glass 5.L*
lourd   heavy
loyer: un loyer modéré   low
      rent
une lueur   gleam
la lumière   light
lundi   Monday 3.FP2
la lune   moon
une lutte   fight, struggle
      en lutte   struggling
      la lutte pour la vie   the
      struggle for survival

M

mâcher   to chew
machinalement   unconsciously
un magazine   magazine 2.FP1
un magnan   red ant
maigre   skinny 1.FP1
main: sous la main   at hand,
      available
la main-d'oeuvre   labor,
      manpower

maintes   many, several
le maire   mayor
la mairie   city hall 8.FP2
le maïs   corn
maison: une Maison des
      Jeunes   youth center
      8.FP2
une maison individuelle
      single-family house 8.FP2
mal   bad 1.FP4, harm
      mal au foie   abdominal pain
      mal aux dents   toothache
      7.FP4
malade   sick 1.FP4
une maladie   sickness, disease
      7.FP1
une maladie d'enfance
      childhood illness 7.FP1
maladroit   clumsy
une malédiction   curse
maléfique   detrimental
un malfaiteur (une malfaitrice)
      criminal
malgré   in spite of
malheureux (malheureuse)
      unhappy 1.FP4
malicieux (malicieuse)
      inclined to tease, malicious
une mallette   briefcase 5.L*
malpoli   impolite
une manche   sleeve
une manifestation   demonstration
manifester   to show, manifest
manquer   to lack
les maquis   guerilla troops
le maquillage   makeup
se maquiller   to put on makeup
      se maquiller les yeux   to
      apply eye makeup 1.FP2
un marchand   merchant 2.L*
      le/la marchand(e)
      d'antiquités   antique
      dealer 9.L*
marchander   to bargain over
      the price
marche: la marche à pied
      walking
un marché   deal
marcher   to work, function
      4.FP2
      faire marcher   to operate
      (equipment) 4.LC3
      marcher bien   to go well
      marcher sur   to step on
      1.LC3
les marches *f.*   steps, stairs
marécageux (marécageuse)
      swampy
se marier   to get married 9.FP2
marin   marine
un marin   sailor

le marketing   marketing 10.FP1
une marque   designer, brand name
      de marque   important
marrant   funny
marron   brown 1.FP1
le mascara   mascara 1.FP2
massif (massive)   massive
      2.FP3
      massif *m.* de fleurs
      flower bed
mater   to put down
le matériel (pl. matériaux)
      material, equipment
les maths *f.*   mathematics 1.LC1
la matière   material 2.FP3
      la matière synthétique
      synthetic material 2.FP3
maudit   darned
mauvais   bad
le matin   morning 7.FP1
la matinée   morning
la méchanceté   malice
méchant   mean, nasty 2.L*
une mèche   streak, highlight (hair)
méconnu   unrecognized
la Mecque   Mecca
un médecin   doctor 7.FP1
la médecine   medicine (the
      practice of) 10.FP1
le médicament   medicine, drugs
médiocre   average, mediocre
se méfier   to be distrustful
mégarde: par mégarde   by
      accident
mélanger   to mix
      mélanger les colorants   to
      mix dyes
mêlé   mixed together
même   even
Mémé   grandma
mener   to take, lead
la menthe   mint
*mentir: sans mentir   to tell
      the truth, honestly
mention: avec mention   with
      honors
le menton   chin 1.FP1
menu   small
merci   thank you 2.FP2
      merci beaucoup   thank you
      very much 2.FP2
      merci mille fois   thanks a
      million 2.FP2
la messe   (Catholic) Mass
Messire   My Lord
mesurer   to measure 1.FP1
le métal (pl. métaux)   metal
      2.FP3
la météo   weather forecast 3.FP3
un métier   trade
mètre: à 100 mètres   100

meters away **8.FP2**

metteur: le metteur en scène director

*****mettre** to put, place, turn on **6.FP2**

  mettre des sutures to put stitches (in a wound) **7.FP2**

  mettre la table to set the table **2.FP1**

  mettre le couvert to set the table (silverware) **2.FP1**

  mettre le feu to set a fire **3.FP1**

  mettre en garde to warn

  mettre en question to call

meuble: des meubles *m.* **rustiques** rustic furniture **6.L***

le **Mexique** Mexico **5.FP1**

le **micro** microphone **4.FP3**

le **miel** honey

millénaire 1000 years old

un **milliard** one billion

millier: des milliers thousands

mince thin **1.FP1**

miné weakened

minuscule minuscule **2.FP3**

un **miroir** mirror **1.FP2**

mise: une mise en plis a set (hair) **4.FP2**

le **Mississippi** Mississippi **1.LC1**

une **mode** way

modeste modest

modique low, modest

la **moindre** the least, the smallest

un **moine** monk

moins less **6.FP1**

  à moins que unless **10.LC2**

un **mois** month **3.FP2**

la **moitié** half **2.L***

moment: au moment où just as **3.LC2**

mondain social, of fashionable society

la **monnaie** change

les **monnaies** *f.* coins

la **mononucléose** mononucleosis **7.FP1**

monter to get on (train) **5.FP2**; to bring up, carry up **6.FP2**

  monter une garde vigilante to keep watchful guard

  monter: avoir + monté to have taken or carried something up **3.LC1**

  monter: être + monté(e) to have gone up **3.LC1**

montrer: montrer du doigt to point at **8.L***

un **montreur (une montreuse)** exhibitor

se **moquer de** to make fun of

un **morceau (pl. morceaux)** piece

morfondu upset

la **mort** death

un **mot** word **6.L***

  mou (molle) soft **2.FP3**

un **moucheron** gnat

un **mouchoir** handkerchief **1.L***

  un mouchoir en papier paper tissue **4.FP1**

mouillé wet **2.FP3**

un **moulin** coffee grinder

*****mourir** to die **9.FP2**

  mourir de faim to die of hunger

la **moustache** moustache **1.FP1**

le **moyen** means

moyen (moyenne) average; average size **10.FP2**

  en moyenne on the average

le **Moyen Âge** Middle Ages

  au Moyen Âge in the Middle Ages

muet (muette) silent **7.L***

*****mugir** to roar

multinational multinational **10.FP2**

un **mur** wall

murmurer to murmur, say in a low voice

un **musée** museum **8.FP2**

la **musique** music **10.FP1**

musulman Moslem

N

nager to swim **3.FP1**

naguère in the past

*****naître** to be born **9.FP2**

la **nature** nature **3.FP1**

naturel: il est naturel que it is natural that **2.LC2**

la **nausée** nausea **7.FP1**

une **navette** shuttle train

un **navire** boat, ship

  ne . . . aucun no, not any **5.LC1**

  ne . . . jamais never **3.LC1**

  ne . . . ni . . . ni neither . . . nor **5.LC1**

  ne . . . nulle part nowhere **5.LC1**

  ne . . . pas encore not yet **3.LC1**

  ne . . . personne no one, nobody **RC**

  ne. . . plus no longer, not

anymore **1.L***

  ne. . . point not (at all)

  ne . . . que only

  ne . . . rien nothing **RC**

la **neige** snow **3.FP3**

nerveux (nerveuse) nervous **7.FP1**

le **nettoyage** cleaning **2.FP1**

nettoyer to clean **2.FP1**

neuf (neuve) brand new **2.FP3**

un **neveu (pl. neveux)** nephew **R.L***

le **nez** nose **1.FP1**

  ni . . . ni neither . . . nor

un **nid** nest

niveau: de niveaux at the same level

  le niveau de vie standard of living

la **noblesse** nobility

les **noces** *f.* marriage

nocif (nocive) harmful

noir black **1.FP1**

  il fait noir it's dark **3.FP3**

  il fait nuit noire it's pitch black

nombreux (nombreuses) numerous

se **nommer** to be called, named

normal: il est normal que it is normal that **2.LC2**

la **Norvège** Norway

notable important, notable

la **note** bill **6.FP2**

*****nourrir** to feed

nouveau: de nouveau again **1.L***

les **nouvelles** news

la **Nouvelle Écosse** Nova Scotia

se **noyer** to drown **3.FP1**

nu naked, nude

un **nuage** cloud **3.FP3**

*****nuire à** to ruin, damage

nul (nulle) zero. nothing

O

l' **objectif** *m.* lens (focus) **4.FP3**

obligatoire compulsory

obliger to oblige, do a favor

l' **obscurité** *f.* darkness **4.L***

obsédé obsessed

observer to observe **3.FP1**

*****obtenir** to get, obtain

occasion: d'occasion second-hand, used **2.FP3**

l' **occident** *m.* Western world

occidental (occidentaux) western

occupé busy **2.FP2**

s' **occuper de** to be busy, take care of **1.LC4**
un **oculiste** ophthalmologist **7.FP1**
un **oeil (pl. yeux)** eye **1.FP1**
l' **oeuvre** *f.* work (of art)
***offrir** to offer, give
un **oiseau (pl. oiseaux)** bird **2.FP1**
l' **ombre** *f.* shadow
　faire de l'ombre to cast a shadow
　ondulé wavy **2.FP3**
　ongle nail **1.FP2**
　opérer to work, operate
　opprimé oppressed
l' **or** *m.* gold **R.L***
un **orage** storm **3.FP3**
un **orchestre** band
un **ordinateur** computer **10.FP3**
une **ordonnance** prescription **7.FP1**
les **ordures** *f.* garbage **2.FP1**
une **oreille** ear **1.FP1**
un **oreiller** pillow **6.FP2**
les **oreillons** *m.* mumps **7.FP1**
l' **orgueil** *m.* pride **7.LC1**
l' **origine** *f.* background
　orner to decorate, embellish
un **orphelin** orphan
　oser to dare
　ou or **5.LC1**
l' **ouate** *f.* cotton **4.FP1**
les **oubliés** *m.* forgotten people
un **ouragan** hurricane **3.FP3**
un **ours** bear
un **outil** tool
　outre: en outre in addition
　outre-mer overseas
un **ouvrier (une ouvrière)** worker **R.L***
　les ouvriers working class
***ouvrir** to open
　ovale oval **1.FP1**

P ▬▬▬▬▬▬

un **paillasson** doormat **1.L***
la **paille** straw
une **paillote** straw hut
le **pain** bread **2.FP1**
　paisible peaceful, quiet
la **paix** peace
un **palais** palace
un **pansement adhésif** bandage **4.FP1**
　faire un pansement to dress a wound **7.FP2**
une **pantoufle** slipper
la **papeterie** stationery store **4.FP1**

le **papier** paper **2.FP3**
　le **papier à lettres** stationery paper **4.FP1**
　le **papier hygiénique** toilet paper **4.FP1**
un **paquet** package **4.FP1**
un **parachute** parachute **2.FP3**
paraître** to appear **7.L
　il paraît que it seems that
le **parapente** parasailing
un **parc** park **8.FP2**
***parcourir** to travel through
　parfait perfect **3.L***
le **parfum** perfume **1.FP2**
　parier to bet **7.L***
　parler: parler anglais to speak English **10.FP3**
　parmi among
　part: à part entière one hundred percent
le **partage** division
　partager to share
　parterre: les parterres de fleurs flower beds
un **parti** political party
***partir** to leave **5.LC2**
　à partir de from
　partir à (en, pour) to leave for (destination) **5.LC2**
　partir de to leave from (place) **5.LC2**
　partout everywhere **3.L***
un **pas** step
　pas mal a lot; not bad
　pas possible! impossible! **3.FP2**
un **passant** passerby
un **passeport** passport **5.FP1**
　passer to pass
　passer (un vêtement) to put on
　passer l'aspirateur to vacuum **2.FP1**
　passer la nuit to spend the night **6.FP1**
　passer par to go through **5.FP2**
　passer: avoir + passé to have spent (time) **3.LC1**
　passer: être + passé to have passed by **3.LC1**
se **passer** to happen **3.FP2**
un **passionné** real devotee
une **pastille** tablet (medicine)
　pâté: le pâté de cochon type of meatloaf
la **patrie** native land
un **patron (une patronne)** boss **10.FP1**
la **paume** palm
　pauvre: Mon (Ma)

　pauvre! . . . My poor . . . ! 10.FP1
un **pays** country **5.FP1**
un **paysage** landscape
un **paysan (une paysanne)** peasant, farmer
un **péage** toll (highway)
la **peau (pl. peaux)** skin
　dans sa peau in one's skin
une **pêche** peach **8.L***
　pêcher to fish **3.L***
un **pêcher** peach tree **8.L***
un **pêcheur (une pêcheuse)** fisherman
le **peigne** comb **1.FP2**
se **peigner** to comb one's hair **1.FP2**
***peindre** to paint
　peiné hurt
la **peine** effort, trouble; sorrow
　à peine hardly **2.IC**
　faire de la peine to make sad, upset
la **peinture** painting
un **pèlerinage** pilgrimage
une **pèlerine** cape
une **pellicule** film **4.FP1**
　une pellicule en noir et blanc black and white film **4.FP1**
　une pellicule-couleurs color film **4.FP1**
une **pelote** ball (of string) **4.FP1**
la **pelouse** lawn **2.FP1**
　pendant during **3.LC2**
　pendant que while **3.LC2**
pendre** to hang (up) **10.L
　pénible painful
　pension: la pension complète full room and board **6.FP1**
　la demi-pension room with breakfast and dinner **6.FP1**
un **pensionnaire** boarding student
une **pépite** nugget
***perdre: perdre l'équilibre** to lose one's balance **3.FP1**
*se **perdre** to get lost **3.FP1**
　perfectionner to improve
　périr perish, die
une **permanente** hair perm **4.FP2**
***permettre** to allow
　permis: un permis de conduire driver's license **5.FP1**
　perplexe perplexed **1.FP4**
la **perruche** parakeet **2.FP1**
　peser to weigh **1.FP1**
　petit small, short **1.FP1**
　peuplé populated
la **peur** fright

préposé assigned

près: de près closely, from close up **4.L***

présenter to present, show **5.FP2**

se présenter to show up

presque almost

pressé in a hurry

se presser to hurry

prêter: prêter serment to pledge allegiance

prétexte: un prétexte quelconque some pretext or other

un prêtre priest

la preuve proof

*prévenir to warn **3.L***

*prévoir to plan ahead for

prier to pray

je t'en prie you're welcome **2.FP2**

une prière prayer

une princesse princess **1.LC1**

la prise taking; electrical plug **4.FP3**

le prix prize

prochain next **5.FP2**

proche close

*produire to produce

*se produire to happen

profiter de to take advantage of **1.L***

la proie prey

le prolongement extension

promener to walk **2.FP1**

*se promener to take a walk **1.FP3**

*promettre to promise

propre own; clean

la propreté cleanliness, hygiene

un propriétaire owner **R.L***

prosterné prostrate, face to the ground

*protéger to protect **3.FP1**

provoqué caused, provoked

la psychologie psychology **10.FP1**

la publicité advertising **10.FP1**

une puce microchip

puis then **3.FP2**

puisque since **3.L***

puissant powerful

un pupitre school desk

pur fresh

Q

le quai platform **5.FP2**

quand when **5.LC2**

quand même anyhow **3.L***

la quantité quantity **4.FP1**

qu'est-ce que. . . : qu'est-ce qu'il y a? what's wrong? **1.FP4**

qu'est-ce qu'il y a eu? What happened? **3.FP2**

qu'est-ce que tu as? what's the matter? **1.FP4**

qu'est-ce qui. . . : qu'est-ce qui a eu lieu? what happened? **3.FP2**

qu'est-ce qui est arrivé? what happened? **3.FP2**

qu'est-ce qui ne marche pas? what doesn't work? **4.FP3**

qu'est-ce qui ne va pas? what's wrong? **7.FP1**

qu'est-ce qui s'est passé? what happened? **3.FP2**

quant à as for

le quartier neighborhood, district **8.FP2**

que whom, that, which **9.LC1**

quel (quelle) what, which **4.FP1**

quel dommage! too bad! **9.FP1**

quel est le problème? what is the problem? **4.FP3**

quel genre? what kind, type? **6.FP1**

quelle bonne nouvelle! what good news! **9.FP1**

quelle malchance! what bad luck! **9.FP1**

quelle que soit whatever

quelle sorte de what type of **5.FP2**

quelques some, a few **4.LC1**

quelqu'un someone, somebody **RC**

quelque chose something **RC**

quelque chose à déclarer something to declare **5.FP1**

quelque chose d'autre something else **4.FP1**

quelque part somewhere **5.LC1**

quelques-un(e)s some, a few **4.LC1**

se quereller to quarrel, have a fight **9.FP1**

question: question de because of

quête: en quête de in search of

faire la quête to pass the hat

queue: une queue de cheval ponytail **1.FP1**

qui who, that, which **9.LC1**

un quiproquo misunderstanding

quitter to leave (place/person) **5.LC2**

quoi: quoi de neuf? what's new? **3.FP2**

quoi que ce soit whatever it is

quoi qu'il arrive whatever happens

quoi qu'il lui en coûte whatever it may cost her

quoi qu'il y ait although there is (are)

quotidien (quotidienne) daily, common

R

la racine root

raconter to tell (what happened) **3.FP3**

une radio x-ray

faire une radio to x–ray **7.FP1**

une rafale gust of wind

raide straight

raison: la raison de vivre aim in life

*ralentir to slow down **7.L***

un ramage song

ramasser to pick up **7.L***

une rame oar

ramener to bring back **3.L***

une randonnée long hike

une randonnée pédestre hiking

un rang row

rangé clean, put-away **2.FP1**

ranger to put away **2.FP1**

rappeler to remind

se rappeler to remember, to recall **1.LC4**

un rapport connection, relation **9.FP1**

bons rapports good relations **9.FP1**

mauvais rapports bad relations **9.FP1**

rapporter to equal, match, relate **3.IM**

se raser to shave **1.FP2**

le rasoir shaver **1.FP2**

rater to flunk; to miss (bus) **5.FP2**

rattrapé caught

se rattraper to catch up with

ravi delighted **7.LC1**

rayé striped

un rayon department (in store) **4.FP1**

*réagir to react

un réalisateur (réalisatrice) movie director

recensé registered

le récepteur receiver

la réception reception desk 6.FP1; gala, party

le/la réceptionniste receptionist, secretary 6.FP2

*recevoir to get, receive

recherche: la recherche scientifique scientific research 10.FP2

recherché sought after

rechercher to research; to look for, search for 10.FP2

récif: le récif de corail coral reef

un récit story

une récolte crop

faire la récolte to harvest

récompenser to reward 4.L*

*se réconcilier to make up 9.FP1

la reconnaissance gratitude

reconnu recognized

*reconstruire to rebuild

recouvert: recouvert de covered with

récréatif (récréative) recreational

rectangulaire rectangular 1.FP1

recueilli adopted, taken in

reculé remote

récupérer to get back, recuperate 5.L*

*redécouvrir to rediscover

redonner to give back

redoubler to repeat a grade

une référence reference 10.FP3

réfléchir to think things over; to reflect on 7.L*

un réfrigérateur refrigerator 2.FP3

un regain renewal

un regard glance, look

réglé: réglé par structured according to

le règlement rule

le regret regret 7.LC1

regretter to regret 2.FP2

la reine queen 1.LC1

les reins *m.* kidneys

*se réjouir to be happy 9.FP1

relâché released

les relations *m.* relations 9.FP1

les relations publiques public relations 10.FP2

relié linked

se remarier to remarry 9.FP2

remarquer to notice 2.L*

remercier to thank 2.FP2

remettre to put back 9.L*

se remettre to get back (into shape), restart

une remise shed

remonter to put back together; to go back (in time); go up

rempli filled

remplir to fill 2.FP1

un renard fox

rencontrer to meet by chance, run into (person) 8.FP1

se rencontrer to meet each other 8.FP1

un rendez-vous appointment, date 7.FP1

se rendormir to go back to sleep 10.L

*rendre grâce to give thanks

rendre service to do a favor 2.FP2

*se rendre to go, to render oneself

se rendre compte to realize 2.L*

un renfort reinforcement

renoncer to give up

un renseignement information

renvoyé fired

renvoyer to send away, send back

*se répandre to spread

répandu spilled

réparer to fix, repair 4.FP3

repasser to iron 2.FP1

*répondre to respond 10.FP3

se reposer to rest 1.FP3

repousser to grow back

repousser du pied to kick away

un(e) représentant(e) representative 10.FP1

la représentation performance

se représenter to retake (the exam)

repris: un repris de justice prison inmate

une requête request 8.L*

une réservation reservation 5.FP2

réserver to reserve 6.FP1

une résidence apartment complex

*résoudre to solve, resolve

le respect respect 9.FP1

respecter to respect 3.FP1

respirer to breathe

une responsabilité responsibility 10.FP2

*ressentir to feel (pain or emotion) 1.FP4

le ressort spring (in watch) 4.FP3

rester: il ne reste que . . .

there is/are only . . . left 10.L*

il reste . . . there is/are . . . left 8.L*

il vous reste . . . you have . . . left

rester au lit to stay in bed 7.FP1

un resto restaurant

retard: en retard late 5.FP2

une heure de retard one hour late 5.FP2

retentissant big, huge

*retentir to resound

retirer to withdraw (money)

se retourner to turn around 7.L*

se retrouver to meet each other 8.FP1

réuni reunited

*se réunir to unite, get together

un rêve dream

un réveil alarm clock

réveiller to wake (something, someone) 6.FP2

se réveiller to wake (oneself) up 1.FP3

revenir to come back 1.L

rêver to dream

*revoir to see again

révolu long past

un rhume a cold 7.FP1

un rhume des foins hayfever 7.FP1

ricaner to laugh

rien: de rien you're welcome 2.FP2

rien à déclarer nothing to declare 5.FP1

rien à voir (avec) nothing to do (with)

rien que only

rigolo amusing 3.L*

le rimmel mascara 1.FP2

*rire to laugh

une rive bank, shore

robe: une robe de chambre bathrobe

le robinet faucet

rocambolesque incredible, fantastic

le roi king

le Roi du Ciel King of Heaven

romantique romantic

rompre to break 7.L

rompre (avec) to break up (with) 9.FP1

rond round 1.FP1

la roue wheel 4.FP3

rouge red 1.LC1

le rouge à lèvres lipstick
1.FP2
la rougeole measles 7.FP1
rougir to blush 4.L
un rouleau (pl. rouleaux) roll (of
paper towels) 4.FP1
rouler to roll; to travel, drive
roux (rousse) red-headed
1.FP1
un royaume kingdom
un ruban ribbon
la rubéole German measles
7.FP1
une rubrique column
rude rough
rugueux (rugueuse) rough,
uneven 2.FP3
rupestre on rock walls
la Russie Russia 5.FP1
rustre boorish, lacking good
manners

S

le sable sand
un sac bag 5.FP1
un sac à dos backpack
un sac à provisions
shopping bag
sacré "cursed"
la sagesse wisdom
saigner to bleed 7.FP1
saigner du nez to get a
nosebleed 7.FP1
sain healthy, sain
saint holy
saisi seized, taken
saisir to seize, take 9.L
*se saisir to seize, take
un salaire salary 10.FP2
sale dirty 2.FP1
une saleté something gross, dirty
une salle hall
la salle d'armes fencing
hall
la salle d'attente waiting
room 5.FP2
la salle d'exercices
exercise gym 6.FP1
la salle de bains bathroom
6.FP1
un salon show
une salopette overalls
saluer to salute, greet, take
one's leave of
samedi on Saturday 1.LC1
le samedi on Saturdays
1.LC1
le sang blood
sanglant blood-stained
un sanglier wild boar

sans (que) without 10.LC1
sans bouger without
moving
sans cesse unceasingly
sans trêve unceasingly
les sans-abri m. homeless people
la santé health
en bonne santé in good
health 7.FP1
le saucisson sausage
sauf except
sauter to jump 1.L*
sauvage wild
sauver to save 5.L*
se sauver to escape
savant trained
un savant scientist
la saveur taste
le savon soap 1.FP2
un scénario script
scène: sur scène on the stage
une scie saw 2.FP3
science: les sciences f.
économiques economics
10.FP1
les sciences f. politiques
political science 10.FP1
un(e) scientifique scientist 10.FP1
le scotch scotch tape 4.FP1
un seau (pl. seaux) bucket
sec (sèche) dry 2.FP3
un sécateur shrub clippers 2.FP1
se *sécher to dry (oneself) 1.FP2
se sécher les cheveux to
dry one's hair 1.FP2
une sécheresse drought
le séchoir (hair) dryer 1.FP2
secouer to shake 10.L*
*secourir to help
secours: crier au secours to
call for help
un secrétaire writing desk
un(e) secrétaire secretary 10.FP1
section: la section fumeur
smoking section 5.FP2
la section non-fumeur
non-smoking section 5.FP2
séduisant attractive 7.L*
séduit attracted, seduced
le seigneur lord
un séjour stay
faire un séjour to go on
holiday, spend some time
5.FP1
séjourner to stay, lodge 6.FP1
semaine week 3.FP2
sembler to seem, to appear
1.FP4
la semoule semolina
le sens sense, direction, meaning
le sens des contacts

humains ability to
network 10.FP3
la sensation feeling
un sentier trail
*sentir to smell 1.FP4
*se sentir to feel
comment te sens-tu? how
do you feel? 1.FP4
se sentir chez soi to feel at
home
ne pas se sentir de joie to
be beside oneself with joy
se séparer to separate (husband &
wife) 9.FP2
un serpent serpent 3.FP1
serré held tightly, close
together
serrer to clutch
serrer la main de to shake
hands with
service: le service dans les
chambres room service
6.FP1
la serviette towel 1.FP2; napkin
*servir to serve 6.FP2
*se servir de to use 10.FP3
seul alone, lonely
le seul the only
un seul only one
le shampooing shampoo 1.FP2
un shampooing a shampoo
(hair salon) 4.FP2
si if 5.LC2
un siècle century
un siège a seat 5.FP2
siffler to whistle 3.L*
sifflet: un sifflet à roulette
whistle 3.L*
un signe sign
la signification meaning
signifier to represent, signify
sillonner to travel across
un singe monkey
singulier (singulière) strange
situé: bien situé well located
6.FP1
mieux situé better located
6.FP1
une société society, company
10.FP2
soigner to treat (medical)
7.FP1
soignez-le (la)! pay careful
attention to it!
se soigner to take care of one's
health
le soir evening 7.FP1
soit all right, so be it
le sol floor 2.FP1
des soldes sale
le soleil sun

le **soleil levant** rising sun

solliciter to solicit, ask for 10.FP3

solide solid 2.FP3

sombre black, somber

le **sommeil** sleep

un **son** beat

sonner to ring; to blow

sonnerie: la sonnerie de clairon bugle call

le **Sopalin** paper towels (brand name) 4.FP1

la **sorcellerie** witchcraft

un **sorcier (une sorcière)** witch doctor

le **sort** fate

la **sortie** exit 5.FP2

*****sortir** to take (something) out; to go out 2.FP1

    sortir la poubelle to take out the trash 2.FP1

    sortir: avoir + sorti to have taken something out 3.LC1

    sortir: être + sorti to have gone out 3.LC1

un **sot (une sotte)** stupid person

souche: de souche native born

un **souci** concern, worry

souffler to blow out 10.L*; to blow 3.FP3; to prompt

*****souffrir** to suffer

souhaiter to wish 2.LC2

soupir: un soupir de soulagement sigh of relief

la **source** spring

sourd deaf

souriant smiling

*****sourire** to smile

un **sourire** smile

une **souris** mouse

*****soustraire à** to protect from

*****soutenir** to support

un **souvenir** memory

    en souvenir de in memory of 8.L*

souvent often 3.LC1

*****se souvenir (de)** to remember

spacieux (spacieuse) roomy 6.FP1

se spécialiser en to specialize, major in 10.FP1

un **spécialiste** specialist 7.FP1

    un(e) spécialiste de données data processor 10.FP1

    un(e) spécialiste de logiciel software specialist 10.FP1

    un(e) spécialiste de marketing marketing

specialist 10.FP1

spirituel (spirituelle) witty

un **square** public garden

un **stage** training session, internship

    faire un stage to do an internship

un **standard** operator 6.FP2

station: une station thermale hot springs resort

une **station-service** gas station 8.FP2

statue: la Statue de la Liberté Statue of Liberty 2.FP3

une **stèle** stele (stone marker with an inscription) 6.L*

le **steward** steward 5.FP2

une **strophe** verse

stylo: un stylo à bille ball point pen 4.FP1

subit sudden

*****subvenir** to meet

    subvenir aux besoins to meet the needs

une **subvention** subsidiary

se succéder to follow one another

succomber to die, succumb

la **sueur** sweat

*****suffire** to be sufficient

    il suffit . . . it is sufficient . . .

    il suffit d'y penser you just have to think about it

la **suite** series, sequence

    à la suite de right behind; as a result of

suivant according to; next 5.FP2

*****suivre** to take (a class); to follow

une **supérette** convenience store 4.FP1

supporter to bear, stand 2.L*

supprimé abolished

sûr safe, sure

    bien sûr of course 2.FP2

surprenant surprising

*****surprendre** to surprise 9.L*

surpris surprised 7.LC1

sursaut: en sursaut with a start

la **survie** survival

susceptible touchy

sympa nice, kind 2.FP2

la **sympathie** instinctive liking 9.FP1

syndicat: le Syndicat d'Initiative Chamber of Commerce 6.LC1

T ▬▬▬▬▬▬▬▬▬▬

la **table** table 2.FP1

un **tableau (pl. tableaux)** painting

    le tableau d'affichage billboard 5.FP2

une **tablette** bar

un **tabouret** stool 4.L*

une **tache** spot, stain

    les taches *f*. de rousseur freckles 1.FP1

la **taille** height, size (person) 1.FP1

    de taille moyenne average size 1.FP1

tailler to prune, trim 2.FP1

*****se taire** to be quiet, shut up 1.LC4

un **talon** heel (of shoe) 4.FP3

talonné followed close on one's heels

le **tambour** drum

la **Tamise** Thames (River)

une **tanière** lair

tant: tant de so many; so much

    tant que as long as

    tant pis! too bad! 2.LC2

un **tapis** rug 1.L*

la **tapisserie** tapestry

tard late 3.LC1

tas: des tas tons, a lot

un **technicien (une technicienne)** technician 10.FP1

le **teint** complexion

la **teinte** color

le **teinturerie** the cleaners 4.FP3

le **téléobjectif** telephoto lens 4.FP3

le **téléphone** telephone 6.FP1

téléphoner to telephone, call 10.FP3

la **télévision** television 6.FP1

tel (telle) such

    tel qu'on le connaît as we know him

tellement so much 4.L*

    pas tellement not that much

téméraire bold

un **témoin** witness

la **température** temperature 2.FP3

la **tempête** storm 3.FP3

    une tempête de neige snowstorm 3.FP3

le **temps** time 2.FP2

    le beau temps nice weather 3.FP3

    le mauvais temps bad weather 3.FP3

    de temps en temps from

time to time **4.L***

tendre** to hand, give **7.L

tendu tense, uptight **1.FP4;**
stretched out

tenir** to hold **3.L, to have;
present

  tenir à to hold dear, cherish
9.L*

  tenir compagnie to keep
company **9.L***

  tenir un langage parler

  qu'a cela ne tienne that
won't matter

**tentative: une tentative
d'évasion** escape attempt

tenter to tempt **9.L***

terne dull **2.FP3**

la **terre** land, earth, soil

  la terre d'asile land of
asylum

  la terre ferme solid ground

  par terre on the ground

  sous terre underground

  la Terre Sainte Holy Land

  Terre-Neuve Newfoundland

un **testament** will

un **têtard** tadpole **3.L***

tête: tête à tête face to face

  en tête leading

une **thèse** thesis, essay

tiède warm **2.FP3**

un **tiers** one-third

le **tiers-monde** third world

une **tignasse** unruly mop (of hair)
4.L*

un **timbre** stamp

tiré fired

tirer to take out; to derive

  tirer au sort to choose at
random

  tiré de based on

le **tissu** fabric

la **toile** canvas

le **toit** roof

une **tombe** tombstone

  tomber to fall **3.FP1**

  **tomber amoureux
(amoureuse) de** to fall in
love with

  tomber dans l'eau to fall in
the water **3.FP1**

  tomber malade to get sick
9.FP2

une **tondeuse** lawn-mower **2.FP1;**
clippers **4.L***

***tondre** to mow, cut very short
2.FP1; to clip very short
4.L*

le **tonnerre** thunder **3.FP3**

tonte: la tonte des moutons
sheep-shearing

tort: à tort wrongly

une **tortue** turtle

tôt early **3.LC1**

toujours still

un **tour** turn; trick

  faire des tours to do tricks
3.L*

  faire le tour to go around

  faire un tour to walk
3.FP1

une **tour** tower, high-rise **8.FP2**

  la Tour Eiffel Eiffel Tower
2.FP3

le **tournage** making (of a film)

une **tournée** tour

tourner to film

se **tourner** to turn around

tousser to cough **7.FP1**

tout any

  tout à fait completely

  tout à l'heure in a little
while **4.FP3**

  tout court directly

  tout d'un coup all of a
sudden

  tout de même nevertheless

  tout de suite immediately

  tout le temps all the time,
always

  tous les . . . every

  toutes les 4 heures every
four hours **7.FP1**

  tout petit very young

  tout près nearby **8.FP2**

une **toux** cough

***trahir** to betray

une **trahison** betrayal

un **train** train **5.FP2**

un **trait** feature

un **traité** treaty

traîtrise treachery

une **trame** plot

tranquillement safely

traqué tracked, hunted down

le **travail (pl. travaux)** work
2.FP1

  les travaux domestiques
housework **2.FP1**

  les travaux des champs
farm work

travailler to work **9.FP2**

travers: à travers across,
through **1.L***

  de travers in a strange way

traverser to cross

**tremblement: un tremblement
de terre** earthquake

trempé soaking wet

triangulaire triangular **2.FP3**

tricher to cheat

tricolore blue, white, red

le **tricot** knitting **9.L***

triste sad **1.FP4**

la **tristesse** sadness **7.LC1**

un **trombone** paper clip **4.FP1**

se **tromper** to make a mistake
1.LC4

trôner to occupy a place of
honor

trop too **3.LC1**

un **trottoir** sidewalk **9.L***

un **trou** hole

  **trousse: la trousse de
toilette** toiletry kit **1.FP2**

trouver to find **9.FP2**

se **trouver** to be (located); to find
oneself

un **tube** tube **4.FP1**

tuer to kill

tuméfié swollen

tuyau: le tuyau d'arrosage
garden hose **2.FP1**

un **type** guy, person

U

usagé worn **2.FP3**

usé worn out, old **4.FP3**

une **usine** factory **10.FP2**

utile: il est utile que it is
useful that **2.LC2**

utiliser to use **10.FP3**

V

la **vaisselle** dishes **2.FP1**

la **valeur** value

une **valise** suitcase **5.FP1**

***valoir** to be worth **3.IC**

  il vaut mieux que it is
better that **2.LC2**

valoriser to emphasize the
value of

valser to waltz

vaniteux (vaniteuse) boastful

se **vanter** to boast

la **varicelle** chicken pox **7.FP1**

vase: un vase de Venise
Venetian glass vase

un **vassal (pl. vassaux)** subject

une **vedette** star

la **végétation** vegetation **3.FP1**

veille previous day

veilleuse low (light)

un **vélodrome** bicycle racetrack

velours: le velours côtelé
corduroy

un **vendeur (une vendeuse)**
salesperson **10.FP1**

venger to avenge

***venir** to come

  faire venir to bring

un **verger** orchard **8.L***

le **verglas** sheet ice **3.FP3**

véritable true

vernis: le vernis à ongles nail polish **1.FP2**

un **verre** glass **2.FP1**

les **verres de Bohême** Bohemian glasses

les **verres de contact** contact lenses **1.FP1**

vers towards; at, about **1.FP3,**

verser to pour **3.L***

vert green **1.FP1**

le **vertige** dizzy spell, vertigo **7.FP1**

les **vêtements** *m.* clothes **2.FP1**

un(e) **vétérinaire** veterinary doctor **10.FP1**

vêtu dressed

une **victime** victim, casualty

vide empty **2.FP3**

vider to empty **2.FP1**

la **vie** life **R.V**

la **vie courante** daily life

un **vieillard** elderly man

***vieillir** to grow old **9.FP2**

le **vieillissement** aging

vieux (vieille) old **2.FP3**

vif (vive) bright

vif d'esprit alert

la **ville** the city

vingt: vingt et un coups de canon 21-gun salute

la **Virginie** Virginia **1.LC1**

le **visage** face **1.FP1**

une **vitamine** vitamin **4.FP1**

la **vitesse** speed

en vitesse quickly

une **vitre** window pane **2.FP1**

la **vitrine** store window **9.L***

vivant living

***vivre** to live

une **voie** way

voilà there you go **4.FP1**

voile: un voile de dentelle lace veil

une **voile** sail

***voir** to see

faire voir to show 4.LC3

la **voiture** car **2.FP1**

voix; à mi-voix in a low voice

un **vol** flight **5.FP2;** theft

volé stolen

voler to steal **5.L*** to fly **9.C**

les **volets** shutters **8.IC**

un **voleur (une voleuse)** thief **5.L**

la **volonté** will **7.LC2**

volontiers! sure! with pleasure! I'd love to! **2.FP2**

volumineux (volumineuse) voluminous, large in volume **2.FP3**

vomir to throw up **7. FP1**

***vouloir** to want, to wish **2.LC2**

vouloir bien to want (used to accept an offer), to accept, agree **4.FP1**

vouloir dire to mean **10.L***

***voyager** to travel **5.FP1**

un **voyage** voyage, trip

vrai true

à vrai dire to tell the truth **8.L***

Vraiment? Really? Truly? **3.FP3**

une **vue: une belle vue** a nice view **6.FP2**

w ▬▬▬▬▬▬▬▬▬▬▬▬▬▬

un **wagon** car (train) **5.FP2**

un **wagon-lit** sleeping car (train) **5.IM**

un **wagon-restaurant** dining car (train) **5.IM**

y ▬▬▬▬▬▬▬▬▬▬▬▬▬▬

y: j'y vais there: I'm going (there) **4.LC1**

les **yeux** *m.* **(un oeil)** eyes **1.FP1**

z ▬▬▬▬▬▬▬▬▬▬▬▬▬▬

les **zébrures** *f.* stripes, welts **9.IC**

VOCABULAIRE: Anglais—Français

The English—French vocabulary contains active and passive words from the text, as well as words introduced in the *Mots utiles* sections of the Lectures.

The numbers and letters following an entry indicate the first unit section in which the words or phrase are activated. The following abbreviations have been used:

R   Reprise
L   Lecture
IM   Info magazine
IC   Interlude Culturel
FP   Français pratique
TA   Teacher's Annotation
LC   Langue et communication
A   Appendix

The number after the section abbreviation indicates the unit *Partie* in which the vocabulary word is introduced.

An Asterisk (*) after the unit reference indicates that the word or phrase is presented in the *Mots Utiles* section of the reading.

Nouns: If the article of a noun does not indicate gender, the noun is followed by *m. (masculine)* or *f. (feminine)*. If the plural is irregular, it is given in parentheses.

Verbs: Verbs are listed in the infinitive form. An asterisk (*) in front of an active verb means that it is irregular. (For forms, see the verb charts in the Appendix.)

Words beginning with an **h** are preceded by a bullet (•) if the **h** is aspirate; that is, if the word is treated as if it begins with a consonant sound.

A

ability: ability to network   le sens des contacts humains **10.FP3**
abroad   à l'étranger **5.FP1**
accident   un accident **3.FP2**
accomplice   un(e) complice **5.L***
accountant   un(e) comptable **10.FP1**
accounting   la comptabilité **10.FP1**
acquaintance   une connaissance, un(e) camarade **9.FP1**
across   à travers **1.L***
   across from   en face de **8.FP1**
adhesive: adhesive bandage   un pansement **4.FP1**
admiration   l'admiration *f.* **9.FP1**
to **admit**   avouer **2.L***
advertising   la publicité **10.FP1**
affection   l'affection *f.* **9.FP1**
after   au bout de **8.L***; après **3.FP2**
afterwards   après **3.FP2**
aftershave   l'après-rasage *m.* **1.FP2**
again   de nouveau **1.L***
ago   il y a **3.FP2**

to **agree**   *être d'accord **9.FP2**
   to agree to meet   se donner rendez-vous **8.FP1**
agreed   entendu **8.FP1**
air conditioning   l'air *m.* conditionné **6.FP1**, la climatisation **6.FP1**
airport   l'aéroport *m.* **5.FP2**
aisle   un couloir **5.FP2**
all: all the more that   d'autant plus que **9.L***
allergy   une allergie **7.FP1**
Alps   les Alpes *f.* **1.LC1**
already   déjà **3.LC1**
aluminum   l'aluminium *m.* **2.FP3**
alumnus   un ancien élève **8.L***
amazement   l'étonnement *m.* **7.LC1**
amazing   étonnant **6.LC1**
ambition   l'ambition *f.* **10.FP3**
amplifier   un ampli **4.FP3**
amusing   rigolo **3.L***
and   et **5.LC1**
anger   la colère **7.LC1**
angry   en colère **1.FP4**
animal   une bête **3.L***, un animal (pl. animaux) **2.FP1**
animosity   l'animosité *f.* **9.FP1**

ankle   la cheville **7.FP2**
another, another one   un autre **4.LC1**
antenna   une antenne **4.FP3**
antibiotic   un antibiotique **7.FP1**
antipathy   l'antipathie *f.* **9.FP1**
antique: antique dealer   le/la marchand(e) d'antiquités **9.L***
anyhow   quand même **3.L***
anything   n'importe quoi **7.L***
apartment   un appartement **8.FP2**
to **appear**   *paraître **7.L***
appearance   l'apparence *f.* **2.FP3**
to **apply: to apply eye make up**   se maquiller les yeux **1.FP2**
appointment   un rendez-vous **7.FP1**
to **approach**   s'approcher (de) **1.LC4**
aquarium   l'aquarium *m.* **2.FP1**
arch: Arch of St. Louis   l'Arche *f.* de Saint Louis **2.FP3**
argument   une dispute **9.FP1**
arm   le bras **7.FP2**
around   autour de **9.L***
to **arrest**   arrêter **5.L***
as: as if   comme si **8.L***
   as soon as   aussitôt que, dès

que 5.LC2
aspirin   l'aspirine *f.* 4.FP1
asthma   l'asthme *m.* 7.FP1
astonished   étonné 7.LC1
at: at about   vers 1.FP3
   at last   enfin 3.FP2
   at the end of   au bout de 8.L*
athletic   athlétique 1.FP1
atmosphere   une ambiance 10.FP2
to attach   attacher 5.FP2
attractive   séduisant 7.L*
average: average size   de taille moyenne 1.FP1, moyen (moyenne) 10.FP2
aversion   l'aversion *f.* 9.FP1
to avoid   éviter 3.FP1
to avow   avouer 2.L*

B

bad   mal 1.FP4
bag   un sac 5.FP1
baggage   les bagages *m.* 5.FP1
   baggage claim   la livraison des bagages 5.FP2
baggage-check   la consigne 5.FP2
balcony   un balcon 6.FP1
bald   chauve 1.FP1
   bald head   la boule à zéro 4.L*
ball (of string)   une pelote (de ficelle) 4.FP1
   ball point pen   un stylo à bille 4.FP1
balloon   un ballon 2.FP3
bank   la banque 10.FP2
banker   un banquier (une ban-quière) 10.FP1
bath   un bain 1.FP3
bathroom   la salle de bains 6.FP1
   bathroom sink   le lavabo 2.FP1
battery   une pile 4.FP1
to be alone, undisturbed   *être tranquille 1.L*
   to be bitten by mosquitos   *être piqué par des moustiques 3.FP1
   to be born   *naître 9.FP2
   to be busy   s'occuper de 1.LC4
   to be called, named   s'appeler 1.LC4
   to be happy   *se réjouir 9.FP1
   to be in good health   se porter bien 7.FP1
   to be present at   assister à 3.FP2
   to be qualified   *faire l'affaire 10.FP3
   to be quiet   *se taire 1.LC4
   to be sad, in pain   *avoir de la peine 3.L*
   to be scared   *avoir peur 7.LC1
   to be seasick   *avoir le mal de mer 3.L*
   to be upset   se fâcher 9.FP1
to bear   supporter 2.L*
beard   une barbe 1.FP1
bearded   barbu 1.FP1
to beat   *battre 7.L*
beauty: beauty mark   un grain de beauté 1.FP1
because of   à cause de 7.L*
before   avant de 10.LC1
to begin to   *se mettre à 3.L*
to believe   *croire 7.LC1
bellboy   le groom 6.FP2
to belong to   *appartenir à 2.L*
besides   d'ailleurs 8.L*
to bet   parier 7.L*
big   grand 1.FP1
bill   la note 6.FP2
billboard   le tableau d'affichage 5.FP2
biology   la biologie 10.FP1
bird   un oiseau (pl. oiseaux) 2.FP1
black   noir 1.FP1
   black and white film   une pellicule en noir et blanc 4.FP1
blanket   une couverture 2.L*
to bleed   saigner 7.FP1
blond   blond 1.FP1
to blow   souffler 3.FP3; (out) souffler 10.L*
blue   bleu 1.FP1
to blush   *rougir 4.L*
to board (plane)   embarquer 5.FP2
   boarding: boarding pass   une carte d'embarquement 5.FP2
to boil   *faire bouillir 4.LC3
bookcase   une bibliothèque 8.FP2
boss   un patron (une patronne) 10.FP1
bothered   énervé 1.FP4
bothersome   gênant 3.L*
bottle   une bouteille 2.FP3
box   une boîte 4.FP1
boyfriend, (girlfriend)   un copain (une copine) 9.FP1
bracelet   un bracelet 9.L*
brakes   les freins *m.* 4.FP3
branch: branch office   une branche d'activité 10.FP2
brand: brand new   neuf (neuve) 2.FP3
Bravo!   Bravo! 9.FP1
bread   le pain 2.FP1
to break   casser 3.FP1, *rompre 7.L*; (body part) se casser 3.FP1

to break a leg   se casser la jambe 3.FP1
   to break up (with)   *rompre (avec) 9.FP1
brick   une brique 2.FP3
briefcase   une mallette 5.L*
to bring (object)   apporter 6.L*; (person) emmener 3.L*
   to bring back   ramener 3.L*
   to bring down   *descendre 6.FP2
   to bring up, carry up   monter 6.FP2
broken   cassé 4.FP3
bronchitis   la bronchite 7.FP1
broom   un balai 2.FP1
brown   brun 1.FP1, châtain foncé (hair) 1.FP1, marron 1.FP1
to brush (one's hair, one's teeth)   se brosser (les cheveux, les dents) 1.FP2
   to brush one's teeth   se brosser les dents 1.FP2
burden   une charge 2.L*
burglary   un cambriolage 3.FP2
to burn oneself   se brûler 7.FP2
business   les affaires *f.* 2.L*
   business (small)   un commerce 8.FP2
   business   le commerce 10.FP1
   business class   classe affaires 5.FP2
   businessman, woman   un homme (une femme) d'affaires 10.FP1
busy   occupé 2.FP2
button (on camera)   le bouton 4.FP3
to buy   acheter 5.FP2
   to buy (oneself)   s'acheter 1.FP3

C

cage   la cage 2.FP1
to call   appeler 6.FP2
calm   calme 1.FP4
camera   l'appareil-photo *m.* 4.FP3
   camera flash   le flash 4.FP3
Canada   le Canada 1.LC1
canary: Canary Islands   les îles Canaries *f.* 5.FP1
to cancel   annuler 5.FP2
canceled   annulé 5.FP2
candle   une chandelle 6.L*
capacity   la capacité 2.FP3
car   une voiture 2.FP1; (train) un wagon 5.FP2
cardboard   un carton 2.FP3
carrot   une carotte 2.FP1

carry-on: carry-on luggage un bagage à main **5.FP1**

cat le chat **2.FP1**

catastrophe un désastre **4.L***

to **catch** attraper **3.FP1**

cavity une carie **7.FP2**

certain: certain ones certain(e)s **4.LC1**

chamber: Chamber of Commerce le Syndicat d'Initiative **6.LC1**

to **change: to change one's mind** changer d'avis **7.L***

check: (paid) by check par chèque **6.FP1**

to **check (luggage)** enregistrer **5.FP2**

chemistry la chimie **10.FP1**

chest la poitrine **8.L***

chestnut (hair) châtain **1.FP1**

chicken: chicken pox la varicelle **7.FP1**

childhood: childhood illness une maladie d'enfance **7.FP1**

chin le menton **1.FP1**

to **choose** *choisir **9.FP2**

circular circulaire **2.FP3**

city: city hall la mairie **8.FP2**

civil: civil servant un(e) fonctionnaire **10.FP1**

civil service la fonction publique **10.FP2**

to **claim (luggage)** chercher **5.FP2**

classmate un(e) camarade **9.FP1**

clean, put-away rangé **2.FP1**

to **clean** nettoyer **2.FP1**

cleaners le teinturier **4.FP3**

to **clear** débarrasser **2.FP1**

to clear the table débarrasser la table **2.FP1**

to **clip: to clip very short** *tondre **4.L***

clippers une tondeuse **4.L***

closely, from close up de près **4.L***

cloth: cloth rag un chiffon **2.FP1**

clothes les vêtements m. **2.FP1**

cloud un nuage **3.FP3**

cold froid **2.FP3**; un rhume **7.FP1**

color: color film une pellicule-couleurs **4.FP1**

comb le peigne **1.FP2**

to **comb: to comb one's hair** se peigner **1.FP2**

to **come: to come back** *revenir **1.L***

to come closer s'approcher (de) **1.LC4**

comfortable confortable **6.FP1**

communication la communication **10.FP2**

company une entreprise, une compagnie **10.FP2**

to **complain about** *se plaindre de **7.LC1**

complete, full (sold out) complet (complète) **5.FP2**

computer un ordinateur **10.FP3**

computer specialist un informaticien (une informaticienne) **10.FP1**

condition l'état m. **2.FP3**; la condition **2.FP3**

to **confirm** confirmer **5.FP2**

to **congratulate** féliciter **9.FP1**

Congratulations! Félicitations! **9.FP1**

connection, relation un rapport **9.FP1**; (plane) une correspondance **5.FP2**

consistency la consistance **2.FP3**

contact: contact lenses les lentilles f. de contact, les verres m. de contact **1.FP1**

to **contact (someone)** *joindre **9.L***

convenience: convenience store une supérette **4.FP1**

to **cook** *faire cuire **4.LC3**

copper le cuivre **2.FP3**

cotton l'ouate f. **4.FP1**

cotton swab un coton-tige **4.FP1**

to **cough** tousser **7.FP1**

to **count** compter **6.FP1**

counter le comptoir **5.FP2**

countess la comtesse **7.L***

country un pays **5.FP1**

course: course of study des études **10.FP1**

crazy fou (folle) **3.L***

credit: credit card une carte de crédit **6.FP1**

crew: crew-cut les cheveux en brosse **1.FP1**

crutch une béquille **7.FP2**

to **cry** pleurer **1.L***

curly, frizzy frisé **1.FP1**

customs la douane **5.FP1**

to **cut** couper **2.FP1**; (into pieces) découper **8.L***; (oneself) se couper **1.FP2**

cut my hair short coupez-les-moi courts **4.FP2**

to cut one's hair se couper les cheveux **4.FP2**

to cut one's hand se couper à la main **7.FP2**

to cut very short *tondre **2.FP1**

dance un bal **8.L***

darkness l'obscurité f. **4.L***

data processing l'informatique f. **10.FP1**

data processor un(e) spécialiste de données **10.FP1**

day after le lendemain **6.L***

day before yesterday avant-hier **3.FP2**

day off un jour de congé **4.L***

date un rendez-vous **7.FP1**

delighted ravi **7.LC1**

dentist un dentiste **7.FP1**

deodorant le déodorant **1.FP2**

department (in store) un rayon **4.FP1**

to **deplore** déplorer **7.LC1**

depressed déprimé **7.FP1**

detergent la lessive **4.FP1**

to **develop (photos, personality)** développer **4.FP3**

devoted dévoué **7.L***

to **die** mourir **9.FP2**

dignified digne **8.L***

dimension, size la dimension **2.FP3**

to **dine, have dinner** dîner **3.LC1**

diploma un diplôme **10.FP3**

diplomat un(e) diplomate **10.FP1**

direct (flight) direct **5.FP2**

director un directeur (une directrice) **10.FP1**

dirty sale **2.FP1**

to **disappear, go away** *disparaître **5.L***

disappointed, deceived déçu **1.FP4**

to **disembark, land** débarquer **5.FP2**

dishes la vaisselle **2.FP1**

distance: distance from . . . à + distance **8.FP2**

dizzy spell, vertigo le vertige **7.FP1**

to **do, make** fabriquer **3.L***

to do a favor rendre service **2.FP2**

to do housework faire le ménage **2.FP1**

to do laundry laver le linge **2.FP1**

to do tricks *faire des tours **3.L***

does it hurt you? ça vous fait mal? **7.FP2**

doctor un médecin **7.FP1**, un docteur **1.LC1**

doctor's office un cabinet de médecin **7.FP1**

dog   le chien 2.FP1
door, boarding gate   la porte 5.FP2
doormat   un paillasson 1.L*
to dress a wound   faire un pansement 7.FP2
driver's license   un permis de conduire 5.FP1
drop   une goutte 7.FP1
to drown   se noyer 3.FP1
dry   sec (sèche) 2.FP3
dryer (hair)   le séchoir 1.FP2
to dry (oneself)   se sécher 1.FP2
  to dry one's hair   se sécher les cheveux 1.FP2
  to dry one's hands   s'essuyer les mains 1.FP2
dull   terne 2.FP3
during   pendant 3.LC2

E

ear   une oreille 1.FP1
early   tôt 3.LC1, en avance 5.FP2
to earn: to earn one's living   gagner sa vie R.L*
economics   les sciences f. économiques 10.FP1
Eiffel Tower   la Tour Eiffel 2.FP3
electrical plug   la prise 4.FP3
electronics   l'électronique f. 10.FP2
eldest   l'aîné R.L*
elevator   un ascenseur 6.FP1
employee, clerk   un employé (une employée) 10.FP1
employment, job   un emploi 10.FP1
empty   vide 2.FP3
to empty   vider 2.FP1
engineer   un ingénieur 10.FP1
engineering studies   les études f. d'ingénieur 10.FP1
enormous   énorme 2.FP3
enough   assez 3.LC1
envelope   une enveloppe 4.FP1
evening   le soir 7.FP1
event   un événement 3.FP2
ever   déjà 3.LC1
every: every four hours   toutes les 4 heures 7.FP1
everywhere   partout 3.L*
to examine   examiner 7.FP1
to excuse oneself, apologize   s'excuser 1.FP3
exercise gym   la salle d'exercices 6.FP1
to exhibit   exposer 9.L*
exit   la sortie 5.FP2
to explain   expliquer 2.L*
exquisite   exquis 7.L*

extent   l'ampleur f. 4.L*
eye   un oeil (pl. yeux) 1.FP1
eyeliner   l'eye-liner m. 1.FP2
eyeshadow   le fard à paupières 1.FP2

F

fabric   l'étoffe f. 2.FP3
face   la figure 1.FP1, le visage 1.FP1
fact   un fait 3.FP2
factory   une usine 10.FP2
fair   juste R.L*
to fall   tomber 3.FP1
  to fall in love with at first sight   avoir le coup de foudre pour 9.FP1
  to fall in the water   tomber dans l'eau 3.FP1
far, far away   loin 8.FP2
farm   une ferme 6.L*
farmer   un cultivateur (une cultivatrice) 8.L*
fear   la crainte 7.LC1
to fear, be afraid of   craindre 7.LC1
to feed   donner à manger à 2.FP1
to feel (pain or emotion)   *ressentir 1.FP4
  to feel nauseous   avoir mal au coeur 7.FP1
  to feel sorry for   *plaindre 7.LC1
fever   la fièvre 7.FP1
field   un champ 6.L*
to file   classer 10.FP3
to fill   remplir 2.FP1
film   une pellicule 4.FP1
filter   le filtre 4.FP3
finally   finalement 3.FP2
finance   la finance 10.FP2
to find   trouver 9.FP2
to finish   finir 3.LC1
fire station   une caserne de pompiers 8.FP2
firm (company)   une firme 10.FP2
first, at first   d'abord 3.FP2
  first class   la première classe 5.FP2
to fish   pêcher 3.L*
to fix, repair   réparer 4.FP3
to fix   arranger 4.L*
flat   plat 2.FP3
flexible   flexible 2.FP3
floor   le sol 2.FP1
flower   une fleur 2.FP1
flu   la grippe 7.FP1
fog   la brume 3.FP3
to fold (up)   plier 3.L*
forbidden   défendu 3.L*

forehead   le front 1.FP1
foreign languages   les langues étrangères 10.FP1
forest   la forêt 3.FP1
form   la forme 2.FP3
to fracture   se fracturer 7.FP2
frame   le cadre 10.L*
freckles   les taches f. de rousseur 1.FP1
free   libre 2.FP2
French (language)   le français 1.LC1
friend   un ami (une amie) 9.FP1
friendship   l'amitié f. 9.FP1
fringe benefit   un avantage social 10.FP2
frog   une grenouille 3.L*
from time to time   de temps en temps 4.L*
frozen   gelé 3.FP3
to fry   faire frire 4.LC3
full room & board   la pension complète 6.FP1
full-time employment   un emploi à plein temps 10.FP3
to function, work   fonctionner 4.FP3; marcher 4.FP3
furious   furieux (furieuse) 1.FP4

G

gang   une bande 5.L*
garbage   les ordures f. 2.FP1
  garbage can   la poubelle 1.L*
garden hose   le tuyau d'arrosage 2.FP1
gas station   une station-service 8.FP2
gasoline   l'essence f. 6.L*
general delivery   la poste restante 4.FP1
German measles   la rubéole 7.FP1
to get a nosebleed   saigner du nez 7.FP1
  to get a sunburn   attraper un coup de soleil 3.FP1
  to get angry   se mettre en colère 1.LC4
  to get back, recuperate   récupérer 5.L*
  to get bored   s'embêter 1.LC4
  to get dressed   s'habiller 1.FP3
  to get engaged   se fiancer 9.FP2
  to get hurt, injure oneself   se faire mal 3.FP1; se blesser 3.FP1
  to get impatient   s'impatienter 1.LC4

in disorder   en désordre **2.FP1**
   in a bad mood   de mauvaise humeur **1.FP4**
   in a good mood   de bonne humeur **1.FP4**
   in a little while   tout à l'heure **4.FP3**
   in back   derrière **4.FP2**
   in cash   en espèces **6.FP1**
   in front   sur le devant **4.FP2**, (of) devant **8.FP1**
   in good health   bien portant **7.FP1**
   in memory of   en souvenir de **8.L***
   in order to   pour **10.LC1**
   in shape   en forme **1.FP4**
   in steps (hair), uneven   des échelles **4.L***
   in the distance   au loin **6.L***
   in two days' time   dans deux jours **4.FP3**
   in your opinion   à votre avis **R.A.**
inclination for responsibility   le goût des responsabilités **10.FP3**
indigestion   l'indigestion *f.* **7.FP1**
industry   l'industrie *f.* **10.FP2**
inexpensive hotel   un hôtel bon marché **6.FP1**
to **inherit**   hériter (de) **8.L***
initiative   un esprit d'initiative **10.FP3**
inn   une auberge **6.FP1**
to **insist**   exiger **2.L***
   to **insist that**   insister pour que **2.LC2**
instinctive liking   la sympathie **9.FP1**
insurance agent   un agent d'assurances **10.FP1**
international company   une compagnie internationale **10.FP2**
interview   un entretien **10.FP3**, une entrevue **10.FP3**
to **iron**   repasser **2.FP1**
iron (for clothes)   un fer à repasser **2.FP1**; (metal) le fer **2.FP3**
is there something else?   autre chose? **4.FP1**
it is better that . . .   il vaut mieux que . . . **2.LC2**
   it is essential that   il est essentiel que **2.LC2**
   it is fair that   il est juste que **2.LC2**
   it is good that   il est bon que **2.LC2**
it happened   c'est arrivé **3.FP2**

it is important that   il est important que **2.LC2**
it is indispensable that   il est indispensable que **2.LC2**
it is natural that   il est naturel que **2.LC2**
it is normal that   il est normal que **2.LC2**
it is too bad that   il est dommage que **2.LC2**
it is useful that . . .   utile: il est utile que . . . **2.LC2**
it's dark   il fait noir **3.FP3**
it's your turn   c'est votre tour **4.FP1**
item   un article **4.FP1**

J

jealousy   la jalousie **9.FP1**
jewel, jewelry   un bijou (pl. bijoux) **9.L***
journalism   le journalisme **10.FP1**
joy   la joie **7.LC1**
judge   un(e) juge **10.FP1**
to **jump**   sauter **1.L***
just as   au moment où **3.LC2**

K

to **keep company**   *tenir compagnie **9.L***
   kiss   un baiser **7.L***
to **kiss**   embrasser **1.L***
knee, lap   un genou (pl. genoux) **7.L***
knife   un couteau (pl. couteaux) **2.FP1**
knitting   le tricot **9.L***
to **knock (on door)**   frapper **1.L***

L

to **land**   atterrir **5.FP2**
to **last**   durer **2.L***
   last   dernier (dernière) **3.FP2**
   last night   hier soir **3.FP2**
   late   tard **3.LC1**; en retard **5.FP2**
   one hour late   une heure de retard **5.FP2**
to **launch**   lancer **4.L***
laundry room   la lingerie **2.FP1**
law enforcement   la police **8.FP2**
lawn   la pelouse **2.FP1**
lawn-mower   la tondeuse **2.FP1**
lawyer   un avocat (une avocate) **10.FP1**
   lawyer's office   un cabinet d'avocat **10.FP2**
lead   le plomb **2.FP3**
to **lead**   *conduire **3.L***

to **lean**   appuyer **10.L***
to **leave**   laisser **R.L***; partir **5.LC2**
   to leave my hair long (haircut)   laissez-les-moi longs **4.FP2**
   to leave (place/person)   quitter **5.LC2**
   to leave from (place)   partir de **5.LC2**
   to leave for (destination)   partir à (en, pour) **5.LC2**
length: length of time from . . .   à + length of time **8.FP2**
lens (camera)   la lentille **4.FP3**
lens (focus)   l'objectif *m.* **4.FP3**
less   moins **6.FP1**
letter   une lettre **4.FP1**
   letter of recommendation   une lettre de recommandation **10.FP3**
library   une bibliothèque **8.FP2**
license plate   une plaque d'immatriculation **5.L***
light   léger (légère) **2.FP3**
to **light**   allumer **10.L***
   to light a fire   allumer un feu **2.L***
lightening (flash of)   un éclair **3.FP3**
to **like**   aimer **2.LC2**
   to like   aimer bien **9.FP1**
lipstick   le rouge à lèvres **1.FP2**
liter   le litre **1.LC1**
literature   la littérature **10.FP1**
to **live, lodge**   loger **2.L***
long   long (longue) **1.FP1**
to **look for, search for**   rechercher **10.FP2**
to **lose one's balance**   perdre l'équilibre **3.FP1**
loud   fort **6.L***
loudspeaker   le • haut-parleur **4.FP3**
to **love**   aimer **9.FP1**
low   bas (basse) **2.FP3**
   low-income housing   un HLM (Habitation à Loyer Modéré) **8.FP2**
luggage   les bagages *m.* **5.FP1**
luxury hotel   un hôtel de luxe **6.FP1**

M

madman/woman   un fou (une folle) **7.L***
magazine   un magazine **2.FP1**
magnifying glass   une loupe **5.L***
mail   le courrier **4.FP3**
to **make a cast (broken bone)**   faire un plâtre **7.FP2**

to make a mistake   se tromper 1.LC4
to make an appointment/date with   donner rendez-vous à 8.FP1
to make an appointment, date   prendre rendez-vous 7.FP1
to make friends   se faire des amis 9.FP2
to make sure   s'assurer 8.L*
to make the bed   faire le lit 2.FP1
to make up   se réconcilier 9.FP1
mall   un grand centre commercial 8.FP2
to manage to   arriver à 4.L*
management   la gestion 10.FP1
manager   le/la gérant(e) 6.FP2
marketing   le marketing 10.FP1
marketing specialist   un(e) spécialiste de marketing 10.FP1
to marry   épouser 2.L*
mascara   le mascara 1.FP2, le rimmel 1.FP2
massive   massif (massive) 2.FP3
match   une allumette 4.FP1
material   le matériel 2.FP3
mathematics   les maths f. 1.LC1
mean, nasty   méchant 2.L*
to mean   *vouloir dire 10.L*
measles   la rougeole 7.FP1
to measure   mesurer 1.FP1
medicine (the practice of)   la médecine 10.FP1
to meet each other   se rencontrer 8.FP1
to meet by chance, run into (person)   rencontrer 8.FP1
merchant   un marchand 2.L*
metal   le métal (pl. métaux) 2.FP3
Mexico   le Mexique 5.FP1
microphone   le micro 4.FP3
minuscule   minuscule 2.FP3
minor news event   un fait divers 3.FP2
mirror   un miroir 1.FP2; la glace 1.FP2
to miss (bus)   rater 5.FP2
Mississippi   le Mississippi 1.LC1
Monday   lundi 3.FP2
mononucleosis   la mononucléose 7.FP1
month   un mois 3.FP2
mood   l'humeur f. 1.FP4
more   plus 6.FP1
morning   le matin 7.FP1
most of   la plupart de 4.LC1
most of them, the majority   la plupart 4.LC1

moustache   la moustache 1.FP1
mouth   la bouche 1.FP1
to move toward   se diriger vers 8.L*
to mow   *tondre 2.FP1
multinational   multinational 10.FP2
mumps   les oreillons m.pl. 7.FP1
museum   un musée 8.FP2
music   la musique 10.FP1
must   devoir 4.FP1
My Goodness!   Mon Dieu! 3.FP2
My poor . . .   Mon (Ma) pauvre . . . 9.FP1

N

nail (metal)   le clou 2.FP3
nail   un ongle 1.FP2
nail polish   le vernis à ongles 1.FP2
narrow, tight   étroit 2.FP3
nature   la nature 3.FP1
nausea   la nausée 7.FP1
nearby   tout près 8.FP2
neck   le cou 1.FP1
neighborhood, district   le quartier 8.FP2
neither . . . nor   ni . . . ni 5.LC1
nephew   un neveu (pl. neveux) R.L*
nervous   nerveux (nerveuse) 7.FP1
never   ne . . . jamais 3.LC1
next   suivant 5.FP2; ensuite 3.FP2
next   prochain 5.FP2
nice, kind   sympathique 2.FP2
no longer, not anymore   ne . . . plus 1.L*
no one, nobody   ne . . . personne RC
no, not any   ne . . . aucun 5.LC1
noisy   bruyant 6.FP1
non-smoking section   la section non-fumeur 5.FP2
nose   le nez 1.FP1
not yet   ne . . . pas encore 3.LC1
notebook   un carnet 4.FP1
nothing   ne . . . rien RC
nothing to declare   rien à déclarer 5.FP1
to notice   remarquer 2.L*; apercevoir 6.L*
nowhere   ne . . . nulle part 5.LC1
nurse   un infirmier (une infirmière) 7.FP1

O

to observe   observer 3.FP1
of course   bien sûr 2.FP2
often   souvent 3.LC1

O.K.   d'accord 2.FP2
old   vieux (vieille) 2.FP3
former   ancien (ancienne) 2.FP3
on foot   à pied 8.FP2
on his own account   à son propre compte 10.FP2
on time   à l'heure 5.FP2
on Saturday   samedi 1.LC1
on Saturdays   le samedi 1.LC1
on the sides   sur les côtés 4.FP2
on top   sur le dessus 4.FP2
once   une fois 7.FP1
one hundred meters away   à 100 mètres 8.FP2
one week from now   d'ici une semaine 4.FP3
one-way ticket   un aller simple 5.FP2
the one who(m), the one that   celui (celle) qui 6.LC2
to operate (equipment)   faire marcher 4.LC3
operator   un standard 6.FP2
opportunity for promotion   la possibilité de promotion 10.FP2
opposite   en face de 6.L*
ophthamologist   un oculiste 7.FP1
or   ou 5.LC1
orchard   un verger 8.L*
other ones   d'autres 4.LC1
ouch!   aïe! 7.FP1
outside   dehors 3.FP2
oval   oval 1.FP1
oven   un four 1.L*
overcast   couvert 3.FP3
overwhelmed   bouleversé 7.L*
to owe   devoir 4.FP1
to own, possess   posséder 9.L*
owner   un propriétaire R.L*

P

package   un paquet 4.FP1; un colis 4.FP1
pad: pad (of paper)   un bloc 4.FP1
pain, suffering   une douleur 7.FP2
painful   douloureux (douloureuse) 7.L*
paper   le papier 2.FP3
paper clip   un trombone 4.FP1
paper tissue   un mouchoir en papier 4.FP1
paper towels (brand name)   le Sopalin 4.FP1
parachute   un parachute 2.FP3

parakeet   la perruche **2.FP1**
park   un parc **8.FP2**
to **pass by**   passer **3.LC1**
passport   un passeport **5.FP1**
   passport check   un contrôle
      des passeports **5.FP1**
peach   une pêche **8.L***
   peach tree   un pêcher **8.L***
to **peel**   éplucher **2.FP1**
pencil   un crayon **4.FP1**
perfect   parfait **3.L***
perfume   l'eau *f.* de toilette **1.FP2**;
   le parfum **1.FP2**
perplexed   perplexe **1.FP4**
pharmaceutics (practice of)   la
   pharmacie **10.FP1**
pharmacy   la pharmacie **4.FP1**
pharmacist   un pharmacien (une
   pharmacienne) **10.FP1**
philosophy   la philosophie **10.FP1**
photocopy   une photocopie **4.FP1**
photographer   le photographe
   4.FP1
physics   la physique **10.FP1**
to **pick up**   ramasser **7.L***
picture slide   une diapo **4.FP1**
pillow   un oreiller **6.FP2**
pill (medicine)   un comprimé
   7.FP1
pilot   le pilote **5.FP2**
pin   une épingle **4.FP1**
pitiful   pitoyable **4.L***
plant   une plante **2.FP1**
plastic   en plastique (adj.)
   2.FP3; le plastique (n.)
   2.FP3
platform   le quai **5.FP2**
to **please**   faire plaisir à **8.L***
pneumonia   une pneumonie
   7.FP1
pocket   une poche **1.L***
to **point: point at**   montrer du doigt
   8.L*
pointed   pointu **2.FP3**
police: police detective   un
   inspecteur de police **5.L***
   police station   le poste de
      police **8.FP2**; une
      gendarmerie **8.FP2**
polished   poli **2.FP3**
   political science   les sciences *f.*
      politiques **10.FP1**
to **pollute**   polluer **3.FP1**
ponytail   une queue de cheval
   1.FP1
Portugal   le Portugal **5.FP1**
postcard   une carte postale **4.FP1**
post office   la poste **4.FP1**
pot, pan   une casserole **1.L***
to **pour**   verser **3.L***
precisely at that moment

   justement **8.L***
to **predict**   prédire **3.FP3**
to **prefer**   préférer **2.LC2**
prescription   une ordonnance
   7.FP1
to **present, show**   présenter **5.FP2**
to **prevent, keep from doing**
   empêcher de **1.L***
pride   l'orgueil *m.* **7.LC1**
princess   une princesse **1.LC1**
private eye   un détective privé **5.L***
professional experience
   l'expérience *f.* professionnelle
   10.FP3
proud   fier (fière) **3.L***
provided, on condition that   à
   condition que **10.LC2**
to **prune, trim**   tailler **2.FP1**
psychology   la psychologie
   10.FP1
public: public garden   un jardin
   public **8.FP2**
   public relations   les relations *f.*
      publiques **10.FP2**
to **punch (ticket)**   composter **5.FP2**
to **put, place, turn on**   mettre
   6.FP2
   to put away   ranger **2.FP1**
   to put back   *remettre **9.L***
   to put stitches (in a wound)
      mettre des sutures **7.FP2**

Q ━━━━━━━━━━━━━━━━

quantity   une quantité **4.FP1**
to **quarrel, have a fight**   se quereller
   9.FP1
queen   la reine **1.LC1**

R ━━━━━━━━━━━━━━━━

rabbit   un lapin **2.FP1**
raconter   to tell (what happened)
   3.FP2
rain   la pluie **3.FP3**
to **raise (children)**   élever **2.L***
raised, high   élevé **2.FP3**
rash (skin)   l'eczéma *m.* **7.FP1**;
   des boutons **7.FP1**
real estate   l'immobilier *m.*
   10.FP2
   real estate agent   un agent
      immobilier **10.FP1**
Really?   Vraiment? **3.FP2**
to **realize**   se rendre compte **2.L***
reception desk   la réception
   6.FP1
receptionist, secretary   le/la
   réceptionniste **6.FP2**
recreation center   un centre de
   loisirs **8.FP2**

rectangular   rectangulaire **1.FP1**
red   rouge **1.LC1**
   redhead   roux (rousse) **1.FP1**
reference   une référence
   10.FP3
to **reflect on**   réfléchir **7.L***
refrigerator   le réfrigérateur
   2.FP3
regret   le regret **7.LC1**
to **regret**   regretter **2.FP2**
relations   les relations *f.* **9.FP1**
   good relations   bons rapports
      9.FP1
   bad relations   mauvaises
      relations **9.FP1**
to **remarry**   se remarier **9.FP2**
to **remember, recall**   se rappeler
   1.LC4
representative   un(e)
   représentant(e) **10.FP1**
request   une requête **8.L***
research laboratory   un
   laboratoire de recherche
   10.FP2
researcher   un chercheur (une
   chercheuse) **10.FP1**
to **reserve**   réserver **6.FP1**
reservation   une réservation
   5.FP2
respect   le respect **9.FP1**
to **respect**   respecter **3.FP1**
to **respond**   répondre **10.FP3**
responsibility   une responsabilité
   10.FP2
to **rest**   se reposer **1.FP3**
résumé   un curriculum vitae
   10.FP3
to **retire**   prendre sa retraite **9.FP2**
to **reward**   récompenser **4.L***
ring   une bague **R.L***
roll (of paper towels)   un rouleau
   (pl. rouleaux) **4.FP1**
room   de la place **5.FP2**
   room service   le service dans
      les chambres **6.FP1**
   room with breakfast, dinner
      la demi-pension **6.FP1**
roomy   spacieux (spacieuse)
   6.FP1
rough, uneven   rugueux
   (rugueuse) **2.FP3**
round   rond **1.FP1**
   round-trip ticket   un aller et
      retour **5.FP2**
rounded, arched   courbé **2.FP3**
rubber   le caoutchouc **2.FP3**
   rubber band   un élastique
      4.FP1
rug   un tapis **1.L***
to **run**   *courir **1.L***
Russia   la Russie **5.FP1**

rustic furniture   des meubles *m.* rustiques **6.L***

S

sad   triste **1.FP4**
sadness   la tristesse **7.LC1**
safe   un coffre **R.L***
safety pin   une épingle de sûreté **4.FP1**
salary   un salaire **10.FP2**
sales person   un vendeur (une vendeuse) **10.FP1**
to **save**   sauver **5.L***
saw   une scie **2.FP3**
scar   une cicatrice **1.FP1**
to **scare**   faire peur **3.FP1**
schedule   un horaire **5.FP2**
scientist   un(e) scientifique **10.FP1**
scientific research   la recherche scientifique **10.FP2**
scissors   les ciseaux *m.* **1.FP2**
scotch tape   le scotch **4.FP1**
to **scream**   pousser des cris **3.L***
seat   un siège **5.FP2**; une place **5.FP2**
   seat belt   une ceinture de sécurité **5.FP2**
   second class   la deuxième classe **5.FP2**
   second-hand, used   d'occasion **2.FP3**
secretary   un(e) secrétaire **10.FP1**
security check   un contrôle de sécurité **5.FP2**
see you (date, time)   à + date, time **8.FP1**
to **see**   assister à **3.FP2**
to **seem, appear**   sembler **1.FP4**
to **seize, take**   saisir **9.L***
to **separate: to separate (husband & wife)**   se séparer **9.FP2**
serpent   un serpent **3.FP1**
to **serve**   *servir **6.FP2**
set (hair)   une mise en plis **4.FP2**
to **set a fire**   mettre le feu **3.FP1**
   to set the table (silverware)   mettre le couvert **2.FP1**
   to set the table   mettre la table **2.FP1**
to **settle**   s'installer **8.L***
several   certain(e)s, plusieurs **4.LC1**
to **shake**   secouer **10.L***
shampoo   le shampooing **1.FP2**
   a shampoo (hair salon)   un shampooing **4.FP2**
to **shave**   se raser **1.FP2**
shaver   le rasoir **1.FP2**
shaving cream   la crème à raser **1.FP2**

sheet: sheet (bedding)   un drap **6.FP2**
   sheet ice   le verglas **3.FP3**
to **shine**   briller **3.FP3**
shiny   brillant **2.FP3**
shirt   une chemise **2.FP1**
to **shiver, shudder**   frissonner **9.L***
shoe repairer   le cordonier **4.FP3**
shop   une boutique **4.FP1**; un commerce **8.FP2**
to **shorten (hair)**   dégager **4.FP2**
shot of novocaine   une piqûre de novocaïne **7.FP2**
to **show**   *faire voir **4.LC3**
shower   une douche **1.FP3**
shrub   un arbuste **2.FP1**
   shrub clippers   un sécateur **2.FP1**
to **shut up**   *se taire **1.LC4**
sick   malade **1.FP4**
sickness, disease   une maladie **7.FP1**
side   un côté **4.L***
sideboard   un buffet **1.L***
sidewalk   le trottoir **9.L***
silent   muet (muette) **7.L***
silver   l'argent *m.* **R.L***
since   puisque **3.L***
   single-family house   une maison individuelle **8.FP2**
to **sit down**   *s'asseoir **1.LC4**
   to sit down to eat   se mettre à table **1.FP3**
skinny   maigre **1.FP1**
skull   le crâne **4.L***
to **slip**   glisser **3.FP1**
to **slow down**   *ralentir **7.L***
small, short   petit **1.FP1**
   small sofa   un canapé **1.L***
to **smell**   *sentir **1.FP4**
smoking section   la section fumeur **5.FP2**
smooth   lisse **2.FP3**
to **sneeze**   éternuer **7.FP1**
snow   la neige **3.FP3**
snowstorm   une tempête de neige **3.FP3**
so much   tellement **4.L***
   so that   pour que **10.LC2**
soap   le savon **1.FP2**
social worker   un(e) assistant(e) social(e) **10.FP1**
soft   mou (molle) **2.FP3**
   software specialist   un(e) spécialiste de logiciel **10.FP1**
something else to do   autre chose à faire **2.FP2**
to **solicit, ask for**   solliciter **10.FP3**
solid   solide **2.FP3**
some, a few   quelques **4.LC1**; quelques-un(e)s **4.LC1**;

certain(e)s **4.LC1**
someone, somebody   quelqu'un **RC**
something   quelque chose **RC**
   something else   quelque chose d'autre **4.FP1**
   something to declare   quelque chose à déclarer **5.FP1**
somewhere   quelque part **5.LC1**
very sorry, sad   désolé **2.FP2**
to **speak English**   parler anglais **10.FP3**
to **specialize, major in**   se spécialiser en **10.FP1**
specialist   un spécialiste **7.FP1**
to **spend (time)**   passer **3.LC1**
to **spend the night**   passer la nuit **6.FP1**
to **spoil**   gâter **7.L***
sponge   une éponge **2.FP1**
to **sprain**   se fouler **7.FP2**
spring (in watch)   le ressort **4.FP3**
spy   un espion (une espionne) **5.L***
square   carré **1.FP1**
to **stand**   supporter **2.L***
to **start**   *se mettre à **3.L***
   to start one's own business   créer sa propre entreprise **10.FP2**
stationery store   la papeterie **4.FP1**
   stationery paper   le papier à lettres **4.FP1**
Statue of Liberty   la Statue de la Liberté **2.FP3**
to **stay, lodge**   séjourner **6.FP1**
   to stay in bed   rester au lit **7.FP1**
to **steal**   voler **5.L***
steel   l'acier *m.* **2.FP3**
stele (stone marker with an inscription)   une stèle **6.L***
to **step on**   marcher sur **1.LC3**
steward   le steward **5.FP2**
stewardess   l'hôtesse *f.* de l'air **5.FP2**
to **sting**   piquer **3.FP1**
stockbroker   un agent de change **10.FP1**
stone   une pierre **2.FP3**
stool   un tabouret **4.L***
to **stoop, bend down**   se baisser **7.L***
to **stop, prevent oneself from**   s'arrêter **1.FP3**; s'empêcher (de) **4.L***
stopover, connection   une escale **5.FP2**
store window   une vitrine **9.L***
storm   la tempête **3.FP3**; un orage **3.FP3**

straight   lisse 1.FP1

   straight, upright   droit 2.FP3

stranger   un inconnu 7.L*

strep throat   l'angine *f.* 7.FP1

string   la ficelle 4.FP1

strong   fort 1.FP1

to study   étudier 10.FP1, faire des études (de) 9.FP3

suitcase   une valise 5.FP1

summer job   un job d'été 10.FP3

sunny   clair 6.FP1

to sunbathe   prendre un bain de soleil 3.FP1

super   chouette 3.L*

surgeon   un chirurgien (une chirurgienne) 7.FP1

to surprise   *surprendre 9.L*

surprised   surpris 7.LC1

to swallow   avaler 7.FP1

to sweep   balayer 2.FP1

to swim   nager 3.FP1

swimming pool   une piscine 6.FP1

synthetic material   la matière synthétique 2.FP3

T

table   la table 2.FP1

tablet (medicine)   un cachet 7.FP1

tadpole   un têtard 3.L*

to take   *prendre 5.FP2

   to take a blood sample   faire une analyse de sang 7.FP1

   to take a boat trip   faire une promenade en bateau 3.FP1

   to take a walk   se promener 1.FP3

   to take advantage of   profiter de 1.L*

   to take care of   s'occuper de 1.LC4

   to take off (plane)   décoller 5.FP2

   to take off, remove   enlever 4.FP3

   to take one's blood pressure   prendre la tension 7.FP1

   to have taken or carried something up   monter: avoir + monté 3.LC1

   to take out the trash   sortir la poubelle 2.FP1

   to take place   avoir lieu 2.L*

to tan oneself   bronzer 3.FP1

tear   une larme 7.L*

technical knowledge   les connaissances *f.* techniques 10.FP3

technician   un technicien (une technicienne) 10.FP1

telephone   le téléphone 6.FP1

to telephone, call   téléphoner 10.FP3

telephoto lens   le téléobjectif 4.FP3

television   la télévision 6.FP1

temperature   la température 2.FP3

temporary employment   un emploi temporaire 10.FP3

to tempt   tenter 9.L*

ten minutes early   dix minutes d'avance 5.FP2

tense, uptight   tendu 1.FP4

to thank   remercier 2.FP2

   thank you   merci 2.FP2

   thank you very much   merci beaucoup 2.FP2

   thanks a million   merci mille fois 2.FP2

that   que 9.LC1

   that doesn't matter   ça n'a pas d'importance 10.L*

   that of, the one belonging to   celui (celle) de 6.LC2

   that's all?   c'est tout? 4.FP1

   that's not for real!   ce n'est pas croyable! 3.FP2

   that's unbelieveable!   c'est incroyable! 3.FP2

then   puis 3.FP2

there is/are . . . left   il reste . . . 8.L*

there is/are only . . . left   il ne reste que . . . 10.L*

thick   épais (épaisse) 2.FP3

thief   un voleur (une voleuse) 5.L*

thin   mince 1.FP1

things will be okay   ça s'arrangera 9.FP1

this happened, took place   ça a eu lieu 3.FP2; ça s'est passé . . . 3.FP2

   this one   celui-ci (celle-ci) 2.L*

   this one, the one   celui (celle) 6.LC2

   this will be ready   ce sera prêt 4.FP3

through   à travers 1.L*

to throw   *jeter 3.FP1

   to throw up   *vomir 7.FP1

thunder   le tonnerre 3.FP3

ticket   un billet 5.FP2

   ticket window   le guichet 5.FP2

   ticket-punching machine   le composteur 5.FP2

time   le temps 2.FP2

tire   la roue 4.FP3

tired   fatigué 1.FP4

to the end   jusqu'au bout 7.L*

toilet paper   le papier hygiénique 4.FP1

toiletry bag   la trousse de toilette 1.FP2

too   trop 3.LC1

too bad!   tant pis! 2.LC2; quel dommage! 9.FP1

tooth   une dent 7.FP2

   tooth filling   un plombage 7.FP2

   toothache   mal aux dents 7.FP4

   toothbrush   une brosse à dents 1.FP2

   toothpaste   le dentifrice 1.FP2

tourist class   la classe économie 5.FP2

towel   la serviette 1.FP2

tower, high-rise   une tour 8.FP2

town centre, downtown   le centre-ville 8.FP2

trade   le commerce 10.FP1

traffic   la circulation 6.L*

   traffic regulations   le code de la route 8.FP2

train   un train 5.FP2

   train door   une portière 7.L*

   train station   la gare 5.FP2

travel agency   une agence de voyages 5.FP2

to travel   voyager 5.FP1

traveler's check   un chèque de voyage 6.FP1

to treat (medical)   soigner 7.FP1

triangular   triangulaire 2.FP3

truly   drôlement 4.L*

trust   une confiance 9.FP1

to trust   avoir confiance 9.FP1

to try in vain   avoir beau essayer 4.L*

   to try to   chercher à 10.L*

tube   un tube 4.FP1

to turn: to turn around   se tourner 4.L*

   to turn down, lower   baisser 6.FP2

twice a day   deux fois par jour 7.FP1

U

unexpected   inattendu 8.L*

unfair   injuste R.L*

unhappy   malheureux (malheureuse) 1.FP4

United Nations building   le bâtiment des Nations Unies 2.FP3

United States   les États-Unis *m.* 1.LC1

unless   à moins que 10.LC2

unruly mop (of hair) la tignasse 4.L*

until now jusqu'ici 4.L*

    until when jusqu'à quand 6.FP1

upset fâché 3.L*; énervé 1.FP4

to **use** utiliser 10.FP3; *se servir de 10.FP3

V

to **vacuum** passer l'aspirateur 2.FP1

vegetable un légume 2.FP3

vegetation la végétation 3.FP1

very much beaucoup 3.LC1

veterinary: veterinary doctor un(e) vétérinaire 10.FP1

    veterinary studies les études f. vétérinaires 10.FP1

view une vue 6.FP1

Virginia la Virginie 1.LC1

vitamin une vitamine 4.FP1

volume la capacité 2.FP3

voluminous volumineux (volumineuse) 2.FP3

W

to **wait** attendre 5.FP2

    waiting room la salle d'attente 5.FP2

to **wake up (something, someone)** réveiller 6.FP2

to **wake (oneself) up** se réveiller 1.FP3; s'éveiller 10.L*

    wakefulness l'éveil m. 10.L*

to **walk** faire un tour 3.FP1; promener 2.FP1

to **want** *vouloir 2.LC2

    wardrobe, closet une armoire 1.L*

    warm tiède 2.FP3

to **warn** *prévenir 3.L*

to **wash** laver 2.FP1

    to **wash (oneself)** se laver 1.FP3

    to **wash one's face** se laver la figure 1.FP2

    to **wash the dishes** faire la vaisselle 2.FP1

    wash cloth un gant de toilette 1.FP2

    wastepaper basket, trash la corbeille 2.FP1

wavy ondulé 2.FP3

weak faible 1.FP1; fragile 2.FP3

wealth les biens m. 2.L*

to **wear glasses** porter des lunettes 1.FP1

    bad weather le mauvais temps 3.FP3

nice weather le beau temps 3.FP3

    weather forecast la météo 3.FP3

week une semaine 3.FP2

to **weigh** peser 1.FP1

weight le poids 1.FP1

well, good bien 1.FP4

    well-being le bien-être 10.L*

    well-built, solid costaud 1.FP1

    well located bien situé 6.FP1

wet mouillé 2.FP3

what quel (quelle) 4.FP1

    what bad luck! quelle malchance! 9.FP2

    what doesn't work? qu'est-ce qui ne marche pas? 4.FP2

    what good news! quelle bonne nouvelle! 9.FP2

    what happened? qu'est-ce qu'il y a eu? 3.FP2; qu'est-ce qui a eu lieu? 3.FP2; qu'est-ce qui est arrivé? 3.FP2; qu'est-ce qui s'est passé? 3.FP2

    what is the problem? quel est le problème? 4.FP3

    what kind, type? quel genre? 7.FP1

    what type of quelle sorte de 5.FP2

    what's new? quoi de neuf? 3.FP2

    what's the matter? qu'est-ce que tu as? 1.FP4

    what's wrong? qu'est-ce qu'il y a? 1.FP4; qu'est-ce qui ne va pas? 7.FP1

when lorsque 3.LC2; quand 5.LC2

which quel (quelle) 4.FP1; que 9.LC1

while pendant que 3.LC2

whim un caprice 8.L*

whistle un sifflet à roulette 3.L*

to **whistle** siffler 3.L*

who, that, which qui 9.LC1

whom que 9.LC1

whooping cough la coqueluche 7.FP1

wide large 2.FP3

wind le vent 3.FP3

window pane une vitre 2.FP1

to **wipe** essuyer 2.FP1

    to **wipe (oneself) dry** s'essuyer 1.FP2

wisdom tooth une dent de sagesse 7.FP2

to **wish** souhaiter 2.LC2; désirer 2.LC2

with one bed à un lit 6.FP1

with pleasure avec plaisir 2.FP2

without sans (que) 10.LC1

to **witness** être témoin 3.FP2

to **wonder** se demander 8.L*

wood le bois 2.FP3

word un mot 6.L*

work le travail (pl. travaux) 2.FP1

to **work** travailler 9.FP2

    worker un ouvrier (une ouvrière) R.L*

worn usagé 2.FP3

    worn out, old usé 4.FP3

to **worry** s'en faire 4.L*

worried préoccupé 1.FP4

worse pire 7.L*

to **wrap** envelopper 7.L*

wrist le poignet 7.L*

X

to **x-ray** faire une radio 7.FP1

Y

to **yell, shout** crier 1.L*

yesterday hier 3.FP2

you're kidding! tu plaisantes! 3.FP2

    you're the boss! c'est vous le patron (patronne)! 2.LC2

    you're welcome de rien 2.FP2; je t'en prie 2.FP2; il n'y a pas de quoi 2.FP2

yet déjà 3.LC1

youth center une Maison des Jeunes 8.FP2

    youth hostel une auberge de la jeunesse 6.FP1

INDEX

43153000558615

Photo Credits

Front Cover
Background: Port Al-Kantaoui, Sousse, Tunisia, José Fuste Raga/zefa/Corbis
Inset: PhotoDisc/Getty Images

Back cover
Level 1a: *background* Palace of Versailles, Versailles, France, Fernand Ivaldi/Getty Images; *inset* PhotoDisc/Getty Images

Level 1b: *background* Martinique, Jake Rajs/Getty Images; *inset* PhotoDisc/Getty Images

Level 1: *background* Eiffel Tower illuminated at night, Paris, France, Paul Hardy/Corbis; *inset* Digital Vision/Getty Images

Level 2: *background* Chateau Frontenac, Quebec Old Town, Quebec, Canada, nagelestock.com/Alamy; *inset* AGE Fotostock

Level 3: *background* Port Al-Kantaoui, Sousse, Tunisia, José Fuste Raga/zefa/Corbis; *inset* PhotoDisc/Getty Images

Interior: All photos by Tom Craig /© D.C. Heath, except:
i: Lawrence Migdale/PIX; **iii:** John Henebry/© D.C. Heath; **v & vi:** Giraudon/Art Resource, NY; **vii:** Laurie Platt Winfrey, Inc.; **viii:** Jean-Loup Charmet; **ix:** Giraudon/Art Resource, NY; **x:** Laurie Platt Winfrey, Inc.; **xi** *tr:* Sygma; **xii:** Hector Hyppolite. Courtesy of Selden Rodman. Owned by Patricia & Maurice Thompson, Wilton CT; **xiii:** The Metropolitan Museum of Art, The Michael C. Rockefeller Memorial Collection, Gift of Nelson A. Rockefeller, 1965; **xiv:** Art Resource, NY.; **xv:** Pierre Valette; **2** *b:* E. Morelli/Peter Arnold, Inc.; **4** *bkgd:* Y. Levy/© D.C. Heath; **6** *bkgd:* O. Franken/© D.C. Heath; **6:** Stuart Cohen; **7** *t:* VPG/© D.C. Heath; *b:* Yves Levy/© D.C. Heath; **8** *bkgd:* J. Charlas/© D.C. Heath; **10, 11** *tl:* M. Heron /© D.C. Heath; **11** *t:* Owen Franken; *bl:* D. Donne Bryant/DDB StockPhoto; *tml:* R. Lucas/Image Works; *tr:* Francois Perri/Cosmos/Woodfin Camp; *tmr:* Melina Freedman; *mbl:* Brian Vikander; *bmr:* Lee Snider/Photo Images; *br:* Tony Freeman/PhotoEdit; **16–17:** O. Franken/© D.C. Heath; **19, 20, 21, 22:** © D.C. Heath; **26:** Yves Levy/© D.C. Heath; **32:** Stuart Cohen; **34** *r:* Ken O'Donoghue/© D.C. Heath; **35** *tl:* Giraudon/Art Resource, NY; *tml & tmr:* Art Resource, NY; *bml:* Erich Lessing/Art Resource, NY; *bl:* The Metropolitan Museum of Art, Gift of Mr. and Mrs. Klaus G. Perls, 1991. (1991.17.146); *tr, bmr & br:* Giraudon/Art Resource, NY; **36–37** *bkgd:* O. Franken/© D.C. Heath; **36–37:** M. Heron/© D.C. Heath; **38** *all:* © D.C. Heath; **38–39** *bkgd:* Henebry Photography/© D.C. Heath; **42** *t & b;* © D.C. Heath; **41, 42–43** *bkgd,* **43:** M. Heron/© D.C. Heath; **46–47** *bkgd:* © D.C. Heath; **48–49** *bkgd,* **48** *mr, tr,* **49** *mr:* M. Heron/© D.C. Heath; **49** *tl:* Henebry Photography/© D.C. Heath; **49** *tr:* Yves Levy/© D.C. Heath; **49** *b,* **50:** M. Heron/© D.C. Heath; **51:** Liaison International; **52–53:** M. Heron/© D.C. Heath; **56:** Eva Rudling/Sipa Press; **60:** © Photo R.M.N.; **61** *tr:* Pierre Auguste Renoir (French, 1841-1919), *Bal à Bougival,* 1883. Oil on canvas, 181.8 x 98.1 cm. Picture Fund, courtesy of Museum of Fine Arts, Boston; *br:* detail, Berthe Morisot (French, 1841–1895) *READING (La Lecture),* 1888, oil on canvas, 29 1/4 x 36 1/2". Museum of Fine Arts, St. Petersburg, FL. Given in memory of Margaret Acheson Stuart by family and friends; *tl: & bl:* © Photo R.M.N.; **62** *tr:* Musée Marmottan-Claude Monet.; *mr:* Archives Monet-Musée Marmottan/Jean-Loup Charmet; *ml:* Claude Monet (French, 1840–1926), *Arrival of the Normandy Train, Saint-Lazare Station,* oil on canvas, 1877, 59.6 x 80.2 cm, Mr. and Mrs. Martin A. Ryerson Collection, 1933.1158. Photograph © 1994, The Art Institute of Chicago, All

Rights Reserved; *br:* Claude Monet, *Rouen Cathedral, West Facade, Sunlight,* 1894, oil on canvas, 1.002 x .660 (framed). Chester Dale Collection © 1994 National Gallery of Art, Washington; **63** *tl:* De Casseres/Photo Researchers Inc.; *tr: Pierre-Auguste Renoir, Monet Painting in His Garden at Argenteuil, 1873.* Wadsworth Atheneum, Hartford. Bequest of Anne Parrish Titzell.; *bl:* Farrell Grehan/Photo Researchers Inc.; *mr:* Claude Monet (French, 1840–1926), *Waterlilies and Japanese Bridge,* 1899, oil on canvas, 90.5 x 89.7 cm. The Art Museum, Princeton University. From the Collection of William Church Osborn, Class of 1883, Trustee of Princeton University (1914–1951), President of the Metropolitan Museum of Art (1941–1947); gift of his family; **64** *tl:* Vincent van Gogh, *The Starry Night.* (1889). Oil on canvas, 29 x 36 1/4". The Museum of Modern Art, New York. Acquired through the Lillie P. Bliss Bequest. Photograph © 1994 The Museum of Modern Art, New York; *bl:* Henri Rousseau, *The Sleeping Gypsy.* 1897. Oil on canvas, 51" x 6'7". The Museum of Modern Art, New York. Gift of Mrs. Simon Guggenheim. Photograph © 1994 The Museum of Modern Art, New York; *r:* Erich Lessing/Art Resource, NY; **65** *t:* Jean-Loup Charmet; *br & tr:* Giraudon/Art Resource, NY; *bl:* photo © Bruno Jarret/ADGAP and La Petite Chatelaine© Camille Claudel/SPADEM, #S1007 courtesy of Musée Rodin, Paris.; **66** *tr:* Phototèque René Magritte-Giraudon/Art Resource, NY; *m:* Duane Michals; *b:* René Magritte, *The Blank Signature,* 1965, oil on canvas, .813 x .651 (framed). Collection of Mr. and Mrs. Paul Mellon, © 1994 National Gallery of Art, Washington. Photo by Jose A. Naranjo; **67–68** *bkgd:* Stock Editions; **67–68:** Roger-Viollet; **69** *tl:* © D.C. Heath; *br:* Ted Russell/Image Bank; **74–75:** M. Heron/© D.C. Heath; **77** *b:* Harold V. Green/Valan Photos; **79** *bl,* **84** *bkgd,* **85** *tr,* **86, 90–91, 91–92:** M. Heron/© D.C. Heath; **99** *tr:* Bibliothèque Nationale, Paris/The Bridgeman Art Library, London; *l:* Mary Evans Picture Library; *br:* Giraudon/Art Resource, NY; **103** *b:* Edimedia; **104** *b:* Musée de Bayeux/Michael Holford; **106** *t:* Lee Snider/Image Works; **109:** DeRichemond/Image Works; **110** *b:* Ginies/Sipa Press; *t:* Jacques Witt/Sipa Press; **111** *b:* Alex Farnsworth/Image Works; **112** *t:* O. Franken/© D.C. Heath; *bkgd, tm:* M. Heron/© D.C. Heath; *mb, b:* DeRichemond/The Image Works; **113** *tl:* P. Pipard/© D.C. Heath; *m, tr & bl,* **114, 117:** M. Heron/© D.C. Heath; **115:** O. Franken/© D.C. Heath; **120** *t:* Bebert/Sipa Press; *bl & br:* A.Tannenbaum/Sygma; *bl:* **122** *t:* Bullaty Lomeo/Image Bank; *b:* Alain Choisnet/Image Bank, **124–125** *bkgd,* **125** *b:* M. Heron/© D.C. Heath; **126–127** *bkdg:* O. Franken/© D.C. Heath; **127 & 131:** M. Heron/© D.C. Heath; **133:** The Bettmann Archive; **140:** Philippe Chardon/Option Photo; **141** *t:* Photo R.M.N.; *tr:* Giraudon/Art Resource, NY; *br:* Laurie Platt Winfrey, Inc; **142:** Ken O'Donoghue/© D.C. Heath; **143 & 145** *all:* B. Barbier/Sygma; **147** *tr:* David W. Hamilton/Image Bank; *tmr:* Weinberg/Clark/Image Bank; *bmr, tml, bml, bl:* Lee Snider/Image Works; *br:* O. Franken; **151** *mr:* M. Heron/© D.C. Heath; *bl:* S. Reiter/© D.C. Heath; *ml:* O.Franken/© D.C. Heath; *tl:* DCH; **152–153:** Palmer/Brilliant/© D.C. Heath; **152** *bl:* Lawrence Migdale/PIX; **154** *inset,* **155** *m & b:* © D.C. Heath; **157** *t:* M. Heron/© D.C. Heath; **157** *b,* **158** *bl & br:* © D.C. Heath; *tr:* M. Heron/© D.C. Heath; **159** *tl, tr, ml & br:* © D.C. Heath; **166–67** *bkgd:* Adine Sagalyn/© D.C. Heath; **169** *l, br & tm:* © D.C. Heath; *tr, bl & bm:* M. Heron/© D.C. Heath; **176** *bl:* Giraudon/Art Resource, NY; *br:* Jean-Loup Charmet; **177** *l:* Jean Guichard/Sygma; *ml:* Ledru/Sygma; *mr:* P. Vauthey/Sygma.; *r:* Alain Denize/Liaison International; *b:* Keystone/Sygma; **178** *t:* J. Andanson/Sygma; *b:* UPI/Bettmann Newsphotos;

179 *tl:* Bassignac/Liaison International; *tr:* Corbis/Craig Davis; *mr:* Alain Benainous/Liaison Agency; *bl:* © D.C. Heath; *br:* Jeremy Bembaron/CORBIS SYGMA; **180** *l:* F. Camhi/Stills; *r:* Courtesy of the Martinique Development and Promotion Bureau; **181** *t:* Francois Darmigny/Sygma; *m:* Ken O'Donaghue/© D.C. Heath; **182** *m:* D. Doug Bryant/DDB Stock Photo; *t:* Miranda Shen/Keystone Press Ltd; **182** *b:* Kindra Clineff/The Picture Cube; **183:** Jean F. Leblanc/Keystone Press Ltd.; **184** *t:* Laurie Platt Winfrey, Inc.; *b:* Edimedia; **185** *t:* Winnie Klotz. Courtesy of the Metropolitan Opera Association Inc.; *b & m:* Edimedia; **190** *t:* M. Heron/© D.C. Heath; **191** *br:* Lawrence Migdale/PIX; **193:** George S. Zimbel; **194:** Ray Stott/Image Works; **195:** Nicholas Fievez/SIPA; **196–197** *bkgd:* Henebry Photography/© D.C. Heath; **197** *tl:* Courtesy of Air France; **198** *tr:* M. Heron/© D.C. Heath; **198–199** *bkgd:* O. Franken/© D.C. Heath; **200, 206:** M. Heron/© D.C. Heath; **217** *t & bl:* Giraudon/Art Resource, NY; **217** *tl:* Art Resource, NY; **218:** Jean Loup Charmet; **219** *tl:* O. Franken; *tr:* Lee Snider/Photo Images; *bl:* Roger-Viollet; *br:* Art Resource, NY.; **220:** Henebry Photography/© D.C. Heath; **221** *tl:* Roger-Viollet; *tr:* © D.C. Heath; *ml:* George S. Zimbel; *mr:* O. Franken; *b:* Jean-Loup Charmet; **223** *t:* Jean-Loup Charmet; *b:* Edimedia; **224** *b:* Giraudon/Art Resource, NY; **225** *b:* Art Resource, NY; **227** *tr:* O. Franken; *br:* Ray Stott/Image Works; **232–233** *bkgd:* O. Franken/© D.C. Heath; **235 & 243:** M. Heron/© D.C. Heath; **245** *t:* DeRichemond/Image Works; *m:* Ray Stott/Image Works; **252** *t:* Giraudon/Art Resource, NY.; *m:* ND-Roger-Viollet; *b:* John Henebry; **253** *t & m:* Harlingue-Viollet; *b:* M. Pelletier/Sygma; **254** *l:* UPI/Bettmann; *r:* Sygma; **255** *t:* UPI/Bettmann Newsphotos; *m:* Roger-Viollet; *bl:* Roger-Viollet; **256** *tr:* Jean-Loup Charmet; *l:* Roger-Viollet; *b:* Jeanne Louise Bulliard/Sygma; **257:** Laurie Platt Winfrey, Inc.; **258** *t:* © Fabian, Sygma; *b:* Jeanne Louise Bulliard/Sygma; **259** *all:* Jeanne Louise Bulliard/Sygma; **261** *t:* Jose L. Pelaez/The Stock Market; *b:* Tom Stewart/The Stock Market; **267:** M. Heron/© D.C. Heath; **268** *t:* Y. Levy/© D.C. Heath; **269:** © D.C. Heath; **276** *tr:* Courtesy of Médecins Sans Frontières; *bl,* **281:** A. Sagalyn/© D.C. Heath; **293** *tr:* Pascal la Segretain/Sygma; *tml:* Robert Fried; *bml:* P. Pipard/© D.C. Heath; *br:* Lawrence Migdale/PIX; **294** *r:* Sygma; *b:* Micheline Pelletier/Sygma; **295** *tl:* Gerard Schachmes/Sygma; **299** *b:* M. Antman/Image Works; *t :* S. Reiter/© D.C. Heath; **300** *tr:* Sygma; *bl:* Reuters/Bettmann; **303** *t:* Roger-Viollet; **305:** Owen Franken; **306–307** *bkgd:* O. Franken/© D.C. Heath; **306** *b,* **307, 309:** © D.C. Heath; **310** *tr:* Owen Franken; *tl, ml & mr:* Lee Snider/Photo Images; **311** *tr:* Lee Snider/Photo Images.; *tl:* David Sailors/Stock Market; **313** *t:* Henebry Photography/© D.C. Heath; *bmr:* Yves Levy/© D.C. Heath; *tl inset, tr, both, l & br,* **314** *br:* Henebry Photography/© D.C. Heath; *bl:* O. Franken/© D.C. Heath; **318:** © D.C. Heath; **319** *bm:* S. Reiter/© D.C. Heath; *br, bl:* M. Heron/©

D.C. Heath; **321:** K. Preuss/Image Works; **323, 324:** M. Heron/© D.C. Heath; **336** *t:* ND-Viollet; *b:* Courtesy of the Martinique Development and Promotion Bureau; **338:** Harlingue-Viollet; **339:** Alvis Upitis/Image Bank; **340** *l:* H. Obin. Courtesy of Selden Rodman. Owned by William & Denise Feldman, Wayne, NJ; *r:* Salnave Philippe-Auguste. Courtesy of Selden Rodman; **341** *tl:* Préfet Duffaut. Courtesy of Selden Rodman. Owned by Sara Danzig, NY; *tr:* Dieuseul Paul. Courtesy of Selden Rodman. Owned by Reynald Lally, Haiti; *bl:* Hector Hyppolite. Courtesy of Selden Rodman. Owned by Patricia & Maurice Thompson, Wilton, CT; *br:* Pauleus Vital, 1981. Courtesy of Selden Rodman; **342:** D. Fineman/Sygma; **343** *tr:* Francois Lehr/Sipa Press; *bl, mtr, tl:* Photofest; *br:* Courtesy, Unifrance Film, French Film Board; **344:** Stuart Cohen; **348–351** *bkgd:* M. Heron/© D.C. Heath; **358** *all:* O. Franken/© D.C. Heath; **360–361** *bkgd:* O. Franken/© D.C. Heath; **360** *inset;* Julio Donoso/Woodfin Camp & Associates/Contact Press Images; **361** *b:* *Jean Bruneau/*Valan Photos; **363:** Giraudon/Art Resource, NY; **364:** M. Heron/© D.C. Heath; **372** *t:* © by WARA, Centro Camuno di Studi Preistorici. 25044 Capo di Ponte, Italy; *b:* The Granger Collection, New York; **373** *t:* The Metropolitan Museum of Art, The Michael C. Rockefeller Memorial Collection, Gift of Nelson A. Rockefeller, 1965; **375** *t:* Timothy Beddow/Hutchison Library; *bl:* Maurice Harvey/Hutchison Library; *br:* Nik Wheeler; **376** *t:* Hutchison Library; *b:* Margaret Courtney-Clarke; **377:** UPI/Bettmann; **378** *t:* Courtesy of Présence Africaine; *b:* Liba Taylor/Hutchison Library; **379** *mr:* Musée des Arts Africains et Océaniens, Paris/Giraudon; *r:* Amedo Modigliani, *Head of a Woman,* Chester Dale Collection, © National Gallery of Art, Washington; *l:* © Service Documentation Photographique, Musée National D'Art Moderne, Paris; *mr:* Giraudon/Art Resource, NY.; *br:* Photo R.M.N; **382:** Stuart Cohen; **385** *b:* Jacques Witt, Sipa Press; **386–387** *bkgd:* O.Franken/© D.C. Heath; **387** *t:* Andrew Brilliant/© D.C. Heath; *b:* O. Franken/© D.C. Heath; **388, 389:** M. Heron/© D.C. Heath; **394–395** *bkgd:* P. Pipard/© D.C. Heath; **396–397:** O. Franken/© D.C. Heath; **399** *b:* M. Heron/© D.C. Heath; **400:** Lee Snider/Image Works; **401:** © D.C. Heath; **402:** Canapress Photo Service; **410** *tl:* Richard Pasley; *tmt:* Claudia Dhimitri/Viesti Associates; *tmb:* Margaret Flanagan; *b:* National Archives of Canada/Valan Photos; *tr:* Andrew Brilliant; **411:** National Archives of Canada/Valan Photos; **412, 413** *t & m:* The Bettmann Archive; **413** *b:* The Granger Collection, New York; **414:** Art Resource, NY; **415:** Stock Montage, Inc.; **416:** UPI/Bettmann Newsphotos; **418** *r:* Kindra Clineff/The Picture Cube; **419:** Les Riess; **420:** Kennon Cooke/Valan Photos; **PA10:** Bettmann/Corbis; **R2:** O. Franken/© D.C. Heath; **R3** *tl:* P. Pipard/© D.C. Heath; *bl & tr:* M. Heron/© D.C. Heath; **R6** *t & b:* O. Franken/© D.C. Heath; **R7** *t:* Henebry Photography/© D.C. Heath; *tm & bm:* M. Heron/© D.C. Heath; *b:* Adine Sagalyn/© D.C. Heath.

Illustration Credits

Francis Back: 102–103, 140–141, 183, 326–332, 410, 411, 412, 419

Pierre Ballouhey: 36, 37*t*, 80, 125, 126, 140, 141, 165, 167, 325

Jean-Louis Besson: 54, 57–59, 91*t*, 129, 130, 273, 303, 317

Dave Clegg: 18*t*, 187, 192, 201

Véronique Deiss: 47, 67, 132, 149, 150, 243, 316, 322, 350*c,b*, R3

Chris Demarest: 135*t*, 136

Patrick Deubelbeiss: 27–30, 93–96, 105*b*, 216, 217

Philippe Dumas: 68, 366–370

Jacques Ferrandez: 209–215

Caroline Finadri: 42*b*, 43, 91*b*, 119, 126, 152, 154, 160, 263, 264*bl*, 270, 275, 278, 304, 318, 320–321, 359, 401, R11, R13

Michel Garneau: 5, 6, 9, 12, 13, 16–17, 22, 23, 37c, 38, 44, 50, 53, 71, 72, 76, 78, 81, 117, 162, 168, 188, 197, 198t, 205, 228b, 234, 236, 238–239, 244, 267, 272, 274, 346, 349, 350t, 351, 355, R4, R5, R9

Paul Giambarba: 15

Laurie Gilburne: 228c

Marsha Goldberg: 387

Tama Hochbaum: 337

Carol Inouye: 176, 335

Louise-Andrée Laliberte: 378, 380–381

Diana Maloney: 315

Mapping Specialists, Ltd.: R34, R36–R37

Winslow Pinney Pels: 402–408

Mike Reagan: 92, 104t, 105t, 220, 222, 282, 292, 297, 334, 373, 374b, 412, 417

John Rumery: 14, 195, 262

Lauren Scheuer: 170-174

Élisabeth Schlossberg: R12

Dave Shepherd: 18b, 42t, 90, 104c, 198br, 218, 219, 232t, 254, 335t, 361b, 392–393, 395, 420

Lorraine Silvestri: 283–290

Anna Vojtech: 98, 146, 374t, 377

Laura Wallace: 77

Fabrice Weiss: 106–107, 224–225, 247–250

Yayo: 33, 164, 352, 388, 390

MW01200144